SOME PASTORS
AND TEACHERS

SOME PASTORS AND TEACHERS

*Reflecting a Biblical Vision of What
Every Minister is Called to Be*

SINCLAIR B. FERGUSON

*And he gave some, apostles; and some, prophets; and some, evangelists; and
some, pastors and teachers; for the perfecting of the saints, for the work
of the ministry, for the edifying of the body of Christ: till we all come
in the unity of the faith, and of the knowledge of the Son of God, unto
a perfect man, unto the measure of the stature of the fullness of Christ.*
—EPHESIANS 4:11-13

THE BANNER OF TRUTH TRUST

THE BANNER OF TRUTH TRUST

3 Murrayfield Road, Edinburgh, EH12 6EL, UK
PO Box 621, Carlisle, PA 17013, USA

❦

ISBN
Print: 978 1 84871 789 3
Epub: 978 1 84871 790 9
Kindle: 978 1 84871 791 6

❦

Typeset in 10.5/13.5 Adobe Garamond Pro
at The Banner of Truth Trust, Edinburgh

Printed in the USA by
Versa Press Inc.,
East Peoria, IL.

❦

CONTENTS

INTRODUCTION

THE title of *Some Pastors and Teachers* comes from Paul's words in Ephesians 4:11. Echoing Psalm 68:18, he says that the ascended Christ has given certain gifts for the upbuilding of the church in unity and love. In particular, he mentions various ministries of the word of God that were exercised in the New Testament church. In the dignified language of the Authorized (King James) Version in which I first memorized the words: 'He gave some, apostles; and some, prophets; and some, evangelists ...'. These are foundational ministries (as Paul indicates in Eph. 2:20). But Christ has also made provision for the church's ongoing growth and at its heart are 'some, pastors and teachers' (Eph. 4:11 KJV). Their ministry forms the theme, in one way or another, of the following pages.

Every book, no matter how recondite—even one on modal logic or pure mathematics—is part of the narrative of its author's life. *Some Pastors and Teachers* is no exception, since most of my own life has been devoted to being a pastor and teacher, sometimes one more than the other, and sometimes both simultaneously. During these years I have often been asked to contribute essays or chapters to a wide variety of books—sometimes when my main task has been that of seminary teaching, but often while I have been serving in pastoral ministry. This volume contains a selection of these writings that reflect particularly on being a pastor and teacher, and on doctrines and themes especially relevant to the preaching of the gospel.

Many of these chapters were first published in relatively obscure places. But just as the main screens in major airports rearrange departure information, and we see the various flights arranged in order, so, one day these essays seemed to self-select and rearrange themselves in my mind into a coherent whole.

One particular motivation lies behind *Some Pastors and Teachers* seeing the light of day. Many—probably most—of these chapters were written in the context of busy pastoral ministry, either in Scotland or in the United States—preaching, teaching, pastoral visiting, personal meetings, crises in the lives of individuals and sometimes the whole church, administrative responsibilities, and the wide and wonderful variety of activities that make up the average minister's life. And since virtually all the essays were written by request, their writing has been squeezed into, or out of, an occasional hiatus in the sheer busy-ness of ministry life and the constant preparation involved in preaching anywhere between three and six times in the week. So, at some point in the writing of almost all these chapters I have heard an inner voice ask, 'Whatever possessed you to agree to do this?' Yet, however far short these various pieces fall, in each case the preparation of them did me good, enlarged my understanding a little, and fed into the day to day work of pastoral ministry. I hope, therefore, that these pages will encourage other ministers to allow themselves to be stretched a little beyond their normal pulpit or lectern preparation. There is no doubt that the wider reflection, reading, study and stretching involved can only strengthen and enrich long-term ministry.

Such stretching produces growth. Sometimes ministers can 'waste' the privileged time they have by studying only in relation to their next sermon. This does produce some growth, of course; but perhaps not growth that is constantly putting down deeper roots and producing richer fruit. Preachers need to be reading and studying more widely, and reflecting theologically if that is to be the case. For only then will our ongoing ministry be deepened and enriched.

Thus, in one sense at least, the undergirding message of these diverse chapters is: if you are a preacher, accept invitations or create opportunities to study, speak, or write on subjects outside of your usual diet of preparation. Yes, you may find yourself under a little pressure; but pressure can produce diamonds! You will grow personally as a result, and, God-willing, Paul's exhortation will be fulfilled in your ministry:

Devote yourself to the public reading of Scripture, to exhortation, to teaching. Do not neglect the gift you have ... Practise these things, devote yourself to them, *so that all may see your progress*. Keep a close watch on yourself and on the teaching. Persist in this, for by so doing you will save both yourself and your hearers (1 Tim. 4:13-16).

It can be an unnerving question to ask oneself, 'Has anyone in the congregation ever thought, far less said, about me, 'He is making progress'?

There is a further consideration. I remember as a student reading a wise letter John Newton wrote to a younger Christian who was puzzled why one man's ministry was more helpful to him than another's. Newton well knew that the young and immature are prone to rank such preachers as Paul, Peter and Apollos (and usually in that order!). Some men may be more gifted than others, he explained; but that does not mean they are more sanctified. Further, God in his providence shapes ministers in different ways, with different gifts, impressing on them various aspects of the single burden of the gospel. While all must preach Christ crucified, some are stronger teachers than exhorters and *vice versa*; some have a special gift in exposing sin, while others excel in comforting the afflicted. The important thing is that each has his own gift, sovereignly distributed. So 'use the gift Christ has given to you' is Paul's counsel (Rom. 12:6).

In those far-off student days, I began to believe that just as members of the body of Christ in general differ in their gifts, the same is true in some measure of 'pastors and teachers'. All need to be able to teach. But Christ shapes each of us, by his word, through his Spirit, and in his providential dealings, to enable us to say to each other 'the Lord Jesus has given me something to give to you'. That is as true of the brotherhood of pastors and teachers as it is of the whole body of Christ. Should we not therefore ask ourselves, 'What gift has the Lord Jesus given to me *for my fellow ministers?*'

So, in this sense *Some Pastors and Teachers* is simply a way of saying, 'These are some of the gifts that the Lord has given to me for others who have an interest in and a concern for the ministry of the gospel. I know the parcels are small; but I hope there will be something inside them that will be a blessing and an encouragement to you.' And perhaps I may be allowed to add, 'You also have received something from the Lord that you could give to other pastors and teachers, saying to them, "The

Lord gave me this—it is for you; I am your servant for Jesus' sake" (2 Cor. 4:5).' Thus, I hope these pages will encourage brother ministers to say, 'I think I could do something like that too'—whether by writing or speaking.

While this is a *big* book, it only seems long! For each chapter is an entity on its own. Readers can enter and leave at any point they choose. No chapter is completely dependent on the previous chapter, or for that matter on any other chapter in the book. I hope, therefore, that it may be a volume that readers will enjoy dipping into, here and there. Yet, as will be clear from the contents pages, it does have an overall shape, progressing from studies of three great pastors and teachers who have influenced me, to reflections on specific doctrines, and then on to the work of preaching and teaching the gospel. In this way, the book covers many, if by no means all, of the themes and tasks of Christian ministry.

Hidden underneath every book lies a network of its author's connections and relations. Behind *Some Pastors and Teachers* lie all the joys and sorrows of life and ministry in three congregations and two theological seminaries, lived out of several different homes, in two continents and in three different states of the USA. To those who welcomed us in each of these ministry contexts I am deeply grateful.

The prospect of having one's name attached to a book of this nature and size inevitably brings with it a fair share of self-doubt on the one hand and the fear of misplaced egotism on the other. Why, after all, would anyone think that essays one had published in the past deserve to be rescued from their obscurity and gathered into a more permanent form? I am therefore very grateful to the publishers and especially to my editor Jonathan Watson for their enthusiasm and encouragement. In addition, the whole project would have been impossible without the willingness of various publishers to allow it to come to fruition. I am grateful to them for their kindness and considerable generosity. They are separately acknowledged at the end of the book.

Many fellow pastors and teachers have been faithful friends and wise counsellors to me. Their encouragement has meant more to me than any of them knows or perhaps could imagine. When faced as a young teenager with the claims of Christ I wondered if following him would mean losing friends. I knew the Lord's promise that we give up nothing for him without receiving a hundredfold, with eternal life (even if with persecutions, Mark 10:28-30). That promise has been abundantly fulfilled. While an inadequate expression of my gratitude, these pages are a way of saying, 'Here are some of the leftovers from the abundance of good food the Lord has given us in his word.'

I owe an unrepayable debt of love and gratitude to my wife Dorothy, to our four children, David, Peter, John and Ruth and to their families. Their love, acceptance and loyalty have meant more to me than words can express. And beyond this stands the debt of debts owed to the One who has given me the privilege of being a 'pastor and teacher'. He is the One

> who is able to do far more abundantly
> than all that we ask or think,
> according to the power at work within us,
> to him be glory in the church
> and in Christ Jesus
> throughout all generations,
> forever and ever. Amen.
> (Eph. 3:20-21)

SINCLAIR B. FERGUSON
September 2017

I. PASTORS AND TEACHERS: THREE JOHNS

CHAPTER ONE

JOHN CALVIN: PASTOR-TEACHER

J OHN CALVIN ranks as one of the most significant figures in the
history of the Christian church. Unlike his older contemporary
Martin Luther or the later John Wesley, he did not 'found' a
denominational tradition as such, yet his impact on history in general
and the history of the church in particular has been incalculable. From
his influence on French literature to his contribution to democracy,
he has been hailed as a pioneer. He bequeathed to later generations a
small library of written material, but more than that, he exhibited an
approach to Scripture, the gospel, and the life of the Christian that has
inspired both scholarship and martyrdom. He was scholar, pastor, social
and ecclesiastical reformer, political influencer, preacher, letter writer,
theologian, and faithful friend.

Calvin is increasingly well served by the number of biographical
studies in print.[1] In this brief chapter, we can touch on only a small

[1] Among the more recent are: Alexander Ganoczy, *The Young Calvin* (1966),
trs. David Foxgrover and Wade Provo (Philadelphia: Westminster Press, 1987);
T. H. L. Parker, *John Calvin: A Biography* (London: Darton, Longman & Todd, 1975);
William J. Bouwsma, *John Calvin: A Sixteenth Century Portrait* (New York: Oxford
University Press, 1988); Alister E. McGrath, *A Life of John Calvin* (Oxford: Blackwell,
1990); Bernard Cottret, *Calvin: A Biography* (1995), tr. M. Wallace McDonald (Grand
Rapids: Eerdmans, 2000); Bruce Gordon, *Calvin* (New Haven, CT.: Yale University
Press, 2009); W. Robert Godfrey, *John Calvin: Pilgrim and Pastor* (Phillipsburg, NJ:
P&R, 2009); Herman Selderhuis, *John Calvin: A Pilgrim's Life* (Downers Grove,
IL: InterVarsity Press, 2009). At various points Calvin's biographers disagree with
one another, especially where the evidence is thin, for example concerning the exact
pattern of his early education.
The ensuing narrative, being introductory in intent, presumes rather than argues
for a position on these debates. Readers who wish to investigate the disagreements
further will find the different positions identified within the biographies.

selection of themes. In particular, we will focus attention on his family life, the events surrounding his conversion, his early ministry, his friendships, and some applications to be made from the life and providences of this magisterial Reformer.

Early life

Jean Cauvin[1] was born on July 10, 1509, in the town of Noyon, some fifty miles north-east of Paris. He was the third of the four sons of Girard Cauvin,[2] an official in the local cathedral. Girard appears to have been a rather difficult man. Calvin's mother, Jeanne, on the other hand, was reputed to be both a physically attractive and pious woman. Calvin later recalled times when she took him on pilgrimages as a small boy. He remembered kissing a relic. However, his mother died when he was about six years old.

It does not require profound psychological insight to suspect that this early loss left an indelible impression on Calvin. Simply from the personal point of view, it meant that he lacked the balance of his parents' personalities. The impression certainly arises from Calvin's writings that his relationship with his father was dutiful but not particularly affectionate. That said, it is noteworthy how reticent Calvin was throughout his life to entrust his inner emotional life to writing, and then only within the context of his deepest and most secure friendships.

Two particularly significant privileges arose from Girard's position as the legal adviser to the chapter of the Noyon Cathedral. The first was that his connections with the Montmor family provided young John with a private education alongside the Montmor children. For a child of Calvin's precocity of mind, this was indeed a privilege. It led, in turn, to his beginning further studies with them in Paris in his early teens.

The second was that young Calvin had access to what was essentially the medieval equivalent of a college scholarship. This was accomplished through the practice of granting benefices. Thus, while a student, Calvin was appointed to the 'livings' of several congregations. Of course, none of the pastoral responsibilities devolved on him. But he received the

---

[1] He did not adopt the formal Latin name Johannes Calvinus until the period in his life when aspirations to scholarship emerged.

[2] His brothers were Charles, Anthony, and Francis.

income remaining after someone had been employed to fulfil those duties. By the time he graduated from the University of Paris, he would be 'pastor' of three congregations.

Arriving in Paris in the early 1520s (the precise year is debated), he spent his first few months studying at the Collège de la Marche. Providentially, his instructor there was Maturin Cordier, one of the finest Latinists of his time. Later in life, Calvin would dedicate his commentary on 1 Thessalonians to him, writing:

> When my father sent me, while yet a boy, to Paris, after I had simply tasted the first elements of the Latin tongue; Providence so ordered it that I had, for a short time, the privilege of having you as my instructor, that I might be taught by you the true method of learning, in such a way that I might be prepared afterwards to make somewhat better proficiency. For, after presiding over the first class with the highest renown, on observing that pupils who had been ambitiously trained up by the other masters, produced nothing but mere show, nothing of solidity, so that they required to be formed by you anew, tired of this annoyance, you that year descended to the fourth class. This, indeed, was what you had in view, but to me it was a singular kindness on the part of God that I happened to have an auspicious commencement of such a course of training...
>
> I derived so much assistance afterwards from your training, that it is with good reason that I acknowledge myself indebted to you for such progress as has since been made. And this I was desirous to testify to posterity, that, if any advantage shall accrue to them from my writings, they shall know that it has in some degree originated with you.[1]

In that same dedication, Calvin also remembered the darker side of education in the Collège de la Marche. He noted that he was removed from Cordier's tutelage through the less-than-tender care of 'an injudicious man, who regulated our studies according to his own pleasure, or rather his caprice'.[2]

---

[1] John Calvin, 'The Author's Epistle Dedicatory to Marturinus Corderius', dated February 1, 1550, in *Commentaries on the Epistles to the Philippians, Colossians, and Thessalonians*, tr. John Pringle (Edinburgh: Calvin Translation Society, 1851), p. 234.
[2] *Ibid.*

5

From there, Calvin soon transferred to the Collège de Montaigu. Father Calvin's aspiration was that his son should enter the priesthood, and de Montaigu was a kind of monastery for teens who intended to become priests.

Calvin recalled two things in particular about college life: first, the food was terrible (he later believed it contributed to the ruin of his own health and that of a number of his fellow students). Second, the college exacted enormous discipline. Classes began at 4 a.m. and continued (with some intermission) until at least 8 p.m. in the winter and 9 p.m. in the summer.

Calvin was a sponge for learning. His preparatory training in Latin, followed by studies in philosophy and rhetoric, led to a spoken and written style marked by simplicity, clarity, delicacy of phrasing, and powerful analytical argument.

Although his masterwork, the *Institutes of the Christian Religion*, evolved into a very large four-book treatise, Calvin early developed an unusual ability in and love for brevity and clarity.[1] Clear communication was one of the passions of his life, whether he was writing letters, theological treatises, or commentaries, or preaching in his native French language. His clear, economic use of language, unburdened with complicated phrasing, allowed his message to come alive to those who read his works or listened to him preach.

Life at college meant lessons, exercises, and minor inquisitions, as well as bad food. But during that time, Calvin practised a rigorous self-discipline. Indeed, it may have been at this early time that he began a practice that would irritate his friends when he became a law student. At the end of every day, he made it a habit to review what he had learned during the day; then, the next morning, he would not rise from bed until he was sure that he remembered everything he had learned the previous day. In many ways, Calvin's self-discipline explains his vast productivity in later life. Though the young man was not yet a believer, he was later

[1] In the dedication of his Romans commentary to Simon Grynaeus, he recalled a conversation with him in which they were of one mind that 'the chief excellency of an expounder consists in lucid brevity'. John Calvin, *Commentary on the Epistle of Paul to the Romans*, tr. John Owen (Edinburgh: Calvin Translation Society, 1849), p. xxiii.

conscious of the extent to which God was building into his life habits on which he would draw in order to minister to the glory of God.

By the time Calvin graduated from college, his father had left the cathedral. He was about to be excommunicated in 1528, and, later—were it not for intervention from the family—would have been buried in an unconsecrated grave. In the uncharacteristically autobiographical introduction to his *Commentary on the Psalms*, Calvin guardedly recorded how his father changed his mind and decided that young John should study law rather than prepare for the priesthood. The reason—or at least the one that was given—was, Calvin says, that Girard now believed the legal profession held much better prospects for his son than the church. So Calvin dutifully went to study law, first at the University of Orléans and later at the University of Bourges.

At this time, Calvin says in the introduction to his *Commentary on the Psalms*, he was 'addicted to the papacy'. By this, he doubtless meant he had a prejudicial acceptance of and commitment to the medieval Roman Catholic Church with its sacramental way of salvation, and that he lived in conformity to its teaching and obedience to its authority.

Though Calvin does not say so, during his time in college he must have been exposed to the new gospel of the Lutherans. Indeed, he surely would have known of Luther's tracts since they had been under examination by theological professors of the Sorbonne in the early 1520s. No doubt student fascination with the current trends of the academy marked early sixteenth-century Paris as much as it did the Sorbonne of the mid-twentieth century. It is virtually inconceivable that Calvin did not have strong opinions. Indeed, he virtually admits as much, as we see in his admission in the introduction to his *Commentary on the Psalms*. But this was to change.

Calvin's conversion

Calvin studied law at the University of Orléans and at the University of Bourges (where he also studied Greek literature with Melchior Wolmar, with additional classical studies in Paris). As a post-graduate student, he now came under the spell of the new humanist movement with its motto of *ad fontes*—returning to the literature of antiquity and to the study of its languages. All of this, in Calvin's case, bore fruit in his earliest publication, a commentary on Seneca's work *De Clementia*, published in 1532. It would be, he hoped, the first step on the ladder of academic advance. He was to be disappointed. Perhaps it would be more accurate to say God providentially would disappoint him. Neither humanism nor a career in academia could answer the needs in Calvin's mind and heart.

Calvin's stubborn allegiance to the Roman Catholic Church now found itself under the pressure of evangelical influences, not least from the entourage of remarkable friends who surrounded him. They shared his passion for learning the old languages, but also—earlier than Calvin—they were developing an interest in and love for the Christian faith in its more primitive New Testament form. Erasmus' *Greek New Testament* had been published in 1516, and some of Calvin's friends were studying it carefully. They were coming to realize that Luther's views on justification were not, after all, idiosyncratic and heretical, but in fact were founded on basic New Testament teaching.

This 'crack' led to the growing realization that the late medieval Roman Catholic Church's theology of salvation could never lead to spiritual certainty. While the church's position was not codified until the Council of Trent (1545–63), the teaching enunciated by that council simply underlined the current view that the only way to have assurance of salvation was by canonizable levels of holiness or by a special divine revelation. Cardinal Robert Bellarmine, perhaps the most formidable Roman Catholic theologian of the sixteenth century, gave striking expression to this when he claimed that assurance was the greatest of all Protestant heresies.

The way of salvation, according to the Roman Church, was dependent first on the grace given at baptism, then progressed through a person's various life experiences governed by the sacraments of the Church. One did what one could (*facere quod in se est*) until one's faith was (through the grace of the sacraments) fully formed in perfect love for God (*fides formata caritate*). At this point, 'by grace' (i.e. through the sacramental system) a person became actually righteous in himself and therefore could be accounted righteous in God's sight. Justification in this sense was claimed to be 'by grace', but it was not 'by faith alone'. Rome regarded any different teaching (such as Luther's doctrine of the justification of the ungodly in his ungodliness) as a 'legal fiction'. Thus, for Rome, grace involved the *infusion*, not the *imputation*, of righteousness; sinners were justified because grace made them justifiable.

This system rendered assurance virtually impossible. How could one know one had 'done enough'? The system left ordinary men and women without certainty of faith. Without assurance, the people were bound to the sacramental system of the Church, fair game for the sale of indulgences, and deprived of all joy in salvation.

Judging by the emphasis Calvin would later place (in various contexts) on certainty in the Christian life, it seems likely that coming to an assured knowledge of God and the forgiveness of sins in Christ was a major element in his conversion. Now he and his young friends were beginning to read in the pages of their Greek New Testament of ordinary men and women who abounded in pardon, assurance, joy and freedom, certain that nothing could separate them from the love of God in Christ Jesus. In the New Testament, people experienced the love of God poured into their hearts by the Holy Spirit from the very beginning of the life of faith.

Some of Calvin's friends were beginning to speak more openly about their new discoveries. One of them was Calvin's cousin, Pierre-Robert Olivétan, whose diligence in study rivalled Calvin's own. Eventually Olivétan would translate the Bible into French—and his cousin John would write the preface (1534). Calvin also was beginning to move in the circles of reform of which King Francis's sister, Marguerite of Navarre, was the guardian, and which included her confessor, Gérard Roussel.

Another friend was Nicholas Cop, who would deliver the Rector's Address at the University of Paris in November 1533. Theodore Beza, Calvin's colleague and successor in Geneva, and an early biographer, believed that Calvin himself was the author of the speech. The speech is interesting for its combination of the old and the new. It expresses the movement toward New Testament Christianity; but while there is protest, there is not yet Protestantism. In any event, Calvin fled Paris in the maelstrom that followed. In 1534, the incident of the Placards (when anti-Roman placards were posted throughout Paris—including, reportedly, on the king's bedchamber door) meant that Paris was a city permanently closed to Calvin. He was beginning to preach now and even to write model sermons, but all of the implications of the pathway on which he had started were not yet clear.

What happened to bring him fully into the Reformation movement? All we know from Calvin's own hand is that God subdued him to docility by a sudden (or unexpected) conversion. It is tempting to think that he was referring to what we would call his 'conversion experience', but perhaps it is a description only of its beginnings, in which his stubborn spirit became teachable. Certainly his full confession of being an '*évangélique*' would wait for his forfeiture of his benefices in the realization that since others were giving their lives for the gospel he must not remain hidden, even if he still aspired to the life of a scholar. He had, at last, grasped what would be a central motif in his developed theology—everything we need is provided for us in Christ, plus nothing.[1]

Scholars have discussed what passage of Scripture most influenced Calvin's conversion. Ford Lewis Battles, who translated the 1960 English edition of the *Institutes*, argued that it was Romans 1:18-32 because of the way the *Institutes* is divided into the knowledge of God the Creator and the knowledge of God the Saviour in Jesus Christ.[2] Romans 1 certainly did have a profound influence on Calvin's theology. But Calvin may also have been influenced by Paul's letter to the Philippians. Certainly he keeps returning in his writings to the theme that the Christian loses everything for Christ but gains everything through him. Whether we live or die, Christ is ours (Phil. 1:21; 3:7-11). From one standpoint, Calvin lost everything by giving himself in faith to Jesus Christ.

By whatever means, whether slow or sudden, Calvin's conversion took place. His stubborn addiction to the papacy was broken and his heart subdued. From that time forward, the great motto of his life became, 'Lord, I offer my heart to thee, promptly and sincerely.' His personal symbol (apparently designed by himself) was an open hand with a heart between the letters J and C. Still in his twenties, he now clearly belonged to Christ.

[1] See his exposition in *Institutes of the Christian Religion*, ed. John T. McNeill, tr. Ford Lewis Battles (Louisville: Westminster John Knox, 1960), II.xvi.

[2] See Ford Lewis Battles, *The Piety of John Calvin* (Grand Rapids: Baker, 1978), p. 48.

He was part of a widespread movement involving many young people. It is easy to forget just how young they actually were. Many of them were arrested for their faith; numbers were executed. One of those who was put to death was Calvin's landlord in Paris. Calvin's own room was searched. He and his friends became hunted criminals. By the time he was twenty-six, he was a man on the run; he had become a pilgrim and would live the rest of his life as a refugee. His ambition remained solitude and study; but now there also burned within him a passion to serve his fellow believers.

In 1536, the *Institutes of the Christian Religion* came from the press. It was at first a six-chapter catechetical work which only gradually grew into the substantial work of theology with which we are familiar today. The final (Latin) edition was printed in 1559 (French translation, 1560).

Calvin's first concern was merely to produce a work that would edify Christians and, to some extent, serve as an apology for the Reformed faith. In the face of criticism and hostility, he wanted to prove that fidelity to Scripture characterized the new evangelicals. He wrote an extensive prefatory letter to King Francis I of France, defending the Reformation against a whole series of false accusations.

Calvin's ministry

Calvin was on the run. In a relatively short time, he traversed Europe, moving through Italy and Switzerland. He returned briefly to Noyon in 1536 to gather members of his family and some friends to accompany him to Strasbourg, where he could continue his scholarly life. But they could not go directly there because of troop movements. Instead, they decided to enter Switzerland near Geneva. The plan was to stay for a night before moving on to Strasbourg.

Paradoxically, one of Calvin's friends, Louis du Tillet,[1] let slip that the young man travelling through Geneva was in fact the author of the *Institutes of the Christian Religion*. William Farel, who had come to Geneva to lead the work of reformation, sought Calvin out. Geneva had recently embraced the Reformation, but it had not yet been transformed into an

---

[1] 'Paradoxically', since du Tillet later returned to the Roman Catholic Church. In God's providence, the remarkable ministry of Calvin in Geneva was thus in part effected by someone who rejected the ministry for which Calvin stood.

evangelical city, and Farel believed Calvin was the man Geneva needed. Calvin resisted Farel's appeal. The story is best told in his own words:

> I had resolved to continue in the same privacy and obscurity, until at length William Farel detained me at Geneva, not so much by counsel and exhortation, as by a dreadful imprecation, which I felt to be as if God had from heaven laid his mighty hand upon me to arrest me. As the most direct road to Strasburg, to which I then intended to retire, was shut up by the wars, I had resolved to pass quickly by Geneva, without staying longer than a single night in that city. A little before this, Popery had been driven from it by the exertions of the excellent person whom I have named, and Peter Viret; but matters were not yet brought to a settled state, and the city was divided into unholy and dangerous factions. Then an individual who now basely apostatised and returned to the Papists, discovered me and made me known to others. Upon this, Farel, who burned with an extraordinary zeal to advance the gospel, immediately strained every nerve to detain me. And after having learned that my heart was set upon devoting myself to private studies for which I wished to keep myself free from other pursuits, and finding that he gained nothing by entreaties, he proceeded to utter an imprecation that God would curse my retirement, and the tranquillity of the studies which I sought, if I should withdraw and refuse to give assistance, when the necessity was so urgent. By this imprecation I was so stricken with terror, that I desisted from the journey which I had undertaken.[1]

So Calvin stayed in Geneva. On more than one occasion in the years that followed, he might have believed that by staying in Geneva he was experiencing rather than avoiding the curse of God! The Genevans had separated from the Roman Church, but they were not 'set apart for the gospel of God' (Rom. 1:1).

The ministry there was far from being a sinecure. The early years (1536–38) proved to be a nightmare. Many were opposed to the preaching of the word of God. During Calvin's sermons, there were all

[1] John Calvin, *Commentary on the Book of Psalms*, tr. James Anderson (Edinburgh: Calvin Translation Society, 1845), I:xlii-xliii.

kinds of unseemly noises, as well as irritating chattering and mockery of the preacher. Even later, the Register of the Consistory of Geneva reads like a chronicle of spiritual indifference on the part of church members.

As the word of God came forth from the pulpit in Geneva, stressing the urgency of faith, repentance, and sanctification, opposition intensified. People would shoot their guns outside Calvin's residence while he was trying to sleep. They would set their dogs on him in the street— indeed, some of them named their dogs after him (without affection). Near-constant friction developed between the ministers and numbers of the citizens, and also between the ministers and the city government.

The crisis point was reached on Easter Sunday of 1538, when Calvin and other ministers preached but then refused to serve the Lord's Supper. They were told to leave the city when replacements could be found. A few days later, they were told to leave without delay. By the end of the week, Calvin was in exile again. In his own words, 'I was banished from Geneva.'[1]

It is not difficult to imagine how low Calvin must have sunk at that point. 'Naturally of a timid, soft, and pusillanimous disposition',[2] and now with what must have felt like a disastrously brief ministry, it is not surprising that he had little taste to begin again. What he most needed was a wise minister to come alongside him, put his hand on his shoulder, and say: 'Join me here. Watch how we do things here. Pick up the vibrations of what ministry means. Learn all over again. We will give you opportunity, we will encourage you, we will pray for you, and we will minister to you.'

That is exactly what Martin Bucer, the seasoned pastor of Strasbourg, did for Calvin. But Calvin did not bend easily. Like Farel before him, Bucer encountered resistance to his proposal. Bruised and wounded, he simply wanted to go back to his books. But Bucer had exactly the biblical model to bind Calvin's conscience—Jonah:

> That most excellent servant of Christ, Martin Bucer, employing a similar kind of remonstrance and protestation as that to which Farel had recourse before, drew me back to a new station. Alarmed by the

[1] Calvin, *Comm. Psa.*, I:xlii-xliii.
[2] *Ibid.*

example of Jonas, which he set before me, I still continued in the work of teaching.[1]

Bucer encouraged Calvin to lead a congregation of French refugees, which numbered about five hundred. That may well be the ideal size for a church: everyone can know everyone else in such a congregation; the pastor can know his sheep by name; everyone can know the pastor; and a wide variety of gifts is likely to be present. Calvin grew as he preached God's word and ministered to his new people. He also thought through many issues of worship and church life.

At this stage Calvin was single, and seems to have had little thought of marrying, and had a great desire for privacy. His friends, however, were determined to find him a wife. Calvin respected their authority, as they introduced him to one woman after another. Indeed, they went so far as to fix a wedding date for Calvin and a young lady of their choice. Calvin might have married were it not for the fact that he learned more about the lady. When he did, he wrote that he would have needed to have lost his mind to have married her!

In August 1540, Calvin married Idelette de Bure, the widow of an Anabaptist convert. She had a little boy and girl. They enjoyed a happy, but short, marriage. In July 1542, she bore him a son, Jacques. He was a premature baby and died in infancy. In the grief of that loss, Calvin wrote about the Fatherhood of his God and bowed to confess that he knows best what is for the good of his children. But the sense of loss remained with him throughout his life.

Although Calvin's closest male friend at this time was his brother Antoine, who shared the house, there is little doubt that Idelette was his heart. Her health was precarious, however, and after a few years of illness, she died in 1549. Calvin deeply grieved her loss. He wrote to Viret with stark simplicity: 'I have been bereaved of the best companion of my life ... she was the faithful helper of my ministry.'[2]

The Strasbourg period was perhaps the happiest in Calvin's life. But in the sixteenth century, no one was ever far from pain and loss. In one

---

[1] Calvin, *Comm. Psa.*, I:xlii-xliii.

[2] John Calvin, *Letters of John Calvin*, 4 vols, tr. David Constable, ed. Jules Bonnet (Philadelphia: Presbyterian Board of Publication, 1858), II:216.

year of his sojourn there (1538), Calvin nursed his friend Farel's nephew prior to his death from the plague, and lost his friend and blind fellow pastor Elie Couraud, who had worked with him in Geneva, and his brilliant cousin Olivétan. But exercising iron discipline in this season of great loss, he accomplished two significant things. While growing into pastoral ministry, he revised the *Institutes*, expanding it from a small volume to a large book. He also conceived what we might call 'The Calvin project'—a one-man production of a biblically rooted theology (the *Institutes*) accompanied by a series of commentaries on the entire New Testament. He began with the book of Romans.

Calvin realized that the new Reformation church needed doctrine that could be taught and applied clearly, and that men and women needed to understand how the message of the gospel derives from, and is shaped by, Scripture. At the same time, he saw how the Scriptures could be expounded in the form of commentaries. It is remarkable, given the workload he carried (preaching five, six, or seven times each week, lecturing, writing letters, working on various writing projects, studying, attending many meetings, counselling), that he almost succeeded in completing his New Testament exposition (only 2 and 3 John and Revelation lack comment). Thus, as people studied Scripture, Calvin reasoned, they would have two kinds of works to help them: a volume of theology that would teach them the contours of the gospel and provide a road map, and commentaries that would demonstrate how the doctrine was both constituted and confirmed from divine revelation. The goal of the project was to produce all-Bible and all-doctrine Christians, whose lives were transformed by the renewing of their minds (Rom. 12:1-2).

Although Calvin was exiled from Geneva during this time, he continued to have contact with the Genevans, even though the relationship remained strained and difficult. In March 1539, the Genevans received a letter from the Roman Catholic Cardinal Jacopo Sadoleto. He was deeply scathing about the Reformation, but graciously invited the Genevans to return to the fold of Rome. They had no local resources adequate to answer Sadoleto, so they asked Calvin to respond. His reply to the cardinal is one of the small masterpieces of Reformation writing. Sadoleto had spoken about the judgment seat. Calvin's response expounded the privileges of grace that marked the confession an evangelical believer could make at that judgment seat.

In 1540, he was asked to return to Geneva. His response was predictable. He wrote to Farel on March 29, 1540: 'Rather would I submit to death a hundred times than to that cross on which one had to perish daily one thousand times over.'[1] Nevertheless, he eventually agreed to go, but only on loan for six months. He returned to the pulpit, made a few remarks, and then began preaching on the same passage he had left off expounding a few years before. In a profound sense, it was the first day of the rest of his life.

Calvin remained in Geneva and gave himself to its people and its transformation over the quarter century that followed until his death in 1564. All was not plain sailing. But he was a more seasoned minister now. He knew better how to lead, how to pastor, how to care, and, not least, how to endure to the end. The result was what John Knox called 'the most perfect school of Christ on earth since the days of the apostles.'

Lessons from the life of Calvin

During most of his time in Geneva, Calvin lived on the edge. The edge in this case was enormous political pressure. He was not a citizen of Geneva; he was a refugee until a few years before he died. He had no formal political power. In addition, for many years he faced an underlying hostility to his presence and his ministry. As late as the 1550s, Calvin remained convinced he would have to leave Geneva again. Only in 1555 did the city fathers give the church the right of excommunication, thereby ceding spiritual authority. He also laboured under great personal pressure due to attacks from his enemies, some of whom had originally enticed him to come back to Geneva.

There were other trials, too, such as 'The Servetus Affair' in 1553. Michael Servetus, who had a history with Calvin, had already been condemned and placed under sentence of death for heresy throughout Europe, and he soon was charged in Geneva, especially for his anti-trinitarian teaching. A deeply unstable figure, he seems to have come to Geneva deliberately to challenge Calvin to refute his views. He was

---

[1] Calvin, *Letters*, I:75.

offered the opportunity to return to France to be tried as a heretic, but he begged to be tried in Geneva, perhaps hoping that Calvin would refuse to deal with the issue in the light of the ongoing insecurity of his position. Nonetheless, the Council of Geneva convicted Servetus of heresy and ordered him to be burned at the stake. Calvin argued for a more humane death, but his request was refused.

Another difficulty Calvin had to deal with was Jérôme-Hermès Bolsec, a strange and unstable former Carmelite father. He was a physician (and spy) in the court of Renée of Ferrara. He settled near Geneva in 1550. While he expressed appreciation for much of Calvin's teaching, he had a deep distaste for the biblical doctrine of predestination.

On Fridays, Calvin met in what was essentially a group Bible study for local ministers and others, known as *les Congrégations*.[1] At one of these meetings, Bolsec brought up the subject of predestination, critiquing Calvin full-on. He did not realize that Calvin was at the meeting and was listening to the whole performance. Needless to say, Calvin was not greatly impressed or pleased. Bolsec became an implacable enemy from that time on. He wrote much against the Reformer that was libellous and destructive. Calvin was haunted by such attacks, as well as the less sophisticated but ongoing opposition to the gospel and the Reformation.

How, then, was the work in Geneva transformed from a quasi-political reformation to a genuine gospel reformation?

First, prayer changed the city. One of the first things Calvin did on his return from Strasbourg was to institute a weekly day of prayer. While there was regular preaching each weekday, Wednesdays were set aside for prayer from 8 a.m. to 10 a.m. At these times, as well as in the regular private prayers of the congregation and the regular prayers in the worship services, the people and the ministers prayed for the benediction of God on the city and on the growing number of churches that were being planted outside of Geneva.

The second thing that transformed Geneva was the ministry of the word of God. Sermons were preached on Sunday mornings and afternoons. On weekdays, Calvin preached three times during the week (and when his strength allowed it, he preached every day). Beza says about

---

[1] *Les Congrégations* had been inaugurated by Farel in 1536.

a thousand people crowded into the cathedral in Geneva to listen to this frail, asthmatic man as he preached the word of God. He worked the word of God like a potter into the clay of God's people in Geneva, sometimes preaching ten times a week, perhaps forty minutes or more each time. Besides that, he gave three lectures on the Old Testament to students each week, went to Consistory meetings on Thursdays, and participated in the Congregation. (Imagine having Calvin at your group Bible study!)

Clearly Calvin's mind was always at work, always fertile. But his life was not only a constant round of sermon preparation, prayer, lectures, writing, and conferences. Earlier in his ministry life, in a note to Farel (1539), he wrote:

> When the present messenger wished to carry along with him the beginning of my book, there were still twenty leaves, which it required me to revise. In addition, there was the public lecture and I also had to preach; four letters were also to be written; some disputes to settle, and to reply to more than ten interruptions in the meantime. You will therefore excuse if my letter should be both brief and inaccurate.[1]

With such enormous pressure, it makes sense that several years later (1551), Calvin wrote to Heinrich Bullinger, 'I am so much exhausted by constant writing, and so greatly broken down by fatigue, that I frequently feel an almost positive aversion to writing a letter.' At that point, Calvin was given secretaries to take down his dictation.[2]

Space forbids further elaboration of the life of this remarkable man whom God raised up. Calvin was far from perfect. But often the measure of a man is to be assessed not so much by his height as by the obstacles he overcomes in order to grow. By that canon of assessment, Calvin was even more remarkable. During most of his ministry, he was a sick man. He suffered from malaria and tuberculosis; he also had a heart problem, gout, migraines, and kidney stones (the remedies being almost worse than the stones themselves). He had digestive problems and often suffered from insomnia. Yet Calvin was constantly critical of himself

[1] Calvin, *Letters*, I:132.
[2] *Ibid.*, II:304.

and his shortcomings. He lived physically and spiritually on the edge. At times he could be irritable. It was a wonderful reality, then, to this tightly wound man, living under such great pressure, that Jesus Christ was so kind.

That thought—the kindness of Christ—serves as a fitting reminder of Calvin's deep Christ-centredness. It would be difficult to exaggerate the extent to which this was true. He had found in Christ the wisdom, righteousness, sanctification, and redemption he needed. Indeed, he found all he needed in Christ, and urged others to search nowhere else. It is therefore not difficult to imagine that he may indeed have been involved in the writing of the only hymn (in distinction from metricized psalms) that has ever been attributed to him:

> I greet Thee, who my sure Redeemer art,
> My only trust and Saviour of my heart,
> Who pain didst undergo for my poor sake;
> I pray Thee from our hearts all cares to take.
>
> Thou art the King of mercy and of grace,
> Reigning omnipotent in every place;
> So come, O King, and our whole being sway;
> Shine on us with the light of Thy pure day.
>
> Thou art the life, by which alone we live,
> And all our substance and our strength receive;
> O comfort us in death's approaching hour,
> Strong-hearted then to face it by Thy power.
>
> Thou hast the true and perfect gentleness,
> No harshness hast Thou, and no bitterness;
> O grant to us the grace we find in Thee,
> That we may dwell in perfect unity.
>
> Our hope is in no other save in Thee;
> Our faith is built upon Thy promise free;
> Come, give us peace, make us so strong and sure,
> That we may conquerors be, and ills endure.

CHAPTER TWO

JOHN OWEN: PASTOR AND TEACHER

A pastor, a scholar, a divine of the first magnitude; holiness gave a divine lustre to his other accomplishments, it shined in his whole course, and was diffused through his whole conversation.[1]

—David Clarkson
Funeral Sermon for John Owen
September 4, 1683

THE year of his birth—1616—was the year of William Shakespeare's death.

On January 31, 1649, still only thirty-two, he preached before the English Parliament. It was not for the first time, but on this occasion, King Charles I had been publicly executed less than twenty-four hours before.

At the age of thirty-six, he was appointed to be vice-chancellor of the University of Oxford (in American terms, the president) by the English general and future Lord Protector Oliver Cromwell.

In 1662, along with around two thousand other ministers, he was ejected from the Church of England for refusing to conform to the use of the Book of Common Prayer in church services.

Thereafter, under the threat of arrest, he served as the pastor of Nonconformist congregations. During the last period of his life, he pastored a congregation in London.

---

[1] Peter Toon, *God's Statesman: The Life and Work of John Owen* (Exeter: Paternoster Press, 1971), p. 173.

He died in 1683, leaving behind him a legacy of writings that now occupy twenty-four large volumes, averaging around six hundred pages each.

His name was John Owen. In his own time, he was England's greatest living theologian. Now, more than three hundred years after his death, many still regard him as such. But who was he?

Early life

John Owen was born in Stadham (now Stadhampton), about ten miles southeast of Oxford. His father, Henry, was the minister of the local congregation.[1] He had an older brother, William (who also became a minister[2]), and two younger brothers, Henry (who entered the military) and Philemon (who was killed while on military duty in Ireland in 1649), and a sister whose name is unknown.[3]

The Owens were a Puritan family. 'I was bred up from my infancy under the care of my father', Owen wrote, 'who was a Nonconformist all his days, and a painful [hard-working] labourer in the vineyard of the Lord.'[4]

Scholars have long debated what constitutes a 'Puritan'. The term describes a wide variety of individuals, ranging from Anglicans who simply wanted to see the Church of England purified from some of its unbiblical features to individuals who, in their opposition to the Church of England, stood on the margins of Christian orthodoxy. Henry Owen, as his son John would later do, stood in the mainstream of biblical orthodoxy and was perhaps concerned only to see biblical guidelines

[1] Henry Owen later became minister at Harpsden, and he died there on September 18, 1649. He is buried in the chancel of the church.

[2] William was minister in Ewelme in Oxfordshire and died in 1660 at age 48.

[3] She married John Hartcliffe, minister of Harding in Oxfordshire and later canon of Windsor. He died in 1702.

[4] *The Works of John Owen*, ed. W. H. Goold, 24 vols (Edinburgh, 1850–53), XIII:224. Vols I-XVI were reprinted 1965–68, and vols XVIII-XXIV reprinted in 1991 (Edinburgh: Banner of Truth Trust). The reprint edition omits Owen's Latin works published in vol. XVII of the original Goold edition, and transfers to vol. XVI Owen's Posthumous Sermons (1854) and transfers Three Sacramental Discourses (1798) to vol. XVI:423-451. For convenience, subsequent references to Owen refer to the available reprint edition.

followed in the worship and governance of the church. In any event, he was a faithful gospel minister and father. As Calvin said of Timothy, so we could say of Owen: he 'sucked in godliness with his mother's milk'.[1]

Having received his early education from his father, when he was around ten years old, thanks to a generous uncle, both he and his elder brother, William, were sent to a small school in Oxford to prepare for entry to Queen's College in Oxford University.

Students at Oxford in the seventeenth century were by and large either gentlemen or scholars, but rarely both. In many ways, the university served as a kind of educational finishing school for the upper classes, many of whom would neither take exams nor graduate. Owen, however, entered the university with a view to study, and he graduated with a Bachelor of Arts alongside his brother in 1632, at age fifteen or sixteen. In essence, the Bachelor's degree was merely preparatory to the Master's degree studies that followed. He duly graduated with a Master of Arts in 1635.

Owen's education was classical: logic, philosophy, mathematics, ancient history, astronomy, Greek, and Hebrew. Latin was the *lingua franca* of the academic world (from college sermons to lectures and debates). Against that background, it is perhaps not surprising that Owen had as much facility in Latin as in English—indeed, perhaps more, since much of his written English scarcely masks its deep Latin influences.

Clearly, Owen benefited enormously from his studies. He had an outstandingly able academic tutor in Thomas Barlow.[2] And he did not neglect the Latin maxim *mens sana in corpore sano* (a healthy mind in a healthy body[3]). He ran, threw the javelin, and enjoyed playing the flute (he later appointed his teacher Thomas Wilson to the chair of music

---

[1] John Calvin, *Commentary on 2 Corinthians, 1 and 2 Timothy, Titus, Philemon*, ed. D. W. and T. F. Torrance, tr. T. A. Smail (Edinburgh: Oliver and Boyd, 1964), p. 292.

[2] Carl Trueman has underscored various ways in which Owen's education and thinking may have been directly influenced by Barlow (1607–91), who, although he conformed and became bishop of Lincoln, remained a lifelong friend of Owen. See Carl R. Trueman, *John Owen: Reformed Catholic, Renaissance Man* (Farnham: Ashgate, 2007), especially chapter 2.

[3] The expression appears to have been first used by the Roman satirist Juvenal, *Satires*, X.356.

in the university). Clearly, he was a serious student, and he disciplined himself to the extent that he often took only four hours of sleep.[1]

On graduation, Owen's intention was to engage in the prolonged studies required to attain the Bachelor of Divinity degree (then a seven-year programme). But Oxford University had fallen under influences alien to Owen's Puritan background. William Laud had been appointed university chancellor in 1630 en route to becoming archbishop of Canterbury some three years later. King Charles I had already forbidden debates on the Calvinistic themes of election and predestination, and Laud followed this through with the catholicizing of the ethos of college life and the reintroduction of high liturgy in chapel worship, all mingled with Arminian theology.

The signs did not look auspicious for a Puritan student in divinity, and after a further two years of study, Owen left to become family chaplain and tutor in the home of Sir Robert Dormer in Ascot, shortly thereafter accepting a similar position in the house of Lord Lovelace at Hurley. Here, presumably, his duties were not onerous, and he had leisure to continue his studies. Lord Lovelace, however, was a supporter of the king in his increasing conflict with Parliament, and in 1642, Owen moved on to take up residence in London.

New beginnings

The year Owen arrived in London, the English Civil War broke out.[2] Now in the capital, Owen was able to follow the crucial events of the day at first-hand. More important, however, was a more personal experience that was to change his life permanently.

By all accounts, Owen developed into a warm and genial individual. But he rarely gave himself away in his writings. If he kept journals, as

---

[1] Like others before and since, when in ill health in later life, Owen regretted the punishment he had given his physical resources as a younger man.

[2] The First and Second Civil Wars (1642–45 and 1648–49) were part of a prolonged conflict between the English Parliament and Charles I, and came to a climax with the execution of Charles on January 30, 1649. A Third Civil War (1649–51) saw the replacement of the monarchy by a Commonwealth (1649–53) and from 1653–59 by the protectorate of Oliver Cromwell. On the failure of Cromwell's son Richard, the monarchy was restored by the English Parliament in 1660.

many Puritans did, they were presumably destroyed at the time of his death. But what seems clear at this stage in his life—he was now in his mid-twenties—is that while he was committed to Puritan principles, he had no settled assurance that he belonged to Christ. On occasion in his published works, he gives scarcely veiled hints that he experienced deep spiritual distress.

One Sunday in 1642, he went with his cousin to hear the celebrated Presbyterian minister Edmund Calamy preach at St Mary's, Aldermanbury. But Calamy was unable to preach, and his substitute was a little-known minister. Despite his cousin's prompting, Owen had no heart to go elsewhere. As a result, he heard a sermon on Christ's words to the disciples after the calming of the storm: 'Why are you afraid, O you of little faith?'[1] He was immediately brought into a new sense of peace and assurance. The imagery of the text, as we shall see, would later echo throughout his writings.

Later that same year, he began his career as an author with the publication of a polemical work, *A Display of Arminianism*.[2] The book was dedicated to the Committee of Religion, which had begun its work as a kind of theological watchdog two years earlier. In turn, the Committee appointed him the following year to serve the church at Fordham in Essex.

Now settled in pastoral ministry, Owen met and married Mary Rooke, who would bear him eleven children, only one of whom survived into adulthood. By 1646, however, his ministry at Fordham came to an end. His original appointment had been the result of the sequestration of the previous incumbent. Now the appointment of his successor reverted to the original (and non-Puritan) patron.

But John Owen had already come to public attention. He had recently been invited to preach before Parliament.[3] Now he was appointed to serve the congregation of St Peter's, Coggeshall, also in the county of Essex.[4] This was a large congregation that had recently enjoyed the

[1] Matt. 8:26.
[2] In *Works*, X:1-137.
[3] On April 29, 1646. His sermon is reprinted in *Works*, VIII:2ff.
[4] On August 18, 1646.

distinguished ministry of Obadiah Sedgwick.[1] Here, Owen both ministered within the parish church and also gathered a fellowship along Congregationalist lines. His thinking had now developed from the more Presbyterian perspective he had earlier adopted when he had written *The Duty of Pastors and People Distinguished*[2] for his Fordham congregation.

Owen employed a wise and good principle whenever he thought through any controversial issue: he studied the strongest and best exposition of the view he opposed. In the case of church government, he had read the Congregationalist John Cotton's book *The Keyes of the Kingdom of Heaven* and found it convinced him.[3] His precise views in later life have been debated, but the indications are that he held to something like a loose form of Presbyterian-Congregationalism that both recognized that a congregation is the church in any particular place, yet, as such, wisely consults with other congregations in matters of common interest or concern.[4]

Stepping on to the national stage

As events in the Civil War began to move inexorably to their climax, Owen found himself further caught up into national life. At the same time, his career began to intersect with that of Oliver Cromwell, the charismatic general who would later rule as Lord Protector of the Commonwealth of England, Scotland, and Ireland.

In the summer of 1648, the nearby city of Colchester[5] was under siege by General Thomas Fairfax and the Parliamentarians' New Model Army. Owen was invited to preach to the troops[6] and became a personal friend

[1] Sedgwick (1600–58) had also been a student at Queen's College, Oxford, and would later serve as a member of the Westminster Assembly.

[2] In *Works*, XIII:3ff.

[3] John Cotton, who was minister in both Boston, Lincolnshire, and later in Boston, Massachusetts, was one of the most significant and influential figures in the Puritan brotherhood. Owen's account of his change in ecclesiology is found in *Works*, XIII:222-23.

[4] The author of the first (anonymous) memoir of Owen noted, 'I heard him say, before a person of quality and others, he could readily join with Presbytery as it was exercised in Scotland.' Cited in Andrew Thomson, *Life of Dr Owen*, in *Works*, I:xcviii.

[5] The towns are some ten miles apart.

[6] His sermons on Habakkuk 3:19 were later published as one under the title

of some of the officers, including Henry Ireton, Cromwell's son-in-law.[1] Step by step, Owen was becoming a public figure.

The next year, as we have seen, he preached before Parliament the day after Charles I's execution.[2] Rather than engaging in triumphalism, Owen instead preached on the call to humility and steadfastness in the face of suffering. Three months after that momentous occasion, he was invited to preach before Parliament once again,[3] with Cromwell in the congregation.

The following day, Owen visited the home of General Fairfax. While Owen waited to be seen, Cromwell and a number of his officers arrived. Recognizing Owen, Cromwell put his hand on his shoulder and said, 'Sir, you are the man I must be acquainted with.' Owen's (quick-thinking) response was to say, 'That will be much more to my advantage than to yours!' 'We shall soon see that!' Cromwell replied. He immediately invited Owen to join him in Ireland and to serve both as his chaplain and as a visitor to Trinity College, Dublin. Owen's younger brother, Philemon, already served in the army and persuaded him to accept the challenge.

Thus, Owen accompanied some twelve thousand psalm-singing soldiers in the New Model Army. Cromwell laid siege to the city of Drogheda, Ireland, which had become the focal point of resistance to the invading army. When the city refused to accept terms of surrender, Cromwell's army showed no quarter in taking it. Students of history have discussed and debated both the number of civilian casualties and the ethics of Cromwell's action ever since. Owen was almost certainly not an eyewitness of the event, but his intimate knowledge of it stirred him to both high eloquence and passionate appeal when he preached before Parliament on his return:

Ebenezer: A Memorial of the Deliverance of Essex County, and Committee, in *Works*, VIII:73.

[1] Owen would later preach his funeral sermon in 1651. See *Works*, VIII:345-63.

[2] Printed in *Works*, VIII:127-62. Owen has been both vilified and praised for his sermon. Perhaps the most striking feature of it is its total lack of specific reference to the events of the previous day. The sermon was, however, considered worthy to be publicly burned at Oxford on July 21, 1683, within weeks of his death.

[3] This sermon, 'The Shaking and Translating of Heaven and Earth', is found in *Works*, VIII:244ff.

> How is it that Jesus Christ is in Ireland only as a *lion staining all his garments with the blood of his enemies, and none to hold him out as a lamb sprinkled with his own blood to his friends?*

He pleaded with the Members of Parliament, that

> the Irish might enjoy Ireland so long as the moon endureth, so that Jesus Christ might possess the Irish. ... I would that there were for the present one gospel preacher for every walled town in the English possession in Ireland. The land mourneth, and the people perish for want of knowledge. ... The tears and cries of the inhabitants of Dublin after the manifestations of Christ are ever in my view.[1]

Later in 1649, Owen became an official preacher at the Palace of Whitehall,[2] and the following year he was with Cromwell again, this time on an expedition north of the border to subdue the Scots. Here Owen preached and debated repeatedly—on one occasion, according to local tradition, finding himself at least matched, if not bettered in discussion by the brilliant young theologian and minister Hugh Binning. Cromwell was sufficiently impressed to ask for his name, and discovering it was 'Binning' (which may have been pronounced more like 'Bunning'), he commented with a sharp pun, 'He hath *bound* well, indeed', and then, putting hand to sword, added, 'But *this* will *loose* all again!'[3]

Oxford and Cromwell—again

In 1651, Owen became dean of Christ Church, Oxford, and in September the following year (contrary to Owen's personal wishes), Cromwell appointed him the university's vice-chancellor (the executive head of the university). He preached regularly in his college and also on alternate Sundays with his friend Thomas Goodwin at St Mary's Church.[4] When

---

[1] *Works*, VIII:235-36. It seems that Owen's preaching had led to the conversion of some in Dublin.

[2] The royal residence in London during the sixteenth and seventeenth centuries.

[3] Hugh Binning (1627–53) was minister of Govan (now part of the city of Glasgow) and an outstandingly gifted thinker and preacher. Despite his short life, he left a remarkable collection of work, which was published posthumously.

[4] Both John Owen and Thomas Goodwin had been appointed heads of colleges (Goodwin of Magdalen [pronounced 'Modlin']), and both were awarded the degree of Doctor of Divinity in December 1653. Owen used the title Doctor reluctantly.

not preaching at St Mary's, he seems to have preached to familiar friends at Stadham.

It is to a sermon series from this period that we owe one of the books for which Owen is best known today, *On the Mortification of Sin.*[1] On reading this paperback-length book for the first time, most contemporary Christians are left feeling they have never read anything quite like it. That impression is deepened by the realization that Owen's profound spiritual analysis is simply the edited version of messages he had preached to a congregation composed, in large measure, of teenage students. Perhaps memories of his own earlier spiritual struggles underlined for him how important it is to go deep as early as possible. There are few things more important in the Christian life than learning to overcome sin.

We all have in our mind's eye a picture of a Puritan. It is often a distorted one.[2] Owen apparently did not resemble the dark misrepresentation. Indeed, the contemporary caricature of him—however overdrawn it may have been by his enemies—sought to demean him by drawing him in bright colours. According to Anthony Wood's famous description, he—

> instead of being a grave example to the university, scorned all formality, undervalued his office by going in quirpo like a young scholar, with powdered hair, snakebone bandstrings, lawn bands, a very large set of ribbons pointed at his knees, and Spanish leather boots with large lawn tops, and his hat mostly cock'd.[3]

Yet even Wood was forced to acknowledge, doubtless with a touch of cynicism:

In 1654, he represented Oxford in Parliament (he was presumably the best-qualified person to do so) but was forced to withdraw because he was an ordained clergyman. Presumably, as a Nonconformist and an academic rather than strictly speaking a pastor, Owen did not think of himself as governed by the regulation forbidding ministers from serving as Members of Parliament.

[1] *Works*, VI:1-86.

[2] For a helpful corrective, see Leland Ryken, *Worldly Saints* (Grand Rapids, Mich.: Zondervan, 1986).

[3] Anthony Wood, *Athenae Oxonienses* (London, 1691), 3rd ed., ed. Philip Bliss (London, 1813–20), IV, col. 98. Cited by Thomson, *Life of Dr Owen*, in *Works*, I:xlviii-xlix.

His personage was proper and comely and he had a very graceful behaviour in the pulpit, an eloquent elocution, a winning and insinuating deportment, and could, by the persuasion of his oratory … move and win the affection of his admiring auditory almost as he pleased.[1]

Oxford was in a state of disarray at the end of the Civil War. Five of the colleges were deserted; some had been used largely to quarter military personnel. Owen referred to 'the despised tears and sobs of our almost dying mother, the University'.[2] But his administration brought fresh life into the institution, new and distinguished faculty members, and a period in which a variety of influential students would pass through its corridors of learning.[3]

His major regret from his decade in academia seems to have been that his literary output was not greater. Yet it was during this time that he published several of his most substantial works, including *The Doctrine of the Saints' Perseverance* (1654)—in essence a book review of John Goodwin's Arminian treatise *Redemption Redeemed* but one that extends to some 666 pages in the Goold edition of his *Works*. In a steady stream of literary output, there followed his defence of orthodox Christianity against Socinianism[4] in *Vindiciae Evangelicae* (which he dedicated

---

[1] Wood. Cited by Toon, *God's Statesman*, p. 55.

[2] William Orme, *Memoirs of the Life, Writings, and Religious Connexions of John Owen, D.D.* (London, 1810), p. 170.

[3] Owen's Fifth Oration, delivered at the university convocation on October 9, 1657, is a wonderful testimony to both his Christian commitment and his administrative abilities. See *The Oxford Orations of Dr John Owen*, ed. Peter Toon (Callington: Gospel Communication, 1971), pp. 40-46. The list of students at Oxford during Owen's vice-chancellorship includes John Locke, the philosopher; William Penn, founder of Pennsylvania; Christopher Wren, the great architect of the rebuilding of London; Thomas Ken, author of 'The Doxology'; and many others, some of whom would lay the foundations for the Royal Society. Owen certainly held the view that Christians have a cultural mandate to explore God's creation.

[4] Socinianism was a sixteenth- and seventeenth-century form of what we today would call Unitarianism, named after two of its leaders, Lelio Sozzini (1525–62), who knew and corresponded with Calvin, and his nephew Fausto Sozzini (1539–1604). Socinianism developed particularly in Poland, and its leaders expressed their beliefs in *The Racovian Catechism* (1605). An English version was produced by John Biddle and published in 1652. The catechism was burned two years later under Cromwell's

to Cromwell, 1655), *Of the Mortification of Sin in Believers* (1656), *Of Communion with God the Father, Son and Holy Ghost* (1657), *Of Schism* (1657), and *Of Temptation: The Nature and Power of It* (1658). He must also have been working on his extensive Latin work *Theologoumena Pantodapa* (*Theology of All Kinds*, 1661).

The reasons for viewing himself as a literary 'under-achiever' were not sloth or indifference. As he himself hinted, much of his time was taken up with affairs of state. Not only was he called on to preach before Parliament and on other civic occasions, but he also served as one of the 'triers' charged with assessing fitness for gospel ministry, and was frequently consulted by both politicians and pastors, and by Cromwell in particular, on matters of national and ecclesiastical importance.[1] He served in a variety of ways as a 'negotiator and trouble-shooter'.[2]

Owen's star as vice-chancellor would, however, soon be on the wane. The Parliament that had held out so much hope to him of a nation led by genuinely Christian and Reformed leaders had, to his mind, grown spiritually tepid.

In particular, Owen was deeply troubled by and opposed to the proposals being aired in 1657 that Cromwell should become king. Cromwell was offered the throne earlier in the year and wrestled with the decision for a number of weeks thereafter. In early May, he seemed to be on the verge of accepting it when his son-in-law Charles Fleetwood, Thomas Pride (who had signed the death warrant for Charles

administration. Owen saw Socinianism as a major enemy of the gospel and especially expounded and defended the doctrine of the priesthood of Christ against it.

For the discussion of Owen's response to the Socinian rejection of the central importance of Christ's priestly ministry, see chapter 16.

[1] These gatherings included one convened by Cromwell himself to discuss the question of the legal residence of Jews in England. Cromwell, partly motivated by a desire for their conversion as well as their widely recognized business acumen, was in favour of allowing the Jews to remain. Owen shared Cromwell's understanding of Romans 11:25-32, although he resolutely declined to speculate on how it would take place. See *Works*, IV:440 and also XVIII:434 (this is vol. I of his Hebrews commentary).

Cromwell made a speech to the Council of State on December 4, 1655, on this subject that one hearer said was 'the best speech he ever made'. Antonia Fraser, *Cromwell, Our Chief of Men* (London: Weidenfeld and Nicolson, 1975), p. 565.

[2] For a full account, see Toon, *God's Statesman*, pp. 80-102.

I), and others approached him personally with their objections. They
called Owen into service in order to draw up a petition opposing his
enthronement, and Cromwell immediately declined the throne. This
marked the end of any royal aspirations Cromwell may have had. It also
marked the end of Owen's ease of access to him and influence on him.
More than a decade later, Owen was personally attacked by the Anglican
minister George Vernon in *A Letter to a Friend concerning Some of Dr
Owen's Principles and Practices* (1670). Accused of promising Cromwell
during his last illness that he would be raised up, Owen replied, 'I saw
him not in his sickness, nor in some long time before.'[1] Although not
involved in the installation of Cromwell as Lord Protector, he was
present at his funeral service.

Thus, Owen's leadership of the university as a whole came to an end
in 1657, although he remained as dean of Christ Church until the restoration of the monarchy in 1660.

Despite his differences with the Lord Protector, Owen's speech on
the occasion of the election of Cromwell's son, Richard, to the office of
chancellor of Oxford abounds in graciousness:

> There is no need to expatiate now on his [Oliver Cromwell's] merits
> or to recount his benefactions when all are eager to acknowledge
> their debt to him for all their blessings. ... Therefore, it is delib-
> erately that I refrain here from giving any formal appraisal of the
> wisest and most gallant of all the men whom this age, rich in heroes,
> has produced. In whatever direction England finally moves it will
> go down to the ages that she had a ruler who had the glory of this
> island and the respect for religion close to his heart.[2]

George Vernon also accused Owen of 'being the instrument in the
ruining of his [Oliver Cromwell's] son' and in the failure of the protectorate in which he followed his father. Owen was certainly close to a
group of men who shared a common desire for a republic rather than
a protectorate (corporately described as 'the Wallingford House Group'
because of their meeting place), but he denied the charge: 'with whose

---

[1] *Works*, XVI:273-74.
[2] Toon, ed., *The Oxford Orations of Dr John Owen*, p. 47.

[Richard Cromwell's] setting up and pulling down I had no more to do than himself.'[1]

In October 1658, during his closing years at Oxford, Owen participated in a gathering of representatives of around one hundred Independent churches meeting at the Savoy Palace in London. Here, as an expression of doctrinal unity—and to a degree as a defence against the often-expressed criticism that Independency, in advocating local congregational control and rejecting church hierarchies, was a form of sectarianism that wounded the church of Christ[2]—the Independents drew up a declaration of faith with a lengthy preface probably largely written by Owen.

In great measure, the *Savoy Declaration of Faith and Order* adopts the text of the *Westminster Confession of Faith* of 1647. Its most substantial changes were in its discussion of repentance (chapter 15); the addition of an entirely new chapter 20: 'Of the Gospel, and of the Extent of the Grace Thereof'; a rewriting of an entire section on the limits of the authority of the magistrate with respect to the church (chapter 24, section 3); and a new writing of sections 2 and 5 in the chapter on the church (chapter 26).

Perhaps the most interesting change in relation to our theme is the way in which chapter 2, 'Of God and of the Holy Trinity', was revised to conclude with these additional words, one of Owen's most profound convictions: 'Which doctrine of the Trinity is the foundation of all our communion with God, and comfortable dependence upon him.'[3]

The Restoration and the Ejection

After the execution of Charles I, Parliament abolished the monarchy and declared England to be a Commonwealth. But after Richard Crom-

---

[1] *Works*, XVI:274.

[2] When a copy of the declaration was presented to Richard Cromwell on October 14, 1658, Thomas Goodwin noted in his speech, 'We [desired] in the first place to clear ourselves of that scandal, which not only some persons at home, but of foreign parts, have affixed upon us, viz. that Independentism (as they call it) is the sink of all Heresies and Schisms.' Quoted by A. G. Matthews in his introduction to *The Savoy Declaration of Faith and Order 1658*, ed. A. G. Matthews (London: Independent Press, 1959), p. 12.

[3] Matthews, p. 79.

well failed to continue his father's success as Lord Protector, Parliament removed him and restored the monarchy in 1660. King Charles II, son of the king whom Parliament had executed, was crowned on April 23, 1661, at Westminster Abbey.

The Restoration ushered in difficult times for Owen and his fellow Nonconformists. A new religious settlement was now put in place and undergirded by the acts of the Clarendon Code, which placed heavy restrictions on Nonconformists:

- The Corporation Act of 1661 prohibited Nonconformists from holding civic office.

- The Act of Uniformity of 1662 excluded them from office in the church. This act led to the expulsion of some two thousand ministers from the Church of England, the event known as the Great Ejection.

- The Conventicle Act of 1662 made Nonconformist meetings illegal.

- The Five Mile Acts of 1665 prohibited Nonconformist ministers from living within five miles of any place where they had once ministered.[1]

Owen declined to conform, and thus, his service to the University of Oxford was brought to an end. He withdrew to his small estate at Stadhampton and sought to continue to minister to gathered groups of believers there and elsewhere, in contravention of the law. He did not lack opportunities to conform (he may well have been offered a bishopric) or to serve elsewhere (he was invited to follow John Cotton at the First Congregational Church of Boston, Massachusetts). He remained with others who suffered for the sake of their convictions. While not exposed to the same privations as some of his brethren, Owen and his family found it necessary to move from one house to another where they would be protected guests. For a man who had grown accustomed to the corridors of power, these must have been days of profound humiliation.

[1] The Clarendon Code was named after Edward Hyde, Lord Clarendon, the lord chancellor during whose administration its various laws were enacted, although he was not directly responsible for them. Cf. J. P. Kenyon, *Stuart England*, 2nd ed. (London: Penguin Books, 1985), pp. 215-16.

In 1665, England experienced the most severe outbreak of plague since the Black Death struck Europe in the fourteenth century. In London, about fifteen percent of the population died, including more than seven thousand in one fateful week. The plague finally ended in 1666, which was also the year of the Great Fire of London. These events were thought by many to be a divine judgment for the treatment of the Nonconformists. In any event, Owen joined many of his Puritan brethren in ministering to the needy in the city. He took this opportunity to plead for toleration in his works *Indulgence and Toleration Considered* and *A Peace Offering* (both published in 1667). He continued to work behind the scenes to secure relief for his fellow Independents. Indeed, on one occasion, he was forced to defend his actions for receiving a considerable sum of money from the Duke of York (a Roman Catholic) to alleviate the privation of suffering Dissenters. Although arrested or close to arrest on a number of occasions, he was never imprisoned.

Owen knew and greatly esteemed the suffering 'Tinker-Preacher' John Bunyan, and indeed appears to have been the go-between to make arrangements for his own publisher, Nathaniel Ponder, to publish Bunyan's great work *The Pilgrim's Progress*. According to both Bunyan's and Owen's biographers, the king once asked Owen why he so appreciated an uneducated tinker like Bunyan, to which he replied, 'Could I possess the tinker's abilities for preaching, please your majesty, I would gladly relinquish all my learning.'[1]

Faithful to the end

In 1673, the little congregation to which Owen privately ministered united with the church fellowship of which the Westminster divine Joseph Caryl had been pastor. During this last decade of Owen's life, his time would be spent writing, preaching, and giving counsel. His first wife, Mary, died in 1675. He was married again eighteen months later, to Michel, the widow of one Thomas D'Oyley. Her companionship must have filled a great void in his life and at the same time brought much comfort in days of ongoing sickness.

Throughout these years, Owen suffered from severe asthma and gallstones, and at times was too sick to preach. He nevertheless continued

---

[1] Toon, *God's Statesman*, p. 162.

to publish (almost two dozen items issued from his pen during this last decade). Even in his dying months, he was working on what by any reckoning is a classic work of theology filled with spiritual sensitivity and personal devotion, *Meditations and Discourses on the Glory of Christ.*[1] No account of his life, however brief, would be complete without including a section of the letter he wrote to his friend Charles Fleetwood on the day before his death, and a conversation he had with a colleague on the next morning. To Fleetwood he wrote:

> I am going to Him whom my soul hath loved, or rather who hath loved me with an everlasting love; which is the whole ground of all my consolation. The passage is very irksome and wearysome through strong pains of various sorts which are all issued in an intermitting fever. All things were provided to carry me to London today attending to the advice of my physician, but we were all disappointed by my utter disability to undertake the journey.
>
> I am leaving the ship of the church in a storm, but whilst the great Pilot is in it the loss of a poore under-rower will be inconsiderable. Live and pray and hope and doe not despair; the promise stands invincible that he will never leave thee nor forsake thee.[2]

How fitting that in almost his last recorded words there should be a final appearance of imagery from the text that had brought him into the assurance of Christ he had now long enjoyed!

The next day, he confirmed his sense of assurance with even greater force when William Payne,[3] a minister from Saffron Waldon, visited to tell him that his *Meditations on the Glory of Christ* was at that very hour going to press. The dying Owen's response was memorable: 'I am glad to hear it; but O brother Payne! the long-wished-for day is come at last, in which I shall see that glory in another manner than I have ever done, or was capable of doing in this world.'[4]

By the evening of that day, August 24, 1683, St Bartholomew's Day—twenty-one years after the ejection of two thousand ministers from the

---

[1] *Works*, I:273-415.

[2] Peter Toon, *Correspondence of John Owen* (Lutterworth: James Clarke, 2000), p. 174.

[3] Biographers differ on Payne's Christian name. Orme gives it as Thomas (p. 448).

[4] Thomson, *Life of Dr Owen*, in *Works*, I:ciii.

Church of England in 1662, and on the anniversary of the St Bartholomew's Day Massacre of 1572, when between five thousand and thirty thousand French Protestants were slaughtered—John Owen was with Christ. On the 4th of September, followed by a long line of stately carriages, his body was taken to Bunhill Fields, the Nonconformist burial ground then just outside the City of London. There, with the mortal remains of friends and fellow labourers in Christ—John Bunyan, David Clarkson (once his assistant), his friend Charles Fleetwood, and many others—the dust of John Owen, pastor of Christ's flock, preacher of Christ's gospel, teacher of Christ's universal church, awaits the glory of the resurrection.

There can be no doubt, for all his massive intellect and prodigious self-discipline (how does one man write twenty-four volumes using seventeenth-century writing materials?), that the secret of Owen's life lay not in his natural gifts but in his deep devotion to God—Father, Son, and Holy Spirit. Perhaps the summary of his life that most matched his own aspirations is found in these words from a defence of Owen's character and work, *Vindication of Owen by a Friendly Scrutiny*.

> His general frame was serious, cheerful, and discoursive, his expressions savouring nothing of discontent, much of heaven and love to Christ, and saints, and all men; which came from him so seriously and spontaneously, as if grace and nature were in him reconciled, and but one thing.

To this day, the words of Thomas Gilbert's epitaph can be found on his gravestone:

> *Et, missis Caeteris, Coluit ipse, Sensitque,*
> *Beatam quam scripsit, cum Deo Communionem*

> And, disregarding other things, he cherished and experienced
> That blessed communion with God about which he wrote.

CHAPTER THREE

JOHN MURRAY: TEACHER OF PASTORS

JOHN MURRAY'S life spanned the first three-quarters of the twentieth century. Born on October 14, 1898, and reared on a Scottish highland croft near Bonar Bridge, he can also be numbered among those who 'drank in godliness with his mother's milk' (to use words from John Calvin of which he would have approved). His father, Alexander Murray, a member of the Free Presbyterian Church of Scotland, set before him a lasting example of true Christian manhood. Following his father's death in 1942, John wrote: 'There were few men in the Highlands of Scotland whose life and memory were surrounded by such fragrance, and whose life of consistent godliness claimed such veneration and respect. To be his son is a great privilege but also a tremendous responsibility.'[1] Alexander Murray was the embodiment of the catechetical teaching John received in childhood, especially the principle that 'to glorify God and to enjoy him for ever' is the chief end of man.

Educated locally at Bonar Bridge Primary School and then at Dornoch Academy, John Murray enlisted towards the end of World War I (April 1917) in the Royal Highlanders (Black Watch). Serving in France in 1918, he was struck by shrapnel during the last German offensive and permanently lost sight in his right eye. Honourably discharged, he entered the University of Glasgow the following year and graduated with a Master of Arts in 1923.

Murray's desire was to enter the ministry of his own denomination. The Free Presbyterian Church did not maintain a theological seminary, but used the old tutorial method of ministerial training. Happily for

[1] Iain H. Murray, *The Life of John Murray* (Edinburgh: Banner of Truth Trust, 1984), p. 82.

the Christian church at large, Murray's tutor was the wise and able Donald Beaton of Wick, who, recognizing his new student's academic prowess, made the very unusual suggestion that he be sent to Princeton Theological Seminary with a view to future service as a theological tutor in the Free Presbyterian Church.

Thus Murray enrolled at Princeton in 1924, doubtless without a clue as to the way in which the seminary's impending crisis would affect his whole future. The older emphases on Reformed orthodoxy and experiential piety, exemplified in Charles Hodge and B. B. Warfield, no longer stood unquestioned in the wider seminary constituency. Indeed, J. Gresham Machen had written that Old Princeton had died with Warfield in 1921. Nevertheless, the presence of Caspar Wistar Hodge, Oswald T. Allis, Geerhardus Vos, and Machen on the faculty must have thrilled the young Scot, even if Machen's recently published *Christianity and Liberalism* (1923) already hinted at the division that would soon take place.

Murray was an outstanding student. The *Princeton Seminary Bulletin* would later say, 'Few students have maintained as high a level of scholarship as did Mr Murray during his seminary course.' He graduated in 1927 and returned to Scotland, still with the expectation of entering the pastoral ministry.

The way ahead was, however, blocked by a disagreement over the use of public transport on the Lord's Day. Murray did not believe that his church had the right to bar from the Lord's Table anyone who used public transport in order to attend worship on Sunday. So, instead of proceeding to ordination, he took advantage of the Gelston-Winthrop Scholarship he had been awarded at Princeton to do postgraduate study at New College, Edinburgh. While there, he received an invitation from Caspar Wistar Hodge to serve on the faculty at Princeton. This he agreed to do for the year 1929–30, little realizing that by the time of his arrival Machen, Allis, Robert Dick Wilson, and soon Cornelius Van Til, along with some fifty students, would have begun Westminster Theological Seminary in Philadelphia, determined to maintain the biblical orthodoxy of the Old Princeton tradition. (The fact that the neo-orthodox Emil Brunner would later come as a guest professor to succeed Hodge and then be invited to remain permanently simply confirmed the conviction that a theological drift was under way.)

The following year (1930) Murray himself moved to Westminster, where he was to spend the greater part of the rest of his life as a professor of systematic theology, first in the seminary's mid-city location on property owned by Allis (a stark contrast to the Scottish croft!), and thereafter in the pleasant surroundings of the suburban campus on the northern outskirts of Philadelphia. Here he stood with Machen following his dismissal from the Presbyterian ministry and he assisted him in both his private and public ministries. One of Machen's last acts before dying suddenly on January 1, 1937 was to send his younger colleague a telegram alluding to a topic which they had discussed at length and on which Murray's thinking had profoundly influenced him. It read: 'I'm so thankful for the active obedience of Christ. No hope without it.'[1]

Murray now committed himself to the Orthodox Presbyterian Church, which Machen had been instrumental in founding, and was ordained in 1937. His evangelistic concern found expression in his service as chairman of the committee for the propagation of the Reformed faith in New England and his decade-long work as secretary of the committee of local evangelism. The same concern led him to conduct Bible studies on board ship whenever he travelled between the United States and his home country.

As a professor Murray employed (and was deeply committed to) the lecture method. While he deplored self-assurance, in his final report to the seminary's accrediting association (perhaps with a view to antici-pated criticism of his old-fashioned pedagogy, which allowed little time for questions and class discussion), he hinted that if his lectures, which reflected thirty years of teaching experience, were not already answering his students' questions, they were probably not asking the right questions. He believed that the lecture method helped students to feel the weight and authority of biblical doctrine, and that the exercise of thinking and writing that was involved in recording notes aided the process of learning.

[1] I. H. Murray, *Life of John Murray*, p. 64.

Murray's students remember the sense of *gravitas* which characterized his presence in the lecture room, yet both his prayers and his teaching were also marked by a rich and lively verbal animation. While, no doubt, his piety and manner might have seemed austere, even severe to some, no one who knew him failed to recognize what could only be called a serious joy and an energy for the gospel which commanded both respect and admiration. The affection in which he was held is perhaps best illustrated by the answer which new students always received when they inquired which was the glass eye—'It's the one that has a twinkle.'

John Murray's influence on his students was profound, particularly his model of combining exegetical care with biblico-theological insights in expounding systematic theology. His wider ministry, largely in writing, may be dated from the 1950s, when a steady stream of influential works flowed from his pen. It was characteristic of his reticence that his publications date from his sixth and seventh decades. Several of these works remain standard studies and required reading in their field.

A bachelor throughout the whole of his seminary ministry, in 1966 Murray was heard to say on the Westminster campus (no doubt to the astonishment of some of his hearers, for more than one reason!): 'If I marry in the next year, I will be younger than my grandfather was at his marriage.' And this was precisely what he did, marrying a longtime friend, Valerie Knowlton, who had been a student at Westminster in the 1950s. Having earned a doctorate at Harvard, she became a professor of anatomy at the Woman's Medical College of Pennsylvania. Settling in Scotland on the family croft, they had two children, the second of whom was to survive her father by only a few months.

On his retirement and return to Scotland in 1966, Murray was free to engage in an extensive speaking ministry throughout the United Kingdom. He served as a speaker in churches, at Inter-Varsity gatherings, and perhaps most notably in a regular ministry at the increasingly significant Leicester Ministers' Conference, which was organized by the Banner of Truth Trust, of which he was a trustee.

In his last years, Murray was asked to take pastoral oversight of the Free Church of Scotland congregation at Ardgay, some two miles from his home. Thus, to his great joy, at the end of his life came a taste of the work which in earlier years he had assumed would dominate the whole of it. Now an internationally respected theologian and author, he found his highest joy in expounding God's word to the congregation of some two dozen people who gathered with him on the Lord's Day.

In 1975, cancer was diagnosed. According to his biographer, Murray bore his terminal illness with Christian grace and with the qualities which had marked his long Christian life:

> We do not know how many copies of the Greek New Testament John Murray wore out—he left several in that condition among his books—but in the last one which he used he had written inside the covers in the closing weeks of his life:
>
> > O Lord, all that I do desire
> > is still before thine eye,
> > And of my heart the secret groans
> > not hidden are from thee.[1]

He died in faith on May 8, 1975. As Cornelius Van Til, his colleague of thirty years, was later to comment, 'Humble boldness marked John's every doing.'

A systematic and biblical theologian

John Murray came to be widely regarded as one of the most significant orthodox Reformed theologians of his generation in the English-speaking world. Reared, as we have seen, in the Calvinistic theology and piety which flourished in the Reformed congregations of highland Scotland, he had a profound sense of the majesty of God, human depravity, and the glories of the person and work of Christ. From childhood he had been taught to think both biblically and systematically about these truths. At Princeton, under Hodge, Machen, and particularly Geerhardus Vos (who had himself taught dogmatic theology prior to his appointment as Princeton's first professor of biblical theology),[2] these skills had been fine-tuned to prepare him to make important contributions to the expo-

[1] I. H. Murray, *Life of John Murray*, p. 156. The stanza quoted is the *Scottish Psalter* rendering of Psa. 38:9.
[2] See Richard B. Gaffin Jr, ed., *Redemptive History and Biblical Interpretation: The Shorter Writings of Geerhardus Vos* (Phillipsburg, NJ: P&R, 1980), pp. ix-xxiii.

sition, defence, and development of the Reformed faith. Indebted to the theology of Calvin (in which he was an expert) and to the Puritan tradition, best represented by John Owen, Murray's work is reminiscent of both: it marries theology with spirituality in such a way that the latter suffuses the former and is not merely an *addendum* to it; and it combines careful scholarly exegesis with a theological systematizing which advances the understanding of Christian truth. Evidence of this is his commentary on Romans, which, at least in length and period of preparation, is his *magnum opus*.

Like Warfield, whom he so admired, Murray's contribution lies in his exposition of and insight into aspects of theology, elements in the individual *loci*, rather than in a lengthy systematic presentation of the whole. Doubtless his respect for Charles Hodge and his three-volume *Systematic Theology*, and the fact that Warfield himself had not produced such a work, made Murray reluctant to engage in that task himself. In retrospect, we may also note that in some respects Murray represents a transition in the method of Reformed systematics, highlighting the role of biblical theology and demonstrating its applications rather than producing a comprehensive treatise. This new emphasis is evident both in the amount of exegetical work in which he engaged as he forged doctrine, and in his understanding of the nature and task of systematic theology.

While Murray (apparently to his regret)[1] did not give extensive attention to questions of prolegomena and methodology, he did publish two seminal essays in 1963 in the *Westminster Theological Journal* (of which he had been a founding editor in 1938). Here he crystallized the core of his thinking: 'The task of systematic theology is to set forth in orderly and coherent manner the truth respecting God and his relations to men and the world. This truth is derived from the data of revelation.'[2] This meant not only that theology, when interpreting the universe, must regard the general revelation as well as the special inscripturated

---

[1] I owe this information to Murray's colleague the late Robert D. Knudsen, professor of apologetics at Westminster Seminary.

[2] John Murray, *Collected Writings*, 4 vols (Edinburgh: Banner of Truth Trust, 1976–83), IV:1. For the convenience of the reader, citations from Murray are, wherever possible, taken from this collection.

revelation as normative, but also that systematic theology, with its logical method, must be informed by biblical theology, which deals with the same data (special revelation), but from the standpoint of the historical. Here Murray's guiding light was the Dutch-American Geerhardus Vos, who had taught him at Princeton and whom he later described as 'the most penetrating exegete it has been my privilege to know'.

In many ways Vos had been ahead of his time in his pioneering work in biblical theology and especially in his appreciation of the significance of the eschatological for understanding the apostolic message. Vos had emphasized the epochal character of the overall structure of special revelation, and the principles of continuity, accumulation, and advance that are evident therein. Systematic theology needed to take note of and be informed by this. Thus Murray argued that systematic theology is rooted in biblical exegesis, but also that 'biblical theology is regulative of exegesis. It coordinates and synthesizes the whole witness of Scripture in the various topics with which it deals.'[1] Murray's approach to every theological *locus* and issue was determined by these principles. Though he was well aware of the advances in the area of the history of ideas, his own contributions, when not specifically historical-theological in character, were heavily freighted with biblical exegesis and theology. It is noteworthy that when Ned B. Stonehouse, the first editor of the *New International Commentary* series, allotted the volume on Romans, he approached John Murray, who so obviously possessed the necessary exegetical tools and skills.

The biblical doctrine of Scripture

Against this background it is not surprising that Murray gave special attention to the unfolding of the biblical doctrine of Scripture, rejecting the neo-orthodox supposition that Scripture is not itself the word of God, but only becomes so by the special action of God when it is heard or read. Scripture, in the neo-orthodox view, was simply the witness to the word of God. Following Warfield's weighty defence of the orthodox doctrine of inspiration and authority, Murray contended against the theory of limited inspiration as well as the romantic notion of inspiration, and

---

[1] Murray, *Collected Writings*, IV:19.

for 'the view entertained of Scripture by our Lord and his apostles'.[1] On the basis of passages such as 2 Timothy 3:16 and 2 Peter 1:16-21 he argued that all the revelation that God inspires reflects his own qualities of reliability. That this was Jesus' view Murray demonstrated by referring to such passages as Matthew 26:53-54; Luke 24:25-27; and John 10:33-36, which he saw as evidence of our Lord's 'attitude of meticulous acceptance and reverence'.[2]

While Murray recognized that, technically, the New Testament references he cited have the Old Testament canon in view, he employed a threefold argument to confirm the equal applicability of plenary inspiration to the New Testament:

(1) the greater glory of the New Testament required a no less plenary and real inspiration for the New than for the Old;

(2) the New Testament writers give evidence of a consciousness of divine authority (e.g., 1 Cor. 2:10-13; 14:37, 38; 2 Thess. 3:12-14); and

(3) the New Testament writers refer to other parts of the New Testament in the same way they refer to the Old (e.g., 2 Pet. 3:15-16).

Reject these considerations, and the view of biblical authority which is implied by them, Murray argued, and it becomes logically impossible to appeal to the Scripture as reliably authoritative on other subjects. If it is fallible in its teaching on its own nature, it cannot be relied on when it speaks of the nature of things (or people) other than itself. Note that Murray did not say that Scripture would therefore be useless, but simply that it would no longer be reliable.[3] He insisted that Scripture must provide its own guidelines for the way in which its infallibility or inerrancy (terms he regarded as theologically synonymous) is to be understood: 'artificial and pedantic canons of errancy or inerrancy' he resisted:

---

[1] Murray, *Collected Writings*, IV:42-43. Significantly, Murray devoted his inaugural lecture as professor of systematic theology (Nov. 16, 1939) to the topic of inspiration.

[2] *Ibid.*, IV:47.

[3] *Ibid.*, IV:56.

We may not impose upon the Bible our own standards of truth-fulness or our own notions of right and wrong. It is easy for propo-nents of inerrancy to set up certain canons of inerrancy which are arbitrarily conceived and which prejudice the whole question from the outset. And it is still easier for the opponents of inerrancy to set up certain criteria in terms of which the Bible could readily be shown to be in error. Both attempts must be resisted. This is just saying that we must think of inerrancy concretely and our criterion of inerrancy must be divested of the *a priori* and often mechanical notions with which it is associated in the minds of many people, particularly those who are hostile to the doctrine.[1]

The 'jot and tittle' inerrancy of which Jesus speaks (Matt. 5:18), Murray added, needs to be understood aright:

> He is not speaking of jot and tittle inspiration in abstraction, for the simple reason that what represents a jot is no longer a jot if it exists in abstraction. ... Jesus is thinking of jot and tittle in construction and combination with relevant words, clauses and phrases.[2]

Thus, Murray contends, 'it is not with words in abstraction that we are concerned, but with words in relationship'.[3] Careful exegesis done in the light of biblical theology will alone determine what inerrancy means *in concreto*.

Murray further argued that the doctrine of inerrancy is a continu-ation of and consistent with the teaching of the Reformers and especially Calvin. One of the great controversies evoked by the neo-orthodoxy which had encroached on twentieth-century Presbyterianism was the question of the degree to which seventeenth-century Protestant orthodoxy had continued the teaching of Calvin. If Reformed orthodoxy was a distortion at this point, it, of course, could no longer claim to be a true heir of the Reformation. Here, in expounding Calvin, the exegetical care and mastery of the text which marked Murray's exposition of Scripture stood him in good stead. Over against the contentions of Charles A. Briggs and others that Calvin, Luther, and other Reformers

[1] Murray, *Collected Writings*, IV:26.
[2] *Ibid.*, IV:25.
[3] *Ibid.*, IV:28.

recognized errors in the Scriptures,[1] Murray denied that this was Calvin's position either in general or on particular details. Calvin did indeed speak of 'mistakes' in regard to the text of Scripture; but, as Murray was able to demonstrate, in such cases the Reformer had in view the matter of textual transmission, not accuracy of content. Calvin also fully recognized the difficulties and even apparent tensions within Scripture. Sometimes Murray regarded the Genevan Reformer's resolutions of these problems as 'ill advised'.[2] But the very manner in which Calvin sought such resolutions was, as Murray recognized, an indication of his conviction of Scripture's inerrancy.

Continuity with Calvin is also evident in Murray's view of the Holy Spirit's role in attesting Scripture. Contrary to neo-orthodoxy, Murray, with Calvin, argued that the internal testimony of the Spirit does not give authority to Scripture, but witnesses to the authority Scripture already inherently possesses. The Spirit does not affect Scripture, but those who read and hear it. The difference between these two positions Murray regarded as 'the most important cleavage within Protestantism today'.[3] Against the view that it is 'the ever-recurring act of God that is the authority-constituting fact', Murray argued that Scripture's authority rests on its God-breathed quality, on its divine authorship. This is a finished activity, of which the Spirit's ongoing testimony convinces our darkened minds. Here Murray stood in the great tradition of Calvin and Owen, applying to the threat which he saw emerging to biblical Christianity in his own day the biblical teaching they had recognized and utilized in their day.

In connection with the doctrine of Scripture (and indeed all doctrines), Murray stressed that theology is a creaturely activity. When we have stretched our intellectual powers to their capacity, our

---

[1] For Briggs's contention see Murray, *Collected Writings*, IV:159; Briggs has, of course, been followed by Calvin scholars since his day, but by no means all Calvin experts subscribe to his position. Indeed, Murray's view also enjoys a good deal of support.

[2] *Ibid.*, IV:175.

[3] John Murray, 'The Attestation of Scripture', in *The Infallible Word*, ed. Ned B. Stonehouse and Paul Woolley, 3d rev. ed. (Philadelphia: Presbyterian and Reformed, 1967), p. 43.

heightened understanding of revelation discloses as well our limitations. Our inability to solve all the problems connected with the doctrine of Scripture must be viewed in this light. Here the knowability and the incomprehensibility of God, the former a divine attribute, the latter essentially a limiting concept, coalesce. For Murray, standing on the high tower of revelation, the realization of our inadequacy led primarily to adoring worship. The very nature of Scripture served as a reminder that God is God:

> It must be freely admitted that there are difficulties connected with the doctrine of biblical infallibility. ... The conscientious student has ... great difficulty sometimes in resolving problems raised by apparent contradictions....
>
> It might seem that this confession of ... inability to resolve seeming discrepancy is not compatible with faith in Scripture as infallible. This is, however, at the best, very superficial judgment. There is no doctrine of our Christian faith that does not confront us with unresolved difficulties here in this world, and the difficulties become all the greater just as we get nearer to the centre. It is in connection with the most transcendent mysteries of our faith that the difficulties multiply. The person who thinks he has resolved all the difficulties surrounding our established faith in the Trinity has probably no faith in the triune God. The person who encounters no unresolved mystery in the incarnation of the Son of God and his death on Calvary's tree has not yet learned the meaning of 1 Timothy 3:16. Yet these unanswered questions are not incompatible with unshaken faith in the triune God and in Jesus Christ, the incarnate Son. The questions are often perplexing. But they are more often the questions of adoring wonder rather than the questions of painful perplexity.
>
> So there should be no surprise if faith in God's inerrant word should be quite consonant with unresolved questions and difficulties with regard to the content of this faith.[1]

---

[1] Murray, 'The Attestation of Scripture', in *The Infallible Word*, pp. 7-8.

Theological monographs

The Covenant of Grace

Reformed theology is covenantal in character. Indeed, according to Warfield, covenant theology is the 'architectonic principle' of the *Westminster Confession*. This is the theology in which Murray had been nourished since childhood. It is not surprising, therefore, that he would explore the biblical and historical materials which undergird it.

Murray's 1954 publication *The Covenant of Grace* bore the subtitle *A Biblico-Theological Study*, which indeed it was. In it he traced the nature of the divine covenants in Scripture, distancing himself in the process from the tendency in scholastic Reformed theology to define 'covenant' as a compact or agreement, and arguing instead that in Scripture a covenant is 'a sovereign administration of grace and promise'.[1] In view of the present-day interest in the scriptural concept of covenant, it may be difficult for the coming generation of students to appreciate the degree to which this slim monograph proved to be a significant landmark. For two decades it served as the basic evangelical work on the doctrine of the covenant. In its own way it set a new standard for the use of biblical theology in systematic theology.

Murray's exposition was innovative in several ways. His starting point was not a comparison with the compacts or contracts of seventeenth-century mercantilism, but the biblical use of the term *berith* ('covenant'). Accordingly, he insisted that the highly charged question of whether the covenant was conditional or unconditional could not be resolved 'without a reorientation in terms of a revised definition of the biblical concept of covenant'.[2] Furthermore, his view that in Scripture divine covenants were restorative in nature inevitably raised the question of whether Reformed orthodoxy's description of the relationship between God and Adam as covenantal is accurate. Murray's response was to reject the term 'covenant of works'.

[1] John Murray, *The Covenant of Grace* (London: The Tyndale Press, 1954), p. 30. It is of interest that the biblical and historical doctrine of the covenant had been the subject of Vos's rectoral address at the Theological School of the Christian Reformed Church (now Calvin Seminary); see Gaffin, ed., *Redemptive History*, pp. 234-67.

[2] Murray, *Collected Writings*, IV:217.

The Imputation of Adam's Sin

While rejecting the classic Reformed terminology, preferring the expression 'Adamic administration' to 'covenant of works', Murray nevertheless held firmly to the classic doctrine that the sin of Adam was imputed to all of his posterity. This issue had figured largely in American Presbyterianism, and had been a topic of special interest to the Hodges. Murray in fact took Caspar Wistar Hodge's course on the doctrine of imputation and would himself address the subject directly during a sabbatical leave in 1955 and 1956. The fruit of his studies appeared in 1956 and 1957 in a series of articles in the *Westminster Theological Journal*. These were later published as *The Imputation of Adam's Sin*.[1]

Against the background of previous debate and discussion, Murray set forward his own understanding of Romans 5:12-21. This passage, he argued, requires the doctrine of the immediate imputation of Adam's sin to all of his posterity. Murray offered four proofs:

(1) the immediate conjunction of the sin of Adam and the death of all (verses 12, 15, 17);

(2) the immediate conjunction of the sin of Adam and the condemnation of all (verses 16, 18);

(3) the immediate conjunction of the sin of Adam and the sin of all (verses 12, 19); and

(4) the nature of the analogy between Christ and Adam.

The Imputation of Adam's Sin, which in some respects espouses a view somewhat different from that of Charles Hodge, is generally recognized as Murray's most difficult work. The reason is not the abstruseness of his style, but the depth to which he penetrates the logic of the Pauline teaching in Romans 5, so alien to the twentieth-century Western mind, and therefore not amenable to easy analysis. The essence of Paul's teaching lies in two of its emphases: on the one hand, the plight of sinful humanity, and, on the other, the nature of the atonement (which

---

[1] John Murray, *The Imputation of Adam's Sin* (Grand Rapids: Eerdmans, 1959). This material may have been prepared in conjunction with the first volume of his commentary on Romans, which appeared the following year.

is actually the reversal of what took place in Adam). Murray is deeply sensitive to the fact that Romans 5:12-21 highlights the latter. He recognizes that the passage sheds light not only on atonement as obedience, but also on the inseparability of justification and sanctification, for both are based on union with Christ—a point that Murray was at constant pains to emphasize.

Redemption—Accomplished and Applied

The emphasis of Reformed theology on divine sovereignty in salvation is often attributed exclusively to the nature of its doctrine of God. But to do so is to ignore the crucial factor of anthropology. Like Calvin, Murray recognized that divine sovereignty in salvation is necessitated by the nature and effect of human sin. Since in Adam we are spiritually dead and altogether incapable of spiritual good, we can neither achieve salvation through obedience, nor come to faith by a decision of our own will in its natural condition. Here Murray concurred heartily with the *Westminster Confession* that 'man, by his fall into a state of sin, hath wholly lost all ability of will to any spiritual good accompanying salvation' (IX.3).

To be sure, Murray believed that fallen humans possess the power of *alternative* choice (i.e., they are able to choose between A and B). He vigorously contested, however, the view common in nineteenth- and twentieth-century evangelicalism that *with respect to salvation* the human will is free in the sense of possessing the power of contrary choice (i.e., free to choose the spiritually good rather than the spiritually evil). Murray's point is that, in whatever we choose, we are 'under an unholy necessity of sinning'.[1] Inability to choose spiritual good is not a denial of free agency, Murray argued, but rather the tragic form free agency takes in sinners. We act in keeping with our character and without any absolute compulsion from the outside. Such is our depraved nature that we are necessarily incapable of willing that which pleases God or of willing in a manner that pleases him. Therefore, we are dependent on the sovereign activity of God not only for the objective provision of redemption, but also for its subjective reception.

[1] Murray, *Collected Writings*, II:64.

To expound what is central to these themes, Murray penned his most popular and widely read study, *Redemption—Accomplished and Applied*. Here he distilled his understanding of the work of Christ and its implications. While it has been commonplace to employ the concepts of sacrifice, propitiation, reconciliation, and redemption in expounding the work of Christ, Murray believed that the concept of obedience 'supplies us with an inclusive category in terms of which the atoning work of Christ may be viewed'.[1] Obedience points to 'the capacity in which Christ discharged all phases of his atoning work'.[2] Tracing this motif back to Isaiah 53, Murray detected references throughout the New Testament to Christ's obedience, not least in Romans 5:12-21, which specifically contrasts his obedience with Adam's disobedience. This obedience may conveniently be viewed as both active and passive, so long as we understand that no part of obedience is merely passive. Rather, the formula points to both what he achieved and what he suffered. He obeyed both by fulfilling the law and by accepting its sanctions against the sins of those for whom he died.

Murray was particularly anxious to bring to the fore the biblical teaching on the progressiveness of Christ's obedience, an aspect where he thought orthodoxy had been weak. The concept of learning obedience through suffering (Heb. 5:8) implies such progress, from the perfect boyhood obedience of Jesus to the climactic adult obedience of his death on the cross (Phil. 2:8). This safeguards the biblical emphasis on what Murray calls 'corresponding degrees of complacency on the Father's part'.[3] In Luke's terms, Christ grew in favour with God (2:52). This personal relationship between the Father and Son must be emphasized if the nature of the incarnation and Christ's obedience is to be fully appreciated:

> Obedience ... is not something that may be conceived of artificially or abstractedly. It is obedience that enlisted all the resources

[1] John Murray, *Redemption—Accomplished and Applied* (Grand Rapids: Eerdmans, 1955; London: Banner of Truth, 1961), p. 24 (citations are from the 1961 ed.). This work was a development of a series of articles that appeared in the *Presbyterian Guardian* in 1952–54.
[2] Murray, *Collected Writings*, II:151.
[3] *Ibid.*, II:153.

of his perfect humanity, obedience that resided in his person, and obedience of which he is ever the perfect embodiment. ... And we become the beneficiaries of it, indeed the partakers of it, by union with him. It is this that serves to advertise the significance of that which is the central truth of all soteriology, namely, union and communion with Christ.[1]

Further reference must be made to the centrality of the theme of union with Christ, but no exposition of Murray's understanding of the work of Christ would be complete without some mention of his convictions about the extent of the atonement. On this issue Murray held to the classic Reformed teaching, which was by no means popular among his academic peers or in evangelicalism generally. He averred that Christ died specifically for the salvation of the elect. Though numerous benefits flow to the world in general from Christ's work, he bore God's wrath against sin to redeem specific persons.[2]

Unless we hold to full-orbed universalism, Murray argued, we are bound to hold to some limitations in the purpose, accomplishment, or application of the atonement. If its purpose were universal, then its efficacy must be limited; for if some perish for whom Christ died, the atonement made for them cannot have been efficacious. Reformed theology has always objected to this view on the grounds that it disrupts the harmonious purpose and power of the Trinity; the Father, Son, and Spirit are rendered incapable of accomplishing exactly the same ends. Murray was anxious to safeguard what he saw as the biblical emphasis on the efficacy of Christ's work and the honour of the triune God.

Murray did not base his view on autonomous logical or theological arguments, but appealed to a wide variety of textual and exegetical considerations. He argued, for example, that expressions like 'world' and 'all' rarely imply an all-inclusive universalism. Further, the New Testament's teaching on the work of Christ consistently stresses its efficacy: Christ actually redeems, reconciles, and propitiates. Efficacy is written into the nature of the atonement.[3] Murray found his strongest evidence

---

[1] Murray, *Redemption*, p. 24; see also Murray, *Collected Writings*, II:161.

[2] See Murray, *Redemption*, pp. 59-75; Murray, *Collected Writings*, I:59-85; IV:106-12.

[3] This was precisely the point at issue in fellow Scotsman John McLeod Campbell's *Nature of the Atonement* (1856), which argued against the evangelical interpretation

in John 10:7-29, where Jesus teaches that he will die for his sheep, who are carefully distinguished from those who are not his sheep.[1]

Murray was aware of the standard objection to such teaching: it enervates evangelism and dismembers the gospel. How can we preach the gospel if we cannot tell people indiscriminately that Christ died for them? Unlike those who raised this objection, Murray, from the preaching he had heard since childhood, had come to the understanding that the doctrines of election and particular redemption present no barrier to the full preaching of the gospel in faithful New Testament terms. He pointed out that the phrase 'Christ died for you', which many of his contemporaries regarded as so essential to the proclamation of the gospel, was not part of the New Testament language of proclamation! They erroneously identified the mode in which the gospel had come to be presented as the way in which it had in fact been expounded by the apostles. It is not, however, the benefits of Christ that are offered in the gospel, but Christ himself; the warrant for faith is not 'Christ died for you', but Christ's promise to be the Saviour of those who come to him.[2] Thus Murray sought to obviate hyper-Calvinism on the one hand and Arminianism on the other.[3] It must be said that hearing him preach would have dispelled any notion that his understanding of the biblical teaching was a barrier to impassioned proclamation of the gospel.

We have already noted that, in Murray's view, union with Christ is 'the central truth of the whole doctrine of salvation'.[4] In union with Christ not only do we enter into the grace of justification through his obedience (Rom. 5), but we simultaneously participate in sanctification (Rom. 6). In contrast to both Lutheran theology and popular evangelicalism, where justification dominates and sanctification serves as a codicil confirming or advancing its reality, for Murray justification

---

of the atonement as penal substitution. If this were the nature of the atonement, its efficacy would by necessity be limited to the elect. Campbell therefore felt compelled to deny the classic Reformed teaching and to revise completely the doctrine of the nature of the atonement.

[1] Murray, *Collected Writings*, I:74.

[2] *Ibid.*, I:82.

[3] See Murray, 'The Message of Evangelism', in *Collected Writings*, I:124-32, especially pp. 130-32.

[4] Murray, *Redemption*, p. 170.

and sanctification are inseparably linked to one another because both are the effect of union with Christ. Indeed, when we recognize that they are different dimensions of the Christian's existence (technically, justification is an *act* of God on our behalf, sanctification a *work* of God upon our lives), we may say that justification and sanctification begin simultaneously, both being part of the one eschatological reality of our union with Christ.

Here again Murray captured and echoed Calvin's finest emphases.[1] But in one respect at least he advanced the Reformer's thought, providing what was probably the most lucid English-language exposition of Romans 6 to date.[2] The union with Christ which lies at the foundation of justification also means, wrote Murray, that we have died to sin and have been raised to newness of life in him. In fact, the New Testament perspective of sanctification is not so much that it is an ongoing process, but an already accomplished reality, a decisive breach with the dominion of sin and an entry into the reign of grace. For this concept Murray coined the expression 'definitive sanctification'. But far from suggesting that the Christian is therefore free from the struggle with sin (a perfectionist view), he recognized and stressed the biblical teaching that the Christian is to wage war on sin from the position of strength in Christ. The church's failure to grasp this point Murray saw as the source of great ethical weakness:

> We are far too ready to give heed to what we deem to be the hard, empirical facts of Christian profession, and we have erased the clear line of demarcation which Scripture defines. As a result we have lost our vision of the high calling of God in Christ Jesus. Our ethic has lost its dynamic and we have become conformed to this world. We know not the power of death to sin in the death of Christ, and we are not able to bear the rigour of the liberty of redemptive emancipation. 'We died to sin': the glory of Christ's accomplishment and the guarantee of the Christian ethic are bound up with that doctrine. If we live in sin we have not died to it, and if we have not died to it we are not Christ's. If we died to sin we no longer live in

[1] See Calvin, *Institutes*, III.i.1; and also his commentary on Rom. 8:13.
[2] John Murray, *Principles of Conduct* (Grand Rapids: Eerdmans, 1957), pp. 202-21; Murray, *Collected Writings*, II:277-93.

it, for 'we who are such as have died to sin, how shall we still live in it?' (Romans 6:2).[1]

Murray saw a further implication of union with Christ, one of great significance for the whole ethos of the Christian life: union with Christ brings with it, as its highest benediction and 'the apex of redemptive grace and privilege', adoption by God.[2] By the twentieth century this doctrine had fallen into desuetude in evangelical thought. In the pristine theology of Calvin it had been a dominant motif, although never treated as a distinctive locus or given a separate chapter in his *Institutes*. The English Puritan theologians tended to treat the topic of adoption similarly, although it was given specific exposition in the *Westminster Confession* (XII) and fine treatment by such authors as John Owen and Thomas Watson. But, perhaps through the influence of Francis Turretin on later Reformed thought, it fell into decline and was viewed as no more than the positive aspect of justification. Furthermore, the emphasis of liberal theology on the universal fatherhood of God and brotherhood of man considerably weakened evangelical emphasis on the benefits of being adopted by God as a concomitant of salvation.[3]

By contrast, under the influence of the *Westminster Confession* and *Catechisms*, Murray refused to regard adoption 'as simply an aspect of justification or as another way of stating the privilege conferred by regeneration. It is much more than either or both of these acts of grace.'[4] While adoption is a judicial act, it points to the Christian's being sustained in a relationship to God which transcends justification. The Christian is an adopted child of God, and thereby becomes heir to all the privileges of the family of God. This determines the whole ethos of the Christian life, and reflects particularly on the character of Christian obedience, which is thereby rendered filial rather than servile. Adoption, Murray wrote with feeling, 'staggers imagination because of its amazing condescension and love. The Spirit alone could be the seal of it on our hearts.'[5]

---

[1] Murray, *Principles of Conduct*, p. 205.
[2] Murray, *Collected Writings*, II:233.
[3] See below, Chapter 29, 'The Reformed Doctrine of Sonship'.
[4] Murray, *Redemption*, p. 132.
[5] *Ibid.*, p. 134.

Ethical writings

One final area of Murray's theology must be mentioned, namely, his long-standing interest in the Christian ethic. This emerged in a series of six articles on divorce which were published in the *Westminster Theological Journal* from 1946 to 1949 and appeared in book form in 1953. With his characteristic care Murray worked through the biblical teaching stage by stage. His view was that divorce is legitimate on only two grounds: adultery and desertion of a believer by an unbeliever. In both cases he believed Scripture teaches that the wronged party is free to marry again. The book concludes with a series of case studies in which Murray seeks to apply the biblical teaching. It is noteworthy that, in keeping with his recognition of the limits of systematic theology, Murray concludes in one case study that 'we are not able to answer [concerning the legitimacy of remarriage] dogmatically one way or the other'.[1] On the other hand, contemporary society evinces so much legal confusion in this general area that the church should give serious consideration to recognizing divorce on biblical grounds.

In 1955 Murray gave the Payton Lectures at Fuller Theological Seminary; these were published in expanded form in 1957 under the title *Principles of Conduct*. Here the same exegetical concern already displayed in the volume on divorce is evident. But Murray now spells out his agenda more deliberately:

> One of the main purposes of the lectures and of this volume is to
> seek to show the basic unity and continuity of the biblical ethic.
> I have attempted to apply to the ethic of Scripture something of
> the biblico-theological method, understanding 'biblical theology' in
> the sense defined by Geerhardus Vos as 'that branch of exegetical
> theology which deals with the process of the self-revelation of God
> deposited in the Bible'.[2]

In identifying with Vos, Murray deliberately distanced himself from the brand of biblical theology that had been characteristic of the

---

[1] John Murray, *Divorce* (Philadelphia: Committee on Christian Education, Orthodox Presbyterian Church, 1953; Philadelphia: Presbyterian and Reformed, 1961), p. 115.

[2] Murray, *Principles of Conduct*, p. 7.

history-of-religions school as well as from the much-vaunted biblical-theology movement of his own times. His position was that 'the presentation given in the Scripture is the true transcript of what the history of revelation and redemption really was. The unity which we find in the Bible reflects the organic unity of the process of divine revelation of which the Bible itself is the depository.'[1] In particular, Murray treated Genesis 1-3 as a historical record with remarkable implications for a biblico-theological understanding of the Christian ethic.

Adhering to a characteristically Reformed view of God's covenant, Murray sees the Decalogue as essentially built on God's original design for creation. The commandments are expressed negatively because they are set in the context of human depravity. Furthermore, Murray argues in detail that Old Testament and New Testament, grace and law, law and love, cannot be regarded as antithetical. In Scripture they are complementary and indeed essential to one another. A study of the creation ordinances is therefore foundational to a proper understanding of the Christian ethic. These ordinances, as set forth in the opening chapters of Genesis, are marriage and family life, labour, and the Sabbath day. In addition, Murray sees the sanctity of life and of truth adumbrated in the creation narrative.

Murray's exposition, rigorous in detail and replete with exegetical and theological insight, is particularly trenchant in discussing law and grace. Here his commitment to the principle that biblical theology yields insight in particular exegesis produces a rich harvest. A notable instance is his comment on Paul's statement in Romans 6:14 that Christians are not under law but under grace:

> A good deal of the misconception pertaining to the relation of the law to the believer springs from a biblico-theological error of much broader proportions than a misinterpretation of Paul's statement in Romans 6:14. It is the misinterpretation of the Mosaic economy and covenant in relation to the new covenant. ... The demand for obedience in the Mosaic covenant is principially identical with the same demand under the gospel. ... Obedience belongs here no more 'to the legal sphere of merit' than in the new covenant.[2]

[1] Murray, *Principles of Conduct*, pp. 8-9.
[2] *Ibid.*, pp. 195, 200.

The Mosaic economy, Murray is here contending, is itself an expression of grace. Consistently throughout Scripture the claims of law and the specific commands of God, which are rooted in his character, are motivated and effected in us by grace. Moreover, appealing to John 14:15 ('If ye love me, keep my commandments', kjv) and Deuteronomy 6:5 ('Thou shalt love the LORD thy God ...', kjv), Murray argues that law and love, far from being antithetical, are harmonious. Love itself is in fact a command of God! Thus all forms of antinomianism (including situation ethics, as he was later to demonstrate)[1] fail to meet basic biblical considerations. The law for Murray is not simply an academic matter; it is spiritually vital:

> It is only myopia that prevents us from seeing this, and when there is a persistent animosity to the notion of keeping commandments the only conclusion is that there is either gross ignorance or malignant opposition to the testimony of Jesus.[2]

Following a fine chapter on 'The Dynamic of the Biblical Ethic', in which he sets forward in some detail the import of union with Christ and gives hints of the concept of 'definitive sanctification', Murray concludes his ethical studies, significantly, with a chapter on the fear of God, which he characterizes as 'the soul of godliness ... the sum of piety',[3] and the fruit of the indwelling of the Spirit of Christ, who himself was endued with the Spirit of the fear of the Lord (Isa. 11:2-3). The ethical integrity which Murray sees the church summoned to by the biblical teaching he has expounded 'is grounded in and is the fruit of the fear of God'.[4] This fear is twofold: 'the dread or terror of the Lord and ... reverential awe'—terror in view of our sinfulness set in the light of his holiness; awe in the sense of filial reverence, which takes its origin not from our sinfulness, but from God's inherent glory.[5] It is this reverential awe which Murray considers the soul of godliness. Deterioration here is evidence of spiritual decline and the root of an inevitable moral collapse,

---

[1] John Murray, 'Situation Ethics', *Banner of Truth*, Issue 226 (July 1982), pp. 7-16.
[2] Murray, *Principles of Conduct*, p. 182.
[3] *Ibid.*, p. 229.
[4] *Ibid.*, p. 230.
[5] *Ibid.*, p. 233.

because it is the truest expression of that God-consciousness which lies at the heart of seriously committed holiness of life. Murray is at his most eloquent when describing this fear of God, putting into words the very piety which others saw in his life:

> The fear of God could be nothing less than the soul of rectitude. It is the apprehension of God's glory that constrains the fear of his name. It is that same glory that commands our totality commitment to him, totality trust and obedience. The fear of God is but the reflex in our consciousness of the transcendent perfection which alone could warrant and demand the totality of our commitment to him.[1]

Principles of Conduct abundantly realizes Murray's stated goal: to demonstrate 'how fruitful ethical studies conducted along this line can be and how in this field, as well as in others, we may discover the organic unity and continuity of divine revelation'.[2] But this volume does more—it shows John Murray to have been a theologian who *felt* what he believed.

Much more could be written about Murray's other works: his seven-hundred-page exposition of Romans as well as his studies on such subjects as the theology of Calvin and baptism.[3] He liked to think of himself and his contributions to the Christian church as embodying an old saying: a dwarf seated on the shoulders of a giant is able to see farther than the giant can. As one of the community of saints called to press farther on into the unfolding riches of the grace of God in the gospel, he sat on the shoulders of giant theologians, especially those in the Augustinian tradition like Calvin and Owen. Among North Americans, Jonathan Edwards, the Hodges, Warfield, and, of course, the unsung Geerhardus Vos, were his theological fathers. Reared on a Scottish highland croft and serving Christ far from home, John Murray proved to be their worthy heir.

---

[1] Murray, *Principles of Conduct*, p. 242.

[2] *Ibid.*, p. 7.

[3] John Murray, *The Epistle to the Romans*, 2 vols (Grand Rapids: Eerdmans, 1960, 1965); Murray, *Calvin on Scripture and Divine Sovereignty* (Grand Rapids: Baker, 1960); Murray, *Collected Writings*, IV:158-204; Murray, *Christian Baptism* (Philadelphia: Presbyterian and Reformed, 1952).

II. JOHN CALVIN
PASTOR-TEACHER

CHAPTER FOUR

A HEART FOR GOD

I call 'piety' that reverence joined with love of God which the knowledge of his benefits induces. For until men recognize that they owe everything to God, that they are nourished by his fatherly care, that he is the author of their every good, that they should seek nothing beyond him—they will never yield him willing service. Nay, unless they establish their complete happiness in him, they will never give themselves truly and sincerely to him.[1]

—JOHN CALVIN

JOHN CALVIN was one of the most reserved of Christian men, rarely disclosing in public the inner workings of his heart. Only occasionally did he lift the veil, as for example in his preface to his *Commentary on the Psalms*. There he acknowledged himself to have been 'of a disposition somewhat unpolished and bashful, which led me always to love the shade and retirement'.[2]

How, then, did a reserved, studious, tightly wired young humanist scholar of the late 1520s and early 1530s become such a powerful force in the service of the gospel?

The simplest answer is found in a letter he wrote in 1564 to his friend and colleague Guillaume Farel: 'It is enough that I live and die for Christ, who is to all his followers a gain both in life and death.'[3] The echo

---

[1] Calvin, *Institutes*, I.ii.1.

[2] Calvin, *Comm. Psalms*, p. xli.

[3] Calvin, *Letters*, IV:364. The letter was written on May 2, 1564. Calvin died on May 27.

of Paul's testimony is unmistakable: 'For to me to live is Christ, and to die is gain' (Phil. 1:21). Hence the motto always associated with Calvin: 'I offer my heart to you, Lord, promptly and sincerely' (*Cor meum tibi offero, Domine, prompte et sincere*).[1]

Calvin seems to have been conscious of two things that shaped him: God's sovereign renewal of his life, and his progressive transformation into the likeness of Christ.

Powerful renewal

Scripture teaches that renewal by the Holy Spirit involves the understanding, the will, and the affections. So it proved to be with Calvin:

> ... since I was too obstinately devoted to the superstitions of Popery to be easily extricated from so profound an abyss of mire, God by a sudden conversion subdued and brought my mind to a teachable frame, which was more hardened in such matters than might have been expected from one at my early period of life. Having thus received some taste and knowledge of true godliness I was immediately inflamed with so intense a desire to make progress therein, that although I did not altogether leave off other studies, I yet pursued them with less ardour.[2]

The shape and burden of an individual's ministry often emerge from the influences and atmosphere in which his conversion took place. These seem at times to leave a permanent birthmark on an individual's life. This was true for Calvin. Whatever he means by the much-discussed phrase 'by a sudden conversion' (*subita conversione*), the rich and emotive vocabulary he uses to describe that conversion provides us with a transcript of the principles that shaped his Christian life. His language here is strikingly different from that of contemporary evangelicalism. It is hard to imagine him speaking about 'letting Jesus into my heart' or 'praying to accept Jesus'; indeed, for Calvin, the movement of conversion is not 'getting Christ in' but 'getting into Christ'.

---

[1] Cf. the language in his letter in August 1541 to Farel as he prepared to return to Geneva: 'Had I the choice at my own disposal, nothing would be less agreeable to me than to follow your advice. But when I remember that I am not my own, I offer up my heart, presented as a sacrifice to the Lord.' Calvin, *Letters*, I:280-281.

[2] Calvin, *Comm. Psalms*, p. xl.

In Calvin's conversion, two things stand out: First, his pre-conversion condition was marked by a 'hardened' and resistant ('unteachable') mind, and, by implication, a distaste for true godliness (later reversed into an 'inflamed ... desire'). This, of course, was the informed biblical analysis of one who believed that the fallen human mind is 'a perpetual factory of idols',[1] and therefore deeply resistant to the iconoclasm of grace.

Second, for Calvin, conversion to Christ meant not only a transition from condemnation to justification but from ignorance to knowledge and from arrogant rebellion to a humbled heart.[2] His mind was thus softened and brought 'to a teachable frame'. From this flowed powerful new affections. He now was 'inflamed' with 'intense ... desire' to make progress in 'true godliness'. Thus, to have a heart for God meant to have a desire to grow in the 'knowledge of the truth, which accords with godliness' (Titus 1:1).

Progressive transformation

Calvin's description of the events that followed his 'sudden' conversion gives us a further clue to his spiritual progress:

> I was quite surprised to find that before a year had elapsed, all who had any desire after purer doctrine were continually coming to me to learn, although I myself was as yet but a mere novice and tyro.[3]

His distinctive genius, present virtually from his conversion, was a God-given ability to penetrate to the heart of the meaning of the text of Scripture. But these words also indicate in passing that his early progress was set in the context of an interconnected—and somewhat underground—fellowship of like-minded young men, first in Paris and thereafter throughout Europe. Such brotherhoods are often God's chief instruments in stimulating holy living and advancing the gospel.

Calvin had been a student in Paris in the aftermath of the Sorbonne doctors' scrutiny of Martin Luther's works. Out of that cauldron of spiritual unrest came a loose-knit group of younger men who became

[1] Calvin, *Institutes*, I.xi.8.
[2] Note in this connection his approval of a remark in one of Augustine's letters that the essence of the Christian life is humility. *Ibid.*, II.ii.11.
[3] Calvin, *Comm. Psalms*, p. xli.

leaders of the new churches of the Reformation. It was from this school of prophets that Calvin emerged as the leading young theological scholar of his generation, evidenced by the publication of the first, and comparatively brief, edition of his *Institutes of the Christian Religion* in 1536. Its subtitle underlined the young Calvin's daring vision: *Summa Pietatis*,[1] or '*the Sum of Piety*'. His goal from the first was not merely knowledge, but an understanding of the gospel that impacted the heart and the will, and in turn transformed lives.

This marriage of learning and piety marked the whole of Calvin's ministry and reflected his understanding of what it means to know Christ, to serve God, and to live in the power of the Spirit. 'I call piety', he writes, 'that reverence joined with the love of God which the knowledge of his benefits induces.'[2] *Piety* has a family ring about it (devotion to one's father being its most common human expression). Alongside it in sheer frequency of use, Calvin employs another family term to describe the Christian life: *adoptio*—adoptive sonship. While he never made either concept a separate locus in the *Institutes*, together they virtually summarize what is involved in being a Christian and growing in likeness to Jesus Christ. Piety is an expression of adoption—reverence for God, living with a single eye to his glory. This is what the children of God are called to do and to be.[3]

A theological transcript

Living the Christian life is a theme that runs throughout the *Institutes*, but it is the central theme of Book III, which is entitled: 'The mode of obtaining the grace of Christ. The benefits it confers, and the effects

[1] The title of the first edition was: *Christianae religionis institutio tota fere pietatis summam ... complectens.*

[2] Calvin, *Institutes*, I.ii.1.

[3] Cf. the beautiful words in Calvin's French Catechism of 1537 describing piety as 'a pure and true zeal which loves God altogether as Father and reveres him truly as Lord, embraces his justice and dreads to offend him more than to die' (John Calvin, *Instruction in Faith*. tr. Paul T. Fuhrmann [Louisville, KY: Westminster John Knox Press, 1949], 22). The abundance of Calvin's references to *pietas* is often masked by its translation in English versions as 'godliness'. Similarly, his intense focus on the Christian life as a life of adopted sons has been little recognized simply because he did not treat adoption as a separate locus for exposition in the *Institutes*.

resulting from it.' Calvin's exposition has a distinctive (some have thought idiosyncratic) order, as a glance at the chapter headings will indicate. To some extent, this underlines the way in which his greatest work is simultaneously a trinitarian theology, an expression of, and *apologia* for, the gospel, and a transcript of his own spiritual life.

Nowhere in Calvin's writings can we take his spiritual pulse more easily than in his exposition of the Christian life in *Institutes* III.vi-x. Its themes are germane to Calvin's own experience, and we cannot read his heart without some reference to them.[1]

Centrality of Jesus Christ

For Calvin, the gospel is not predestination or election, the sovereignty of God, or even the five points of doctrine with which his name is so often associated. These are aspects of the gospel, but the gospel is Jesus Christ himself. That may seem a truism—who would think anything else? But this truth takes on fresh significance in Calvin's understanding.

By the time of the second (1539) and subsequent editions of the *Institutes*, Calvin's ongoing study of Scripture had brought a new depth to his understanding of the gospel (he completed his commentary on Romans in the same year). With this new understanding, he insisted that salvation and all its benefits not only come to us through Christ but are to be found exclusively in Christ. Union with Christ brings the believer into fellowship with Christ, crucified, resurrected, ascended, reigning, and returning.

Two considerations followed. First, Calvin realized that through faith in Christ all the blessings of the gospel were his. Second, he saw that his life must be rooted and grounded in fellowship with Christ. Perhaps it was the personal realization of this that led him to wax lyrical at the climax of his exposition of the Christological section of the Apostles' Creed:

> We see that our whole salvation and all its parts are comprehended in Christ [Acts 4:12]. We should therefore take care not to derive the least portion of it from anywhere else. If we seek salvation, we

[1] This material appeared in earlier form in the second edition of the *Institutes* in 1539 and was separately published in 1549 in an English translation by Thomas Broke under the title *The Life and Communicacion* [sic] *of a Christian Man*. It has often been republished as *The Golden Booklet of the Christian Life*.

are taught by the very name of Jesus that it is 'of him' [1 Cor. 1:30].
If we seek any other gifts of the Spirit, they will be found in his
anointing. If we seek strength, it lies in his dominion; if purity, in
his conception; if gentleness, it appears in his birth. ... If we seek
redemption, it lies in his passion; if acquittal, in his condemnation;
if remission of the curse, in his cross [Gal. 3:13]; if satisfaction, in his
sacrifice; if purification, in his blood; if reconciliation, in his descent
into hell; if mortification of the flesh, in his tomb; if newness of
life, in his resurrection; if immortality, in the same; if inheritance
of the heavenly kingdom, in his entrance into heaven; if protection,
if security, if abundant supply of all blessings, in his kingdom; if
untroubled expectation of judgment, in the power given to him to
judge.[1]

Calvin had made a great discovery, one that dominated both his
theology and his life: if Christ is our Redeemer, then Christ was formed
in the incarnation in order to deal precisely, perfectly, and fully with
both the cause of our guilt and the consequences of our sin. Union with
Christ was the means by which the Spirit applies this to us.

Likeness to Christ: gentle Calvin, meek and mild?
One statement from Calvin's exposition of the Apostles' Creed can serve
as a case study in his personal struggles for sanctification and the measure
of progress he made: 'If we seek ... gentleness, it appears in his birth.'[2]
   This is the man who reputedly had been known by his fellow students
as 'The Accusative Case', the youth of tense and nervous disposition,
conscious of a certain shortness of temper. But he realized that God
had made provision for this in Christ—even to make John Calvin
gentle. Intriguingly, the same theme reappears in the hymn sometimes
attributed to him, 'I Greet Thee Who My Sure Redeemer Art',[3] in the
words:

[1] Calvin, *Institutes*, II.xvi.19.
[2] *Ibid.*
[3] The hymn appeared in the Strasbourg Psalter of 1545. Calvin versified a number of
psalms, but appears to have taken a low view of his gifts as a poet and his work did
not reappear in the Genevan Psalter. Certainly the sentiment of this hymn is pure
Calvin, whether penned by the Reformer himself or by someone deeply influenced
by his teaching.

> Thou hast the true and perfect gentleness.
> No harshness hast Thou, and no bitterness.

This is the *ipsissima vox* ('the very voice', or convictions), if not the *ipsissima verba* ('the very words') of Calvin, wonderfully expressing that all that we lack is now ours in Jesus Christ. Calvin writes, 'In short, since rich store of every kind of good abounds in him, let us drink our fill from this fountain, and from no other.'[1]

How well Calvin drank of Christ with respect to personal gentleness and tenderness is indicated in several incidental ways:

1. In his restraint of personal malice to those who opposed him. Calvin could use strong language and regret it.[2] But Giovanni Diodati records how Johannes Eck was surprised, when he visited the Genevan Reformer, to have the door opened by a kind and modest-living Calvin himself, who refused with grace the offers of preferment in Rome if he would return to the fold.

2. In his empathy for those who suffered. His correspondence expresses his deep affection for his friends, but also his deep compassion for his brothers and sisters in Christ who were sick or bereaved. His extant letters to some of the young men he had schooled for martyrdom express a tender kindness mingled with fortitude that is deeply moving and impressive.

3. In his concern to show respect to others. On one occasion, his secretary, Charles de Jonvilliers, remonstrated with him to dictate his letters rather than write them in his own hand. Calvin was concerned lest the recipients of his letters should in any degree feel slighted that he himself was not the penman.

4. In his gracious attitude toward others. In his biography of Calvin, Theodore Beza, Calvin's colleague and successor, writes that Calvin never put 'weak brethren to the blush'.[3] There is something touching about Beza's comment. This Calvin had learned from the Christ who would not break a bruised reed or quench a faintly burning wick (Isa.

---

[1] Calvin, *Institutes*, II.xvi.19.

[2] See Calvin's letter to Farel on Oct. 8, 1539, in which he describes his agonies with respect to this. Calvin, *Letters*, I:151-57.

[3] Theodore Beza, *Life of Calvin*, in *Tracts and Treatises*, 3 vols, ed. and tr. Henry Beveridge (Edinburgh: Calvin Translation Society, 1841–51), I:xcvii.

42:3). Thus Calvin concludes his exposition of that text with a comment on ministry styles:

> Following this example, the ministers of the gospel, who are his deputies, ought to show themselves to be meek, and to support the weak, and gently to lead them in the way, so as not to extinguish in them the feeblest sparks of piety, but, on the contrary, to kindle them with all their might.[1]

Clearly Calvin, 'The Accusative Case', became in measure a Christ-like pastor. Illustrations of other graces might be multiplied.

Life under the cross

'Howbeit, you must remember', Calvin wrote to a correspondent, 'the cross of Jesus Christ will follow us.'[2] He well understood that cross-bearing is central to the Christian life. Compulsory flight from persecution while in his mid-twenties early introduced him to the implications of union with Christ: sharing in the death of Christ involves not only inward mortification (*mortificatio interna*) leading to sanctification, but also outward participation in sufferings (*mortificatio externa*), whether personal, or in the way of persecution and even martyrdom:

> For whomever the Lord has adopted and deemed worthy of his fellowship ought to prepare themselves for a hard, toilsome, and unquiet life, crammed with very many and various kinds of evils. It is the heavenly Father's will thus to exercise them so as to put his own children to a definite test. Beginning with Christ, his firstborn, he follows his plan with all his children.[3]

This sentiment could be cited a hundred times from Calvin's writings.

These principles were written on a large scale in his own life as a gospel minister. Geneva was no sinecure. Effectively banished from the city in April 1538, Calvin wrote to his friend Pierre Viret when he was invited to return, 'There is no place under heaven of which I can have a

---

[1] John Calvin, *Commentary on Isaiah*, tr. William Pringle (Edinburgh: Calvin Translation Society, 1850), III:288.

[2] Calvin, *Letters*, I:230.

[3] Calvin, *Institutes*, III.viii.1.

greater dread.'[1] But return he did. Often vilified, he was sustained in his ministry precisely by the conviction that it is through tribulation that we enter the kingdom, and that God uses it to transform his children into the likeness of Christ.

Calvin also knew personal suffering. Married in 1540, he had lost his wife and his son Jacques before the end of the decade. The brevity of his comment to Viret on Jacques's death is starkly eloquent: '[God] is himself a Father, and knows what is best for his children.'[2]

Beyond this, the closing years of his ministry were marked by a series of debilitating illnesses. He matter-of-factly describes one incident to his friend Heinrich Bullinger:

> At present, I am relieved from very acute suffering, having been delivered of a calculus [i.e., a 'stone'] about the size of the kernel of a filbert [i.e., a hazelnut]. As the retention of urine was very painful to me, by the advice of my physician, I got upon horseback that the jolting might assist me in discharging the calculus. On my return home I was surprised to find that I emitted discoloured blood instead of urine. The following day the calculus had forced its way from the bladder into the urethra. Hence still more excruciating tortures. For more than half an hour I endeavoured to disengage myself from it by a violent agitation of my whole body. I gained nothing by that, but obtained a slight relief by fomentations with warm water. Meanwhile, the urinary canal was so much lacerated that copious discharges of blood flowed from it. It seems to me now that I begin to live anew for the last two days since I am delivered from these pains.

Remarkably, but somewhat typical of Calvin's sheer determination to focus on God's work, his next words are: 'Of the state of France, I should have written to you with more details if I had been at leisure.'[3] What is the explanation for this pattern of divine working? Calvin explains in words that we may readily apply to him:

---

[1] Calvin, *Letters*, I:231.

[2] *Ibid.*, I:344.

[3] *Ibid.*, IV:320-21. A letter to Farel in 1540 indicates that his sickness was longstanding, while simultaneously giving insight into the tension under which he lived. *Ibid.*, I:204ff.

But even the most holy persons, however much they may recognize that they stand not through their own strength but through God's grace, are too sure of their own fortitude and constancy unless by the testing of the cross he bring them into a deeper knowledge of himself.[1]

Living for the future

It is commonplace today in Reformed theology to recognize that the Christian lives 'between the times'—already we are in Christ, but a yet more glorious future awaits us in the final consummation. There is, therefore, a 'not yet' about our present Christian experience. Calvin well understood this, and he never dissolved the tension between the 'already' and the 'not yet'. But he also stressed the importance for the present of a life-focus on the future.

Calvin sought, personally, to develop a balance of contempt for the present life with a deep gratitude for the blessings of God and a love and longing for the heavenly kingdom. The sense that the Lord would come and issue his final assessment on all and bring his elect to glory was a dominant motif for him. This, the theme of his chapter 'Meditation on the Future Life',[2] was a major element in the energy with which he lived in the face of the 'not yet' of his own ailments and weakness. When he was seriously ill and confined to bed, his friends urged him to take some rest, but he replied, 'Would you that the Lord, when he comes, should find me idle?'[3] By living in the light of the return of Christ and the coming judgment, Calvin became deeply conscious of the brevity of time and the length of eternity.

This sense of eternity overflowed from his life into his work. It was so characteristic of him that it emerged very naturally in his prayers at the conclusion of his lectures. Here we see the wonderful harmony of his biblical exposition, his understanding of the gospel, his concern to teach young men how to live for God's glory, and his personal piety.

---

[1] Calvin, *Institutes*, III.viii.2. Here Calvin's exposition of such passages as 2 Cor. 4:10-12 and Phil. 3:10 may be consulted with profit.

[2] *Ibid.*, III.ix.

[3] Quoted in 'Translator's Preface', in John Calvin, *Commentaries on the Book of Joshua*, tr. Henry Beveridge (Edinburgh: Calvin Translation Society, 1854), p. vi.

A fragment of one of these prayers, chosen almost randomly, fittingly summarizes this all-too-brief reflection on the heart for God that Calvin expressed in his learning and leadership:

> May we be prepared, whatever happens, rather to undergo a hundred deaths than to turn aside from the profession of true piety, in which we know our safety to be laid up. And may we so glorify thy name as to be partakers of that glory which has been acquired for us through the blood of thine only-begotten Son. Amen.[1]

---

[1] John Calvin, prayer after Lecture 16 on Daniel, *Commentaries on the Prophet Daniel*, tr. Thomas Myers (Edinburgh: Calvin Translation Society, 1852), I:242.

CHAPTER FIVE

MANIFESTED IN THE FLESH: JOHN CALVIN ON THE REALITY OF THE INCARNATION

THE question of whether there is a central theme in John Calvin's theology has long been debated and will surely continue to be so. The options placed on the table of Calvin scholarship have varied from the now *passé* assumption that he was obsessed with predestination to more recent attempts to place Christology at the centre and core. Insofar as Calvin was a remarkably sensitive biblical (and not a narrowly systematic) theologian, this diversity of perspective is not surprising. An analogous diversity of answers is found among contemporary biblical scholars when asked what the central motif of the Old Testament is. It was part of Calvin's wisdom that he did not commit himself to view biblical revelation through a single controlling principle.

This essay does not attempt to resolve these long-standing issues, but simply pursues a motif which was certainly central to Calvin personally, as a Christian believer: Jesus Christ, God's incarnate Son, clothed in the garments of the gospel. With Paul he held that 'the knowledge of Christ so far surpasses everything else by its sublimity that, compared with it, there is nothing that is not contemptible'.[1]

Calvin did not view this in isolation from the rest of his theology: the knowledge of God and his sovereignty, the wonder of his providence, the reliability of his revelation, and the importance of belonging to the Christian community. But his knowledge of the person of Christ, and

---

[1] John Calvin, *The Epistles of Paul to the Galatians, Ephesians, Philippians and Colossians*, tr. T. H. L. Parker, ed. D. W. and T. F. Torrance (Edinburgh: St Andrew Press, 1965), p. 272.

particularly his humanity, seems increasingly to have played an important role in shaping his sense of the sheer privilege of belonging to the Lord. This, in turn, created the distinctive atmosphere of the Christian life which he himself sought to live as a 'practical Calvinist'.[1]

Calvin's teaching on the work of Christ incarnate as Saviour can be readily explored in three stages: the necessity of the incarnation; the precise nature of the incarnation; and the relationship between the incarnation and the atonement.

The necessity of the incarnation

In an arresting passage in the *Institutes*, Calvin distinguishes between the pre- and post-fall mediation of Christ: 'Even if man had remained free from all stain, his condition would have been too lowly for him to reach God without a Mediator.'[2] Now, however, that man has sinned and lapsed from the divine glory, there is (to express it technically) a consequent contingent necessity for the incarnation. It is *consequent upon*, yet not logically determined by the fall. It is *necessary* insofar as God has determined to save fallen man. The incarnation has no *a priori* necessity attached to it (e.g. in the nature of God); rather it is a free action of God, determined by his own will. In this sense

> Christ suffered by his appointment and not by necessity [i.e. of a logically *a priori* kind] because, being 'in the form of God' he could have escaped this necessity, but nevertheless he suffered 'through weakness' because he 'emptied himself'.[3]

A mediator adequate for man's needs must be both divine and human. The atonement required can come only from man. But fallen man is disqualified from making atonement. God the Son incarnate is alone free from sin and able to offer himself as an atoning sacrifice.

---

[1] That Calvin viewed his theology as 'practical' is beautifully expressed in *De Vita Hominis Christiani*, first published in 1550, material drawn from the *Institutes*. See *A Guide to Christian Living* (Edinburgh: Banner of Truth Trust, 2009).

[2] Calvin, *Institutes*, II.xii.1. Cf. his comments on Gal. 3:19 in *Comm. Galatians*, p. 62.

[3] John Calvin, *Commentary on The Second Epistle of Paul to the Corinthians and the Epistles to Timothy, Titus and Philemon*, tr. T. A. Smail, ed. D. W. and T. F. Torrance (Edinburgh: St Andrew Press, 1964), p. 172. Cf. *Institutes*, II.xii.1.

Stylistically, Calvin delights to express this in a mode which illustrates a deep-seated pattern in his theological thinking, what Hermann Bauke called a *complexio oppositorum*.[1] This pattern of thought is so deeply embedded in Calvin's thinking about Christ that it frequently surfaces even in the basic structure of his sentences, as the following characteristic statement indicates:

> [Christ's] task was so to restore us to God's grace as to make
>
> of the **children of men**,
>> *children of God*;
> of the **heirs of Gehenna**,
>> *heirs of the heavenly kingdom*.
>
> Who could have done this had not
>> the self-same **Son of God**
>> become the *Son of Man*,
> and had not
>> so taken **what was *ours***
>> as to impart ... *what was his* to us,
> and
>> to make *what was **his*** **by nature**
>>> ours by grace?[2]

What is so significant here is the extent to which salvation, and consequently the confidence of faith, are derived from the fact that the antithesis/oppositeness between what we are and what Christ is, has been turned through 180 degrees. Thus everything lacking in us is given to us by Christ, everything sinful in us is imputed to Christ, and all condemnation merited by us is borne by Christ.

Faith unites us directly with Christ thus clothed in his gospel and relieves us instantaneously from condemnation. Faith properly exercised drinks deeply from these springs of grace and sees that Christ is not only perfectly equipped to become the Saviour, but actually is *my* Saviour.

Calvin seems instinctively to have recognized the proclivity (often unspoken) in the faithful to seek assurance *apart* from faith in Christ.

[1] Hermann Bauke, *Die Probleme der Theologie Calvins* (Leipzig: J. C. Hinrichs Buchhandlung, 1922), p. 16.
[2] Calvin, *Institutes*, II.xii.2.

There is a native tendency (and perversity) to ask: 'How can I enjoy assurance even if I am not exercising faith?' His answer is that it cannot be done. We cannot have the assurance that comes from Christ on a *remoto Christo* principle (Anselm) in which we place Christ in abeyance and rest on other grounds! Assurance is possible only through Christ; Christ is known and received only through faith. There is no alternative to this correlation. Assurance is, after all, the assurance of faith in Christ.

This helps to explain why Calvin devotes so much detailed attention to the way in which Christ has really taken our flesh and accomplished our redemption. He thereby portrays Christ as so perfectly suited to our need for salvation, that Christ so portrayed effects faith and brings the conviction that in Christ one cannot but be saved.

As we have noted, Calvin holds, with Anselm and others, that reparation in atonement must be made from among those who owe it (humanity); but humanity lacks the resources to do this. Since all have sinned and fall short of the divine glory, what is due from below can now be effected only from outside of corrupt humanity. Thus an impasse is reached. But this insolvable dilemma is divinely resolved: the Son comes from outside into our humanity to do for us what we cannot accomplish for ourselves.

In his exposition of the assumption of our humanity by the divine *Logos*, Calvin clearly stands on the shoulders of Athanasius in his conviction that the doctrine of the incarnation must be formulated soteriologically. Thus, in contrast to Osiander, he argues that had Adam not fallen, the Son never would have become incarnate.

But the incarnation *per se* is not saving. While Calvin's theology reflects the most biblical elements of Eastern theology's stress on the healing of humanity through Christ, for him the redemption of man is not to be viewed as a transformation of our flesh by the mere fact of its assumption and resurrection by the Holy Son. The ultimate consummation of salvation (which will be seen in the healing of our flesh involved in the final resurrection glory) is grounded in Christ's obedience as incarnate. This obedience of the incarnate Christ is in the whole course of his life and in his atoning death—in what he experienced and accomplished in our flesh—not simply in the taking of and living in our flesh in and of itself.

The controlling principle of the work of Christ in Calvin's thought is the concept of exchange. In order to restore fallen man to sinless God, the Son must take what is ours (sin, guilt, bondage, condemnation, death) and deal with it in such a way that what was ours becomes his and what is his also becomes ours. But what does this involve?

Christ appeared in 'the name and the person of sinners' in order genuinely and righteously to accomplish what we could not do for ourselves:

> That is why it is here narrated to us that not only our Lord Jesus Christ has been willing to suffer death and has offered himself as a sacrifice to pacify the wrath of God his Father, but in order that he might be truly and wholly our pledge, he did not refuse to bear the agonies which are prepared for all those whose consciences rebuke them and who feel themselves guilty of eternal death and damnation before God. Let us note well, then, that the Son of God was not content merely to offer his flesh and blood and to subject them to death, but he willed in full measure to appear before the judgment seat of God his Father in the name and in the person of all sinners, being then ready to be condemned, inasmuch as he bore our burden.[1]

Because Christ bears our name and our nature even the weakest believer may look to Christ and find assurance of grace and salvation in him. Here Calvin's exposition of the Gospels' testimony is profound and telling: Jesus' ministry reveals to us the humanity of a Saviour who can be trusted, who understands, and who is able to bring reassurance of the adequacy and fittingness of his grace. Much of what he does and experiences is intended to show us how near to us he came. The revelation of his frailty and weakness is all intended to assure us that he is one with us and has taken our place.

Calvin places great stress on the fact that the atonement was offered by Christ in his humanity:

> We know that the two natures of Christ were so conformed in one person that each retained what was proper to it; in particular the

---

[1] *Sermons on the Deity of Christ*, selected and translated by Leroy Nixon (Grand Rapids: Eerdmans, 1950), p. 52.

divinity was silent (*quievit Divinitas*) and made no assertion of itself whenever it was the business of the human nature to act alone in its own terms in fulfilment of the office of mediator.[1]

While this is stated explicitly in connection with Christ's confession of ignorance in Matthew 24:36, it is a principle which surfaces throughout Calvin's writings.[2] True, were he not God, Christ could not have accomplished all that was necessary for reconciliation. Nevertheless, 'it is certain that he carried out all these acts according to his human nature'.[3] Calvin regularly strikes an additional note in his comments on the Saviour's life and work: Christ did not need to experience what he did. He did so to persuade us that he knows, understands and sympathizes with us in our weakness. He can be trusted to support us in our times of darkness:

> It was not because the Son of God needed to experience it to become accustomed to the emotion of mercy, but because he could not persuade us that he is kind and ready to help us, unless he had been tested by our misfortunes. ... Whenever, therefore, all kinds of evils press upon us, let this be our immediate consolation, that nothing befalls us which the Son of God has not experienced himself, so that he can sympathize with us; and let us not doubt that he is with us in it as if he were distressed along with us.[4]

In other words, the key to salvation and assurance lies in the extent to which the Son of God has come near to us in his incarnation, actually entering into our situation, tasting our experience from the inside, and exchanging his strength and confidence for our fears and frailties. This sense—that Christ enters into our life and bears the cursed condition from underneath, as it were, so that we may make the faith-discovery that all that is lacking in us is to be found in Christ—is nowhere in all Christian literature given more exquisite expression than in these words:

[1] *Harmony of the Gospels, Matthew, Mark and Luke*, tr. A. W. Morrison, ed. D. W. and T. F. Torrance (Edinburgh: St Andrew Press, 1972), III:99.

[2] See, e.g. his commentaries on Luke 2:40; 19:41; Phil. 2:7; cf. also *Institutes*, II.xiv.3.

[3] *Institutes*, III.xi.9. Cf. his commentaries on Isa. 42:1 and Heb. 5:1.

[4] *Commentary on Hebrews*, tr. W. B. Johnston, ed. D. W. and T. F. Torrance (Edinburgh: St Andrew Press, 1963), p. 33 (on 2:17). Cf his comments on Heb. 4:14, *ibid.*, p. 55.

We see that our salvation and all its parts are comprehended in Christ (Acts 4:12). We should therefore take care not to derive the least portion of it from anywhere else. If we seek salvation, we are taught by the very name of Jesus that it is 'of him' (1 Cor. 1:30). ...

If we seek strength it lies in his dominion; if purity, in his conception; if gentleness, it appears in his birth. For by his birth he was made like us in all respects (Heb. 2:17) that he might learn to feel our pain (cf. Heb. 5:2) ... in short, since rich store of every kind of good abounds in him, let us drink our fill from this fountain, and from no other.[1]

But what, exactly, was involved in the *Logos* assuming our human nature?

The nature of the incarnation

The Son of God's motivation in assuming humanity was to redeem us. Calvin has shown that the precise way in which he assumes humanity brings Christ within trusting distance, as it were.

What, then, was the nature of the humanity the *Logos* assumed?

It was, first and foremost, our flesh he took in the Virgin Mary's womb. Calvin had no time for a theology without a genuine incarnation.[2] Christ was genuinely conceived in the womb of Mary—she was not merely a conduit for a humanity forged in heaven (*contra* Menno Simons who taught that the *Logos* became man 'not of the womb, but in the womb' of Mary).[3] He thus came near to us, says Calvin, 'indeed touches us, since he is our flesh'.[4]

Such flesh was like ours. In it Christ grew in wisdom and knowledge because, as a man, he was 'subject to ignorance' (albeit voluntarily, not necessarily like ourselves). Calvin thus starkly accepts what some of the Fathers had found so difficult to come to terms with: if the *Logos* really took human nature, then in that nature he experienced an innocent ignorance akin to that of Adam before the fall. 'He freely took that

---

[1] Calvin, *Institutes*, II.xvi.19.
[2] *Ibid.*, II.xiii.1.
[3] *Ibid.*, II.xiii.3.
[4] *Ibid.*, II.xii.1.

which cannot be separated from human nature.'[1] This included all the emotions and affections of our common humanity in its weakness and infirmity. Commenting on Jesus' response of inner groaning at the grave of Lazarus, Calvin notes:

> When the Son of God put on our flesh he also of his own accord put on human feelings, so that he differed in nothing from his brethren, sin only excepted. ... Our feelings are sinful because they rush on unrestrainedly and immoderately; but in Christ they were composed and regulated in obedience to God and were completely free from sin.[2]

Christ is not 'an idle spectator'[3] of the human condition, but a participant in it. Indeed so much is this the case, Calvin argues, that if we did not recognize the significance of Christ's humanity we would, like the Jews, find it an immense stumbling block that he took on a 'lowly and earthly body subject to many infirmities'.[4] In a word, the *Logos* became real flesh. Thus Calvin comments on John 1:14 ('the Word became flesh ...'):

> This word [*sarx*] expresses his [John's] meaning more forcibly than if he had said that he was made man. He wanted to show to what a low and abject state the Son of God descended from the height of his heavenly glory for our sake. When Scripture speaks of man derogatorily it calls him 'flesh'. How great is the distance between the spiritual glory of the Word of God and the stinking filth of our flesh. Yet the Son of God stooped so low as to take to himself that flesh addicted to so many wretchednesses.[5]

Elsewhere Calvin can speak of Christ joining the infinite glory of God 'to our polluted flesh so that the two become one',[6] and of the

---

[1] Calvin, *Institutes*, II.xii.1.

[2] John Calvin, *Commentary on The Gospel according to St John*, 11-21, tr. T. H. L. Parker; ed. D. W. and T. F. Torrance (Edinburgh: St Andrew Press, 1961), p. 12 (on John 11:33).

[3] *Ibid.*, p. 13 (on John 11:36).

[4] Calvin, *Comm. Colossians*, pp. 314-15 (on Col. 1:22).

[5] Calvin, *Comm. John*, 1-10, pp. 10-20 (on John 1:14).

[6] Calvin, *Comm. Timothy*, p. 233 (on 1 Tim. 3:16). Calvin's language here (*cum*

'weakness' and 'abasement' of the flesh which the Son assumed.[1] It had 'the appearance of being sinful' and 'a certain resemblance to our sinful nature'.[2] He saves from within, underneath, and surrounded by this humanity, flesh of our flesh, bone of our bone.

Undoubtedly the most striking exposition of this in Calvin appears in his understanding of the experience of our Lord in Gethsemane (which he thinks of as a village). Alongside, perhaps even beyond Christ's admission of ignorance, the nature of Christ's suffering in Gethsemane and the apparent ambivalence of his will had long been seen as an intractable difficulty for those who believed in his absolute divinity. Calvin summarizes the struggles of the church's theologians to come to terms with this. Since it 'seems to be below the dignity of Christ's divine glory that he was affected with panic and sorrow, many interpreters are vehemently concerned to find a way out'.[3]

Calvin's response to these interpreters is illuminating:

> Their efforts were thoughtless and fruitless; if we are ashamed of his fear and sorrow, our redemption will trickle away and be lost. … Those who pretend the Son of God was immune from human passions do not truly and seriously acknowledge him as man.[4]

In a sermon on Gethsemane, preached towards the end of his own life, Calvin justifies the theological coherence of his exegesis at this point on the grounds that men are creatures who experience affections that do not belong by rights to God.[5] And in his *Harmony of the Gospels* he writes with similar vigour:

> But within the capacity of a sane and unspoiled human nature, he was struck with fright and seized with anguish, and so compelled to

---

hac nostra carnis putredine) is characteristically strong, conveying the notion of something that has gone rotten.

[1] Calvin, *Comm. Philippians*, p. 248 (on Phil. 2:7).

[2] John Calvin, *Commentary on The Epistles of Paul the Apostle to the Romans and to the Thessalonians*, tr. R. Mackenzie, ed. D. W. and T. F. Torrance (Edinburgh: St Andrew Press, 1972), p. 159 (on Rom. 8:3). Calvin is at pains however to point out that 'the flesh of Christ was unpolluted by any stain'.

[3] Calvin, *Harmony of the Gospels*, III:147 (on Matt. 26:37).

[4] *Ibid.*

[5] *Sermons on the Deity of Christ*, p. 58.

shift (as it were) between the violent waves of trial from one prayer to another. This is the reason why he prays to be spared death, then holds himself in check, submits himself to the Father's command, and corrects and revokes the wish that had suddenly escaped him. ... This was no rehearsed prayer of Christ's, but the force and onset of grief wrung a cry from him on the instant, which he at once went on to correct. The same vehemence took from him any thoughts of the decree of heaven, so that for a moment he did not think how he was sent to be the Redeemer of the human race. Often heavy anxiety clouds the eyes from seeing everything at once. ...

Yet,

> As various musical sounds, different from each other, make no discord but compose a tuneful and sweet harmony, so in Christ there exists a remarkable example of balance between the wills of God and of man; they differ without conflict or contradiction.[1]

The point of such quotations is not necessarily to defend every part of Calvin's exegesis, or the self-consistency of the whole as a theological construct, but to underline the seriousness with which he took the incarnation. For Calvin, Christ really can act for us because he is one with us, sin apart. We should not be alarmed to discover Christ's weakness, since the Saviour held it in such check. But we should learn to recognize that the extent to which he is able to save us is correlative to the extent to which he became fully like us, while 'pure and free from all vice and stain'[2] because of his sanctification by the Spirit in the womb of the virgin Mary at the moment of his generation.[3]

Incarnation and atonement

The Son of God took our human nature in order to redeem us. It is axiomatic with Calvin that unless Christ is really one of us, united to us by a common nature, and that his human nature is identical to ours

---

[1] *Harmony of the Gospels*, III:149-51 (on Matt. 26:37-39).

[2] *Institutes*, II.xiii.4.

[3] See *The Catechism of the Church of Geneva* (1541), questions 53 and 54 in which the sanctifying ministry of the Spirit in the conception of Christ is spelled out. Cf. his comments in *Institutes*, II.xiii.4 and also on Luke 1:35 in the *Harmony of the Gospels*.

(sin apart), he cannot be our Saviour. This explains his problem with the Lutheran doctrine of the ubiquity of the resurrected humanity of Christ (which lies behind the Lutheran view of the real presence of Christ in the Lord's Supper)—it no longer remains authentic humanity.[1] The one who possesses it could not save us because he is not really one of us.

But the Son goes beyond assuming our nature; he also assumes our name and place, so that we see 'the person of a sinner and evildoer represented in Christ'. Commenting on Galatians 3:13, Calvin notes:

> He took our place and thus became a sinner and subject to the curse, not in himself indeed, but in us; yet in such a way that it was necessary for him to act in our name.[2]

What Calvin additionally emphasizes, however, is that while Christ's saving work climaxes in his death and resurrection, this bearing of our name and nature is to be traced back to the very beginning of his life: 'from the time he took on the form of a servant, he began to pay the price of liberation in order to redeem us'.[3] Again,

> How has Christ abolished sin, banished the separation between us and God, and acquired righteousness to render God favourable and kindly toward us? To this we can in general reply that he has achieved this for us by the whole course of his obedience.

His obedience is an obedience unto (even *into*) death, as well as in death.[4]

But, in addition to this ongoing (active) obedience, Christ accomplished our salvation 'more exactly'[5] on the cross when he bore the judgment curse of death as sin's wages. Here again we see him bearing the name and person of Adam. Calvin brings this out in the remarkable way in which he treats the gospel passion narrative as a theological as well as an historical drama. Christ is explicitly charged with the two great Adamic sin-crimes: *blasphemy*, in that he sought to be equal with God; and *treason*, in that he rebelled against his lawfully constituted authority.

---

[1] Calvin, *Institutes*, IV.17.17.

[2] Calvin, *Comm. Galatians, Ephesians, Philippians and Colossians*, p. 55.

[3] Calvin, *Institutes*, II.16.5. Cf. III.8.1 and also his *Comms.* on John 17:19, Rom. 5:19, and Gal. 4:4-5.

[4] Calvin, *Institutes*, II.16.5.

[5] *Ibid.*

This is what it means for Christ to bear 'our person', as Calvin so often puts it. Taking the character of a sinner, he undergoes the just judgment of God against our sins. Repeatedly pronounced innocent before human tribunals—as he is before every tribunal in heaven and earth—yet he is executed as though he had the character of a sinner under the law of God. This is the ultimate explanation for his trembling in Gethsemane:

> It was not simple horror of death, the passing away from the world, but the sight of the dread tribunal of God that came to him, the Judge himself armed with vengeance beyond understanding. ... No wonder if death's fearful abyss tormented him grievously. ... There is nothing more dreadful than to feel God as Judge, whose wrath is worse than all deaths. When the trial came on Christ in this form, that he was now against God and doomed to ruin, he was overcome with dread ... as though under the wrath of God, he were cast into the labyrinth of evil.[1]

But when Calvin has said that the life and death of Christ involved obedience and bearing the penalty of sin, he has not spoken his final word. That word has been spoken only when he has added that all this was *pro nobis*, for us. It was substitutionary (for us) as well as penal (for sin). Grasp this and we grasp both the wonder of God's love and receive the assurance of salvation. For Calvin, one cannot read the passion narrative without being confronted by the substitutionary nature of what is happening and by the soteriological implications it carries. Here, on the stage of history an exchange is being played out. Thus, in commenting on Matthew's passion narrative he highlights the fact that a theological transaction is taking place.

The powerful combination of chiasmic rhythm and contrasting statements underlines the wonder of the great exchange involved in the work of atonement. First he comments on Christ being spat upon:

(A) The *face* of Christ,
   (B) marred with *spittle* and *blows*
(A) has restored to us that *image*
   (B) which sin had *corrupted*, indeed *destroyed*,[2]

[1] *Harmony of the Gospels*, III:148, 207-8 (on Matt. 26:37 and 27:46).
[2] *Ibid.*, p. 168 (on Matt. 26:67).

Calvin continues:

(A) Christ *said nothing*
    (B) when the priests *pressed* Him from every side,

(A) in order to open our mouths by His *silence.*
    (B) Hence the glorious *freedom* which Paul acclaims that

(A) we can call out with a *full voice* 'Abba, Father.'[1]

(A) Thus He was
    (B) reckoned worse than a *thief,*

(A) to
    (B) bring us into the company of the *angels.*[2]

(A) Whatever might be
    (B) Pilate's *purpose,*
    (B) God *wishes*
        (C) his Son's *innocence*
            (D) *attested* in this way,
            (D) that it might be more *clear*
        (C) that our *sins*
            (D) were *condemned* in Him.[3]

(A) So the
    (B) *ugliness*
        (C) He once endured on *earth*
        (C) now wins us grace in *heaven,*
    (B) and also restores the *image* of God,
        (C) which had not only been *polluted* with the filth of sin,
        (C) but almost *effaced.*

(A) So also
    (B) God's inestimable mercy *upon us* shines out,
        (C) in *lowering*
        (C) His only-begotten Son to these *depths,*
    (B) for *our sake.*[4]

---

[1] *Ibid.*, p. 179 (on Matt. 27:11).
[2] *Ibid.*, p. 184 (on Matt. 27:15).
[3] *Ibid.*, p. 187 (on Matt. 27:24).
[4] *Ibid.*, p. 189 (on Matt. 27:27).

(A) God willed
    (B) His Son to be *stripped*
        (C) that we should *appear freely*, with the angels,
    (B) in the *garments* of His righteousness and fullness of all good
        things,
        (C) whereas formerly *foul disgrace*,
    (B) in torn *clothes*,
        (C) *kept us away* from the approach to the heavens.
(A) Christ Himself allows
    (B) His *raiment* to be torn apart like booty
        (C) *to make us rich* with the riches of His victory.[1]

Here, for Calvin, is the solid ground on which salvation rests. In the fact that Christ has entered our life, shared our nature, taken our place, borne our sin, received our judgment, lies the foundation of our justification and acceptance with God.

But in addition, the manner in which this is accomplished encourages assurance. For the manner in which he has made the exchange—so evidently taking our place, bearing our guilt, facing our judgment, dying our death, rising for our triumph in our flesh—assures us that what he has done is both for us and suited to our needs. For here, in the climactic display of Jesus' love (John 13:1ff.) we are given the clearest demonstration of:

- *The love of God for us in his not-spared Son.* If he gives his Son for us, he will give to us everything necessary to effect the purposes for which he gave his Son (Rom. 8:32). Calvin believes that this apostolic logic, and behind it the logic of God, is irrefutable.

- *The forgiveness of sins.* The fact that in the Gospels we see Christ bearing sins before our eyes (as it were placarded before us, Gal. 3:1) leaves us in no doubt that our guilt has been objectively removed, our judgment absorbed in Christ. The sense of guilt, and the uncertainty it fosters, must yield to this solvent.

- *The hope of glory.* The Innocent One who appears in silence before

[1] *Ibid.*, p. 194 (on Matt. 27:35).

the earthly tribunal thereby accepts the condemnation of the Heavenly One. His mouth is shut; he is held to be guilty before God (Rom. 3:19). Because of his silence before the divine tribunal, we will be able to say 'Abba, Father' there.

For Calvin, nothing is more relevant than this to being a practical Calvinist. For the most practical Calvinists will be those who know such trust in, love for, and assurance of, Jesus Christ. The assurance that he is their Saviour sets them free to serve him in a life whose *leitmotif* is grace.

Against this background, it does not require vivid imagination to transport oneself to the congregation gathered in St Peter's Church, Geneva, on Wednesday, June 29, 1558. The asthmatic, disease-ridden Calvin, now some twenty minutes into his sermon, momentarily clears his throat, and makes his moving appeal:

> Since then there is in us nothing but spiritual infection and leprosy and that we are corrupt in our iniquities, what shall we do?
>
> What remedy is there?
>
> Shall we go to seek help from the angels in Paradise?
>
> Alas! They can do nothing for us.
>
> No, we must come to our Lord Jesus Christ, who was willing to be disfigured from the top of his head even to the sole of his feet and was a mass of wounds, flogged with many stripes and crowned with thorns, nailed and fastened to the cross and pierced through the side.
>
> This is how we are healed; here is our true medicine, with which we must be content, and which we must embrace wholeheartedly, knowing that otherwise we can never have inward peace but must always be tormented and tortured to the extreme, unless Jesus Christ comforts us and appeases God's wrath against us. When we are certain of that, we have cause to sing his praises,[1] instead of being capable of nothing but trembling and confusion.[2]

[1] In the light of this exploration of Calvin's thinking, it is difficult to avoid the conclusion that the hymn *Je te salue, mon certain Rédempteur* ('I Greet Thee Who My Sure Redeemer Art') was indeed written by Calvin himself (to whom it has been attributed) or by someone both intimately acquainted with his theology and sharing much of his personal experience.

[2] John Calvin, *Sermons on Isaiah's Prophecy of the Death and Passion of Christ*, tr. and ed. T. H. L. Parker (London: James Clarke, 1956), p. 75.

CHAPTER SIX

JOHN CALVIN:
COMMENTATOR FOR PREACHERS

C ALVIN'S Old and New Testament commentaries differ from each other in style.[1] More than half of the former have their immediate origin in his classroom lectures to his students, while the latter were all specifically written as commentaries, although no doubt his New Testament lectures and his comments at *Les Congré-gations* (the weekly pastors' meetings in Geneva) lie in the background. More accurately, many of the New Testament commentaries were probably dictated by Calvin from his bed—on which he spent long hours, physically weakened, but mentally vigorous!

The publication of an entire series of commentaries was clearly already on the still-young Reformer's mind while he was working on the second edition of his *Institutes* in 1539. He wrote to his readers, explaining his programme:

> If, after this road has, as it were, been paved, I shall publish any interpretations of Scripture, I shall always condense them, because I shall have no need to undertake long doctrinal discussions, and to digress into commonplaces. In this way the godly reader will be spared great annoyance and boredom[!] ...[2]

Calvin was probably already well through the preparation of his first commentary—on Romans—as he wrote; the impact of his concentrated

---

[1] For background to Calvin as a biblical commentator, see T. H. L. Parker's *Calvin's New Testament Commentaries* (London: SCM Press, 1971) and his later *Calvin's Old Testament Commentaries* (Edinburgh: T. & T. Clark, 1986).
[2] 'John Calvin to the Reader', *Institutes*, pp. 4-5.

study of the epistle is evident in various ways in the 1539 and later editions of the *Institutes*.

The Romans commentary was published in 1540. From hints he gives in later commentaries it is clear that the plan was to complete the exposition of the Pauline corpus, and thereafter the whole of the New Testament. And the Reformation public were hungry for the vision to come to fruition. But he was often hindered in this task. The second volume, on 1 Corinthians, did not appear until 1546. But during the last ten years of his life he completed the entire series, with the exception only of Revelation (which it is often said he claimed not to understand) and 2 and 3 John. Given his other activities and his tenuous health, it is a mark of his singular genius and determination that he was able to accomplish so much.

By a preacher for preachers

But Calvin for preachers? Can one expect much help from a master theologian (and, to those who have not read him, a rather intimidating one) when one is a preacher?

Perhaps it is as well to note what we do not get. There is little in the way of technical introduction and apparatus on display. Calvin cleared his work bench of the shavings before he presented his finished work. 'Lucid brevity' is his goal.[1] In contrast to the philosophy of recent commentary writing, Calvin self-consciously aimed for clutter-free volumes.

Again, there is little of major structural analysis—usually only a brief outline of the theme. For these, insofar as they prove valuable to interpreting Scripture, we need to look elsewhere.

But we do get some great and important things. For one thing, these are commentaries written by a preacher for preachers. Indeed the distinction between his commentaries and his sermons is largely a matter of form and context. For that reason alone, there is a great deal in Calvin's commentaries that translates easily into preaching.

Furthermore, since Calvin's great burden as an interpreter of Scripture is always to seek out the *scopus* of the text, his work is invaluable in

---

[1] The phrase is Calvin's own. See the dedicatory letter to Simon Grynaeus in his *Commentary on Romans*.

helping us get to the point (still a *sine qua non* of good preaching!). From this foundation, Calvin then provides us with solid theological and doctrinal instruction which grounds his rich application.

But, for most preachers, what gives real value to a commentary is a sometimes less easily defined quality: its ability to stimulate, to prime the pump for our own work on a passage, sometimes giving us a jump start when the batteries have begun to run low. Calvin does exactly this, occasionally in surprising ways. All this and more we discover in the *Commentary on the Gospel of John.*

The *Commentary on John* was published in 1553 and translated into French in the same year. In English it amounts to some 500 pages.[1] We cannot examine it exhaustively here, but in introducing it as an aid to preachers, three foci will give us a taste of its usefulness.

1. General characteristics

For Calvin the gospel is 'the glad and joyful message of the grace revealed to us in Christ, to teach us to despise the world and its transient riches and pleasures'.[2] This is a note which he strikes again and again.

The distinctiveness of John's Gospel is seen to be twofold:

First, John 'fills in' what the other Gospel writers omit—a relatively simple view of their inter-relationship.

Second, the Synoptic Gospels narrate more fully the history of Jesus' life and ministry. John, by contrast, has a focus on Christ's office (prophet, priest and king). Calvin puts it memorably, 'the first three exhibit his body, if I may be permitted to put it like that, but John shows his soul.'[3] Hence, for Calvin, as we read Scripture as a unified testimony to Christ, the Gospel of John provides the theological key by which we are to read the Synoptics. This becomes a basic hermeneutical principle.

Calvin had been educated in the context of French humanism. Its impact on him was already evident in his 1532 Commentary on Seneca's

---

[1] All references are from *Calvin's Commentaries: The Gospel according to St John*, 2 vols, tr. T. H. L. Parker, eds. D. W. and T. F. Torrance (Edinburgh: St Andrew Press, 1959; 1961). For convenience of reference the text on which Calvin is commenting is also given.

[2] I:5 ('The Theme').

[3] I:6 ('The Theme').

De Clementia. Now he added to his grammatical-historical exegetical instincts a strong theological and Christological sensitivity. Combining these, he typically will do several things as he works his way through the text.

1. He provides a simple statement of the *scopus* of the pericope, and where necessary adds some grammatical comments.

2. He expounds the theological significance of the passage, and, in particular within the context of John's Gospel, its Christological importance.

3. He shows its relation to and consistency with other parts of Scripture, providing harmonization where necessary.

4. On occasion he will suggest various possible interpretations, and indicate his disagreement with other commentators. Interestingly in his *Commentary on St John*, Augustine is a discussion partner with whom he regularly disagrees—an indication of his ability to appreciate the great Father's theological exposition of grace (in the *Institutes* Augustine is 'wholly ours'), while he is not always so comfortable with his exegesis!

5. He moves gracefully from exegesis to theology, but equally readily to practical application. Here the metaphor of the mirror, which is used in various ways in the Calvin corpus, is called into strategic service. Christ's dealing with one individual thereby becomes a paradigm for and an insight into his dealings with contemporary individuals and the entire church.

2. *Theological strengths*

One of the gains of contemporary Gospel scholarship is that the theological character of the Gospels is widely recognized. They are not merely an amalgamation of biographical facts (although they are not thereby fictional). For Calvin that perspective is so obvious as scarcely to require special stress. It would take us far beyond the boundaries of one brief study to explore the theological contribution of his *Commentary on St John* as an aid to preachers. But a few hints may be sufficient to underline its value.

John's Christology

John's Christology is magnificently expounded, and in particular there is a sensitivity to the full, real, and true humanity of Christ that outstrips almost everything in the Christian literature that preceded it. Calvin throbs with the robust, insightful, and sensitive expression he gives to what it meant for the Word to be made flesh. For example:

> the Son of God stooped so low as to take to himself that flesh addicted to so many wretchednesses. 'Flesh' here is not used for corrupt nature (as in Paul), but for mortal man. It denotes derogatorily his frail and almost transient nature.[1]

It is refreshing to sense that he actually believes in what he says and delights to express it so that he may himself contemplate it.

In this same area, it is salutary to observe so robust an exponent and defender of the deity of Christ seeking to listen in total silence to what the text is actually saying about him. Rather than stretching passages which speak of the oneness of Father and Son to turn them into proofs of Christ's absolute deity as such, Calvin sees several of the passages employed in the earlier patristic debates as expressions of the harmony between the Father and the incarnate Mediator rather than straightforward proof-texts for his deity. While he admires and defends the theology of the Fathers, his desire to be absolutely dictated to by the text of Scripture comes to the surface very evidently. His approach helps to illustrate the difference between rightly believing that something is a truth of Scripture and wrongly insisting that it is the truth of a particular passage which in fact states something different.

But, most of all, Calvin helps the preacher to see that preaching from a Gospel must be preaching full of Christ. That may seem to be an obvious and trivial thing to say, but a little reflection will indicate how easily preaching from the Gospels can focus more on 'what this passage says about us' than on 'what this passage says about Christ'. We all too easily leapfrog over the Scriptures to ourselves and our own situation and needs without giving adequate attention to expounding the character and work of Christ. Here Calvin becomes a companion to keep our eyes

---

[1] I:20, on John 1:14.

fixed on Christ 'clothed in the garments of his gospel'[1] (to use his own
beautiful expression).

Harmonization

Calvin approaches the question of harmonization with great sanity. In
principle he does not feel bound to be able to harmonize everything.
There is, after all, much that we do not know that might explain why
there are different perspectives in the Gospels. But when he does seek to
harmonize he does so with simplicity and modesty.[2]

Christ and the law

As readers of the *Institutes* would expect, he excels in the balance with
which he expresses the relationship of the old and new covenants, the
Old and New Testaments. He is especially good (in my view) on the relationship of the law to Christ and the incompleteness of the old order—
aspects of John's Gospel which even a swift-footed exposition of it is
bound to encounter.[3]

Practical Christian living

Deeply embedded in Calvin's theology is the correlation of (i) Christ's
work, (ii) the Spirit's ministry as the one who brings all of Christ's
resources to the Christian, and (iii) faith as the bond of union the Spirit
forges between the believer and Christ. The important statement opening *Institutes* Book III: 'as long as Christ remains outside of us, and we
are separated from him, all that he has suffered and done for the salvation of the human race remains useless and of no value to us'[4] is, in
John, given positive explication. Indeed, this is the significant nexus in
Calvin by means of which Christology and practical Christian living are
related.[5]

---

[1] *Institutes*, III.ii.6.
[2] For example, his approach to the temple cleansings, I:51, on John 2:12-17.
[3] For example, I:24-25, on John 1:17; I:137-9, on John 5:37-39; I:143, on John 5:46, 47.
[4] *Institutes*, III.i.1.
[5] For example, I:199, on John 7:38.

Divine sovereignty and election

Calvin, predictably, pays careful attention to John's emphasis on divine sovereignty and predetermination. Here he is helpful in ways that may surprise the new reader. In the *Institutes*, he is providing a guide to biblical theology for Christians. Yet even there his major focus on predestination lies within the context of his exposition of how we receive the grace of Christ (Book III). Indeed it seems to be deliberately located at the end of Book III as one of three ultimate mysteries in Christian experience—divine election, prayer, and the resurrection.

In the *Commentary on St John*, however, Calvin is able to expound election in the context of the teaching of our Lord. This gives him (and other preachers) two advantages. The first is that it is the teaching of Jesus himself he is expounding. Some of the emotional difficulties (prejudices?) Christians experience with election begin to dissolve when we hear it taught from the lips of Jesus. Secondly, it becomes clear that Jesus taught this doctrine largely within two contexts: (i) the need for his disciples to be encouraged; (ii) his own rejection by the religious unconverted. This does not diminish the full blown divine sovereignty to which Calvin is committed, but it enables him to set it within a personal, spiritual, moral context rather than an abstract metaphysical one.[1]

Exposure of hypocrisy

This last note brings us to a further striking aspect of Calvin's treatment. He is especially powerful in his exposing of hypocrisy. He well grasps the thread running through the first half of John's Gospel of ongoing opposition to and hatred of Jesus by those who wore the mask of true religion. And since he sees continuities between the old and new covenant churches, Calvin is able to apply this in a contemporary way with considerable rigour. He speaks from very painful and profound experience at this juncture. But his exposition is not a sudden blast of vituperation. He very carefully works God's word under the skin of hypocrisy and irresistibly unmasks it. 'Even if the whole world should boil over in rage, we must proclaim God's glory' is his watchword.[2]

[1] For example, I:160ff., on John 6:37-39.
[2] I:120, on John 7:9; cf. also I:183-84, on John 7:9-13; II:108, 113-14, on John 15:23 and 16:2.

The burdens of ministry

Finally, Calvin's exposition is full of telling passages and a substantial number of one-liners which leap out of the page at the preacher to indicate that here is a man who has sat where he sits, struggling with the great task of leading the flock of Christ, bearing with their infirmities and seeking to lead them to maturity and fruitfulness through the ministry of the word. Not only is his understanding of the labyrinth of the human heart profound, but his empathy with the burdens of the minister of the gospel is enormously encouraging.[1]

3. Particular illustration

The best brief way to demonstrate the value of Calvin for preachers is to examine one particular chapter of the commentary as a kind of *hors d'oeuvre* to whet the appetite. While John's Gospel will be preached through perhaps only once during years of ministry, for most preachers Easter comes round once a year, with its concentration of sermons on one theme. John chapter 20 should therefore provide us with a test case broadly applicable sooner rather than later.[2]

In what follows, Calvin's exposition will be filtered in order to indicate the suggestiveness of what he writes. He will not write your sermons for you (and ought never to be allowed to!), but he does sit down alongside you in your preparation, like a teacher saying: 'See that? See this? What can you make of this aspect, and that, of the text?'

His comments fall fairly naturally into four sections:

The discovery of the resurrection, John 20:1-10

(i) Calvin draws our attention here to the sheer abundance of evidence for the resurrection. Like Paul (1 Cor. 15:5-8), he is impressed by the force of the resurrected Christ's appearances.

But why did Jesus appear first to women, whose position in contemporary society was so low? Calvin's response is not to deny the presupposition but to reject the implied deduction: Precisely(!)—this is the way God works (1 Cor. 1:28).

(ii) He deals with the question of the relationship between this account

---

[1] For example, II:64, on John 13:20; II:104, on John 15:17; II:218-21, on John 21:15-17.
[2] II:191-214, on John chapter 20.

and that of the other Gospels, and with a whole series of harmonization 'problems': the number of women; the difference in time—when did Jesus appear to Mary (which he resolves in terms of different narrative functions); the nature of communications between Mary and John and Peter (in John's Gospel) and Mary and the eleven (in the Synoptic Gospels).

It would be a dreary Easter sermon that explained how problems of harmonization in the Easter narrative are to be resolved, and a foolish man who preached it! But the positive side of what Calvin does is the way he pieces together the fragments as a whole to provide one unified account of an extraordinary morning. Thinking through these issues with him strengthens the sense of the reality and wonder of the events themselves.

(iii) But it is when Calvin looks at the narrative from the perspective of its lessons for us that his commentary comes into its own. Noting how remarkable it is that the disciples even went to the tomb, he views it as an illustration of the way in which the seed of faith can be smothered, yet brought to life by an action of the Spirit set within the context of a providential work of God. This drove the disciples back to the Scriptures (e.g. Isa. 55:3 interpreted in terms of Acts 13:34; Psa. 16:10; 110:1; Isa. 53:8) which they had known but did not well understand. Here is one of those instances when an event becomes a 'mirror' of the characteristic working of God—as is also true, for Calvin, of the way in which Peter is slower than John in reaching the tomb, but enters it first—many have more given to them at the end than appears at the beginning!

(iv) There is a striking note on the significance of the linen cloths; they are 'so to say, the slough, which would produce faith in Christ's resurrection'.[1] With solid common sense Calvin comments that you do not strip a body if your intention is to steal it! In John's observation that the napkin which had covered Jesus' head and face lay separate from the linen shroud (John 20:7), Calvin finds interesting grounds here for the refutation of such relics as the Turin Shroud.

In different ways these comments surely help to prime most pumps!

---

[1] II:193, on John 20:5; 'slough' in the sense of skin shed by a snake.

Encounter with Mary, John 20:11-18

In harmonizing the resurrection accounts, Calvin concluded that other women were present with Mary, but he rejects the idea that the reason John does not mention their presence is that they fainted. Wise man! Indeed, he chastises the women for their useless weeping.

Primarily, however, this encounter with Mary becomes in Calvin's hands a mirror of divine calling. It illustrates the point that Jesus never deals with people merely in terms of surface relationships. What we have is a paradigm of what Christ does now through the Spirit.

(i) Mary's understanding is veiled. Christ presents himself to her, but he is not yet recognized. Similarly our minds are covered in folly; we are bewildered spiritually. Mary (like us) is concerned with earthly things (Jesus' body). Like us, there is no room for resurrection in her thinking. So she does not, indeed cannot, recognize him.

(ii) Illumination is given. Jesus' physical appearance is unchanged. But he now assumes the character of Master, and speaks with a sovereign accent. This precisely mirrors the more didactic form of the same truth in John 10: Jesus is the Good Shepherd who knows his sheep and calls them by name in such a way that the sheep recognize his voice and follow him (John 10:3-4, 14). Thus, (a) Jesus calls Mary by name; (b) His voice penetrates inwardly, awakening recognition; (c) Recognizing Christ as risen, she trusts and honours him.

But if Mary has come to faith, why the insistence on not touching him—especially in view of Matthew 28:9 ('They … clasped his feet …'), and the invitation given to Thomas later in John 20:27? Calvin answers: the grip of Matthew 28:9 was the grip of worship, not of possessiveness. Here Mary's zeal was misplaced, a holding on to his earthly body, a return to the pre-resurrection world. The purpose of the resurrection is not that he should remain thus in this world, but that he should enter into his kingdom and from his throne govern the church through the Spirit.

(iii) A commission is received. The women return to tell others. Does this ground an argument for women's office in the church, asks Calvin in passing? No, he responds, and provides us with one of his many well-crafted one-liners: Christ never intends what is 'done by a single privilege to be taken as an example'.[1]

---

[1] II:200, on John 20:17.

Understanding veiled, illumination given, commission received. The movement from reading the passage with Calvin's help to formulating a progressive series of points or stages in exposition and application is—at least in this case—almost painless!

Two interesting further points should be touched on here. Calvin treats the words 'my Father and your Father … my God and your God' not as underlining the differentiation between Christ and believers, but rather their adoption into the family of God, whereby they partake of all the blessings that are in Christ. In addition he notes how expressive of God's grace it is that Mary, from whom Jesus cast out seven demons, should be the first human witness of his resurrection. Calvin sees in this God bringing her 'out of the deepest hell to raise her above heaven'.[1]

Breathing of the Spirit, John 20:19-23

This third section is a well-known crux in Johannine studies. In general Calvin notes the providence of God in gathering the disciples together; but suggests that the closed doors show their lack of faith. Incidentally, he does not believe that John suggests that Jesus passed through a closed door. And further, he rejects the popular idea of Christ now having 'rich wounds, yet visible above, in beauty glorified'.

Here three questions are faced which almost invite homiletical formulation:

(i) What is the significance of the event? It is Christ's appointing of the apostles to their extra-ordinary future office. He had been their teacher: now, as his 'sent ones', they are to have the same function, role, and authority.

(ii) What is the meaning of the breathing? It is a symbolic act by which Christ institutes the apostles into their new ministry, putting forth the power of the Spirit. The whole event is a stage *en route* to Pentecost. This was a sprinkling, that an outpouring of the Spirit.

On a polemical note with a contemporary ring, Calvin points out that this breathing belongs to Christ alone, not to men or bishops—who 'boast of making sacrificing priests when they belch over them'! All they do, Calvin notes with obvious relish, is to 'change horses into asses'.[2] It

[1] II:200, on John 20:17.
[2] II:204-6, on John 20:22-23.

is not too difficult to deduce what his comments might be on analogous practices today.

The overall principle to be emphasized is clear: when Christ ordains to ministry he furnishes with all necessary gifts. The word and the Spirit are conjoined, as always for Calvin.

(iii) In what sense could the apostles pardon sins? Calvin notes that in this context Jesus is commissioning them to preach the gospel; since pardon is the fruit of their preaching, it must be the means implied. Not auricular confession but gospel proclamation is the instrument of forgiveness. What we need is 'Not confessors who speak in low mutters but heralds who speak up and seal in hearts the grace of the atonement.'[1]

Confession of Thomas, John 20:24-29

In this final section, Calvin draws attention to the *scopus* of the narrative of Thomas's unbelief: it serves to confirm the faith of the godly.

Thomas is seen as obstinate, proud, and wise in his own eyes. Yet Jesus condescends to him, not just for Thomas's own sake, but for us. Thomas represents faith buried, which in God's grace is revived—like David's faith was until Nathan came.

Undergirding this lies another principle. God holds, restrains, and keeps his elect by a secret bridle, although in themselves they are as guilty as if they had renounced the faith.

This leads to his comments on Thomas's confession, 'My Lord and my God.' The doubter's recognition of Jesus' incarnate identity leads to a confession of eternal deity. Here Christology from below meets Christology from above! But, Calvin adds, we cannot confess Christ truly as Lord without recognizing him as God.

Here again Calvin's 'mirror principle' for drawing application from a narrative passage of Scripture is evident. It should be carefully distinguished from a moralistic and even an exemplary use of the text. It is in fact a Christocentric use. He does not move in his exposition immediately from Thomas to us. Rather, he begins with Christ. He then moves from Christ to Thomas, from Thomas to Christ, and then to us *via* the principle that Christ sends the Spirit to continue the very ministry he

---

[1] II:208, on John 20:23.

had thus begun (cf. John 14:16; 16:7-11). He does not say: Look at the passage, see yourself. Rather the dynamic of his application is: Look at the passage, see Jesus; understand the Spirit's ministry: now see yourself. This is a helpful hermeneutical safeguard against the unhealthy aspects of a tendency to either moralism or naked exemplarism.

Calvin concludes with notes drawn from the promise of blessing which is given to believing without seeing. First, to clear the ground of any naive misunderstanding, he harmonizes this saying with Matthew 13:16. Secondly, he draws from this principle the conclusion that the doctrine of and belief in transubstantiation are frivolous.

Conclusion, John 20:30-31

He closes with comments on verses 30-31: many other signs given to that age were not recorded for us according to John 20:30. For Calvin—and indeed for the Catholic Church—miracles acted as confirmation of revelation. That was why, in the Address to King Francis I, which prefaced the *Institutes*, he had found it necessary to defend his cessationist position over against the Roman criticism that the Reformation gospel had no attesting miracles. Here, as there, he defends the Reformation by pointing out that the gospel is already sufficiently attested.[1] The fact that these miracles have been recorded assures us in an age when miracles are not given that the gospel has already been abundantly confirmed once and for all.

The Gospel of John was written that we might believe and have life. This, then, says Calvin, is the chief head of John's teaching: outside of Christ we are dead; by his grace we are restored. The Gospel as a whole, and each chapter in it, should be read and expounded in this light. Precisely this is what he helps us to do in his treatment of chapter 20, and indeed of the whole Gospel. Calvin is not a quick fix, but he is an invaluable companion in the lifelong adventure of preaching the word!

---

[1] Prefatory Address by John Calvin to Francis I, King of France, *Institutes*, p. 17.

CHAPTER SEVEN

CHRISTOLOGY AND PNEUMATOLOGY: JOHN CALVIN, THE THEOLOGIAN OF THE HOLY SPIRIT

A T the time of the four-hundredth anniversary of the birth of John Calvin in 1909, one of his most distinguished disciples, B. B. Warfield, famously described his mentor as 'pre-eminently *the theologian of the Holy Spirit*'.[1] At the end of the intervening century, marked as it has been by claims that the Holy Spirit is 'the neglected' or 'the forgotten' person of the Trinity, Warfield's words remind us how easy it is to live the Christian life on an island isolated from all that God has done in the church of the previous nineteen centuries. It is one aspect of the calling of the church historian to remind us of the past in order that we may see the present and the future with greater clarity. The Holy Spirit has not always been 'forgotten'.

John Calvin and the Holy Spirit?

Despite Warfield, the combination continues to raise eyebrows. In the church at large it is still with other, usually regarded as darker, themes that Calvin's name tends to be connected. The word associations for 'Calvin' tend to be 'predestination', 'theocracy', or 'Servetus'. Even (especially?) in the academy, in the period before the First

---

[1] B. B. Warfield, 'John Calvin: The Man and His Work', *Calvin and Calvinism, Works of Benjamin B. Warfield*, 10 vols (New York: Oxford University Press, 1927–32), V:21. I. John Hesselink notes a predecessor in Charles Lelièvre in 1901, but dates Warfield's comment by the publication of his collected writings. See Herman J. Selderhuis, *The Calvin Handbook* (Grand Rapids: Eerdmans, 2009), p. 299. Warfield had probably entertained the thought for many years.

World War, any note of grace and graciousness in Calvin's theology was relatively little appreciated. He was not often associated with the beautiful words of the hymn attributed to him, 'I Greet Thee Who My Sure Redeemer Art'. Consequently it was astonishing that B. B. Warfield should state with such confidence (as he did on more than one occasion)[1] that Calvin was 'the theologian of the Holy Spirit'. It is clear, however, that Warfield's judgment can be vindicated as both sound scholarship and a considerable insight into Calvin's trinitarian theology—for at least two reasons:

Pervasive in his theology

The role and ministry of the Holy Spirit pervade Calvin's theology as a whole. They are notably evident in his thinking in the following areas:

1. In the creation and divine governing of the world in general and the people of God in particular.

2. In the special providence of the miraculous.

3. In the giving of Scripture and in the church's reception of the knowledge of God from Scripture.

4. In the life and ministry of Jesus.

5. In relation to union with Christ, where the Spirit is instrumental in our entering into all the benefits of Christ's work and the blessings of grace.

6. In the context of the mystery of the sacraments of baptism and the Lord's Supper.

This is not to argue that the central motif in the theology of Calvin is the role of the Holy Spirit. But it is to say that unless we recognize his role in Calvin's theology we will never come fully to appreciate Calvin as a theologian, and we will have little sense of his heartbeat as a Christian.

---

[1] Cf. *John Calvin: The Man and his Work*, p. 21. Originally an article printed in *The Methodist Review* in October 1909 and reprinted as a pamphlet. Also published in *Calvin and Calvinism* in *Works of Benjamin B. Warfield*, V:3-26.

Interwoven in encyclopedia

A second reason for speaking of Calvin as the theologian of the Holy
Spirit is that he does something new in a systematic way in his theology. While there are some outstanding exceptions, major works on the
person and work of the Holy Spirit are relatively sparse in the history of
theology. The *De Spiritu Sancto* of Basil of Caesarea and the *De Proces-
sione Spiritus Sancti* of Anselm of Canterbury provide the bookends of
patristic through scholastic thinking.[1] John Owen's great *Pneumatologia*
was clearly the dominant work in post-Reformation thought.[2] Calvin
himself did not write a dogmatic treatise on the Spirit. For that matter,
of course, neither did he write one on the fatherhood of God or the
person and work of Christ; but he did give locus-style attention to these
themes in the *Institutes*.

At first glance, then, we might guess that Calvin was simply following
in the normal, if not normative, tradition of refraining from writing on
the Spirit as a locus of theology, since the Spirit always brought glory to
Christ and not to himself. Or perhaps he refrained simply because he
thought he had nothing distinctive to contribute to the discussion of the
person and work of the Spirit, since the fundamental issues concerning
the deity of the Spirit, and the formulation of the trinitarian dogma, had
been long since settled.

But, in fact, there is a deliberateness in the way Calvin does not lock
up the Holy Spirit in one locus of theology. After all, he seems very
intentional in the creedal-trinitarian structure which the later editions
of the *Institutes* possess.[3] In that context an extensive treatment of the
locus *De Spiritu Sancto* would surely have been in keeping with the
overall plan of his *opus magnum*. By holding a high view of the Spirit's

---

[1] Basil's treatise, published in 374–75, was stimulated by the controversy he evoked
in September 374 by pronouncing the doxology 'Glory to the Father, with the Son,
with the Holy Spirit' [rather than the customary 'Glory to the Father in the Son
through the Holy Spirit']. Anselm wrote his treatise following his participation in
the Council of Bari which involved both Eastern and Western theologians.

[2] See John Owen, ΠΝΕΥΜΑΤΑΛΟΓΙΑ or *A Discourse Concerning the Holy Spirit*,
Works, III.

[3] Book I, God the Father, Book II, God the Son, Book III, the Application of
Redemption (and by implication, therefore, the special role appropriated by the
Spirit), Book IV, the Church and Sacraments.

person and work, yet refraining from a specific locus exposition, Calvin thus demonstrates that the Spirit's personal influence must pervade all theology, and touch it at every point precisely because he is the executive member of the Godhead.

In this way Calvin serves as the great bridge between the Reformation theology of the sixteenth century and the Puritan and evangelical theology of the seventeenth century onwards, with its stress on the necessity of the Spirit's ministry for the application of redemption and the experience of salvation in Christ.[1] Calvin, therefore, is the theologian of the Spirit because he sets the tone for so much future theological development.

The context of his exposition

Of course, Calvin did not develop or expound his doctrine of the Spirit in a vacuum. It is evident that his thinking developed within a polemical as well as a theological context. In particular he self-consciously opposed two different emphases in sixteenth-century theology.

The first was Roman Catholicism. From his perspective Rome had locked up salvation in the institutions and instruments of the church. Under the *magisterium* of the Church salvation was effected in a sacramental and apparently *ex opere operato* fashion. This meant not only an adding to Scripture but also, where the efficacy of grace was distributed sacramentally, through the physical channels of the Church, the Holy Spirit was replaced and his role usurped. In this sense Calvin stresses a neglected '*sola*' of the Reformation, namely *solus Spiritus*, which for him must be the constant companion of *solo Christo*. Consequently,

1. For all practical purposes the priesthood effected sacramentally what Calvin saw in Scripture was effected only by the Holy Spirit.

2. The *magisterium* of the Church usurped the internal ministry of the Spirit in persuading people of the authority of God's word and illuminating to them its saving message.

[1] Most notably in the extensive treatment by John Owen, *Works*, vols III and IV, and by Thomas Goodwin, *The Works of Thomas Goodwin*, vol. VI (Edinburgh: James Nichol, 1863).

3. Adherence to the institution of the Church became the only hope of security, in the Roman system. By contrast Calvin saw in Scripture a testimony of the Spirit bringing freedom, joy, assurance, and release from a spirit of bondage. Thus—and this was a remarkably simple insight—in Calvin's estimation, Roman theology was not only an offence against the sole mediation of Christ, but also against the sole executive of salvation, the Holy Spirit.

If this first malevolent influence involved *replacing* the Spirit by the Church, the second involved *dividing* the Spirit from the word. Here we find Calvin in polemical opposition not only against Rome, but now against sectarian groups within the Protestant movement itself. If he accused Catholicism of institutionalizing the Spirit, then he in turn needed to distinguish his teaching from those who in their emphasis on the Spirit ignored or neglected the word. This further involved Calvin in defending his teaching from the attack that he was biblicizing the Spirit, thus binding the church to a formal biblicism which emphasized the letter and not the Spirit, and thus tended to legalism rather than the freedom of the Spirit.

In response we find Calvin frequently emphasizing—as a refrain in his teaching—that we can never separate the Spirit from the word, precisely because the Spirit is the author of the word, and executes the will of God in covenantal consistency with the word of God. Thus, for example, he writes that those who forsake the word for the Spirit are guilty of 'fatal fantasies in which fanatics entangle themselves when they abandon the word and invent some sort of vague and erratic spirit'.[1] A recurring theme in Calvin's thought, therefore, is that Christ, the Spirit, and the word are not to be separated. For the Scriptures are the sceptre by which Christ rules over the church as its Lord.

Debate continues as to exactly how much real knowledge Calvin had of some of these movements in sixteenth-century Europe. What is clear is that he was familiar with claims of groups in the Netherlands and France to be living by the Spirit, which claims he believed were not accompanied with careful submission to the word of God, and led

---

[1] John Calvin, *Commentary on the Acts of the Apostles*, 1-13, tr. J. W. Fraser *et al.*, eds. D. W. Torrance and T. F. Torrance (Edinburgh: T & T Clark, 1965), p. 317.

inevitably to libertinism and antinomianism. This prompted him to write his 1545 work, *Against the Fantastic and Furious Sect of the Libertines, Called Spirituals.*[1]

By 1544 refugees from the Netherlands had acquainted Calvin with the teaching of an early leader in this group by the name of Quintin Thiery. But Calvin himself had contact earlier with both Thiery and one of the other leaders, Antoine Pocquet, who had at one time lived in Geneva, and later in 1542 had actually sought Calvin's backing. Some of Calvin's comments on the 'Spirituals' probably reflect that personal encounter. Furthermore, Calvin had already written what appears to be a polemic against them as early as the 1539 *Institutes.*[2]

The 'Quintinists' were, Calvin thought, basically a sixteenth-century revival of elements of early Gnostic and Manichean teaching. It was theologically inevitable, therefore, that their doctrine would lead to antinomianism. That is not to say that everyone who showed interest in their views would be guilty of all kinds of immorality, but that the *tendenz* of their teaching was in that direction. In a manner reminiscent for Calvin of elements in the church at Corinth, their focus was on the Spirit; they held that the resurrection was a spiritual work that had already taken place in them; and their dualism between flesh and spirit opened the way for an antinomianism in which it was argued that the activity of the flesh could not destroy the new holiness of the Spirit. Indeed, their teaching seemed to contain elements of potential if not actual pantheism.

Calvin complains, interestingly, that they are always talking about the Spirit. They cannot, he says, speak two sentences without mentioning him—a statistic which the 'Spirituals' took to be a mark of maturity, but Calvin saw as a sign of spiritual neuroticism and serious imbalance. With such people it is impossible to reason, since their final court of appeal is the Spirit apart from the word. Thus what presents itself as a

---

[1] John Calvin, *Contre la secte phantastique et furieuse des Libertins, qui se nomment Spirituelz.* See John Calvin, *Treatises Against the Anabaptists and Against the Libertines,* tr. Benjamin Wirt Farley (Grand Rapids: Baker, 1982), pp. 161-326. See also Wulfert de Greef, *The Writings of John Calvin, Expanded Edition,* tr. Lyle D. Bierma (Louisville: Westminster John Knox Press, 2008), pp. 155-57.

[2] Calvin, *Institutes,* I.ix.1.

recovery of the ministry of the Spirit in effect leads to a rejection of the distance between God and man, a rejection of the authority of Scripture, and a rending apart of justification and sanctification.

Calvin contends everywhere that the Spirit and the word must not be separated from each other:

> For as soon as the Spirit is severed from Christ's word the door is open to all sorts of craziness and impostures. Many fanatics have tried a similar method of deception in our own age. The written teaching seems to them to be of the letter. Therefore they were pleased to make up a new theology consisting of revelations.[1]

But he sees another, even more fundamental correlation which explains this—that between the Spirit and Christ. After all, the Spirit is the Spirit of the Son. So while his theology is set against the background of this double polemic against Rome and against the Spirituals, undergirding all is Calvin's passion to uphold what he views as the biblical teaching on the correlation between the Spirit and the incarnate Christ. To this, the central theme of this essay, we now turn.

The Spirit and the ministry of Jesus

The relationship of Christ to the Spirit lies at the foundation of all that Calvin has to say about the effects of the Spirit's ministry. Foundational in all of Calvin's thinking about salvation is the role of Christ as mediator. Nothing is received in salvation that is not first accomplished in and through Jesus Christ; everything that is accomplished in Christ is done so, not for his own sake, but for ours. Moreover, everything that has been accomplished for us in Christ is to be applied to us and in us by the Holy Spirit. The correlations between the work of Christ and the work of the Spirit, and subsequently between the work of the Spirit and the faith of the believer, are of the most comprehensive and intimate kind.

Calvin summarizes this in the well-known passage in *Institutes* II.xvi.19, at the close of his exposition of the Christological section of the Apostles' Creed:

> We see that our whole salvation and all its parts are comprehended in Christ [Acts 4:12]. We should therefore take care not to derive

[1] Calvin, *Comm. John*, II:121.

the least portion of it from anywhere else. If we seek salvation, we are taught by the very name of Jesus that it is 'of him' [1 Cor. 1:30]. If we seek any other gifts of the Spirit, they will be found in his anointing. If we seek strength, it lies in his dominion; if purity, in his conception; if gentleness, it appears in his birth. For by his birth he was made like us in all respects [Heb. 2:17] that he might learn to feel our pain [Heb. 5:2]. If we seek redemption, it lies in his passion; if acquittal, in his condemnation; if remission of the curse, in his cross [Gal. 3:13]; if satisfaction, in his sacrifice; if purification, in his blood; if reconciliation, in his descent into hell; if mortification of the flesh, in his tomb; if newness of life, in his resurrection; if immortality, in the same; if inheritance of the heavenly kingdom, in his entrance into heaven; if protection, if security, if abundant supply of all blessings, in his kingdom; if untroubled expectation of judgment, in the power given to him to judge. In short, since rich store of every kind of good abounds in him, let us drink our fill from this fountain and from no other.

Within the polemical context, Calvin adds:

Some men, not content with him alone, are borne hither and thither from one hope to another; even if they concern themselves chiefly with him, they nevertheless stray from the right way in turning some part of their thinking in another direction. Yet such distrust cannot creep in where men have once for all truly known the abundance of his blessings.

While Calvin thus underscores the objectivity of the gospel—our whole salvation is found in Christ—he is equally emphatic that the realization of salvation requires a union between Christ and ourselves. Thus he opens *Institutes* Book III by emphasizing that all Christ has done for us remains of no value to us unless we are united to Christ. It is this union that is effected by the Holy Spirit.

Correlation between Christ and the Spirit

In essence, then, the task of the Spirit is to correlate our need and the salvation which is embodied in Jesus Christ. It is only through him that all that is for us in the head is diffused throughout the whole body, and

Christ, clothed in the gospel, becomes ours existentially through faith. Thus when the Spirit sanctifies us (i.e., sets us apart for God and transforms us in regeneration) he is simply bringing to us what is already found in Christ, so that we are formed into his image by the Spirit's hidden operation.

The key to this correlation lies in the fact that, for Calvin, Christ was first the recipient of the Spirit in the fulfilment of his Messianic ministry, in order that he might, as exalted Lord, become bestower of the same Spirit upon his people. The Spirit who dwelt on Christ, sanctifying him through what Calvin calls 'the whole course of his obedience', is given by Christ to us, with the authority of the Father, to reproduce in us what he first produced in Christ himself.[1]

Calvin sees Christ's reception of the Spirit typified already in the ritual of the Old Testament. The priesthood and the tabernacle in the Old Testament were sprinkled with the sacrificial blood as a shadow of the redemption that was to come in Christ's death; but they were also consecrated with oil, as a sign of the anointing of the Holy Spirit on Jesus who is the antitype and fulfilment of both the priesthood and the tabernacle. His body is the true temple of God; he is consecrated as the meeting place between God and man, not with the symbol of oil, but with the power and sanctification of the Holy Spirit. It is this, ultimately, that he sees is in view in the anointing of the holy thing/place at the close of the 'seventy weeks' of Daniel 9:25, and fulfilled in our Lord's words in John 17:19, that he is consecrated, or sanctified, for the sake of his people.

But—and here is a critical point in Calvin's thinking—Christ is bearer of the Spirit not for his own sake but for ours. He bore the Spirit in order to bestow the Spirit; he receives the Spirit in order to accomplish his work so that the Spirit may communicate him in the virtue of his accomplished work to all who believe. The Spirit chose Christ as his seat so 'that from him might abundantly flow the heavenly riches of which we are in such need'.[2] Thus the anointing Christ receives flows over him, like the oil flowing over Aaron's beard to all the members of

[1] Calvin, *Institutes*, III.xvi.5.
[2] *Ibid.*, III.xvi.1.

his mystical body. 'Outside of Christ, nothing is worth knowing', says Calvin;[1] but Christ, *totus Christus*, becomes ours through the gift of the Holy Spirit to us.

The Spirit and the Messianic ministry

Calvin traces the framework of the relationship between Christ and the Spirit back to the prophecies of Isaiah, especially to chapter 11. Here Isaiah prophesies that Jesus will receive the Spirit in order to establish a spiritual kingdom. He receives the gift of the Spirit in the fullness of his gifts in our nature, in order to bestow them on the whole church.

Jesus is thus the anointed one, the Christ; we in turn are called Christians because he receives us into fellowship with himself. Thus, the gifts of the Spirit dwell first in him, and then through him come to his people. Better, the gifts dwell in him, and in union with him we together and severally come to share in them.

Thus, for example, Christ is endowed with shrewdness and discernment in order to govern his people and rule over them in perfect wisdom. Here Calvin nicely alludes to Isaiah's use of the sense of smell to express the idea of the acuity of Christ's discernment:

> Christ will be so shrewd that he will not need to learn from what he hears, or from what he sees; for by smelling alone he will perceive what would otherwise be unknown.[2]

In relation again to the kingly office, Calvin points to the fact that the blessings we receive from it are not carnal but spiritual: we are furnished with the gifts of the Spirit, which we lack by nature.

Calvin waxes eloquent about these benedictions:

> Such is the nature of his rule that he shares with us all that he has received from the Father ... he arms and equips us with his power, adorns us with his beauty and magnificence, enriches us with his wealth. These benefits then give us the most fruitful occasion to glory, and also provide us with confidence to struggle fearlessly against the devil, sin and death.[3]

[1] Calvin, *Institutes*, I.xvi.1.
[2] John Calvin, *Commentary on Isaiah*, tr. William Pringle (Edinburgh: Calvin Translation Society, 1850), I:376.
[3] Calvin, *Institutes*, II.xv.4.

There is, however, a clear order in this work. Christ receives the Spirit from the Father in order to fulfil his role as mediator. He then sends the Spirit; as mediator he sends him from the Father, as Son he sends him himself. The Spirit then works to transform us into the image of Christ and to restore us to the kingdom.

In order to follow this pattern, we must examine three things:

(i) the Spirit in the life of Christ,

(ii) the promise and the gift of the Spirit at Pentecost,

(iii) the work of the Spirit in uniting us to Christ by creating faith.

Calvin stresses that Christ accomplished our salvation 'by the whole course of his obedience'. Calvin realizes that the atonement was accomplished not by incarnation but in the crucifixion of Christ; but he refuses artificially to separate Christ's death and resurrection from the rest of his life. Christ, he says, began to pay the price of our redemption 'when he took on the form of a servant'.[1] Calvin (unfortunately for us) does not give us a coherent, extended exposition of this theme, important although it is to him. But we can trace his thinking through the course of Christ's own ministry.

In the incarnation, Mary was overshadowed by the Spirit with a view to the conception of Christ. The overshadowing not only indicates the presence of the Spirit in the miraculous nature of the conception of Christ but also the secrecy of the work, covering it, as it were, from the sight and understanding of man:

> as though a cloud should intervene and cover over the sight of men's eyes. As God, in publishing his miracles, keeps back from us the means of his working, so on our part we must adore with restraint, what he wishes to keep hidden from us.[2]

In fact, for Calvin this is paradigmatic of the Spirit's operation in the creation. There is always mystery attached to his working—hence the frequent occurrence, especially in the commentaries, of phrases like 'the secret impulse of the Spirit'. Characteristic of Calvin's thinking

---

[1] Calvin, *Institutes*, II.xvi.5.
[2] Calvin, *Harmony of the Gospels*, I:28.

here is that if Scripture provides no illumination as to how precisely the conception of Christ took place, it is illegitimate speculation to inquire. Where God makes an end of teaching, the Christian must needs make an end of learning.[1]

The Spirit is also present at the incarnation in order to keep Christ pure from the beginning. But again Calvin sees this not only in Christological terms (the impeccability of the Son), but in soteriological terms. It was 'not merely that he should abound in holiness unto himself alone, but rather that he should make others holy'.[2]

Although no specific mention is made of the Spirit by Luke in the context of Christ's hidden years, his commentary on Jesus' teenage years is significant. Jesus has come to share our lives. He experiences ignorance and weakness, but for him this reality is voluntarily assumed and sustained; for us it is a necessity we cannot avoid. It was necessary, therefore, that Jesus grow not only physically, and in favour with man, but spiritually, and in favour with God. Our Lord, notes Calvin,

> in the degree and process of his age ... according to his human nature increased in the free gifts of the Holy Spirit, that from his fullness he might shower them upon us, for we draw grace from his grace.[3]

Once again it is the soteriological motif that is dominant in Calvin's thinking.

In the baptism in the Jordan, according to the Evangelists, the Spirit comes upon Christ. The effect is, according to Calvin, that Jesus, in his humanity, received deep assurance, from an objective source, of his Messiahship and the nature and goal of his coming ministry. Calvin sees the ministry of Christ as a 'campaign' against the forces of darkness, and in that light, the Spirit comes upon Christ to defend him by his unique power: 'he had, insofar as his humanity required it, need of the defence of the Spirit's unique power, in embarking on such a rigorous campaign'.[4]

[1] See Calvin, *Institutes*, III.xxi.3.
[2] Calvin, *Harmony of the Gospels*, I:29.
[3] *Ibid.*, I:107.
[4] *Ibid.*

Two interesting questions are faced here by Calvin:

First, why did the Spirit descend *then* on Christ when the Evangelists' testimony leads us to think that the Spirit *already* rested on Jesus?

The answer Calvin finds in part in Isaiah 61:1. Until this time our Lord lived as a private individual; his experience of the fullness of the Spirit extended to that manner of life. But now he emerges to fulfil the public office of Redeemer. For this he is equipped with new power, but not for his own personal sake as a private individual. He did not need a further outpouring of the Spirit in order to live a life of perfect holiness and obedience to God. But in order to fulfil his task as Messiah, as a public person, as the representative of all the people of God, and to procure salvation for them in such a way that it might be conveyed to them, the Spirit is given and received. Here again, note the insistence of Calvin that Christ does not act *for himself*, but *for others*. It is precisely because of the goal of his work—he acts with a view to his work being communicated personally to others—that the Spirit must be given to him.

Second, why did the Spirit descend on him in the form of a dove, and not in the form of fire? Would this not have been more appropriate and in keeping with John's prophecy that he would baptize with the Spirit and with fire?

Here Calvin gives a surprising answer—all the more surprising in view of the almost universally unbalanced public image of both his theology and his person. He says that the Spirit comes in the form of a dove to symbolize Christ's gentleness in calling sinners to himself, 'in kind and soft tones to hope for salvation'. The dove is a pledge of the sweet consolation that is to be found in Christ, for Christ meets us 'not in the dread power of the Spirit, but wearing his lovable and pleasant grace'.[1]

Curiously, Calvin says disappointingly little about the significance of Christ being driven out by the Spirit to be tempted by the devil, except that in doing so, the Spirit is preparing him by such fierce conflict for a

---

[1] Calvin, *Harmony of the Gospels*, I:132. This and other expressions of Calvin's sensitivity to Christ's grace render more rather than less likely some close association between Calvin himself and the hymn often attributed to him, 'I Greet Thee Who My Sure Redeemer Art'.

ministry of unique glory. His ministry from the beginning is seen as a conflict with the powers of darkness.

In the Nazareth synagogue, Jesus identifies himself as the one on whom the Spirit rests, underlining that he does nothing by his own instinct or design, but his whole life is under the direction of the Spirit of God—evidenced by the fact that his words of grace show 'the evident power and favour of the Holy Spirit'.[1] The same divine power is displayed in a different way in the Capernaum synagogue, where 'the power of the Spirit shone out in Christ to compel even the profane and unfeeling hearers to admiration'.[2]

Calvin famously recognizes that the passion of Jesus is a trial before human judges that illumines the fact that he is standing in our place and taking our guilt before the Eternal Judge. As he faces the tribunal of God's judgment against our sin which he bears, he is overcome by dread as he stares death in the face—not as the end of life but as the specific wages of sin—but he again overcomes by the power of the Spirit. However, when he comes to comment on Hebrews 9:13 (Christ offered himself to the Father by the power of the eternal Spirit), Calvin searches out a deeper mystery yet. It is true and necessary, he acknowledges, that Christ suffered as a man. But his death is to be regarded

> not from its external act but from the power of the Spirit. Christ suffered as man, but in order that his death might effect our salvation it came forth in the power of the Spirit. The sacrifice of eternal atonement was a more than human work. He calls the Spirit eternal so that we know that the reconciliation which he effects is eternal.[3]

These words are particularly illuminating because, as we noted, the cross is for Calvin not to be isolated from the whole life of Christ. The cross is the climax of his work, and also the paradigm of the principle of the whole of Christ's work. He is God-Man, the Mediator. But apparently we are not to think so much of his work being effected by his humanity depending on his deity, as by him as man depending entirely on the help of the Holy Spirit. So there is, in the strict sense,

[1] Calvin, *Harmony of the Gospels*, I:149.
[2] *Ibid.*, I:160.
[3] Calvin, *Comm. Hebrews*, p. 121.

no *communicatio idiomatum* here. Rather there is in the God-Man a *communio idiomatum*, the natures being hypostatically united, not possessing transferable characteristics.[1] It is because of the union of the human and divine natures in the one person of the Son of God that the person of Christ is the Reconciler: but insofar as atonement is made by Christ in his humanity, it is through the power of the Spirit that the atonement made has a more than finite quality.

Just as he is in the continual resurrection experienced by believers, Christ was, in his resurrection, declared to be the Son of God by the Spirit. Here, again, Calvin is quick to draw the soteriological connection. Our resurrection to newness of life is testimony in our hearts to the 'stupendous power of the Spirit' which Christ manifested in his resurrection through the Spirit. His resurrection is a blueprint for our resurrection and 'a specimen of the power that belongs to the whole body of the church'.[2]

The ascension forms the point at which Christology and soteriology merge in Calvin's thinking. For Calvin, ascension and Pentecost are not only *integrally related*, in the sense that the former is the *a priori* for the latter; they are also *correlative*, in the sense that all that is taken up to God in the ascension of Jesus—that is to say, embodied in Jesus himself, crucified, resurrected, exalted—is brought down again to man by the outpouring of the Holy Spirit. It will be more appropriate, therefore, to handle Calvin's teaching under the further heading of the promise and the gift of the Spirit.

The Spirit and Pentecost
In the 'Farewell Discourse' (John 13–17) Christ teaches that his departure from the disciples is a necessary prerequisite to the Spirit coming to them. It is to their advantage that he goes away (John 16:7). The Spirit is the gift of the Father, but, Calvin emphasizes, he is freely given to us at

---

[1] This is consistent with Calvin's driving Christological principle that the humanity assumed by Christ must be the same as ours in nature (sin apart, which is an accretion on our created existence). To the extent Jesus deviates in his humanity from our humanity, to that extent he is disqualified from functioning as our Saviour.

[2] John Calvin, *The Epistles of Paul the Apostle to the Romans and the Thessalonians*, tr. Ross Mackenzie (Edinburgh: Oliver and Boyd, 1960), p. 165.

the expense of Christ, and through his prayers. He asks the Father, and in response the Spirit is sent as another Paraclete.

Calvin sees two things here: First, our condition apart from the Spirit is that we are 'orphans'. We are exposed to deceit and injustice; we are incapable of governing our own lives; we are unfit to do anything ourselves. We are separated from Christ, and in bondage to sin. This is why the effect of the Spirit's coming is to show us that outside of Christ sin reigns.[1] The Spirit of God is promised to relieve this condition, because apart from Christ this world is a spiritual orphanage.

This further helps to explain a much overlooked facet of Calvin's thought. His favourite title for the Holy Spirit is 'Spirit of adoption'. Indeed, he holds that this is the 'first' title of the Spirit,[2] by which he clearly does not mean 'chronologically first' but 'title of primacy'. This in turn alerts us to his widespread use of adoption (*adoptio*) as a key term for understanding the nature of the believer's relationship to God and the character of the whole Christian life. The Spirit who comes from the Father and the Son, as the Spirit of the Son, brings us into the fellowship of the Father and Son in union with the Son, as those who are adopted into God's family.

Second, the Spirit who comes to us is the economic equivalent of Christ coming to us. This is why it is better for the disciples (and us) that Christ should be bodily absent from us, in order that the Spirit may be present with us.[3] Jesus must leave if the Spirit, as the Spirit of Jesus incarnate, obedient, crucified, risen, and exalted, is to come. Thus for Calvin the act of ascension is of great significance in understanding the role of the Spirit.

The importance of the ascension

This is a principle with wide-ranging implications in Calvin's thinking, and explains, for example, why he is so insistent that the Roman Catholic doctrine of the church and sacraments demeans dominical teaching and minimizes the ministry of the Spirit. It focuses on the localization of the physical body of Christ. This is precisely the danger against which

[1] John 16:9.
[2] Calvin, *Institutes*, III.i.3.
[3] John 16:7.

Jesus warned the apostles when he insisted that it was necessary for him to go, in order that he might come again to them in the new mode of the Spirit. But, says Calvin, 'because we are carnal, nothing is harder than to tear from our minds this foolish attitude by which we drag down Christ from heaven to us'.[1]

Only when we see that the ascension is the correlate of the gift of the Spirit does the fact of the ascension fill us with joy. For then, as Calvin points out, again from the farewell discourse, we come to know the sacred union of the Son with the Father, and the believer with the Son, 'when he pours his life into us by the secret efficacy of the Spirit'.[2] This is what Jesus means when he says 'I will come to you' (John 14:18). He is not thinking so much of the resurrection as of the ascension and the gift of the Spirit.

In the light of what Calvin has said about the ministry of the Spirit in Christ's ministry, it becomes clear why the coming of the Spirit is the coming of Christ to the church. 'In that day' focuses on not just the resurrection but Pentecost.[3] Yet it is not limited to Pentecost, according to Calvin, but is 'the uninterrupted course of the one day from the time when Christ put forth the power of the Spirit until the last resurrection'.[4] In this general sense, Christ baptizes the church daily with his Spirit, and the Spirit bestows on the church nothing except what is to be found in the incarnate, crucified, risen, and ascended Christ.

This leads us to consider the significance of Pentecost as an expression of the work of Christ, an indication of the relationship of the Spirit to Christ, and an aspect of the fruit of Christ's work in believers through the gift of the Spirit.

The Day of Pentecost

Calvin preached at length on Pentecost in his mammoth series of 189 Sunday sermons on Acts from 1549–54.[5] In briefer and more focused

---

[1] Calvin, *Comm. John*, II:115.
[2] *Ibid.*, II:84.
[3] John 14:20.
[4] Calvin, *Comm. John*, II:84.
[5] Unfortunately the majority of these sermons are now lost. Originally turned into manuscript form by the indefatigable Denis Raguenier and catalogued in four

compass, there are discussions of the significance of Pentecost in two commentaries written in the last decade of his life: the Joel lectures, published in 1559, and the Acts commentary dating from a year later.

Calvin argues that the Spirit was already given to the people of God in the Old Testament period, but Joel's prophecy points us towards two epochal developments in his ministry, both ushered in by Pentecost: first, there is an *outpouring* of the Spirit in great abundance. Certainly the Spirit was present under the law, but not in the same plenitude. Second, there is a new *universality* in view in the Messianic reign. The Spirit is poured out on 'all flesh'.

In Joel the presence of the Spirit is signalled and expressed in terms of the gift of prophecy. Calvin maintains that prophecy here should be understood as the expression of the knowledge and understanding of God. Dreams and visions were the means by which this knowledge of God was disclosed and received. In the days of the old covenant, while there were colleges of the prophets, the prophets themselves were few in number, and the knowledge of God they enjoyed was rare. But now this is to be changed. Sons and daughters are to prophesy, old men and young men will see visions and dream dreams—that is to say, the knowledge and understanding of God given to prophets and disclosed in dreams and visions will become the universal experience of all of God's people.

The promise that all will prophesy, therefore, should not be confused with the notion that each believer will receive the gift either of public exposition or the specific gift of being a prophet in the church. Calvin takes Paul's assumption that not all are prophets as the hermeneutical clue to understanding what is being said here.[1] It is characteristic of Old Testament prophecy to describe the phenomena of Christ's kingdom in terms of the experiences of the prophets' contemporaries. The prophets 'comprehend, under figures which were familiar to people of the time,

---

volumes, only the volume containing 44 sermons on Acts 1-7 remains extant, and it—sadly—lacks perhaps as many as 15 sermons on the whole of the section Acts 1:3–2:35 on which Calvin would have preached between September 1 and December 15, 1549. The extant sermons have been published as John Calvin, *Sermons on the Acts of the Apostles, Chapters 1–7*, tr. Rob Roy McGregor (Edinburgh: Banner of Truth Trust, 2008).

[1] 1 Cor. 12:29.

the same things which we now see set forth in a different guise'.[1] The promises of God's work in the future are given in a manner of speech accommodated to the contemporary level of apprehension among the people. The fact that there were neither visions nor dreams on the Day of Pentecost when the prophecy was fulfilled underscores the principle. In other words, this promise of widespread prophecy is not speaking of the office of prophet at all, but of those who, as Calvin says,

> were endued with so much of the light of truth, that they might be compared with the prophets, and certainly the knowledge which flourished in the primitive church was such, that the meanest were in many respects equal to the ancient prophets.[2]

Indeed, in terms of the content of their knowledge, Calvin holds that the predictions of the Old Testament prophets are hardly worth comparing with the wisdom that is made known to us in the gospel. Thus, he writes, 'Faith then, after the coming of Christ, if rightly estimated according to its value, far excels the gift of prophecy.'[3]

In the Joel commentary, Calvin takes the extension to manservants and maidservants to mean that even those who were gifted by the Spirit under the old would be yet more fully equipped by the Spirit under the new covenant. The exposition of the Day of Pentecost in the commentary on the Acts, although published only a year later (1560), is, as one would expect, much more detailed.

Prior to the ascension, Christ had urged his disciples to wait for the promised Spirit. For although Christ daily baptizes the elect of the Father, Calvin sees Pentecost as the most memorable token of the Spirit's power. Calvin notes, however, that the kingdom baptism of the Spirit brings a restoration different from the disciples' initial hopes. They are to receive power in order to be witnesses, not in order to enjoy material prosperity; and as such witnesses they are called to be partakers of Christ's death in order that they may live together with him. Already, then, Calvin's exposition of the Spirit's coming has in view the theme

---

[1] Calvin, *Comm. Acts*, I:58.

[2] John Calvin, *Commentary on Joel*, *The Twelve Minor Prophets*, tr. John Owen (Edinburgh: Calvin Translation Society, 1846–49), II:94. Cf. Jesus' words in Matt. 11:11.

[3] Calvin, *Comm. Joel*, II:95.

that underlies so much of his thinking in *Institutes* Book III, namely union and communion with Christ in his death and resurrection.[1]

Calvin sees the significance of the time of the baptism with the Spirit as programmatic rather than in biblico-theological terms. His own focus is different from Augustine's development of the typology of the giving of the law. Calvin rather sees the chief significance of Pentecost lying more in the sheer numbers of people present for the feast, just as later Paul wants to be in Jerusalem at Pentecost,

> not on religious grounds but because of the greater profit to be gained from larger numbers (Acts 20:16). Therefore in the choice of the day God had regard to the usefulness of the miracle; that the news of it might, in the first place, be more widely talked of in Jerusalem … and secondly, be spread abroad to the remotest lands.[2]

The Spirit is given publicly at Pentecost, therefore, for two reasons: first, so that the gospel would be exalted in Jerusalem, and second, so that it could be quickly disseminated by those who attended the feast from other parts of the world.

At Pentecost, the Spirit came with external, sensory manifestations, to awaken the disciples' senses of sound and vision, and to stir them from their sloth.

- The violent sound of the mighty wind tames the confidence of the flesh.

- The appearance of tongues forms a visual prelude to the nature and immediate effects of Christ's work, just as his appearance as a dove at Jesus' baptism had pointed forwards to the character of Jesus' ministry.

- The division of the tongues Calvin sees as an indication that through Pentecost Christ will no longer be confined to the Jewish people. Though all speak different languages, in another sense Calvin sees that the prophecy of Isaiah 19:18 will be fulfilled, that all will speak the language of Canaan and call on one God as Father. Thus not

[1] Calvin, *Comm. Acts*, I:31-32.
[2] *Ibid.*, I:49-50.

only does the division of tongues act as a harbinger and confirmation of the calling of the Gentiles; the miracle of Pentecost also evidences that the gospel is of divine origin.

- The fire, related to the tongues, Calvin then sees as a token of the efficacy of the preaching of the gospel. Without the power of the Spirit the disciples' voices would have merely 'beaten the air ineffectually. The Lord shows therefore that their voice is to be as fire, to kindle the hearts of men, for the burning up and consuming of the vanity of the world and the purging and renewing of all things.'[1]

- How then does Calvin understand the speaking in tongues that the Spirit wrought at Pentecost? He argues that the miracle is one of speech, not one of hearing. He suspects that it is possible, but unnecessary, to think that when Peter preached there was a miracle of hearing. He assumes that most of those who came to Jerusalem would have been able to follow the message had he and the other apostles spoken their own language.

More important than these external symbols, of course, is the reality itself. Calvin sees the function of the Spirit's coming as the repair of the church from its ruined condition—'restoration' is the term he uses in connection with the prophecy of Joel. In other words, Pentecost has a restorative function in the context of the continuity of God's covenant purposes. It is axiomatic to him that Pentecost is not the inauguration of salvation, for under the law the fathers shared the same grace. Indeed, since the beginning of the world, all the godly have shared the same spirit of understanding, righteousness, and sanctification. But:

(i) Only a few have enjoyed that knowledge by comparison with the many who will share it in the wake of Christ's coming and the gift of the Spirit.

(ii) The knowledge possessed under the old dispensation was obscure and slender by comparison with the knowledge we enjoy now that Christ has shone on us in his perfect brightness. Understanding

---

[1] Calvin, *Comm. Acts*, I:51.

under the old covenant had the aroma of the pedagogy of the law; by comparison, understanding through the revelation of Christ breathes the intimacy of the children's knowledge of their father.

As in the Joel lectures, so in the exposition of Acts, Calvin understands that the idea of prophecy is to be resolved into that of the knowledge and understanding of God. Pentecost is simply the fulfilment of Jeremiah 31:34. The exhortation 'know the Lord', which in many ways was the real heart of the ministry of special prophets, as their peculiar intimacy of knowledge and understanding was passed on to the people, will no longer be necessary, because all will be endued with the Spirit of the knowledge of God.

Calvin describes the hermeneutical principle driving his exegesis with such clarity that it is worth quoting him at length:

> it was a common custom of the prophets to foreshadow the kingdom of Christ under images appropriate to their own day. When they speak of the worship of God they name the altar, the sacrifices, the offering of gold, silver, and frankincense. Yet we know that altars now have passed, and that the sacrifices which were used under the law are abolished, and that the Lord requires at our hands some higher thing than earthly riches. This is true indeed; but the prophets, in adjusting their style to the fashion of their own time, comprehend under figures which were familiar to people of the time, the same things which we now see set forth in a different guise; just as elsewhere when he promises to make priests of Levites, and Levites of the common people (Isa. 66:21), he means simply this, that in the kingdom of Christ every man, however mean, shall have an honourable standing. To gain the true and accurate meaning of this passage therefore we must not take too literally words which are derived from the old economy of the law, but we must seek the simple truth, shorn of metaphor. And that truth is that the apostles through the sudden inspiration of the Spirit discoursed prophetically, that is, under divine influence and exceptionally, concerning heavenly mysteries. The word 'prophesy' therefore signifies simply the rare and excellent gift of understanding: as if Joel should say that under the kingdom of Christ

there should not be merely a few prophets to whom God would reveal his secrets, but that all men should be endowed with spiritual wisdom to the extent of excelling in prophetic gifts. As it is written also in Jeremiah: 'Every man shall no longer teach his neighbour, because they shall all know me from the least up to the greatest' (Jer. 31:34).[1]

Calvin understands 'manservants and maidservants' to refer to the true worshippers of God. In the Joel commentary he had also suggested this means that even those who are gifted in understanding the ways of God will increase in knowledge; now he understands it as a description of the elect, and takes it to mean that the gift of the Spirit and the knowledge of God are exclusively given to the people of God.

Calvin picks up several elements of theological importance for understanding the significance of Pentecost and the role of the Spirit from the exposition Peter gives in his Day of Pentecost sermon:

• Pentecost is the fruit of the resurrection and the ascension of Christ in his role as mediator. Both in creation and recreation, the Spirit is the Lord and giver of life. It is inconceivable, then, that a buried Christ could give the Spirit to the church. It is as victor that he gives the Spirit, and this is the real explanation for Peter's proclamation of the resurrection. It not only vindicates Christ; it has soteriological and therefore pneumatological significance. Christ 'did not rise for his own sake alone, but by pouring out his Spirit to make the whole church partaker of his life'.[2]

• Pentecost is also the fruit of the ascension, in which as mediator, man before God for us, Christ has asked the Father for the promised Holy Spirit, whom he now delivers into our hands. In this way both the force and the fruit of Christ's resurrection are sealed to us by the Spirit. Christ goes from the church bodily, but returns in the Spirit, and so 'is present with us in a better way'.[3]

• Pentecost is a display of the recreating and restoring power of the Spirit. Those who heard Peter preach experienced the power of

[1] Calvin, *Comm. Acts*, I:58-59.
[2] *Ibid.*, I:73.
[3] *Ibid.*, I:74.

the Spirit to effect repentance in their hearts. This, rather than the tongues, is the real significance of Pentecost. Tongues are impermanent, repentance is permanent in the church. Calvin states this forcefully both in the context of Pentecost itself and in his comments on the coming of the Spirit in the home of Cornelius.

In the latter context he writes:

> Certainly the gift of tongues and other things of that kind have long since ceased in the church, but the Spirit of understanding and regeneration thrives and will always thrive. And the Lord unites him with the external preaching of the gospel so as to keep us in reverence of his word, and obviate the fatal fantasies in which fanatics entangle themselves, when they abandon the word and invent some sort of vague and erratic spirit.[1]

And, commenting on Acts 2:38, and the way in which the gift of the Spirit is there related to the ongoing administration of baptism, he explains more fully the difference between the external manifestations of the Spirit, and the permanent life-giving ministry:

> He promises them the gift of the Spirit, of which they saw an example in the diversity of tongues. Therefore this does not strictly apply to us. For since it was the inauguration of his kingdom that Christ meant to set forth by these miracles, they lasted only for a time. ... For although we do not receive the Spirit to the end that we may speak with tongues, or be prophets, or cure the sick, or work miracles, yet is he given us for a better use, that we may believe with the heart unto righteousness, that our tongues may be trained to true confession (Rom. 10:10), that we may pass from death to life (John 5:24), that we who are poor and empty may be made rich, and that we may sound victorious against Satan and the world. Therefore the grace of the Spirit will always be conjoined to baptism, unless a hindrance arise on our part.[2]

---

[1] Calvin, *Comm. Acts*, I:317.
[2] *Ibid.*, I:81-82.

The Spirit and the believer—Institutes *Book III*

These considerations provide, for Calvin, the underpinning of the Spirit's ministry in the life of the believer, the topic with which he deals in *Institutes* Book III. At this juncture Calvin has already dealt with the knowledge of God the Creator, and the subsequent fall of man into sin and alienation. In *Institutes* Book II, he has expounded the doctrine of Christ as Mediator and Redeemer. Now he turns to what he calls 'the way we receive the grace of Christ'.

We have already seen the pattern of Calvin's thinking: all that is in Christ is to be made ours by the Holy Spirit. Christ brings us into his kingdom. The Spirit effects deliverance from the kingdom of darkness and his chief work now is to restore us to the image of God, which he does as he conforms us to the rule of life in his kingdom.

In terms of the ministry of the Spirit, then: he is given to Christ in order that redemption may be accomplished; he is bestowed on us by the Father in order that we may enter into the fullness of Christ's redemption. To effect this, not only has Christ become one flesh with us in the incarnation, but following his ascension and our baptism with the Spirit, we become one Spirit with Christ,[1] and, forsaking this world, we ascend to the life of the world to come more and more.

The heavenly riches flow to us from Christ that, ultimately, we may be made like him, reformed, as Calvin says, 'to the image of God'.[2] This is the harbinger of the restoration of the final order of things; already in the present a microcosm of it begins to exist in us. Thus, says Calvin,

> all virtues, all good and well-regulated affections, proceed from the Spirit, that is from the grace of God and the renewed nature which we have from Christ. As if he had said: 'Nothing but evil comes from man; nothing good comes but from the Holy Spirit.'[3]

Already we are constituted righteous, and sanctification is inaugurated in our hearts, giving us hope for the full renewal of our lives, since the Holy Spirit (who will accomplish the final transformation) already dwells in us.

[1] 1 Cor. 6:17. John Calvin, *Commentary on 1 Corinthians*, tr. J. W. Fraser, ed. D. W. Torrance and T. F. Torrance (Edinburgh: Oliver and Boyd, 1960), p. 131.

[2] Calvin, *Harmony of the Gospels*, II:134.

[3] Calvin, *Comm. Galatians*, p. 105.

Calvin sees the various titles given to the Spirit as representing a kind of survey of his multifaceted ministry. We have already noted that chief among them is 'Spirit of adoption', but he is also the guarantee and seal of redemption, life because of righteousness; the water that cleanses us, but chiefly makes us fruitful in the service of the kingdom; the anointing that restores us to life and spiritual vigour; the fire that consumes sin and enflames our hearts with zeal for Christ.[1]

Yet the chief work of the Spirit, Calvin holds, is to effect faith in our hearts. Thus Book III of the *Institutes* is essentially an exposition of the correlation between the Spirit and faith, in which the prior and foundational correlation between Christ and the Spirit is worked out into our lives. All blessings are ours in Christ, effected in and through him in the power of the Spirit, and now, likewise, effected in us by the power of the same Spirit. He brings us to be partakers of Christ.

This, at least in part, helps to explain the structure of Book III. It is not structured in the characteristic style of the later Reformed *ordo salutis*. Faith, not order, is the key to Calvin's exposition of the reception of Christ and all grace and graces in him. This may be why *Institutes* Book III closes on the themes of prayer, election, and the resurrection. For these are simultaneously the furthest reaches of faith, and faith grasping its choicest privileges. For prayer is access by the Spirit of sonship, which enables us to call God 'Abba, Father'. Predestination grounds our security in the knowledge that the Father chose us in Christ before the foundation of the world. Resurrection spells out the ultimate triumph of the gospel and of faith, since it means that the end of the good work he has begun will be the transformation not only of our souls, but of our whole beings, into the image of God to share in the renewal of the cosmos. It is as though Calvin were saying, we do not really appreciate the riches of faith, the blessings that are ours in Christ, until the Spirit of God has led us to the final perimeter of the things that have been revealed, and that belong to us and to our children.

Thus he writes, God

> sanctifies us by reforming our corrupt nature by his Spirit, and so sanctification has to do with regeneration … the blood of Christ

---

[1] Calvin, *Institutes*, III.i.3.

is the cause of our cleansing; from his death and resurrection we obtain righteousness and sanctification. But since the cleansing which Christ has carried out and the obtaining of righteousness are of no benefit to any except those who have been made to share in these blessings by the power of the Spirit along with Christ, Paul is quite right in speaking of the Spirit along with Christ. Christ, therefore, is the source of every blessing to us; it is from him that we obtain everything. But Christ himself, with all his blessings, is communicated to us by the Spirit. For we receive Christ by faith; and it is by faith that his benefits (*gratiae*) are applied to us. The author of faith is the Spirit.[1]

Here, then, is the correlation to which we have alluded, which in turn holds the key to *Institutes* Book III. Christ is and possesses all blessing; the Spirit brings *totus Christus* to us; faith is wrought in us by the Spirit, and takes hold of Christ, clothed in all his benefits. This is how we receive grace.

Space forbids exploring the way in which we find in Calvin's sacramental theology, especially his eucharistic theology, essentially what we have found here. Salvation is ours only in Christ; this is one and the same as saying that salvation is ours only by faith; and this, in turn, is the same as saying that salvation is ours only through the Spirit, because it is the Spirit who brings Christ to us, and brings in Christ to us all that is in Christ for us. It is by the Spirit that faith in Christ is effected in us by means of the Supper so that all that is his is experimentally realized in us. All that is planned by the Father and fulfilled in the Son comes to us through the Holy Spirit.[2]

It is simply because Calvin explored in such depth what was planned by the Father, and expounded in such detail what had been fulfilled in the Son, that inevitably he was driven on to such full exposition of the work of the Spirit, and thus merits the title Warfield has given him: 'The theologian of the Holy Spirit.'

---

[1] Calvin, *Comm. 1 Cor.*, pp. 126-27.
[2] This is explained at greater length in 'Calvin on the Lord's Supper and Communion with Christ'. See Chapter 9 below.

CHAPTER EIGHT

CALVIN AND CHRISTIAN EXPERIENCE: THE HOLY SPIRIT IN THE LIFE OF A CHRISTIAN

T HE century since the four-hundredth anniversary of the birth of John Calvin has witnessed many developments in the story of the Christian church, but few have been more striking than the avalanche of new interest in the ministry of the Holy Spirit. It might be thought that this interest provides the major stimulus for a chapter that might exhaust the (presumably) little that Calvin had to say on the subject. But it would be a mistake, on more than one count, to imagine that Calvin's references to the Spirit were sparse. Indeed, already in 1909, B. B. Warfield was prepared to venture the thesis that Calvin was 'preeminently the theologian of the Holy Spirit'.[1]

Warfield may have been one of only a few voices crying in the wilderness, but his assessment is vindicated in a number of ways, for Calvin's writings abound in references to the person and ministry of the Spirit. For such a profoundly biblical theologian, it could not be otherwise. As Calvin worked his way through biblical revelation, he emphasized the multidimensional character of the Spirit's role. His understanding of the Spirit's work ranged from his involvement in the creating and governing of the universe, to the giving and authenticating of Scripture to believers, to his presence in the ministry of our Lord Jesus Christ. Then, since the Holy Spirit is the bond of union between Jesus Christ and the whole church as well as the individual believer,

---

[1] B. B. Warfield, *Calvin as a Theologian and Calvin Today*, p. 5. Warfield's view was shared by very few theologians of his day.

Calvin further traced his activity in the application of the redemption that Christ accomplished.[1] Thus, throughout his biblical commentaries and the *Institutes of the Christian Religion*, he underscored that the Holy Spirit is the key to the church's communion with the Lord Jesus, not least (as we shall see) in the Lord's Supper.

This is not to claim that the work of the Holy Spirit is the central motif in Calvin's theology; 'all-pervasive' would be a better description of the reality.

It might be objected that while the *Institutes* contains sections on the work of God the Father (Book I) and the person and work of Jesus Christ (Book II), there is no distinct treatment of the Holy Spirit and his work. To some extent, this is explained by the fact that Calvin understood that the Holy Spirit does not bring glory to himself but to the Father and to the Son.[2] Thus, references to the Holy Spirit and his work are present throughout the entire encyclopedia of Calvin's thought rather than localized in one particular area of it. Indeed, such was the extent of his interest in this theme that it might be claimed that Calvin paved the way for the attention to the Spirit's ministry that would later mark evangelical theology. He, probably more than any other Reformer, bequeathed to the Reformed tradition the deep interest in the role of the Spirit that would come to prominence in such *magna opera* as John Owen's and Thomas Goodwin's monumental studies in the Puritan era.[3]

In this context, it is necessary to limit comments to only a few aspects of Calvin's teaching.

The polemical context
To understand what Calvin says about the ministry of the Spirit, we should first consider the polemical context in which he was writing.

On the one hand, he faced the necessity of dealing with Roman Catholic theology. In the late medieval Church, salvation for a regular church member—if attainable at all—was dependent on the institutions of the Church. In the view of the Reformers, for all practical purposes,

---

[1] See Calvin, *Institutes*, III.i.3. Cf. Calvin, *Comm. John*, II:121, on John 16:14.

[2] 'The Spirit bestows on us nothing apart from Christ.' Calvin, *Comm. John*, II:122.

[3] Owen, *Pneumatologia, Works*, III-IV; Goodwin, *The Work of the Holy Ghost in Our Salvation, Works*, VI.

the *magisterium* had replaced the Holy Spirit in his work of authenticating the Scriptures to the believer (the *testimonium internum Spiritus Sancti* so beloved of Calvin[1]). Rome claimed that the Church had created the canon of Scripture; therefore, the Church authenticated Scripture and was its sole interpreter. By contrast, Calvin argued that the Scriptures were given by the Spirit and therefore were canonical from their moment of origin.[2] Furthermore, the Spirit continued to authenticate them to believers.[3] No merely human testimony can ever be adequate to bear witness to the divine nature of God's word. Only God can give testimony to himself, Calvin says, echoing Hilary of Poitiers.[4]

The tragedy of the medieval Church, from Calvin's point of view, was not only the distortion of the gospel of free justification, but the usurpation of the ministry of the Holy Spirit in the application of redemption, replacing his dynamic activity with a static and formal sacramental *ordo salutis*. In that system, the ordinary Christian might hope to progress in grace, from being baptized into the Church, through participating in the various Church sacraments that would sustain him in life, so that one day he would become the kind of righteous person—his faith fully formed in unadulterated love for God (*fides formata caritate*)—whom God could then justify because he was in fact righteous.[5]

From within this system of justification, the Roman Catholic Church accused the Reformers of teaching a legal fiction (the justification of the *unjust*). Calvin both demonstrated the biblical basis for such justification and the fact that rather than constituting a legal fiction leading to licence, its actual effect through the Spirit was to spur the justified on to greater godliness.[6]

Since, for Calvin, the justification of the ungodly is based solely on the justification accomplished in Jesus Christ acting for us, the great work of the Holy Spirit is to unite us to Christ, in whom this justification

[1] See Calvin, *Institutes*, I.vii.4.
[2] *Ibid.*, I.vii.1.
[3] *Ibid.*, I.vii.4.
[4] *Ibid.*
[5] *Ibid.*, III.xv.7.
[6] Calvin, *Comm. Romans*, p. 121.

is grounded, and in union with whom sanctification is effected and develops. Moral licence is impossible, for the Spirit unites us to Christ as Saviour and Lord—to have him as one but not the other is, as Calvin puts it, 'to rend Christ asunder'.[1]

Thus, we might add to the customary *solas* of the Reformation the principle that the salvation that is in Christ alone, by grace alone, by faith alone, is also 'by the Spirit alone'.

If this first aspect of Calvin's polemic dealt with the way the Roman Church *replaced* the Spirit's ministry with the sacramental system, the second aspect involved the radical groups of the so-called 'left wing' of the Reformation, whom Calvin saw falling into the error of *dividing* the Spirit from the word. These groups separated the Spirit from the word by emphasizing that God reveals himself through the Spirit apart from the word. Calvin speaks of their 'fatal fantasies in which fanatics entangle themselves when they abandon the word and invent some sort of vague and erratic spirit'.[2]

The refrain that runs through Calvin's teaching in this context is that the Spirit is never to be separated from Christ, nor should he be separated from the word. In 1545, Calvin wrote a sharply worded tract, *Against the Fantastic and Furious Sect of the Libertines Called Spirituals.* The tell-tale sign of their imbalance was that they could speak scarcely a few sentences without referring to the Holy Spirit and the leading or revelation he gave. Calvin viewed such language as a distortion of biblical teaching that resulted in harmful confusion about the Spirit's ministry:

> For as soon as the Spirit is severed from Christ's word the door is open to all sorts of craziness and impostures. Many fanatics have tried a similar method of deception in our own age. The written teaching seems to them to be of the letter. Therefore they were pleased to make up a new theology consisting of revelations.[3]

This supposed mark of higher spiritual maturity is actually a sign of spiritual neuroticism, because it severs the Spirit from the word. What Calvin emphasized in contrast is the close union of the Father with the

---

[1] *Ibid.* See also Calvin, *Comm. Romans*, pp. 166-67.
[2] Calvin, *Comm. Acts*, I:317.
[3] Calvin, *Comm. John*, II:121.

Son, the Son with the Spirit, and the Spirit with the word, so that the ministry of all three persons of the Godhead is expressed through the word as the Spirit brings believers into genuine union and communion with the Father and the Son.

The theological context

In the *Institutes*, Calvin emphasizes the deity of the Spirit in a manner consonant with the teaching of the Fathers and creeds of antiquity. While in earlier life he seems to have wanted to keep within the confines of purely biblical language when expressing the mysteries of the gospel, he came to realize that the technical vocabulary of the early church provided a means by which doctrinal parameters could be set and an appropriate theological shorthand employed.[1]

The Spirit is a person of divine essence. He is a distinct centre of personal existence within the single essence of the being of God. He reveals his divinity by participating in creation and providence, in sending prophets, and in the inspiration of Scripture. The Spirit possesses infinite knowledge of God. God is known exhaustively only to himself; the depths of God are known by the Spirit.[2] When the New Testament speaks of believers corporately or individually as temples of God, it is because they are indwelt by the Holy Spirit. The inherent logic in those statements implies the absolute deity of the person of the Holy Spirit.[3]

The baptismal formula, Calvin argues, expresses not only the unity-in-trinity of God's being but the specific deity of the Spirit. The unity of God's name implies the unity of the persons in the triune God.[4]

Perhaps Calvin's most significant contribution to the development of the doctrine of the Trinity lay in his insistence on the auto-theistic nature of the Son—while the Father is the personal fountain of the Trinity in terms of the diversity of persons, the Son possesses his deity (as does the Father) in an underived fashion. The Father is not the author of the deity of the Son. It follows, then, that the Holy Spirit is also auto-theistic; his deity is not derived from the Father and from the Son. He

---

[1] See Calvin's discussion in *Institutes*, I.xii.3. Cf. Calvin, *Comm. 1 Corinthians*, p. 79.
[2] Cf. 1 Cor. 2:10-11.
[3] Calvin, *Institutes*, I.xiii.14-15.
[4] Calvin, *Harmony of the Gospels*, III:253.

is himself very God.[1] The Spirit is common to both the Father and the Son. He is one essence with them, and is the same eternal deity while proceeding personally from both. Citing Romans 8:9, Calvin says the Spirit is as truly the Spirit of the Son as he is truly the Spirit of the Father. He proceeds personally from both the Father and the Son within the internal union and communion of the Trinity.[2] This reality is expressed by revelation when at Pentecost the Spirit is sent from both the Father and the Son to believers in the church.

The maxim *opera ad extra trinitatis indivisa sunt*[3] applies to his ministry in the believer. When the believer receives the Spirit, he also receives the Father and the Son. The Trinity is indivisible in all of God's activities beyond himself, although for Calvin each person of the Trinity has specific roles in God's external relationship to the universe (the so-called doctrine of 'appropriations').

Calvin traces the role of the Spirit not only in creation but through the old covenant into the new. In *Institutes* II.11, he shows the contrast between the Spirit's roles in the Old Testament and New Testament epochs. But he also emphasizes that the Spirit who ministered to the saints under the old covenant and brought them to hope for redemption in Jesus Christ is the same Spirit who ministers to the saints under the new covenant and brings the consummation of that redemption to believers. Whether under the law or through its fulfilment in Jesus Christ, the Holy Spirit applies the work of the Mediator. The words of the prologue to John's Gospel, that the law came through Moses while grace and truth came through Jesus Christ (John 1:17), do not point so much to a radical antithesis between two dispensations with different agents in the application of redemption but to two dispensations of the same redemptive historical stream, the one finding its fulfilment and consummation in the other.[4]

[1] See Calvin, *Institutes*, I.xiii.16-20.

[2] Calvin thus subscribes to the *filioque* clause in the Western form of the Nicene Creed. See *Institutes*, I.xiii.18.

[3] The *ad extra* works of God are those he does in relation to his creation, not those which are within the trinity of persons in the Godhead. The meaning of *opera ad extra trinitatis indivisa sunt* is that all God's external works are joint undertakings of the three persons.

[4] See Calvin's discussion in *Comm. John*, I:24-25.

The Holy Spirit applies the work of Jesus Christ to those who believe in him, whether they see him opaquely in terms of promise or live (as we do) in the light of the historical reality of the death of Jesus. The Holy Spirit bridges the gap in space and time between the historical anticipation and the actual accomplishment of our Lord Jesus Christ's saving ministry and the present time, in which God justifies sinners and transforms them into saints. So while the Holy Spirit worked through the old covenant, his ministry came to marvellous consummation in the new covenant.

Against this general background, there are four areas in which Calvin particularly emphasizes the Spirit's ministry in the life of the Christian believer: *illumination, regeneration, adoption,* and *communion.* The dividing lines between these themes are thin, for they are tributaries feeding into one marvellous unity in Calvin's thinking.

Illumination

The Spirit who gives us Scripture also convinces us of the truth of Scripture through that truth. We do not stand outside of Scripture to be convinced of its authority as the word of God. Thus, for Calvin, we are ultimately persuaded that Scripture is God's word not by the use of arguments extraneous to Scripture, nor by any of its impressive external characteristics, but by the reading and exposition of Scripture itself. The Holy Spirit uses the very Scriptures that we read to persuade us that what we are reading is the very word of God. His testimony is not separate from the word, but comes *with* and *through* the word.[1] There is no substitute for this.

The implication of what Calvin is saying is that while Christians can commend the Bible in all kinds of ways, the fundamental need is for people to hear it or read it for themselves. '*Tolle lege*' ('Take up and read') is the watchword that will lead to the conversion of many, in addition to Augustine!

Calvin insists, then, that Scripture itself, through the ministry of the Spirit, brings inner certainty that it is the very voice of God, 'as if there the living words of God were heard'.[2] That is why the fruit of the Spirit's

---

[1] Calvin, *Institutes*, I.vii.4.
[2] *Ibid.*, I.vii.1.

ministry is that we give to Scripture the reverence that we give to God himself, because it is his own word.

For Calvin, illumination involves more than understanding what Scripture says; it is an *internal persuasion of* and a *yielding to* its truth.

This perspective was rooted in Calvin's experience. At one time, of course, he was a convinced Roman Catholic ('stubbornly addicted' to the Roman Catholic Church is his own way of describing his earlier life[1]). However, as the Scriptures were illumined to him by the Holy Spirit, Calvin began yielding to a greater authority than the Church or his own prejudice. But he also learned that inner illumination is not a substitute for external and objective revelation. Indeed, it is impossible apart from it, for the Spirit must never be separated from the word, since the Spirit gives the word so that he might illumine the word, breaking down the stubborn prejudices of our nature, which, as Calvin says, is 'a perpetual factory of idols'.[2] The Spirit engages in a demolition and reconstruction process in the mind as light enters into it from the teaching of Scripture. This is what happened to the disciples on the road to Emmaus (Luke 24:13-35). Jesus opened the Scriptures to them. There was both light (illumination) and heat (burning hearts).[3]

The Spirit's work in illumination is an integral aspect of regeneration. Those who are born again 'see' the kingdom of God (John 3:3). The Spirit enlightens the mind, reveals Christ, subdues the heart, and makes the heart burn. Being convinced of the Scriptures this way is not merely a scholastic conviction. Rather, the testimony of the Holy Spirit is so intertwined with the grasp of the truth of the gospel that it is indistinguishable from it in actual subjective experience.

The Spirit of illumination is therefore also the Spirit of regeneration. But this, for Calvin, is a broad category and requires separate consideration.

---

[1] See Calvin's comments in his introduction to his *Commentary on the Book of Psalms*, where he describes himself in this way: 'Since I was too obstinately devoted to the superstitions of Popery to be easily extricated from so profound an abyss of mire, God by a sudden conversion subdued and brought my mind to a teachable frame, which was more hardened in such matters than might have been expected from one at my early period of life.' *Comm. Psalms*, I:xl.

[2] Calvin, *Institutes*, I.xi.8.

[3] Calvin, *Harmony of the Gospels*, III:238.

Regeneration

Here contemporary readers of Calvin may misread him. The progression of Calvin's exposition of 'The Way in Which We Receive the Grace of Christ' in *Institutes* Book III contrasts with the order of exposition characteristic of later Reformed theology. There, regeneration is viewed as the prerequisite for faith, justification, adoption, sanctification, and perseverance, and therefore is given priority over them in the order of exposition (as well as in the *ordo salutis*).

Against this background, the reader who comes to Calvin as the fountain of the Reformed understanding of the *ordo salutis* is likely to experience something of a shock. He essentially deals with sanctification before he deals with justification, and in that context he uses the expression 'regeneration by faith'. This, to modern Reformed ears, has a distinctly Arminian ring!

What is Calvin about in Book III of the *Institutes* that might help to explain this? Two things in particular are of interest at this point.

First, part of Calvin's motivation in discussing the Christian life *prior* to discussing justification is to provide theological grounding for his conviction that there is no such thing as a justified person who is not also a sanctified one. Justification is never grounded in sanctification. Justification must never be confused with sanctification. But neither can justification ever exist without sanctification. In the Roman polemic (to which Calvin was extremely sensitive from the very beginning of his ministry), free justification of the ungodly by grace alone through faith alone inevitably leads to libertinism. Since the same accusation was levelled against Paul (Rom. 6:1ff.), its reappearance in the sixteenth century simply confirmed to Calvin that his gospel was faithful to the apostolic teaching.[1] It need hardly be said that Calvin did not advocate, nor did his gospel encourage, antinomianism any more than did the apostle Paul.

Second, and more fundamentally, Calvin uses the term *regeneration* in a different way from the customary usage of later Reformed theology. For him, the regeneration that comes through faith is repentance.[2] Repentance, in turn, is that lifelong mortification and vivification, both

---

[1] See Calvin, *Comm. Romans*, pp. 63-64.
[2] Calvin, *Institutes*, III.iii.

internal and external, that characterizes the whole of the Christian life.

In a word, Calvin has a much more unified idea of what happens in regeneration than later theologians, who tend to speak about regeneration as the inauguration point in the Christian life, an initial and instantaneous work of God rather than an ongoing transformation. But for Calvin, regeneration or repentance is much more than the event of a moment; it is the ongoing restoration of a person's whole being into the image of God. In this, Calvin echoes the first of Martin Luther's Ninety-five Theses: 'When our Lord Jesus Christ said "repent" he meant that the whole of the Christian life should be repentance.'

This helps us make sense of a number of things Calvin writes. For example, in his discussion of John 1:12 ('as many as received him, to them gave he power to become the sons of God ...'), he speaks of regeneration preceding faith and also of regeneration following faith.[1] Does Calvin speak with a forked tongue? No, he means that the regenerating activity of God the Holy Spirit is absolutely essential to the birth of faith in our lives, the sovereign ministry of illumination through the word of God, conviction of its truth, and the enflaming of the heart. We must be born from above. But divine regeneration, which is sovereignly inaugurated, is also continued in the Christian life by the way of faith, because what God has in view is the regeneration of our entire lives—which ultimately will be climaxed in that *vivificatio externa* (external vivification) that will take place in the final resurrection of the body. Thus, regeneration is consummated in final Christlikeness and glorification. It is an ongoing process in the Christian life. It takes place *in my life* in a way that engages my being, so that I actually *am made new and become new* in every aspect of life. In this sense, there is both divine monergism and also a kind of synergism in the actual experience of salvation. The person who is made new actually does new things—they do not simply 'happen' above his head.[2]

Calvin's commentary on John 1:13 makes it clear that this is how he understands regeneration. The Holy Spirit, in essence, unites us by faith with the Lord Jesus Christ so that we become one with him and his life comes to expression in ours.

[1] Calvin, *Comm. John*, I:18-19.
[2] Cf. Calvin, *Comm. Philippians*, pp. 253-56.

We share in Christ by participation. This language is significant for Calvin, because salvation comes to us not only *from* Christ as its source, or *through* Christ as the channel, but *in* Christ. Indeed, the prepositional distinction is so significant for Calvin that on more than one occasion he writes in such terms as:

> I prefer however to retain Paul's words *in* Christ Jesus rather than to render with Erasmus *by* Christ Jesus, because this conveys more clearly the ingrafting by which we are made one with Christ.[1]

For Calvin, we do not gain the blessings of the Christian gospel merely *through* Christ, as though they were entities somehow capable of impersonal abstraction from him. Rather, all of the blessings come in him.

In essence, Calvin is emphasizing here that it is Jesus Christ—not justification, regeneration, sanctification, glorification, or adoption as such—that we need. None of these is the object of Spirit-wrought faith. Rather, through the Holy Spirit, faith unites us to Jesus Christ in a spiritual but real union, and we receive all these blessings in him, not apart from him. This is everything to Calvin.[2]

But the fact that this is the work of the Spirit does not mean that spiritual blessings come from a mystical Christ. Rather, they are embodied for us in the incarnate, crucified, buried, raised, ascended, and glorified Christ who forever retains our humanity. He is the one to whom we are united. We are not united to the Holy Spirit. We are united by the Holy Spirit to the person of our Lord Jesus Christ.

This is the key to what Calvin writes about the Spirit's ministry, especially in *Institutes* Book III. The role of the Holy Spirit is to bring us into union with the Lord Jesus, to keep us in that union, and to see that union flourish in communion with him. Calvin makes this clear in his commentary on Psalm 133. He writes: 'The peace that springs from Christ as the head, is diffused through the whole length and breadth of the church.'[3] The blessings that are in Christ flow over onto his body, the church, much as the anointing oil flowed over Aaron's head onto

---

[1] Calvin, *Comm. Romans*, p. 128 (emphasis added). See also Calvin, *Comm. 1 Corinthians*, p. 21.

[2] See Calvin, *Institutes*, II.xvi.19.

[3] Calvin, *Comm. Psalms*, V:165.

his beard and body. The anointing first comes on the Lord Jesus Christ. Then the Holy Spirit gathers all the ingredients of that oil that flows over Christ and brings it to the body so that Christian believers who are regenerated may participate in Jesus Christ's graces.

For Calvin, the union with the Lord Jesus that comes through the Holy Spirit involves—as has already been noted—mortification and vivification. Both of these are twofold. Regeneration includes an internal and an external mortification, as well as an internal and external vivification. Just as we are united by the Spirit to a whole Christ, we are united as whole individuals. The Spirit works in us to conform us to the Lord Jesus, incarnate and resurrected. Mortification of sin takes place in the Christian life, but so does a mortification of the body in suffering and ultimately in death.

Vivification of our spirit is involved in regeneration, but this is not restricted to the 'inner man'. It ultimately has in view the vivification of the whole person in the resurrection, when the Lord Jesus will transform the Christian's body of lowliness from its state of humiliation to be like his body of glory. The Spirit does not unite us to Spirit so that in the end we may become disembodied spirit. Rather, he unites us to the Son of God incarnate in our flesh. The hallmark of the Spirit's work, therefore, is ongoing conformity to Christ crucified and raised, causing us to share his death in order to share his resurrection, to taste his suffering in order that we might also taste his glory. The Spirit implants the seed of this at the beginning of the Christian life and nourishes it to the end.[1]

Adoption

Calvin opens *Institutes* Book III with a striking comment on the importance of union with Christ.

> We must understand that as long as Christ remains outside of us, and we are separated from him, all that he has suffered and done for the salvation of the human race remains useless and of no value to us.[2]

---

[1] Calvin deals with this in three paragraphs: *Institutes*, III.vii-ix.
[2] *Institutes*, III.i.1.

Union with Christ becomes ours through faith. But, argues Calvin, we must go deeper than this in our analysis, for not all exercise faith. Thus, 'reason itself teaches us to climb higher and to examine into the secret energy of the Spirit'.[1]

This leads Calvin to a discussion of the titles of the Spirit. Here, he makes the remarkable statement that, in fact, 'the first title' of the Holy Spirit is *Spirit of adoption*.[2] This title appears in the Scriptures only in Romans 8:15. In what sense, then, can it be 'the first title'? It is first not in the sense of chronological but of theological priority.

The issue here transcends the question of whether Calvin is accurately assessing the biblical titles for the Spirit—for he is stressing that this is so within his own theology (of course because he believes this is true in Scripture).

This is the single most important description of the Spirit because, in Calvin's view, sonship is the most basic and comprehensive rubric for understanding the nature of the Christian life.[3] This is all of a piece with the fact that Calvin places strong emphasis on the gospel as the means by which we come to know the fatherhood of God, in which he brings us into his family and makes us his children. It is therefore something of a paradox that in some strands of the Reformed tradition believers have been discouraged from enjoying any assurance of their sonship. What good father in this world would want to bring his children up without the assurance that they are his children? Would the Father of lights (James 1:17) do that?

The model for all true fatherhood is rooted in the fatherhood of God. Calvin considers this truth to be a glorious liberation, in some senses his own parallel to Luther's appreciation of justification. The God of all glory not only becomes our Father, but wishes to assure his children that this is so. That is why Calvin says in *Institutes* III.ii.7 that we possess a

---

[1] *Ibid.*

[2] *Ibid.*, III.i.3.

[3] *Adoptio*—sonship—which Calvin frequently uses, serves virtually as the summary term for what it means to be a Christian. See *Institutes* III.i.3; III.ii.22; III.vi.3; III.xi.6; III.xiv.18; III.xvii.6; III.xviii.2; III.xx.36; III.xxi.7, etc. Cf. also the discussion of God's fatherhood in Brian A. Gerrish, *Grace and Gratitude* (Minneapolis: Fortress Press, 1993), pp. 87-123.

right definition of faith only when we think of it as 'a firm and certain knowledge of God's benevolence towards us'.

This definition of faith has evoked considerable controversy, especially when contrasted with the emphasis of later Reformed writers that assurance is *not* of the essence of faith. But it should be remembered here that Calvin is defining faith; he is not describing the Christian life as, for example, the Westminster divines were to do.

For Calvin, faith in its essence is a joyful assurance. It is joyful because it has Jesus Christ in its sights and nothing else. But Calvin also recognizes that experience is not always identical to definition, as the rest of *Institutes* III.ii demonstrates. We are living in the rough and tumble of an eschatological tension in which the Spirit has 'already' united us to Christ but 'not yet' consummated that work. Faith experiences the joy of the 'already' but also tastes the struggles of the 'not yet'. Furthermore, life in the Spirit is lived out within the context of conflict with the flesh. The Spirit's ministry takes place not in a hermetically-sealed laboratory where definitions of faith are written, but, as Calvin makes clear, in the nitty-gritty of the Christian life, where 'the Spirit helps us in our weakness' (Rom. 8:26).

Communion

The adopted children of God have the witness of the Spirit of sonship and cry, 'Abba! Father!' (Rom. 8:15). In their darkest moments, Christians cry out to their heavenly Father and experience this remarkable indication that they know themselves to belong to the Lord.[1]

But how does the Holy Spirit further enrich our lives within the context of our communion with Christ? Here it may be worth noting how the Lord's Supper ('the Communion service') fits into Calvin's theology as a whole.

In the aftermath of the painful split at the Marburg Colloquy between Luther and Ulrich Zwingli over the meaning of the Supper, Calvin argued that at the Lord's Supper the church does in fact have communion with Christ, but he is not located in the *res* (the actual things) of the Supper, the bread and the wine.

[1] Calvin, *Comm. Romans*, pp. 167-71.

Calvin thus distances himself from both Rome and Luther in the way he understands the presence of Christ at the Lord's Supper. He denies the presence of Christ's humanity 'in' the bread and the wine, since he has ascended to the right hand of the Father. Yet he does not want to withdraw into a 'memorialist' doctrine in which all that is actually present is the believer's reflections on the death of his Saviour.

Calvin admittedly describes that presence in ways that have disturbed some of the best Reformed theologians. He writes about the virtue or power that is communicated to us in the Lord's Supper being infused into ('poured into') us from the flesh and blood of Jesus Christ. This can easily strike readers as overly materialistic language.

The key to understanding Calvin's position is to remember the importance of the role of the Holy Spirit. All the resources for our blessing to which he has access are found in the incarnate, crucified, buried, raised, ascended, reigning, and returning Lord Jesus Christ. There are no other resources for the transformation of our lives because there is no mystical Christ, only the incarnate Christ. There is nothing else the Spirit can do, therefore, than bring us resources from the incarnate flesh of the Saviour.

The Holy Spirit therefore brings us to receive from the real (i.e. the incarnate) Jesus:[1] 'Christ's body is the only food to invigorate and enliven our soul.'[2] There is no other Jesus. At the Lord's Supper, then, we have communion with Jesus in the Spirit, not communion with a spiritual Jesus.[3]

The role of the Holy Spirit, therefore, is to bring us to where the Lord Jesus is. He 'closes the gap' in the space–time continuum between ourselves and Christ. This is the function of the *sursum corda* at the Lord's Supper: 'Lift up your hearts' (to which we respond, 'We lift them up to you, O Lord'). Calvin insists on this because true worship of and communion with Christ cannot be merely earthly worship; it is heavenly worship, and is offered and experienced where Christ is, at the right

[1] See, for example, Calvin, *Institutes*, IV.xvii.31.
[2] *Ibid.*, IV.xvii.2.
[3] 'I am not satisfied with those persons who, recognizing that we have some communion with Christ, when they would show what it is, make us partakers of the Spirit only, omitting mention of flesh and blood.' *Ibid.*, IV.xvii.7.

hand of God.[1] By the ministry of the Spirit, we are lifted, as it were, to heaven, where we find the incarnate Christ now glorified and have communion with him.

Calvin's teaching on the Supper is therefore integrated with his teaching on the work of the Holy Spirit, and is in turn embedded in his teaching about the person and work of the Lord Jesus. For it is on Christ the Spirit shines, and to him we come by that same Spirit. Since everything we need is found in him, it is into union and communion with him that the Spirit brings us and keeps us.

This is why Calvin eloquently affirms:

> We see that our whole salvation and all its parts are comprehended in Christ [Acts 4:12]. We should therefore take care not to derive the least portion of it from anywhere else. If we seek salvation, we are taught by the very name of Jesus that it is 'of him' [1 Cor. 1:30]. If we seek any other gifts of the Spirit, they will be found in his anointing. If we seek strength, it lies in his dominion; if purity, in his conception; if gentleness, it appears in his birth. For by his birth he was made like us in all respects [Heb. 2:17] that he might learn to feel our pain [Heb. 5:2]. If we seek redemption, it lies in his passion; if acquittal, in his condemnation; if remission of the curse, in his cross [Gal. 3:13]; if satisfaction, in his sacrifice; if purification, in his blood; if reconciliation, in his descent into hell; if mortification of the flesh, in his tomb; if newness of life, in his resurrection; if immortality, in the same; if inheritance of the heavenly kingdom, in his entrance into heaven; if protection, if security, if abundant supply of all blessings, in his kingdom; if untroubled expectation of judgment, in the power given to him to judge. In short, since rich store of every kind of good abounds in him, let us drink our fill from this fountain and from no other.[2]

The Spirit then, as the bond of union between the Father and the Son, is also the bond of union between the Son and his people. It is through his ministry that all that is in Christ for us becomes ours; indeed, Christ himself 'clothed in the gospel'[3] becomes ours.

---

[1] *Institutes*, IV.xvii.36.
[2] *Ibid.*, II.xvi.19.
[3] *Ibid.*, III.ii.6.

The Spirit thus glorifies Christ, and in due season transforms us from one degree of glory to another. For 'it is only under the guidance of the Spirit that we come into possession of Christ and all his benefits'.[1]

In his remarkable vision for the unity of biblical theology, the being of God the Trinity, and the harmony of the three persons of the Trinity, Calvin portrays the Holy Spirit as the executive of the Godhead in bringing us into union and communion with Christ through illumination, regeneration, adoption, and communion. All this is ours through the Spirit alone. To the extent that Calvin grasped this, and so eloquently expressed it as perhaps the supreme exponent of these truths, Warfield was surely saying no more than was warranted when he described the Genevan Reformer as, indeed, 'the theologian of the Holy Spirit'.

[1] Calvin, *Comm. 2 Corinthians*, p. 177.

CHAPTER NINE

CALVIN ON THE LORD'S SUPPER AND COMMUNION WITH CHRIST

As long as Christ remains outside of us, and we are separated from
him, all that he has suffered and done for the salvation of the human
race remains useless and of no value to us.

SO Calvin notes in a famous passage at the beginning of *Institutes*
Book III, and adds that this saving union with Christ takes place
only through 'the secret energy of the Spirit, by which we come to
enjoy Christ and all his benefits'.[1]

Central to this understanding of the role of the Holy Spirit in our
salvation is the principle that the Spirit takes what belongs to Christ and
makes it known to us (John 16:14). The same Spirit who accompanied
Jesus from conception to ascension descends on the church at Pentecost
in his specific identity as the Spirit of Jesus Christ. For the correlation
between the Spirit and Christ is now such that all that Christ has done
for us lies in the possession of the Spirit, and is brought from Christ to
the church by him. Thus the empty mouth of faith eats and drinks Christ
and the empty hands of faith are filled with every spiritual blessing.[2]

Furthermore, for Calvin the 'first' or supreme title of the Spirit is
'Spirit of sonship'.[3] Consequently, through his work believers come to
experience the assurance of God's fatherly benevolence and experience
communion with God.[4]

[1] Calvin, *Institutes*, III.i.1.
[2] See, for example, Calvin's *Short Treatise on the Lord's Supper* (Geneva, 1541), 10; tr.
J. K. S. Reid, *Calvin: Theological Treatises* (London: SCM, 1954), p. 148.
[3] Calvin, *Institutes*, III.i.3.
[4] Cf. *Comm. 1 Corinthians*, p. 60 (on 1 Cor. 2:12).

Preaching and sacraments

The objective channels through which this communion and assurance come are the word of God (particularly, but not exclusively, the preached word) and the sacraments of baptism and the Lord's Supper. Standing as he does in the Augustinian tradition, Calvin sees significant parallels between the audible word expounded in preaching and the visible word received in the sacraments.[1] Just as Christ is the *scopus*, the goal and, indeed, the focus of the Scriptures, so he is also the *scopus*[2] as well as the focus, the matter and substance[3] of the sacraments. Thus, for example, baptism is into the name of Christ, because he is its *scopus*. Its whole strength (*virtus*) lies in him. In this dynamic relation between the sacrament and Christ, a double movement takes place in which the meaning of the sacrament opens out towards Christ and in that event Christ makes himself known to and communicates (engages in communion) with the believer.

In the preached word, then, Christ speaks to us and we respond in faith to his living voice. This in itself is enough for us; but God recognizes that our faith is weak and in need of his strengthening. So he further provides the visible words of baptism and the Lord's Supper where Christ puts his grace on display in order to bring us into a more assured communion with him through the Spirit's work and our responding faith.[4]

Focus on Christ himself

Here already we have a hint of the theme which constantly underlies Calvin's thinking and gives rise to the polemical thrust in his teaching: Christ himself is the heart of the sacraments. They should not be expounded in terms of the *res* (the element in itself—water, bread or wine), but in terms of the *persona* (the person who is presented to us, i.e. Jesus himself). If attention is focused on the sacramental 'thing' (water, bread and wine), and hearts are not lifted beyond the sign to the person of Jesus signified in the sign and revealed by the Spirit through the sign, then the true meaning of the sacraments is bound to become distorted.

[1] Cf. Calvin, *Institutes*, IV.xiv.6.
[2] Cf. *Comm. Acts*, I:319 (on Acts 10:48): 'Christ is the proper goal of baptism' (*proprius Baptismi scopus*).
[3] Calvin, *Institutes*, IV.iv.16.
[4] *Ibid.*, IV.xiv.8.

This understanding of how sacraments 'work' explains Calvin's concern to expound the role of the Spirit in their administration. It is directly analogous to his role in preaching. The Spirit does not transform the words of the Bible but employs them to bring us to Christ; so too, in the administration of the sacraments, the elements are not transformed, but rather employed by the Spirit to realize in us all that is symbolized to us. Nothing 'changes' the elements.

This note is particularly dominant in Calvin's teaching on the Lord's Supper. For, in his view, while men can employ the *res* of the Lord's Supper, breaking the bread and offering the wine, only the divine Spirit is qualified to communicate the person of Jesus Christ to us by these means.

A Christo-dynamic view of the Supper

For Calvin, then, sacraments are not mere or bare signs (*signa nuda*) but, like the audible 'signs' of the words of Scripture, when received in faith they function as communicative signs. By means of them the very realities they symbolize are actually communicated to and experienced by the recipients as they respond in faith. The Spirit is the connection, the bond (*vinculum*) between the *res* (bread and wine), the *persona* (Jesus himself), and ourselves as the recipients.

If we fail to grasp this, error and confusion follow: either (i) the sign is confused with the thing signified, and an *ex opere operato* doctrine of the sacraments results, as though we could receive Christ simply by the act of eating and drinking; or (ii) the sign is divorced from what it signifies (Jesus Christ, clothed in the gospel) and the Supper thus tends to be little more than an *aide-mémoire*, falling far short of Spirit-given communion with Christ.

Calvin's Christo-dynamic view of the sacraments (if we may thus describe it) constantly seeks to turn the recipient's eyes to Jesus Christ himself. The communion in view is with Christ, and the feasting is on Jesus himself. What the sacramental signs externally signify is internally effected by the Spirit.[1]

This understanding protects us from the implications of the two errors noted above:

---

[1] See Calvin, *Comm. Titus*, pp. 382-83 (on Titus 3:5).

(1) It prevents us from adorning the sign (possibly even adoring it!), as though the sign itself were or could become the reality it represents (the danger of an *ex opere operato* view, in which the priest's action is sufficient of itself to make Christ present, apart from the free, sovereign and dynamic activity of the Spirit).

(2) It safeguards us from emptying the sign of its ability to bring us to Christ when so employed by the Spirit. This is the danger of *signa nuda*, reducing the bread and the wine to 'bare signs', in which human faith alone is active and nothing is attributed to the Spirit.

Calvin here distances himself from Rome on the right and the Anabaptists on the left, but also by implication from both Luther and Zwingli. Self-consciously he provided a *via media* between the latter two. He did so, however, not by adopting the common factors between them, but by expounding what he saw as a biblical, that is a pneumatic (Holy Spirit-empowered), doctrine of the sacraments. Only this, he believed, preserves the biblical conjunction of the sign and the reality of the thing (or better, *person*) signified, and safeguards the necessity of the Spirit's ministry and also of our faith. Without this inner dynamic in the Supper, the biblical correlation between Christ, the sacramental symbols, and our faith collapses.

Thus he believes that the Roman Church (papal *magisterium* and priestly acts) has usurped, whereas Zwingli and Luther have minimized, the ministry which belongs to the Holy Spirit.

Polemical emphases

Because Calvin expounds the doctrine of the Supper in a variety of polemical contexts, his teaching is contextualized in different ways.

(1) When dealing with those who boast in the sign, he tends to stress the emptiness of the sign in and of itself.

(2) When addressing the criticisms of both Rome and the Anabaptists (one stressing the necessity of priestly ordination and power, the other stressing the personal status of the administrant), he stresses the essential insignificance of the human administrant.

(3) When addressing believers he stresses the dynamic connection of the sign with what it signifies—the so-called sacramental union.

But in each of these reactions, Calvin returns basically to the same central theme: the efficacy of the sacraments depends on the dynamic ministry of the Holy Spirit uniting the recipients to the reality which the sacraments objectively signify, namely the person of Jesus Christ clothed in the garments of salvation. He enlightens the mind with faith, he seals in the heart the adoption of God, he regenerates us to new life, and he grafts us into the body of Christ so that we come to live in him and he in us.[1]

The display of Christ, the substance of the Supper

The function of the sacraments, then, can be summed up in two Latin terms Calvin employs:

(1) Exhibere

The signs display or exhibit Christ to the eyes and to the sense of vision, just as the word displays Christ to the ears and to the sense of hearing as the Spirit takes what belongs to Christ and shows or exhibits it to us. In this sense Calvin sees sacraments as appendices to the promise of the gospel, confirming it to faith.[2] Pictures may display what the weak in faith are not able to read easily in the word. They thus help to remove our ignorance and doubt of God's grace toward us, and strengthen our weak faith.

In this respect, it is important to notice the way Calvin balances the famous definition of faith he had given earlier in his *Institutes*[3] by what he says here about faith's existential weakness:

> God's truth is of itself firm and sure enough. ... But as our faith is slight and feeble unless it be propped on all sides and sustained by every means, it trembles, wavers, totters, and at last gives way. Here

---

[1] Cf. Calvin, *Comm. Hebrews*, p. 149.

[2] Calvin, *Institutes*, IV.xiv.5-6.

[3] *Ibid.*, II.ii.7: 'We shall possess a right definition of faith if we call it a firm and certain knowledge of God's benevolence towards us, founded upon the truth of the freely given promise in Christ, both revealed to our minds and sealed upon our hearts through the Holy Spirit.'

our merciful Lord, according to his infinite kindness, so tempers himself to our capacity that, since we are creatures who always creep on the ground, cleave to the flesh, and do not think about or even conceive of anything spiritual, he condescends to lead us to himself, even by these earthly elements, and to set before us in the flesh a mirror of spiritual blessings.[1]

Calvin is therefore very far from the quasi-perfectionism he detected in some left-wing Reformation thinking that viewed the sacraments as unnecessary for those who had real faith and could feed inwardly on Christ.[2] Rather, he holds that through the visible words of the sacraments, the Spirit penetrates our hard hearts, moves our jaded affections and opens our souls to receive the Christ who is exhibited by means of the signs.

(2) Substantia

Calvin contends that the sacraments communicate to believers the 'substance' of Jesus Christ, in his saving humanity. The precise manner in which this takes place is, as we shall see, one of the most significant and distinctive elements in Calvin's teaching on the Lord's Supper, and one that has provoked considerable comment. We shall return to it.

The 'real' presence of Christ

As with all the magisterial Reformers, the central controversy of the Lord's Supper (and subsequently the context in which Calvin enlarged on the role of the Holy Spirit) was the question of the nature of the presence of the body and blood of Christ and the manner of our communion with him. Here he seeks to avoid two opposite, if not quite equal, errors:

(1) That our communion is with the flesh and blood of Christ localized in the bread and wine of the Supper.

(2) That our communion is not with the actual body and blood of Christ, but is merely a spiritual one, in the sense that the

[1] *Ibid.*, IV.xiv.3.
[2] For example, Caspar Schwenckfeld. See G. H. Williams, *The Radical Reformation* (Philadelphia: Westminster Press, 1962), pp. 106ff.

Supper prompts us to reflect back on our conversion and enables us to meditate on what Jesus Christ has done for us, or on our commitment and love to him. The Supper, thus conceived, has a rather subjective orientation.[1]

Against both these positions, Calvin argues that we have true communion with the actual flesh and blood of Christ, whose *virtus*, strength, is ours by Spirit-born faith. Christ who is in heaven thus feeds those who are on the earth from his own flesh. All this is accomplished—admittedly mysteriously—through the Spirit. This, for Calvin, is the true partaking of the flesh and blood of Christ. In fact, he says, in this ministry the Spirit is like a channel 'through which all that Christ himself is and has is conveyed to us'.[2]

It is here that we can see how central to Calvin's thinking about the Supper is the way he views the distinctive role of the Holy Spirit. On the one hand (over against Rome), he asserts the permanent bodily presence of Christ in heaven, and denies his physical presence in the bread and wine; but equally (over against a mere memorialism) he insists that the substantial presence of Christ, in the event of the Supper as a whole, is experienced through the power of the Spirit.

Implications

Three important consequences emerge as a result of Calvin's thinking:

(1) The body and blood of Christ are not, and cannot be, shut up (*inclusus*) in the bread and the wine of the Lord's Supper. The ascension of Christ is a real, physical, once-for-all, irreversible, redemptive-historical event. Whatever is meant, therefore, by our communion with the body and blood of Christ, they cannot be thought of as locally present in the elements of the Supper since they are at the right hand of God, in heaven, where Jesus has ascended. Calvin regards this much as clear on the basis of Acts 3:21 ('He must remain in heaven until the time comes for God to restore everything').

It would be a major departure from the Scriptures to hold, as Rome did, that, as a result of the priestly words *Hoc est corpus meum* ('This is

---

[1] Calvin, *Institutes*, IV.xvii.7.

[2] *Ibid.*, IV.xvii.12.

my body'), an act of transubstantiation takes place so that the bread and wine are changed as to their substance into the body and blood of Christ which are consequently contained by and located within the bread and the wine. Calvin's fundamental objection to the idea that, while the *accidents* or properties of bread and wine remain, their *substance* has become the flesh and blood of Christ, is that it compromises the heavenly glory of Christ, and fails to give due weight to the significance of the ascension.

Rather the exhortation appropriate to communion, 'lift up your hearts' (*sursum corda*), indicates that we look beyond the physical eating and drinking to enjoy communion with an ascended and glorified Lord in the flesh and blood he assumed and continues to possess.[1]

(2) On the other hand, to adopt the Lutheran (so-called consubstantiation) view was an equal error. Luther held, in the light of his doctrine of the ubiquity (omnipresence) of the resurrected humanity of Christ, that his body and blood could be received 'in, with, and under' the bread and the wine. To Calvin this was essentially to deny the reality of Christ's humanity and its real identity with ours. For ubiquity is not a property of humanity as such. If Christ's humanity is ubiquitous, it cannot truly be 'our' humanity, and the grammatical rules which make the incarnation a saving event have been transgressed: a humanity so unlike ours cannot be the means of the salvation of the humanity which is ours.

The seriousness of the flaw in the Lutheran view, as far as Calvin is concerned, is that ultimately it undermines orthodox Christology (which stated that the two natures were united in one person, not united directly in such a way that their properties mingled with each other). The Christ of this doctrine would be a 'phantasm', and this, for Calvin, meant that a consistent soteriology and a genuine sacramental theology would become impossible. Theologically what was at stake here was not merely the doctrine of the sacraments or even the finer points of Christology, but the very possibility of salvation itself. For only one who is truly one of us can become a Saviour for us.

(3) But again, over against a reactionary memorialism which reduces the action in the Supper to that of the recipient, Calvin insists that the

---

[1] *Institutes*, IV.xvii.36.

Spirit works in order to give believers a genuine share in Christ's real body and blood, not because of its local presence, nor by its infinite extension in space, but by the power of the Spirit. This pneumatological dimension of the Supper is one which Calvin believes his opponents essentially ignore. For him, however, it is the key to the whole thing.

True communion with Christ

How then does communion with Christ take place? In Calvin's view, the space–time gap between believers and Christ is bridged by the Holy Spirit. It is his office to unite believers on earth to Christ in heaven, bringing together realities which are spatially distanced.[1] Through the Spirit we are raised up into the heavenly presence of Christ and feed on him. This is the secret and wonderful work of the Spirit. We cannot measure it; indeed it would be sinful to try. Calvin himself admits this is incredible. It is beyond our understanding that the Spirit should join together things separated spatially; but nevertheless we experience the reality of it even if we do not comprehend the mystery of it. Here, far from being coldly rationalistic, Calvin subscribes to the view that certain aspects of grace are, apparently, 'better felt than telt'.

Calvin's eucharistic doctrine, therefore, in denying the local, enclosed presence of Christ, emphasizes what is sometimes called his spiritual presence. But here being present 'spiritually' means 'the presence of the incarnate and exalted Son of God *by the Spirit*'. Unwilling to surrender to Rome's claim that only by transubstantiation can believers enjoy the 'real presence' of Christ in the eucharist, Calvin affirms that it is only by the Spirit that believers can know Christ's real presence in the sense of his 'true presence' as a body-and-blood-presence.

Calvin's concern here is to expound the mystery of personal communion with a physical (flesh-and-blood), but glorified, Christ. For him there is no other Christ, and the polemic in his sacramental teaching draws its violence from the fact that his opponents' errors distort a true biblical Christology. After all, communion with a person does not involve eating their body carnally, but communion with that person-in-flesh-and-blood personally. Since Christ is a person, we

---

[1] Cf. *Comm. 1 Corinthians*, pp. 246-47.

enjoy fellowship with him in an embodied-person to embodied-person manner—through the ministry of the Spirit.

Thus our communion is not merely with the Spirit, but with the ascended, bodily Christ, not merely with Christ's benefits, but with Christ himself. 'Christ's flesh, separated from such great distance', says Calvin, 'penetrates to our flesh',[1] so that although it dwells in heaven, our spiritual life is drawn from his flesh:

> It is declared in my writings more than a hundred times, that so far am I from rejecting the term substance, that I ingenuously and readily declare, that by the incomprehensible agency of the Spirit, spiritual life is infused into us from the substance of the flesh of Christ. I also constantly admit that we are substantially fed on the flesh and blood of Christ, though I discard the gross fiction of a local intermingling.[2]

Language like this is now so rare that to modern ears it sounds unexpectedly realistic, even shocking. Here, and in the *Institutes* where he similarly speaks about life being 'infused into us from the substance of his flesh',[3] Calvin is obviously struggling to express in words the mystery of what the Holy Spirit actually accomplishes in the Supper. It is just at this point that he has sometimes been criticized by theologians within the very Reformed tradition to which he gave birth. William Cunningham, for example, regarded Calvin's formulation as both incomprehensible and impossible.[4] R. L. Dabney thought it 'as real a violation of my intuitive reason in this doctrine as when transubstantiation requires me to believe that the flesh of Christ is present, indivisible, and unextended in each crumb or drop of the elements'.[5] It is, consequently, rare to find Calvin's teaching expressed today.

---

[1] *Institutes*, IV.xvii.10.

[2] These words are drawn from Calvin's 1561 treatise, *The Clear Explanation of Sound Doctrine Concerning the True Partaking of the Flesh and Blood of Christ in the Holy Supper to Dissipate the Mists of Tileman Heshusius*, in Beveridge, *Tracts and Treatises*, II:502.

[3] Calvin, *Institutes*, IV.xvii.4.

[4] See William Cunningham, *The Reformers and the Theology of the Reformation* (Edinburgh, 1862), p. 240. Cunningham calls Calvin's views here 'perhaps, the greatest blot in the history of Calvin's labours as a public instructor'.

[5] R. L. Dabney, *Lectures in Systematic Theology* (1878; repr., Edinburgh: Banner of Truth Trust, 1985), p. 182.

While one might hesitate to say dogmatically that Calvin's teaching has been misunderstood, it may be that the vigorous language in which he expresses himself has obscured the point he is making. For he makes it clear that Christ's flesh as such is not mingled with ours, but rather that, by the Spirit, Christ breathes his new life into us from the substance of that flesh, that is from all that he, the Son of God, now is in our humanity. This is Calvin's way of saying that as the last Adam who has become life-giving Spirit and Lord of the Spirit (1 Cor. 15:45; 2 Cor. 3:18), Christ gives to us both himself and all he has gained for us.

The essential point for Calvin here is that, at the end of the day, this is the only Christ there is. The Christ from whom all spiritual blessings flow is Christ physically risen and ascended, bearing our flesh albeit now glorified. If salvation and blessing are to be found only in Christ (Eph. 1:3ff), then this Christ, flesh and blood as he remains, is the only possible source from which the Spirit can bring salvation and the only Saviour to whom he can unite us.

The general point made earlier, namely that the key to understanding Calvin's doctrine of the Lord's Supper is found in his doctrine of the correlativity of the ascended yet still incarnate Christ and the descending Spirit, here comes into its own. Grasp this, Calvin believes, and the realism of his doctrine of the Supper becomes less problematic.

What we find in Calvin's eucharistic theology is essentially what we find again and again in his writings: salvation is ours only in Christ incarnate, crucified, buried, raised, ascended, and reigning in our flesh.[1] This salvation is ours only by faith, and this, in turn, is the same as saying that salvation is ours only through the Spirit, because it is the Spirit who brings from Christ to us all that is in Christ for us, and it is the Spirit who creates the faith in Christ, by means of which all that is his is experientially realized in us. All that is planned by the Father and fulfilled in the Son comes to us through the Holy Spirit.

Drawn into the Reformation eucharistic debates as he was, Calvin makes statements both about the nature of Christ and about our fellowship with him which may seem to be less heavily accented elsewhere in his writings. Nevertheless his Christology is one and the

---

[1] A point made most graphically and in lyrical style in Calvin, *Institutes*, II.xvi.19.

same. Only one who is genuinely incarnate, sharing our flesh and blood, is qualified to be our Saviour. There are no other resources in heaven or earth for our salvation than those which are possessed by this Saviour wearing and possessing our flesh. There is, therefore, no other source from which salvation can be brought to us by the Holy Spirit than from that glorified flesh of Christ. Faith communion through the ministry of either word or sacraments is communion with the enfleshed but now glorified Christ and none other.

Calvin's Christ is a substantial flesh-and-blood Christ. For Calvin, salvation is a substantial, not merely a forensic, matter; hence his thoroughgoing emphasis on Christ's union with us in our flesh, and the resultant salvation-transformation of our flesh in final salvation. Here he seems to combine elements of the emphases of the Greek as well as the Latin Fathers of the church. It should not surprise us if his view of the Lord's Supper reflects this substantial Christ.

Calvin's Christologically-focused eucharistic theology found its way into the blood-stream of the Church of Scotland in the sixteenth century. Thus, in his famous 1589 sermons in St Giles, Edinburgh, Robert Bruce expressed the point perfectly when he noted that we do not get a different or better Christ at the Supper than we get in the preaching of the word; but because the Supper-sign is added to the word preached, by God's grace and the Spirit's ministry we may get the same Christ better, and, sensing the firmness of his grasp of grace on us, get a firmer grasp on him.[1]

It is this Calvin–Bruce tradition that Horatius Bonar so well expressed in the nineteenth century:

> Here, O my Lord, I see Thee face to face;
>   Here would I touch and handle things unseen,
> Here grasp with firmer hand the eternal grace,
>   And all my weariness upon Thee lean.

Thus we experience Christ gripping us in the word and the same Christ—incarnate, crucified, raised, ascended, glorified, reigning, and returning—made known at the Table, and there sometimes better grasped.

[1] See Robert Bruce, *The Mystery of the Lord's Supper*, ed. T. F. Torrance (Edinburgh: Knox Press, 1958), p. 64.

III. PURITANS:
PASTORS AND TEACHERS

CHAPTER TEN

PURITANS: MINISTERS OF THE WORD

F EW, if any, epochs in the history of the Christian church can boast so many outstanding examples of pastoral ministry as the Puritan period of the late sixteenth and seventeenth centuries. Even a little knowledge of the history of the cure of souls underscores the impressiveness of the example of men such as William Perkins, Richard Sibbes, John Bunyan, Richard Baxter, Thomas Goodwin, John Owen, Thomas Watson, and many others who, though less well known now, were revered in their own day for the power and fruitfulness of their ministries.

To turn to the work of the Puritans today, against the background of contemporary popular Christian literature, is to enter a markedly different order of reality. For those unacquainted with their writings, a first encounter with their literature can be like entering a world where people seem bigger, wiser, and years older.

To read and study the Puritans is akin to standing in a familiar house and noticing there is an extra door one had never noticed. Press it open and a large basement full of unimagined resources comes into view. Here one may linger often, and from here Christians—and not least Christian pastors—may return to the world of their daily service with renewed vigour, with a greater sense of the gospel and its power, deeply challenged to live for their chief end: 'to glorify God, and to enjoy him for ever.'[1]

Here we find ourselves in a world of men with a clear vision of the nature of true pastoral ministry, and an unreserved commitment to it,

---

[1] The answer to the first question in the *Shorter Catechism* produced by the Westminster Assembly.

whatever the personal cost. This is an environment of clear-sightedness, single-mindedness, and a deep love of God which if applied to the work of the pastor today would have a profound, if at times a disturbing, impact on our understanding of the real task of the ministry.

The Puritan view of the ministry

What lay at the heart of this Puritan view of the ministry? It was the vision of seeing godly, learned preachers and spiritual shepherds replacing the spiritually impoverished pastoral ministries which had come to characterize much of the church in late sixteenth-century England. So successful were they in this that within half a century the quality of English clergy in general had became a byword.

Puritan ministers were, of course, varied in personality, gift, burden and sphere of calling. Indeed while they shared the same heartbeat, and while the family likeness in their ministries is obvious, there was great diversity of style among them. The insight in Phillips Brooks's notion that preaching is 'the bringing of truth through personality'[1] can be abundantly illustrated in Puritan preachers. The dramatic features of a John Rogers of Dedham, who at times would virtually 'act out' his preaching in a dramatic way, involved a different use of the imagination from the preaching of, for example, the story-telling of a John Flavel, or the deep-reasoning John Owen. But the Puritans shared a common perspective on what pastoral ministry ought to be. It was the work of men who were, first, godly and learned; second, men whose task was preaching; and who, third, in the deepest sense cared for their people.

But we can find more colourful descriptions in their own writings. None better exists than the famous word-portrait of the Puritan minister which John Bunyan gives us in Part One of *The Pilgrim's Progress*.

Christian comes to Interpreter's House where he sees a picture:

> Christian saw a picture of a very grave person hang up against the wall, and this was the fashion of it: it had eyes lift up to heaven, the best of books in its hand, the law of truth was written upon its lips, the world was behind its back; it stood as if it pleaded with men, and a crown of gold did hang over its head.

[1] Phillips Brooks, *Lectures on Preaching* (New York: E. P. Dutton & Company, 1878), p. 5.

Interpreter provided the artistic exegesis and commentary:

> The man whose picture this is, is one of a thousand; he can beget
> children, travail in birth with children, and nurse them himself
> when they are born. And whereas thou seest him with his eyes lift
> up to heaven, the best of books in his hand, and the law of truth
> writ on his lips, it is to show thee that his work is to know, and
> unfold dark things to sinners even as also thou seest him stand
> as if he pleaded with men; and whereas thou seest the world
> as cast behind him, and that a crown hangs over his head, that
> is to show thee that slighting and despising the things that are
> present, for the love that he hath to his Master's service, he is sure
> in the world that comes next to have glory for his reward … this
> is the only man whom the Lord of the place whither thou art
> going hath authorized to be thy guide in all difficult places thou
> mayest meet with in the way.[1]

All the ingredients of the Puritan view of the ministry can be seen
in this single portrait: the basic qualification of personal godliness and
giftedness coupled with single-minded learning in the interpretation of
Scripture; a spirit of prayerfulness; a deep care for the people of God;
and the ability to unfold the mysteries of the gospel in a manner which
reached into men's hearts and touched their consciences—and all set
within the context of a prayerful dependence on the Lord.

This style of ministry is never without cost. That was certainly true
of the Puritans. Their lot was far from ideal. The sixteenth and seventeenth centuries were no times to be committed to biblical ministry if
earthly comforts featured high on one's list of priorities—or, perhaps
as importantly, on one's wife's list. Many of them suffered materially
for their faithfulness to the gospel. True, some Puritans—such as John
Owen—seem to have been comfortably endowed, on occasion through
marriage. But these were the exception, not the rule.

Secular historians suggest that fewer than ten per cent of churches
provided a salary remotely commensurate with the Puritan minister's
educational qualifications. Add to this the struggles which would, in

---

[1] John Bunyan, *The Pilgrim's Progress* (1678; 1685; repr. Edinburgh: Banner of Truth
Trust, 2017), pp. 26-27.

1662, lead to the ejection of some 2,000 ministers of Puritan conviction from their livings and it becomes clear that however competent these men were, intellectually and spiritually, they did not look to, or live for, this present world. Middle-class comfort was by no means their aspiration in life.

What, then, did mark these men and their ministries?

The Puritan minister

The marriage of true learning and personal godliness lay at the heart of the Puritan vision. A recurring note in their thinking was the apostolic injunction, 'Pay careful attention to yourselves' (Acts 20:28); 'keep a close watch on yourself ...' (1 Tim. 4:16). Personal godliness was the great essential. The chief misery of the church, argued Richard Baxter, lies in the fact that there are too many men who are ministers before they are Christians.

And so the Puritan pastor was marked, first and foremost, by his personal growth in grace: his reading, study, knowledge of, and obedience to God's word in his own life.

But, unlike many of their predecessors and a growing number of their contemporaries, especially the so-called 'mechanik preachers', the Puritans sought to marry learning to their spirituality.

In those days, theological college was as yet no part of ministerial training. Perkins, Preston, Manton, Sibbes, Cotton, Goodwin, Owen—none of these men had what we would regard as a theological education. But they were university-educated men, benefiting from a system which had incorporated the study of Latin, Greek, and Hebrew into the curriculum at Oxford and Cambridge Universities early in the fifteenth century. Young men had further equipped themselves by personal study undertaken while serving as tutors and chaplains in wealthy homes. Often they apprenticed themselves to well-tried gospel ministers, at times lived with them, and breathed-in the atmosphere of ministry by observation and personal discussion in a way that echoed the schools of the prophets in the days of Elijah and Elisha, and imitated the pattern of Paul and Timothy.

This practical training was extended on occasions when ministers would gather—often on market day—for times of public preaching and thereafter to 'combine', that is, to share a fellowship meal in which younger men could eavesdrop on the rich and experienced conversation of older ministers.

In many ways these gatherings, known as 'prophesyings', were rooted in the practice of the weekly '*Congrégations*' which John Calvin had developed in Geneva, when the local ministers and others met for Bible study, often concluding with Calvin himself leading them into the meaning, significance, and application of the passage set for study. As for Calvin, so for the Puritans, 'prophesying' was, in essence, an exposition and application of God's word in the power of the Spirit. Thus for all practical purposes these regular gatherings became seminars in faith and preaching skills for younger men.

It would be mistaken, however, to think that in lacking a seminary, theological college, or divinity faculty education these men lacked a biblical and theological education itself. Their learning in areas of biblical study and theology would have left most of them unembarrassed in the company of a modern graduate in theology. Indeed, a seminary graduate sharing the ordination exam of the young ministerial candidate (later a Westminster divine) John Carter might be taken aback by his answer to the question 'Have you read through the Bible?' 'Yes', Carter replied, 'I have read the Old Testament twice through in the Hebrew, and the New Testament often through in the Greek.' That may have been somewhat exceptional, but Carter was by no means unique.

Of course these men lacked the benefit of the three hundred years of biblical interpretation which have passed since their time, and it would be a mistake to discount those advances. But the style of their training well illustrates the principle that it is often what takes place outside of the classroom that really determines the quality of preparation for ministry. Their intense familiarity with, and love for, Scripture provided them with an understanding of the grace of God and of the human heart which we might well envy.

That is well illustrated today by the widespread reading of such a work as John Owen's searching little book *On the Mortification of Sin*.[1] Today regarded as strong meat for mature Christians with substantial

---

[1] Owen, *Works*, VI:1-86. The work was first published in 1656.

appetites, Owen actually preached the material to students at Oxford University, many of them presumably in their late teens.

The Puritans were also well capable of highly technical biblical studies. John Owen, for example, published a commentary on Hebrews of extraordinary sophistication. But this work, which is perhaps the zenith of Puritan biblical exegesis, also abounds in practical applications. It therefore underscores the fact that the great interest lay—to coin a term on the basis of Paul's language in 2 Timothy 3:16—in the *ophelimostic* qualities of Scripture.[1] Their burden was not the explanation of the syntax of the texts on which they preached, but the fact that Scripture is useful in its power to transform character and life. Thus study of it was not for purely professional reasons, such as the writing of the academic literature of which they were eminently capable, or even the writing of sermons. Rather they studied *to know God*. For them theology was the art of living well, and it was out of the rich fullness of the biblical knowledge they developed that they were able to speak so powerfully.

The Puritan preachers possessed a diversity of gifts—academic as well as pastoral, controversial as well as conscience-striking and comforting. But the centre of their task was offering Christ and wooing men and women to him. To this they devoted the very best of their energies and imaginative powers. Preaching, as one of them said, is the chariot that carries Christ to the world.

This Christocentric element in their thinking has often been neglected in the study of the Puritans. One only needs to think of Richard Sibbes's wonderful portrayal of a Christ who does not break the bruised reed;[2] or of Thomas Goodwin's mighty descriptions of the unveiled heart of Christ as mediator;[3] or of John Owen's awe-inspiring and loving exposition of the glories of Jesus Christ,[4] to realize that these were Christ-full preachers.

---

[1] Paul speaks about the God-breathed Scripture being 'profitable' or 'useful' (*ophelimos*) for the very practical functions of teaching, reproof, correction, and training in righteousness.

[2] *Complete Works of Richard Sibbes*, ed. Alexander Grosart (Edinburgh: J. Nichol, 1862-64); I:42-101. The work was first published in 1630.

[3] Goodwin, *Works*, IV:93-150. The work was first published in 1651.

[4] Owen, *Works*, I:1-461. The expositions were first published posthumously in 1684 and 1691.

Much modern preaching and popular evangelical teaching has a tendency to give its best energies and strongest imaginative powers to exploring man, his world, and his self-improvement—witness the themes of much evangelical literature and seminars. Little more than lip-service is given to the apostolic principle to preach Christ, the whole Christ, and nothing but Christ and him crucified. The 'wondrous cross' is all too little surveyed today. But that was not so with the Puritans.

The Puritan minister's chief task, then, was the preaching of the word of God, of which he was an appointed interpreter. But he was first and foremost a pastor: his first task was to feed and defend his sheep; the means by which he did this was preaching. The Puritan preacher's focus therefore never lay in the personal satisfaction he gained from study, preparation, and delivery. Rather it lay in the provision of spiritual food for his flock.

For that reason, Puritan manuals on the ministry focused on how to handle the word of God both privately and publicly in such a way that hearers would be spiritually helped and nourished. While their preaching was informative and in general educative, its central function was not the communication of information but the effecting of transformation. They therefore developed their own form of rhetoric.

The Puritan plain style

Puritan preaching is often described as exemplifying the so-called 'plain style'—one unadorned by developed rhetorical skills. In general terms this is true, albeit preachers' styles varied from the rugged and bare to the naturally eloquent and aesthetically pleasing. But common to all forms of this style was the adoption of Paul's principle: 'we have renounced disgraceful, underhanded ways. We refuse to practise cunning or to tamper with God's word, but by the open statement of the truth we would commend ourselves to everyone's conscience in the sight of God' (2 Cor. 4:2). This *phanerōsis*, the setting on display of the truth, was their goal. The wisdom of this world, the enticing aesthetics of the schools of oratory and acting, were thus eschewed. No rhetorical interest or effect should stand between the hearer and the truth of the gospel.

Consequently three features were characteristic of the Puritan sermon from the time of William Perkins and became dominant throughout the seventeenth century:

(1) First the text was 'opened'. The preacher would briefly explain its meaning in its context in Scripture.

(2) Secondly, it was 'divided'. As a diamond merchant might cut precious stones, so the preacher would separate out from the text the specific doctrines he would teach, and then verbally hold them up before the eyes of the congregation.

(3) Thirdly, 'uses' were expounded. Great practical questions were asked and answered: 'How does this apply to me?' 'How do I know these things are true of me?' 'How can I make this mine?'

Puritan preaching therefore required three fundamental skills of the preacher himself: exegetical insight, a solid grasp of systematic theology (the 'body of divinity'), and spiritual wisdom (in order for his exegetical and theological work to be applicable to the body of Christ in the world). The Puritans believed themselves to be called to be exegetes, but their preaching was not merely a retelling of the text. They were theologians, but their aim was not the display of philosophical erudition, for they believed that all Scripture, and therefore all theology, belonged to all the people of God. They were also spiritual counsellors, but they believed that the best counsellor is the Holy Spirit, who applies the word of God to our minds, consciences, emotions, dispositions, and affections especially through preaching. They saw themselves as spiritual surgeons whose calling was to use the cleanest, sharpest, most appropriate instruments available to them to enable them to do a profound work through spiritual incisions that might lead to healing.

This aspect of their thinking is of great significance. The Puritan movement did not set preaching and counselling over against one another as alternatives. For them preaching was counselling, and the most fundamental and best counselling was done in preaching. Such preaching also inevitably brought to the surface specific needs which might require further counsel, and so many of them spent long hours engaged in personal conversations. A further common feature of Puritan churches was a more general, public, counselling meeting in which ministers and mature leaders might deal with 'cases of conscience', expounding biblical teaching on Christian patterns of behaviour and especially encouraging and strengthening the weak.

The Puritans would have found passing strange any 'Christian' preaching that did not bring counsel that was both biblically rooted and practically applicable. They would equally have found strange any 'Christian' counselling that did not place a fundamental emphasis on constantly sitting under a biblical ministry. Healing neuroses was not their goal; a transformed life for the glory of God was.

The Puritan pastors believed that through applicatory preaching the Holy Spirit works, without further limited human mediation, to apply the word of God to individual situations. The effectiveness of their work is evidenced by the accusations, made against some of them by members of their congregations, that they had hired paid informers to tell them the secrets of their hearers!

Much could be said about this. But it is worth noting that the Puritans also never divorced counselling from the life of the fellowship of the church. It was, in their view, of the essence of a congregation's life that it would be not only an army in the battles of the Lord, but also a hospital for the war-wounded.

Preaching grids

The Puritans applied their exposition to many different needs. Here they took a lead from Jesus' parable of the sower and the soils.[1] The Puritan pastor knew that those who listened to him belonged to different categories of condition and need. Here, as in other respects, they took their lead from the 'preaching grid' which they found first in Jesus: the pathway, the rocky soil, the weed-infested soil, the good soil.

A more sophisticated 'grid' was found in a developed contemporary form in the great William Perkins's work *The Arte of Prophecying*.

The Arte of Prophecying had been published in 1592 in Latin—an indication that it was intended for an educated audience. It was translated into English by Thomas Tuke and published in 1606 a few years

[1] Mark 4:1-20.

after Perkins's death. The influence of this little book[1] flowed partly from its own seminal character, but largely from the well-deserved reputation of its author as a preacher of unparalleled power and fruitfulness.

Such was the impact of Perkins's preaching and indeed of his very presence in the university city of Cambridge, that when the young John Cotton heard the church bell tolling at Perkins's death he rejoiced that his conscience would never again be smitten by Perkins's sermons. Little did he know!

Ten years later, when the twelve-year-old Thomas Goodwin came up to Cambridge (in 1613), 'the town was then filled with the discourse of the power of Mr Perkins's ministry'.[2]

Perkins divided hearers into seven categories.

1. Ignorant and unteachable unbelievers.

2. Ignorant but teachable.

3. Knowledgeable but unhumbled.

4. The humbled, either partly or thoroughly.

5. Those who are already believers.

6. Backsliders of various kinds.

7. Congregations containing a mixture of believers and unbelievers.

What is significant here is not so much the precise details of Perkins's preaching grid—we might want to use different ones today. Rather it is his consciousness of, and sensitivity to, the differing spiritual conditions of those to whom he ministered the word of God. He was far from having a needs-orientation in his preaching (he was more interested in *creating* a sense of need through deep conviction of sin than in pandering to what his hearers superficially might think of as their 'needs'). Yet he clearly shaped his application of Scripture to the *specific* conditions, and to *all of* the conditions, of his hearers.

---

[1] For a modernized version see *The Art of Prophesying*, including Perkins's powerful two-part tract on *The Calling of the Ministry*, ed. Sinclair B. Ferguson (Edinburgh: Banner of Truth Trust, 1996).

[2] Robert Halley, 'Memoir of Thomas Goodwin, D.D.', in Goodwin, *Works*, II:xiii.

Richard Sibbes wrote in similar vein of the preacher's responsibility: 'Ministers ... are *to learn their duty hence, to observe the dispositions of people, and what bars they lay to their own salvation*'[3] in order that through the ministry of the word they might deal with them faithfully.

Puritan ministers thus realized that this aspect of preaching—bringing it home to the hearers—was, as they expressed it, the most 'painful' (i.e. painstaking) aspect of both preparation and delivery. It demanded the greatest knowledge of the human heart and its foibles. Furthermore, it laid greatest demand on their imagination since it indicated the extent to which they had placed themselves under the word.

The 'ripping up the conscience' of which Perkins and others were exponents was a hallmark of the Puritans' mastery of pastoral skills. But they did not simply berate or beat their sheep into greater self-effort. Rather, they led them on, showed them the way, held them as they took their first steps, encouraged them with gospel grace, wooing them always to Christ. They knew that emotionally powerful sermons can be preached by those who grasp what the law demands. But life-transforming sermons can be preached only by those who also have a firm grasp on how the wonder of grace operates.

The best brief summary of such 'plain style' preaching as a central aspect of the pastoral calling is, undoubtedly, found in *The Directory for Publick Worship of God* composed by the great assembly of divines that met at Westminster Abbey in the 1640s and, over a period of four years or so, produced the documents that have been foundational ever since to Presbyterian churches. These were *The Confession of Faith*, *The Larger Catechism*, *The Shorter Catechism*, *The Directory for Church Government* and *The Directory for Publick Worship*. It may be helpful here to say something about the context of the Westminster Assembly and its work.

The Westminster Assembly

On June 12, 1643, the English Parliament 'thought fit and necessary to call an Assembly of learned, godly, and judicious Divines' (i.e. ministers, although laymen were also present). It had three specific aims in view:

(1) To reform the worship, discipline and government of the Church

---

[3] Sibbes, *Works*, VII:481.

of England;

(2) To promote church unity among the churches in England, Scotland, and the Continent;

(3) To clarify the doctrine, and revise the Thirty-nine Articles of the Church of England.[1]

What lay behind this remarkable vision, and why was it felt to be so necessary in the first place?

The historical origins of the Westminster Assembly lie, in very simple terms, in the difference between the English and Scottish Reformations. The reformation in England was not only the fruit of a widespread movement of spiritual awakening and revival in the early sixteenth century; it was also intertwined with the personal life of the monarch Henry VIII, and particularly his marital status. At one time created *Defensor Fidei* by the Pope (a title the British monarch still carries), Henry would eventually resist the authority of Rome rather than bow to its judgments on his marital infidelity. The reformation in England, subsequently, took the form of a balancing act between the new wine of the Reformation gospel, and the old wine bottles of the unreformed church.[2]

Undoubtedly a further difference in the two reformations involved the personalities of the leaders of the churches in England and Scotland. There is no impersonal theology! Simply put, Scotland had John Knox.

John Knox 'the chief priest and founder'

John Knox was born in Haddington probably around 1514. He studied in St Andrews and, in 1536, became a priest. Sometime in the 1540s he seems to have come under the influence of Thomas Guilliame and was converted to the Reformed faith. He thereafter became a friend, and sometime bodyguard, of his contemporary George Wishart. Wishart was arrested and executed in St Andrews in 1546. In a bloody event,

---

[1] See the 'Ordinance ... for the calling of an Assembly of learned and godly Divines, and others ...' often printed with *The Confession of Faith*.

[2] For a detailed, scholarly account in the context of a major biography of one of the central players in the drama, see D. MacCulloch, *Thomas Cranmer: A Life* (London: Yale University Press, 1996).

vividly related by Knox in his *History of the Reformation in Scotland*,[1] Wishart's death was avenged and a group of reformers gathered in St Andrews Castle whither Knox and some of his pupils came in 1547.

Despite apparent differences in temperament, Knox shared with John Calvin a desire to pursue learning, teach others, and be a faithful encourager of other leaders. But in the Castle congregation his gifts were soon recognized, and he was called to the ministry. Despite a literal flight in tears, he soon became the leader of the embryonic new Scottish Church.

Besieged by French gunboats called into service by Mary of Guise, Queen Regent during the early years of Mary Stuart, Queen of Scots, the Castle congregation was forced into surrender and Knox became a slave on French galleys for some eighteen months. By now he was developing into a feisty and single-minded leader.

Freed in 1549, Knox returned home to minister in Berwick-upon-Tweed, and in 1551 in Newcastle-upon-Tyne. On the death of King Edward VI in 1553 and the accession of 'Bloody' Mary Tudor, he fled to the Continent where he spent time ministering and studying with Calvin in Geneva (which he believed to be 'the most perfect school of Christ on earth since the days of the apostles').

He also ministered in Frankfurt-am-Main, and there, in the context of controversy, sought to reform the church from having an 'English face' to be a church that was fully reformed according to Scripture. For Knox this meant that only what was mandated by Scripture could be mandated in congregational worship. In 1555 he spent time in Scotland where he was being increasingly looked to as the church's most experienced, and perhaps best-connected, leader. He returned briefly to Geneva in 1556 (meanwhile being burnt in effigy at Edinburgh Cross). Urged in 1557 to return, he came back finally to his homeland in 1558.

A man of radical biblical conviction, extraordinary drive, and deep passion, for the next fourteen years John Knox led the very remarkable reformation that has left its imprint on the Scottish nation ever since. Absolutely convinced that the Scriptures are 'the mouth of God', he

---

[1] John Knox, *Works*, 6 vols (Edinburgh: 1846–64), I-II. For a modernized and edited version, see also John Knox, *History of the Reformation in Scotland*, ed. C. J. Guthrie (1898; repr. Edinburgh: Banner of Truth Trust, 2010).

sought to apply their authority to every aspect of the church's life, not least to worship, to which he applied what has come to be known as the Puritan regulative principle, namely that only what God commands can carry authority in the organization, structure, and worship of the church. Knox's own explanation of the success of his labours was simply that 'God gave his Holy Spirit to simple men in great abundance'.

As we have noted, Knox had for a period ministered in England. His opposition to aspects of the 1552 Prayer Book led to the last-minute inclusion of the so-called 'Black Rubric' affirming that kneeling at communion carried no Roman significance. In some respects this was more of a rebuttal of Knox than a victory for him. He opposed kneeling during communion either with or without explanation. Having been appointed to the team of royal chaplain preachers in 1551, in one sermon before the king he had used the occasion 'freely to attack kneeling at the Lord's Supper'. To that extent the Black Rubric (so-called because it had been printed at the last minute in black rather than the customary red) underscored the difference between the vision of an archbishop (Cranmer) and that of plain 'Mr' Knox. That notwithstanding, Knox at one point was offered the bishopric of Rochester.

Knox and his friends were never able to establish his regulative principle in the life of the Church of England. Failure, however, did not bring about the demise of desire. Convictions about the regulative principle lingered on, took root in the lives of many in England, and effected a desire for such further reformation. All this simply confirms that there is some insight in Thomas Carlyle's comment that it is actually John Knox who was the 'chief priest and founder' of English Puritanism.[1]

The 'Puritans' who shared Knox's vision (a 'purifying' of the national church) were stubbornly resisted by Elizabeth I from 1558 onwards. They were to be further disappointed when, following the union of the Crowns in 1603, James VI of Scotland (and now James I of England)—despite his rigorous education at the hands of Scottish Calvinists—resisted the Puritan movement vehemently. His position was famously summarized in one of his statements at the Hampton Court Conference of 1604:

---

[1] Thomas Carlyle, *Heroes and Hero Worship* in *The Works of Thomas Carlyle* (London, 1907), V:143.

> If you aim at Scottish Presbytery, it agreeth as well with monarchy
> as God and the Devil. Then Jack and Tom and Will and Dick shall
> meet and censure me and my Council ... My Lords the Bishops, if
> once you were out and they in, I know what would become of my
> supremacy, for No Bishop, No King. I will make them conform
> themselves, or I will harry them out of the land, or else do worse.

James at least knew the stomach of the people; his son, Charles I,
reared by his father in the divine right of kings doctrine, was altogether
less sensitive. His national and foreign policies, in addition to his Roman
Catholic wife and his personal lifestyle, led to increasing tensions in the
nation which, coupled with the spread of the Puritan movement and its
influence in Parliament, led eventually to the Civil War.

The assembly

It was in the context of such political and social tension, indeed virtually as part of it, that the idea of a reforming assembly was first mooted.
Charles eventually forbade it, but the assembly at Westminster nevertheless convened—albeit minus the presence of Archbishop James Ussher
and others who shared his Episcopalian perspective.

Strictly speaking the assembly was a parliamentary advisory body. A
list of potential participants had been drawn up more than a year earlier
(two ministers from each English county, the two English Universities,
and one for each Welsh county, plus four from the city of London,
with a further fourteen others named by the Lords. In addition twenty
laymen from the House of Commons and ten from the House of Lords
were chosen). Despite the royal proclamation on June 22, 1643 prohib-
iting the assembly, Parliament proceeded with its own ordinance. And
so the assembly held regular meetings at Westminster Abbey in London,
gathering at first in Henry VII's Chapel, until, with the onset of winter,
the plenary sessions were moved to the Jerusalem Chamber (which
boasted a fireplace!).

Later in the year a group of Scottish ministers and elders arrived to
assist in the work. Although they were never technically members of
the assembly, in many ways they were the most powerful single group
participating in it and virtually became a kind of approval committee for

the work that was transacted. They included several of the most famous Scottish ministers of the seventeenth century: Alexander Henderson, Samuel Rutherford, and the remarkably gifted young George Gillespie.

The progress of the assembly, recorded in its minutes and in other extant materials written by participants, was marked by tension among the various ecclesiastical parties (Presbyterians of various stripes, Independents who resisted the strong connectionalism of the former, and a group of Erastians who held a strong view of state authority in relationship to the church). The Scots Commissioner Robert Baillie in particular found the devotion to detailed argument a drain on his patience: 'nothing in any Assemblie that was in the world except Trent, like to this in prolixitie', he wrote home to Scotland![1]

In the first weeks of the assembly much attention was given to the task of revising the Church of England's Thirty-nine Articles. The divines had proceeded to discuss about one-third of these when The Solemn League and Covenant was entered into as a religious bond between Scotland and England. It then became clear that something more comprehensive than a mere revision would be necessary. Parliament now instructed the divines to proceed immediately to the production of directories for both church government and public worship. Having begun with the former, the latter was discussed at various times during 1644. Once completed the *Directory of Publick Worship* was approved by the General Assembly of the Church of Scotland in February 1645.

It is one of the ironies of the entire assembly that while the Scots made various compromises of their own traditions, by and large the impact of the assembly on the English Church was minimal whereas it marked Scottish church life for centuries to come.

The regular pattern of the assembly was for the divines to meet in plenary sessions in the mornings. They then divided into three committees for the purpose of drafting materials which would then be debated on the floor of the entire gathering. Debate on various points of doctrine and liturgy stretched over several days on some occasions as the assembly sought to express biblical teaching in a manner that carried the wide agreement of the whole body. We often think of 'compromise

---

[1] *Letters and Journals of Robert Baillie* (Edinburgh, 1842), II:164.

wording' as a feature of liberal theology, but, clearly, one of the challenges facing the divines at Westminster was to create statements of doctrine and practice that placed most emphasis on major elements of agreement and minimized differences over matters that did not so obviously belong to the heart of biblical teaching, or involved more abstract reasoning. What was true in areas of doctrinal expression was also characteristic of their approach to liturgy.

The Directory for Publick Worship

The Directory for Publick Worship was intended to produce a more uniform ethos in worship. It covered such matters as the behaviour of the congregation, conduct of worship, prayers, forms of administration of baptism and communion, marriage, pastoral visitation of the sick, burial of the dead, fasting, thanksgiving and praise.

There were 'worship wars' in the seventeenth century as well as in our own. Some of them were fought out behind the scenes of the assembly. Frequently issues arose about the proper application of the Puritan regulative principle which reduced elements of acceptable worship to what is prescribed or necessarily deducible from Scripture alone. Disagreements over how communion should be served, patterns of devotion, and other details abounded. The final document is in many ways a fine example of compromise on non-essentials set within the context of agreement on essentials.

Without doubt one of the *Directory*'s most relevant sections is its discussion of preaching. The chairman of the committee to whom the drafting of the *Directory* was given was Stephen Marshall (*c.* 1594–1655), himself one of the greatest of the Puritan preachers. The *Directory* was finally approved by Parliament in January 1645.

The *Directory*'s outline of what is involved in the exposition of Scripture could fruitfully be engraved on to the desk of every preacher of the gospel. Wisely, their instruction was framed in a way that made it applicable to a whole range of preaching methods and styles (a range, incidentally, to which the Puritans themselves gave rich expression. Homiletical cloning was not their purpose any more than it should be ours):

This method is not prescribed as necessary for every man, or upon every text [he is likely to be a homiletical cripple who does not realize or has not heard evidence of the fact that some sermons of startling power seem to break most homiletical rules!]; but only recommended, as being found by experience to be very much blessed of God, and very helpful for the people's understandings and memories.

These principles were, in their view, as applicable to preaching from one text, an entire passage, or on a key doctrinal statement, as they were to preaching systematically through a section or entire book of Scripture.

A brief introduction should lead the preacher to a summary or paraphrase of the preaching segment and to the principal burden of the exposition. Sensitive to the mental capacity of his hearers, the preacher should feed them well but never overload them. In particular the following three rules were seen to be fundamental:

(1) What is taught must be biblical truth. But more than that, it must be drawn from the text or passage being expounded, so that people can see for themselves that it is biblical and how they themselves can draw that truth from the same Scripture.

These men recognized that, as a general rule, the way Christians read the Bible privately is shaped by the model of exposition they regularly hear from the pulpit. That is why this principle is not only essential to the integrity of pastoral preaching but central to the whole ethos of a congregation's life.

(2) The teaching on which the passage focuses should then be highlighted, expounded and illustrated, and honest and relevant difficulties (intellectual or practical) dealt with.

The preacher is not a purveyor of novelties, nor is his task to titillate some in his congregation with the latest deviation in the evangelical world, nor to set on display his own erudition. He is behind the 'sacred desk' to teach and to nourish the flock. As a general principle, whatever is not edifying and spiritually nourishing should be no part of the preacher's message.

(3) Stage three brings the preacher in the study to his knees. He must not only make clear the burden of the passage, but also, in the words of

the Westminster divines,

> bring it home to special use, by application to his hearers … a work
> of great difficulty to himself, requiring much prudence, zeal and
> meditation, and to the natural and corrupt man … very unpleasant;
> yet he is to endeavour to perform it in such a manner, that his
> auditors may feel the word of God to be quick and powerful, and a
> discerner of the thoughts and intents of the heart; and that, if any
> unbeliever or ignorant person be present, he may have the secrets of
> his heart made manifest, and give glory to God.

How is this to be done? The Westminster masters stressed three
further things:

(1) In the light of the grace of God in the gospel, the Puritan minister
spelled out the 'duties' found in Scripture. 'Duty' is a much-mis-
understood term in our modern culture and carries with it the aroma of
legalism. In contrast the Puritan minister realized that grace always leads
to and commands duties; he was a Paulinist in this sense—all his imperatives were rooted in the indicatives of grace; but every indicative of grace
gave rise in his preaching to an imperative of grace-filled obedience.

So far have contemporary Christians slipped in grasping the shape
and logic of the gospel that when they discover that some forty per
cent of the *Shorter Catechism* is taken up expounding the law, the cry
of 'legalism' is often heard. But the Puritan pastor saw that it is in the
fulfilment of the duties of grace that grace comes into its own. So he
laboured to make clear how these duties may be fulfilled in love and
joy suffused with a glorious pleasure in walking with God in ways that
honour him. After all, the Scriptures teach us how to live for God's glory
and in doing so how to enjoy him.

(2) The gospel minister further must unveil the true nature of sin with
its misery, danger, and remedy. Virtually every sermon will strike this
note in one form or another. Anselm's words to Boso, the theological
stooge in the former's famous *Cur Deus Homo*, echoed from every
Puritan pulpit in the seventeenth century: 'You have not yet considered
the greatness of the weight of sin.'[1]

---

[1] Anselm, *Cur Deus Homo*, chap. xxi.

The Puritans treated this as a pastoral as well as a theological formula: grace makes sense to us only in the light of the sin to which it provides the remedy. Consequently, the more sensitive we are to sin, misery, and danger, the more clearly we will grasp the wonder of God's salvation. Grace is only 'amazing' when we see that it is 'a wretch like me' it saves. Only sinners seek Jesus as a Saviour!

Nor did the Puritan stop there. To borrow William Gurnall's words, the Christian needed to be equipped with 'complete armour'[1] against temptation. This the preacher furnished from Scripture, in addition to providing comfort and encouragement for the afflicted and assailed heart. He took human problems seriously, analyzed them in the light of Scripture and resolved them from the same source.

(3) Puritan preachers also gave what they called 'notes of trial'. Here the Westminster divines' description of this aspect of preaching illumines the practical value of reflecting on the 'categories' of William Perkins mentioned earlier:

> It is sometimes requisite to give some notes of trial (which is very profitable, especially when performed by able and experienced ministers, with circumspection and prudence, and the signs clearly grounded on the holy scripture,) whereby the hearers may be able to examine themselves whether they have attained those graces, and performed those duties, to which he exhorteth, or be guilty of the sin reprehended, and in danger of the judgments threatened, or are such to whom the consolations propounded do belong; that accordingly they may be quickened and excited to duty, humbled for their wants and sins, affected with their danger, and strengthened with comfort, as their condition, upon examination, shall require.

This, then, was the Puritan preaching 'method'. As we have noted, they did not regard it as an unbreakable preaching rule, or a method of cloning preachers—no one familiar with their sermons would confuse John Owen with Thomas Watson, for example! So long as the Scriptures were truly expounded and applied—by whatever method—the key lay in the extent to which the preacher himself was given over to, and

---

[1] The expression is drawn from the title of William Gurnall's famous work *The Christian in Complete Armour* (London, 1655–62).

himself sat under, the word. As Owen wrote, 'No man preacheth that sermon well to others that doth not first preach it to his own heart.'[1]

What did this imply? These seven things:

(1) A commitment to the hard work of studying, meditating on, and applying to oneself the truth of Scripture.

(2) A concern to speak God's truth to all of God's people, however simple they might be. The great Puritans were well-educated and highly intelligent ministers; but they knew that the concealment of art is also an art.

(3) Preaching the whole counsel of God, for the conversion of men and women, for the glory of God alone in whose presence both great and obscure must be exposed as sinners.

(4) Manifesting wisdom in teaching and applying the word of God, as well as the grace of God, in the very spirit of the preaching without 'passion or bitterness'.

(5) Doing so with a sense of the *gravitas* which ought to characterize a servant of God. This influenced the minister's physical demeanour and even the use of his voice. The preacher is neither joker nor trifler. He is not sent by God to entertain and amuse, for life is more of a tragedy than a comedy. Message and manner must harmonize or the message itself will be trivialized. Emotions and affections in preaching must be consistent with and expressive of the very substance of the text which is being expounded.

(6) Neither is the minister to be lugubrious and censorious, but rather filled with a loving affection for those to whom he ministers and preaches. Nothing is better calculated to win hearers than their knowledge that their minister has 'a hearty desire to do them good'. The Puritans recognized that people will take a great deal from such a man.

(7) All this is to be backed up by a life which is consistent both in private and in public with the message that is preached.

---

[1] Owen, *Works*, IX:455.

All this, the Puritans emphasized, should ordinarily be anchored in a local context where the preacher fed a flock he had come to know and love.

Local ministry

There were three obvious reasons why it was essential to the Puritans that a minister should be *resident* among his people, not absent from them.

(1) The calling of the Puritan minister was to feed the flock in his charge through the ministry of the word.

(2) In apostolic fashion that was always coupled with prayer, without which the wheels of the chariot in which Christ was conveyed to the congregation (i.e. the preaching) would not run on smooth ground.

It is impossible to overstress the importance of this principle in Puritan practice. Apostolic ministry must exemplify the apostolic principle: 'we will devote ourselves to prayer and to the ministry of the word' (Acts 6:4). For them the order was important. If the pastor was not a man of prayer he was not a true pastor. This was why Robert Traill was able to write:

> Ministers must pray much, if they would be successful ... Some ministers of meaner gifts and parts [i.e. abilities] are more successful than some that are far above them in abilities; not because they preach better, so much as because they pray more. Many good sermons are lost for lack of much prayer in study.[1]

A further evidence of this in Puritan ministry was seen in the importance they placed on prayer in the lives of their fellowships. Richard Baxter was by no means unique in seeing it as so central that he spent one night every week gathering young people together in order that they might learn what it is to pray.

(3) The need to particularize pastoral ministry, one aspect of which was to pray for the people, was then taken one stage further: the minister was also called to apply biblical truth to his congregation individually in personalized instruction and evangelism.

---

[1] Robert Traill, 'By What Means May Ministers Best Win Souls?' (sermon preached in October 1682 at the Cripplegate Morning Exercise), *Works* (Edinburgh, 1810), I:246.

How was this accomplished? The Puritan answer was twofold. Part of it was by meeting with members of the congregation corporately outside of the context of worship. Again Baxter is an obvious example. Every Thursday night at home he gathered a group who would go over his sermon of the previous Lord's Day, and discuss its meaning and application.

In the recovery of biblical exposition that has marked the church in our own time, it has not always been recognized that in addition to such exposition the Reformers and Puritans placed great stress on catechizing. We tend to think of this as children learning catechetical questions and answers by rote. But what the Puritans had in view was in many ways a more profound exercise. They saw the need to build into the thinking of all their people frameworks of reference, grids that would help them receive, understand, digest, and apply the biblical teaching given from the pulpit.

This is an essential ingredient in the recovery of biblical Christianity. Neither the Reformers nor the Puritans envisaged their task of the public exposition of Scripture without finding ways of anchoring what was heard in the minds and memories of their hearers. Without the framework of doctrine provided in some such pedagogical tool as a catechism a person might find it extremely difficult to assimilate all they were being taught. And without the personal probing of catechetical questions they might never work the public exposition through into practical understanding and application.

The Baxter plan

Richard Baxter had two catechists in Kidderminster to share in what was in part a sophisticated, well-grounded kind of seventeenth-century Evangelism Explosion. But it was more. It was also a Pastoral Explosion with a fully-orbed Pauline goal: to present every man mature before God.

It was in large measure due to his vision for this work that Baxter wrote his justly famous work *The Reformed Pastor*. His concern was to share with his ministerial brethren the necessity of pastoral visitation and personal instruction and evangelism.

The experiences which brought him to this conviction are telling. 'It hath oft grieved my heart', wrote Baxter, 'to observe some eminent able preachers, how little they do for the saving of souls, save only in the pulpit; and to how little purpose much of their labour is, by this neglect.'[1] In fact Baxter had come to the sobering personal discovery that many of his hearers were taking in far less of what he said than he imagined. He realized that he needed to speak with them one by one to help them understand the message of the gospel and to help them work out its significance for their lives. In a moment of tremendous candour, he writes:

> For my part, I study to speak as plainly and movingly as I can … and yet I frequently meet with those that have been my hearers eight or ten years, who know not whether Christ be God or man, and wonder when I tell them the history of his birth and life and death, as if they had never heard it before. And of those who know the history of the gospel, how few are there who know the nature of that faith, repentance, and holiness which it requireth, or, at least, who know their own hearts? … I have found by experience, that some ignorant persons, who have been so long unprofitable hearers, have got more knowledge and remorse of conscience in half an hour's close discourse, than they did from ten years' public preaching.[2]

It was this discovery that led Baxter to arrange for every family in his parish area to have a catechism. Then, together with his two assistants, he spent two days of each week, from morning until evening, moving from house to house in his parish, teaching, gently quizzing, and with great sensitivity leading people to Christ and to the Scriptures.

The effect on the town during Baxter's fifteen-year ministry was revolutionary. He states that when he was installed as rector at Kidderminster perhaps one family in each street was devoted to the Lord and honoured him in family worship; when he left there were streets where only one family did not do so.

---

[1] Richard Baxter, *The Reformed Pastor* (1656; ed. William Brown, London, 1829), pp. 178-79.
[2] *Ibid.*, p. 196.

Doubtless Baxter's gifts were unusual and perhaps the blessing of God was exceptional; but it is evident that he and others felt that the instrument of catechizing was utterly essential to the work of the pastoral ministry.

Baxter knew that there would be objections to such activity. Perhaps we might be inclined to say that in Baxter's day, 'He had all the time in the world.' But not so. He tells us that when he began this work he was already fully employed (think of his well over one hundred published works, of the great folio volumes of his writings, of his magnificent *The Saints' Everlasting Rest*, whose massive length might seem to require experience of its title to complete a reading!). No, Baxter saw catechizing as a work of necessity, not as an additional luxury. Furthermore he recognized that beginning such an activity would cause all kinds of disturbance, but argued that anything new has that effect. Nothing ventured, nothing gained.

With Baxter, the Puritans in general realized that we cannot build for eternity with wood, hay and stubble; we must build with precious stones that will last. That may be by the use of a catechism or by some similar means. By whatever means, access must be gained to the minds, hearts and homes of the people by those who are the pastors of the flock. After all, the Good and Great Shepherd catechized his little flock regularly in order to test, confirm and strengthen the effect of his ministry. Something of the same order, however contemporary its garb, is surely needed today.

The heart of the matter

It is not surprising, then, since establishing such a preaching ministry was their goal, that so many of the Puritan ministers note the sheer costliness of this task, and echo the cry of Paul, 'Who is sufficient for these things?' They rested their souls on the apostle's answer: 'our sufficiency is from God' (2 Cor. 2:16; 3:5).

Yet, for all the costliness of such a ministry, Puritan ministers were tremendously conscious of the privilege of the high calling they had received.

One such was Herbert Palmer (1601–47), the gifted upper-class bachelor who became one of the Assessors of the Westminster Assembly. He was widely believed to be its best catechist.

Palmer himself knew what it was to be catechized. Asked when he was only a five-year-old what he wanted to be, he replied that he hoped to be a minister. When others tried to dissuade him by telling him that ministers were 'hated, despised, and accounted as the off scouring of the world', little Palmer nobly replied, 'It was no matter for that; for if the world hated him, yet God would love him.'[1]

Perhaps more than anything else, this was the heartbeat of Puritan ministry at its best. The love of Christ constrained them to be ambassadors. That constraint invested their preaching with impassioned appeal. The fact that their ministry was that of an ambassador drove them to the study of their Sovereign's message. The knowledge that their Master was the Sovereign Lord gave them confidence that their mission would not, indeed could not, in the last analysis, fail. This was the spirit that had gripped little Palmer from his earliest days.

Well might we pray today, 'Lord, will you not raise up Herbert Palmers in our day too?'

---

[1] Samuel Clarke, *The Lives of Thirty-Two English Divines* (London, 1677), 3rd ed., p. 184.

CHAPTER ELEVEN

JOHN OWEN AND THE DOCTRINE OF THE PERSON OF CHRIST

But had we the tongue of men and angels, we were not able in any just measure to express the glory of this condescension; for it is the most ineffable effect of the divine wisdom of the Father and the love of the Son,—the highest evidence of the care of God towards mankind.[1]

S TUDYING the work of John Owen underlines the principle that when one is able to master the writing of a great theologian, much in contemporary theological literature seems superficial or even superfluous. Certainly that is true of Owen's teaching on the person of our Lord Jesus Christ, which is worthy of examination for at least these two reasons.

1. A distinctive approach

The first is the rather obvious one of the distinctiveness and indeed genius of Owen's approach. There is a considerable amount of literature available today in the area of Christology. But very little of that material comes out of deeply evangelical and biblical convictions, and an even smaller proportion breathes the kind of spirit that is characteristic of Owen's work. We find in him the all too rare combination of the sharpness of intellect required in the academy, with the largeness of heart and spirit required for growth in the knowledge of our Lord Jesus Christ.

Of course we should never despise the importance of technical knowledge in the work of the gospel ministry. But merely technical

---

[1] Owen, *Works*, I:330.

knowledge carries its own danger—a danger Owen managed to avoid. He never lost sight of the fact that the doctrine of the person of Christ is not so much a doctrine as it is an exposition of the character of a person. The personal dimension to his Christology shines through and indicates the extent to which he placed his intellectual learning in tribute to his pursuit of a personal knowledge of the person of Jesus Christ.

Owen was well able to write within a polemical context, as he does in his *Vindiciae Evangelicae*,[1] a critical and devastating response to John Biddle's version of *The Racovian Catechism*. He writes at enormous length because he sees the need to undermine false foundations, and to remove theological rubble, in order that he might plant Jesus Christ truly in the hearts and minds of those for whom he writes.

But Christ is not for Owen a subject for technical analysis. He is a person, coming to us 'clothed with his gospel' as Calvin put it.[2] He is the focus of the Bible's story in order that first he may be known and, second, that he may be worshipped. There is constantly in Owen, even when we are in the thick of him (and some of his writing is dense indeed), a doxological motive and motif. If we can persevere with his style (which becomes easier the longer we persevere), he will not fail to bring us to the feet of Jesus Christ.

2. A balanced perspective on Owen's theology

The second reason why it is helpful to focus on Owen's Christology is because doing so enables us to get a more balanced view of his theology as a whole.

John Owen is a theologian who has been recovered from obscurity only relatively recently. Until the reprinting of his *Works* in the mid-1960s, there would have been very few ministers in the western world who either possessed a volume of Owen, or would even have recognized his name. Now many thousands do.

Yet probably most attention has been paid to his polemical writing, such as his early work, *The Death of Death in the Death of Christ* (1647), or the striking, and in its own way important, work on the *Mortification*

[1] *Vindiciae Evangelicae* (Oxford, 1655), in *Works*, XII:1-590 is an exhaustive critique of Socinianism.
[2] *Institutes*, III.ii.6.

of Sin (1656). Many readers come to Owen through these books and are perhaps tempted therefore to think that this is Owen in his entirety.

But we need to remember that when he wrote *The Death of Death* in 1647, Owen was only thirty or thirty-one years old. Furthermore the material in the *Mortification of Sin* was not originally prepared for mature or adult Christians. In fact it was probably the material of a series of sermons Owen preached to students in the University of Oxford. These were, essentially, addresses to teenagers! He did not view the material as the strong meat for well-tried Christians as we tend to do. Rather it was basic milk, foundational principles for every Christian believer. It is a sign of the times that we find the *Mortification of Sin* nourishment for serious spiritual athletes!

These two works taken in isolation might therefore give the impression that Owen's great concern was with polemics over the question of the extent of the atonement on the one hand and concern about the mastery of sin in the life of the believer on the other. Deeply concerned though he obviously was about both of these issues, he was far more concerned about their foundation in (a) wholesome trinitarian theology and (b) knowledge of, trust in, and love for, the Lord Jesus Christ. Argument without adoration interested him not at all.[1] Focus on sin, without a greater focus on Christ and grace, he recognized, would in fact eventually disable Christian ministry. It could point to the need there is in the human heart but never provide the gospel remedy for it.

For this reason it is an extremely valuable historical-theological exercise for us to focus on the person of Jesus Christ, the centre and goal of all his theology. Indeed, it is not insignificant that the book on which he had been working shortly before his death was *Meditations on the Glory of Christ*.[2] He turned then, instinctively, to the central things of the gospel; and nothing was more central to him than the One who had brought him into fellowship with the Father and with the Holy Spirit.

This theme runs throughout Owen's work, but there are several pieces in his corpus that focus specific attention on Christology.

---

[1] *Works*, XII:52.

[2] This work ('*Meditations*' was Owen's own description) was written originally for his own benefit and then for the encouragement of a private group to whom he preached. It was first published in 1684, in the year following his death.

The first of these is his 1655 publication *Vindiciae Evangelicae*. Here, at the request of the Council of State,[1] he sets out to defend Christian orthodoxy over against the perceived threat of Socinianism. He does this to the extent of some 600 closely argued pages, reviewing John Biddle's[2] version of the *Racovian Catechism* (1605)—probably one of the longest book reviews ever written in the history of the Christian church!

More positively and broadly, he turned his attention to the person of Christ, and the glory and the beauty of Christ, in what must rank among his greatest works, *Communion with God* (1657).[3] This, like so much else, arose out of his preaching ministry (from around 1650). It is a deeply trinitarian exposition of the character of the Christian life. Owen underlines that being a Christian is at its very root trinitarian in character and that every aspect of our salvation has ultimately to be traced back to the design of the Trinity. Salvation is enjoyed within the context of a distinct communion with each person of the Trinity, with respect to the distinctive aspects of that person's work in the accomplishment of our redemption.[4]

These themes are given more detailed exegetical attention in various places in his mammoth *Exposition of the Epistle to the Hebrews* (1668, 1674, 1680, 1684).[5] Both in the essays ('exercitations') which precede the commentary proper, and in the exposition of the text itself, Owen expounds the centrality of the priesthood of Christ in the work of reconciliation. Then in his great work *Christologia* (1679)[6] he sets out in a more formal way to give expression to the doctrine of Christ's person, and again in a more meditative, contemplative fashion in the posthumously published *Meditations on the Glory of Christ*.[7] The production of any

[1] The Council of State was formed after the British Isles were declared a republic and became a Commonwealth. It was the executive body of the new one-chamber Parliament. It was chaired by the Lord Protector Oliver Cromwell.

[2] Biddle (1616–62), an Oxford graduate and a teacher, was a central figure in spreading Socinian anti-trinitarian views in England. He spent much of his life in jail as a result.

[3] *Works*, II:1-274.

[4] Sometimes referred to as the doctrine of appropriations.

[5] Vols XVIII-XXIV in the original Goold edition of the *Works*.

[6] *Works*, I:1-272.

[7] Part 1, 1684; Part 2, 1689; *Works* I:274-463.

one of these volumes would have marked Owen out as a theologian of substance; to have produced all of them marks him as a truly great one. Taken together, they give us real insight into the passion that John Owen held for the person of his Lord Jesus.

This Christological focus can in fact be traced back to Owen's first pastorate in Fordham in Essex. He was installed there in 1642, when he was no more than 26 years old. Three years later, we find him as a young pastor writing to his congregation, deeply burdened by the need to help them to understand the gospel. He is concerned, Paul-like, for their salvation. His desire is to hold back nothing that would be profitable to them and to expose them to the whole counsel of God. As a direct result, for their use—and for the use of the people of God in general—he wrote two catechisms.

The title page of this brief work is interesting—it will seem less humorous when we remember that seventeenth-century books did not advertise their contents on dust-jackets. Hence the extended title of these catechisms reads: *Two short catechisms, wherein the principles of the doctrine of Christ are unfolded and explained. Proper for all persons to learn before they be admitted to the sacrament of the Lord's Supper, and composed for the use of all congregations in general.* The year of their publication (1645) means that they preceded the publication of the *Shorter* and *Larger Catechisms* of the Westminster Assembly and helps explain why Owen did not simply use these better-known educational tools.

Interestingly, like the Westminster divines and the whole school of Puritan catechists, Owen recognized how important it was as a pastor to have a spiritual concern for the children under his care, and also for those of simple mind, as well as to provide more solid meat for the mature. In both cases Owen was troubled by the fact that many of his parishioners were 'grossly ignorant'[1] of Christ and the gospel. In that sense Owen's burden developed around the same time, and in a manner analogous to, the concern which led Richard Baxter to engage in his great catechetical labours in Kidderminster.[2]

In a way that echoes Owen's burden, Baxter tells us in *The Reformed Pastor* why this work is so essential:

[1] The words are from his dedicatory letter to the catechisms; cf. *Works*, I:465.
[2] Richard Baxter, *The Reformed Pastor* (1656) chronicles this vividly and at length.

> For my part, I study to speak as plainly and movingly as I can, (and next to my study to speak truly, these are my chief studies,) and yet I frequently meet with those that have been my hearers eight or ten years, who know not whether Christ be God or man, and wonder when I tell them the history of his birth and life and death, as if they had never heard it before. And of those who know the history of the gospel, how few are there who know the nature of that faith, repentance, and holiness, which it requireth, or, at least, who know their own hearts? ... I have found by experience, that some ignorant persons, who have been so long unprofitable hearers, have got more knowledge and remorse of conscience in half an hour's close discourse, than they did from ten years' public preaching ...[1]

With that Baxter-like burden, Owen was driven on to do something, however basic and simple, to help his people understand the character of Christ and the glory of the gospel. In fact, his central burden in these two catechisms is specifically and explicitly the knowledge of Jesus Christ, his person and work.

Interestingly Owen also indicates that he had the intention, unfulfilled as far as there is evidence, of writing further catechisms, which would cover the Lord's Prayer, the Ten Commandments, and the articles of the Apostles' Creed. But in these preliminary pieces he focuses on the main essentials: the person of Jesus Christ.

His catechism for younger ones contains thirty-three questions, eight of which give basic teaching on Christology. The catechism for adults contains twenty-seven chapters, each with several questions. One-third of the chapters are on the Trinity, and therefore by definition include aspects of Christology. Chapters 9-14 focus directly on the person of our Lord Jesus Christ. Here in this larger catechism we find a basic framework which comes to fuller expression throughout Owen's future ministry.

1. Jesus Christ is God and man united in one person.

2. Christ fulfils his saving ministry in a two-dimensional way.

 • In his fulfilment of a threefold office, Prophet, Priest and King.

---

[1] *The Reformed Pastor*, p. 196.

- In his experience of a twofold state, the state of humiliation and the state of exaltation.

3. He does this specifically for the sake of the elect.

Already here are the themes he will unravel in his later and greater works; the distinction being that in his later writings he expands on these in a more obviously technical, theological way, in a more clearly expository way, and in a more thoroughgoing devotional way.

Of course, Owen's writing is historically determined. That is most clearly evident in his *Vindiciae Evangelicae*. But what is most striking about it is his conscious sense that he is expounding a perennial theology, and that the context in which Christology is under attack is essentially the same in every age. Thus when he introduces his exposition in *Christologia*, he does so in terms of Peter's confession and the way in which it immediately came under Satanic attack.[1]

In fact Owen sees this as a kind of paradigm of the whole of church history, coming to expression in different ways and contexts, from the time of Stephen to the time of Constantine in the early church, and thereafter constantly repeated over and again.

This in itself helps to bridge the gap between Owen's work in the seventeenth century and our own times. A common strand runs through all periods of church history—the ongoing antithesis between the kingdom of God and the kingdom of darkness, the heavenly Jerusalem and the earthly Babylon, the powers of light and the powers of darkness. That was the context in which the incarnate Christ was first confessed by Peter; it remains the context in which we seek to witness to Jesus Christ. Consequently, just as the patterns of Satanic temptation in Scripture are repeated in our individual lives, so the patterns of Satanic attack on the person of Jesus Christ will be repeated in one form or other in every age. These attacks Owen sees as basically threefold:

1. A theology which denies the role of Christ.

2. A rejection of our Lord's divine nature.

3. A rejection of our Lord's hypostatic union; two natures united in one *hypostasis*, or person.

[1] *Works*, I:29. See Matt. 16:13-23.

In Owen's own day, these attacks took particularized historical form in:

(i) Socinianism which denied the deity of Christ.

(ii) Rationalism and Naturalism that denied the necessity of either his deity or his saving humanity.

(iii) The burgeoning 'inner-light' movements which had already troubled the magisterial Reformers in the previous century.

These last emphasized the personal indwelling of Christ by the Holy Spirit, rather marginalizing the historical work of Christ in his flesh, on the cross, in the resurrection, and in his ascension to the right hand of the Father. Existential experience thus swallowed up the objective work of Christ producing a truncated gospel at best and a subjective morass of individually experienced revelations at worst.

If I am not mistaken, although we find ourselves in a different context, we constantly face exactly the same basic critical issues. For this reason, as we try to master Owen's orthodoxy, we discover that his work has an immediate relevance to the times in which we ourselves live.

What, then, is Owen's response? How does he provide a positive exposition of the person of Christ? Here we must confine ourselves to four themes which can be expressed in a series of questions:

1. How does Owen establish the deity of Christ from Scripture?

2. How does Owen think of Christ's relationships within the Trinity?

3. How does Owen understand the nature of the incarnation?

4. Recognizing that for Owen the person and work of Christ are inseparable, what does he have to say about the character of his work?

1. The deity of Christ

Owen's approach is generic to orthodox Christology and can be dealt with briefly. He suggests that there are four basic lines of evidence.

1. Many Old Testament testimonies, in their original context clearly describing the one and only God, are applied in the New Testament

specifically to Christ. Owen provides several illustrations; but here one will suffice. Psalm 102:25-27 is cited in Hebrews 1:10 and applied specifically to the Son. Thus an Old Testament statement about the character of the deity is equally applicable to the person of the Lord Jesus.

2. The acts that Christ performs are specifically and exclusively divine. Thus in John 1:3 creation is attributed to the *Logos* who is himself specifically excluded from belonging to the category of the created.

3. The attributes Christ possesses are exclusively those of God. For example, in majesty and glory he is one with the Father (John 5:23).

4. Owen notes how some titles given to Jesus in the New Testament are those exclusively attributable to the deity.

Here, then, he is simply following the lines of classical orthodoxy in seeking to establish exegetically from Scripture testimonies to the absolute deity of Jesus Christ.

In his Christology Owen places great stress on the necessity of Christ's deity for the fulfilment of his offices. Here is his Calvin-like consciousness that deity and genuine soteriology belong together in an indivisible way; loosen our grip on one and we inevitably lose our grasp on the other. This is because the deity of Christ relates in Owen's thinking to the character of the obedience of Christ and its power to effect salvation.

We can clarify this point by analyzing what Owen has to say in five ways:

1. Owen argues that any obedience rendered in a substitutionary way to save sinners, must bring more honour to God's holy character than the dishonour that is reflected on that character by the fall. It must not only bring man back, as it were, to square one in Eden, but forwards to final acceptance with God. This Owen argues is impossible for a mere man, for the simple reason that God cannot be more pleased with the obedience of one man than he was displeased and dishonoured by Adam's fall. Only an infinite person can give infinite value to an otherwise finite obedience.

Furthermore, while one man may act for another man, no single man can offer obedience adequate to substitute for a multitude of men. In order to give that obedience a quality beyond the obedience of one human being, it must be rendered by one who is an infinite person.

2. 'The obedience of a mere man could not substitute for the failure of others for the simple reason that it would be required of that man for himself: it ... could have no influence at all on the recovery of mankind, nor the salvation of the church. For whatever it were, it would be all due from him, *for himself*, and so could only profit and benefit himself. ... He then, that performs this obedience, must be one who was not originally obliged thereunto, on his own account, or for himself.'[1] This Owen argues must be a divine person. Every man offering a perfect obedience owes that perfect obedience. To put it crudely, he has no obedience left over to cover anyone else's failure to render that obedience. Supererogation is impossible for mere man. Hence it is necessary, Owen argues, for one who does not owe that obedience to God in terms of the basic relationship between the two, to offer that obedience in the place of others.

3. Given the innumerable multitudes of the redeemed and the sins from which they need deliverance, which Owen says are 'next to absolutely infinite',[2] and the fact that these sins are committed against an infinite majesty and therefore have something reductively infinite about them (the terminology is his), only an infinite person could provide satisfaction.

4. Since man cannot fulfil the office of prophet, priest and king, essential for salvation, only a divine person could.

5. Fallen man must be restored to his original state; indeed Owen argues, it seems 'agreeable unto the glory of the divine excellencies in their operations, that he should be brought into a better and a more honourable condition than that what he had lost'.[3]

[1] *Works*, I:201.
[2] *Ibid.*
[3] *Ibid.*, I:203.

But, Owen argues, echoing the discussions of the older theologians, anyone who redeems becomes the master of those he redeems. It is therefore unthinkable that we should be redeemed to have any other as our Lord, than the Lord God himself. It was, therefore, morally necessary for redemption to be accomplished by a divine person. To hold that Christ is less than God, to hold that he is a mere man, contradicts a moral principle basic to the logic inherent in our idea of salvation. So redemption is by necessity brought through the infinite wisdom of God in the incarnation of his Son who is himself divine.

Interestingly, here the doctrine of God, the doctrine of man's condition, and the doctrine of Jesus Christ, are all integrally connected in Owen's theology. Just as pulling a loose thread may unravel an entire garment, so pull one of these strands from the whole fabric of the gospel and we will soon be left with no gospel at all.

But Owen's Christology is not limited to this soteriological dimension.

2. Relationships within the Godhead

What is the relationship of Christ within the Godhead to the other persons of the glorious Trinity?

It is worth repeating frequently in today's climate that Owen, with his high Christology and deep passion for practical Christianity, is also a deeply trinitarian theologian. This is, in fact, an expression of his profoundly catholic theology. One might say about Owen—it is certainly evident in his *Works*—that he was first of all a catholic Christian, and then secondly a Puritan, which for him meant simply a consistent biblically-rooted Christian.

Owen, like many of his contemporaries, was more conscious than we tend to be of the stream of unity that flows through the history of the church.[1] Of course he was aware of the streams of diversity that flow through the history of theology, and he struggled to contain and sometimes resist them. But as he wrestles with the doctrine of the person of Christ, he understands very clearly the importance of the

---

[1] Thus for all his closer affinity with Calvin than with Augustine, like other major Puritan figures, Owen cites the bishop of Hippo several times more frequently than he does the reformer of Geneva. And references to the Fathers punctuate many of his writings. His extensive personal library included many of their works.

early Christological and trinitarian discussions and draws extensively from them. In his own way he takes these discussions a little further. In his study of *Communion with God* there is, whatever one thinks of his exegesis, an extraordinary further development of the deep-seated trinitarianism of both Calvin and the Fathers. It is certainly against the background of this trinitarianism that we should seek to understand his Christology.

There is a lesson here, surely, for Reformed and evangelical Christians today, not least within the context of the rediscovery of the Puritans. It is all too easy to be caught up in the applicatory end of their theology and to lose sight of the grand trinitarian and Christological vision which formed its foundation. It is equally easy to lose sight of their sense of the continuity of the Christian church, warts and all. It was, after all, the Reformation, not the incarnation, that took place in the sixteenth century!

Divine incomprehensibility

How are we to understand the relationship between Christ and the Godhead? Here Owen begins by underlining the important principle of the incomprehensibility of God. Within that context, nothing is more incomprehensible than the way God most fundamentally is in his inner eternal triunity. There is a fine statement of this early in his *Christologia*:

> God in his own essence, being, and existence, is absolutely incomprehensible. His nature being immense, and all his holy properties essentially infinite, no creature can directly or perfectly comprehend them, or any of them. He must be infinite that can perfectly comprehend that which is infinite; wherefore God is perfectly known unto himself only. ... The subsistence of his most single and simple nature in three distinct persons, though it raises and ennobles faith in its revelation, yet it amazeth reason which would trust to itself in the contemplation of it—whence men grow giddy who will own no other guide, and are carried out of the way of truth.[1]

---

[1] *Works*, I:65.

As an aside, Owen's catholicity is illustrated here by his citing with approval Dionysius the pseudo-Areopagite, emphasizing the absolute, total incomprehensibility of God.[1]

As in all areas of his theology, so in this area, we find the necessity of the divine condescension, if the incomprehensible God is to be made known to finite man. Within that context Owen understands the relationship between the Son and the Spirit in terms of Western classical orthodoxy, happily subscribing to the *filioque* clause of Augustinian Christology (that the Spirit proceeds from the Father *and from the Son*). He argues this in part on the basis of the analogy between the being of God and the revelation of that incomprehensible God in redemptive history. If the incarnation is a genuine revelation of the inner being of God, then, as in redemptive history, so in the very being of God, the Spirit proceeds from both the Father and the Son.[2]

With respect to the relationship between the Son and the Father, while Owen is committed to the *filioque* clause it is important to say more:

> His distinct personality and subsistence was by an internal and eternal act of the Divine Being in the person of the Father, or eternal generation—which is essential unto the divine essence—whereby nothing anew was outwardly wrought or did exist. He was not, he is not, in that sense, the effect of the divine wisdom and power of God but the essential wisdom and power of God himself.[3]

Here Owen is addressing an issue with which Calvin and others before him had wrestled very deeply. How, in our understanding of the inner relationships in the Godhead, do we emphasize the Fatherhood of God in relationship to the Son, without inherently suggesting that the Son, and correspondingly the Holy Spirit, fall into a kind of second (and even third) rank within the Godhead?

---

[1] Dionysius the pseudo-Areopagite was a mystical, neo-platonic, and, probably, Syrian theologian of the fifth or sixth century. Until the Renaissance and Reformation he was often wrongly assumed to be Dionysius the council member of the Areopagus who became a Christian (Acts 17:34).

[2] See e.g. *Works*, II:226; 3.60-1.

[3] *Ibid.*, I:45.

Calvin's way of doing this was to emphasize the autotheistic nature of the Son. His deity is not derived from the deity of the Father. Yes, there is a mutual interdependence in terms of personal relationship; you cannot be a son unless there is a father, but nor can there be a father unless there is a son. Calvin was very insistent that we escape from the incipient subordinationism of the history of the Christian church by emphasizing the autotheistic nature of the Son.[1]

While it may be a question how closely Owen follows Calvin's concerns in this area, he is wrestling with the same issues. While committed to eternal generation, he emphasizes that eternal generation produces nothing new within, nor anything external to, the being of God. Indeed, the eternally begotten Son is not to be thought of as the effect of the wisdom and power of God. He is himself the essential wisdom and power of God. Here, then, Owen seeks to hold together on the one hand the patristic doctrine of the eternal generation of the Son from the Father with this Calvinian principle of the absoluteness of the deity of the Son.

Against that background it is interesting to notice that particularly in *Vindiciae Evangelicae*, but also elsewhere, Owen argues that Proverbs 8:22ff., a *locus classicus* of early Christological and trinitarian discussion, actually is a reference to the Son of God.[2] What is said here, he argues, cannot be applied to another, and is in fact fulfilled in the description of Christ given in the opening verses of the prologue to John's Gospel. The Son and the Father mutually indwell one another in a unity of essence, and commune with one another in a distinction of persons. That, in a nutshell, is what Owen is seeking to underline.

Within this eternal relationship, the Father and the Son take counsel together in the fellowship of the Spirit. The axiom *opera trinitatis ad extra sunt indivisa* is consistently maintained. The external actions of God are indivisible in the sense that there is no action of any single person of the Trinity in which the other persons of the Trinity are not simultaneously engaged.

---

[1] B. B. Warfield's magisterial study remains the best guide here. See *Calvin and Calvinism* in *Works*, V:189-284.

[2] See e.g. *Works*, I:54ff.; II:390; XII:243-5, 501; XIX:58-60 (*Comm. Heb.*, vol. II).

This undergirds not simply Owen's trinitarianism but his Christology in particular. For him the intimacy, the absoluteness of the relationships between the Son and Father in terms of eternal generation, and with the Spirit in terms of eternal procession, ground the principle that when this One comes to save, it is the trinitarian God who is doing the saving. In Christ we discover what God is really like, how God is disposed to us, and what God will do for us, because in him we have seen the Father. There is nothing therefore veiled, nothing sinister hidden in God to take us by surprise. This is why it is so very important for Owen, in the context of his doctrine of the incomprehensibility of God, to emphasize that the One who is in the bosom of the Father really has made him known, and has the credentials to make him known as fully as we are capable of knowing him, because he is the eternal Son of the eternal Father.

The Son shared in glory with the Father from all eternity, before all worlds. It is this fellowship, in the communion of the Spirit, that upholds the pillars of the earth, otherwise this planet would cease to be. It is within this fellowship that both creation and recreation were planned in the context of mutual personal love and delight.[1] Indeed within the Trinity there is not only self-existence and self-sufficiency; there is also endless self-delight and satisfaction.

Christology stands as the entrance gate into this communion, for it is Christ who brings us (in intercession and ultimately in reality) to see, and then to share in, the glory of God. It was to this end that the Son of God assumed our humanity.[2]

This note leads us directly to Owen's focus on the nature of the incarnation.

3. *The nature of the incarnation*

Here there are four basic areas which Owen addresses:

(i) The appropriateness of the incarnation of the Son.

(ii) The nature of the incarnation as such.

---

[1] See e.g. *Works*, I.144ff.
[2] *Ibid.*, I:287ff.

(iii) The condescension that is involved in the incarnation

(iv) The love that is expressed by the incarnation.

We have already reflected on the necessity of the incarnation. When he turns to its nature he raises first a question about the reasons for the second person becoming incarnate.

(i) The appropriateness of the Son's incarnation
Why did the Son, in distinction from either the Father or the Spirit, become incarnate? Owen suggests three reasons.[1]

(1) Through the fall we have lost acceptance with God and the divine image thereby has been lost. It is therefore, in terms of Hebrews 1:1ff., fitting that the restoration of that lost image should be accomplished by the one who is in himself the essential image of the God whose image we have 'lost'.

(2) We were created to be sons of God with the prospect of a glorious inheritance. It is therefore fitting that the one who is himself the eternal Son of God, through whom all things were made, and for whom they came into existence, the heir of all things, should take upon himself the task of restoring us to sonship with God and bringing us into the divine inheritance.

(3) It is fitting that the order of divine subsistence be followed in the order of divine operation. As the Son comes, as it were, from the Father's love in eternal generation, so he is sent to us, in that same love, in the historical event of the incarnation.

So in general terms Owen sees that there is an extraordinary appropriateness about the second person becoming the Redeemer. In particular terms, he finds himself dazzled by the 'infinite wisdom and sovereign counsel of the divine will' that fashioned and fulfilled such a redemptive scheme.[2]

---

[1] *Works*, I:218-20.
[2] *Ibid.,* I:218.

(ii) The nature of the incarnation

In the hypostatic union two natures are united in the one divine person of the Son of God. In this act, Owen says, the Son takes our human nature in the womb of the virgin into personal subsistence with himself in an act of power and grace. This principle, easier to state than to analyse, is the bedrock of Owen's Christology. Unless the Son takes human nature into his person, uniting human and divine natures in that one person, that human nature could not really, fully, truly and permanently be his.[1]

We see Owen echoing earlier Christology—the incarnation is not a conversion of one nature into another, but an assumption of human nature by the divine person so that it truly and permanently becomes his own nature. He shares our human nature but in such a way that it becomes the human nature of this particular divine person. The humanity of Jesus is not an appendage. Jesus is not conceived as a divine person with a divine nature and a human nature stuck on, as it were, by some kind of incarnational superglue.

Here we have to confess that we reach the limits of our ability further to conceptualize the implications of biblical teaching. We have no analogy to this. But what Owen rightly insists on is that the human nature of Christ is assumed into union with the person of the Son in such a way that it becomes permanently his. We are not to think that the humanity of Christ becomes redundant on his ascension as though he were, at the end of the day, a divine person with a human bit temporarily added in order to effect the atonement. As becomes clear in his exposition of the high priestly ministry of Christ, human nature is so really and permanently Christ's, that he will never exist without it.[2]

There is a broader dimension to this assumption of human nature: in so far as it is an act of God, it is an external act of the Trinity. Father, Son and Holy Spirit participate in this action that will bring redemption.

Firstly, it is an act of authoritative designation in which the Father sends the Son.

Secondly, it is an act of divine formation in which the union is the effect of the secret work of the Holy Spirit (Luke 1:35).

[1] *Works*, I:223-35.
[2] *Ibid.*, XXI:422-24.

Thirdly, it is an act of sovereign assumption by the Son. He—and not the Father or the Spirit—is the one who assumes the human nature into his own person.[1] But in that act of incarnation with its permanent repercussions, Father and Spirit are engaged and involved, because the redemption of humanity is an act of the eternal Trinity.

What is the effect of this union, this incarnation? Here again Owen stands on the shoulders of the giants of earlier years (although he himself became a giant). This union of the divine person with our human nature by the incarnation takes place without change in the person who assumes the nature. Further, though the natures are distinct, they are not separated but united in the one person. But in that union in the person of the Son, there is no mixture or confusion of the natures. Both natures are possessed personally by the Son, not, as it were, accidentally as appendages. This means for Owen that *communicatio idiomatum*, the communication of the properties of the two natures, would better be expressed by the notion of *communio idiomatum*, a communion of the natures in the one divine person. This, he believes, safeguards three principles fundamental to our salvation:[2]

(1) Each nature, united in the person of the Son, preserves its own essential properties, so there is no direct communion between the two in such a way that would lead inevitably to one (the human) becoming subservient to the other nature (the divine). There are two whole, perfect natures, divine and human, united in the one *person*.

(2) Each nature therefore operates in accordance with its essential properties: the divine nature knows all things, upholds all things, rules all things, and acts by its presence everywhere. The human nature was born, yielded obedience, died and rose again. But it is the same person, the same Christ who does all these things, the one nature being no less active than the other.[3]

(3) The work of Christ, then, is not an act of one nature or the other nature, but an act of the whole person (*totus Christus*) in whom these two natures are united.

[1] *Works*, I:225.
[2] *Ibid.*, I:234.
[3] *Ibid.*, I:234.

This principle serves as a hermeneutical key to the way in which we read the New Testament. There some things are spoken of Christ in which what is stated is verified in respect to one nature only; other things are spoken of the person which belong not distinctly or originally to either nature, but to the person as a whole, and so on. Thus we interpret such language as men crucifying the Lord of glory, or the blood of God being the purchase of the church, against the background of a hermeneutic that emerges from a Christology formulated to be consistent with all the data of Scripture. The essential key here is the hypostatic union in which the two natures are not confused, mixed or diminished, but possessed hypostatically in and by the person of the Son.[1]

(iii) The condescension of the incarnation

But this is not all. Owen also emphasizes the condescension that is involved in the incarnation. The fact of the incarnation creates mental giddiness in those who seek to understand it, because it is an event without analogy, but also because it expresses an awe-inspiring condescension on the part of God.

There is an infinite distance between the being of God and that of his creatures. He is infinitely self-sufficient while we are lowly and utterly dependent.

> All being is essentially in him, and in comparison thereunto all other things are as nothing. And there are no measures, there is no proportion between infinite being and nothing,—nothing that should induce a regard from the one unto the other. Wherefore, the infinite, essential greatness of the nature of God, with his infinite distance from the nature of all creatures thereby, causeth all his dealings with them to be in the way of condescension or humbling himself.[2]

For Owen, creation is an act of divine humbling. All the more then is redemption in the incarnation an act of divine humbling.

But what is the nature of this humbling? It is not the laying aside of the divine nature. The Son was in the form of God. He participated

---

[1] *Works*, I:234-35.
[2] *Ibid.*, I:324.

fully in deity. Yes, he took the form of a servant, and was made man, but he did not thereby, Owen argues, cease to be God. He did indeed become what he was not, but in doing so he did not cease to be what he ever was. So in his own way, Owen stresses and affirms the so-called *extra-calvinisticum*: while Christ lay in the manger he continued as the Son of God to uphold the universe by his divine power. So there is great condescension, but that does not imply abnegation of his personal being. Nor was the divine nature exchanged for the human, changed into the human, or mixed with the human.[1]

How, then, do we describe it? Owen says that the divine nature was veiled during the incarnation. The Son did not cease to be what he always was, but he veiled that which he fully was from all eternity, so much so that far from believing him to be God, his contemporaries did not even believe that he was a good man.

Such was the self-veiling of the Son of God—humbling himself, as Owen says, following Scripture, to become a worm and no man. Here he waxes lyrical:

> But had we the tongue of men and angels, we were not able in any just measure to express the glory of this condescension; for it is the most ineffable effect of the divine wisdom of the Father and of the love of the Son,—the highest evidence of the care of God towards mankind. What can be equal unto it? what can be like it? …
>
> We *speak* of these things in a poor low broken manner—we *teach* them as they are revealed in Scripture,—we labour by faith to adhere unto them as revealed; but when we come into a steady, direct view and consideration of the *thing itself,* our minds fail, our hearts tremble, and we can find no rest but in a holy admiration of what we cannot comprehend. Here we are at a loss, and know that we shall be so whilst we are in this world; but all the ineffable fruits and benefits of this truth are communicated unto them that do believe.[2]

God is incomprehensible in himself. There is something incomprehensible in the hypostatic union, something incomprehensible about

[1] *Works*, I:229.
[2] *Ibid.*, I:330.

the condescension of the incarnation. But what we cannot comprehend we may nevertheless apprehend. And so we have nothing to fear from either the will or the power of God because both of these are exercised towards us in Christ by means of the condescension of the incarnation.

(iv) The love expressed in the incarnation

It is clear now that the incarnation is a mighty expression of the love of God, set against the backcloth of the Father's electing grace to the unworthy and the defiled. Christ's first act of love, Owen says, arises as he views us in our sinfulness and under judgment. It is an act of pity and compassion. He viewed us as recoverable in the light of his death, and his love delights in what we will become by his grace.

Against that background Owen sees the way of salvation being proposed to the Son in the covenant of redemption.[1] This was a task of immense difficulty, requiring the Son to assume our humanity, and requiring of him an unparalleled act of love which would, at the same time, be an act of his whole being in obedience to his Father. Nevertheless the Son displays this love with respect to both natures, each acting in accordance with its own distinct properties. His love is always the love of one and the same person, never of merely one or other nature. This brings us to our fourth major emphasis.

4. The character of Christ's work

Here we move seamlessly from considering the person of Christ in his work to considering the work of Christ as a revelation of his person. We must limit our focus to one aspect of Owen's teaching which particularly helps us grasp the magnitude of his Christological vision.

What is the character of Christ's work? In the history of the church there has been a tendency to play off against each other various theories and interpretations of the atonement as though the work of Christ were one-dimensional. Owen, by contrast, while stressing the significance of the substitutionary nature and obedience-orientation of the atonement, also recognizes that the work of Christ is multidimensional in form and

---

[1] Sometimes called 'the covenant of the Mediator or Redeemer'. See *Works*, XVIII:78; XXI:230. See further, Sinclair B. Ferguson, *John Owen on the Christian Life* (Edinburgh: Banner of Truth Trust, 1987), pp. 25-27.

multivalent in function. But the background to every aspect of it is that it is an act of divine recapitulation in which Jesus Christ comes as the second man and the last Adam, first to restore individual sinners and an entire people to fellowship with God, and then to bring a restored, reconstituted, and glorious universe into being—one that surpasses creation in its original form. It is particularly fascinating to see the way in which Owen here resurrects and seeks to perfect biblically a motif normally associated with the early church father Irenaeus.[1]

Owen expounds this against the background of Paul's teaching in Ephesians 1:20-22 and Colossians 1:15-20. He is convinced from his reading of Scripture that in the original creation God brought into being two families distinct from each other:

(1) a family in heaven of archangels, angels, cherubim and seraphim, and

(2) a family on earth consisting of human beings.

These two families, distinct from each other, were united only in so far as their obedience was owed to God himself.[2] But (as Owen reads Scripture), part of the family of heaven and all of the family on earth sinned and fell. As a consequence God cut off the angels who had fallen and, by contrast, decreed to preserve the unfallen angels and to save a remnant of those who had fallen in the human family. His plan was to accomplish this now, not in terms of the original creation, but in terms of a new creation in which those two families would be united as one. One part (angelic) would be preserved from sinning, the other part (human) delivered from the guilt and power and eventually the very presence of sin.

This, for Owen, is the vision of which Paul speaks when he envisages everything in heaven and earth being headed up in Christ. Thus both the family in heaven and the family on earth are indebted to the incarnation, death, resurrection, exaltation, heavenly ascension, and final

---

[1] Irenaeus, bishop of Lyons during the late second century, expounds his teaching on the reversal of Adam's fall in the incarnation and obedience of Christ in various sections of his *Against Heresies* (e.g. II.22.4; III.xviii.1,7.)

[2] *Works*, I:369-70.

return of the incarnate Son—albeit not in identical ways. Christ thus comes to save sinners, to restore the universe to its stability, and to fill it with glory, and hence to bring the two families together as one glorious fellowship of which he himself is the head.

How does the Son of God do this? He does it, Owen argues, *principally* by atonement as obedience. He became obedient to the law of God as he discharged his threefold office in terms of a substitution of his obedience for our disobedience. His obedience was perfect. It was notably accomplished, not in the context of an unfallen world, but in the context of a fallen, decaying and disintegrating world. That contrast is emblematized in biblical history by the fact that while Adam failed in a garden, Jesus was tempted in a wilderness. By contrast with Eden—the garden in which Adam met with God in the evening—it was in dark Gethsemane that Jesus met with God, experiencing it as a place of crying and tears.

It is against this background of a cosmic reconciliation, the *anakephalaiōsis*, that the work of Christ is seen to be glorious by believers, and the majesty of Christ himself becomes clearer.

> How glorious is the Lord Christ on this account, in the eyes of believers. When Adam had sinned, and thereby eternally, according unto the sanction of the law, ruined himself and all his posterity, he stood ashamed, afraid, trembling, as one ready to perish for ever, under the displeasure of God. Death was that which he had deserved, and immediate death was that which he looked for. In this state the Lord Christ in the promise comes unto him, and says, Poor creature! how woful is thy condition! how deformed is thy appearance! What is become of the beauty, of the glory of that image of God wherein thou wast created? how hast thou taken on thee the monstrous shape and image of Satan? And yet thy present misery, thy entrance into dust and darkness, is no way to be compared with what is to ensue. Eternal distress lies at the door. But yet look up once more, and behold me, that thou mayest have some glimpse of what is in the designs of infinite wisdom, love, and grace. Come forth from thy vain shelter, thy hiding place. I will put myself into thy condition. I will undergo and bear that burden of guilt and punishment which should sink thee eternally into the bottom of hell. I will pay that which I never took; and be made *temporally*

a curse for thee, that thou mayest attain unto *eternal* blessedness. To the same purpose he speaks unto convinced sinners, in the invitation he gives them to come unto him.[1]

This, then, says Owen, is the Lord Jesus Christ who is set before us in the gospel. The Son of God, in infinite grace, laid aside infinite dignity, in an act of infinite condescension, revealing infinite love, and all with a view to producing infinite glory.

The knowledge of the person of Jesus Christ was never an academic matter for Owen. On the last day of his life he was visited at home in the (then) 'quiet village of Ealing'[2] by his friend William Payne. Payne was seeing his *Meditations on the Glory of Christ* through publication, and called to tell him the work was beginning to roll off the press. But Owen's eyes were already seeing beyond his own meditations. He responded,

> I am glad to hear it; but, O brother Payne! The long wished for day is come at last, in which I shall see that glory in another manner than I have ever done, or was capable of doing, in this world.[3]

Owen saw a great deal of that glory in this world. His deathbed testimony simply underlines how much more glorious he expected the actual reality to be than his efforts to express it.

It would be to miss the whole point of Owen's teaching if we failed to ask ourselves the obvious questions arising from any reading of his Christology. But perhaps it is important to spell them out simply:

1. How seriously do I pursue the knowledge of Christ?

2. How central is Jesus Christ in our preaching and worship?

3. How can it be—if these are the riches of Christ—when we too possess these riches, that the church today is so silent and embarrassed about its Saviour?

---

[1] *Works*, I:341-42.
[2] *Ibid.*, I:cii.
[3] *Ibid.*, I:ciii.

CHAPTER TWELVE

JOHN OWEN ON
THE GLORY OF CHRIST

THE seventeenth-century mini-biographer Anthony Wood famously described John Owen, when vice-chancellor of the University of Oxford, in these sneering words:

> While he did undergo the said office, he, instead of being a grave example to the university, scorned all formality, undervalued his office by going in quirpo[1] like a young scholar, with powdred hair, snakebone bandstrings (or bandstrings with large tassels), lawn band, and a large set of ribbons pointed, at his knees, and Spanish leather boots, with large lawn tops, and his hat mostly cock'd.[2]

Doubtless the portrayal was overdone. The author's complaint was, essentially, that Owen should have looked more like a distinguished cleric. Instead Wood was describing a Puritan, some might even say *the* Puritan *par excellence*, at least as far as Christian theologians are concerned. And why should one's attire not reflect the freedom, reality, colour and even joy of Christian doctrine?

---

[1] From the Spanish *cuerpo*, body. Cf. the Latin *corpus*. The suggestion here is that Owen walked around without a cloak or outer garment, so that the shape of his body was visible. Perhaps the author used the somewhat recondite expression because it stretched to the notion of being naked—suggesting in Owen an intolerable flaunting of etiquette and thus being a deeply insulting comment to make about him.

[2] Anthony Wood, *Athenae Oxonienses: An exact history of all the writers and bishops who have had their education in the University of Oxford, to which are added the fasti, or annals, of the said university* (London: 1691–92), II:556.

John Owen

John Owen was born in 1616 the son of a Church of England minister, graduated from the University of Oxford, and served two congregations as an Anglican minister. In 1649, still only thirty-two, he was appointed to preach to the British Parliament the day after the execution of Charles I. A one-time confidant of Oliver Cromwell, he fell out of favour with the Lord Protector when the latter was considering accepting an offer of the throne. Forced out of the Church of England in 1662, he continued to exercise an influential public role in both church and state. He was a prolific author: Anthony Wood required more space to list his published works than to describe his life. He died in 1683, leaving behind already published and posthumously published writings that now fill twenty-four volumes of approximately six hundred pages each.

By any measure Owen was the greatest Puritan theologian; in the esteem of some, probably the greatest English theologian since the Reformation.

But perhaps the most remarkable fact about Owen is this: today more Christians possess and read his works than ever before, whether in small paperback editions or hefty six-hundred-page multi-treatise volumes. If you read or 'listen' carefully between the lines, and sometimes actually on the lines, of many authors or preachers today who are serious 'thought-leaders' of younger generations of ministers, you may well hear the influence of John Owen. It is safe to say that he goes down deeper, stays down longer, and comes up with greater spiritual riches than can be found in the vast bulk of contemporary Christian literature. Speaking only for myself, whenever I return to something written by Owen, I wonder if I am wasting my time reading lesser works.

So if you want to develop strong roots in Christian thinking and living, then climb Mount Owen and breathe in its rich and healthy atmosphere—and if you are a preacher, or teacher, or pastoral counsellor, or for that matter simply finding ways to serve the Lord in his church and world, Owen will help you.

But confronted by twenty-four substantial volumes, where do you start? Actually as with most great authors it is not too difficult to suggest: 'Try this one' or 'Try that one, and see how you get on.'

The Glory of Christ

In John Owen's case it is not such a bad idea to begin *at the end!* The day Owen died a friend visited him to tell him that his last book was now going through the press. Sure enough it was published in 1684 with the title (it was an era when titles took the place of wording on dust-jackets): *Meditations and Discourses on the Glory of Christ in his Person, Office, and Grace: with the differences between faith and sight; applied unto the use of them that believe.* It is usually referred to simply as *The Glory of Christ.*

The title says it all. The book's theme is Jesus Christ. He is, says Owen, 'the principal object of our faith, love, delight, and admiration'.[1] This, the first sentence of Owen's preface, is already enough to give one pause. His second sentence is a lament that we understand and experience so little of it.

There is food for thought here.

Think about yourself first. What do you think about when you do not have much on your mind? Do you know enough about Christ to find your mind almost unconsciously admiring his actions and character and love for you? Or do you 'dry up' after a minute or two?

Then think about the preaching and teaching you hear (or provide). Is its best energy, its most insightful exposition of Scripture, its rich variety, its emotional atmosphere, full of Jesus Christ—or, despite everything, does it focus only on our own lives—perhaps even subtly, albeit seriously, focused horizontally, on sin, repentance, and even mortification? Owen has much to teach us about all three—he wrote about them at length—but never apart from his central focus on who Jesus Christ is and what he has done and is doing for his people and the world.

Owen wants to change our focus. He wanted to see it changed in himself, and then in the Christians he served. So his book on the glory of Christ is the refined echo of personal meditations on Scripture, which he preached probably in private homes. Now more than three centuries later *The Glory of Christ* still retains its freshness and power. That is the chief reason to read the book yourself.

Here, to encourage you to begin, is what Owen does.

---

[1] Owen, *Works*, I:275.

Foundations

Owen's starting place is John 17:24—Jesus' prayer that his people will see him in the glory the Father has given him. This is his 'High Priestly Prayer' and in many ways his 'Last will and testament'. In this prayer (contrast Gethsemane) his words are not 'If it is possible ... Nevertheless not my will but yours ...'. Rather, as the eternal Son of God, Jesus is coming to the Father who has promised him the nations for his inheritance and saying: 'Father ... you promised ... I will ....'

What is the Saviour's desire? He wants us to see him in his glory. That is everything. And it will be enough. Because for Owen (sitting at the feet of the apostles) this is: (i) the Christian's highest privilege; (ii) the means by which we are transformed into Christ's likeness, as Paul notes in 2 Corinthians 3:18; and (iii) the Christian's ultimate destiny, as John notes in 1 John 3:1-2: when we see Christ as he is, we will be forever made like him. This—beholding and becoming like Christ—gives us comfort now as we view him by faith and promises us perfect joy then when we view him by sight.

Owen then more fully expounds and explains the glory of Christ by means of a penetrating analysis of biblical teaching.

Christ—God's representative

Glory is seen in Christ because he is God's representative to his people. Sin has rendered the human race blind to and ignorant of the glory of God (Rom. 3:23). Only in Christ is God's glory restored and revealed. Thus, for example, only in him do we see the wisdom of God clearly expressed and the love of God convincingly displayed. True, people tell us they believe that God is love (it is the one axiom that unites everyone from liberal theologians, through Unitarians, to those whose letters appear in the correspondence columns of the newspapers). But Owen acutely observes,

> The most of the natural notions of men about it [God's love] are corrupt, and the best of them weak and imperfect. Generally, the thoughts of men about it are, that he is of a facile and easy nature, one that they may make bold withal in all their occasions, as the Psalmist declares, Psa. 50:21.[1]

[1] *Works*, I:301.

Owen's words are as relevant to the twenty-first century as they were to the seventeenth. His point is well taken. What people 'believe in' is not a God of love at all, but a superior being made largely in their own image, who tolerates them doing and being anything they want to be, including being wholly indifferent to him. That, however, is not *love*.

Would you know who God really is, and what it means to admire and experience the overwhelming reality of his love and glory? Then you must fix your gaze diligently on Christ as he is described in the Scriptures. Alas, 'the most of those who at this day are called Christians, are strangers unto this duty'.[1] Can that be true? Then beware, Owen warns us, for 'slothful and lazy souls never obtain one view of this glory'.[2]

Christ's person

Christ's glory is also seen in his person, presented to us in three ways in Scripture: first, by specific and direct descriptions; second, by means of prophecies; and third, by means of the typology of Old Testament worship and liturgy. We therefore turn to Scripture like the man in Jesus' parable (Matt. 13:45-46), seeking spiritual pearls of all kinds. But when we find Christ in Scripture we know we have discovered the pearl of great price.

If this is so then meditation on Scripture is essential. Only by such means will thoughts about the Christ we find there become habitual, accompanied as they should be by *'admiration, adoration, and thanksgiving'*.[3]

Condescension

Christ's glory is then seen in the way in which he became, and remains, the Mediator between the thrice-holy God and sinful man. He took our flesh in condescension and love. There is an infinite distance between God and man—yet the Son came among us; there is an infinite self-sufficiency in God, and yet God's Son humbled himself by taking our nature—not by *laying aside* the divine nature but by *taking* our human nature:

[1] *Works*, I:303.
[2] *Ibid.*, I:306.
[3] *Ibid.*, I:320.

Had we the tongue of men and angels, we were not able in any just measure to express the glory of this condescension; for it is the most ineffable effect of the divine wisdom of the Father and of the love of the Son,—the highest evidence of the care of God toward mankind.[1]

Love

Not only do we see here the wisdom of God in the incarnation, but also his amazing love. It is utterly free and undeserving. Nothing either foreseen in us, or accomplished by us, constrains it.

This is a counter-intuitive thought for sinners. We love because love's object draws forth that love. By contrast God's love is manifested in Christ to sinners, weak and helpless, not constrained by our virtue. Further, Christ is the way God the Father manifests his love for us, not the cause of it. Indeed,

In this love he is glorious; for it is such as no creatures, angels or men, could have the least conceptions of, before its manifestation by its effects; and after its manifestation, it is in this world absolutely incomprehensible.[2]

It is not merely by mastering this biblical revelation, but by its mastering us through our loving meditation on it, that the sheer incomprehensibility of God's love for us in Christ is seen by us as glorious and we are overwhelmed by it, 'lost in wonder, love, and praise'. With this in mind Owen traces out Christ's work for us through its various stages: his obedience to God's law; the fact that this was for us, not for himself; that it was universal (without the least exception) and perfect (without the least defect). He was obedient in a context of opposition and difficulty, not of comparative comfort (the First Adam lost the battle against Satan in a garden, blessed, and standing in front of a tree; the Last Adam conquered him in the wilderness of Calvary, and hanging by nails from a tree).

[1] *Works*, I:330.
[2] *Ibid.*, I:338.

Exaltation

Christ's mediatorial ministry does not finish at the cross, or even in the resurrection and ascension. It continues in his present exaltation in glory. There his humanity is

> *filled with all the divine graces and perfections* whereof a limited, created nature is capable. It is not deified, it is not made a god;—it doth not in heaven coalesce into one nature with the divine by a composition of them;—it hath not any essential property of the Deity communicated unto it, so as subjectively to reside in it;—it is not made omniscient, omnipresent, omnipotent; but it is exalted in a fullness of all divine perfection ineffably above the glory of angels and men. It is incomprehensibly nearer God than they all—hath communications from God, in glorious light, love, and power, ineffably above them all; but it is still a creature.[1]

Such eloquent outbursts of Christ-centred and exalting admiration and adoration, in the high rhetoric of someone familiar with what he describes, may leave us staggering a little in Owen's footsteps. But strain to follow the logic and the language and Owen becomes like a father lifting a child on to his shoulders, enabling us to see what he sees. For we must be lifted up, Owen insists, because

> They who endeavour not to see the glory of Christ in this world, as hath been often said, shall never behold him in glory hereafter unto their satisfaction; nor do they desire to do so, only they suppose it a part of that relief which they would have when they are gone out of this world.[2]

I am reminded of a programme I once heard on BBC Radio in which a variety of well-known people were asked how they envisaged heaven. But as the programme continued a consistent pattern developed in their answers. It was maintained throughout the half hour: *not one person mentioned the presence of Christ in heaven!* This is Owen's point: think little or not at all of Christ's glory *now* and at best we regard the Lamb on the throne as a necessary inconvenience to be, if possible, tolerated.

[1] *Works*, I:345.
[2] *Ibid.*, I:346-47.

But this is a religious illusion, not saving faith. The genuine Christian believer is someone increasingly gripped by Christ and the great exchange he has made with his people: "'O blessed change! sweet permutation!" as Justin Martyr speaks', notes Owen.[1] In the sight of both men and angels Christ is glorious because in him heaven's justice and heaven's love have met ('the one in punishing ... the other in pardoning').[2]

An appreciation of these gospel truths prompts in us a deep longing to live apprehending this and in dying fully and everlastingly to enjoy it.

Implications?

But does this make any practical difference to my life (and to the impact of my preaching or teaching if that is my calling)? Or is this simply deep theology? We have surely become a generation detached from apostolic Christianity if there is any seriousness in our asking that question. Was not Philippians 2:5-11, among the profoundest Christological statements in the New Testament, written in order to deal with the practical issues of pride and potential disunity in the church? Does not the Saviour's prayer in John 17, overheard by the apostles, deal with the deep things of God in a context in which the disciples desperately needed practical comfort and hope? In reality, claims Owen, the deeper the theology, the stronger the foundations for practical Christian living:

> *This is that glory of Christ whereof one view by faith*
> *will scatter all the fears,*
> *answer all the objections,*
> *and give relief against all the despondencies, of poor tempted souls;*
> *and an anchor it will be unto all believers,*
> *which they may cast within the veil,*
> *to hold them firm and steadfast in all trials, storms, and temptations*
> *in life and death.*[3]

The wonder is this: all that is treasured up in Christ, communicated to him by the Father, is in turn brought to us by the Spirit. He takes what

---

[1] *Works*, I:358.

[2] *Ibid.*, I:359.

[3] *Ibid.*, I:359; the quasi-poetic setting is mine. Owen is not, after all, always obscure, abstruse, or prosaic.

belongs to Christ and reveals it to us (John 16:14-15). Indeed the Spirit who was given to the Son by the Father is now through the Son given to believers so that as 'in his incarnation he took our nature into personal union with his own; so herein he takes our persons into a mystical union with himself. Hereby he becomes ours, and we are his.'[1]

Consummation

Ultimately this glory we already see in Christ will be fully and finally manifested in '*the recapitulation of all things in him*, after they had been scattered and disordered by sin'.[2] The fulfilment of this hope[3] will display the glory of Christ in ways most Christians have never imagined. For example, Owen directs us to the fact that the 'union between the two families of God—human and angelic—was disturbed, broken, dissolved by the entrance of sin'.[4] Now, where sin abounded grace has super-abounded. For in Christ something greater than the separate restoration of these two families has been accomplished. Now the angelic and the human families are gathered *into one* in their common head to whom belongs all authority in both heaven and earth.

No wonder Owen comments,

> Who can declare this glory of Christ? who can speak of these things as he ought? I am so far from designing to set forth the whole of it, that I am deeply sensible how little a portion I can comprehend of the least part of it. Nor can I attain unto any satisfaction in these Meditations, but what issues in an humble adoration.[5]

And so Owen closes his study with an extended discussion of the difference between beholding the glory of Christ in this world by faith and in the world to come by sight.[6]

Surely this brief summary whets the appetite for more. And Owen has more to give us, for after his death two further chapters, written in his own hand, were discovered among his papers: another forty-plus

---

[1] *Works*, I:365.
[2] *Ibid.*, I:367.
[3] See Eph. 1:8-10.
[4] *Works*, I:370.
[5] *Ibid.*, I:374.
[6] *Ibid.*, I:374-415.

pages[1] of application, first to those who are 'strangers to Christ', and then for those who are anxious to know how they may recover from spiritual decay.

Even a cursory reading of *The Glory of Christ* leaves one asking 'Do I own another book quite like this—for richness of exposition, for profundity of meditation, and for fullness of application?'

Owen is reminiscent of such Fathers of the church as Irenaeus, Athanasius, and others. Their passionate love for Christ demanded that they should describe their Saviour in a manner that was as detailed as possible and as biblical as their understanding allowed. It was not philosophical interests, or academic reputations they sought. They would no more have countenanced our slack and indifferent approach to describing their Lord and Saviour fully than fathers are willing to tolerate indifference in their own children in describing the mother who gave them birth. To lack this devotion, not to be interested in a true description of the Lord Jesus would have been for Owen, as for the Fathers, an unnatural and monstrous breach of trust.

Owen—worth reading

When the young John Owen wrote his 'To the Reader' prefacing what has become his most famous work, *Salus Electorum, Sanguis Jesu; or The Death of Death in the Death of Christ*, he commented:

> If thou intendest to go farther, I would entreat thee to stay here a little. If thou art, as many in this pretending age, *a sign or title gazer*, and comest into books as Cato into the theatre, to go out again—thou hast had thy entertainment; farewell![2]

True, Owen realized his works would never appeal to the superficial reader in search of a quick fix, to the person who thinks that the Christian faith is lived largely if not exclusively at the emotional level, or who naively imbibes the mantra that doctrine divides while experience unites. If we are like that then Owen bids us goodnight. But he farewells

---

[1] *Works*, I:419-61.

[2] *Ibid.*, X:149. Owen wrote this when he was no more than thirty years old, and perhaps the sharpness of his words needs to be set within the context of his youthful idealism! The Roman consul Cato the Elder (234–149 BC) was known as 'The Censor'.

us as people destined to know little about Christ (and who will tend
to see him as serving our own ends rather than God's glory), as people
who have slight thoughts of heaven and eternal glory and therefore live
ephemeral lives here on earth.

The same would be true, by implication, of pastors and teachers.
Not to want to know Christ better, not to pursue a sense of his glory
approximating to the understanding Owen displays, not to want to be
like Paul and say 'Him we proclaim … struggling with all his energy
that he powerfully works within me' (Col. 1:28-29)—surely this would
be inexcusable in a preacher of the gospel?

But if we want to know Christ, and to make him known, clothed in
the wonder of the gospel and the effulgence of his exalted glory, Owen
is our man. We can sit at his feet and learn, or better, be lifted up on his
shoulders and begin to see what he saw. This is what *The Glory of Christ*
does for us.

We began at the end of Owen's life. But not quite. The friend who
called on Owen on the morning of August 24, 1683 was William Payne,
a minister in Saffron Walden. 'Doctor', he said for his encouragement,
'your book on the *Glory of Christ* is in the process of publication.' Owen
gave the reply which constitutes his last recorded words:

> I am glad to hear it; but, O brother Payne! The long wished for day
> is come at last, in which I shall see that glory in another manner
> than I have ever done, or was capable of doing, in this world![1]

Until then, however, his *Glory of Christ* remains one of the fullest glimpses of that glory you will ever read.

[1] *Works*, I:ciii.

CHAPTER THIRTEEN

JOHN OWEN ON
THE PRIESTHOOD OF CHRIST

O WEN'S work on the priesthood of Christ may present some readers with a greater reading challenge than his other works such as on the *Glory of Christ*, the *Holy Spirit*, or *Communion with God*. But the effort will prove to be immensely worthwhile. For this is a significant work on a major biblical doctrine. Owen himself believed it was probably the most substantial work to date on the theme. While it is now 350 years old its burden addresses issues that remain vitally important today. Yet for Owen these 350 pages amounted to what nowadays would be referred to as an *excursus* in a much larger work!

Who was this John Owen who was capable not only of writing these pages but more than twelve thousand besides?—*The Priesthood of Christ* accounts for only part of one volume in an immense corpus of works.

In brief, John Owen was born in a vicarage in Stadhampton, near Oxford, in 1616. His early education was followed by studies at Oxford University (graduating B.A. in 1632), time spent as a private tutor, pastoral service in two congregations, first in Fordham in Essex and then at Coggeshall (a congregation of over 2,000), service as a chaplain to Oliver Cromwell, a period as vice-chancellor of Oxford University (in American terms, the President), ejection from the Church of England in 1662 as a 'Nonconformist', and finally a period towards the end of his life when he served in pastoral ministry in a gathered congregation in Leadenhall Street, London. He died in Ealing (then a pleasant village, now a London suburb) in 1683.

A man of immense learning, Owen's collected *Works* extend to twenty-four substantial volumes. They fall, essentially, into four categories:

(1) expositions of specific doctrines;

(2) pastoral and practical teaching;

(3) writings dealing with controversies;

(4) biblical exposition.

Dominating this last category is a massive exposition of the Letter to the Hebrews, well over 3,000 pages in length. 'It is', wrote Thomas Chalmers, 'a work of gigantic strength as well as gigantic size; and he who has mastered it is very little short, both in respect to the doctrinal and the practical of Christianity, of being an erudite and accomplished theologian.'

The Priesthood of Christ (originally entitled *Concerning the Sacerdotal Office of Christ*) forms one of a series of introductory essays ('Exercitations' in Owen's now disused language). These contain material which nowadays might appear in a series of appendices in which the author might review or further develop material which would be inappropriate in the body of the text, or be too extensive for a footnote.

In Owen's hands these exercitations are advanced expositions in which he discusses important theological issues, and points up their relevance. In relation to his commentary on Hebrews they serve a similar role to the one Calvin's *Institutes* plays in relation to his commentaries, enabling him essentially to say to the reader, 'For further discussion see the exercitations.'

Owen wrote for serious readers. ('If you have come like Cato into the theatre,' he greets his readers on one occasion, 'Farewell, you have had your entertainment'!). Thus this 'precursus' on Christ's priestly ministry is a work of such substance that it stretches the powers of a culture more accustomed to the three- or four-sentence, multi-paragraph pages of contemporary books. But the dividends of thoughtful reading are immense.

It may help us as readers if two things are available to us before we set out on the journey on which Owen will lead us: (1) A road map to provide some sense of direction to the journey, and (2) some basic knowledge of the major individuals and theological controversies singled out by Owen in his discussion.

(1) A map for the road

Owen develops his theme in a logical and theological order. The exposition begins with a discussion of the origin of priestly ministry. Its necessity arises from the presence of sin:

> A supposition of the entrance of sin, and what ensued thereon in the curse of the law, lie at the foundation of the designation of the priesthood and sacrifice of Christ.[1]

Owen does not mean that the plan of redemption is a divine afterthought, a poor Plan B cobbled together because of the failure of Plan A. Rather it is rooted in eternity in the inter-personal purposes of the Father and the Son, together with the Spirit. Readers of *Communion with God* will recognize here Owen's profound interest in the inner relations in the Trinity and their far-reaching implications.

There were, Owen argues, 'eternal transactions' between the Father and the Son with respect to the work of redemption. These were of a covenantal or federal nature.[2]

Owen shared with the earlier Scottish theologian, Robert Rollock, the view that all of God's relations with respect to creation and redemption are covenantal in nature. In particular he viewed God's work in history unfolding in terms of four covenants:

(i) a covenant of works made with Adam in creation;

(ii) a covenant of grace, made with Adam following the fall and fulfilled in the work of Christ;

(iii) a covenant made through Moses, which he believed had aspects of both the covenant of works and the covenant of grace; and

(iv) an inner-trinitarian covenant between the Father and the Son, the covenant of redemption.

---

[1] Owen, *Works*, XVIII:41.

[2] 'Federal' from the Latin *foedus* (stem *foeder*) is a covenant or treaty. Owen's exposition here, as in a number of places, provides the reader with a series of mini-seminars on important theological themes. Pausing on them, without being frustrated that the argument does not move with contemporary rapidity, will add to the riches of the study.

While it often comes as a surprise to readers of Owen to discover that his federal theology was not simply a reiteration of, for example, *The Confession of Faith*, he was by no means unique in holding the four-covenant view, nor in particular the mixed-covenant view of Sinai.[1]

In view in these covenant purposes is the salvation of sinners for the glory of God—demonstrated in the manner in which he displays his wisdom, justice, and grace in the gospel of Christ.

This plan then raises the question: What did this involve for the Son? Two things:

(i) obedience (he becomes the Servant of the Lord), and

(ii) sacrifice (he becomes the Suffering Servant who bears God's judgment on man's sin).

The covenant of grace, the covenant of redemption, the coming of Christ—these are all necessary for our salvation. Yet they remain the free act of God. The justice of God and the mercy of God are not opposed to one another (as though the former were an involuntary necessity while the latter is an act of voluntary condescension). God freely performs that which is necessary for man's salvation; he freely exercises the judgment against man's sin that his nature necessarily requires.

In the light of the fact that God has committed himself to our salvation in all persons of the Trinity, Owen continues, Christ had to suffer what we deserve (it was an action of consequent absolute necessity given the prior commitment to save):

> The Lord underwent the punishment due unto our sins in the judgment of God, and according to the sentence of the law; for how did God make our sins to meet on him, how did he bear them, if he did not suffer the penalty due to them, or if he underwent some other inconvenience, but not the exact demerit of sin?[2]

---

[1] This is all the more striking in the light of the fact that Owen was involved in the composition of *The Savoy Declaration* which simply echoed the *Westminster Confession of Faith* at this point. It does not seem to have been a matter for which he would have gone to the stake.

[2] *Works*, XVIII:127.

The Father lovingly sent the Son in our place. Christ then became our substitute; the Father punishes our sin even when it is borne before him by his own beloved Son. For God hates sin, and not to judge it would impeach his own glory. Herein lie the heart and wonder of the cross— 'heaven's love and heaven's justice meet'.[1]

This is what makes the priesthood of Christ a necessity. He must become both sacrificing priest and sacrificial lamb. Owen argues—surely rightly—that without this perspective the cross cannot be the foundation for a coherent theology. Priestly, substitutionary, penal substitution is of the essence of the atonement. Any perspective on the atonement that denies or lacks the notion of penal substitution must fail to provide a rationale for redemption from the guilt and power of sin.

Thus, for Owen, any theology of the atonement that reduces the work of Christ to either the kingly role (Christ conquers our enemies) or the prophetic role (Christ reveals the Father's love to overwhelm us and turn us from sin, or as an example to us of how to live in sacrificial love) disembowels the gospel. It cannot provide an adequate grounding for the cry of dereliction. The cross becomes either inessential, or too high a price for the blessing purchased by it. The cross cannot be fully explained in terms of Jesus identifying himself with us in our need in order to show us the love of God. For, as James Denney pointed out long ago, if I see a man drowning in a river, I do not demonstrate my love for him, nor do I rescue him, by jumping in and drowning with him. No, the wonder of the love of God at the cross is that while we were sinners Christ died for us in order to justify us and save us from the wrath of God (Rom. 5:8-10). The cross is a revelation of love only because there God made Christ to be sin for us (2 Cor. 5:21), and a curse (Gal. 3:13).

Substitutionary self-sacrifice (eye for eye, tooth for tooth, man for man) is therefore essential to Christ's priesthood. He comes to act for the church before the face of God. His life, with its slow but divinely ordained journey to Calvary, constitutes his preparation for this ministry; his bearing our sin, his sacrificial slaying and his oblation in his shedding of his precious blood are forerunners of his representation as he stands on our behalf before the throne of God.

---

[1] Words taken from the hymn 'Beneath the Cross of Jesus' by Elizabeth Cecilia Clephane.

Charitie Lees de Chenez was therefore right, after all:

> Before the throne of God above
> I have a strong, a perfect plea…
>
> When Satan tempts me to despair,
> And tells me of the guilt within,
> Upward I look and see Him there
> Who made an end of all my sin.
>
> Because the sinless Saviour died,
> My sinful soul is counted free;
> For God, the Just, is satisfied
> To look on Him, and pardon me.

There Christ serves us as intercessor—not, in Owen's view, so much by formal representation of our needs in words audibly spoken to his Father and ours, but in a virtual manner (i.e. real and powerful way).[1]

But, Owen notes, Christ came 'in the fullness of time'. What of before? He provides the standard Augustinian biblical-theological answer: God prefigured the work of Christ in the priestly sacrifices of the Old Testament period, whether those offered before the law of Moses or according to it. In the providence of God, priestly ministry was exercised prior to Sinai (cf. Exod. 19:22, 24) as well as according to the pattern given at Sinai. By means of the Old Testament priesthood, old covenant saints looked forward in faith, by way of promise, to that priesthood of Christ to which we look back in faith.

Here—it may seem both curiously and unexpectedly—Owen bids farewell to his readers.[2] Ordinary humanity momentarily interrupts his massive, driving intellect. In essence Owen thinks the *excursus* is already long enough, although (as ever!) there is still much to say. But—we could not have guessed—he is in fact feeling unwell, and the printer is knocking at his door for a complete manuscript. We will—he hopes—excuse him if he leaves further exposition for later!

Indeed we will.

---

[1] Owen is using the term in its Latin sense: *virtus*, strength or power.
[2] *Works*, XVIII:259.

But just before setting out on the reading journey, it may be helpful to provide further orientation—this time to some of the individuals and issues Owen addresses.

(2) People to meet, issues to face

There are some historical and theological landmarks in his work on the *Priesthood of Christ* that may not be wholly familiar to contemporary readers, and a few comments about them may provide helpful orientation to what follows.

Given Owen's context (he is writing in 1668) we might expect him to comment on Roman Catholic teaching.

Owen's grandparents were alive at the time of the Spanish Armada (1588)—an invading force calculated to bring England back to subservience to the papacy. He was born less than a hundred years from the date when Luther's Ninety-five Theses exploded on to the church of early sixteenth-century Europe. The reign of 'Bloody Mary' (1553–58), when large numbers of Protestants had been executed, was within living memory. The Stuart monarchy of Owen's own day had taken a decided Rome-ward direction in the eyes of many. Roman Catholicism was not merely a religious issue; it was a political one. So we find here a critique of Roman Catholic theology.

Owen also lived during the period when the Quaker movement appeared to be gaining momentum. Here too he had issues (it should not be forgotten that while 'Quaker' today may convey the idea of a pacifism and quietism, the nomenclature was originally expressive of a very different aspect of radical religious life). While by no means a homogeneous group, the nickname 'quakers' was descriptive of some of the more radical groups. In addition, such theologically significant figures as the Lutheran Andreas Osiander (1498–1552) and the Dutch lawyer-theologian Hugo Grotius (1583–1645) also make cameo appearances in these pages.

But throughout this work (and it is not alone in his corpus of writings) it is Socinianism that Owen chiefly has in his crosshairs.

Socinianism?

Socinianism was in some respects similar to Arianism in the early church and Unitarianism today. Its distinctives included denying the eternal deity of Christ, the doctrine of the Trinity, and the centrality of penal substitution. For all practical purposes it saw Jesus as a unique man given supreme authority and (at least in its earlier forms) to be worshipped only as a kind of representative symbol of God. It taught that salvation (insofar as it was necessary for those not totally depraved) came through repentance and good works. Many of its emphases would reappear in developed form in, for example, the teaching of Lord Herbert of Cherbury (1583–1648), elder brother of the great metaphysical pastor-poet, George Herbert.

The rise of this theology at the time of the Reformation is traced back to Lelio Sozzini (Latin: *Laelius Socinus*), an Italian, and his nephew Fausto (Latin: *Faustus Socinus*). Born in Sienna in 1525, Lelio was a man of unusual charm and free spirit, with an enquiring but restless mind. Underwritten by his father, he was able to travel widely and came into contact with the burgeoning groups of men whose intelligent minds and eager hearts had been captured by the evangelical reformation. Sozzini's attractive personality and inquisitive mind gave him an entrée to such luminaries as Luther's colleague and friend Philip Melanchthon, Heinrich Bullinger, and John Calvin.

At various times Sozzini questioned Calvin on such matters as predestination, the resurrection of the body, and the grounds of salvation. Calvin's correspondence with him is partially extant, and in it he reveals the two sides of Sozzini he had obviously experienced. Thus he wrote to him in 1551:

> The word of God ... is my only guide, and to acquiesce in its plain doctrines shall be my constant rule of wisdom. Would that you also, my dear Lelio, would learn to regulate your powers with the same moderation! You have no reason to expect a reply from me so long as you bring forward those monstrous questions. If you are gratified by floating among these aerial speculations ... I am very greatly grieved that the fine talents with which God has endowed you, should be occupied not only with what is vain and fruitless,

but that they should also be injured by pernicious figments. What I warned you of long ago, I must again seriously repeat, that unless you correct in time this itching after investigation, it is to be feared that you will bring upon yourself severe suffering. I should be cruel towards you did I treat with a show of indulgence what I believe to be a very dangerous error ...

Adieu, brother very highly esteemed by me; and if this rebuke is harsher than it ought to be, ascribe it to my love to you.

A year or so later, following the trial and death of the anti-trinitarian Michael Servetus, Sozzini's own mind turned to the issue of the Trinity itself, which he would likewise come to reject.

Sozzini died in 1562, a couple of years before Calvin. But he had by that time exercised considerable influence on his young nephew Fausto who both imbibed and developed his uncle's thought. More than that, he published his anti-trinitarian views and as a result, Calvin's fears for the uncle were fulfilled in the nephew, who was persecuted and physically abused. From 1579 until his death in 1604 he lived in Poland, and it was there that his influence became virtually institutionalized.

Several of Fausto's leading colleagues seem to have been involved in both 'perfecting' the catechism he had prepared (later published as the *Racovian Catechism*) and disseminating their unitarian and Socinian views. These included Johannes Crellius (1590–1631) who became Rector of the University of Cracow, Johannes Volkelius (d. 1618) who may have acted as an amanuensis to Socinus, and Valentinius Smalcius, all of whom, along with Ludwig Woolzogenius, Owen both mentions and vigorously critiques.

This was not the first time Owen had dealt with Socinianism. In 1652 an Englishman, John Biddle, had translated and published the *Racovian Catechism* (it was condemned by Parliament in April 1652, and all copies were to be burned).[1] Indeed Parliament had requested Owen's help to deal with Socinianism and in 1655 he published an extensive and devastating critique in *Vindiciae Evangelicae*.

In the *Priesthood of Christ*, however, Owen's central concern with Socinianism is that it reduces the priesthood of Christ to his roles as

---

[1] Biddle also translated a *Memoir of the Life of Faustus Socinus* in 1653.

prophet and king and thus destroys both its centrality and its distinctive significance. In Socinianism Christ's death amounts to little more than a revelation of God's heart of love; it is not therefore a substitutionary sacrifice made for our sins. While Owen by no means denies that all of Christ's offices belong together, and may be exercised simultaneously, nor ignores the fact that God does reveal his love at the cross, he insists that something was definitively accomplished on the cross to procure our salvation. Otherwise it does not reveal the heart of God. As in other areas, Owen recognizes that behind the Socinian view lies an inadequate view of God, an unbiblical diminution of the gravity of sin, and an inevitable down-playing of the reality of the judgment and wrath of God.

Relevance to today?

But why should Owen's exposition of Christ's priesthood and his polemic against Socinianism have relevance to today's church? Because we live in times of theological thought at both the academic and popular levels when the chilling waters of Socinianism continue to flow.

There is no doubt a very pressing need for us to understand that Christ's ministry was a revelatory one (the prophetic office) and the establishing of a new order in his kingdom (the kingly office). But to see the *Christus Victor* motif—Christ the Conquering King, or the lordship of Christ, or even for that matter the kingdom of Christ—as central to the New Testament's gospel without emphasizing the essential role of his priestly ministry in his vicarious sacrifice and substitutionary death under the judgment and wrath of God as the heart of our salvation, is a fatal blunder for theology, pastoral ministry, and world evangelism.

It will be said that the earliest Christian confession was 'Jesus is Lord' and not 'Jesus is priest'. But that is not the point. The point is that it is as Saviour, as substitute, as penalty-bearer, crucified and risen, that he now is Lord—not apart from that. His power to bring deliverance is not naked power but atoning power (as Heb. 1:1-4; 2:5-18 clarifies).

Years ago the Swedish Lutheran theologian Gustav Aulén famously argued in his book *Christus Victor*[1] that Martin Luther saw the kingship of Christ, not his penal substitutionary death (priesthood), as central to

---

[1] First published in Swedish in 1930 and in English in 1931.

the gospel. Aulén's own theology, however, made it clear that this was by no means an unbiased conviction. Penal substitution was not central in his own exposition of the work of Christ.[1]

More recently among some adherents of the so-called 'New Perspective on Paul' a similar argument for the central role of Christ's kingship and the centrality of the *Christus Victor* motif (Jesus is Lord) has been made to the diminution, if not exclusion, of the gravity of sin as guilt, the righteous judgment of God on sin, and the reality of divine wrath. In emerging and emergent ecclesiastical circles echoes of the same have been heard.

Owen will have none of this. Probably no theologian in the English language has ever rivalled him in stressing the absolute centrality of Christ's penal substitution, and therefore his role as priest. The point is that Christ is not victor unless he is first substitute. The deliverance he brings requires that he deal with both the guilt of sin and the wrath of God as well as our bondage to the powers of darkness.

For that reason alone the *Priesthood of Christ* is worth all the time it takes to read it with humility, care, and reflection. Written as it was in the mid-seventeenth century, and providing a vigorous theological workout for many readers, there are important points at which it remains a tract for the times.

So, with some quick map reading, and a little warning that you may meet strangers on the way, and have some hard thinking to do, it is time for your journey to begin. I hope that, even if the road sometimes calls for perseverance, the walk will be bracing, and at the end you will be grateful to Owen that you are stronger spiritually and theologically than you were at the beginning. So, to borrow words that proved so significant in the life of Augustine of Hippo: *tolle lege*—pick up and read John Owen on the priesthood of Christ!

---

[1] As his *Faith of the Christian Church* (Swedish, 1923; English, 1948) demonstrated. See below, Chapter 24, '*Christus Victor et Propitiator*'.

CHAPTER FOURTEEN

JOHN OWEN AND
THE DOCTRINE OF THE HOLY SPIRIT

Oftentimes they go for water to the well, and are not able to draw ...
They seek to promises for refreshment, and find no more savour in
them than in the white of an egg; but when the same promises are
brought to remembrance by the Spirit the Comforter, who is with
them and in them, how full of life and power are they![1]

THE doctrine of the Holy Spirit was of crucial theological importance to John Owen. His great work *Pneumatologia* covers two
volumes of his *Works* in the Goold Edition,[2] almost 1,200 pages
in all. Its size and breathtaking vision give eloquent expression to his
sense of the need for a thorough biblical exposition and a comprehensive
theology of the Holy Spirit. The work—really an entire series of books—
began to be published in 1674 when Owen was fifty-eight years old. The
final volumes appeared posthumously in 1693. It represents the mature
mind of a very great systematic thinker who was also an outstanding
pastoral theologian.

Owen himself recognized the historical significance in his work. It is
easy to forget that a man born in 1616 could theoretically have known
an elderly man who, in his youth, had listened to the preaching of John
Calvin. The centenary of the Reformation had not yet taken place.
And central to that revolution had been a recovery of an understanding
and experience of the role of the Holy Spirit in the church and in the
individual. Indeed Edmund Campion, the famous Jesuit missionary

[1] Owen, *Works*, XI:347.
[2] *Ibid.*, III and IV.

to England,[1] said on one occasion that the great dividing line between Rome and Geneva lay along the axis of the doctrine of the person and work of the Holy Spirit.

Such a statement from a Counter-Reformation figure like Campion simply confirmed what especially Calvin (and later Owen and others) recognized. The Roman Catholic Church had sequestered for the church's *magisterium*, priesthood and sacramental administration what properly belonged exclusively to the Holy Spirit. He alone can bring men to Christ, keep them in Christ, and assure them that through faith they belong to Christ and will be finally saved by God's free grace. In keeping with this, the learned Robert Bellarmine, the greatest theologian of the Roman Catholic Counter-Reformation movement, wrote that assurance is the greatest of all Protestant heresies.[2]

Against this historical background John Owen became increasingly conscious of the strategic importance of expounding the ministry of the Holy Spirit. He does this in essentially three dimensions, working simultaneously on several fronts.

1. Constructive exposition

First of all Owen wants constructively and comprehensively to expound the ministry of the Holy Spirit within a solid biblical theology. He introduces his work on this note: 'I know not any who ever went before me in this design of representing the whole economy of the Holy Spirit with all his adjuncts, operations, and effects.'[3]

Owen was very conscious that he was constructively contributing to the theology, not only of his own era, but also of the entire Christian church. Of course a number of the church Fathers had written on the

---

[1] Edmund Campion (1540–81), along with Robert Parsons (1546–1610), came to England from the Continent in 1580 to spearhead the Jesuit English Mission. Campion was arrested and executed at Tyburn in 1581.

[2] *De Justificatione* III.2.3. Cardinal Robert Bellarmine (1542–1621) was a Jesuit scholar and personal theologian to the pope. He was canonized in 1930 and made a Doctor of the Church. He is the Counter-Reformation theologian most frequently cited by the Puritans and regarded universally by them as the most formidable. The Council of Trent's Decree on Justification (Session VI, chapter 9) implies a similar perspective.

[3] Owen, *Works*, III:7.

doctrine of the Holy Spirit,[1] but their focus tended to be on his personal divine identity. Owen's vision was larger as well as being more obviously orientated to soteriology and its pastoral implications. And it is out of this context that he wrote the monumental exposition of the Holy Spirit with which we are familiar.

2. Defensive polemic

But not only did Owen work constructively; he also engaged in polemic. He seeks to expound and define biblical teaching over against a whole series of errors:

1. Over against Rome and the way in which it had usurped the Spirit's role and replaced it with the magisterial authority of the church and the ministry of the sacraments.

2. Over against the increasing influence of a rationalism which regarded Christianity merely as an external behavioural pattern of which the natural man is capable.

3. Over against those forms of spirituality that stressed the immediacy of the Spirit's presence in the giving of continuing revelation. That had already been an ongoing burden to Calvin; if anything it had become a more critical issue by the time of Owen.

The theology of the magisterial Reformers had sought to stress the harmony of the Spirit with the word. Over against this, elements in the radical reformation tended to bypass the written word of Scripture and claimed the immediate revelation and leading of the Holy Spirit. Calvin himself had complained about the impossibility of discussion with people who punctuate every paragraph they utter with references to what the Spirit had told them.[2]

It is sometimes said, by way of whimsical summary of the Reformation's teaching, that if we emphasize the word without the Spirit then

---

[1] Owen's familiarity with the work on the Holy Spirit of, e.g., Cyprian (*c.* 200–258), Didymus the Blind (*c.* 309–398), Basil the Great (329–379), Ambrose (339–397), Chrysostom (*c.* 344–407) and others is evident in the course of his exposition.

[2] See e.g. his *Contre la secte phantastique et furieuse des Libertins qui se nomment Spirituelz* in *Treatises Against the Anabaptists and Against the Libertines*, pp. 161-326.

we will *dry up*, if we emphasize the Spirit without the word we will *blow up*(!); but if we emphasize the Spirit and the word we will *grow up*. Owen had his own version of this: 'He that would utterly separate the Spirit from the word had as good burn his Bible.'[1]

It is worth noting in passing that the context in which Owen was seeking to build a biblical doctrine of the Holy Spirit was not dissimilar to the context in which we minister the word of God today: a rationalism that denies the reality of the supernatural and in its ecclesiastical garb sees either liturgy or decency as equivalent to Christianity; an increasing interest in mystical and sacerdotal religion; a context in which a healthy orthodox evangelical biblicism is giving way to a denial of the sufficiency of Scripture interpreted and applied by the Spirit, replacing written revelation with immediate revelation as the canon of the Christian's decision-making process. If we can get revelation from God directly, it is psychologically inevitable that we will find less enthusiasm for serious Bible study. There is, therefore, an impressive relevance about what Owen said so many generations ago.

3. Experimental focus

Owen also writes with a concern for Christian experience. He had, after all, a deep personal reason to expound the role of the ministry of the Holy Spirit in the believer.

One of the axioms that Owen returns to again and again as a preacher of the gospel is that there is a difference between the knowledge of the truth and the knowledge of the power of the truth. That was a distinction carved out of personal experience. For he himself had possessed a knowledge of the truth since childhood (his own father was a minister with Puritan leanings). Yet he had at one time a deep consciousness that he lacked real experience of the power of the truth of which he had so much knowledge.[2] For the later Owen it became axiomatic that it is the presence of the Spirit of God that transforms our bare knowledge of the truth into our experience of the power of the truth. He lived and breathed for this. As David Clarkson[3] would say later, in his funeral

---

[1] *Works*, III:192.
[2] See e.g. *Ibid.*, I:xxv-xxvi, xxix-xxx.
[3] David Clarkson (1622–86), Fellow of Clare Hall, Cambridge 1645–51, and then,

address after Owen's death, it was for the promotion of Spirit-given holiness that all of John Owen's significant intellectual powers were laid in tribute at the feet of his Lord Jesus Christ.[1]

There is an embarrassment of riches to be explored in Owen's doctrine of the Holy Spirit. Here we must restrict ourselves to two central aspects of his thought. Taken together they will help us to catch the flavour of his approach to the role and power of the Holy Spirit in the life of the believer. He explores the relationship of the Spirit first to Christ, and then to the believer.

Although Owen gave unequal attention to these themes in terms of length of treatment, they are integrally related in his theology, the first providing the framework for the second.

1. The Holy Spirit in communion with Christ

Evangelical theology has long had a tendency to leapfrog over redemptive history and head directly to personal experience of salvation. Put in technical terms, it has often ignored the significance of the being and activity of God in favour of subjective experience of God, bypassing *historia salutis* in favour of an interest in *ordo salutis*.[2]

Owen manfully resisted that tendency. In his Pneumatology in particular he emphasizes that, in order to understand the significance of the work of the Holy Spirit, we must first explore his relationship to the life and ministry of our Lord Jesus Christ.

Owen refers in this connection to the prophetic Psalm 45: '... you have loved righteousness and hated wickedness. Therefore God, your God, has anointed you with the oil of gladness beyond your companions' (Psa. 45:6-7). He raises two questions with (in his view) obvious answers:

(i) About whom does the psalmist speak? Answer: the use of these words in Hebrews 1:9 makes it clear that he speaks of the Lord Jesus Christ.

---

until the Great Ejection in 1662, curate of Mortlake, Surrey. He became colleague to the then-ailing Owen in 1682 and succeeded him in ministry until his own death.

[1] The whole sermon, published in 1720, is reprinted in William Orme, *Memoirs of the Life and Writings of John Owen*, in *The Works of John Owen*, ed. T. Russell (1826), I:411-22.

[2] See the comments of H. N. Ridderbos, *Paul: An Outline of his Theology*, tr. J. R. de Witt (Grand Rapids: Eerdmans, 1975), pp. 14ff.

(ii) Of what does the psalmist speak when he says: 'God, your God, has anointed you with the oil of gladness beyond your companions'? Answer: the words of John 3:34 make clear that he is looking forward to the anointing of Jesus Christ with the Spirit without measure.

Owen's understanding of the believer's experience of the Holy Spirit rests upon this foundation. Jesus Christ, who gives the Spirit to his people on the Day of Pentecost, and who bestows the same gift on all those who trust him, does so as the one upon whom that Spirit was first and foremost bestowed.

Thus Owen understands that Jesus was the recipient and bearer of the Spirit both *prior to* our becoming the recipients of the Spirit and also *with a specific view to* our reception of the Spirit. Furthermore, the relationship formed between the divine Spirit and the incarnate mediator is determinative of the character of the ministry of the Holy Spirit to all believers. So, says Owen, Christ, who was conceived under the aegis of the Holy Spirit, was, from the moment of conception in his mother's womb right through to his resurrection and exaltation, also borne by the Spirit, and in turn bore the Spirit, in order that after his ascension he might give the very Spirit who was upon him to all who believe in him.

Owen sees four critical stages of our Lord's relationship to the Holy Spirit in connection with his ministry to him as the Messiah.

1. The incarnation
Wherever we turn in Owen's theology we encounter various applications of the patristic axiom: *opera Trinitatis ad extra sunt indivisa*.[1] This is certainly true of his doctrine of the incarnation proper. The Father prepares a body for his Son and sends him. Simultaneously the Son takes hold not of the seed of angels but of the seed of Abraham (Heb. 2:16). This work of the Father and this act of the Son both take place in and through the power of the Holy Spirit.

Our Lord's conception has all the characteristic marks of the Spirit's work. As the Spirit overshadowed the first work of creation, and at Pentecost overshadowed the first moments of recreation, so when the

---

[1] e.g. *Works*, III:162.

author of that first creation became the head of the new creation in the womb of the virgin Mary, the Holy Spirit again acted as the executive of the Godhead. It was through the Holy Spirit that the Holy One was conceived in the virgin's womb. By that same act in the mystery of virgin conception, the humanity which the Son assumed in the womb of the virgin Mary was sanctified. Thus the 'thing' (Luke 1:35 KJV) that was conceived in her was simultaneously fully human and fully holy.[1]

Thus by the power of the Spirit our Lord, the second person of the Trinity, became the second man and the last Adam.[2] The striking result of this, for Owen, is that here uniquely, by this work of God's grace, there emerges one among us in whom grace and nature meet in harmony.

2. The ministry

Owen further develops this train of thought by moving from the Spirit's ministry in Jesus' conception and birth to his ministry throughout the course of his life. For Owen it is axiomatic that, although our Lord lived in the power of the Spirit, he 'acted grace as a man';[3] that is, as a man, fully man, truly man and in every aspect of his humanity. This is expounded in two ways:

(i) Jesus' human development

The reality of Christ's humanity carries with it an important implication. It means that there is, by definition, a progress in our Lord's humanity and correspondingly progress in his holiness—not from sin to holiness as such, but from holiness to holiness, in a manner commensurate with the natural progress within his humanity. This is implied in the statement of Luke 2:52 that as he grew in stature and in favour with men, he also grew in favour with God as he grew in wisdom.[4]

As Owen points out from the Messianic prophecies (Isa. 11:1-3), this wisdom is the distinguishing feature of the individual who is full of the

---

[1] *Works*, III:162-64.

[2] It is significant that the chapter title Owen chooses in this context speaks of the 'work of the Holy Spirit with respect unto the head of the new creation'. The last-Adam Christology is of considerable significance in the pattern of his thought.

[3] *Ibid.*, III:169. The entire section is important for Owen's Christology as well as his Pneumatology.

[4] *Ibid.*, III:169-70.

Holy Spirit. As his natural capacities developed so the Spirit of God worked in the Lord Jesus, gradually and incrementally training him in the development of perfect godliness at each stage of his life.

In this sense Jesus obeyed the law of God perfectly and did so in the power of the Holy Spirit, 'naturally' in the sense of 'in a fully and truly human way'. There was nothing inhuman, a-human, or super-human about the obedience of Jesus. The Spirit of God led him into a full, perfect and 'natural' humanity. Correspondingly the mind of the Lord Jesus, under the influence of the Holy Spirit, was illumined by the Scriptures to guide him on each step of his way, as he lived in the general obedience to God required of man as creature, and the specific obedience to God required by Jesus as Messiah:

> In the representation, then, of things anew to the human nature of Christ, the wisdom and knowledge of it [his human nature] was *objectively* increased, and in new trials and temptations he *experimentally* learned the new exercise of grace. And this was the constant work of the Holy Spirit on the human nature of Christ.[1]

To put Owen's point in blunt terms: the Messiah who died on the cross did not come immediately from heaven to the cross. Rather, he developed from his (literally) embryonic condition in the womb, through the natural processes of growth, accompanied by the development of holiness in the power of the Spirit, to become a mature man in his thirties. In him, uniquely, ongoing growth in obedience and in the fruit of the Spirit were perfectly commensurate with the natural development of all human characteristics:

> This was the constant work of the Holy Spirit in the human nature of Christ. He dwelt in him in fullness; for he received not him by measure. And continually, upon all occasions, he gave out of his unsearchable treasures grace for exercise in all duties and instances of it. From hence was he [Jesus] habitually holy, and from hence did he exercise holiness entirely and universally in all things.[2]

---

[1] *Works*, III:170.
[2] *Ibid.*, III:170-71.

(ii) The public ministry

Jesus grew strong in the Holy Spirit during the hidden years from twelve to thirty. But at his baptism, according to Owen, he entered into the fullness of the Spirit, not for progress in holiness, but to be equipped to fulfil his Messianic ministry. The baptismal descent of the Spirit was specifically related to a new stage in his *ministry* as Messiah, not to a new stage in his *humanity* in its ordinary development. Gifts were now given to him by the Spirit, in order that he might don the armour of God to engage in the ages-old conflict between the kingdom of God and the powers of darkness.[1] In his battle against Satan he took the sword of the Spirit, which is the word of God, in order to overcome the kingdom of darkness. In his use of Scripture he simultaneously obeyed his Father, maintained his own integrity, and under the Spirit's guidance caused Satan to flee.

Already then, at this stage in Jesus' ministry, Owen is hinting that the ministry of the Spirit in the life of our Lord will serve as the paradigm for the ministry of the Spirit in the life of the believer. Here the great axiom in Calvin's theology, that word and Spirit must never be separated, is given very practical expression. The Lord Jesus himself as second Man becomes a living embodiment of obedience to, and fulfilment of, the word of God.

3. The sacrifice

Here, for Owen, the key text is Hebrews 9:13-14. It was 'through the eternal Spirit' that our Lord 'offered himself without blemish [as a sacrifice] to God'. There is an expressed contrast here. The sacrifice of the blood of bulls and goats was inherently inadequate to take away the sins of human beings. Christ, by contrast, offered himself, and did so through the eternal Spirit.

There is an exegetical crux to be resolved here. Is the referent to the human spirit of Jesus or to the Holy Spirit? Owen's view oscillates between the two. There seems to be explicit contrast between Old Testament sacrifices and the sacrifice of Christ: 'the blood of bulls and goats' – 'offered *himself*'. The former sacrifices were made on the altar of

---

[1] *Works*, III:174.

tabernacle and temple; the latter was made by Christ's eternal Spirit, but also, not on a material altar but in the power of the Holy Spirit.[1]

It is interesting to see what Owen is doing here with the text. He is setting the blood of bulls and goats within its redemptive-historical context of temple sacrifice as *type*, and seeing the fulfilment of it, the *antitype*, in the sacrifice of Jesus. On what altar did Jesus make himself the sacrifice? Owen believes that the author of Hebrews (in his view, Paul) is teaching us that no earthly altar can support the weight of an infinite sacrifice. Only the eternal Spirit could bear the weight of an eternal person bearing the weight of human sin.

Owen does not mean to deny the Protestant watchword that Calvary is our only altar. But he wishes to stress that it is the Holy Spirit alone who is capable of bearing the weight of an infinite sacrifice in order that it might be placed before God. While fire consumed the whole burnt offerings of the temple, Christ's true and final sacrifice expressed the kindling of the Spirit, the zeal for the glory of God that consumed him.[2]

Christ thus offers himself in his own eternal Spirit. But at the same time, the eternal Holy Spirit was concursively active in him.

1. He must, first of all, be seen as supporting Jesus in his decision to offer himself to the Father throughout the whole course of his life, with a view to his sacrificial death.

2. He must be seen as the Spirit who sustained Jesus as he came near to the gate of the temple when, in the garden of Gethsemane, he caught sight at close range of the bloody altar that awaited him.

3. That same Spirit held Jesus up in the breaking of his heart and the engulfing of his soul as he experienced the dereliction of Calvary.[3]

But even here Owen is not finished. He adds a deeply moving touch by asking the question: If, on the cross, our Lord Jesus Christ committed his spirit into the hands of his Father, to what did he commit his body? Externally, says Owen, his lifeless body was guarded by the holy angels,

[1] *Works*, XXII:307. In both *Works* III and XXII Owen recognizes the appropriateness of understanding 'eternal Spirit' in Heb. 9:13-14 being either Christ's spirit or the Holy Spirit.
[2] *Ibid.*, III:178.
[3] *Ibid.*, III:176-77.

mounted as a watch over the garden tomb. But internally the Spirit preserved it from corruption in the darkness of Joseph's tomb, just as it had been preserved from corruption by that same Spirit in the darkness of the womb of the virgin Mary.[1] From womb to tomb the devotion of the Spirit to the enfleshed Son was constantly evident. This brings us to a fourth aspect of our Lord's communion with the Spirit.

4. *The exaltation*

The ministry of the Spirit in the life of our Lord is also revealed at the point of our Lord's exaltation. Here again Owen notes that the external works of the Trinity are indivisible. The Father raised up the Son (Acts 2:32); and yet the New Testament also teaches that the Son has power to lay down his life and to take it up again (John 10:17-18). Here Father and Son are together both active in the exaltation of the resurrection.

But Owen also notes the New Testament hints at the role of the Holy Spirit in the resurrection-exaltation of our Lord.[2] The Spirit declared him Son of God with power through the resurrection; the Spirit thereby vindicates him. Nor is this merely a work of resuscitation; it is a work of transformation and of glorification. As Owen puts it, 'He who first made his nature *holy*, now made it *glorious*.'[3] Not only, then, from womb to tomb is the Spirit present powerfully in the life of our Lord, but, we might say, from womb to glory the Spirit has been the companion of every moment of his human experience.

What is the significance of this theology?

For Owen, this communion between the Spirit and the Son, the Son and the Spirit, gives expression to a basic New Testament principle: the Spirit is not to be known apart from Christ, just as Christ cannot be known by us apart from the Spirit. This is true for two reasons:

First, the source of the Spirit's ministry in the believer is Jesus Christ. Jesus the bearer of the Spirit has now become the bestower of the Spirit. And he is the bestower of the Spirit as the one who has been the bearer of the Spirit. To put it otherwise: it is the very Spirit he has borne as

---

[1] *Works*, III:180-81. The whole passage is remarkable for its meditative tenderness.
[2] *Ibid.*, III:181-83.
[3] *Ibid.*, III:183.

incarnate, *and no other*, whom he pours out upon the church on the Day of Pentecost.

Second, because of this intimate relationship between the Spirit and the incarnate Son, the identity in which the Spirit comes to the church and the believer is defined by his intimate relationship to the life of the incarnate Saviour. The Spirit is able to take from what is Christ's and make it known to us, because he has been dynamically active in Christ's incarnate life and ministry. He is intimately knowledgeable about Christ. He is therefore able to bring to believers, from the now-exalted Christ, all the riches of the grace embodied in his humanity. It follows that, if this is the dynamic of his ministry, its goal will inevitably be to transform us into the likeness of Christ. The Spirit takes from the fullness of Christ and brings it to us in order that we may be transformed by his ministry into the likeness of Christ.

This brings us to our second major consideration.

2. The Holy Spirit in communion with the believer

In his farewell discourse, Jesus said that it was to the advantage of his disciples that he was leaving them; in his place the Spirit would come (John 16:7). With an eye to Roman Catholic polemic, shrewdly and somewhat amusingly Owen notes that Reformed believers possess two things Rome denies they have. They have the Vicar of Christ on earth and a priceless relic given to them by Christ—the Holy Spirit! He comes to us shaped, as it were, by Jesus' history and ministry. He is in that sense another Comforter (*alios parakletos*). Having been with Jesus throughout his life and ministry, he can be subjectively to us all that Jesus objectively was. He can bring to us from the fullness of Christ and, therefore, minister to us as the Vicar of Christ. His presence in our lives is the great relic that the Lord Jesus has bestowed upon the church.

Owen is one of relatively few theologians who have spelled out the implications of Peter's words on the Day of Pentecost.[1] Explaining the significance of that event, Peter says—speaking about Christ—that having been exalted to the right hand of God, he has received from the Father the promise of the Holy Spirit (Acts 2:33). Theologians have characteristically noted that Christ is exalted to the right hand of the

[1] *Works*, III:185.

Father and then pours out the Spirit upon the church. What they have not noted is the relationship between these two events: at the point of exaltation a further transaction takes place within the Godhead between the Father and the Son, one prophesied by Jesus: '*I will ask the Father, and he will give you another Helper, to be with you for ever*' (John 14:16). Owen recognizes here the fulfilment of a whole raft of prophecies that run through the Old Testament Scriptures, from God's promise to Abraham that in his seed the nations would be blessed (Gen. 12:3), to, for example, Psalm 2:8: 'Ask of me, and I will make the nations your heritage.'

Here the covenant between the Father and the Son reaches its climactic fulfilment. The Son, having fully obeyed the stipulations of the covenant of redemption, now, on his ascension, returns to the Father and says, 'Father, you promised ... You promised that if I were obedient to death, then I would be exalted and rewarded with a people.' Owen held that now, on his ascension, our Lord Jesus asked for this, in the understanding that only the outpouring of his Spirit could bring it to pass. Only the one who had dwelt upon Jesus could produce a people like Jesus. For this reason, like the true and wise Solomon he is, on his coronation at the right hand of the Father, Jesus asks for the Holy Spirit.

It is upon this gift of the Spirit, asked for, received, and bestowed by Christ, that virtually everything in the Christian life depends. The Spirit is the agent of illumination, the author of regeneration, the sanctifier, the author of spiritual gifts, the Christian's consolation in affliction.[1]

What then is the nature of this ministry of the Spirit? Owen has two ways of answering that question. The first is what we might call the biographical way, tracing the dimensions of the Spirit's ministry in applying redemption in terms of the *ordo salutis*. He uses the example of Augustine as a paradigm of how the Spirit works in bringing us to saving faith.[2] The second answer, on which we will concentrate, is thematic. Here Owen traces not so much the pattern of the application of redemption as the chief characteristics of the believer's communion with the Spirit.

---

[1] Owen deals with these themes throughout *Works*, III and IV.
[2] *Ibid.*, III:337-66.

He believes there are four ways in which the Spirit evidences his presence and power in the believer: indwelling, unction, earnest, and seal. For all practical purposes, he regards unction and earnest as aspects of indwelling. Thus we can reduce his perspective to two essential aspects: indwelling and sealing.

1. Indwelling of the Spirit

The Spirit indwells every believer mysteriously.[1] But he does so, Owen recognizes, personally as the Spirit of Christ.[2] Owen makes a distinction, which he shares with other Puritan writers on this theme, between the indwelling of the Holy Spirit as the Spirit of holiness and his self-manifestation as Comforter. The former is a constant ministry. The Spirit is always, under all circumstances, at all times making us holy. He uses every situation—joys, trials, successes, and failures—to conform us to the image of God's Son.

But the manifestation of the Spirit as Comforter, Owen argues, is a ministry of an intermittent character. While he acts in all circumstances to sanctify us he does not similarly act to bring us a conscious sense of the comforts of the gospel.[3] The point is an important one for Owen, for the simple reason that he believes we need to distinguish between the indwelling of the Spirit (a constant), and the manner in which he manifests that identity in, and to, the consciousness of the individual believer (a variable). One obvious implication of this arises in the doctrine of assurance—in the distinction between assurance that is provided in the gift of Christ, and the manifold sense of it in the believer's conscience.

Nevertheless, Owen holds that the indwelling of the Holy Spirit brings with it several distinct blessings.

(i) The Spirit comes to give the believer direction and guidance[4]— a guidance that is moral and extrinsical, in the sense that the Spirit gives it to us objectively in the word he has indited; a guidance that is internal and efficient as the Holy Spirit illuminates our understanding

---

[1] *Works*, IV:383.

[2] *Ibid.*, XI:333.

[3] He does, of course, provide this comfort to believers 'at all times, and on all occasions wherein they really stand in need of spiritual consolation'. *Ibid.*, IV:379.

[4] *Ibid.*, XI:342-46.

of the Scriptures. In addition he enables us to embrace the teaching Scripture gives us as well as the providences that govern our lives under the sovereign hand of God.

This, for Owen, is tantamount to what the New Testament means when it speaks of the anointing of the Spirit (1 John 2:20, 27). Christian believers do not need teachers in this context because they have received the anointing that enables them to apply Scripture.

(ii) The Spirit comes to give support; in terms of Romans 8:26ff., he helps us in our infirmities.[1] He does this by the application of the Scriptures, illumining their force, relevance, and practical application to us:

> And this he doth every day. How often, when the spirits of the saints are ready to faint within them, when straits and perplexities are round about them, that they know not what to do, nor whither to apply themselves for help or supportment, doth the Spirit that dwelleth in them bring to mind some seasonable, suitable promise of Christ, that bears them up quite above their difficulties and distractions, opening such a new spring of life and consolation to their souls as that they who but now stooped, yea were almost bowed to the ground, do stand upright, and feel no weight or burden at all! Oftentimes they go for water to the well, and are not able to draw; or, if it be poured out upon them, it comes like rain on a stick that is fully dry. They seek to promises for refreshment, and find no more savour in them than in the white of an egg; but when the same promises are brought to remembrance by the Spirit the Comforter, who is with them and in them, how full of life and power are they![2]

In addition the Spirit brings consolation by storing up graces to enable believers to cope. Here Owen appeals to Romans 5:3-5. The Spirit pours out God's love into our hearts, and thereby 'sets all our graces to work'.[3]

(iii) Even more significantly, the Spirit comes to exercise an ongoing but internal restraint on Christians' lives, and in Owen's quaint phrase, 'drops an awe upon their spirits'[4] to safeguard them against running

---

[1] *Works*, XI:346-48.
[2] *Ibid.*, XI:347.
[3] *Ibid.*, XI:348.
[4] *Ibid.*, XI:349.

headlong into sin. The Spirit brings a gladness to obedience, banishing our native sluggishness. Peter is the paradigm here: 'Peter was broken loose, and running down hill apace, denying and forswearing his Master', but Christ restrained him.[1] This, in turn, becomes for Owen a paradigm of the work of the other Comforter, the Holy Spirit, who inwardly 'drops an awe' upon our spirits that causes this holy restraint in order that we may not fall into sin.

A question of conscience

Against that background, Owen raises a strategically important question. How do we distinguish between the directions of the Spirit of grace in his guiding and governing of our lives, and the delusions of the spirit of the world and of our own sinful heart? How do we distinguish the promptings of the Holy Spirit from the promptings of our own inclinations? He suggests four marks of the leading of the Spirit, by which it is to be contrasted to the instinct of the flesh or the leading of the world.[2]

(i) The leading of the Spirit, he says, is *regular*—in the literal sense: according to the *regulam*—the rule (of Scripture). It is axiomatic for Owen that the Spirit does not work in us to give us a new rule of life, but to bring us light on the rule contained in Scripture and new power to obey its injunctions. In that sense for Owen the fundamental question to ask about guidance will be: Is this course of action consistent with the word of God?

(ii) The commands of the Spirit, the directives with which the Spirit prompts us through the teaching of Scripture, are *not grievous* (1 John 5:3). They are in harmony with the word, and the word is in harmony with the new creation. To that extent, the Christian believer consciously submitted to the word of God will find pleasure in obeying that word, even though there be attendant pain.

(iii) The 'motions' or actions of the Spirit, Owen says, are *orderly*. Just as the covenant of God is ordered in all things and secure (2 Sam. 23:5), so the chief gift of that covenant, the indwelling Spirit, is orderly in the way in which he deals with us. Owen translates this into flesh and blood terms. Here is someone, Owen envisages, who claims frequently

---

[1] *Works*, XI:349.
[2] For what follows see *Ibid.*, XI:363-64.

that the Holy Spirit is leading them, but whose life is characterized by a deep instability.

> We see some poor souls to be in such bondage as to be hurried up and down, in the matter of duties, at the pleasure of Satan. They must run from one to another, and commonly neglect that which they should do.

One can almost see particular members of the congregations Owen pastored in his mind's eye as he continues:

> When they are at prayer, then they should be at the work of their calling; and when they are at their calling, they are tempted for not laying all aside and running to prayer. Believers know that this is not from the Spirit of God, which makes 'every thing beautiful in its season'.[1]

(iv) The 'motions' of the Spirit always tend to *glorify God* according to his word.

The Spirit, who thus indwells and leads believers, is given as an earnest, a pledge, a down-payment on final redemption. This means that the Spirit of Christ is here and now *both* the foretaste of future glory, and *also* an indication of the incompleteness of all present spiritual experience.

This principle is a major clue to Owen's response to the influence of the 'inner light' teaching in his own day (which is not without parallels in our day). He placed great emphasis in his teaching on the struggle of the believer to overcome indwelling sin. In response to antithetical appeals to a supposed liberty of the Spirit which set the Christian free from such low-level spirituality, it was enough for Owen to point out that the Spirit, who is the earnest of our inheritance, is the one who causes our groanings: 'we ourselves, who have the firstfruits of the Spirit, groan inwardly as we wait eagerly for adoption as sons, the redemption of our bodies' (Rom. 8:23). The recognition of this simultaneity of groaning and anticipating stabilizes the Christian in the context of misleading teaching.

---

[1] *Works*, XI:364.

2. *The sealing of the Spirit*

Owen was intensely interested in what Scripture means when it speaks about believers being sealed with the Spirit (Eph. 1:13; 4:30). He was conscious also that the Reformed tradition he inherited had not always exegeted Paul's thought here with complete unanimity.[1] Indeed, as late as 1667 Owen wrote about the sealing of the Spirit: 'I am not very clear on the certain particular intendment of this metaphor.'[2]

Here it is worth noting, in parenthesis, that if Owen had the wisdom and courage to say 'I am not completely certain what this text of Scripture means', we should not be slow to share his modesty. Indeed, it is one of the blessings of Reformed theology's sense of the incomprehensible greatness of God that it recognizes we do not know all of the answers!

In his great work on *Communion with God*, published in 1667, Owen reasoned that it is the promises of God, not the persons who receive them, that are in view in the first instance in this sealing: God seals his promises to the believer. And so he concludes that we are sealed when we enjoy a fresh sense of the love of God within us and a comfortable persuasion of acceptance with God. The promises of God—the promises of grace in salvation—are sealed to us and we, correspondingly, enter into the enjoyment of him. The objective produces the subjective.

But in his posthumously published work on the Holy Spirit as Comforter,[3] which emerged from the presses in 1693, ten years after his death, Owen writes, it would seem, more confidently and definitively on the sealing of the Spirit. He notes that

> The *effects of this sealing* are gracious operations of the Holy Spirit in and upon believers; but *the sealing itself* is the communication of the Spirit unto them.[4]

The effects of this sealing are the gracious operations of the Holy Spirit in the believer; the sealing itself is the communication of the Spirit to the believer. Here, conscious of discussions that had taken place, not

---

[1] For further discussion see Sinclair B. Ferguson, *John Owen on the Christian Life* (Edinburgh: Banner of Truth Trust, 1987), pp. 116-24.
[2] *Works*, II:242.
[3] *Ibid.*, IV:353-419.
[4] *Ibid.*, IV:404 (emphasis added).

least among highly-esteemed members of the Puritan brotherhood (such
as Richard Sibbes, John Preston, and Thomas Goodwin, who regarded
the sealing as 'a second work' of grace giving an immediate assurance of
salvation), Owen goes on to note:

> It hath been generally conceived that this sealing with the Spirit is
> that which gives assurance unto believers,—and so indeed it doth,
> although the way whereby it doth it hath not been rightly appre-
> hended; and, therefore, none have been able to declare the especial
> nature of that act of the Spirit whereby he seals us, whence such
> assurance should ensue. But it is indeed not any act of the Spirit in
> us that is the ground of our assurance, but the communication of
> the Spirit unto us.[1]

Here is a wise and mature man dealing sensitively with a difficult
theological and pastoral issue. His basic distinction is clear enough. He
is saying the sealing of the Spirit does indeed bring assurance, but the
sealing of the Spirit is not to be thought of as a specific act of the Spirit,
so much as the act of the communication of the Spirit to us. In essence,
for Owen *the Spirit himself is the seal.* In that context—and here we come
near to the entry point of our discussion—he moves back to the basic
principle that the Lord Jesus Christ is the one whom the Father sealed
(John 6:27). This can only mean that the Father communicated the
Spirit to him without measure. What was true of Christ then, *mutatis
mutandis*, becomes true of believers.

Clearly in this context Owen is anxious not to diminish the role of
the Spirit in giving a powerful assurance of salvation in Jesus Christ
through his indwelling. He is simply making the exegetical point that
this is not the precise meaning of the Scriptures to which appeal is made.
Rather the Spirit is himself the seal. As he ministers, assurance of grace
and salvation follow. The testimony of the Spirit, to put it in these terms,
is an effect of the presence of the Spirit as seal and activates the believer's
sense of assurance; it is not the seal itself.

Owen provides a vivid and colourful word-picture of this in
his exposition of communion with God. While it is nuanced in a

[1] *Works*, IV:405. Cf. his earlier comments, pp. 400-1.

distinctively Owenian way, his thinking is characteristic of many of his Puritan brethren:

> The soul, by the power of its own conscience, is brought before the law of God. There a man puts in his plea,—that he is a child of God, that he belongs to God's family; and for this end produceth all his evidences, every thing whereby faith gives him an interest in God.

The issue is clear: Is this man a believer? He responds: 'I am a believer. Here is the basis of my conviction that I belong to God's family; here are the evidences. These are the things that faith has wrought.' But, says Owen,

> Satan, in the meantime, opposeth with all his might; sin and law assist him; many flaws are found in his evidences; the truth of them all is questioned; and the soul hangs in suspense as to the issue. In the midst of the plea and contest the Comforter comes, and, by a word of promise or otherwise, overpowers the heart with a comfortable persuasion (and bears down all objections) that his plea is good, and that he is a child of God. ... When our spirits are pleading their right and title, he comes in and bears witness on our side ...
>
> When the Lord Jesus Christ at one word stilled the raging of the sea and wind, all that were with him knew there was divine power at hand, Matt 8:25-27. And when the Holy Ghost by one word stills the tumults and storms that are raised in the soul, giving it an immediate calm and security, it knows his divine power, and rejoices in his presence.[1]

In a word, Owen is saying the Spirit does in us as seal what Christ did for the disciples as Saviour.

This final reference to Matthew 8:25-27 is particularly telling and poignant to those who are familiar with the biography of John Owen. Here, for a moment, in this magisterial work of rich trinitarian theology, like a great artist he paints himself into a small corner of his own masterwork. For it was through a sermon on this text, preached

[1] *Works*, II:241-42.

by an unknown substitute for the great Edmund Calamy (whom the young Owen had hoped to hear), that his years of spiritual struggle were brought to an end. He had then emerged from the grey areas of uncertainty to a deep and lasting assurance. Here, as it were, is the theological formulation of the reality Owen had experienced in a memorably personal way.

It is fitting for us to conclude our brief consideration of Owen's teaching on the Holy Spirit on this note. In that life-defining experience the knowledge of the truth had become the knowledge of the *power* of the truth.

Summary of Owen's teaching

In summary, then, the ministry of the Spirit will always affect believers in these three ways:

(i) Since the Holy Spirit is the third person of the Godhead, the one who proceeds from the Father and the Son, the Eternal Spirit, *he is to be worshipped, loved, and adored.* Owen well understood that the Holy Spirit, in relationship to Christ, does not bring glory to himself but to the Son. But the Spirit's commitment to bring glory to the Son does not justify our failure to give glory to the Spirit as well as to the Son. The role of the Spirit within the trinitarian economy does not minimize his full deity, nor does it exempt us from admiration, adoration, praise, and devotion to the one who so lovingly shines on the Son and comes to believers as the Spirit of grace. Here Owen's trinitarianism needs to be recovered. And this means learning to worship, as well as to engage in fellowship with, the Holy Spirit.

(ii) The Holy Spirit's work is to *reproduce in us the holiness of Christ.* We must therefore never resist him in this ministry. Rather, as Owen expounds in detail in his great work on the mortification of sin,[1] by the power of the Spirit we are to put to death all that remains in us that is alien to our Lord.

(iii) If as the *Eternal* Spirit he is to be worshipped, and as the Holy Spirit he reproduces the holiness of Christ, then as the indwelling Spirit he is *not to be grieved* (Eph. 4:30). To grieve someone, says Owen, is to

---

[1] *Works*, VI:1-86.

display the unkindness of unrequited love. In the case of the Spirit it is the 'defect of an answerable love unto the fruits and testimonies of his love which we have received'.[1]

To grieve the Holy Spirit is by our lives to disappoint him who has loved us with an eternal love. And so Owen pleads with us: We are the recipients of signal mercies; will we not return to him the holy love he seeks from our hearts, the full obedience he desires to work in our lives?

Such grieving of the Holy Spirit, Owen believes, is heightened precisely because of the intimacy of the Spirit with the Son and the intimacy of the Spirit with the believer. He who dwells in us loves our Saviour; he who dwells in us loves us, because Christ is our Saviour. Those who love us most are most grieved by us when we fail. So it is, says Owen, with the Spirit.

Or to use the words of a greater even than Owen, 'And do not grieve the Holy Spirit of God, by whom you were sealed for the day of redemption' (Eph. 4:30).

[1] *Works*, IV:414.

CHAPTER FIFTEEN

JOHN OWEN ON CHRISTIAN PIETY

WHEN John Owen passed from this world into the immediate presence of Christ, on August 24, 1683, his physicians ascribed the lingering character of his death 'to the strength of his brain'. There is a sense in which their words epitomize the common view of his life! To pick up his seven-volume commentary on Hebrews, for example, is to be impressed by the magisterial nature of his scholarship. To read his work on perseverance—an extended book review which stretches to some 700 pages—is to be staggered by his massive intellectual persistence.

But to see only this would be to misunderstand John Owen. At least he would have thought so. This is how he puts it himself:

> What am I the better if I can dispute that Christ is God, but have no sense of sweetness in my heart from hence that he is a God in covenant with my soul? What will it avail me to evince, by testimonies and arguments, that he hath made satisfaction for sin, if through my unbelief, the wrath of God abideth on me? ... Will it be any advantage to me, in the issue, to profess and dispute that God works the conversion of a sinner by the irresistible grace of his Spirit, if I was never acquainted experimentally with the deadness and utter impotence to good . . . which is in my own soul by nature? ... It is the power of truth in the heart alone that will make us cleave unto it indeed in an hour of temptation. Let us, then, not think that we are any thing the better for our conviction of the truths of the great doctrines of the gospel ... unless we find the power of the truths abiding in our own hearts.[1]

[1] Owen, *Works*, XII:52.

These words, and many like them with which the writings of Owen abound, are sufficient evidence that he was not merely a great theologian. That was never his aspiration. His own desire was to be a true Christian, a living child of God, and not as he saw some men were, simply a walking, talking skeleton in religion. For that reason, as many of his written works bear witness, his great concern in life was the promotion of Christian piety—and a study of what he had to say in this area will indicate, in some measure, the great service that has been rendered to those engaged in pastoral, practical, biblical ministry, by the continuing availability of his works.

Why was Owen so concerned to teach about Christian piety? There is a very simple answer. He was concerned to see it develop in his own heart—and he came therefore to the teaching of it from his own personal search for acceptance with God and perseverance in faith. When he spoke of the difference between the knowledge of truth and the power of the truth, he was speaking about himself.

Born in 1616 the son of a minister of Puritan convictions, Owen went to Oxford at the age of 12, and graduated some four years later as a Bachelor of Arts. But for all his background, he knew no settled peace with God; in fact the anonymous memoir of his life which appeared in 1720, thirty-seven years after his death, hinted that for a period of some five years he had lived through deep melancholy of spirit. Then, going with his cousin to hear the famous Edmund Calamy at Aldermanbury Chapel one day, he discovered to his disappointment that a total stranger entered the pulpit, and preached from Matthew 8:26—'Why are ye fearful, O ye of little faith?' From that day on, while never managing to discover the identity of the messenger of God, Owen knew what it was to enjoy the love of God shed abroad in his heart by the Spirit, and to walk in the assurance of forgiveness and grace. He discovered the difference between the truth and what he so often calls 'the power of the truth in the heart'—and most of what he penned or preached thereafter was marked by a personal concern for Christian piety.

But what did Owen think of as Christian piety? It is essentially *the fruit* of the sanctifying ministry of the Holy Spirit; the obedience of faith; the exercise of spiritual life, which is the outworking of the seed of divine holiness planted in the life of the child of God. To put it in other words, it is the pattern of life produced in the believer by the divine pattern of salvation.

In fact this is virtually a universalizable theological axiom: to a greater or lesser extent every Christian's view of the Christian life, and of Christian piety, is a reflection of his understanding of the nature of the history of redemption. The individual's experience is a microcosmic reflection of the macrocosm of the whole drama of salvation which is expounded in the Scriptures. That was so with Owen. His view of the history of redemption was that God approached man through four covenants: the Covenant of Works, the Covenant of Grace, behind which lay the Covenant of Redemption, and the Covenant at Sinai, which Owen regarded not as the Covenant of Grace, but as a *foedus subserviens*, a republication of the terms of the Covenant of Works under the era of the Covenant of Grace, but not itself the Covenant of Grace. It was logical, and inevitable, therefore, that his whole theology, and his teaching on the nature of Christian piety, should be dominated by this covenant framework.

The result is that when Owen comes to define his teaching, he thinks of sanctification in general as the principle of holiness imparted by the Spirit, producing the fruit of Christian piety because it is attended with 'its exercise in acts and duties of holy obedience unto God'.[1] This seed is the beginning of renewal in the image of God, and enables men, 'from a spiritual and habitual principle of grace, to yield obedience unto God, according unto the tenor and terms of the covenant, by virtue of the life and death of Jesus Christ'.[2]

Now, two basic things emerge from this. (1) The first is that, whether latent or patent, Owen's view of the Christian life is based on his covenant theology. We should therefore anticipate that his teaching will run on what we might call the *indicative/imperative* axis: that is, it is the grace of God which saves a man, sovereignly and freely, and it is out of that grace that all the responsibilities of obedience flow. (2) Furthermore, we should anticipate that his teaching will run on a *negative/positive*

[1] *Works*, III:370.
[2] *Ibid.*, III:386.

axis—just as Christ was put to death in relationship to sin, and was raised to newness of resurrection life and fellowship with God, similarly the pattern of the believer's experience will unite in itself *negatively*, death to sin in its various dimensions, and *positively*, the reception of grace in the fellowship of spiritual resurrection and union with Christ. In fact this is exactly what we find in Owen's teaching.

By way of introduction, we may emphasize four elements:

1. The foundation of Christian piety

At the heart of Owen's teaching on the Christian life lies the tremendous emphasis he places on union with Christ. It is 'the principle and measure of all spiritual enjoyments and expectations'.[1] He is conscious of the glory of this union, because it is based upon Christ's union with us in our frail flesh. That flesh he took, in the virgin's womb, uniting it with his own person, sanctifying it by the Spirit, maturing it as he grew in favour with God in his life of obedience, dying in union with it for our sakes, and, by the gift of the Spirit in his ascended glory, making its perfections available to us for our own sanctification. The divine image is restored for us in Christ: we are united to him in faith through the Spirit; the Spirit, who is the bond of our union with him, consequently transforms us into that same image, from one degree of glory to another.

This image then is restored by union *at regeneration*; it is given as a seed. It is, therefore, out of this seed that the new life begins to grow.

The immediate consequence of this union for the believer is the destruction of the dominion of sin. This is not the same as the banishing of sin's presence—but it is the real destruction of the reign of sin. And while, in common with most of the Reformers and Puritans, Owen struggled to clarify the terminology of Romans 6 and related passages confused, he did grasp the very heart of the matter by seeing that the foundation of sanctification, indeed, sanctification itself, is fundamentally accomplished at regeneration through union with the holy Son of God. It is really quite striking to see that Owen gives germinal expression to the emphasis—which centuries later, John Murray worked out in his

[1] *Works*, XX:146.

266

treatment of definitive sanctification[1]—that while final deliverance from
the presence of sin is still awaited, yet the decisive breach with sin has
already been accomplished. This was Owen's view:

> Indeed, in vocation it [sanctification] seems to be included expressly.
> For whereas it is effectual vocation that is intended, wherein a holy
> principle of spiritual life, or faith itself, is communicated unto
> us, our sanctification radically, and as the effect in its adequate
> immediate cause, is contained in it. Hence we are said to be 'called
> to be saints' [Rom. 1:7], which is the same with being 'sanctified in
> Christ Jesus' [1 Cor. 1:2]. And in many other places sanctification is
> included in vocation.[2]

Similarly, in his work on the Holy Spirit, he puts it like this:

> All the elect are sanctified by the Holy Ghost. And this regeneration
> is the head, fountain, or beginning of our sanctification, virtually
> comprising the whole in itself …[3]

Now, Owen is not saying that the presence of sin has been vanquished.
But he does see the force of Romans 6:14 in these terms: 'That sin which
is *in you* shall not *have dominion over you.*'[4] The *nature* of sin remains
unchanged, but its *status* within the believer is dramatically altered. This
is one of the linchpins in any truly biblical pastoral theology. Owen
found the same pastoral problems as we do, and he puts it like this:
There are two problems we have in connection with sin: the *first* is
persuading those who remain unconverted that they are in fact under its
power and sway. That is the task of evangelism. But the *second* problem
sometimes seems equally intractable—it is the difficulty of persuading
believers that they are not under the dominion of sin! Anyone who has
made some attempt at preaching on such passages as Romans 6:1ff or
Colossians 2–3 will sympathize here with Owen. There is no point of
teaching at which people are more likely to drag in their experience than
this, and to interpret Scripture in the light of that instead of in its own

---

[1] Murray, *Collected Writings*, II:277ff.
[2] *Works*, V:131.
[3] *Ibid.*, III:299.
[4] *Ibid.*, VII:506.

light, to talk to Scripture instead of listening to it. Here then is a word
of encouragement: Owen faced the same problem! And yet, he saw that
this was one of the great secrets of successful Christian living: 'It is the
great interest of a soul conflicting with the power of sin to secure itself
against its dominion, that it is not under its dominion.'[1]

The great danger he saw, as we also see, is that people tend to confuse
the *presence* of sin with the *dominion* of sin; and until we separate these
two things, and distinguish them, it is virtually impossible to grasp hold
of this great truth which lies so near to the heart of Reformed piety. This
is what it means, for Owen, to be in covenant with God: it is his support
in distress:

> He goes to God and saith, 'Thou art my God; thou shalt undertake
> for me. ... I am not in the hand of sin, nor in the hand of my
> enemies' ... He betakes himself to God's covenant, and there he
> finds rest.[2]

Perhaps a word of exhortation here is not out of place. The emphasis
that Reformed theology places upon the irreconcilable war which
takes place in the believer can be preached in such a way that there is a
tendency to ignore what lies at the heart of that war, and what fills the
believer with assurance in it—namely that he has, indeed, died to sin's
dominion. Professor Murray expresses Owen's thrust well:

> We are too ready to give heed to what we deem to be the hard,
> empirical facts of Christian profession, and we have erased the clear
> line of demarcation which Scripture defines. As a result we have
> lost our vision of the high calling of God in Christ Jesus. Our ethic
> has lost its dynamic and we have become conformed to this world.
> We know not the power of death to sin in the death of Christ,
> and we are not able to bear the rigour of the liberty of redemptive
> emancipation.[3]

We are dealing here with the very heart of Reformed piety, and it is
essential for us to see it. The foundation of Christian piety is that a seed

---

[1] *Works*, VII:556.
[2] *Ibid.*, IX:415.
[3] John Murray, *Principles of Conduct* (London: Tyndale Press, 1957), p. 205.

has been planted within us—in which the dominion of sin is broken. Owen stresses two things about this seed:

(1) *It is universal in its influence.* Here we have the obverse of total depravity. Total sanctification; but not total perfection. This sanctification, says Owen, 'is the immediate work of God by his Spirit upon our *whole* nature'.[1] In view is the *universal* renewal of our natures by the Holy Spirit. No part of life may remain unaffected by it.

(2) *It is capable of development.* The whole point of using the metaphor of 1 John 3:9 of the presence of the divine seed, or *sperma*, in the believer is that it lends itself to the idea of progress, growth, and development. Holiness and piety are subject to degrees. Indeed, they are fed by experience: 'Experience is the food of all grace, which it grows and thrives upon.'[2] This thought brings a sense of direction and stability therefore to all the experiences of life:

> All our relations, all our afflictions, all our temptations, all our mercies, all our enjoyments, all occurrences are suited to a continual adding of the exercise of one grace to another, wherein holiness is increased.[3]

In this context it is interesting, and does not go unnoticed by Owen, that the illustrations and metaphors of Scripture for Christian progress are generally horticultural and not in any sense mechanical. Consequently the development and growth of Christian grace and piety are not something to be anticipated with mechanical regularity. Like a plant, the Christian grows, not by constant equal stages of development, but 'by sudden gusts and motions ... so the growth of believers consists principally in some intense, vigorous actings of grace on great occasions'.[4]

And here, in a sense, we return to base. It was suggested earlier that our view of piety is a reflection of our view of salvation. Owen's view was that salvation was not achieved by an evolving process, but by successive interventions of Almighty God in the pursuit of his covenant. So, while we walk in the way of duty constantly, as we will see, God pursues his

---

[1] Owen, *Works*, III:369.
[2] *Ibid.*, III:390.
[3] *Ibid.*, III:391.
[4] *Ibid.*, III:397.

plan in the life of the believer by these intense actings of grace. This work of his is all the more necessary when we turn to a second theme:

2. The opposition to Christian piety

We have seen that Owen makes a clear-cut distinction between the end of the dominion of sin, and the end of the presence of sin. His maxim is this: 'That sin which is *in you* shall not have *dominion over you*.'[1] There is the balance: sin has lost its dominion, but not its potency; it is sin still, says Owen, and it therefore seeks to usurp its former dominion in the experience of the believer; it is his 'inbred traitor'[2] and is altogether and permanently opposed to the progress of God's gracious work in our lives.

Of course, in Owen's teaching, opposition to holiness comes from more than indwelling sin and the flesh. It comes from Satan; it comes from the many sources of temptation we encounter in the world. But the landing-ground for both of these is in the human heart, and in the Christian in the remnants of corruption in indwelling sin.

We ought to focus attention on this area even if briefly.

Indwelling sin manifests itself in what Owen calls 'aversation to God'; it is revealed most clearly, he writes, in the private duties of the spiritual life; it appears in the *affections*, producing a weariness towards the actual exercise of faith; it appears in the *mind*, producing an inability to engage seriously in meditation on God's word, and especially on the Lord Jesus Christ. The great privilege of what Owen calls fixing the mind on Christ and filling the heart with him is squandered under this influence.

But the opposition of indwelling sin appears more directly, in two ways:

1. The brutality of indwelling sin

Indwelling sin, Owen says, is epitomized in Scripture as a lusting and a fighting.

> First, it lusts, stirring and moving inordinate figments in the mind, desires in the appetite and the affections, proposing them to the will. But it rests not there, it cannot rest; it urgeth, presseth, and pursueth

---

[1] *Works*, VII:506.
[2] *Ibid.*, VI:306.

its proposals with earnestness, strength and vigour, fighting, and contending, and warring to obtain its end and purpose.[1]

There is, says Owen, a violent pressure in it, 'like an untamed horse, which, having first cast off his rider, runs away with fierceness and rage'.[2] But sin indwelling is not only brutal in its operations. Owen further emphasizes:

2. *The subtlety of indwelling sin*

Sin deceives men. In several places Owen emphasizes that Scripture warns us to 'be not deceived'. We have already sensed the importance of this in the believer. Indwelling sin may deceive the believer, and confuse him into thinking that *present* sin is *reigning* sin. This subtle but important deception is very wide-ranging. It operates in four stages or degrees:

(1) It deceives by drawing the mind away from its anchor in Christian holiness. It draws the mind from a sense of its own sinfulness, which is one of the great God-given preservatives against sin. It draws the mind away too from those duties which preserve it in a frame of fellowship with Christ—so that it becomes callous and insensitive to the sovereignty of God, the deceitfulness of sin itself, and also to the love of the Father, the grace of the Son, and the power of the Spirit.

(2) When the mind is thus drawn from its duty, the affections are more readily enticed, and, in Owen's words, 'stir up frequent imaginations about the proposed object'.[3] So he puts it:

> Sin, when it presseth upon the soul to this purpose, will use a thousand wiles to hide from it the terror of the Lord, the end of transgressions, and especially of that peculiar folly which it solicits the mind unto. *Hopes of pardon* shall be used to hide it; and *future repentance* shall hide it; and *present importunity* of lust shall hide it; *occasions and opportunities* shall hide it: *surprisals* shall hide it; *extenuation* of sin shall hide it; *balancing of duties* against it shall hide it; *fixing the imagination* on present objects shall hide it; *desperate*

[1] *Works*, VI:195.
[2] *Ibid.*, VI:208.
[3] *Ibid.*, VI:245.

resolutions to venture the uttermost for the enjoyment of lust in its pleasures and profits shall hide it. A thousand wiles it hath, which cannot be recounted.[1]

(3) The third stage is the conception of sin. 'Desire, when it has conceived,' says James, 'gives birth to sin' (James 2:15). The will is invaded by its power. By deceiving the mind no distinction remains clearly engraved in the believer between the pardon which sets us free from sinning, and the pardon which sets us free for sin. When this stage of practical antinomianism is reached in the mind, then the will is loosened from all the right principles which safeguard it from being entangled in the web of sin.

(4) This leads, fourthly, to the accomplishing of sin, and its actual performance. The frightening thing to Owen is that the greatest of men have fallen here: Noah, Lot, David—'not men of ordinary size, but higher than their brethren, by the shoulders and upwards, in profession, yea, in real holiness'.[2] Lot, for example—

> saw, as one speaks, '*hell coming out of heaven*' upon unclean sinners; the greatest evidence, except the cross of Christ, that God ever gave in his providence of the judgment to come. He saw himself and children delivered by the special care and miraculous hand of God; and yet, while these strange mercies were fresh upon him, he fell into *drunkenness and incest*.[3]

So, the alarming thing for the believer who has gazed upon the immolation of his Saviour on the cross is that he may yet turn from that under the deceit of sin, and live as though he himself had not shared in that death by grace and faith. And such leads, says Owen, to 'an obdurate course in sinning, that finisheth, consummates, and shuts up the whole work of sin, whereon ensues death or eternal ruin'.[4]

One unmortified sin weakens every grace!—and the result is that sin 'becomes to the soul like a moth in a garment, to cut and devour the

---

[1] *Works*, VI:249.
[2] *Ibid.*, VI:279.
[3] *Ibid.*, VI:280.
[4] *Ibid.*, VI:216.

strongest threads of it, so that though the whole hang loose together, it is easily torn to pieces'.[1]
It is this situation which lends significance to the third area of our investigation. For one of Owen's great antidotes to the menace of opposition is his emphasis on duty. And this we can consider under the heading:

3. The elements in Christian piety

If we were to ask what the major differences are between the Reformed teaching on Christian piety and much contemporary teaching—one part of the answer would surely be the loss of the fear of God and a sense of duty which is prevalent, if not rampant, in the church today. This was certainly one of Owen's own emphases, for he uses the expression 'duty' very frequently, and employs the idea constantly. And, once again, the reason for this is embedded in his view of the Christian life as an expression of the salvation of a covenant-keeping God: to be in covenant with him is to have unconditional obligations laid upon our lives. This is what he calls *the gospel method*.

> This is the method of the gospel, which the apostle Paul observeth in all his epistles; first he declares the *mysteries of faith* that are peculiar to the gospel, and then descends unto those *moral duties* which are regulated thereby.[2]

The gospel '*grafts all duties* of moral obedience on this stock of faith in Christ'.[3]

Owen underlines four significant characteristics of duties in the Christian life:

(1) *They are consistent with the new nature.* This is the beauty of them. 'There is *no duty of holiness whatever*, but there is a *disposition* in a sanctified heart unto it.'[4]

The true believer loves the duties of his Lord, and this leads, however imperfectly, yet at least consistently, to his delight in them. The law of

[1] *Works*, VI:299.
[2] *Ibid.*, III:279.
[3] *Ibid.*
[4] *Ibid.*, III:485.

273

God is written in his heart, and so there is a correspondence between the external law which gives direction to his life, and the inner law which gives him the spiritual disposition towards it. Duties are part of the inherent harmony and consistency, therefore, of God's operations of covenant grace (Jer. 31:33; Ezek. 36:26-27).

While this is so,

(2) *Duties cannot be performed without the Spirit's aid.* There is no virtue in 'spiritual experiences' if the Christian ceases to be dependent upon the Spirit. The seed of obedience needs to be watered from above, to be nourished and cherished, if it is to grow. It is then 'the way of the Spirit of God to excite us unto special duties'.[1]

(3) *Duties are performed in faith.* This is to repeat what Owen had said in general terms: duties are grafted on to the stalk of faith in Christ. So there is all the difference in the world between the dutiful believer and the legalist. It is not only through faith that duties become evangelical—but wonderfully, through faith they also become enjoyable!

(4) *Duties are defined in Scripture.* The will of God is the rule of man's obedience, says Owen. And he puts it even more clearly: 'all our graces and duties must be tried, as unto any acceptation with God. Whatever pretends to exceed the direction of the word may safely be rejected—cannot safely be admitted.'[2]

This fourth emphasis is highly significant. It is the application of the Puritan view of Scripture to the Puritan view of the Christian life. It is the hallmark of Puritan Christianity. And it helps to explain one of the most striking of all differences between Reformed piety and evangelical piety in many of its contemporary forms. This emphasis on duty, revealed in Scripture, explains why little discussion is to be found in Owen's writings on 'the problem of guidance'. The word 'guidance' in this sense scarcely appears in Owen, and has very little, if any, place in his thought—because at the forefront of his pastoral concern was the desire to bring his people to walk worthily of the Lord according to Scripture. And that major concern delivered him from so many of the minor subjective concerns that tend to dominate our contemporary discussions of divine guidance. And perhaps more importantly, because

[1] *Works*, XX:365.
[2] *Ibid.*, I:143.

Owen was just as familiar with mystical evangelical piety as we are, his teaching delivered his people from a subjective uncertainty into a biblical responsibility. And the service of God in obedience to his word was, for Owen, the enjoyment of perfect freedom.

In more particular terms, Owen suggests throughout his writings that the believer has two special responsibilities by way of duty. The first is to honour Christ, the second to deal with sin.

(i) The duty to honour Christ

The acts and duties of the Christian life, Owen affirms, 'have all their formal nature and reason from their respect and relation unto the person of Christ'.[1] But how then do we honour Christ? In the following three ways:

(a) *By worshipping him.* If union with Christ is the foundation of Reformed piety, for Owen, then, worshipping Jesus is its heart. He is to be honoured with the Father, with honour that is 'divine, sacred, religious, and supreme', and 'with the same faith, love, reverence, and obedience, always, in all things, in all acts and duties of religion whatever'.[2] Owen frequently sees Christ as fulfilling the twin pictures of his work in Revelation 5: he is to be adored, for his incarnation and humiliation as the Lamb of God; and for his exaltation to the throne of God as the Lion of the tribe of Judah.

(b) *By obeying him.* If we love Christ, then we keep his commandments, not merely externally, says Owen, but wholeheartedly.

Christ transforms the concept of obedience into an evangelical grace. This is Owen's understanding of John's reference to the old and new commandment, 1 John 2:7-8. If mediated only by Moses, obedience is legal; when mediated by Christ, obedience to the divine law becomes evangelical, because it is motivated by love, so that,

> there is, and ought to be in all believers, a divine, gracious love unto the person of Christ, immediately fixed on him, whereby they are excited unto, and acted in, all their obedience unto his authority.[3]

[1] *Works*, I:104.
[2] *Ibid.*, I:106.
[3] *Ibid.*, I:140.

This again is, or certainly ought to be, a further hallmark of Reformed piety: love for Jesus.

(c) *By conforming to him.* Christ, says Owen, is not only our Saviour, but he is so as 'the pattern and example of the renovation of the image of God in us, and of the glory that doth ensue thereon'.[1] And this is the pattern to which we are actively to conform ourselves in the fulfilment of all our duties. We are to model ourselves on Christ's whole conversation while he was on the earth, and especially his meekness and self-denial, or as Owen puts it in a phrase strongly reminiscent of Calvin, we are to display in all things a 'readiness for the cross'.[2]

In view of the opposition to piety even within the Christian's heart, it is inevitable that duties also have a strongly negative character to them. Here the chief duty is plain:

(ii) The duty to deal with sin
The actual mortification of sin springs from the believer's union with Christ in his death to sin. That union, says Owen, obliges us always to be mortifying indwelling corruption. This is how he puts it: 'The choicest believers, who are assuredly freed from the condemning power of sin, ought yet to make it their business all their days to mortify the indwelling power of sin.'[3]

But why are we under this obligation? Because we are united to a Saviour who died to sin that we might no longer live in it. Not to mortify sin is tantamount to denying Christ and repudiating both the cross and our union with him on it. It is to deny the Spirit who brings the benefits of Christ and his cross into the heart.

What, then, is mortification? Owen first tells us what it is not.

(a) *It is not to root out and destroy sin.* That is certainly what is aimed at, but it is not accomplishable in this life. Mortification is not eradication.

(b) *It is not dissimulation*—for then a man has 'got another heart than he had, that is more cunning; not a new heart, that is more holy'.[4]

---

[1] *Works*, I:170.
[2] *Ibid.*, I:176; cf. Calvin, *Institutes*, III.viii.
[3] *Ibid.*, VI:7.
[4] *Ibid.*, VI:25.

(c) *Nor is it the development of a quiet and sedate nature,* as Owen puts
it, for outward disposition may belie a heart that is 'a standing sink of
all abominations'.[1]

(d) *Nor is it the diversion of sin, or the merely occasional conquest of sin.*
What then is mortification? It is the constant fighting and contending
with sin, the weakening of it through grace, by the crucifying of the flesh
through the power of the Spirit.

Owen describes the scene vividly:

> As a man *nailed to the cross*; he first struggles, and strives, and cries
> out with great strength and might, but, as his blood and spirits
> waste, his strivings are faint and seldom, his cries low and hoarse,
> scarce to be heard; —when a man first sets on a lust or distemper,
> to deal with it, it struggles with great violence to break loose; it cries
> with earnestness and impatience to be satisfied and relieved; but
> when by mortification the blood and spirits of it are let out, it moves
> seldom and faintly, cries sparingly, and is scarce heard in the heart;
> it may have sometimes a dying pang, that makes an appearance of
> great vigour and strength, but it is quickly over, especially if it be
> kept from considerable success.[2]

If Christ died for all your sins, asks Owen—'Why dost thou not set
thyself against them also?'[3]

In fact Owen has comparatively little to say about the actual deed of
mortification. He puts it like this: 'Set faith … on Christ for the *killing*
of thy sin. … Live in this, and thou wilt die a conqueror.'[4] Direct faith to
'*the death*, blood, and cross of Christ; that is, on Christ as crucified and
slain. Mortification of sin is peculiarly from the death of Christ.' This is
the end of his dying.[5]

But while he has little to say about actual mortification, he recognizes
that success in it depends largely on a right preparation in the believer's
experience. He gives nine preparatory directions:

[1] *Works*, VI:25.
[2] *Ibid.*, VI:30.
[3] *Ibid.*, VI:41.
[4] *Ibid.*, VI:79.
[5] *Ibid.*, VI:83.

1. Examine your heart to see if there are any deadly marks of unmortified sin.

2. Get a clear sense of the guilt, danger, and evil of your own sin.

3. Load your conscience with a sense of the guilt of sin.

4. Pray for a new and stable desire to be delivered from sin's present power: 'Assure thyself, unless thou *longest* for deliverance thou shalt not have it.'[1]

5. Ask if the sin is related to natural temperament. If so, keep the body in subjection in that area so far as possible.

6. Analyse your occasions of sin and avoid them: 'he that dares to dally with occasions of sin', says Owen, 'will dare to sin.'[2]

7. 'Rise mightily against *the first actings*' of sin.[3]

8. Direct your meditation to what will make you most conscious that your God is a consuming fire.

9. Allow yourself no peace of conscience until God speaks it: 'self-healers, or men that speak peace to themselves, do commonly make haste'.[4] Impatience and mortification cannot walk together.

It is these preparations which pave the way in the believer's heart for the great work of mortification by the Spirit: he alone brings the cross of Christ into our hearts with its sin-killing power; for by the Spirit we were baptized into the death of Christ.[5] And it is in the death of Christ that we find the death of sin.

We must now turn briefly to consider one final area. For these duties to honour Christ and to deal with sin are actually productive of Christian character.

---

[1] *Works*, VI:60.
[2] *Ibid.*, VI:62.
[3] *Ibid.*
[4] *Ibid.*, VI:75.
[5] *Ibid.*, VI:86.

4. *The goal of Christian piety*

Christian piety looks to a twofold goal, present and future.

The first and most immediate goal on which we will concentrate here is that of Christian character. What were the leading characteristics of the truly pious man in Owen's view?

(i) *He walks with God.* The Christian life is the progress of the pilgrim. The Christian is marked out by the way he walks, living his life in the presence of God. Enoch was a great prophet and patriarch; he was a mighty preacher of righteousness, but he was singled out for none of these things—instead Scripture gives him this accolade, that 'he walked with God'. But what does this mean? It means, Owen claims, our doing all things for the glory of God; and our aiming in everything, and above everything, at the enjoyment of God. This is 'the only way to preserve and deliver any from the calamities of general apostasies, in wickedness, violence, and destruction'.[1]

(ii) *He walks in humility.* This cannot but be so, since he walks with God—under the law of his grace, which leaves no room for boasting; and also under the law of his providence, which leaves no room for the wisdom of the flesh. Especially in the varying circumstances of his life, the child of God learns to acknowledge the mystery of divine sovereignty, and the greatness of his wisdom:

> Let us lay our mouths in the dust, and ourselves on the ground, and say, 'It is the Lord; I will be silent because he hath done it. He is of one mind, and who can turn him? He doth whatever he pleaseth. Am not I in his hand as clay in the hand of the potter? May he not make what kind of vessel he pleases? When I was not, he brought me out of nothing by his word. What I am, or have, is merely of his pleasure. Oh, let my heart and thoughts be full of deep subjection to his supreme dominion and uncontrollable sovereignty over me!'[2]

(iii) *He walks by faith.* Of course the Christian seeks to emulate Abraham, who gave glory to God as he grew strong in faith. He lived the life of faith, but so does every believer. Weak faith will still carry a man to heaven, says Owen, '*yet it will never carry him comfortably nor pleasantly*

---

[1] *Works*, XVI:503.
[2] *Ibid.*, IX:116-17.

thither. ... The least faith will do its work safely, though not so sweetly'.[1] Yet, even weak faith brings strong consolation: 'A little faith gives a whole Christ.'[2] 'The most imperfect faith will give present justification, because it interests the soul in a present Christ. ... You, who have but a weak faith, have yet a strong Christ.'[3]

Then, finally,

(iv) *The Christian walks by love.* Love, according to Paul, is the bond of perfection, and this is so especially in the fellowship of the church. Owen uses an illustration. He likens the church to a bundle of sticks, of different shapes and sizes—but they can all be carried together at once provided they are tied with a band. So with Christians: they come in different shapes and sizes, spiritually as well as physically, psychologically as well as socially: but they can be bound together by love. But, says Owen, if the band is loosed, 'every one's crookedness will appear, one to be too long, one to be too short; one too big, one too little; one crooked, and one straight; there is no keeping them together'.[4]

Nor is this love to be thought of on a purely natural level:

> It is a fruit of the Spirit of God, an effect of faith, whereby believers, being knit together by the strongest bonds of affection, upon the account of their interest in one head, Jesus Christ, and participating of one Spirit, do delight in, value, and esteem each other, and are in a constant readiness for all those regular duties whereby the temporal, spiritual, and eternal good of one another may be promoted.[5]

So, the Christian walks with God; he walks in humility; he walks by faith; he walks in love. These things are the immediate goal of Christian piety, in the production of Christian character. And this, in fact, as Owen himself confesses, was the purpose he saw in his own ministry: he expresses himself thus, in a rare personal comment:

> I hope I may own in sincerity, that my heart's desire unto God, and the chief design of my life in the station wherein the good

[1] *Works*, IX:28.
[2] *Ibid.*, IX:29.
[3] *Ibid.*
[4] *Ibid.*, XVI:479.
[5] *Ibid.*, IX:259.

providence of God hath placed me, are, that mortification and
universal holiness may be promoted in my own and in the hearts
and ways of others, to the glory of God; that so the gospel of our
Lord and Saviour Jesus Christ may be adorned in all things…[1]

At this point it may be helpful to summarize our discussion thus far.
We have seen that, for Owen, the foundation of Christian piety is rooted
in the Covenant of Grace. The heart of that covenant is that men are
taken into union with Christ, and from that union flow all the blessings
and obligations of the Christian life. The Covenant of Grace, effected
in union with Jesus, transforms all obedience from legal to evangelical.
It is the method of the gospel to graft duties on to faith. Or, to put it
in more modern terms, it is invariably the case that the great indicative
statements of the gospel, which affirm what God has done for us in
Christ, are the foundation for gospel imperatives—what we are to do in
and for Christ.

In particular, we noticed that the Christian has a duty to honour,
worship and obey the Lord Jesus. We also have a duty to deal with the
remnants of corruption in our own hearts. Opposition to that is found
in the work of Satan, the circumstances of life, and most especially, for
Owen, in the power of indwelling sin. Owen calls on his readers always
to be killing sin, or it will be killing them. And this led us to consider
briefly the goal of the Christian life in this world in the development of
Christian character.

So the pattern Owen develops is this:

- There is opposition to sin, on the believer's part. True piety for
  Owen is found in this (a point about which he believed many
  Christians were deceived).

- There is also growth in universal holiness of life; and this takes both
  negative and positive directions.

In what we have already considered, our attention has moved from
the negative aspects of sanctification to the positive. Now we must take
up and develop the more positive framework which Owen gives to
Reformed piety. We have seen that it is based on union with Christ, but

---

[1] *Works*, VI:4.

there is more to it than that, and there is more in it than that. We now turn therefore to consider (1) the nature, (2) progress, and (3) consummation of positive Christian piety.

1. The nature of positive Christian piety

Because it is founded on union with Christ, Reformed piety is characterized by communion with God, which, according to Owen,

> consisteth in his *communication of himself unto us, with our returnal unto him* of that which he requireth and accepteth, flowing from that union which in Jesus Christ we have with him.[1]

This communion is essentially trinitarian. We will find ourselves taken up with it Christologically, and there is no doubt that Owen's teaching here is profoundly, and basically, Christological and Christocentric. But he is also at pains to emphasize that communion with God is trinitarian. Part of what he means by this is that the believer enjoys a quite distinctive communion with each person of the Trinity.

This is a position that has not received a great deal of attention in our Reformed theology, but it is axiomatic with Owen. He bases it partly on 1 John 5:7, and holds that, just as each person of the Trinity is said in that text to bear witness, similarly, in that witness, the believer holds communion with the Father, Son, and Holy Spirit distinctly. That text, as Owen would have known, is suspect, but he also adduces other texts. In 1 Corinthians 12:4-6 emphasis is placed on communion with each person of the Trinity in the special communication of each. Owen holds that Ephesians 2:18 also supports his case, as do other passages in the New Testament.

The question therefore arises: What is distinctive to each person? Owen answers: The Father communicates by original authority. The Son communicates from his purchased treasury. The Spirit communicates in immediate efficacy.

(i) *Communion with the Father* is pre-eminently in love, and if that is to be received, it must first of all be contemplated. It is very striking to notice Owen's pastoral concern in this context:

[1] *Works*, II:8.

How few of the saints are experimentally acquainted with this privilege of holding immediate communion with the Father in love! With what anxious, doubtful thoughts do they look upon him! What fears, what questionings are there, of his good-will and kindness! At the best, many think there is no sweetness at all in him towards us, but what is purchased at the high price of the blood of Jesus. It is true, that alone is the way of communication; but the free fountain and spring of all is in the bosom of the Father.[1]

Owen's point is of immense theological and practical importance. *Theologically* at a stroke it clears Owen's evangelicalism of the accusation that he makes a loving Son placate a reluctant Father, and persuade him to have mercy. No! says Owen, the source and fountain of all our salvation is found in the loving heart of the Father.

Practically, what he says here has far-reaching implications for the doctrine of assurance. There is nothing more inimical to Christian assurance than the thought that Christ is only a 'front' to the Father, and that behind Christ, and sending him, is a God who, in his heart of hearts, would rather destroy us. Of course there is a paradox here, and it has always been recognized in truly Reformed theology: He loved us, even when he hated us, says Augustine—and Calvin quotes him with total approval. This is Owen's position too—and, moreover, he sees that so much of our lack of assurance springs from our basic insecurity about the love of God for us. And lack of assurance always breeds a narrowness of spirit, and a spirit of censoriousness more akin to Pharisaism than the grace of God. That is why Owen stresses the need to recognize the freeness, the fullness, and the universality of the love of God the Father. He too quotes Augustine with approval:[2]

Omnia diligit Deus, quae fecit;
et inter ea magis diligit creaturas rationales,
et de illis eas amplius quae sunt membra unigeniti sui.
Et multo magis ipsum unigenitum.

---

[1] *Works*, II:32.
[2] *Works*, II:33. In fact Owen seems to be quoting the summary of Augustine's Lecture 110 which he found in Thomas Aquinas, *Summa Theologicae*, I.20.3.

> God loves everything he has made;
> And among them, he loves more his rational creatures,
> And among them those who are members of his only begotten.
> And most of all, he loves his only begotten Son.

It is evident that Owen is not denying the distinguishing character of God's love. It would be impossible for him to be doing that in view of his demolition job on Arminianism and universal redemption.[1] But he is emphasizing what he believes to be the biblical logic. Distinguishing love does not contradict the presence of a universal love, but is a category within it.

Now, we may ask, how does Owen put this together, in practical terms? How does he remove the fears of men who see God's distinguishing love but cannot see the full freeness of God's love? Here is his answer:

> Never any one from the foundation of the world, who believed such love in the Father, and made returns of love to him again, was deceived; neither shall ever any to the world's end be so, in so doing. Thou art, then, in this, upon a most sure bottom. If thou believest and receivest the Father as love, he will infallibly be so to thee, though others may fall under his severity.[2]

'Ah', someone may say, imagines Owen: 'If only I could find some response within my own soul to the love of God, then I could believe he loves me.' This is Owen's reply:

> This is the most *preposterous* course that possibly thy thoughts can pitch upon, a most ready way to rob God of his glory. 'Herein is love', saith the Holy Ghost, 'not that we loved God, but that he loved us' first. ... Now, thou wouldst invert this order, and say, 'Herein is love, not that God loved me, but that I love him first'. This is to take the glory of God from him: ... Lay down, then, *thy reasonings*; take up the love of the Father upon a *pure act of believing*, and that will open thy soul to let it out unto the Lord in the communion of love.[3]

---

[1] Cf. *A Display of Arminianism*, *Works*, X, written when Owen was aged about 26!
[2] *Works*, II:36-37.
[3] *Ibid.*, II:37.

(ii) *Communion with Christ the Son* is in grace—in what Owen calls purchased grace and personal grace; purchased grace is what he has done for us by his active and passive obedience; personal grace is what he is in himself as our Saviour.

(iii) *Communion with the Spirit* is in all the ministries which he exercises towards us, in us, and for us. Here Owen thinks of his anointing, his presence in the believer as an earnest of our inheritance, his work as Advocate and Comforter, and also particularly his sealing ministry. Owen has much to say in this connection in volumes II and IV of the *Works*.

We turn now from the nature of Christian piety, with its roots in this threefold communion, to—

2. *The progress of Christian piety*

The essence of progress, positive advance, in the Christian life, is determined by the believer's fellowship with the Lord Jesus Christ. This fellowship, as we have already seen, is in *grace*. Owen recognized that the word 'grace' was used in three different connections in the Scriptures— of free favour, of the quality of graciousness, and of the fruit of the Spirit. He has a very marked tendency to use 'grace' of the graciousness of Christ and the fruit of Spirit, whereas Scripture, in some contrast, tends to use grace in connection with free favour.

There is much that is helpful in Owen's teaching on the benefits of fellowship with the graciousness of Christ. This is what he calls his 'personal grace'. Personal grace is just another way of speaking of the glorious perfections of the humanity of the Lord Jesus. According to Owen, the progress of true religion in the soul depends a great deal on how we respond to him. It is 'The *liking* of Christ, for his *excellency*, grace, and suitableness', and 'The *accepting* of Christ by the *will*, as its only husband, Lord, and Saviour'.[1]

Owen has vast tracts of material on this theme. It is a recurring theme in his writings on the Christian life. One way in which the essence of it can be encapsulated in a summary way is by demonstrating how Owen saw the whole process of developing true fellowship with Christ in terms of the imagery of the Song of Solomon.

[1] *Works*, II:58.

Owen adopted an allegorical approach to the exposition of the Song of Solomon. This does not mean he formulated his doctrine of Christ from its pages. But he did think it was an illustration of the fellowship which believers enjoy with their Lord, and of the vicissitudes of our relationship with Christ. It is, in other words, a transcript of the affections of the child of God: not only piety in the outward behaviour, in moral rectitude, which he emphasizes elsewhere, but piety in the cleansing and substantial healing of the very emotions of the child of God.

The theme of the Song of Solomon (or Canticles) is, essentially:

> This sense of the love of Christ, and the effect of it in communion with him, by prayer and praises, is divinely set forth in the Book of Canticles. The church therein is represented as the spouse of Christ; and, as a faithful spouse, she is always either solicitous about his love, or rejoicing in it.[1]

> In brief, this whole book is taken up in the description of the communion that is between the Lord Christ and his saints.[2]

Owen was really a man of Welsh descent who happened to be born in England! And there is, no doubt, a 'Celtic' flavour to his emphasis here on the importance of the affections and senses. But there is more to it than that. This man, given his massive intellectual equipment, combined with his profound grasp of theology—to what does he aspire most of all? It is the sense of the love of Christ for him. That is what he himself needs if he is to progress in Christian piety. Surely there is something for us to learn here. We reject the false dichotomy between the person of Christ and the Bible which reveals him. We know of no other Christ than the one we meet in the pages of Scripture. But it is possible to search the Scriptures which testify of Christ, and never actually to discover the power of their truth in coming to Christ, and drinking in his love for us.[3] God did not send a theological axiom to die for us; he sent his beloved Son. And it is communion with him which leads to progress in piety. That, after all, is the teaching of Paul—knowledge without this, he says,

---

[1] *Works*, I:116.

[2] *Ibid.*, II:46.

[3] Cf. John 5:39-40. Here again we meet Owen's distinction between the knowledge of the truth and the experience of the power of the truth!

puffs up: it is love which builds up. Owen seems to have been conscious
of the danger of the massive intellectual satisfaction to be gained from
the gospel—that in it all, instead of finding 'Jesus, Lover of my soul',[1] a
man might find himself crying out in spiritual sterility:

> Where is the blessedness I knew,
> When first I saw the Lord?
> Where is the soul refreshing view
> Of Jesus ...?[2]

The theme of Canticles is worked out in this allegorical way:

Christ and the Christian are the two main characters. The *daughters
of Jerusalem* represent 'all sorts of professors'.[3] The *watchmen* represent
office-bearers in the church, and *the city* represents the visible church
itself. But while, occasionally, the corporate aspect of the Christian life
appears in Owen's exposition, the major concentration is on the individual's experience and the communion he enjoys with the Lord Jesus.

Owen develops this theme in several central passages:

2:1-7: Here Christ is seen, describing his own character and significance to the Christian. He is the Rose of Sharon, the Lily of the Valley.
That is, he is pre-eminent in all his personal graces, just as the rose
abounds in perfume, and the lily in beauty. Indeed, the rose is from the
fertile plain of Sharon, in which the choicest herds are reared.

What does all this mean? Christ 'allures'[4] the Christian, says Owen—
there is an irresistible attraction to him; the believer enjoys the scent of
him as the Rose.

But there is more, for Christ goes on in the passage to describe what
the church means to him—she is a lily among thorns (2:2)—and here
Owen draws this lesson. The believer is one with Christ—he is the lily;
but the believer, through faith in Christ, is the lily to Christ. He is the
lily of the valley. But we are the lily among thorns! Christ looks upon
you, in all your trials, in all the opposition there is to you—but do you
not see what he thinks about you? He sees you as his lily!

---

[1] A reference to the hymn 'Jesu', Lover of My Soul' by Charles Wesley.
[2] From the hymn 'O For a Closer Walk with God' by William Cowper.
[3] *Works*, II:55.
[4] *Ibid.*, II:42.

This conversation and communion between the lover and the beloved continues. He is compared to the apple tree (2:3)—it provides fruit for food, and shade for protection. So with Christ; all others are fruitless to the hungry soul, but he provides shelter, 'from wrath without, and refreshment because of weariness from within. ... From the power of *corruptions*, trouble of temptations, distress of persecutions, there is in him quiet, rest, and repose.'[1]

And so in the verses that follow, our communion with the Lord Jesus is delineated for us. It has four characteristics:

(i) *Sweetness of fellowship.* 'He brought me to the banqueting-house' (2:4), where he reveals all the treasures of his grace in the gospel. Indeed, says Owen, we find in this book (1:2) that his love is better than wine—since it is righteousness, peace, and joy in the Holy Spirit. What does wine do? It cheers the heart, it makes us forget our misery; it gives us a glad countenance! And so it is with the wine which flows from the grace of the Lord Jesus, and our fellowship with him.

(ii) *Delight in fellowship.* The maiden is overcome by this, and wants to know more of the love of her beloved. She is 'sick with love' (2:5); 'not (as some suppose) fainting for want of a sense of love', but 'made sick and faint, even overcome, with the mighty actings of that divine affection, after she had once tasted of the sweetness of Christ in the banqueting-house'.[2]

(iii) *Safety.* (2:4)—His banner over her was love—a symbol of protection, and a token of success and victory. There follows Owen's application: Christ's banner stands over the believer—anything that comes upon the believer must first press through the love of Christ. Only what Christ gives to us in his love for us will ever come to us. This is the argument of Romans 8:32—he that spared not his own Son, how shall he not with him also freely give us all things? This is our resting place and safety.

(iv) *Support and consolation.* (2:6)—His left hand is under her head, and his right hand embraces her. What is this? asks Owen. It is the picture of Christ supporting the church, and at the same time cherishing

---

[1] *Works*, II:43-44.
[2] *Ibid.*, II:44.

it and nourishing it! And so (2:7) their fellowship together is continued
and sustained.

He that has much, to him will more be given. There is an increase
in capacity, and in desire for Christ. In a further comment on Song of
Solomon 2:7 Owen describes the effect this has:

> A believer that hath gotten Christ in his arms, is like one that hath
> found great spoils, or a pearl of price. He looks about him every
> way, and fears every thing that may deprive him of it.[1]

In Canticles 2:9 Christ reappears. In the Song, the lover shows himself
through the lattice, and this is interpreted as follows: 'our sight of him
here is as it were by glances—liable to be clouded by many interpo-
sitions'. There is 'instability and imperfection in our view and apprehension of him', that is our present mortal state; 'In the meantime he
looketh through the *windows* of the ordinances of the gospel.'[2] When
the Christian has turned away in heart, Christ comes, searching and
longing for a loving response from our hearts. If he does not receive it, he
will withdraw. It would be impossible within the general framework of
Owen's theology to suppose that this involves severed relationships; but
it does imply disjointed experience and broken fellowship. Christ is still
the Christian's possession and vice versa, but the *sense* of this has gone.

In chapter 3 the spouse discovers that her lover has withdrawn. She
is perplexed. Owen is not clear whether this is the cause or the effect
of the 'night' in which she discovers herself, but points to application:
'in the greatest peace and opportunity of ease and rest, a believer finds
none in the absence of Christ: though he be on his bed, having nothing
to disquiet him, he rests not, if Christ, his rest, be not there'.[3] So the
soul searches for Christ, first of all in its course of *ordinary* duties.[4] But
'This is not a way to recover a sense of lost love';[5] rather there must be
'Resolutions for *new, extraordinary, vigorous,* constant applications unto
God', 'the first general step and degree of a sin-entangled soul acting

[1] *Works*, II:126.
[2] *Ibid.*, I:377.
[3] *Ibid.*, II:128.
[4] *Ibid.*, VI:613.
[5] *Ibid.*, VI:353.

towards a recovery'.[1] It is evident that here the soul has lost its sense of forgiveness, and that the search for its restoration involves two things: first, a search of one's own soul to discover the cause of Christ's absence, and, second, a search of the promises of God to discover the means of his return. Self-examination must be followed by a reapplication to the Covenant of Grace. If this yields no success, the solution is to be found in extraordinary duties, as Owen has already hinted. So the spouse goes about the city (the visible church) looking for her lover. If Christ is not found in private, it is the Christian's duty to make a special search for him in public, through worship, the preaching of the word, and the sacraments. In her search the maiden is found by the watchmen (office-bearers in the church visible)—'it is of sad consideration, that the Holy Ghost doth sometimes in this book take notice of them to no good account. Plainly, chap. 5:7 they turn persecutors.'[2] Owen finds support for this view in Luther's sentiment '*Nunquam periclitatur religio nisi inter reverendissimos*',[3] a reason he gives for his dislike for the title 'reverend'! But in fact in this instance the watchmen take notice of the plight of the spouse. This is the duty of faithful office-bearers. Exactly how Christ is discovered is not indicated in the passage, but Owen detects some significance in this too. When Christ comes, it is in his own mysterious way by the Spirit.

By chapter 5 the spouse has sunk again into sloth and indolence. The shepherd-lover comes to meet with her, but she excuses herself by the unsuitableness of the time and her lack of preparation for her duties.[4] Christ, thus rebuffed, leaves the believer and 'long it is before she obtains any recovery'.[5] He returns later in the chapter and the description given in 5:10-16 provides Owen with a further opportunity to describe what the Christian finds in the Saviour.

Christ is described as being 'white and ruddy'. 'He is *white* in the glory of his *Deity*, and *ruddy* in the preciousness of his *humanity*.'[6] White

---

[1] *Works*, VI:353 (emphasis added).
[2] *Ibid.*, II:130-31.
[3] 'Religion is never so much in danger as amongst the most reverend.'
[4] *Works*, VI:520.
[5] *Ibid.*, VI:346.
[6] *Ibid.*, II:49.

is the colour of glory; red is the colour of man made from the dust of the earth, yet in the image of God. (Owen suggests Adam was so named because of the redness of the earth from which he was made.) So the expression here 'points him [Christ] out as the second Adam, partaker of flesh and blood, because the children partook of the same, Hebrews 2:14'.[1] He is also white in his innocence, and ruddy 'in the blood of his oblation'—'by his whiteness he fulfilled the law; by his redness he satisfied justice'.[2]

Further, the excellence of Christ's administration of the kingdom of God is expressed: he is white with love and mercy to his own people, and red with justice and revenge upon his enemies. This excellence, through the union of the 'white and ruddy', fits him to be the Saviour, and brings salvation through union and communion with him. This is exegesis in the allegorical tradition, and we may note that Owen has gathered the doctrines of the two natures of Christ, his one person, his work as second Adam, in his active and passive obedience, as the source of man's salvation, out of this one phrase! But perhaps his stress on Christ's humanity is most worthy of note.

In the following verses the maiden goes on to describe Christ more fully. His *head* is as fine gold—conveying the splendour and durability of Christ as the head of the government of the kingdom of God.[3] His *locks* are said to be 'bushy' or curled, 'black as a raven'. To first appearance the hair is tangled, but in fact it is well and precisely ordered, thus representing the wisdom of Christ in his mediatorial administration. The *hair* is black to indicate that his ways are past finding out,[4] and, in a natural sense, emphasizing his comeliness and vigour. His *eyes* are like those of the dove—not a bird of prey—indicating the wealth of his knowledge and discernment. They are tender and pure as he discerns the thoughts and intentions of men.[5] His *cheeks* are like beds of spices, sweet of savour, beautiful in their orderliness;[6] so the graces of Christ, in his

[1] *Works*, II:50.
[2] *Ibid.*
[3] *Ibid.*, II:71.
[4] *Ibid.*, II:72.
[5] *Ibid.*, II:73.
[6] *Ibid.*, II:75.

human nature, are gathered by Christians in prayer, from the covenant promises of God which are well ordered (2 Sam. 23:5). These graces are eminent indeed, like 'towers of perfumes' (marginal reading adopted by Owen).[1] His *lips* are like lilies, dropping myrrh—a description of the riches of Christ's word.[2]

His *hands* (verse 14) refers to the work he has accomplished, as the fruit of his love. His *belly* (in the sense of bowels) reminds us of his tender mercy and loving affection. His *legs*, countenance and mouth (verse 15) remind us of the stability of his kingdom, and the grace and faithfulness of his promises. He is completely worthy of the desires and affections of his followers (verse 16) in his birth, life, and death, in the glory of his ascension and coronation, in the supply of the Spirit of God, in the ordinances of worship, in the tenderness of his care, in the justice of his vengeance on his enemies, as well as in the pardon he dispenses to all his people. And this Christ, says Owen, often comes by surprise to the Christian: when he is engaged in ordinary occupations, he finds his mind drawn out in love for Jesus. Weigh these experiences against those times when Satan invades the mind with worldly thoughts, says Owen—lest you be led to despair.

And so the believer is led to the prayer of 8:6, 'Set me as a seal upon thine heart, as a seal upon thine arm; for love is strong as death; jealousy is cruel as the grave.' The worst thought believers have of hell, then, says Owen, 'is that they shall not enjoy Jesus Christ'.[3] Here, as elsewhere, he distinguishes between unbelief and what he calls spiritual jealousy, in which it is the individual's own sense of unworthiness, breeding insecurity, which gives rise to jealousy. Do not only come to love and trust Christ, he counsels, but see that *you are his beloved*; he loves *you*, he adores you as the apple of his eye. He has married himself to *you*!

Here, irrespective of whether we share Owen's allegorical hermeneutic, we glimpse an essential element in his theology. He has something to say to all of us. Owen was a pastor, as well as a scholar. Do not think he was interested in academic theology, but was not interested in Jesus!

---

[1] *Works*, II:76.
[2] *Ibid.*
[3] *Ibid.*, II:140.

This is surely an important observation to make. Owen did not for a moment build his Christology on the Song of Solomon. And in a sense it is of secondary importance how far we follow his exegesis of these passages. What is significant is that at the heart of his teaching on progress in Christian piety lay loving fellowship and company with Jesus. It was *Jesus* he loved—not in some maudlin sentimental sense, but with a sense of our Lord's full deity and glory! This was the great and necessary balance to his mighty intellectual theology. He loved his Lord, and companied with him.

One need hardly point up the application. Is this what ministers are? Is this what they are known for? Is this why people sit under their ministry? Is this what they teach in all the Scriptures? Owen has much to teach us both about piety and about pastoral ministry.

3. The consummation of Christian piety

This leads us, once again, to the same future perspective with which we concluded the part of our study of piety. Now that we have developed the positive aspects of Reformed piety in fellowship with Christ, it should be clear that the ultimate development and consummation of this is not merely the production of Christian character in this world— but the fullness of fellowship with Christ in the world to come. And this is such a consummation that it inevitably must reflect back on to the whole character of the Christian life, for that prospect makes an impact on how we live *now*. This was Paul's teaching: being justified by faith, he says, we rejoice now in our afflictions, because they produce glory. But more: we are able to rejoice now in our afflictions because we rejoice in the hope of sharing the glory of God (Rom. 5:1-5).

Owen's emphasis is no different: the vision of, and the longing for, the future life stamp the present life with a new dimension altogether.

Of course, this was not Owen's only perspective on the future. He held to the view that the glory of God would fill the earth as the waters cover the sea. But he also knew there was something 'far better' in being with Christ. And that is the essence of his view of the consummation of the Christian life. Here, as we have seen, Christ is seen only through the lattice. He comes to us in the ordinances of the gospel—in preaching and praying, in worship and sacraments. But for all the sense of his glory we may have in these, it is but the dim outline of what he really is, and what he will be to the spirits of just men made perfect. For, in the glory, says Owen, all the barriers of sin and the struggles of human experience will be broken down, and believers will be transformed into the likeness of Christ. And this, the final crisis of the Christian life, bringing the Christian from sanctification to glorification, involves a number of factors which Owen expounds enthusiastically:

(1) The mind will be set free from its natural darkness, through sin; and its incapacity in its present state of existence.

(2) A new light—the light of glory—will be implanted within us. We will be changed, says Paul, from one degree of glory to another, and this has a special significance: 'as the *light of grace* doth not destroy or abolish the *light of nature*, but rectify and improve it, so *the light of glory* shall not abolish *the light of faith and grace*, but by incorporating with it, render it absolutely perfect'.[1] But just as we cannot appreciate the light of grace by the light of nature, so we do not fully appreciate the light of glory by the light of grace; we can only here believe that it will form the soul into the image of Christ, so that, as Owen says, 'Grace renews nature; glory perfects grace.'[2]

(3) The body of the believer will also be glorified through union with Christ in the body of his glory. Heaven will more exceed the state of the gospel than the gospel state exceeds the state of the law! In the gospel we see the perfect image of Christ; in the glorified body we will see the perfect substance of Christ. It follows that whatever we see here of Christ will make us long to see him more fully in the future. The Christian life, then, is the planting of a seed, and the growth of the stock. The coming of the flower waits a still future revelation.

It was characteristic of Puritan teaching, as it was of New Testament teaching, that this most heavenly doctrine comes with great practical implications. Thus Owen held that the contemplation of the glorified Christ, through the image of his word, brings a lively experience of grace to the believer. But the experience of the future is yet distinct:

[1] *Works*, I:382.
[2] *Ibid.*, I:383.

our faculties will then be set free from the 'clogs of the flesh',[1] and all its restraints upon our spiritual powers. Christ will be seen, not by faith, but by sight, never to become invisible again, never more to withdraw from sensed fellowship. The vision with which we shall see him will no longer be liable to the defects of our own weakness and the external assaults of the world and the devil. And then, again, here the believer can only gather what Owen calls 'parcels of Christ'; there we will see him, all at once, and for evermore! The transformation will be immediate, total, irreversible, eternal—and yet there will be a continual operation on, and communication to, the saints from the love of Christ. Everything will still depend on his mediation: 'We shall no more be self-subsistent in glory than we are in nature or grace.'[2]

Nothing is more thrilling about Owen's view of Christian piety than that he turned to this theme, as many before and since have done, in the last days of his life. In fact his *Meditations on the Glory of Christ* really represent the substance of his dying ministry to his congregation in London.[3] They contain teaching on Reformed piety at its most testing and glorious time, in the valley of deep darkness. Here especially the contemplation of Christ lies at the heart of all true grace. Contemplation of that glory, says Owen, 'will carry us cheerfully, comfortably, and victoriously through life and death, and all that we have to conflict withal in either of them'.[4]

At such a time, God acts in special wisdom to his children, to bring them a triumphant entrance into his heavenly kingdom. Yet certain duties are still called for, if we are to die confidently in the profession of Christ:

(1) *Special faith must be exercised, to commit the soul to God.* We cannot go into the world beyond without trusting in the glory that is to be revealed. So it was with Christ, who commended his spirit to God in faith. So it was with Stephen, who saw by faith his conquest in Christ's conquest. There is no greater encouragement to believers than the knowledge that it is Jesus who will receive them.

[1] *Works*, I:274.
[2] *Ibid.*, I:414.
[3] *Ibid.*, I:273ff.
[4] *Ibid.*, I:277.

(2) *The Christian must be willing to part with the flesh*, and this, especially for the biblically-instructed believer, takes special understanding. For the body–soul union is peculiar and precious to man; neither angels nor beasts know it. Only man can experience this cataclysmic convulsion of his being. And we, by nature, have 'a fixed aversation from a dissolution'. Only through the knowledge of something that is better yet, can the Christian repose in God:

> He, therefore, that would die comfortably, must be able to say within himself and to himself, 'Die, then, thou frail and sinful flesh: "dust thou art, and unto dust thou shalt return." I yield thee up unto the righteous doom of the Holy One. Yet therein also I give thee into the hand of the great Refiner, who will hide thee in thy grave, and by thy consumption purify thee from all thy corruption and disposition to evil.'[1]

(3) *Believers must learn to comply with the times and seasons that God has ordained for their departure.*

(4) Since the ways and means by which death approaches bring special trials—long illnesses, severe medical treatment, perhaps persecution—*the children of God must learn to resign themselves to the gracious will of God and the infinite perfections of his decree*, in the knowledge that our lives are patterned on the image of him who is the firstborn of many brethren predestined to eternal glory. And thus, says Owen:

> If our future blessedness shall consist in being where he is, and beholding of his glory, what better preparation can there be for it than in a constant previous contemplation of that glory in the revelation that is made in the Gospel, unto this very end, that by a view of it we may be gradually transformed into the same glory?[2]

John Owen himself knew something of this in his own experience. It was during his last days that his great work *The Glory of Christ* was being prepared for the press. On August 24, 1683, William Payne, a Puritan minister at Saffron Walden, who was seeing the work through the various stages of publication, called to tell him that the work was

[1] *Works*, I:283.
[2] *Ibid.*, I:275.

already being printed. Into its composition he had poured the finest of
his spiritual thoughts. But Owen's biographers record his eloquent reply:

> I am glad to hear it; but O brother Payne! the long wished for day is
> come at last, in which I shall see that glory in another manner than
> I have ever done, or was capable of doing, in this world.

That is perhaps the most eloquent argument of all for believing
that John Owen knew what he was speaking of in all his teaching on
Reformed piety. His exposition of salvation and assurance by grace
sprang from his own search for a settled peace with God. Similarly his
teaching on the goal of Christian piety sprang from his love for the Lord
Jesus Christ, and his anticipation of the presence of his glory, where he
trusted he would be received with great joy.

There is therefore a continuing appropriateness in words from Owen's
funeral sermon preached by David Clarkson, one of his assistants, and
himself an erudite theologian and preacher:

> I need not tell you of this who knew him, that it was his great design
> to promote holiness in the life and exercise of it among you: But it
> was his great complaint that its power declined among professors. It
> was his care and endeavour to prevent or cure spiritual decays in his
> own flock: he was a burning and a shining light. Alas! it was but for
> a while; and we may rejoice in it still.[1]

---

[1] *Select Works of David Clarkson*, ed. Basil H. Cooper (London: Wycliffe Society,
1846), p. 452.

CHAPTER SIXTEEN

SOME THOUGHTS ON READING THE WORKS OF JOHN OWEN

J OHN OWEN was born in 1616 and died in 1683. During the course of his life he held pastorates in Fordham and Coggeshall, in Essex, served as vice-chancellor of Oxford University, as army chaplain under Oliver Cromwell, and finally as the minister of a gathered congregation in the city of London. Little is known of his inner life, and biographers have never found it easy to reconstruct the details of his spiritual pilgrimage. It might seem remarkable, therefore, that his works, covering many thousands of closely argued pages, should be kept in print four hundred years after his birth. Owen himself would have been the first to express amazement that so long after his death God's people should continue to discover the value and significance of his writings.

The only possible explanation and justification for this state of affairs is that Owen was one of the foremost, perhaps *the* foremost, theologian England has ever produced. That is not simply the view of an enthusiast. It was recognized by Owen's contemporaries, friends and foes alike, and it has been frequently recognized since. From Thomas Boston, the scholar-pastor of Ettrick, telling us in characteristic manner that he was 'helped by Owen on the Spirit';[1] to a leading modern missiologist describing him as 'perhaps the greatest British theologian of all time' and 'the greatest of Independent theologians'[2], testimonies to his significance abound.

[1] *Memoirs of Thomas Boston*, ed. G. H. Morrison (Edinburgh, 1899), p. 301.
[2] A. F. Walls, *A Guide to Christian Reading* (London: Tyndale Press, 1962), pp. 89, 105.

It is unquestionably for this reason that Owen's works *ought* to be purchased and read. But it is probably true that many find the first of these obligations (purchasing volumes of Owen) easier to fulfil than the second (reading what Owen wrote). There are doubtless many bookcases in the English-speaking world lined with several volumes in their distinctive white and green jackets whose owners would freely confess that they have read too little of the contents, and frankly find Owen very heavy-going. Let it be said that this situation is eminently understandable, and all those who have read Owen will sympathize with others who feel that the initial stages of reading him may be more of a burden than a pleasure. When such eminent Christian men and lovers of Puritan writings as Dr D. Martyn Lloyd-Jones and Dr J. I. Packer have written respectively, 'John Owen on the whole is difficult to read',[1] and 'There is no denying that Owen is heavy and hard to read',[2] lesser mortals may be excused for thinking that such a task is really beyond their capacities.

But this need not be the case, if we approach his writings wisely and intelligently. Owen did not write simply for fellow scholars (although he knew how to do that), but for fellow Christians. His preaching, apparently, was both understandable and eminently helpful, and it would probably be the opinion of those who have found his teaching conducive to spiritual growth, that much of what he wrote is well within the capacity of the serious Christian of average intelligence. While it is a fact that Owen is not universally *easy* to read, it is also true that he is not universally *difficult* to read. We may need some convincing on this point, and it is the function of these paragraphs to attempt to do that, and in measure provide a key which will help to open up the treasures that seem to be locked up behind the heavy door of Owen's length and style of writing. The fact is that Owen wrote some books which nowadays would appear as paperbacks, and it *is* possible to be introduced to him without having to plough through endless subdivisions of material and references to long-dead and almost equally long-forgotten theologians.

[1] D. M. Lloyd-Jones, *Preaching and Preachers* (London: Hodder and Stoughton, 1971), p. 175.
[2] J. I. Packer, Introductory Essay to John Owen, *The Death of Death* (London: Banner of Truth Trust, 1959), p. 25.

Assuming that one possesses some or all (or intends to purchase!) the republished volumes of Owen, what steps can be taken to reap the benefit of such an investment? The first step is to employ the three tools which W. H. Goold, the editor, helpfully supplied, namely:

(1) The division of the works into *Doctrinal* (volumes I-V), *Practical* (volumes VI-IX), *Controversial* (volumes X-XVI) and *Exegetical* (volumes XVII-XXIII, the *Commentary on Hebrews*) sections. These divisions give us a fundamental grasp of the nature and intention of each work.

(2) The introductions to each of the books supplied by Goold, some of which contain outlines and information on the work within very brief compass. It is possible, at least in theory, to have a kind of working knowledge of where Owen will lead you even before you begin the journey. That can serve a very useful function, and it is in fact the *raison d'être* of the introductions.

(3) The indices found at the end of volumes XVI and XXIII, and particularly those on subject matter and Scripture passages. These can be used as a map to Owen's theology in general, and a guide to the exposition of a particular passage or theme. They have a special value for occasional study or reading and preparation.

These three tools will help us to get the 'feel' of Owen's thought before we turn to read him, and a few mornings or evenings spent using them may preserve us from rushing headlong into a volume which we find too long and difficult, and on which we labour to no profit.

But then we will want to read something by Owen himself! The adventure of discovering his rich ministry of God's word and his penetrating knowledge of the human heart can be begun with confidence if we know what pieces are valuable to read as *introductions*, and then, in general terms, what sections of his works we can turn to in the expectation of receiving help and instruction.

With Owen it is probably wise to begin with a work that can be read at one or two sittings, and within a matter of hours. The sense of achievement in doing so, and the thrill of discovering how clearly the teaching speaks to our needs, is something not to be discounted or despised. Once we realize he is not always heavy reading we will want to read on. Depending on personal circumstances, present needs and interests, there are a number of useful starting places.

Sermons

Some readers will find it helpful to begin with a sermon from the collections in volumes VIII, IX, XV, and XVI—and if this is the case, the practical and pastoral sermons in volume IX can be highly recommended, perhaps more so than the statesmanlike addresses in volume VIII. But even in this latter volume, where some of the sermons run to thirty or forty pages, those with an historical interest will find much that is helpful and thought-provoking. Sermon 3, for example, on Jeremiah 15:19-20, was preached the day after the execution of Charles I. It is interesting to reflect on what one might have said oneself if summoned to preach before Parliament on such an occasion, as Owen was! Sermon 4, on Romans 4:20, was preached in connection with his visit to Ireland as an army chaplain, and in it he expresses the desire that the Irish might have peace, and 'might enjoy Ireland as long as the moon endureth, so that Jesus Christ might possess the Irish'.[1] Sermon 5 is the one which led to Owen's first introduction to Cromwell, while sermon 6 was preached in 1650 in Edinburgh and Berwick after the Battle of Dunbar, when the fear-filled Scottish preachers refused to occupy their own pulpits. Volume IX, on the other hand, contains sermons on worship (sermons 3 and 4); spiritual barrenness (14 and 15); the withdrawing of God's presence (24) and dying daily (27-29). Christian ministers will find much help in a sermon on Christ's pastoral care (22), and also series of sermons on the ministry and on the Lord's Supper in the same volume.

Cases of conscience

In volume IX we also find fine examples of a form of teaching and ministry unfamiliar to some readers, but in which all Christians will find great help and blessing. Owen deals with fourteen cases of conscience—for example: What sense of sin and guilt is needed to cause men to look to

---

[1] *Works*, VIII:235.

Christ as Saviour? What are the most certain evidences of conversion? How do we recover from spiritual decline? How should we prepare for the coming of Christ?—all of which speak for themselves as subjects of great personal and pastoral importance. Each is discussed within the scope of a few pages. The study of these in private, or in small groups, would surely have helpful repercussions in any Christian fellowship.

Short books

Others may prefer to begin by reading a whole book, and there are several which can be read without undue weariness to the mind—although it is always wise to read with paper and pencil at hand. Owen's divisions can be perplexing (Goold tells us in volume I, p. xiv, that they are denoted by the numerals I, 1, (1), [1], first and *first!*), and readers will note with some amusement and even relief that the editor indicates in some footnotes that Owen seems to have lost the place. Needless to say such places are few and far between!

The works on temptation and mortification, in volume 6, come within this general category of short works, although both are of outstanding value and probably unsurpassed in their treatment of these respective themes of Christian experience. Each work is less than ninety pages in length. No doubt some difficult passages may be encountered even here, but if so J. I. Packer's suggestion still holds good, that 'the hard places in Owen usually come out as soon as one reads them out loud'.[1] Alternative books might be *The True Nature of a Gospel Church*, in volume XVI, or *The Duty of Pastors and People Distinguished*, in volume XIII. It need hardly be said that such reading should be an exercise in prayerfulness as well as thoughtfulness, for it will be recognized that, however unusual it may be for Christians to read this kind of literature, there can still be a certain carnal *kudos* in having done so. Owen's teaching should be *read* with the same spirit of humility we would commend to those who *listen* to the regular ministry of the word, since we are but servants looking to the Master's hand for mercy and for grace to help in times of need.

---

[1] J. I. Packer, Introductory Essay to *The Death of Death*, p. 25.

Spreading our wings

When we have come thus far, we will want to spread our wings a little, and turn to works of special interest, or that deal with some aspect of Christian living in which we sense our need for further instruction. Owen covers a very wide range of themes, as we would expect:

The doctrine of *God and the Trinity* is discussed in volume 2, where, in *A Brief Declaration and Vindication of the Doctrine of the Trinity*, Owen gave a matter of hours to provide ordinary Christians with a reliable guide to the teaching of Scripture. Earlier in the same volume may be found his work *Of Communion with the Trinity*. In this he describes the particular fellowship which the believer enjoys with *each* person of the Trinity, and thus opens up what may be a fresh avenue of thought for many readers. The section on communion with Christ contains a quite comprehensive, if incomplete, allegorical exposition of the Song of Solomon, with many valuable and spiritual insights. Owen takes the *main characters* to represent Christ and the believer (sometimes the church); the *daughters of Jerusalem* represent 'all sorts of professors'; the *watchmen* are the office-bearers, and the *city* is the visible church. Even those who do not share Owen's allegorical view can find benefit in his comments.

The Person and Work of Christ is covered in volume 1 and elsewhere. Owen's *Christologia*, esteemed by the elder Thomas M'Crie to be second only to Calvin's *Institutes*, is of great value, as is his exposition of John 17:24, on *The Glory of Christ*. The nature and extent of the atonement is dealt with in what is currently Owen's best-known work, in volume 10, *The Death of Death in the Death of Christ*—written when he was only thirty.

While historical circumstances have drawn attention to this last area of his thought, it would be true to say of Owen (as Warfield claimed of Calvin) that he was pre-eminently a theologian of the Holy Spirit. It is clear both from his own statements and the extent of his writing on the theme, that *The Person and Work of the Holy Spirit*, expounded in volumes 3 and 4, and in nine books, lay very close to his heart. It probably remains, in Goold's words, 'The most complete exhibition of the doctrine of Scripture on the person and agency of the Holy Spirit to be found in any language'. It is still claimed that the Reformers and Puritans gave little attention to the Holy Spirit, and many critics have indicated that the *Westminster Confession of Faith* lacks any separate treatment of the doctrine. It is, however, muddle-headed to suggest that the Spirit has been restored from a position of oblivion as 'the forgotten person of the Godhead' only in the present century. Owen's work was but one of a number of massive treatments of the Spirit in seventeenth-century writings. Its contemporary value is out of all proportion to the investment any Christian might make in obtaining volumes III and IV.

Owen provides basic teaching on the Spirit and guides the reader through his work, in the old creation, in the person and work of Christ and his witness to him, in his work in regeneration and conversion, and then in sanctification and holiness. His work in the inspiration of Scripture, as the Comforter, in prayer, and in the exercise of spiritual gifts are all treated at length. Here is wholesome and edifying food for every Christian, and the kind of help and stimulus which serves as a handmaid to the pastor and teacher in public ministry and private counselling. Indeed some may well find that the time spent becoming familiar with the contents of these two volumes will often be repaid by the time saved and the help given to believers in need of counsel simply by commending the reading of some short section which meets their need. In this connection the short works on *Temptation* and *Mortification* should also be mentioned as well as the *Cases of Conscience*. These prepare the way for the teaching in volume VII on *The Dominion of Sin and Grace*, and *The Nature and Power of Indwelling Sin*, and also for the encouragement of the treatment of forgiveness and assurance from Psalm 130, in volume VI.

Students of later expositions of the Reformed doctrine of sanctification may possibly sense a lack of clarity here and there in Owen's definitions of expressions such as 'the old man' (Rom. 6:6), but this does not greatly impair the value of the work, and there are probably few more realistic and pastoral treatments of these themes available today. All in all, it is doubtful whether a young minister could adopt a better study plan than, after working through Calvin's *Institutes*, to turn to volumes III and IV, and VI and VII in Owen's *Works*.

Attention ought also to be drawn to the treatment of *Justification* in volume V. This provides not only a rich exposition of a central biblical doctrine, but also a healthy corrective to aberrations that have recurred at various times since Owen's day, including our own. In volumes IV and XVI Owen briefly gives his understanding of the inspiration and authority of Scripture, and affirms the necessity of faith in it as 'divine, supernatural and infallible' because based upon the testimony of God himself.

The reading of volume XI might seem to demand the grace it expounds—*Perseverance.* It is virtually an extended review of the Arminian teaching found in John Goodwin's *Redemption Redeemed.* Even so, Owen admits that his six hundred-plus pages only deal with a part of Goodwin's book! It was against this same work of Goodwin's that Robert Baillie, a member of the Westminster Assembly and later Principal of Glasgow University, wrote his Scottish *Antidote against the English Infection of Arminianism*! Despite Owen's prolixity there is much valuable exposition here for those with the time and will to find it. It should be said, however, that this is probably not the gate for any young or new reader to enter the city of Oweniana!

Extensive treatment is given to the doctrine of *the Church* in volumes XIII-XVI, where material sometimes overlaps. From a number of important books here perhaps *The Duty of Pastors and People Distinguished* (written when Owen was still Presbyterian), *Eshcol* (scriptural rules for church fellowship), both in volume XIII, and *The True Nature of a Gospel Church*, in volume XVI, may be singled out as specially helpful. Readers who belong to the more or less 'established' churches will find that the careful perusal of these writings will enable them to understand the mind and stance of 'independent' churches in greater measure, and indeed in a heart-searching fashion. The study and discussion of works like these, along with Owen's *Union among Protestants*, in volume XIV, might do much towards a mutual understanding and sympathy amongst evangelical people today.

Attention has already been drawn to Owen's works on the ministry, but mention should also be made of his sermons on *The Lord's Supper.* Volume IX contains twenty-five of these, including five on 1 Corinthians

11:23ff., and volume XVI has three more, published long after Owen's death, but attributed to him on internal grounds. As with other extant sermons preached by Owen at the Lord's Supper, they indicate that he frequently administered the Supper midweek rather than only on the Lord's day.

In these short pieces he draws attention to some of the distinctive features of the Lord's Supper, in the way the believer's concentration is drawn to Christ's body *as sacrificed* and his blood *as shed* rather than to the person or presence of Christ in more general terms. He also shows that in the Supper it is not the Father or the Spirit, but Christ himself who invites us to come to him in faith. Volume XVI also contains an interesting treatment *Of Infant Baptism and Dipping*, both of which Owen discusses in the course of a dozen pages.

Finally, the massive *Commentary on Hebrews* in seven volumes ought to be mentioned. Owen had a special love for Hebrews and this work lay close to his heart. It is marked by great erudition balanced by spiritual insight and theological and practical wisdom. A number of lengthy essays preface the whole work, of which those on The Sacerdotal Office of Christ, and the Day of Sacred Rest (both in volume XIX) may be singled out as of special value.

The words of Thomas Chalmers are adequate commendation of the Hebrews commentary: 'We regard it—as Owen himself did—as his "greatest work": A work of gigantic strength as well as gigantic size; and he who hath mastered it is very little short, both in respect to the doctrinal and practical of Christianity, of being an erudite and accomplished theologian.'[1]

Concluding thoughts

These, then, are some of the riches of Owen's *Works*.[2] They contain the fruit of a lifetime's study of Scripture, and the reader will often find himself thinking that Owen weighed up almost every possible nuance of meaning and application of every verse of the Bible. As with others,

[1] Quoted in *Works*, XVII:xi.
[2] A version of the Latin material published in the original Goold edition has now been published as *Biblical Theology: The History of Theology from Adam to Christ*, edited by Stephen J. Westcott (Pittsburgh: Soli Deo Gloria Publications, 1994).

it is in his almost incidental use of a verse or passage that the fruit of long and deep meditation comes to the surface. That can be overwhelming and almost depressing, but it will be an encouragement as well as a rebuke to us as we read.

What is important, however, is not to *read* much but to *profit* much. That is why regular and regulated study is of value, and leads to a developing ability to read, mark, learn, and inwardly digest the great spiritual lessons Owen expounds. To pastors and teachers there will be a certain value in using the whole set of the *Works* as a constant companion and help, using the Owen *corpus* as a library of pastoral theology. To others the greatest help may come from the specifically practical or doctrinal volumes. But, as W. H. Goold once wrote, *all* Owen's work is marked by the spiritual application of divine truth to human character generally, and to the experience of the saints in particular. It is this experimental dimension in all Owen's teaching that is of universal and permanent value, and brings us nearer to the great goal of his ministry, which was, quite simply, to help his fellow Christians to live according to Scripture.

CHAPTER SEVENTEEN

JOHN FLAVEL AND
THE MYSTERY OF PROVIDENCE

I KNOW the date exactly because it was my twenty-first birthday. The presents included a heavy parcel from two of my closest friends. Inside was the then recently republished six-volume set of *The Works of John Flavel*.[1] Thus I was introduced to a centuries-old, gold-rich mine of biblical and practical Christian wisdom.

Among several outstanding works from Flavel's pen, none speaks with more power than his *Divine Conduct: or, The Mystery of Providence*.[2] The doctrine of divine providence occupies a major place in classical Puritan practical theology and interpretation of the Christian life. It stands out for its insightful, biblical and pastorally-sensitive realism. Here is truly a Puritan and spiritual classic.

A sketch of Flavel's life

Born in 1627, the elder son of a Puritan minister, John Flavel went on to study at the University of Oxford. In April 1650 he was settled as an assistant minister in Diptford, Devon, and ordained to the ministry by the local presbytery some six months later. In 1656 he received and accepted (at some loss of income) a call to Dartmouth. Six years later (1662), along with two thousand other ministers who shared his Puritan convictions, he was ejected from his living. Prohibited by the Five Mile Act

[1] John Flavel, *The Works of John Flavel*, 6 vols (1820; repr. London: Banner of Truth Trust, 1968).
[2] First published in 1678 and reprinted in *Works*, IV:336-497. References are to the *Works* followed by references in the (slightly edited) paperback reprint, *The Mystery of Providence* (London: Banner of Truth Trust, 1963).

(1665) from residing in the area, he continued to minister in whatever way he could. Meanwhile his parents, at that time settled in London, were arrested and confined in Newgate Prison. There they contracted the plague (rampant in 1665), and although bailed, both died of the disease.

Restrictions on Puritan ministers were eased following the Declaration of Indulgence (1672) and Flavel returned to Dartmouth until renewed persecution again took him away from his beloved people. Following the Declaration of Indulgence made by James II and VI in 1687 he was again reunited with them and continued to minister until his death on June 26, 1691. Married four times, he suffered the bereavement of three wives, the first of them in childbirth.

Puritan ministry

Flavel exemplified the Puritan vision of the godly minister and faithful preacher.[1] Sitting under his weekly preaching must have been a rich and nourishing spiritual privilege. He models the preaching method defined by the Westminster divines with its hallmarks:

1. An introduction to the text

2. An analysis of the main points it teaches

3. An exposition of these truths involving:

   • Clear explanation of how the truth arises *from this particular text*

   • A straightforward explanation of the doctrine taught in the text, employing other carefully selected passages to confirm it, if necessary

   • Helpful illustrations of the principle

   • A sensitive dealing with any difficulties that might arise in the minds of hearers

---

[1] Well illustrated in John Bunyan's famous description in *The Pilgrim's Progress* of the picture in Interpreter's House of 'a very grave person … eyes lifted up to heaven, the best of books in his hand, the law of truth … written upon his lips, the world was behind his back; it stood as if it pleaded with men, and a crown of gold did hang over its head'. Bunyan, *Pilgrim's Progress*, pp. 26-27.

4. Application, which may involve:

- Dealing with intellectual error

- Explaining how we should respond to the teaching

- Showing what sins the text reveals and how we are to be delivered from them

- Showing how the text helps Christians who are troubled, fearful, or doubting

- Providing 'notes of trial', i.e., answering the question: 'How do I know that what this text teaches is true for me and of me?'

- This is to be done in plain speech, with wisdom, seriousness of purpose, and love for the congregation.[1]

Divine Conduct, or The Mystery of Providence

All of this comes to fine expression in *The Mystery of Providence*. First published in 1678 it is ostensibly an exposition of Psalm 57:2 ('I cry out to God Most High, to God who fulfils his purpose for me'). The work focuses entirely on the idea that God fulfils his purposes for his people.

Flavel begins with a brief explanation of the text, but his chief interest lies in ransacking the Scriptures to provide a practical, pastoral summary of the doctrine of providence for his readers (and presumably earlier his listeners– -the book still bears some of the marks of originally being a series of spoken addresses). King David's words underline the universal influence of providence in the Christian's life; the efficacy of God's purposes; the beneficial nature of all God does for his people as he fulfils his decrees. With David, believers should reflect on the providences of God in every stage and condition of life.

Of course, our present perception is imperfect and partial. Like the apostle Peter, we do not understand what our Lord is doing, but afterwards we will (John 13:7). We see providence now like the 'disjointed wheels and scattered pins of a watch'—only in glory will we see the

---

[1] See *The Directory for the Publick Worship of God* (London, 1645), printed in *The Confession of Faith* (Inverness: F. P Publications, 1981), pp. 379-81.

complete timepiece. God, by contrast, sees providence as a unified working reality, like an 'accurate Anatomist discerning the course of all the veins and arteries of the body'.[1]

Three aspects of biblical teaching and Christian experience are stressed:

(1) The way in which God's providence operates in every aspect of our lives.

(2) The Christian's responsibility to meditate on God's providences, with practical counsel on how to do so, and on the blessings this brings.

(3) The value of keeping a record of God's providences as an aid to ongoing Christian living.

Providence governs the whole of life

One of Flavel's aims is to press home the privileges that God's providence had showered—as he saw it—on seventeenth-century England. He surveys ten kinds of 'performance' or 'fulfilment' of providence, tracing God's activity from our formation and protection in the womb, through birth, the point in history at which we live, the family in which we are reared, the dangers from which we are preserved, the temptations from which we are protected and finally the ways in which providence enables us to overcome sin and live for the Lord's glory. The chief concern here is to say: 'Do you not realize how blessed you are?'

But the providence of God takes on special significance in our conversion to Christ. Apparently random events lead individuals to faith. A visitor from Ethiopia meets an evangelist in the desert (Acts 8:26-39); a Syrian general has a captured slave girl who knows a secret of which he is ignorant (2 Kings 5:1-4); a woman makes her lonely noon-time journey to the city well and finds a thirsty stranger (John 4:1-42). The same patterns, Flavel believed, could be seen in the contemporary world; for the providence of God is not limited to biblical times. Spanish soldiers going to war enter German cities to conquer them and are brought to faith in Christ; a random piece of paper 'happens' to explain the way

[1] Flavel, *Works*, IV:348 (*Mystery*, p. 22).

of salvation; a romantic attraction brings someone into contact with a truly Christian family; a minister wanders from the main point of his sermon—and through his 'chance' remarks someone is converted; a Christian is imprisoned, and a fellow prisoner is converted through his testimony; Christians are 'tragically' persecuted and scattered, but by this means the gospel spreads. In all this God is absolutely and gloriously sovereign.

Even evil deeds can be the occasion for God's working. Flavel records one particularly gripping personal example. In 1673, a ship returning from Virginia anchored at Dartmouth. A young ship's surgeon, deeply depressed, cut his throat in a suicide attempt. As he lay dying, Flavel went on board and spoke to him about the gospel. It is not difficult to imagine the congregation on the edge of their seats as the story unfolded (it occupies two pages in the written version). The firmness with which Flavel spoke to the young man is itself remarkable. He revisited him and spent many hours with him. The young man was converted and recovered. An attempt at suicide becomes the occasion for conversion. God turns evil to good. Other experiences may not be so spectacular; but they are no less supernatural.[1]

God's providence can also be traced in his ordinary blessings, for example in our employment. Flavel has in view not our self-satisfaction but our eternal blessing: 'If you had more of the world than you have, your heads and hearts might not be able to manage it to your advantage.'[2] This places corresponding obligations squarely on our shoulders: not to be lazy; not to give our calling in this world precedence over our calling to trust and serve the Lord; not to forget that God himself is our ultimate benefactor.

One of the greatest of all God's providences is the blessing of marriage and family life: 'a prudent wife is from the LORD' (Prov. 19:14). God works in his own wonderful and unexpected ways. There are lessons to be learned:

[1] Indeed, Flavel presses home the importance of thinking about this: 'And now suffer me to expostulate a little with thy soul. Reader ... O therefore, set a special mark upon that providence that set you in the way of this mercy.' See *Works*, IV:385-87 (*Mystery*, pp. 70-74).
[2] *Ibid.*, IV:390 (*Mystery*, p. 78).

Not what you projected, but what an higher Counsel than yours determined, is come to pass .... Improve relations, to the end providence designed them: Walk together as co-heirs of the grace of life: Study to be mutual blessings to each other: So walk in your relations, that the parting day may be sweet. Death will shortly break up the family; and then nothing but the sense of duty discharged, or the neglects pardoned, will give comfort.[1]

Flavel spoke from experience. When *The Mystery of Providence* was first published (1678) he had already seen his first wife and their unborn child die while she was in labour. He now had the joy of a second marriage, but his second wife would also predecease him.

Meanwhile he makes some general applications. Never forget the kindnesses God's providence provides; learn not to distrust him in the future or to murmur at new difficulties; do not be discontent; do not neglect to pray; do not worry with sinful anxiety. To do so would be to mistrust the heavenly Father who is the author of all providences.

God also providentially preserves his people from evil, both spiritual and physical. He may do the former by the counsel of another; sometimes by his intervention in creating obstacles in the very things or people that would bring harm; sometimes by illness; sometimes by clearer understanding of the meaning of Scripture; sometimes by death. Flavel finds a striking illustration in the life of the great Puritan John Dod.[2]

Being late at night in his study, he was strongly moved (though at an unseasonable hour) to visit a gentleman of his acquaintance; and not knowing what might be the design of providence therein, he obeyed and went. When he came to the house, after a few knocks at the door, the gentleman himself came to him, and asked him whether he had any business with him? Mr Dod answered, No; but that he could not be quiet till he had seen him. O sir, (replied the gentleman) you are sent of God at this hour, for just now (and

---

[1] *Works*, IV:394-95 (*Mystery*, pp. 84-85).

[2] John Dod (1550–1645), son-in-law of Richard Greenham, was highly esteemed by many of the leading Puritans. William Haller well notes: 'No one probably did more than he to fix by personal influence and example the way of life and style of preaching followed for generations by the rank and file of the Puritan ministry.' W. Haller, *The Rise of Puritanism* (New York: Columbia University Press, 1938), p. 58.

with that takes the halter[1] out of his pocket) I was going to destroy myself. And thus was the mischief prevented.[2]

The Puritans placed great stress on the role of Scripture in finding the guidance of God. Like John Dod, Flavel believed in the ongoing supernatural operations of God in providence, even extending to the subjective 'sense' an individual might have, prompting him to action (analogous to Calvin's 'secret instinct of the Spirit'[3]). But he never dislocated it from the revealed will of God in Scripture.

In his providence God provides special protection for his children. Dartmouth was a busy port and Flavel wrote several works applying this principle to seafarers.[4] Thus he was able to appeal to his own people: 'Many of you have seen wonders of salvation upon the deeps where the hand of God hath been signally stretched forth for your rescue and deliverance.'[5] How important, then, to 'Consider what is the aim of providence in all the tender care it hath manifested for you? Is it not that you should employ your bodies for God, and cheerfully apply yourselves to that service he hath called you to?'[6]

Finally, the providence of God co-operates with the internal ministry of the Holy Spirit to transform our lives, and particularly to enable us to 'mortify' the sin that continues to plague regenerate believers. Here is one of the great themes of Puritan practical theology—'How can I overcome and mortify sin?'[7] While only the blood of Christ can purge us from sin, the application of its power may be effected within the context of the ministry of providential affliction: 'Though a *cross* without

---

[1] That is, the noose with which he intended to hang himself.

[2] Flavel, *Works*, IV:399 (*Mystery*, p. 91).

[3] For example, in *Institutes*, I.xvi.9; commentaries on Matt. 21:8; Luke 19:5; John 19:20; 1 Cor. 11:24, and many other places.

[4] These included his earlier work, *The Seaman's Companion wherein the Mysteries of Providence, relating to Seamen, are opened; their Sins and Dangers discovered; their Duties pressed, and their several Troubles and Burdens relieved. In six practicable and suitable Sermons* (1676), *Works*, V:342-416.

[5] Flavel, *Ibid.*, IV:403 (*Mystery*, p. 95).

[6] *Ibid.*, IV:405 (*Mystery*, p. 97).

[7] John Owen's famous work on *The Mortification of Sin* grew out of sermons he preached in Oxford when many of his hearers must have been teenage boys. Owen, *Works*, VI:1-86.

a Christ, never did any man good, yet thousands have been beholden to the *cross*, as it hath wrought in the virtue of his death for their good.'¹

Thus external providences become the instruments by which God uncovers our indwelling sin, reveals its strength to us, shows us how attached we still are to sinful desires, and motivates us to greater holiness. Flavel expresses this in a wonderfully quaint statement:

> These afflictions have the same use and end to our souls, that frosty weather hath upon those clothes, that are laid a bleaching: they alter the hue, and make them whiter, Dan. 11:35. 'Some of the understanding shall fail, to try them, and to purge, and to make them white.'²

What, then, is our response to be? It is to meditate on God's providence. But how?

How to meditate on the providence of God

Flavel himself was much given to meditation on two things: the word of God and the providences of God. His facility with Scripture is outstanding. In many ways *The Mystery of Providence* is a tapestry woven from biblical principles and history, with additional illustrations and practical application. He seems to know every part, indeed every page, of Scripture well.

Failure to meditate on God's providence is sinful. It diminishes our praises of God. Moreover we deny ourselves benefit from the nourishment our faith would receive. We slight the God who acts. Meditation on God's providence is therefore essential if we are to come to him in prayer and know how to address him. But how are we to learn to meditate?

Answering 'How to?' questions was a major element in Puritan preaching: 'In exhorting to duties, he [the preacher] is, as he seeth cause, to teach also the means that help to the performance of them.'³ Flavel offers the following four principles.

1. *Work hard at remembering and exploring the providence of God toward you.* We should do this *extensively*, tracing his ways through

---

¹ Flavel, *Works*, IV:408, emphasis his (*Mystery*, p. 102).
² *Ibid.*, IV:407 (*Mystery*, p. 101-2).
³ *Directory for the Publick Worship of God*, p. 380.

our life, counting the blessings he has poured out on us. We must do it *intensively* also: 'Let not your thoughts swim like *feathers* upon the surface of the waters, but sink like *lead* to the bottom.'[1] Explore the timing of God's actions, and the care they express. Think about the means he has employed—sometimes a stranger or even an enemy rather than a friend, sometimes an evil act rather than a beneficent one. Consider the way in which 'all things' work together for believers (Rom 8:28): 'a thousand friendly hands are at work for them to promote and bring about their happiness'. In particular we should try to trace the relationship between prayer and providence to see how 'providences have borne the very signatures of your prayers upon them'.[2]

2. *Trace the connection between the providences of God in your life and the promises of God in his word.* This confirms the reliability of Scripture and teaches us what course of action we should adopt in any given set of circumstances. Our decisions should be made on the basis of God's revealed will (in Scripture), not on the basis of his secret will (which comes to expression in providence). As the latter unfolds, we discover that God is always faithful to his promises.

3. *Look beyond the events and circumstances of providence to God himself as author and provider.* Think of the attributes and ways of God (his love, wisdom, grace, condescension, purposes, methods, and goodness). Recognize how he reveals these things in his dealings with you. Remember too that God often works out his purposes through painful trials. He is sovereign in all things, gracious, wise, faithful, all-sufficient and unchanging—this especially we need to know in the darkness of affliction: 'God is what he was, and where he was.'[3]

4. *Respond to each providence in an appropriate way.* Even if their response is sorrow, biblically-instructed believers will always

---

[1] 'Flavel, *Works*, IV:417, emphasis his (*Mystery*, p. 118).
[2] *Ibid.*, IV:418-19 (*Mystery*, p. 120).
[3] *Ibid.*, IV:428 (*Mystery*, p. 132).

experience an element of comfort and even joy. For no element of God's providence should be read as a mark of his enmity against us. After all, 'All your losses are but as the loss of a *farthing*[1] to a prince.' God's 'heart is full of love, whilst the face of providence is full of frowns'.[2] The Christian who realizes that 'the Lord is near' (Phil. 4:5) will see all these things in their proper perspective.

But what are we to do when the providences of God do not seem to coalesce with his promises?

1. *Learn how to resist discouragement.* God is teaching us patience. It may not yet be God's time to act; we may be asking impatiently; he may be increasing our appetite for the blessing for which we long. What are we to do? We need to remember he is bringing about a yet greater blessing—our willingness to depend entirely on God and his good pleasure; he delights to come when we are at the end of our own resources. Furthermore, we may not be ready yet to receive the blessing. If all his mercies are of grace and we do not deserve them, then we need to learn to wait for them.

2. *Learn not to assume you fully and clearly understand God's ways and purposes.* 'There are hard texts in the works, as well as in the word of God. It becomes us modestly and humbly to reverence, but not to dogmatize too boldly and positively about them; a man may easily get a strain by over-reaching.'[3] In Psalm 73, Asaph increased his depression by trying to understand all the intricacies of God's ways; the same can be true for us. This only breeds a sense of suspicion of God, a darkness of spirit, and tempts us to take matters into our own hands. But that would be to distrust providence, and to reject the wisdom and love of God.

Meditating in this way on God's providence leads to an ongoing communion with God, since he 'manifests himself to his *people* by

---

[1] The coin of least value in England until withdrawn from currency in the twentieth century.

[2] *Works*, IV:429 (*Mystery*, pp. 133-34).

[3] *Ibid.*, IV:435 (*Mystery*, p. 140).

providences, as well as ordinances'.¹ It is also a major pleasure of the Christian life to be able to trace the harmony of God's attributes as he expresses them in his providences.

Such meditation also serves to '*over-power and suppress the natural atheism that is in your hearts*'.² Natural atheism? Flavel was a wise enough pastor to know that some true believers are afflicted with doubts about God's goodness and even his very existence. Here our meditations on the providence of God can serve like a bulwark as we trace the clear lines of his loving care and mighty power in our lives.

In this way faith is supported by what we have seen of God in the past (e.g., the young David drew strength for his conflict with Goliath from his memories of the providence of God in his past, 1 Sam. 17:37). Thus a spirit of praise breathes a sweet melody into our lives and Christ becomes more important to us, since all of God's mercies come to us only in and through him. With melted hearts, inward poise in an unstable world, and an increased devotion to holiness, we are thus equipped to face death—in what Flavel realized was sometimes a time of considerable inner turmoil and special temptation from Satan.³ Dying is one of the two most difficult acts of faith (the other is coming to Christ for the first time). But the dying believer who is able to rehearse the blessings of God's providence in his or her life will surely know God's peace.

Questions

Such a perspective on God's providence draws us to a fuller appreciation of his presence and power; it leads us to trust him when fresh difficulties face us; it calls us to renewed consecration to his will. Yet perhaps there are still unanswered questions. Flavel deals briefly with five:

1. *What are we to do when we find it difficult to discern God's will?* While God revealed his will in various ways in the past, he does so now

---

¹ *Works*, IV:436 (*Mystery*, p. 144).
² *Ibid.*, IV:442 (*Mystery*, p. 151).
³ A view he held in common with many other Puritan pastors. Cf. the remarks by Owen in the preface to his *Glory of Christ* (1684), Owen, *Works*, I:280-84, and the vivid descriptions of the Christian's experience in the closing sections to both Parts One and Two of Bunyan's *Pilgrim's Progress*.

through his word: 'all are tied up to the ordinary standing rule of the written word, and must not expect any such extraordinary revelations from God.'[1] If Scripture does not speak directly to our situation, our task is prayerfully to apply its general principles. Admittedly 'God doth give men secret hints and intimations of his will by his providence ... but yet providences in themselves, are no stable rule of duty nor sufficient discovery of the will of God.'[2]

Here is Flavel's counsel:

> If therefore in doubtful cases, you would discover God's will, govern yourself in your search after it by these rules:
>
> • Get the true fear of God upon your hearts; be really afraid of offending him ...
>
> • Study the *word* more, and the concerns and interests of the world less ...
>
> • Reduce what you know into practice, and you shall know what is your duty to practise ...
>
> • Pray for illumination and direction in the way you should go; beg the Lord to guide you in straits, and that he would not suffer you to fall into sin ...
>
> • And this being done, follow providence so far as it agrees with the word, and no further ...[3]

Flavel's emphasis stands in stark contrast to the 'inner light' movements of his time. It stands, too, in contrast with contemporary views of guidance that imply the Christian can bypass Scripture in order to have direct access to the secret will of God.

2. How can we cope when God seems to be slow in working for our relief and blessing? God has his own calendar. 'The Lord doth not compute and reckon his seasons of working by our *arithmetic*.'[4] No doubt Satan

---

[1] *Works*, IV:468 (*Mystery*, p. 186).
[2] *Ibid.*, IV:469 (*Mystery*, pp. 186-87).
[3] *Ibid.*, IV:470-71 (*Mystery*, pp. 188-89).
[4] *Ibid.*, IV:472 (*Mystery*, p. 191).

will seek to make capital out of our uncertainty. So we need to be sure we are relying on the promise of God and not on wishful thinking, and that our motives are truly spiritual, and our wills truly submissive to God's. 'Enjoyment of your desires is the thing that will please you, but resignation of your wills is that which is pleasing to God.'[1] The mercies of God are worth waiting for. After all, he has waited patiently for us! Indeed, our impatience with him is sufficient reason for the 'delay' we experience in his fulfilling his promises to us!

3. *How can we tell whether a specific event in God's providence is an expression of his love—or not?* Events in themselves do not carry with them an infallible explanation of what God means to accomplish through them. We dare not insist that God explain himself in detail to us, as though he were accountable to us. And God's providences often work like medicine—bitter to taste, health-giving in effect. Painful providences may be expressions of God's love designed to deal with specific sinful dispositions and to sanctify us.

On the other hand, pleasant providences are not necessarily evidences of God's love. If they do not come in the context of prayer, if we possess them through sin, if we abuse God's gifts and become proud and self-sufficient, neglect our duty to the Lord, become indifferent to the needs of others—then they are not evidences of his love for us. But if, on the other hand, these mercies humble us, safeguard us from sin, increase our love for God, and never themselves become the objects of our satisfaction, but rather make us sensitive to the needs of others and more concerned to serve the Lord; if they lead us to praise him—then indeed such providences have been sanctified in our lives.

4. *How can we develop stability in our Christian lives when the providences of God are painful for us to bear?* Flavel insists that we need such providences. 'The earth doth not need more chastening frosts and mellowing snows, than our hearts do nipping providences.'[2] But nothing can separate us from the love of Christ, and anything that seems to be

---

[1] *Works*, IV:476 (*Mystery*, p. 195).
[2] *Ibid.*, IV:487 (*Mystery*, p. 209).

able to do so is of temporary duration. Anxiety is fruitless; we need to remember that all things are in our heavenly Father's power and purpose.

5. *How can we learn to be submissive to the will of God?* Remembering that we need tests and trials if we are to grow strong as Christians, five principles are fundamental:

- Recollect how infinitely wise God is, and how limited your own understanding is.

- Realize that anxious thoughts about God's ways are actually sinful as well as harmful.

- Reflect on the examples of submission you find in Scripture— *'shame yourselves out of this quarrelling temper with providence'*.[1]

- Recognize the advantages there are in a submissive will—it creates a perpetual sabbath in the Christian's heart.

- Remember that an insubordinate will is fatal to both our prayers and our profession of faith.

Thus Christians are called to 'lie down meekly at your Father's feet, and say in all cases, and at all times, "*The will of the Lord be done.*"'[2]

It is typical of Flavel that he closes with very basic and very practical advice: learn to record in writing the providences of God in your life. In this way you will preserve the memory of them for future meditation and encouragement:

> Providence carries our lives, liberties, and concernments in its hand every moment. Your bread is in its cupboard, your money in its purse, your safety in its enfolding arms: and sure it is the least part of what you owe, to record the favours you receive at its hands.[3]

Wise counsel indeed from a wise and good shepherd, John Flavel.

---

[1] *Works*, IV:494 (*Mystery*, p. 216).
[2] *Ibid.*, IV:495 (*Mystery*, p. 218).
[3] *Ibid.*, IV:496 (*Mystery*, p. 220).

Reflections

John Flavel's grasp of the doctrine of providence and his pastoral wisdom in expounding and applying it are themselves adequate commendation of this wonderful book. It is easy to read, yet deeply thought-provoking: biblically focused, yet throbbing with a sense of God's ongoing activity; rigorously Puritan, yet wonderfully sensitive to human pain. Written for a generation living in times of social and political upheaval, for people who knew a great deal of the angst which we moderns often mistakenly view as peculiarly post-modern, it speaks to the twenty-first century with the same power as it did to the seventeenth. More than that, it spells out loudly and clearly a number of biblical principles which Christians today desperately need to hear:

- God is in control of his universe.

- God is working out his perfect purposes.

- God is not my servant.

- God's ways are far more mysterious and wonderful than I can understand.

- God is good—all of the time; I can trust him—all of the time.

- God's timetable is not the same as mine.

- God is far more interested in what I become than in what I do.

- Freedom from suffering is no part of the promise of the Christian gospel.

- Suffering is an integral part of the Christian life.

- God works through suffering to fulfil his purposes in me.

- God's purposes, not mine, are what bring him glory.

- God guides me by enabling me to read his providences through the lenses of his word.

- I have few greater pleasures than tracing the wonders of God's ways.

Learning these lessons from John Flavel will transform your life and do you endless and eternal good!

CHAPTER EIGHTEEN

PREACHING THE LAW OF GOD: REFORMERS AND PURITANS

THE subject of the teaching and preaching of the Reformers and Puritans on the subject of the law of God is both vast and exceedingly important simply because it was so central to their understanding of the Bible as a whole, and the gospel in particular.

Whenever the meaning of the grace of God in the gospel has been discovered, the question of the place and significance of the law has arisen. Thus, in Galatians 3, in the light of his exposition of God's gracious covenant with Abraham, Paul raises the question: 'What, then, is the function of the law?' (Gal. 3:19). At the time of Luther and Calvin in the sixteenth century the same issue arose; as it did a hundred years later in the days of the Puritans. After a century of Reformed thought on the matter, Samuel Bolton was still able to write in 1645 that the subject of the law involved 'the greatest knots in the practical part of divinity'.[1]

Bolton's judgment remains valid in our own time, which makes this subject theologically, as well as practically and pastorally, relevant. Decades have now passed since the beginning of an extraordinary upsurge of scholarly interest in the role of God's covenant in Scripture. What had been marginalized by the historical-critical methodology of the previous century now re-emerged as a central dynamic of the revelation of God and the faith of Israel. It should not surprise us that the next question on the agenda would be: How do we understand the role of the law within the context of the New Testament gospel?[2] Thus, today, one can hardly

[1] Samuel Bolton, *The True Bounds of Christian Freedom* (1645; repr. London: Banner of Truth Trust, 1964), p. 51.

[2] It is interesting to note in this connection that just as the 'new view of Paul'

be classed as a cutting-edge New Testament scholar without having made a pronouncement on the subject of Jesus and Paul and the law.

So, this is a subject of immense importance, and it is so from both a theological and a pastoral point of view. Go wrong here and we are in danger of mishandling the Scriptures and the gospel. As John Newton noted, most errors in the Christian life are rooted in erroneous thinking about the law of God: 'Ignorance of the nature and design of the law is at the bottom of most religious mistakes.'[1]

Since it is such a vast subject, however, we will focus here on providing an overview of the structure and inner logic of the Reformed approach to the law of God. While that necessarily means there will be much left unsaid, it will have the virtue of providing a theological anatomy on which the flesh and blood can be built. Certainly, for working pastors, that is the first need.

The Reformers

The teaching of the Reformers and Puritans on the law did not arise *de novo*. They were more conscious of historical continuities in the history of theology than we tend to be. Some of the elements in their thought they received from the groundwork of Thomas Aquinas,[2] or at least developed from the tradition he had fathered. Nevertheless, the dawning of the Reformation in the work of Luther broke new ground, and with him we will begin.

---

precipitated by the work of E. P. Sanders was bubbling under the surface of New Testament scholarship, to emerge in full flood in the next two decades, already in his Essay II on the theology of Romans, appended to his commentary, C. E. B. Cranfield devoted more space to the subject of the Old Testament law than to all aspects of Christology. He did so on the basis that 'there has been widespread misunderstanding of Paul's attitude to the law, which has involved a serious distortion of his theology as a whole and has also bedevilled a good deal of discussion of other matters'. C. E. B. Cranfield, *A Critical and Exegetical Commentary on The Epistle to the Romans*, 2 vols (Edinburgh: T&T Clark, 1975, 1979), p. 845.

[1] *The Works of John Newton* (London, 1820), I:339.

[2] For an accessible introduction, see Stephen J. Casselli, 'The Threefold Division of the Law in the Thought of Aquinas', *Westminster Theological Journal*, 61 (1999), pp. 175-207.

Martin Luther

Martin Luther's theology was quarried out of the interface between his reading of Romans and Galatians on the one hand, and his own personal pilgrimage on the other. Much more of a medieval man than Calvin, Luther seemed to leap from the life of medieval monk to that of Protestant reformer without really passing through the Renaissance to any perceptible level. When in his great hymn *Ein' feste Burg ist unser Gott* he teaches us to sing—

> And were this world all devils o'er,
> And watching to devour us—

Luther is, for all practical purposes, describing the world he believed he inhabited, full of demonic opposition to Christ, grace, the gospel, and the believer—and not least to Luther himself. Thus when in 1520 his powerful early works created such a storm throughout Europe, freedom from alien powers was a sub-theme of both *The Babylonian Captivity of the Church* and *The Freedom of a Christian*.

Luther saw four alien powers ranged against the believer, and he regarded the New Testament's personifications of Sin, Law, and Death as virtual demonizations of them—as a series of alien forces ranged, alongside Satan, against man. The gospel brings freedom from these powers, and therefore frees us from the law. For Luther the law creates bondage and kills; by contrast the gospel brings freedom and new life. The law is accuser, prosecutor, judge, and jailer all in one. The gospel is pardoner, defender, acquitter, and friend all in one. The law and the gospel are opposed to each other. Within this matrix, Luther, generally speaking, holds to a radical antithesis between grace and law.

This principle permeated his whole approach to reading and even translating the Bible. Thus he comments:

> In translating the Holy Scriptures I follow two rules: First, if some passage is obscure I consider whether it treats of grace or law, whether wrath or the forgiveness of sin [is contained in it], and with which of these it agrees better … In theology there are law and gospel, and it must be one or the other.[1]

---

[1] *Table Talk*, in Luther's *Works*, ed. & tr. T. G. Tappert (Philadelphia: Fortress Press, 1967), LIV:42.

Later in his *Table Talk* he adds: 'Anybody who wishes to be a theologian must … understand it must be one or the other.'[1] The importance of this lies in the fact that, 'It's the supreme art of the devil that he can make the law out of the gospel.'[2] Hence the need to be able to distinguish between them:

> If I were able to do this perfectly I would never again be sad. Whoever apprehends this has won. Whatever is Scripture is either law or gospel. One of the two must triumph. The law leads to despair; the gospel leads to salvation. I learn more about this every day … .[3]

The *Commentary on Galatians* is rich with purple passages developing this theme and the freedom the Christian has from the law as a hostile power.

> This is then the proper and true definition of a Christian: that he is the child of grace and remission of sins, which is under no law, but is above the law, sin, death and hell. And even as Christ is free from the grave, and Peter from the prison, so is a Christian free from the law. And such a respect there is between the justified conscience and the law, as is between Christ raised from the grave, and Peter from the prison, so is a Christian free from the law.[4]

But it was not long before Luther's erstwhile student and friend Johannes Agricola (sometimes known as Islebius because he came from Eisleben) drew what seemed, to him, to be the logical implications of the master's teaching: namely, that the Christian has no need whatsoever for law. If love is law's fulfilment (Rom. 13:10) the believer is freed from the law in every respect. Sensing the smoke from the flames he associated with the radical left wing of the Reformation, Luther responded that this was a crass error and a serious misunderstanding of his teaching. It illustrated the problem that people do not know how to distinguish between

[1] *Table Talk*, p. III.
[2] *Ibid.*, p. 106.
[3] *Ibid.*, p. III.
[4] Martin Luther, *Commentary on Galatians*, ed. P. S. Watson (London: James Clarke & Co., 1953), p. 161.

the law and the gospel. Luther himself did not claim fully to understand it![1] But this much he did understand:

> Anybody who abolishes the teaching of the law in a political context abolishes government and domestic life, and anybody who abolishes the law in an ecclesiastical context ceases to have a knowledge of sin. … Away with him who claims that transgressors don't sin against the law but only dishonour the Son of God! Such speculative theologians are the bane of the churches. Without a conscience, without knowledge, and without logical discrimination they teach everything confusedly and say things like this, 'Love is the fulfilment of the law and therefore we have no need of the law.' But those wretched fellows neglect the minor premise: that this fulfilment (namely love) is weak in our flesh, that we must struggle daily against the flesh with the help of the Spirit, and this belongs under the law.[2]

Luther therefore preaches the law to the believer. In general terms it acts as a restraint, within both society and church; more particularly it continues to crush and humble the believer.[3] Thus, in his exposition of the Sermon on the Mount, Luther shows the continuing relevance of the law.[4] So long as the believer is in this world, he will find that the law crushes pride and self-righteousness so that he looks to Christ for grace.

> The law, when it is in his true sense, doth nothing else but reveal sin, engender wrath, accuse and terrify men, so that it bringeth them to the very brink of desperation. This is the proper use of the law, and here it hath an end, and it ought to go no further.[5]

Luther, then, stresses that the proper work of the law is to kill; but in addition, it serves as a guard and restraint on behaviour.

---

[1] *Table Talk*, p. 127.
[2] *Ibid.*, p. 233.
[3] Luther, *Comm. Galatians*, pp. 298ff.
[4] See his treatment of the law in his exposition of *The Sermon on the Mount*, tr. J. Pelikan, in Luther's *Works* (St Louis, MO: Concordia Publishing House, 1968), vol. XXI:67-129.
[5] *Ibid.*, p. 302; cf. p. 303.

John Calvin

As is well known, while Calvin shared Luther's view of the condemning function of the law, his own teaching had a broader base and exudes a different ethos. Calvin was very decidedly a Renaissance scholar; his first published work (1532), a commentary on Seneca's *De Clementia*, already marked him out as a more exacting textual scholar than Luther ever was. Furthermore, his exposition of the law, befitting the fact that his earlier training had been in law, is far less concerned with the law as a power, and far more sensitive to the law as instructor. Less exciting than Luther, and certainly less verbally violent, Calvin's distinction lies in his ability to combine careful textual exegesis with a penetrating sense of the theological import of a passage and an extraordinarily advanced grasp of the flow of redemptive history.

Calvin inherited the traditional formulations of Aquinas. Aquinas had held that the biblical teaching on the law of God can be understood as a series of concentric circles which have their centre in the mind, will, and character of God. In the divine mind is a blueprint for the proper ordering of the created universe.

This comes to expression in creation in natural law and then in what Aquinas calls *old law*. Presupposing natural law, it is realized in the law of Moses with its threefold division of moral law and then ceremonial and civil law, both of which are rooted in the moral law. This old law was given to God's ancient people, Israel. It is shaped for them as God's chosen people. But old law is temporary and looks to, and is fulfilled in, Jesus Christ. New law is written in the heart by Christ through the Spirit.

The new law is continuous with the old; indeed the new is contained in the old as the tree is contained within the seed, virtually. But it is also discontinuous, since the ceremonial aspects of the old law are fulfilled in Christ, and the judicial made void now that the people of God have been constituted as an international community.[1]

Calvin took over this tradition and modified it within the context of the strongly Christ-centred and trinitarian character of his theology.

Three things are important if we are to grasp how Calvin interprets the New Testament's understanding of the role of the law in the gospel,

---

[1] Aquinas devotes Questions 90-108 of his *Summa Theologiae* to these issues.

and especially those passages which seem to present law and gospel in sharp antithesis.

1. Calvin holds that in the history of redemption there is a unity of substance between the old and the new covenants, since both belong to the one covenant of grace. But within that unity there are differences in administration from the time of Adam, through Abraham and Moses until the fulfilment of the covenant in Christ. Some contrasts between Old and New are explicable in this context. Standing, as the New Testament writers do, within the privileges of the epoch of fulfilment, the epoch of Moses (for all its glory) inevitably seems tawdry by comparison: 'these things are not affirmed absolutely of the law or of the gospel, but only in so far as the one is contrasted with the other'.[1]

2. Calvin also holds that sometimes the antithesis between old and new is to be interpreted in terms of the contrast between the letter and the Spirit. This, for him, explains some instances of an apparently negative view of the law in Paul. Legalism, for Calvin, means severing law from the character of the Law-giver. That leads to using law as 'bare law'[2] rather than as law-within-covenant and therefore related to Christ and the work of the Spirit. Calvin understands that *nomos* is used in several different ways in the New Testament, and a true exegesis requires great care in discriminating these different senses.

3. The *telos* (completion or perfection) of the law as well as the *scopus* (scope) of the whole of the Bible is Jesus Christ. He is the end of the law (Rom. 10:4). When it is severed from him its true role in the divine economy becomes incomprehensible. Thus, commenting on Romans 10:4 he notes: 'The law in all its parts has reference to Christ, and therefore no one will be able to understand it correctly who does not constantly strive to attain this mark.'[3]

---

[1] Calvin, *Comm. 2 Corinthians*, p. 42 (on 2 Cor. 3:6).
[2] See, for example, *Institutes*, II.vii.6-14.
[3] Calvin, *Comm. Romans*, p. 222 (on Rom. 10:4).

The law, therefore, according to Paul (Gal. 3:24), serves as a grammarian-schoolmaster which reveals our unrighteousness and in turn leads us by the hand to seek and find Christ. It holds hands with the gospel in order to bring us to faith.

At the same time Calvin sees a distinctive structure in the law of God, and this emerges not only in his teaching in his *Institutes*, but also vividly in his great *Harmony of the Last Four Books of the Pentateuch*. Here he rearranges Exodus, Leviticus, Numbers, and Deuteronomy in order to bring out the theological structure of God's revelation (while recognizing that treating these books as a harmony was bound to cause some irritation to the person reading them in their canonical order!). He saw a fourfold structure:

(1) The revelation of the character of God;

(2) The moral foundations for godly living in the Decalogue;

(3) Supplements or appendages to this moral law. There are two of these:

(i) The first is ceremonial law which concerns pardon for the breach of the relationship with God described in the first table of the law.

(ii) The second governs the way in which the Decalogue is applied in the form of civil law which governs his people as a society. These 'neither change nor detract from the rule laid down in the Ten Commandments; but are only helps …'.[1]

(4) The law then functioned to bring a sense of guilt and need, and thus to point towards its *telos* in Christ.

Thus for Calvin the law reveals God's righteous character, restrains evil in society, and functions as a rule of life to guide Christian believers in the way of life that is pleasing to God. Yes, the law is abrogated in one sense: the ceremonial law is fulfilled in Christ and abrogated—not in effect but in use; the civil law relevant to the Jewish state is now

---

[1] John Calvin, *Commentaries on the Last Four Books of Moses*, tr. C. W. Bingham (Edinburgh, 1852), Preface, p. xvii.

not applicable *simpliciter* to the Gentile world; the moral law no longer condemns us, but nevertheless continues to function as our guide to godliness.[1]

In the late sixteenth century Calvin's *Institutes* became required reading at Oxford and Cambridge. A remarkably steady flow of translations of his works appeared,[2] and this perspective was bequeathed to what later become the Puritan movement, and to this we now turn.

The Puritans

It would not be realistic in this context to provide an historical overview of the Puritan doctrine of the law, or of the Antinomian controversies which dogged the 1640s and 1690s.[3] In fact, it is a little naive to speak of *the* Puritan view of the law. Even in the 1640s when the Westminster divines were crafting the nineteenth chapter of the *Confession of Faith* it is evident from the minutes that they found it extremely difficult to phrase the chapter in such a way as to account for or, at least, to provide an acceptably broad statement of the nature, continuity, and functions of the law.[4]

Puritan preaching employed various preaching grids; the most basic of which was that preaching

(1) unmasked the gospel hypocrite who relied on works rather than on grace,

(2) converted the sinner,

(3) comforted the afflicted, and

(4) built up the saints to equip them to glorify and enjoy God and to prepare them for heaven.

---

[1] See his exposition in *Institutes*, II.vii.2.

[2] See C. D. Cremeans, *The Reception of Calvinist Thought* (Urbana, 1949), p. 60; P. Schaff, *Creeds of Christendom* (New York, 1877), I:603. While Latin was the *lingua franca* of scholars the *Institutes* was already available in 1561 in an English translation by Thomas Norton. It had gone through seven editions by the close of the century.

[3] E. F. Kevan, *The Grace of Law* (London: Carey Kingsgate Press, 1964), remains unrivalled as a theologically sensitive survey of the Puritans' teaching in this area.

[4] In addition to the framing of the chapter at the committee stage, its content and formulation were debated on the floor of the assembly on over a dozen occasions during 1646.

SOME PASTORS AND TEACHERS

Orthodox Puritans regarded the law as a fundamental element in Christian theology and life. Consequently their preaching abounds in discussions of its role.

We will consider three areas—*first*, their biblical theology of law; *second*, their understanding of the present status of the law; and *third*, the use of the law in their preaching and pastoral ministry. The first of these will require more detailed treatment, but without an understanding of it we may be in danger of mimicking the Puritans without actually understanding them.

1. The Puritan biblical theology of law

In keeping with the tradition they inherited from Calvin, the Puritans held that the law of God is a revelation of the character of God ('the image of God's mind'[1] as Thomas Goodwin noted using a phrase the earlier Thomas—Aquinas—might well have employed). As such it was written into the heart of man ('by implantation' as Anthony Burgess puts it[2]) when he was created as the image of God.

> God made man after his image, and so implanted it in him, that that image could not be destroyed, unless man destroyed himself.[3]

What was implanted in man, in creation, then, was nothing less or other than the moral law:

> Thus was the Morall Law written in his heart and what the command is for direction, that he was for conversation ... all must necessarily think, that the Morall Law implanted in his heart, and obedience thereunto, was the greatest part of Adam's happinesse and holinesse.[4]

This was based on a common Puritan interpretation of Romans 2:14-15: 'For when Gentiles, who do not have the law, by nature do what

---

[1] Thomas Goodwin, *Works*, IV:316.

[2] Anthony Burgess, *Vindiciae Legis* (London, 1647; 2nd ed.), p. 113.

[3] *Ibid.*, p. 114.

[4] *Ibid.*, pp. 117-18. Cf. William Perkins, *A Godly and Learned Exposition of Christ's Sermon on the Mount*, in *The Works of William Perkins* (London, 1631), III:33; *The Marrow of Modern Divinity* (1645, 1648), in *The Whole Works of Thomas Boston*, ed. S. McMillan (Aberdeen, 1848–52), VII:173-74.

the law requires, they are a law to themselves, even though they do not have the law.'

While Puritan authors were aware that these words had been applied to Gentile believers (as a number of exegetes apply them today), they were generally convinced that Paul was here affirming that man is constituted with an instinctive knowledge of God's law, which is never wholly obliterated, and manifests itself in various ways. 'There is a law in the minds of men which is a rule of good and evil', writes Stephen Charnock. It is 'universal' and 'is the law of nature'.[1]

In this general connection, the Puritans frequently stressed that this implanted natural law, since it was part of man as divine image, was suited to him; it *fitted* the nature of his humanity. Charnock, again, comments: 'The law and his nature were like two exact straight lines, touching one another in every part when joined together.'[2]

There, in Eden, obedience was *easy* and natural for him, in keeping with man's holy instincts. Thus John Howe notes that the law was 'exactly contempered to his nature, highly approvable to his reason'.[3] And, in addition, in Eden obedience was the twin brother of happiness: 'Thus the law was exactly framed to the nature of man; man had twisted in him a desire of happiness.'[4]

In addition, in order to test, approve, and develop moral fibre and covenant relationship, God added a positive law to natural light. This was a specific divine command which had its rationale exclusively in the fact that God commanded it. This positive law was the command not to eat of the tree of the knowledge of good and evil. It was a *moral* command in the sense that it was commanded by God. But it was a law superimposed upon the moral law written in the heart. The rationale for this command could not be read off the nature of things by Adam. He was called to obey this law for no other reason than that it came from God himself.

When Adam fell, two things happened:

---

[1] Stephen Charnock, *The Complete Works of Stephen Charnock* (Edinburgh, 1864), I:166-67.

[2] *Ibid.*, II:312

[3] John Howe, *The Works of John Howe* (London, n.d.), I:464.

[4] Charnock, *Works*, II:28. Cf. Owen, *Works*, VI:165, 472.

(1) He breached the whole law.[1]

(2) The law-within-the-heart as an instinct to moral obedience was radically damaged. There was a difference of opinion here as to whether it had been entirely obliterated and had actually required some kind of rewriting,[2] or continued to echo in the conscience. In the opinion of the majority, the light of nature within man became both dim and distorted. The law written on his heart was smudged; it remained present, but was less clear. The disposition to obey that law without reservation or shortcoming, and to do so for God's pleasure, and in a way that brought both God and Adam pleasure, was lost. The law now required to be rewritten clearly and externally, while the fallen man himself required to be regenerated.

For the Puritan theology, the rewriting took place, on tablets of stone, at Sinai. The law given there was one and the same for substance with the moral law written in the heart at creation. But it was now written externally and objectively, and came with a series of appendages appropriate to the context in which it was given.

Two considerations arise here:

1. How are we to understand this new context? The law was given at Sinai within the context of God's covenant. This much was clear from Scripture. But what kind of covenant was this?

The language of the *Confession of Faith* in the mid-1640s might give the impression that the Puritan understanding of the law was univocal in every detail. That was hardly the case. For while many, perhaps the majority, regarded Sinai as essentially an expression of the covenant of grace, not a few held that the apparently negative language about Sinai and the law used in the New Testament required a different

---

[1] *Marrow of Modern Divinity, op. cit.*, p. 174.

[2] Thomas Goodwin interestingly comments with reference to Romans 2:14-15: 'That phrase ... where this light is said to be written in men's hearts ... These characters are written, not born with us; we by nature have but *abrasas tabulas*, tables in which everything is razed out; it is the new work of some second hand hath took the pains to write them there.' *Works*, X:101. Goodwin discusses this further within the context of the Prologue to John's Gospel.

interpretation. Some regarded it essentially as a republication of the covenant of works. After all, if Sinai involved a rewriting of the natural law which had been central to the covenant of works, how could it now be the covenant of grace?

Some, however, preferred to see it as a *foedus subserviens*, a rewriting of the covenant of works within the context of the covenant of grace serving the ends of the latter; others viewed it as a *foedus mixtum* with elements of both covenants.[1]

We cannot here enter into a discussion of the relative merits and demerits of these positions. Suffice it to say that however narrowly defined the Sinaitic context was, the law of nature was being set in a new context. For one thing, it was now published for *fallen* man; its commands were therefore phrased negatively. Furthermore, they came to *exodus-delivered* man and therefore were shaped to the society in which he lived with new elements of positive law (hence the references to cattle, slaves, strangers, and the seventh-day Sabbath[2]).

2. But for the Puritans the most obvious difference between the law implanted in man and the law revealed at Sinai lies in the important appendices attached to the moral law in the ceremonial and judicial laws. Herein lies their division of the law into moral, ceremonial, and civil.[3]

This threefold division was, of course, not original to the Reformers or Puritans; it is to be found in Thomas Aquinas and, to a certain extent, was part of a received tradition. In contemporary biblical scholarship it is simply assumed (largely without argument and without reference to the biblical arguments of the Puritans) that this conception is foreign to the Bible.

---

[1] Burgess, *Vindiciae Legis*, p. 213. See Samuel Bolton's discussion in *True Bounds*, pp. 88-101; also Ferguson, *John Owen on the Christian Life*, pp. 20-32.

[2] Burgess, *Vindiciae Legis*, p. 148. For a not untypical example of Puritan sensitivity to understanding the Sabbath within the flow of biblical history, see John Bunyan, *Questions about the Nature and Perpetuity of the Seventh-Day Sabbath* (London, 1685), in *The Works of John Bunyan*, ed. George Offor (Glasgow, 1854), II:358-85.

[3] Perkins, *A Commentarie upon the Epistle to the Galatians*, *Works*, II:251-52; *Works*, III:33, 36. An illustration of how Perkins reasoned in connection with the Puritan principle of the abrogation of the judicial law coupled with the continuation of the application of general equity can be found in his treatment of witchcraft in *Works*, III:650-52.

But the Puritan writers did not simply assume it; they held it to be evident in Scripture. *Inter alia* the fact that the Ten Commandments alone were placed in the Ark of the Covenant underlined that they served as the foundation, and that the ceremonies and judicial instructions were specific (and temporary) outworkings of the principles enshrined in the Decalogue.[1]

Granted the significance of these dimensions of the law would not become crystal clear until the death and resurrection of Christ and the giving of the Spirit; but Puritan theology was convinced that in this division lay an important key to understanding how revelation had a progressive character.

But, as the Old Testament showed, when the law given at Sinai was abstracted from God's revelation, it proved to be just as unsuccessful in establishing righteousness as was the law of nature. A new covenant was required in which the law would be written not on tablets of stone, but once again on the hearts of flesh of men and women (Ezek. 36:26-27).

But how could that restoration take place? In two stages:

Stage one involved the work of Christ in the recapitulation of perfect covenant obedience. For the Puritans the genius of the Old Testament administration of the law was that the permanent moral law was surrounded by temporary scaffolding which both prefigured the work of Christ and preserved the nation from within which he would appear.

Christ fully kept the law of God on behalf of his people; in addition he bore its judgment curses. In doing so he fulfilled the typology of the ceremonial law. Since he did this not merely for the seed of Abraham ethnically viewed, but for all the elect, he entered into the fulfilment of the divine promise: 'Ask of me and I will give you the nations for your inheritance' (Psa. 2:8).

Pentecost then marked his universal lordship, in the outpouring of the Spirit on all flesh. Such an internationalization of the covenant people in and of itself abrogated the mandatory nature of the judicial laws of the Sinaitic covenant which, as the Westminster divines noted, no longer

---

[1] *The Marrow of Modern Divinity*, p. 320. See Bruce K. Waltke in W. S. Barker & W. R. Godfrey, eds, *Theonomy: A Reformed Response* (Grand Rapids: Zondervan, 1990), pp. 70-72 for a distinguished contemporary Old Testament scholar's concurrence.

bind nations except in terms of the general equity of the application of the law of nature exhibited in them.

As Anthony Burgess (whose *Vindiciae Legis* in addition to his personal influence played a major role in the Westminster Assembly's thinking) notes: the judicial laws and the ceremonial laws are explicitly repealed (1 Pet. 2:13 [cf. Gen. 49:10] and Acts 15).

Stage two involved the rewriting of the law in the heart through the power of the Holy Spirit. This takes place in regeneration. Christ himself fulfilled the law in the sense of explaining its true meaning in his preaching. In his life he became the great *prototupon*, writing out the law with his own hands, 'and so set a more perfect copy than ever was extant in the hearts and lives of angels'.[1] Now he does this in us through the Spirit's work of renewal. This, as Stephen Charnock reasons in his great *Discourse on Regeneration*, involves several things:

(1) An inward knowledge of the law and an approval of it in our understanding.

(2) An inward conformity to its requirements.

(3) A strong propensity to be obedient to it.

(4) A mighty affection for it.

(5) An actual ability to obey it.[2]

2. The present status of the law

This brings us to a further question about the Puritan theology: Given this biblical theology, what is the present status of the law? This was one of the most controversial issues they faced, not simply because of their concern with the tide of antinomianism, but because they themselves were familiar with the statements in Scripture that seem to suggest that there is no role for law in the life of the believer. After all, the believer is not under law, but under grace (Rom. 6:14); he is dead to the law and freed from it (Rom. 7:1-6). Indeed this whole question of the relationship between gospel and law, and grace and law, was crucial

[1] Goodwin, *Works*, V:102.
[2] Charnock, *Works*, IV:120ff.

to the way in which they both understood and proclaimed the gospel. How could the law, whose ministry was one of death (2 Cor. 3:7), the law that had been abolished in Christ (Eph. 2:14-15), still have a role in the believer's life?

The question that faced them remains a pressing one for Christians today, and we cannot adequately answer it in a few brief comments. But certain important points should be made:

Hermeneutically, the Puritans stressed the importance of recognizing the various nuances in which the apostolic authors use *nomos*. In particular they explained the negative perspective of passages such as those cited above by viewing the law in two different ways:

1. The law as the specifically Mosaic system of law, composed of the moral law expressed in terms relevant to the Jewish people, with its ceremonial and civil appendages. The abrogation of the Mosaic law, they held, did not abrogate the moral law that historically preceded it and was enshrined within it. Rather it was the specifically *Mosaic form* of law that was abrogated.

2. The law viewed abstracted from grace. Some of course held that the Sinaitic law was, in any case, a covenant of works. Others shared Calvin's view that, at times, the law was spoken of as abstracted from the context in which it was given, law-apart-from-the covenant of grace rather than law-within-the covenant of grace. This sense, essentially equivalent to Calvin's 'bare law', they viewed as a distortion rather than a true understanding of law. For divine law, they held, was always given within the context of divine goodness; indeed they were even prepared to employ the language of grace to describe the context of the pre-fall gift of law.[1]

While the mainstream Puritans held that the moral law continued to bind Christian believers, they denied that it did so as a covenant of works. Even if it were a covenant of works, believers were now released from it as such. But the temporary features of the Mosaic covenant should not be confused with the commandments enshrined in it, whose

---

[1] Many references might be cited here to confirm E. F. Kevan's comment that 'Nearly all the Puritans concurred in the view that whatever good Adam would have received by his obedience was of grace.' *The Grace of Law*, p. 112.

obligation is perpetual. Now, however, the condemnation of the law has been exhausted, the sting of its accusations drawn. There is no condemnation for those who are in Christ.[1]

The function of the gospel, however, is not to destroy the law, but rather to establish the *telos* of that law which includes its rewriting in the hearts of believers, and obedience to it coming to expression in their lives.

The Christian receives the moral law in a new context in Christ. The Puritans debated whether the believer receives the law from the hands of Moses or from the hands of Christ,[2] but however they answered that question, they stressed that no believer receives the law apart from Christ. His obedience to the law was therefore evangelical and not legal.[3]

We must turn finally to:

3. The use of the law in Puritan preaching

The Puritan theologians were first and foremost ministers of the word of God. In closing, then, something needs to be said about the use they made of the law of God in their gospel proclamation.

The abandonment of the Puritan emphasis on the continuing relevance of the Decalogue is one of the hallmarks of our day, including its abandonment among evangelical Christians. A personal memory underlines this point. In a conversation with O. R. Johnston in the early 1970s, when he was the Director of the Nationwide Festival of Light,[4] he told me that the greatest difficulty he found in his task was persuading evangelical ministers of the contemporary relevance of the law of God. The passing of the years would not have made him more sanguine.

---

[1] See, e.g., Bolton, *True Bounds*, pp. 28-44.

[2] See, e.g., the words of Evangelista in *The Marrow of Modern Divinity*, p. 310: The commandments 'have been, and are to be, a rule of life both to the believing Jews and believing Gentiles, unto the end of the world; not as they are delivered by Moses, but as they are delivered by Christ: for when Christ the Son comes and speaks himself, then Moses the servant must keep silence.'

[3] For the differences, see Bolton, *True Bounds*, pp. 141-44.

[4] Originally an organization formed in the early 1970s to counter the influence of the 'permissive society', the NFL later (1983) developed into Christian Action Research and Education (CARE).

Puritan preaching provided a healthy corrective to this almost neurotic fear of the divine law. It was marked, characteristically, by four emphases:

1. The law should be used to convict of sin—but only in the hands of the Spirit.[1] The Gospel pericope of the Rich Young Ruler was a much-favoured illustration of this principle. Here the Puritans believed that Christ himself used the law as a gospel preacher.[2] The law thus exposed the gospel hypocrite, produced a spirit of bondage (cf. Rom. 8:15), and was intended to drive sinners to Christ. In the believer, the law functions in a similar way, to show our need of Christ by bringing us into the cycle of sin-consciousness, guilt-awareness, pardon, and assurance.[3]

2. The law restrains transgressions because it is an expression of the holiness and the will of God. It is part of God's revelation, and as such provides for our spiritual security and well-being in its counsels and admonitions. The Puritans realized that fallen man continues to need objective commands, as well as transformed affections, if he is to live in obedience. Over against antinomian tendencies, they never made the mistake of confusing the matter of obedience (the moral law) with its motivation (God—Creator, Provider, Redeemer—commands us and we trust and love him) or its energizing power (the Holy Spirit received through faith). As a result, Puritan theology at its best never confused law-keeping with legalism.

3. The law restores the notion of duty to the Christian life. This is a much maligned notion largely because it is not well understood that in grace duties are fulfilled with pleasure and delight because of the one for whom they are done. 'As the law was given with evangelical purposes, so it is now kept from evangelical principles', notes Bolton.[4] After all, if the Spirit writes the law in our hearts, why should we think it strange that Christ should place the law in

---

[1] Burgess, *Vindiciae Legis*, p. 199.
[2] Bolton, *True Bounds*, p. 107.
[3] Cf. the conversation between Christian and Faithful in Bunyan, *Pilgrim's Progress*, pp. 77-79.
[4] Bolton, *True Bounds*, pp. 72-73.

our hands?' Burgess adds some wise counsel: 'Suspect all doctrines that teach comfort, but not duty; labour indeed to be a spiritual anatomist dividing between having godlinesse, and trusting in it; but take heed of separating sanctification from justification.'[1] That, as Calvin well said, would be 'to rend Christ asunder by mutilated faith'.[2]

4. The law gives shape to the Christian life. This is the classical *usus normativus legis*. By contrast with moderns, the Puritans recognized that the Ten Commandments covered life comprehensively. When rightly understood and used, they would bring clear direction for the whole of life. This, rather than a spirit of legalism, explains their focus in their catechetical instruction. Two fifths of the *Shorter Catechism* and one third of the *Larger Catechism*, for example, are devoted to a detailed exposition of the law. Far from being legalistic, the Puritans held that this alone provides a framework for the freedom of the Christian believer to live in the confidence that he does the will of God. Of course the Puritans recognized that God's providence could be difficult both to interpret and to experience. But they did not write books specifically on the subject of personal guidance. Having taught the comprehensive implications of the law, they did not need to. Rather, they believed with Samuel Bolton: 'The law sends us to the gospel that we may be justified; and the gospel sends us to the law again to inquire what is our duty as those who are justified. ... The law sends us to the gospel for our justification; the gospel sends us to the law to frame our way of life.'[3]

But if the law is to be used in this way, it must be rightly understood. Hence the Puritans sought to provide clear guidelines for preaching and using the law. As we would expect, none stated these guidelines more clearly than Thomas Watson, surely one of the finest preachers of his own or of any other day. He gives us eight helpful rules:

---

[1] Burgess, *Vindiciae Legis*, p. 48.
[2] Calvin, *Comm. Romans*, p. 167.
[3] Bolton, *True Bounds*, pp. 71-72.

Rule 1: The commands and prohibitions of the moral law reach the heart. They require not only outward actions, but also holy inward affections.

Rule 2: The commandments are given in the form of synecdoche—the part is used for the whole. More is intended than is specifically stated:

(1) Where any duty is commanded, the contrary sin is forbidden.

(2) Where any sin is forbidden, the contrary duty is commanded.

Rule 3: If a specific sin is forbidden in the commandment, the occasion of it is also forbidden. Where murder is forbidden, envy and the anger which may give rise to it are also forbidden.

Rule 4: Where one relationship is mentioned in the commandment, the corresponding relation is involved; e.g. where the child is named, the father is involved.

Rule 5: When greater sins are forbidden, this carries the implication that lesser sins within the same moral category are also forbidden.

Rule 6: The law of God is a unit. The first and second tables belong together. Godliness and righteousness are two aspects of the same response of faith and obedience.

Rule 7: God's law forbids not only that we sin personally, but forbids our being an accessory to, or having any hand in, the sins of others.

Rule 8: Though we cannot, by our own strength, fulfil all these commandments, we should not lose heart. The Lord has provided encouragement for us.

(1) Even although we do not have the ability to obey one command perfectly, in the new covenant God has promised to work in us more and more of what he requires of us.

(2) Although we cannot perfectly fulfil the whole moral law, yet God for Christ's sake mitigates the rigour of the law. He sees our faith, and deals tenderly with us in our failing.

(3) When our personal obedience falls short, God accepts us in Christ. The very service his law might condemn, his mercy crowns, by virtue of the blood of our Mediator.[1]

It is, then, hardly surprising that the Puritans were rightly fond of some words Luther had written in his *Commentary on Galatians* which remain as true today as they did in either the sixteenth or seventeenth century:

> *Qui scit inter Legem et Evangelium distinguere, gratias agat Deo et sciat se esse Theologum.* [Whoever knows how to distinguish between the Law and the Gospel, let him thank God and know that he is a Theologian.][2]

And, we might add, *a true pastor.*

[1] Thomas Watson, *The Ten Commandments*, published in 1692 as part of *A Body of Practical Divinity* (repr. London: Banner of Truth Trust, 1965), pp. 45-48. Cf. *The Marrow of Modern Divinity*, pp. 271-72.
[2] Luther, *Comm. Galatians*, p. 122 (on Gal. 2:14).

IV. THE PASTOR
AND
TEACHING

CHAPTER NINETEEN

HOW DOES THE BIBLE LOOK AT ITSELF?

If the Bible does not witness to its own infallibility, then we have no right to believe that it is infallible. If it does bear witness to its infallibility then our faith in it must rest upon that witness, however much difficulty may be entertained with this belief. If this position with respect to the ground of faith in Scripture is abandoned, then appeal to the Bible for the ground of faith in any other doctrine must also be abandoned. The doctrine of Scripture must be elicited from the Scripture just as any other doctrine should be. If the doctrine of Scripture is denied its right of appeal to Scripture for support, then what right does any other doctrine have to make this appeal?

—John Murray (1946)

I N the final Latin edition of his *Institutes* (1559), John Calvin wrote that 'Scripture exhibits fully as clear evidence of its own truth as white and black things do of their colour, or sweet or bitter things do of their taste. ... Let this point therefore stand: that those whom the Holy Spirit has inwardly taught truly rest upon Scripture, and that Scripture indeed is self-authenticated [*autopiston*].'[1] Few things more characterize the view of Scripture espoused by Calvin's evangelical successors than the assumptions implicit in his words: (1) Scripture bears witness to its own character as God's word; (2) Scripture is the word of God written; and (3) Scripture as written bears the marks of its human authors; as God-given, it bears the marks of its divine origin, namely, uncompromised reliability.

[1] Calvin, *Institutes*, I.vii.2; I.vii.5.

This view is based on several biblical passages, notably 2 Timothy 3:16 and 2 Peter 1:19-21, and on a host of ancillary statements scattered throughout both Testaments. But it has never been regarded as the last word on Scripture. Indeed, it is simply the first word, providing a solid foundation for the rigorous discipline of biblical exposition. For such a conviction about Scripture does not answer in an *a priori* fashion many of the questions we might raise about its teaching. As a biblical doctrine it will influence the interpretation of other passages. But any decision about the *meaning* of a given passage must still be decided on the basis of careful exegetical study. Only when we lapse from such sensitivity to the text does the principle of the self-witness of Scripture become confused with an *a priori* dogmatism about what certain texts must mean.

Implicit in this whole approach to the doctrine of Scripture lies a presupposition which was, in the past, rarely expounded, largely because it was so universally held to be self-evident. It was assumed that we can in fact speak about 'Scripture's view of itself'. Today that assumption is contested and therefore needs to be established as legitimate. Since Scripture could not be a finalized entity until the last of its books had been written, is it not anachronistic to speak of 'Scripture's view of itself'?

The issue is expressed with characteristically pugilistic vigour by James Barr, when he writes:

> According to conservative arguments, it is not only Jesus who made 'claims'; the Bible made 'claims' about itself. The Book of Daniel 'claims' to have been written by a historical Daniel some time in the sixth century BC; the Book of Deuteronomy 'claims' to have been written by Moses; and more important still, the Bible as a whole 'claims' to be divinely inspired. All this is nonsense. There is no 'the Bible' that 'claims' to be divinely inspired, there is no 'it' that has a 'view of itself'. There is only this or that source, like 2 Timothy or 2 Peter, which makes statements about certain other writings, these rather undefined. There is no such thing as 'the Bible's view of itself' from which a fully authoritative answer to these questions can be obtained. This whole side of traditional conservative apologetic, though loudly vociferated, just does not exist; there is no case to answer.[1]

[1] James Barr, *Fundamentalism* (London: SCM, 1977), p. 78.

Barr's powers of debunking are considerable, and well known. Nor have they been directed exclusively against those he regards as fundamentalists. His critique cannot, therefore, be treated in an off-hand fashion. Indeed, it underlines a hiatus in much conservative writing on the doctrine of Scripture. But is he correct in suggesting that we cannot legitimately speak of 'Scripture's view of itself'? If so, he would seem to have destroyed a linchpin in the traditional orthodox view of Scripture and shown that the so-called biblical view is essentially nonbiblical. How can it be claimed that 'Scripture teaches X or Y about Scripture' if such reflection on Scripture as a whole does not (and in the very nature of the case, could not) take place in Scripture itself?

This argument has the appearance of devastating power; but in fact it fails to take account of the direction of the evidence Scripture provides. In what follows, our intention is (1) to demonstrate the legitimacy of speaking of 'Scripture's view of itself', and (2) to expound briefly what this view entails for the doctrine of Scripture.

1. Does the Bible have 'a view of itself'?

Can we really speak about 'the Bible's view of itself' or, with Barr, say only that X (a biblical author) said Y about Z (a section of the Christian canon of Scripture)?

Merely to cite 2 Timothy 3:16 to defend the view that Scripture does indeed have a view of itself is an inadequate response. It begs the question, since (1) Paul here refers apparently to the Old Testament (the 'sacred writings', verse 15), not to the entire Christian canon; (2) evidence must be offered that 2 Timothy 3:16 is itself Scripture, to show that it gives Scripture's view of Scripture; and (3) evidence must be furnished that 2 Timothy 3:16 has the rest of the New Testament canon in view. Only when these conditions are met can this statement justify the claim that it presents Scripture's view of itself.

Is the traditional conservative view of Scripture then justifiable? In the very nature of the case, such justification must rise above the mere citation of proof texts. If one objects that any sophisticated reasoning or pre-understanding would bar the ordinary Christian from reaching the conviction that Scripture claims to be the word of God, the answer is at hand. We are ultimately persuaded of the inspiration and authority of

Scripture not on the basis of coherent arguments in textbooks of doctrine but through 'the inward work of the Holy Spirit, bearing witness by and with the word in our hearts'.[1] It is by reading Scripture under the Spirit's influence, rather than by skill in logic, that trust in God's word is born.

There is no finer illustration of this principle than J. Gresham Machen's experience when exposed in his earlier years to the cream of German liberal theological teaching. It was his reading of the Gospels themselves that strengthened his faith in biblical inspiration and authority.

The function of our discussion here is not to usurp the ministry of the Holy Spirit but to vindicate the inner consistency of the view that Scripture *does* bear witness to its own character. We seek to show that such a conviction is neither incoherent nor irrelevant because of a category mistake.

What, then, are the propositions involved in saying that Scripture bears witness to its own nature? We may note four of them.

First, there is evidence within the Old Testament of a canonical self-consciousness, a recognition that what is written is given by God to rule and direct his people. That is already indicated by the fact that written documentation accompanies the covenant relationship between God and his people and is intended to rule and direct their lives (see Deut. 5:22, 32; 29:9; 30:9-10, 15-16; 31:24-29; Josh. 1:7-8; 8:34). The rest of the books of the Old Testament are written, in various ways, in exposition of this authoritative, canonical, covenant word. The Old Testament grows from this root. Out of this flow, in part, the chronicler's covenantal, canonical interpretation of history and the confidence of the prophetic 'Thus says the LORD'. New Scripture is written in the confidence that it is 'Scripture' only because of its inherent relationship to what God has already given.[2]

Second, there is, in the New Testament, the clear recognition of the divinely given canon we now know as the Old Testament. The New Testament's use of the word *Scripture* and such expressions as 'the law and the prophets', 'it is written', 'God said', and 'Scripture says' abundantly illustrate this fact. Both Jesus and the apostles use Scripture

---

[1] *Westminster Confession of Faith*, I.5.

[2] For an extended discussion of a similar argument, see Meredith G. Kline, *The Structure of Biblical Authority* (Grand Rapids: Eerdmans, 1972), esp. pp. 21-68.

in a normative canonical role. In Jesus' life, Scripture must be fulfilled, simply because it is Scripture. For him, as for the apostles, the appeal to the Old Testament settles all matters, because of its canonical status for God's people. It is 'the mouth of God', by whose every word people are to live (Matt. 4:4).

To the authors of the New Testament, the Old Testament is God's word. But further development of this proposition is required. It must be shown that the New Testament is organically one with the Old, and self-consciously Scripture, to enable us to affirm that this is Scripture's view of Scripture.

Third, there is, in the New Testament, a consciousness among the authors as a whole that the authority of their own writing is on a par with that of the Old Testament and that the content of the revelation given to them is, in some sense, superior to it, not in terms of inspiration, but in the clarity and progress of the revelation recorded (see, e.g., Eph. 3:2-6). This consciousness in the apostolic writings is tantamount to a deliberate addition to the canon in order to bring it to completion in the light of Christ's coming. In this sense, the New Testament as canon is virtually demanded by the coming of Christ. If the older revelation, which was spasmodic and fragmentary (Heb. 1:1), was inscripturated, how much more is inscripturation anticipated of the consummation of revelation?

We find hints of this self-conscious adding to canonical Scripture throughout the New Testament. These are, in the nature of the case, often subtle, but they are almost commonplace. Thus, for example, in keeping with New Testament practice, John's Gospel introduces quotations from the Old Testament with the words, 'it is written' (6:31; 8:17; 12:14; etc.). It is a phrase which 'in the New Testament puts an end to all contradiction'.[1] But a similar expression, 'these are written', marks the rounding off of John's own work (20:31). In John's Gospel the allusion is unlikely to be accidental. Here, as elsewhere, the verb *grapho* (write) seems to retain its quasi-authoritative sense (cf. Pilate's words: 'What I have written I have written', John 19:22).[2] Hebrews 2:2-3 argues from

---

[1] Herman Ridderbos, *Studies in Scripture and Its Authority* (Grand Rapids: Eerdmans, 1978), p. 21.

[2] G. Kittel, G. Friedrich, eds, *Theological Dictionary of the New Testament*, tr. G. W. Bromiley, 10 vols (Grand Rapids: Eerdmans, 1964–76), I:747.

the lesser authority of the law, given through the angels, to the greater authority of the gospel, given through the preaching of the apostles. But if the apostles' spoken word was regarded as the word of God (as they themselves believed it to be, 1 Thess. 2:13), no less will be their written word. No one knows God's thoughts, except God's Spirit. But God's Spirit teaches the apostles to speak the words he teaches (1 Cor. 2:11-13). Those who posses the Spirit therefore recognize the divine canonicity of the apostolic word. Nor is this simply the conclusion of deductive logic. What Paul writes are the Lord's commands, and a mark of a truly spiritual person is that he or she recognizes them as such (1 Cor. 14:37). Disobedience to the teaching given in his letters can lead to excommunication (2 Thess. 3:14). Here Paul aligns his written teaching with the law of the old covenant; rejection of it as canon for life involves the repudiation of the covenant of which it is the canonical record, and then the coming under the divine curse of expulsion from the covenant community. For this reason, apostolic letters are read not only by the church but alongside the sacred writings of the Old Testament, in and to the church (Col. 4:16).

The same inherent canon-consciousness emerges in the opening and closing sections of the book of Revelation. It is assumed that the book will be read in public to the church (1:3). Both reader and hearer are promised 'blessing'—that is, divine, covenantal benediction. In view of this, a similarly covenant-oriented warning closes the book: 'I warn everyone who hears the words of the prophecy of this book: if anyone adds to them, God will add to him the plagues described in this book, and if anyone takes away from the words of the book of this prophecy, God will take away his share in the tree of life and in the holy city, which are described in this book' (22:18-19).

These words are not a naive piece of personal vindictiveness. Rather, they reflect the apex of canon-consciousness in the New Testament. They deliberately echo the warnings of the Old Testament canonical Scripture: 'You shall not add to the word that I command you, nor take from it, that you may keep the commandments of the LORD your God that I command you' (Deut. 4:2; see also verses 5, 14, 40; 12:32). Here, the book of Revelation 'claims' the authority which it assumes for the Old Testament itself. This is nothing less than self-conscious canonicity.

Fourth, in the New Testament we also notice that some sources express a sense not only of their own canonical character but of the existence of a class of literature sharing that status. Admittedly this cross-fertilization does little more than surface in the New Testament documents. But the fact that it does surface is adequate justification for believing that it reflects a wider ecclesiastical consciousness that God was giving a new canon of Scripture for the new age of the gospel.

This sense may be the explanation of the otherwise mysterious citing of words in 1 Timothy 5:18 (from both Deut. 25:4 and Luke 10:7) under the common rubric 'for the Scripture says'. Another interpretation is possible, namely, that the rubric refers only to the first citation, the second being a 'free' *logion* of Jesus. But there is nothing inherently questionable about the first interpretation, and it is in fact the more natural reading of the text. Moreover, given the emergence of the canon of the New Testament and the citation of New Testament documents by the Apostolic Fathers, it would seem inevitable that already in the first century—and especially by Paul, to whom Luke was such a faithful companion—the Gospel of Luke would be cited as 'Scripture'.

More certain yet is the well-known statement of 2 Peter 3:16 regarding Paul's letters. 'There are some things in them that are hard to understand, which the ignorant and unstable twist to their own destruction, as they do the other Scriptures [*tas loipas graphas*].' Here we find confirmation of the fact that Paul's letters are already regarded as Scripture. To refer to his writings in the same category as 'the rest of the Scriptures' assumes their canonicity. Paul's letters, therefore, are placed on a par with the Old Testament. It is possible that Peter has in view in the phrase 'the rest of the Scriptures' (2 Pet. 3:16) other apostolic writings. We have already noted a sufficiently wide-ranging canon-consciousness in the New Testament documents for that to be possible, perhaps even probable. But in strict logic, this statement enables us to affirm only that Peter regarded Paul's letters as canonical Scripture. More, however, may yet be affirmed.

Why does 2 Peter recognize Paul's letters as Scripture? Materially we may here appeal to the testimony of the Spirit. As in the contemporary church, so in the early church the Holy Spirit bore witness to canonical

Scripture. He gave the inner persuasion that it was Sacred Writ. But formally, the answer lies in the recognition of Paul's apostolic office and its significance. Apostleship existed in order to give Scripture to the church.

This is the thrust of several statements of Jesus' farewell discourse in John 13–17. An apostle of Christ is his special representative:

> 'Truly, truly, I say to you, whoever receives the one I send receives me, and whoever receives me receives the one who sent me' (13:20).

> 'But the Helper, the Holy Spirit, whom the Father will send in my name, he will teach you all things and bring to your remembrance all that I have said to you' (14:26).

> 'But when the Helper comes, whom I will send to you from the Father, the Spirit of truth, who proceeds from the Father, he will bear witness about me. And you also will bear witness, because you have been with me from the beginning' (15:26-27).

> 'When the Spirit of truth comes, he will guide you into all the truth … and he will declare to you the things that are to come' (16:13).

All this is part of the same strand of teaching which begins in such passages as Luke 10:16 and culminates in the Great Commission in Matthew 28:20. The apostles were to testify to, and teach, everything that Christ had commanded. They were already prepared to bear their unique witness by their relationship to Jesus and the promise of the Spirit. But implicit in the perspective that their labours will last 'to the end of the age' is the prospect—indeed, the necessity—of the development of a new canonical Scripture flowing from the apostolic circle.

The apostles were called precisely for the purpose of being witnesses of Jesus (note, with the above, Paul's affirmation that he was a witness-apostle to the risen Lord Jesus Christ, 1 Cor. 9:1; see also Acts 1:8, 22; 2:32; 3:15; 5:32; 10:39, 41; 13:31; 22:15; 26:16). They were vehicles of new revelation which was written down (see Eph. 3:2-5) and therefore conscious, to a degree, that they were adding to the already-received canon. This is not to insist that every book in the New Testament was written directly by an apostle; but we have no reason to believe that any book emerged from outside the general apostolic circle.

Such is the relationship, therefore, between apostleship and Scripture that the connection (in 2 Pet. 3:16) between Paul and the 'other Scriptures' (and by parity of reasoning, between the apostles and the 'other Scriptures') is not at all surprising. In a sense it might even be anticipated by the sensitive reader of the New Testament.

In what way, then, do these considerations justify our speaking of 'Scripture's view of itself'? They indicate a consciousness of canonical status within the books of the Old Testament; they emphasize that this canonicity is confirmed by the documents of the New Testament and that they place themselves in the same category as canonical Scripture. The New Testament, then, views the whole of the Old Testament as Scripture, and in the very act of being given to the church by the apostles seals its own canonicity. We may conclude, then, that inherent in the books of our New Testament, as well as the Old, is the self-consciousness of belonging to a divinely given canon.

Clearly there is nothing simple about this reasoning. But it would be a mistake to think that we could or should have a 'simple' explanation. The manner in which God has given Scripture to the church—in space and time, through a variety of human authors—precludes such a simple demonstration of Scripture's self-testimony. Nevertheless, that self-testimony does exist with sufficient clarity for us to speak legitimately of 'Scripture's view of itself'.

2. The Bible's view of itself

Assuming the validity of our earlier considerations, what is 'the Bible's view of itself'? Within the scope of this essay, four features of Scripture's self-testimony call for attention: (1) *inspiration*, (2) *authority*, (3) *reliability*, and (4) *necessity*.

(1) Inspiration

No element is more central to Scripture's testimony to its own nature than the concept of inspiration. Many passages point in this direction, especially Paul's consciously programmatic statement in 2 Timothy 3:16 that 'all Scripture is inspired by God' (NASB).

It has long been realized that the term *inspiration* is problematic and, indeed, an inadequate translation of *theopneustos*.

It is very desirable that we should free ourselves at the outset from influences arising from the current employment of the term 'inspiration'. This term is not a biblical term, and its etymological implications are not perfectly accordant with the biblical conception of the modes of the divine operation in giving the Scripture.[1]

At first glance this may appear an inexplicable statement from one of the greatest of all defenders of the inspiration of Scripture. The words 'Warfield denies Bible is inspired' would make a startling headline! But this would of course be to misconstrue Warfield (and Paul) completely. What is in view here is that *theopneustos* refers not to the in-breathing of God (either into the authors or into the text of Scripture) but to the 'God-breathed' character of the product of the author's writing. What is stressed is not the manner of Scripture's coming into being but its divine source. Paul's language therefore obviates what many readers of the Bible have found to be a stumbling block: large parts of the Bible do not seem very inspiring, and it is difficult to see how the authors of them were in an 'inspired' state of mind when writing them. Paul affirms that the product is God-breathed. But it came into being through a variety of means (careful research and study, ecstatic experience, and even, in the case of some parts, a kind of dictation).

Paul's words require furthur elucidation. Three issues of interpretation arise. *First*, does the anarthrous *pasa graphē* suggest that Paul means 'every Scripture', rather than 'all Scripture'? That meaning is possible. But in fact the point is of minimal importance. If every Scripture is God-breathed, it follows that all Scripture will also be God-breathed. Either translation underlines the inspiration of the entire Old Testament.

Second, should *theopneustos* be taken in an attributive sense ('all God-breathed Scripture is useful …')? If so, it could be taken to limit the extent of inspiration and to imply that some Scripture may not be God-breathed.

In the very nature of the case we cannot demonstrate that every single verse of Scripture is spoken of *seriatim* as God-breathed. But the fact that all sections of Scripture are cited almost randomly in the New Testament, with equal force, emphasizes how far removed such a distinction was

---

[1] B. B. Warfield, 'Inspiration', *Revelation and Inspiration, Works*, I:99.

from the minds of the New Testament writers. So widespread are the New Testament's quotations and allusions from the Old Testament that no distinction surfaces between the 'God-breathed' and the 'man-made'. Such a distinction is alien to the evidence of Scripture itself and cannot therefore have been the apostle's meaning.

Third, should *theopneustos* be taken in an active, rather than a passive, sense (God-breathing, rather than breathed out by God)? While *theopneustos* appears only here in the New Testament, the translation 'all [every] Scripture is God-breathed' is favoured by the testimony of the rest of Scripture. The idea of Scripture as the word of God, that which is carried forth by the breath or speech of God, is commonplace. The notion of Scripture as 'breathing out God' (rather than breathed out by God) is foreign to the statements of Scripture concerning its own nature.

Abundant evidence exists to substantiate this view. Jeremiah's experience may be taken as paradigmatic of biblical writers: 'Then the LORD put out his hand and touched my mouth. And the LORD said to me, "Behold, I have put my words in your mouth"' (Jer. 1:9; cf. Isa. 6:7). Similarly, David's final oracle (the word itself is significant) assumes what is true of all of 'the oracles of God', or 'the very words of God' (Acts 7:38; Rom. 3:2; Heb. 5:12; 1 Pet. 4:11): 'The Spirit of the LORD speaks by me; his word is on my tongue' (2 Sam. 23:2). When Jesus quotes Deuteronomy 8:3 with such manifest approval, he speaks of man's living not by bread alone but by 'every word that comes from the mouth of God' (Matt. 4:4). Again, the way in which God's speech and the words of Scripture are virtually synonymous terms in biblical usage underlines the equation of Scripture with what has been breathed out by God. (See Rom. 9:17 and Gal. 3:8, where 'Scripture' is really equivalent to 'God'; and Matt. 19:4-5 [quoting Gen. 2:24], Heb. 3:7 [Psa. 95:7], and Acts 4:24-25 [Psa. 2:1], where 'Scripture says' and 'God says' are equivalent expressions.) Such evidence, coupled with Warfield's extensive demonstration that the form *theopneustos* is passive rather than active, leaves the issue beyond doubt.[1]

About this inspiration several features should be noted.

[1] B. B. Warfield, 'God Inspired Scripture', *Revelation and Inspiration, Works*, I:229-80.

(i) *Inspiration is given no final explanation.* No doctrine of the exact nature of inspiration is gained from 2 Timothy 3:16. This passage considers, as we have seen, the product of God's powerful working (his 'breath'), not the way in which his Spirit has engaged men's lives and minds in order to create the product of Scripture. The nature of inspiration cannot be determined in an *a priori* fashion from the simple fact of it. Nor, indeed, does 2 Peter 1:21, which speaks of the Holy Spirit's carrying or bearing the biblical authors, shed much light. The mode of inspiration must be discovered exegetically, not dogmatically, in an *a posteriori* manner, by the examination of the whole of Scripture, with special attention to its reflection on the mode of the production of its various parts. This exercise will drive us to the conclusion that we can no more fully explain inspiration than we can explain providence.

In fact, Scripture came into being through a variety of modes. Some passages are the fruit of ecstatic experience; others are the product of historical research and thoughtful interpretation—such as Luke's account of Christ, or the chronicler's account of the history of Israel from a covenantal perspective. There is poetry, much of which must have been the fruit of hard literary labour (only those who have never written poetry assume it is always the result of immediate 'inspiration'); but there is also material which is indeed the immediate fruit of profound experience.

In view of this, two elements characterize the manner of inspiration. The first is *God's general providential superintendence of the lives, experiences, and circumstances of the biblical authors.* 'If God wished to give his people a series of letters like Paul's, he prepared a Paul to write them, and the Paul he brought to the task was a Paul who simultaneously would write just such letters.'[1]

But second, *Scripture is the result of the activity of divine power, through the Spirit.* He works in the lives of the authors specifically in the production of Scripture. He bears them along (2 Pet. 1:21) so that the product of their writing is safeguarded as God's own word. In this sense, God not only governs their lives in equipping them but actually (if mysteriously) teaches them the words they use (see 1 Cor. 2:13).

---

[1] B. B. Warfield, 'Inspiration', *Revelation and Inspiration, Works,* I:101.

(ii) *Inspiration characterizes all Scripture.* We have argued above that Paul did not intend to limit the inspiration in Scripture. Even if 2 Timothy 3:16 were translated 'All God-breathed Scripture is useful …' the connotation that only parts of Scripture are God-breathed is completely absent. Inspiration extends to every section of Scripture.

This point is well illustrated by a glance through the United Bible Societies' edition of the Greek New Testament (which prints citations and allusions from the Old Testament in bold in the text). The index lists some 300 texts from the Old Testament quoted in the New, and more than 1,500 allusions from the Old Testament employed in the New. The pervasive, rather than selective, use of Scripture is manifest. If any part is God-breathed, then the whole is God-breathed.

We must not, however, draw unbiblical deductions from this conclusion. For while there are no degrees of inspiration, there are degrees of revelation. Inspiration is not subject to levels of development, but revelation is—it is progressive and cumulative. It develops through the epochs of redemptive history, reaching several high points before coming to its peak in Jesus Christ. Yet, each stage of revelation, when recorded, is enshrined in an equally inspired Scripture. It is to the embarrassment of those who see different levels of inspiration in the Old Testament that the New Testament writers cite with equanimity the imprecatory psalms (e.g., Psa. 69:25 and 109:8 in Acts 1:20), while they do not directly cite Psalm 23!

The universality of inspiration is epitomized in the notion of *verbal inspiration*, which affirms that the inspiration of Scripture is not limited to its general teaching or to particular doctrines but extends even to the words. This fact Paul affirms of apostolic teaching in 1 Corinthians 2:13. But such words do not stand in isolation from one another, nor do they possess their God-intended meaning apart from each other.[1] Because words express meaning, and a particular word may possess different meanings in different contexts, the meaning communicated depends on the significance of all the words used. If Scripture is God-breathed at all, that inspiration must extend to all the words that are employed. For

[1] See John Murray, 'The Attestation of Scripture', in *The Infallible Word*, 3rd ed., Paul Woolley and Ned B. Stonehouse, eds. (Philadelphia: Presbyterian and Reformed, 1967), p. 23 n.9.

evangelical scholars this teaching is clearly one of the great motives for the pursuit of so-called textual criticism. If inspiration reaches to the words, the identification of what was originally written is a sacred task to be pursued with joy and zeal.

(iii) *Inspiration does not render redundant the necessity of interpretation.* No passage of Scripture discloses its meaning to us apart from actual exegesis. Conviction about the fact of inspiration does not guarantee that we understand even 2 Timothy 3:16 aright or the precise nature of inspiration. Correspondingly, differences of interpretation do not necessarily involve differences in conviction about inspiration.

But if this is so, why is it so important to emphasize Scripture's inspiration? Because our doctrine of inspiration affects our understanding of, and response to, biblical authority.

(2) Authority

If Scripture made no claim to divine inspiration, it could still possess authority—as the unique (and, to that extent, authoritative) witness of the people of God to the acts of God in history and as the source book of all original Christian tradition. It could even be regarded as possessing supreme authority for the faith and life of the church. But it claims more.

The doctrine of plenary divine inspiration implies that Scripture comes to us as an expression of divine authority. It is the 'mouth of God' (Matt. 4:4). What Scripture says, God says. It speaks with his authority. Hence Calvin's famous formulation: 'The Scriptures obtain full authority among believers only when men regard them as having sprung from heaven, as if there the living words of God were heard.'[1] This authority is already evident within the pages of Scripture itself.

(i) *The fact of biblical authority.* Nothing is more characteristic of the New Testament's appeal to the Old Testament as Scripture, and therefore characteristic of Scripture as a class, than the expression 'it is written'. The appeal is not the naive one of 'if it is in a book, it must be true'. Rather, the phrase means: It is written in the document of divine authority, in the canon of the community of God's people. Since what is written there is divinely inspired, appeal to it settles all discussion.

---

[1] Calvin, *Institutes*, I.vii.1.

Such an appeal to Scripture's authority is, it should be stressed, an appeal to Scripture rightly interpreted. Scripture erroneously interpreted is no longer God's word—as Jesus' confrontation with Satan in the wilderness underlines (Matt. 4:1ff.; John 10:34).[1]

Interestingly, precisely in such contexts Jesus gives expression to the final authority of Scripture in his own life. But perhaps even more striking is his use of Scripture immediately before his arrest and immediately after his resurrection. On both occasions, the one under intense duress, the other as Son of God in the power of the new and resurrected humanity (Rom. 1:4), Jesus appeals to the authority of Scripture (see Matt. 26:24, 31; Luke 24:44, 46). If there was any point in his ministry at which it would have been instinctive or appropriate to refer to his own authority instead of the authority of Scripture, these would have been occasions. But precisely in these circumstances he places enormous stress on Scripture's authority.

This use of Scripture and recognition of its authority by Jesus give special significance to his mandate to the apostles to teach whatever he has commanded them to all the world and to every age (Matt. 28:18-20). At the back of the apostles' incessant appeals to Scripture as divinely authoritative lies what they first learned from Jesus himself. The authority of the Old Testament was given the imprimatur of Jesus the Son of God; the authority of the New Testament is anticipated in the words of the Great Commission. On his authority the apostles are to teach throughout the ages what he has taught them. Enshrined in these words is the concept that such teaching must be preserved in Scripture for the church to come.

(ii) *The extent of Scripture's authority.* Already the complexity of this issue is apparent. Simply put, 'The Bible says' ends all questioning—except the great question, 'What does the Bible say?'

---

[1] The fact that Christians sometimes make right decisions on the basis of wrong interpretations of Scripture in no way negates this principle. In such circumstances account must be taken of (1) the providential overruling by God of his people's lives (Rom. 8:28), and (2) the fact that such actions may be consistent with Scripture's teaching generally, even when based on a misunderstanding of one part of Scripture. Such a misunderstanding does not belong to the same category as the repudiation of the teaching of Scripture as a whole.

Scripture is given in the context of ongoing redemptive history, and the authority of its several parts is related to this phenomenon. There is teaching in Scripture which is either further developed or even superseded before the last book of the Bible is written. Thus, to take an obvious example, the dietary laws of the Mosaic legislation and epoch do not carry the final authority for the New Testament Christian that they did for the Old Testament believer (Mark 7:19; Rom. 14:14). All Scripture is authoritative, but its authority is intimately related to its context in the flow of redemptive history.

The authority of God in Scripture is also expressed in an accommodated, phenomenological form, and with specific focus. Not only do the Scriptures actually make us 'wise for salvation through faith in Christ Jesus' (2 Tim. 3:15); that is also their specific intention. They may do other things incidentally; they fulfil this task intentionally. Thus Calvin, commenting on the biblical account of creation, writes: 'He who would learn astronomy [*astrologia*], and other recondite arts, let him go elsewhere.'[1] The Bible is not intended to be an authoritative textbook on physics, chemistry, mathematics, or human biology. The word *heart* in Scripture rarely means the organ in the body! Scripture's focus lies elsewhere: it has been given 'for teaching, for reproof, for correction, and for training in righteousness, that the man of God may be competent, equipped for every good work' (2 Tim. 3:16-17).

Is, then, the authority of Scripture limited? The use of the word *limited* here may be misleading, because it masks a false dichotomy. If we say that Scripture's authority is limited, we are in danger of denying its plenary authority as God's word; if we say that it is not limited, without further explanation of what we mean, we may be in danger of misreading its intentions.

If the Scriptures are God-breathed, they carry God's authority. All they say, on every subject on which they speak, will be authoritative. But they speak on every subject from a particular perspective, not in the intentionally exhaustive fashion of a textbook. That fact does not diminish their authority, nor the universality of their applicability, but provides both with the focus in which they are to be understood and applied.

---

[1] John Calvin, *Commentary on Genesis*, tr. and ed. John King, 2 vols (Grand Rapids: Eerdmans, 1948), I:79.

The Scriptures are like a stone thrown into the water, creating a whole series of concentric circles around the point of entry. Scripture's authority dominates the whole of life, but it does so in different ways through its entry into the human situation. In some areas its authority is immediate and direct, in others it is indirect and mediated. The computer programmer who is a member of God's church sees Scripture as his or her final authority. But that authority functions in different ways. It is not diminished in any sphere. It is one's authority in the fellowship of the church; but one's whole approach to programming will also be dominated and influenced by what God's word says. But we do not read the Scriptures to learn computer programming, because we realize God has not given them in the form of a textbook for such a purpose. Biblical authority is not compromised one iota by recognizing this principle.

(iii) *Authority and sufficiency.* Scripture's authority is intimately related to its sufficiency as our guide to the way of salvation (2 Tim. 3:15). This is the meaning of the Reformation watchword *sola Scriptura*, Scripture alone.

Sola Scriptura did not emerge as an issue only with the Reformation.[1] But at the Reformation it stood over against any principle which either added to or usurped the prerogative of God to speak adequately through his word. In particular, the teaching office of the Roman Church was in view. In this context it remains necessary to insist on *sola Scriptura*.

Today it is also necessary to recognize that *sola Scriptura* contrasts with much current evangelical teaching. In the debates over the question of spiritual gifts, for example, it has not always been realized how central this question is. Involved in the view that such gifts as prophecy and tongues have ceased is the fact that the New Testament regards certain gifts as signs of the apostles and evidence of the apostolic nature of the church (2 Cor. 12:12; Heb. 2:3b-4). But also implied is the conviction that, as *revelatory*, these gifts were exercised prior to the coming into being and universal recognition of the entire New Testament canon. Insofar as prophecy and tongues plus interpretation were regarded as

---

[1] Heiko Oberman, *The Harvest of Medieval Theology* (Cambridge: Harvard University Press, 1963), pp. 201, 361ff., 389.

divine revelation, they served an interim function prior to the inscripturating of the apostolic message. Any contemporary declaration which adds to information given in Scripture and is prefaced by the words 'thus says the Lord' formally implies more than merely illumination. It is a claim to be new divine revelation. This dynamic is not always recognized. In principle, is there any difference between a Protestant claim to give (immediate) revelation in prophecy and interpreted tongues and a Roman Catholic claim to give (carefully thought-out) revelation through the teaching office of the church? Rapprochement between Protestant and Roman Catholic 'charismatic Christians' suggests a similar mindset is often shared quite unconsciously. Debates over the continuation or cessation of certain spiritual gifts will never make headway until it is realized that, to Christians in the Reformed tradition of Calvin, Owen, and Warfield, reservations on the exercise of such gifts are deeply rooted in *sola Scriptura*. To them it is not merely a traditional conviction about the cessation of gifts that is at stake, but 2 Timothy 3:16 itself.

(3) Reliability
'Scripture', said Jesus almost incidentally, 'cannot be broken' (John 10:35). These words appear in the context of a wider *ad hominem* argument. But this part of his statement is not itself *ad hominem* in nature. Jesus is not merely accepting his opponents' point of view for the sake of argument, basing his position on a presupposition shared equally by them—the authority and reliability of the Old Testament. Its authority in this respect, as even Bultmann recognized, 'stands just as fast for him as for the scribes, and he feels himself in opposition to them only in the way he understands and applies the Old Testament'.[1]

But what is claimed when Scripture's reliability (inability to be 'broken') is thus affirmed? It is not only that Scripture in the form of prophecy must be fulfilled (e.g., Matt. 26:24, 31, 54, 56). It is that God's word is truth (John 17:17).

What kind of reliability does this teaching imply? Does Scripture function (as neo-orthodoxy so frequently suggests) like a scratched record? The lyrics can still be clearly heard, even through the distortions.

[1] Rudolf Bultmann, *The Theology of the New Testament*, 2 vols (London: SCM, 1952), I:16.

Is Scripture the fallible word of man, through which can be heard the eternal word of God, who alone is infallible? More than this is claimed in Scripture. We have seen how Jesus assumes that an incidental statement in the Psalms (and by parity of reasoning, the rest of the Scripture) is absolutely reliable and trustworthy. His debate with the Pharisees proceeds on the issue not of Scripture's reliability but of its meaning. This same principle lies behind the conviction that Scripture must be fulfilled—simply because it is Scripture.

The kind of reliability claimed for Scripture, therefore, is an infallible, inerrant reliability, precisely because Scripture is the word of a God who cannot lie. Dewey Beegle calls this position the 'syllogism of inerrancy'.[1] If God is infallible and if Scripture is God's word, then Scripture must also be divinely infallible. Beegle, in keeping with others, questions this 'philosophical assumption'.[2]

But such language simply clouds the issue; it is pejorative, not descriptive, and uses an honourable adjective in a dishonourable and emotive sense. It does not honestly admit what, for Christians who claim Scripture as God's word in any sense, would be the alternative position:

• God is infallible.

• What God says is infallible.

• But what God says through men is not and cannot be infallible.

The assumption here is that human fallibility stubbornly resists the infallible purpose of God. But the biblical witness contains no hint of this position. And with good reason, for this alternative syllogism is tantamount to the denial of Scripture's own statements. Applied universally, this logic would repudiate God's sovereign, teleological rule of a fallen universe for his own perfect purpose (cf. Eph. 1:11b).

Having noted this point, however, our doctrine of Scripture's infallibility requires fine-tuning. It will immediately be said that already the doctrine is exposed to 'the death of a thousand qualifications'. But this is to misunderstand. *Infallibility* is not a biblical term. It belongs to

[1] Dewey Beegle, *Scripture, Tradition, and Infallibility* (Ann Arbor: Pryor Pettengell, 1979), p. 198.
[2] *Ibid.*, p. 85.

the realm of theology as a science and as such requires careful deline-ation and definition. In other sciences such definition or qualification is not a weakness but a matter of accuracy. We do not abandon any other Christian doctrine because it requires precision in its statement and even then retains elements of mystery. One needs to think only of the doctrines of providence, or of the two natures of Christ, or the doctrine of the Trinity, to realize how important is the further eluci-dation, description, and qualification of principial statements. In the same way we need to describe and elucidate our definition of Scripture. How can we further define Scripture's infallibility? What do we mean when we deduce that, as God's word, it is free from error?

Here, again, only a skeletal answer can be given. Three things should be noted.

First, the nature of biblical infallibility cannot be described apart from the actual material of Scripture. As the canon of God's people's lives (not understood in any other category), it lays claim to infallibility. It would therefore be a mistake (made often enough in the past) to discuss whether the Hebrew and Greek of Scripture come to us as examples of perfect grammar. Such a topic is misleading, for grammar is a matter of custom and development, not (normally) a matter of truth and error. In any event, Scripture's infallibility could not be compromised by grammatical infelicities, any more than its meaning is altered by them. The presence of human idiosyncrasy (or eccentricity, for that matter) is not an argument against the infallibility of the product. Thus the young B. B. Warfield wrote:

> No one claims that inspiration secured the use of good Greek in Attic severity of taste, free from the exaggerations and looseness of current speech, but only that it secured the accurate expression of truth, even (if you will) through the medium of the worst Greek a fisherman of Galilee could write and the most startling figures of speech a peasant could invent.[1]

Second, the Bible, which claims such infallibility, speaks phenomeno logically, according to the appearance of things, employing accepted

---

[1] A. A. Hodge and B. B. Warfield, *Inspiration* (Philadelphia: Presbyterian Board of Publication, 1881), p. 43.

customs of speech. In Scripture 'the sun rises'. That no more commits us to a three-decker view of the universe than does our saying, in the early twenty-first century, 'the sun sets'. The person who regards such language as erroneous is insensitive to the complexity of human language, the spheres in which it is used, and to the subtle nuances of human communication. He or she uses this kind of speech all the time!

For some writers, these elements are what Abraham Kuyper called 'innocent inaccuracies'.[1] It is not difficult to understand what Kuyper is saying. Indeed, one may appreciate his desire to allow God's word to stand just as it comes to us. But there is something infelicitous about such a statement in connection with God's word. It brings Scripture to the wrong bar of judgment altogether. Scripture comes to us in the *koinē*, the language of the world of the people. Its statements are to be assessed in that universe of discourse alone.

Third, in the very nature of the case, the Christian cannot prove the infallibility of Scripture. Many biblical statements are not amenable to proof of this kind, or if they were, they are no longer. We cannot prove that 'Christ died for our sins in accordance with the Scriptures' (1 Cor. 15:3) is an infallible statement. We do affirm that such a statement is coherent with itself, the rest of Scripture, and the universe in which we live. We subscribe to biblical infallibility not on the grounds of our ability to prove it but because of the persuasiveness of its testimony to be God's own word and by the ministry of the Holy Spirit.

This position is frequently accused of involving circular reasoning. So be it. We cannot abandon the ultimate authority for our faith when it comes to discussing the nature of that ultimate authority. It should, however, be noted that the argument here is not 'Scripture is infallible because it claims to be infallible' (as, for example, Barr suggests).[2] In fact the reality is quite different: Scripture claims to be infallible because as the word of God it is infallible. The Christian is persuaded of that testimony (through the ministry of the Spirit). On that basis we confess it to be true. We know that the word of God could be nothing less.

---

[1] Abraham Kuyper, *Principles of Sacred Theology* (Grand Rapids: Eerdmans, 1954), p. 457.
[2] Barr, *Fundamentalism*, pp. 72-73.

Belief in the infallibility of Scripture does not imply that we know how to resolve every *prima facie* inconsistency in Scripture. Indeed, we are not under obligation to do this in order to believe in biblical inerrancy, although we will seek to do so for exegetical and apologetic reasons. We believe in the perfect love, righteousness, and sovereignty of God, although we cannot understand their operation in connection with every individual circumstance of life. So too our faith in the inerrancy of Scripture rests on the Bible's own testimony, and in view of the self-consistency of that testimony, we anticipate further resolutions to those passages which as yet we do not fully understand.

We ought not to be driven by the existence of some 'problem passages' into abandoning inerrancy, on the grounds that we are unable to prove it in every conceivable instance. It is important to recognize that 'there are difficulties in Scripture which are at present insoluble and will probably remain so till the last day'.[1] Failure to recognize this limitation has made some grasp at any solution to difficulties, however implausible, or has led others to abandon inerrancy altogether. Nor is it necessary, when a variety of resolutions is open to us, to commit ourselves dogmatically to any of them. One may be correct, or none may be correct. Our conviction of inerrancy does not depend on our possession of final answers to all questions. Does this mean that the inerrantist ignores the 'difficulties' for inerrancy present in Scripture and lives ostrich-like, with head in the sand? On the contrary, in our examination of the text and teaching of the Bible, we find no solid reason to yield up our conviction of Scripture's inerrancy any more than we find reason to yield up our conviction about God's perfect love for us because we cannot harmonize all the ways of the Lord in our own lives.

(4) Necessity

Why, then, is Scripture so necessary? It makes us wise for salvation through faith in Christ Jesus (2 Tim. 3:15). But there is a sense in which the existence of Scripture was not, in terms of strict logic, necessary for salvation. It is Christ and his work, not the Bible and its inspiration, that saves—according to Scripture's testimony.

[1] A. Lecerf, *An Introduction to Reformed Dogmatics*, tr. A. Schlemmer (London: Lutterworth, 1949), p. 314.

Here, we return, therefore, to the practical function of Scripture. Consistently the church has recognized that the Bible is a gift of grace to humankind, who otherwise would forget, distort, and even destroy God's revelation of himself in space and history. The purpose of Scripture is to preserve for all people, in all places, the revelatory word God has spoken. Its function is, in the fullest sense, evangelical and evangelistic.

The perspicuity of Scripture is best understood within this framework. Scripture must be studied with the best tools at our disposal. Many of these are academic in nature (history, geography, foreign languages, etc.), although not necessarily in use. But this should not lead us to conclude that a high level of academic understanding is essential for grasping clearly the message of Scripture. Since Scripture was written for the common people, we should anticipate that its message about the things necessary for salvation is not difficult to understand (in terms of levels of education required): 'The unlearned, in a due use of the ordinary means, may attain unto a sufficient understanding of them.'[1]

This principle of the perspicuity of Scripture is underlined by Jesus and the apostles. It is a source of disappointment to Jesus that the Scripture is misunderstood so seriously (see, e.g., Luke 24:25—'O foolish ones, and slow of heart to believe all that the prophets have spoken!'). Scripture's message is clear enough; people's minds are darkened not by below average intelligence but by sin. The function of the testimony of the Holy Spirit is not to introduce perspicuity to Scripture but to bring illumination to our darkened understanding of it. In this process the Lord of the Scriptures rejoices, knowing that God has hidden the mystery of the kingdom from the wise and understanding and revealed it to babes (Matt. 11:25-27).

If we affirm the inspiration, authority, infallibility, and necessity of Scripture, we are by no means suggesting that to hold 'Scripture's view of itself' is to have all the answers. We have already indicated that these are the first words, not the last word, about Scripture. We have many questions, even puzzles and unreconciled difficulties remaining, which indicate that the continued disciplined exegesis of Scripture is necessary. We therefore have the greatest of motives to learn how to handle God's

---

[1] *Westminster Confession of Faith*, I.7.

word correctly (2 Tim. 2:15). Such study is based on the recognition of what Scripture is: God's mouth, every word from which sustains us in daily life.

Those who study Scripture in such a humble spirit will find that there is yet more truth to break forth from God's holy word. This attitude has never been better expressed than in the words of John Murray:

> There is no doctrine of our Christian faith that does not confront us with unresolved difficulties here in this world, and the difficulties become all the greater just as we get nearer to the centre. It is in connection with the most transcendent mysteries of our faith that the difficulties multiply. The person who thinks he has resolved all the mysteries surrounding our established faith in the Trinity has probably no faith in the triune God. The person who encounters no unresolved mystery in the incarnation of the Son of God and in his death on Calvary's tree has not yet learned the meaning of 1 Timothy 3:16. Yet these unanswered questions are not incompatible with unshaken faith in the triune God and in Jesus Christ the incarnate Son. The questions are often perplexing. But they are more often the questions of adoring wonder rather than the questions of painful perplexity.
>
> So there should be no surprise if faith in God's inerrant word should be quite consonant with unresolved questions and difficulties with regard to the content of this faith.[1]

In such knowledge we rest on the testimony of God's word to itself.

---

[1] Murray, 'Attestation of Scripture', *The Infallible Word*, pp. 7-8.

CHAPTER TWENTY

SCRIPTURE AND TRADITION

M ARTIN LUTHER'S famous Ninety-five Theses sparked a religious fire in Europe that the Roman Catholic Church was unable to extinguish. The theological conflict that ensued has often been characterized as focusing on the four 'alones' of the Reformation: *sola gratia, solus Christus, sola fide, sola Scriptura*[1]— salvation is by grace alone, in Christ alone, by faith alone, and all that is necessary for salvation is taught in Scripture alone. Each of these principles, and certainly all four together, served as a canon by which the teaching of the Roman Catholic Church was assessed and found lacking.

In these great slogans, the nouns—grace, Christ, faith, Scripture— were, and are, of great importance. But in the conflict the qualifying *sola* (alone) was, and is, in some ways even more significant. Rome had always taught that salvation was by grace through faith in Christ, and had always held that the Bible was the word of God—but never *alone*. To speak of *sola Scriptura* was seen in Rome as a prescription for spiritual anarchy. Everyone would create a personalized Bible. The only safeguard against this was the *living tradition* of the church, which was viewed as a separate channel of divine revelation.

Literacy levels were low in the Middle Ages (prior to the printing press, a Renaissance development that brought about widespread access to the Bible). But this alone does not account for the Reformation horror stories about the large-scale biblical ignorance among both priests and people. Nevertheless, it would be uncharitable to extrapolate from those dark days to the present day as though no counter-reformations within Catholicism had taken place in the interim. And Protestants also must

---

[1] Granted that this fourfold summary post-dates the Reformation.

recognize that a widespread interest in the Bible has developed within the Roman Catholic Church in the past century.

Can it be, then, that we now face a new situation in Roman Catholicism? After all, 'common' Bibles are being published for the first time since the Reformation. Moreover, not only within the World Council of Churches (largely dominated by liberal theology) but also within evangelicalism, substantial rapprochement has been viewed as possible in our own time. So it is timely to ask: Has something unprecedented happened within Roman Catholicism's interpretation of the Bible so that the old differences can, at last, be laid to rest?

Between the First Vatican Council (1870) and the publication of the Pontifical Biblical Commission's important work *The Interpretation of the Bible in the Church* (1993), the Roman Magisterium published a series of significant statements on the nature, interpretation, and role of the Bible in the Church. These began in the nineteenth century in the widespread crisis for faith created by the effect of Enlightenment thought, and thereafter by the onslaught of scientific humanism that found its impetus in naturalistic evolutionism. Pronouncements have continued to appear up to the present day, in which the Vatican has sought to wed contemporary historical-critical methods of biblical interpretation to the ancient dogmas of the Church. Each of these statements is of interest on its own account; together they mark a development that has been significant for the work of large numbers of Roman Catholic biblical scholars.

The story of this development is not well known among Protestants. Indeed, probably most Roman Catholics are relatively unfamiliar with it. It is worth narrating, at least in broad outline.

Developments in Rome

In 1893, Pope Leo XIII issued the Encyclical Letter *Providentissimus Deus*. It was the first wide-ranging attempt of the Roman Church to deal specifically with the impact of the critical methodologies that had come to characterize theological scholarship in the latter part of the nineteenth century. These methodologies treated the Bible as an ancient Near Eastern text and assessed it from the standpoint of critical historical investigation and linguistic and religious development. In sophisticated theological terms, Scripture's 'humanity' was explored (and, in fact, its 'divinity' was increasingly ignored and denied).

Against this background, in which the idea of human evolution played a major role, *Providentissimus Deus* insisted on a long-standing principle of Christian orthodoxy: if God is author of both nature and Scripture, these two 'books' of divine revelation must be in harmony with each other. The encyclical emphasized that there could therefore be no ultimate conflict between the Bible and either the natural sciences or historical investigation. It urged both theologians and scientists to respect the limits of their own spheres. In addition, biblical exegetes who employed the fruits of secular scientific and historical studies were counselled to remember the importance of the *analogia fidei* (analogy of faith): the Scriptures should always be interpreted in keeping with the apostolic rule of faith to which the church subscribed. Thus, the last word on what the Bible taught lay with the Roman Magisterium.

Providentissimus Deus was thus characterized by a conservative (some would have said 'reactionary') character, expressed particularly in its negative criticisms of the way in which historical-critical principles were being used. The underlying anxiety of the encyclical was that critical methodologies would prove injurious to the faith of which the church was called to be the guardian, not the destroyer.

Fifty years later, the face of Europe had changed dramatically. The Great War had been fought from 1914 to 1918 and the Second World War of 1939 to 1945 was in full course. The misplaced and anthropocentric optimism of nineteenth-century liberal theology had collapsed, shattered before the enormity of human need; the notion that humanity was evolving from a lower to a higher moral condition had been dealt an embarrassing blow. The 'gospel' of the universal fatherhood of God and the brotherhood of man stood exposed in all of its inherent poverty. There arose a new sense of need for some powerful word from God. In Protestantism, the 'theology of crisis' emerged and what came to be known as 'biblical theology' began to stir.

Significant developments also had taken place within the world of Roman Catholic biblical scholarship. In the wake of *Providentissimus*

Deus, the Pontifical Biblical Commission was created by Leo XIII in 1902. Its earliest responses (*responsa*) to questions of biblical interpretation were characterized by negative reaction to higher criticism. But in due season (it was completely reorganized in 1971 following the Second Vatican Council) it would prove to be a spearhead of the new way of reading the Bible.

In 1943, Pius XII issued his Encyclical Letter *Divino Afflante Spiritu*. It was promulgated during the Second World War, but not until the turn of the decade did its full impact begin to be felt. This time a more positive note was struck. For one thing, Roman Catholic biblical scholars were largely set free from the burden the Church had carried for centuries: the use of the *Vulgate* (Jerome's Latin translation of the Bible). It had been regarded as the authoritative text for ecclesiastical use since the time of the Council of Trent (and even in 1943 it was declared to be 'free from all error in matters of faith and morals').

In a manner reminiscent of the humanists of the Renaissance, with the motto *ad fontes* ('back to the original sources'), Roman Catholic scholars now enjoyed a new freedom and fresh impetus to gain and employ expertise in the biblical languages to enable a true understanding of the text of Scripture. A new value was recognized in the use of such tools as textual, literary, and form criticism. The importance of history, ethnology, archaeology, 'and other sciences' was affirmed. The 'true meaning', indeed the so-called 'literal sense' of Scripture, was to be sought, as well as the 'spiritual significance'. Pre-critical ways of reading the Bible were widely (but not entirely) replaced with the new approach. A clear distinction was made between the 'meaning' of the original text and the contemporary application ('significance') of it. Principles of interpretation that had long been familiar to Protestants were now increasingly recognized as essential to proper biblical exegesis. The historical-critical method had come to stay.

All this was encouraged (it could scarcely have been prevented, but the genius of Rome, unlike Wittenberg and Geneva, has always been its ability to hold opposite tendencies together). The underlying principle was that the Scriptures cannot be charged with error. Supposed errors in Scripture, it was held, could be resolved by a right reading of the text.

Any tensions between Scripture and 'reality' could always be resolved in favour of biblical integrity. Harmonization was an essential key to reading the Bible as a modern Catholic.

Times change, and we change with them. The second half of the twentieth century saw continued movement in Roman Catholic biblical scholarship. This was not without ecclesiastical bloodletting (at one point, professors at the Pontifical Biblical Institute were banned from teaching). But the overall result has been that some of the most erudite biblical studies published during this period carry the imprimatur *Nihil obstat*, which identifies them as the work of Roman Catholic scholars that has been declared 'free of doctrinal or moral error'.

The most recent succinct expression of this development can be seen in the Pontifical Biblical Commission's statement on biblical interpretation, published in 1993. Here the fruits of critical scholarship set within the context of the Church's tradition were warmly welcomed. Indeed, strikingly—in view of the importance of the principle of harmonization at all costs that marked earlier Roman Catholic pronouncements—it was of a Protestant-style fundamentalist approach to Scripture that the Church seemed to have become most critical, and perhaps most fearful.

But why should this development since 1870 be of interest to Protestant Christians? The reason lies on the surface of much of the very best Catholic biblical scholarship. There is, in our day, a clear recognition in Roman Catholic biblical scholarship that there is a gulf—or at least a distance—between what the text of sacred Scripture states and the teaching of the sacred tradition of the Church. There is also recognition that the words of Jesus recorded in John 16:12-15,[1] often taken as a specific promise guaranteeing the truth and infallibility of sacred tradition, do not refer to such a tradition at all.[2] By necessity, therefore, some Roman

---

[1] 'I still have many things to say to you, but you cannot bear them now. When the Spirit of truth comes, he will guide you into all the truth, for he will not speak on his own authority, but whatever he hears he will speak, and he will declare to you the things that are to come. He will glorify me, for he will take what is mine and declare it to you. All that the Father has is mine; therefore I said that he will take what is mine and declare it to you.'

[2] See, for example, Raymond E. Brown, *The Gospel According to John*, 3 vols (Garden City, NY: Anchor Press, 1966), II:714-17.

Catholic interpreters of Scripture have had to develop a novel view of the relationship between Scripture and tradition in order to hold them together: tradition adds to Scripture, but Scripture is 'open' to tradition. Can this contention be readily illustrated from Roman Catholic biblical scholarship?

In critical discussion, it is always a great temptation to treat the most extreme examples of the opposite viewpoint as though they were representative. That is an unworthy tactic, one that often merely hardens prejudices on both sides. In this context, however, the point can readily be illustrated not from the worst historical examples of Roman Catholic biblical interpretation, but—albeit from a necessarily limited sample— by what is widely regarded as its best.

A Roman Catholic scholar on the Letter to the Romans

It would be hard to find a better illustration of the new approach to the Bible in Roman Catholicism than the widely acclaimed commentary on Romans by Joseph A. Fitzmyer (1920–2016). Professor Fitzmyer was a leading Roman Catholic scholar whose outstanding academic gifts pervaded his almost 800-page commentary. While it is often true in the matter of commentaries that 'one man's meat is another man's poison', it is impossible to imagine any student of Scripture failing to find considerable profit from the erudition and stimulus of Fitzmyer's work. Raymond E. Brown, the outstanding American Catholic Johannine scholar, described Fitzmyer as 'the most learned NT scholar on the American Catholic scene'.[1] Elsewhere he says of Fitzmyer's work on Romans that 'It can lay fair claim to being the best commentary on Romans in English.'[2] Even those who might award the palm to someone other than Fitzmyer recognize the value of the commendation.

But it is precisely *because* of the quality of this commentary that its contents are so significant. A desire for careful exegesis coupled with faithfulness to the Magisterium of the Church leads Fitzmyer (a Jesuit) to state, albeit with appropriate sensitivity and discretion, that the teaching of the Scriptures cannot *simpliciter* ('directly') be identified

[1] Raymond E. Brown, *Biblical Exegesis and Church Doctrine* (New York: Paulist Press, 1985), p. 9.
[2] Cited on the dust jacket of Joseph A. Fitzmyer, *Romans* (New York: Doubleday, 1994).

with the teachings of the sacred tradition. The following illustrations will underline this.

In an extensive introductory chapter on Pauline theology, Fitzmyer includes an essay on faith. In the developed theology of the Medieval period, theologians had spoken and written much of *fides caritate formata*, justifying faith that was 'faith formed by love'. This, not 'faith alone', justifies, they said, since now the sinner has become justifiable. This view was confirmed at the Council of Trent (1545–63).

Many of the statements from Trent reveal misunderstandings of the teaching of Luther and the other Reformers; nevertheless, its teaching in this regard is clearly intended as a rejection of the principles the Reformers regarded as central to the gospel. Trent's *Decree on Justification* reads as follows:

> If anyone says that men are justified either by the imputation of Christ's justice alone or by the remission of sins alone, excluding grace and charity that is poured into their hearts by the Holy Spirit [cf. Rom. 5:5] and inheres in them, or also that the grace that justifies us is only the favour of God, let him be anathema.[1]

Rome's great fear has always been that *sola fide* would breed antinomianism and moral licence. Christians, it was held, were preserved from this by the fact that justification takes place through faith that is formed by love; i.e., justification involves personal transformation.

But, comments Fitzmyer, Paul's notion of faith that 'blossoms' in love is to be distinguished from this *fides caritate formata*:

> That is a philosophical transposition of the Pauline teaching— acceptable or not depending on whether one agrees with the philosophy involved—but the genuine Pauline idea of 'faith working itself out through love' is implicit in Romans ... he does not equate faith with love; nor does he ascribe to love what he does to faith (viz., justification, salvation), even though he recognizes the necessity of the two working in tandem.[2]

[1] Council of Trent's *Decree on Justification*, Canon XI in H. Denzinger, *Compendium of Creeds*, P. Hünermann, R. L. Fastiggi, and A. E. Nash, eds (San Francisco: Ignatius Press, 2012), p. 385.
[2] Fitzmyer, *Romans*, p. 138.

Here is an important recognition of the fact that we must distinguish between what the tradition has said and what the Scriptures actually affirm. The idea of faith and love being instrumental in justification cannot be read out of the text as such. It is no part of the exegesis of Paul's words.

Note, however, that Fitzmyer is careful to suggest only that there is distance between what is affirmed by Paul and what is stated in the tradition. He does not affirm that there is any necessary contradiction between Scripture and tradition. More is to follow. Commenting on a central passage regarding the justification controversy, Romans 3:21-26, Fitzmyer states that Paul formulates 'three, or possibly four, effects of the Christ-event [i.e., the work of Christ] …: justification, redemption, expiation, and possibly pardon', and adds,

> It is important to recognize that such effects of the Christ-event are appropriated through faith in Christ Jesus, and only through faith. It is the means whereby human beings experience what Christ has done.[1]

Here again the Pauline text is to be read on its own terms without recourse to post-Pauline developments in the Church. Fitzmyer knows that within the Church there have always been those who have read Paul's words as implying the principle of *sola fide*.

It would be quite wrong, however (indeed naive), to read this distancing of the Church's pronouncements from the statements of the biblical text as a capitulation to the Protestant exposition. Indeed, Fitzmyer gives equal care to articulating the difference between the text and the way in which it has been interpreted within Protestant circles.

Within a page of the previous citation we find Professor Fitzmyer rejecting the interpretation of a Protestant scholar on the grounds that 'that reading would introduce an Anselmian distinction into the Pauline text, which does not warrant it'.[2] But even here the concern is to allow Paul to speak for himself in distinction from reading him through the eyes of the construction of a post-biblical tradition (in this case, one that also appealed to Protestantism). Whether or not Fitzmyer's critique is

[1] Fitzmyer, *Romans*, p. 342.
[2] *Ibid.*, p. 343.

accurate, what is at first sight remarkable is the way in which his recognition of Paul's emphasis on the unique role of faith might easily be mistaken for the comment of a Protestant exegete.

There are other noteworthy illustrations of an exegesis that self-consciously seeks to let the Scriptures speak for themselves apart from the dominance of theological tradition. In this sense, the Roman Catholic scholar is approaching the text in a manner similar to the Protestant. Commenting on the words 'justified freely by his grace' in Romans 3:24, Fitzmyer notes:

> It should be superfluous to stress … that in using *dorean* and *te autou chariti*, Paul is not referring to the efficient cause of justification by the former and the formal cause by the latter (as if *charis* were 'sanctifying grace'). That is anachronistic exegesis, a distinction born of later Medieval and Tridentine [Council of Trent] theology.[1]

Here again, without rejecting the teaching of Trent as such, a distinction is made between what the text itself states and the theology that has developed within the Catholic tradition.

The comments that may strike the Protestant mind as most unexpected are to be found in Professor Fitzmyer's exposition of Romans 3:27-31. It was in his translation of Romans 3:28 in 1522 that Luther's appeal to *sola fide* emerged as seminal for the Reformation understanding of the gospel. Fitzmyer recognizes that this language long predates Luther and can be found in the writings of the early Fathers. He frankly states that 'in this context' Paul means 'by faith alone', although he contends that in the Lutheran sense its use is an extension of what Paul says. This inevitably prompts questions as to the nature of this 'extension' and whether there is any Roman Catholic 'sense' in which justification is genuinely 'by faith alone'. But the admission in and of itself is significant.

The same distance between Scripture and tradition is further indicated when Fitzmyer turns to the exposition of Romans 5:12. The traditional Roman Catholic view of this text is to see here a reference to 'original' sin. This was made explicit by the Council of Trent, which not only set its imprimatur to this exegesis of Paul's words, but also forbade any other understanding of his statement. Fitzmyer comments:

[1] Fitzmyer, *Romans*, p. 348.

This tradition found its formal conciliar expression in the Tridentine *Decretum de peccato originali*, Sess. V, 2-4. ... This decree gave a definitive interpretation to the Pauline text in the sense that his words teach a form of the dogma of Original Sin, a rare text that enjoys such an interpretation.

Care must be taken, however, to understand what Paul is saying and not to transform his mode of expression too facilely into the precision of later dogmatic development. ... Paul's teaching is regarded as seminal and open to later dogmatic development, but it does not say all that the Tridentine decree says.[1]

Again we can hardly avoid noting the caution that emerges with respect to reading the Church's tradition back into Scripture. The dogma as such is not rejected; what is made clear is that it is not to be identified *simpliciter* with the teaching contained in the New Testament.

Next, in commenting on Romans 6:12, Fitzmyer alludes to the teaching of the Council of Trent that what Paul sometimes calls 'sin' (as, for example, in Rom. 6:12) is not described as such by the Roman Catholic Church, but rather is understood as the *fomes peccati*. The allusion here is to one of the most astonishing (and surely embarrassing) statements in the documents of Trent, in the *Decree Concerning Original Sin*:

> Of this concupiscence, which the apostle sometimes calls 'sin' [cf. Rom. 6:12-15; 7:7, 14-20] the holy council declares: The Catholic Church has never understood that it is called sin because it would be sin in the true and proper sense in those who have been reborn, but because it comes from sin and inclines to sin. If anyone thinks the contrary, let him be anathema.[2]

Again we must not make the mistake of thinking that Fitzmyer had ceased to be a faithful son of the Roman Church. For this, he noted (in agreement with the biblical scholar M. J. Lagrange [1855–1938]), 'might be an exact theological transposition', but it is a precision not yet found in the Pauline text.

---

[1] Fitzmyer, *Romans*, p. 408.
[2] Council of Trent's *Decree on Original Sin*, Session V.5 in Denzinger, *Compendium of Creeds*, pp. 373-74.

Our concern here is not to discuss the precision of the theology involved in this statement, but once more to underline the gap—although for Fitzmyer manifestly not an unbridgeable historical gulf—that is fixed between the revelation as it comes to us in Scripture and what the Church has received as its authoritative tradition.

No doubt this whole approach causes anxiety in the hearts of Roman Catholics who are conservative and traditionalist (there are 'fundamentalists' in both Roman Catholicism and Protestantism). They may find some relief in the way Professor Fitzmyer's concurrence with the Roman tradition is given notable expression in his handling of Paul's teaching on justification. Professor Fitzmyer nuances the meaning of *dikaioō* in the direction of 'being made upright'. Here, at perhaps the most critical point, his exegesis harmonizes with the *Vulgate*'s translation of the New Testament's *dikaioō* by *justum facere*.

Despite the presence of Lutheran sympathizers at Trent, the Council committed the Church irrevocably to a transformationist doctrine of justification:

> This disposition or preparation is followed by justification itself, which is not only the remission of sins [*can.* 11] but the sanctification and renewal of the interior man through the voluntary reception of grace and of gifts, whereby from unjust man becomes just, and from enemy a friend, that he may be 'an heir in hope of eternal life'.[1]

Even Fitzmyer's further qualification—he notes that this justification takes place 'gratuitously through God's powerful declaration of acquittal'—does not eliminate a distinctively Tridentine exegesis, as he makes clear: 'The sinful human being is not only "declared upright", but is "made upright" (as in 5:19), for the sinner's condition has changed.'[2]

Much is at stake here. In many areas where sacred tradition is not already present and perspicuous in sacred Scripture, Fitzmyer and other Roman Catholic scholars reduce the gap between what is taught in the biblical text and the dogma of sacred tradition by an appeal to the 'open'

---

[1] Council of Trent's *Decree on Justification*, Session VII.7 in Denzinger, *Compendium of Creeds*, p. 377.
[2] Fitzmyer, *Romans*, p. 347.

character of biblical teaching. In this way, they minimize the force of the Reformation criticism that tradition contradicts Scripture.

Jesus' washing of the disciples' feet with his exhortation to them to imitate him (John 13:1-15) gives an example of this 'open' character of Scripture. Foot-washing might well have developed into a sacrament, in a manner parallel to the development that took place in another 'open' passage, James 5:14. Here, 'under the Spirit-guided development of Tradition' the text became the basis for the sacrament of the anointing of the sick.[1]

No appeal to the theory of Scripture's 'open' character can be of service, however, in relationship to the doctrine of justification. It would simply not be possible for Fitzmyer at this juncture to agree with the Reformation exegesis of justification as declaratory, imputed right- eousness, yet appeal to the 'open' character of Paul's teaching and to the Spirit's continuing work in the Church as bringing out the fullness of meaning in justification as including infused righteousness. These two perspectives stand in direct contradiction to each other.

Nevertheless, Fitzmyer's interpretation is based on an exegetical appeal— to his own exegesis of Romans 5:19: 'Just as through the disobe- dience of one man many were made sinners, so through the obedience of one many will be made upright.'[2] He takes Paul's verb *kathistanai* ('made') in the sense of subjective condition, i.e., in a transformationist sense.

Two things should be said here. *First*, we believe Fitzmyer's interpre- tation of Romans 5:19 can be demonstrated to be mistaken.[3] But *second*, his logic is wrong. Even if *kathistanai* were understood in a subjective- transformationist sense, it does not necessarily follow that Paul's use of *dikaioō* is transformationist rather than forensic and declaratory. To consistently interpret 'justify' in the light of this assumption is an exegetical procedure without justification!

---

[1] J. A. Fitzmyer, *Scripture, The Soul of Theology* (Mahwah, NJ: Paulist Press, 1994), p. 78.

[2] The translation is Fitzmyer's.

[3] See, e.g., Douglas Moo, *Romans* (Chicago: Moody, 1991), I:358-59; Murray, *Romans*, I:205-6, 336-62.

But even here there is a formal recognition of the principle: sacred Scripture must be distinguished from sacred tradition; we should not assume that the latter is an exegesis of the former.

Naturally, Protestants view this distinction through protestantized spectacles. Anyone convinced of the authority and sole sufficiency of Scripture is bound to ask how it is possible for a scholar of integrity to recognize this gap and yet to remain a faithful Roman Catholic.

It is too simple a construction, however, to conclude that there is manifest duplicity here. Rather, the general consistency and clarity with which Fitzmyer's exegesis illustrates the gap between Scripture and tradition highlights why it is that the Protestant appeal to Scripture alone to refute Roman Catholic dogma seems to cut little ice: for Rome, neither Scripture nor tradition can stand on its own. The rationale for this should now be clear: *in the Roman Catholic Church, sacred tradition stands beside sacred Scripture as a valid and authoritative source of divine revelation. In fact, both emerge within one and the same context: the Catholic Church.*

Understanding this principle helps us to see the mindset of the Roman Catholic Church's approach to interpreting the Bible at this juncture.

Scripture and tradition

For Rome, the Bible itself emerges from within the Church. The Church exists prior to the Bible; the Bible is itself an expression of the living voice of the Church—in its own way, it is tradition. In the words of the *Catechism of the Catholic Church*, 'the New Testament itself demonstrates the process of living Tradition'.[1] The New Testament is tradition—the earliest tradition inscripturated in distinction from the living tradition that arises within the ongoing life of the Church in the context of apostolic succession.

This perspective is well attested in the succession of Rome's authoritative doctrinal statements.

Appeal in this context is made to the Profession of Faith composed in connection with the Second Council of Constantinople (553), to the

---

[1] *Catechism of the Catholic Church* (Liguori, MO: Liguori Publications, 1994), p. 26, #83.

Council of the Lateran (649), and to the Second Council of Nicea (787). However, it was in the context of the Counter-Reformation that the Church's position was set in concrete by the Council of Trent:

> The holy ecumenical and general Council of Trent ... clearly perceives that this truth and rule are contained in the written books and unwritten traditions that have come down to us. ... Following, then, the example of the orthodox Fathers, it receives and venerates with the same sense of loyalty and reverence all the books of the Old and New Testament—for the one God is the author of both—together with all the traditions concerning faith and practice, as coming from the mouth of Christ or being inspired by the Holy Spirit and preserved in continuous succession in the Catholic Church.[1]

The implication of this, specifically drawn out by the Council itself, was that no one should dare to interpret Scripture in a way contrary to the unanimous consent of the Fathers, even if such interpretations are not intended for publication:

> Furthermore, to restrain irresponsible minds, it decrees that no one, relying on his own prudence, may twist Holy Scripture in matters of faith and practice that pertain to the building up of Christian doctrine, according to his own mind, contrary to the meaning that Holy Mother the Church has held and holds—since it belongs to her to judge the true meaning and interpretation of Scripture—and that no one may dare to interpret the Scripture in a way contrary to the unanimous consensus of the Fathers, even if such interpretations are not intended for publication ...

> In this regard, as is right, the council wishes to impose a restriction also on printers ... (and) determines that hereafter Sacred Scripture, particularly this ancient Vulgate edition, shall be printed in the most correct manner possible; that no one may print or have printed any books on sacred subjects without the name of the author or in future sell them or even keep them in his possession unless they have first been examined and approved by the Ordinary ...[2]

[1] Council of Trent's *Decree on the Reception of the Sacred Books and on Traditions* in Denzinger, *Compendium of Creeds*, p. 370.

[2] Council of Trent's *Decree on the Vulgate Edition of the Bible and on the Manner of*

Leaving to one side the doubtful concept of the 'unanimous consent of the Fathers', it is clear here why the tradition becomes the master element in the Scripture–tradition liaison. Historically, it has always been the case that a 'living' (in the sense of contemporaneous) word of revelation will become the rule for Christians *de facto* (whatever may be claimed to the contrary). That is virtually a psychological inevitability. In the case of Rome, what may have begun as a limiting concept (the *regula fidei*) developed into the master concept.

This position, with appeal to these very citations, was later confirmed by the Church at the First Vatican Council in the Dogmatic Constitution *Dei Filius* (1870). A quarter of a century later, *Providentissimus Deus* (1893) appealed to the principle of the analogy of faith understood as the *consensus fidelium* as an essential principle for Catholic exposition.

Roman Catholic exegetes were summoned to use critical skills with the specific agenda of confirming the received interpretation. This was stated within the context of Leo XIII's affirmation of the inerrancy and infallibility of Scripture. Such was the continuing impact of modernism, however, that within two decades the Decree *Lamentabili* (1907) was issued to stem the tide of theological corruption. It repudiated and condemned the view that 'The Church's teaching office cannot, even by dogmatic definition, determine the genuine meaning of Sacred Scripture.'[1]

As recently as the International Theological Commission's brief but seminal work *The Interpretation of Theological Truths* (1988), Rome has continued to affirm that any conflict between exegesis and dogma is provoked by unfaithful exegesis. Genuinely Catholic exegesis, by definition, will always seek to find the appropriate harmony between biblical text and ecclesiastical dogma. The Pontifical Biblical Commission comments:

> False paths [i.e., in exegesis] will be avoided if actualization of the biblical message begins with a correct interpretation of the text and continues within the stream of the living Tradition, under the guidance of the Church's Magisterium.[2]

The circle of reasoning here appears to be 'vicious'.

Interpreting Sacred Scripture in Denzinger, *Compendium of Creeds*, p. 371.

[1] J. Neuner and J. Dupois, eds., *The Christian Faith in the Doctrinal Documents of the Catholic Church*, rev. ed. (Staten Island: Alba, 1982), p. 79.

[2] *The Interpretation of the Bible in the Church* (Boston, 1993), p. 121.

In the nineteenth century, the Magisterium rightly recognized that the rise of higher criticism and of theological modernism would endanger the faith of Catholics (as it had already done among Protestants). But Rome faced an additional problem. The view that sacred tradition is also revelation implies that the tradition possesses the attributes of revelation, including infallibility and inerrancy. Consequently, the tradition had to be regarded as infallible. The inevitable correlate of this emerged in Vatican I's Dogmatic Constitution *Pastor Aeternus*, in which papal infallibility was promulgated as a 'divinely revealed dogma'. The pope's *ex cathedra* definitions of faith were stated to be 'irreformable of themselves and not from the consent of the Church' ('I am tradition', commented Pius IX). The *anathema sit* was pronounced on any who might 'contradict this our definition'.

The later pronouncements of the Second Vatican Council continued basically to affirm what was historically regarded as the Tridentine view of the relationship between Scripture and tradition reaffirmed in Vatican I's *Dogmatic Constitution on the Catholic Faith, Dei Filius*. Declared Vatican II,

> This tradition that comes from the apostles develops in the Church with the help of the Holy Spirit. For there is a growth in the understanding of the realities and the words that have been handed down. This happens through the contemplation and study made by believers, who treasure these things in their hearts [cf. Luke 2:19, 51], through a penetrating understanding of the spiritual realities they experience, and through the preaching of those who have received through episcopal succession the sure gift of truth. For as the centuries succeed one another, the Church constantly moves forward toward the fullness of divine truth until the words of God reach their complete fulfilment in her.[1]

Especially significant is the statement made on the relationship between tradition and Scripture. It employed the phraseology of Trent, apparently on papal insistence (presumably in view of the need to hold together the traditionalist and the progressive wings of the Church):

---

[1] *Dogmatic Constitution on Divine Revelation*, II:8 in Denzinger, *Compendium of Creeds*, p. 921.

Hence there exists a close connection and communication between sacred tradition and Sacred Scripture. For both of them, flowing from the same divine wellspring, in a certain way merge into a unity and tend toward the same end. For Sacred Scripture is the Word of God inasmuch as it is consigned to writing under the inspiration of the divine Spirit, while sacred tradition takes the Word of God entrusted by Christ the Lord and the Holy Spirit to the apostles and hands it on to their successors in its full purity, so that led by the light of the Spirit of truth, they may in proclaiming it preserve this Word of God faithfully, explain it, and make it more widely known. Consequently, it is not from Sacred Scripture alone that the Church draws her certainty about everything that has been revealed. Therefore both sacred tradition and Sacred Scripture are to be accepted and venerated with the same sense of loyalty and reverence.

It is clear, therefore, that sacred tradition, Sacred Scripture, and the teaching authority of the Church, in accord with God's most wise design, are so linked and joined together that one cannot stand without the others and that all together and each in its own way under the action of the one Holy Spirit contribute effectively to the salvation of souls.[1]

Theological diversity in the Roman Catholic Church

We ought not to make the mistake of assuming that the Roman Catholic Church is thoroughly monolithic. As we have noted, it too has a conservative and liberal wing. Problems and disagreements arise in tracing and exegeting the tradition as much as in exegeting the Scriptures! Thus, for example, it has become characteristic of many Roman Catholic scholars to re-read the tradition in as ecumenical a fashion as possible.

One of the most interesting developments within this context has been the emergence of a school of thought especially stimulated by the work of the Tübingen theologian J. R. Geiselmann. This school argues that the idea of Scripture and tradition being twin sources of revelation, complementing one another, is a misreading of the teaching

---

[1] *Dogmatic Constitution on Divine Revelation*, II.9-10 in Denzinger, *Compendium of Creeds*, p. 922.

of the Council of Trent. Geiselmann appealed to what he held to be the significant change introduced into the final text of the decree through the influence of Bishop Pietro Bertano of Fano and Angelo Bonucci, the General of the Servites. The draft for the *Decree on Scripture and Tradition* had stated that revealed truth was to be found partly in the books of Scripture, partly in the traditions (*'partim in libris ... partim in ... traditionibus'*). But the final document spoke of this truth being in the scriptural books and in the unwritten traditions (*'in libris scriptis et sine scripto traditionibus'*). Geiselmann argued from this change that Trent did not deny that all saving truth is contained in the Scriptures. The truth of divine revelation is found not partly in Scripture while the remainder is found in the traditions (the draft formulation); it is all in Scripture. It is also all in the tradition. It could be argued therefore that the *sola Scriptura* principle, properly understood, is consistent with Trent.[1]

In response to Geiselmann's position, however, Cardinal Ratzinger (later Pope Benedict XVI) has argued that

> as a Catholic theologian, [Geiselmann] has to hold fast to Catholic dogmas as such, but none of them is to be had *sola Scriptura*, neither the great dogmas of Christian antiquity, of what was once the *consensus quinquesaecularis*, nor, even less, the new ones of 1854 and 1950. In that case, however, what sense is there in talking about the sufficiency of Scripture?[2]

In a word, the deposit of the faith (*depositum fidei*) is contained in both Scripture and tradition, and the task of interpreting it is 'entrusted

[1] The view Geiselmann rejects has been the view of the major Roman apologists since Trent. For a brief account, see J. R. Geiselmann, 'Scripture, Tradition, and the Church: An Ecumenical Problem', in D. J. Callahan, H. A. Obermann, and D. J. O'Hanlon, eds., *Christianity Divided* (London: Sheed and Ward, 1962), pp. 39-72.

[2] J. Ratzinger in K. Rahner and J. Ratzinger, *Revelation and Tradition*, tr. from the German, *Offenbarung und Überlieferung*, by W. J. O'Hara (New York, 1966), 33. The references to 1854 and 1950 are to the bull *Ineffabilis Deus*, promulgating the doctrine of the Immaculate Conception (i.e., the perpetual sinlessness of the Virgin Mary), and to the Apostolic Constitution *Munificentissimus Deus*, which promulgated the bodily assumption into heaven of the Virgin Mary. The term *consensus quinquesaecularis* refers to a theory that the Church was marked by unity and doctrinal purity during the first five centuries.

to bishops in communion with the successor of Peter, the Bishop of Rome'.[1] The recent document of the Pontifical Biblical Commission, *The Interpretation of the Bible in the Church*, continues to affirm this position, if in a less polemical and dogmatic manner and in an ecumenically conscious fashion: 'What characterizes Catholic exegesis is that it deliberately places itself within the living tradition of the Church.'[2] In this context, however, the Commission is careful to add:

> All pre-understanding, however, brings dangers with it. As regards Catholic exegesis, the risk is that of attributing to biblical texts a meaning which they do not contain but which is the product of a later development within the tradition. The exegete must beware of such a danger.[3]

No hint of criticism is made of the fact that sacred tradition requires belief in dogma that is not contained in sacred Scripture. But there is present here a hint that exegetes in the past (and still today) may read the New Testament as though it had been written in the light of the tradition, and thus distort the teaching of sacred Scripture (and by implication perhaps also the function of the tradition). Implicit in this is the recognition of the substance-gap between sacred Scripture and sacred tradition.

The historic Protestant view is that this gap becomes a chasm at certain strategic points. There is an unbearable discrepancy, not merely a healthy tension, between sacred Scripture and sacred tradition in many areas. A wide variety of factors contributed to the Reformation of the sixteenth century. Among the chief was the discovery, fuelled by the Renaissance spirit of *ad fontes* (i.e. back to the sources) that the gap between the clear teaching of Scripture and the tradition was at points so great as to involve not merely development but contradiction.

Conclusions

Roman Catholic scholars such as Professor Fitzmyer have been given the freedom to explore what Scripture teaches. They discover themselves

---

[1] *Catechism of the Catholic Church*, p. 27, #85.
[2] *The Interpretation of the Bible in the Church*, p. 89.
[3] *Ibid.*

looking over their shoulders at the Roman Catholic traditionalists who do not hide their anxiety that such open distancing between Scripture and tradition will be the downfall of the Church. Consequently, their characteristic refrain is that the difference between the content of Scripture and the content of the tradition does not involve contradiction but only development.

What is becoming clearer than ever, however, is that the principle of *sola Scriptura* remains a watershed. As Cardinal Ratzinger as much as admitted in his reaction to Geiselmann, there are major Roman doctrines that simply cannot be found in the Scriptures. In this sense, Scripture alone cannot be regarded as sufficient for the life of the Church.

But we must go further. There are important teachings in the tradition that are not only additional to, but different from, and contradictory to, the teaching of sacred Scripture. These include the very doctrines that were the centrepiece of the Reformation struggle: the nature of justification; the importance of the principle of *sola fide*; the number of the sacraments; the sufficiency of the work of Christ; the effect of baptism; the presence of Christ at the Supper; the priesthood of all believers; the celibacy of the priesthood; the character and role of Mary; and much more. The more that Scripture is exegeted *on its own terms*, the more it will become clear that in these areas sacred tradition does not merely add to sacred Scripture, it *contradicts* it. That being the case, can tradition really be 'sacred'?

A major development has taken place, then, in Roman Catholic interpretation of Scripture. For this we may be grateful. We should not grudgingly minimize the rediscovery of the Bible. Indeed, it might help us greatly if we recalled that responsibility for the confusion in Rome's understanding of justification rests partly on the shoulders of the great Augustine himself, whom we often claim with Calvin as 'wholly ours'.

Having said this, however, it is now clearer than ever (*pace* Geiselmann) that the Roman Catholic Church cannot and will not subscribe to *sola Scriptura*. It *must* deny the sole sufficiency of the Bible. And, as the Reformers recognized, so long as Rome appeals to two sources, or even tributaries, of revelation—the contents of Scripture and the substance of its own tradition—it is inevitable that it will also withstand the message of Scripture and of the Reformation: *sola gratia, solus Christus, sola fide*.

CHAPTER TWENTY-ONE

THE HOLY SPIRIT AND
THE HOLY SCRIPTURES:
INERRANCY AND PNEUMATOLOGY

'MYSTERY is the life blood of dogmatics,' wrote Herman Bavinck.[1] The veracity of his axiom is, of course, related to and rooted in the so-called Creator–creature distinction. God is not a man. He is a different kind of being, underived, independent, infinite, the great 'I AM', one-in-three and three-in-one. As such, he relates to all things in a manner that is different from the creature, even the supreme creature, man—and, indeed, in an unimaginably different manner. Our concepts and language describe this distinction, but can never define it. Our language about God always has an accommodated, creaturely form, legitimated only by the fact that he has made all things to reflect his glory, and has made man, male and female, as his image.

We recognize this to be true in all of our talk about God and in every sphere of theology. The relationship of the Creator to the creature always 'surpasses knowledge', even if, through his self-revelation to us as appropriately created receptors, we are able to grasp it.[2]

God, for example, is omnipresent and eternal. But his presence (which is 'omni') relates to the space–time continuum in a manner altogether different from my relationship to it. The fact that I occupy a

---

[1] Herman Bavinck, *Reformed Dogmatics*, 4 vols, ed. John Bolt, tr. J. Vriend (Grand Rapids, MI: Baker Academic, 2003–08), II:29.

[2] This is a principle Paul employs in relationship to the love of God (Eph. 3:19), but, *mutatis mutandis*, it is applicable to the whole, to every aspect of, the Creator–creature relationship. By parity of reasoning, this may be said about all divine 'attributes', including those sometimes described as 'communicable'.

specific 'space' (say six feet by fourteen inches by five inches) does not delimit his omnipresence (as though it surrounded my space but was excluded from it). This would be a misconceptualization of reality and a misstep in theology. No; God-relationship is an altogether different kind of phenomenon from my creaturely-relationship to any created reality. Because we are not God, there is an inevitability to our limited grasp of his being and actions, both within himself (*opera ad intra Trinitatis*) and beyond himself (*opera ad extra Trinitatis*). This is what we mean when, with Bavinck, we say that mystery is always the starting place, as well as the concluding point, of theology.[1]

Yet the wonder is that God is a revealer of mysteries. We do not fully comprehend them, but nevertheless we may grasp them within the limitations of our creatureliness.

The Holy Spirit

If this is an important general theological axiom, it is certainly true whenever we speak about the person of the Holy Spirit and his mode of operation and relationship to man. To use our Lord's analogy, 'The wind [*pneuma*] blows where it wishes, and you hear its sound, but you do not know where it comes from or where it goes. So it is with everyone who is born of the Spirit' (John 3:8). If this is true of the *sine qua non* of seeing and entering the kingdom of God (John 3:3, 5), then it is surely correspondingly true of all of the Spirit's operations. Indeed, his very title ('Spirit') conveys an atmosphere somewhat distinct from that of either 'Father' or 'Son'. These latter have points of connection with us in terms of human relationships. 'Spirit' also has a connection, but a more mysterious one. If you doubt it, ask someone to define the terms *father* and *son*, and then to define the term *spirit*.

What becomes increasingly clear throughout Scripture, however, are (1) the rich and intimate relationships between the Spirit and the Father and the Spirit and the Son (he is the Spirit 'of' both; Rom. 8:9), and (2) the role the Spirit characteristically plays in the external acts of the Trinity.

[1] In all of our theological thinking, we seek simultaneously to be both 'clothed and in [our] right mind' (Mark 5:15) and yet also 'lost in wonder, love, and praise' (from the hymn 'Love Divine, All Loves Excelling' by Charles Wesley).

The Fathers of the church insisted that the persons of the Trinity never act independently, nor should we ever think of one person abstracted from the others. Yet each person characteristically plays a distinct role: the Father plans, the Son mediates, the Spirit effects and completes. This is true in creation (e.g., Gen. 1:1-3), in providential governing (and restraint) (e.g., Gen. 6:3), in redemptive history,[1] in the incarnation,[2] and in the actual application of salvation to believers (1 Cor. 6:11).

The Spirit occupies a similar role epistemologically. God has acted and revealed himself in creation, providence, and history, culminating in his grand action in Jesus Christ. But how do we have *access* to the facts and to their true interpretation so that we may come to know God as he is and trust and love him because of what he has done? How does he become *our* God in this sense? According to Scripture, the final connecting links are made by the ministry of the Holy Spirit. In the post-apostolic age, those connecting links are, in one form or another, ultimately related to the giving of Scripture.

The God-breathed word

The best-known New Testament text on Scripture, while having in view *its practical effects*, emphasizes the Spirit's originating role by stating that all Scripture is *theopneustos*, or 'breathed out by God' (2 Tim. 3:16).

As Benjamin B. Warfield demonstrated with copious references, the force of this *hapax legomenon* is passive.[3] It refers to Scripture's origin in God ('God-breathed') and not to its activity ('breathing-out God'). Even if there is a sense in which this is what Scripture does, that it does so is a function of its God-breathed quality.

---

[1] This is seen perhaps most strikingly in Isaiah's commentary on the exodus, in which what God does (delivers his people from Egypt) is mediated through the angel of the Lord and executed by the Spirit—against whom, alas, the people rebelled. See Isa. 63:7-19.

[2] Jesus is conceived by the Spirit, anointed with the Spirit, led by the Spirit to defeat Satan, effects his miracles through the Spirit, offers himself as a sacrifice in the Spirit, is raised by the power of the Spirit, energizes his church by the Spirit, and will subdue all things by the power that is at work in him (presumably the Holy Spirit). See Matt. 1:18; 4:1; 12:28; Heb. 9:14; Rom. 1:4; Acts 2:33; Phil. 3:21.

[3] B. B. Warfield, 'God Inspired Scripture', *Revelation and Inspiration, Works*, I:229-80.

While Paul's vocabulary is unique, it simply summarizes a claim evidenced throughout Scripture and confirmed in the New Testament. It can hardly have been accidental that his term is a compound of *theos* ('God') and *pneō*, breathe, hence *pneuma* ('Spirit'), since the Spirit is the breath of God.[1] Scripture comes to us through the ministry of the Holy Spirit. This is a major element in its own teaching about itself.

Scripture 'claims'?

It is said that there is no point at which 'Scripture as a whole' makes this claim about 'Scripture as a whole'.[2] After all, this would virtually necessitate that the last words of the Bible contain a dogmatic statement about the Bible as a whole (perhaps including a statement, akin to those found in a number of confessions of faith,[3] about what actually constitutes the Bible as a whole). But, in fact, in a wide variety of ways, the books of Scripture bear testimony—and, on occasion, a cross-fertilized testimony—to their divine origin. The claim of the editor of 2 Samuel, that David's words constitute an 'oracle of ... the anointed of the God of Jacob', and his record of David's 'last words'[4]—'The Spirit of the LORD speaks by me; his word is on my tongue' (2 Sam. 23:1-2)—provide one of many illustrations of a Spirit-consciousness on the part of the authors of the Old Testament, an understanding that they constituted a line of individuals through whom God breathed out his word. Thus, Hebrews summarizes the entire period of redemptive history until Christ: 'Long ago, at many times and in many ways, God spoke to our fathers by the prophets' (Heb. 1:1). The word comes *from* God; it is spoken *through* the prophets. He is the origin, the ultimate author; they are the speakers or writers through whom he breathes out his word.[5]

---

[1] The parallelisms in Psa. 104:29-30 underscore this relationship within the context of Paul's mindset being structured by the teaching and vocabulary of the Old Testament.

[2] Notably by Professor James Barr in his *Fundamentalism*, p. 78. 'All this', writes Professor Barr, 'is nonsense.' See above, Chapter 19.

[3] For example, the *Gallic Confession*, III (1559), the *Belgic Confession*, Article IV (1561), the *Thirty-Nine Articles*, Article VI (1562), the *Irish Articles*, I (1615), and the *Westminster Confession of Faith*, I.2.

[4] In this context, presumably his last prophetic words, not his dying words.

[5] I have tried to illustrate this conscious awareness in Paul's letters in *From the*

It is noteworthy that when 'God' speaks, he does so through the Spirit. This is the New Testament's understanding, as several references make plain:

> In those days Peter ... said, 'Brothers, the Scripture had to be fulfilled, which *the Holy Spirit spoke* beforehand by the mouth of David concerning Judas ...' (Acts 1:15-16).

'Sovereign Lord, who made the heaven and the earth and the sea and everything in them, who through the mouth of our father David, your servant, *said by the Holy Spirit* ...' (Acts 4:24-25a).

'*The Holy Spirit was right in saying* to your fathers through Isaiah the prophet ...' (Acts 28:25).

The same perspective runs through the letter to the Hebrews:

> Therefore, *as the Holy Spirit says*, 'Today, if you hear his voice, do not harden your hearts ...' (3:7-8a).

But into the second [section of the tabernacle or temple] only the high priest goes, and he but once a year, and not without taking blood, which he offers for himself and for the unintentional sins of the people. By this *the Holy Spirit indicates* that the way into the holy places is not yet opened ... (9:7-8a).

And *the Holy Spirit also bears witness to us, for after saying*, 'This is the covenant that I will make with them ...', *then he adds*, 'I will remember their sins and their lawless deeds no more' (10:15-17).[1]

It has been wisely observed that the strongest confirmation of any particular biblical doctrine is found not so much in the key 'big' or 'proof' texts, but in its pervasiveness throughout Scripture, especially in almost casual references in passages where the central burden is not that particular doctrine. The fact that God speaks by his Spirit is established by these several quotations. In none of them is the doctrine of biblical inspiration the central issue. Yet, *en passant* as it were, the role of the

---

Mouth of God: Trusting, Reading, and Applying the Bible (Edinburgh: Banner of Truth Trust, 2015), pp. 28-30.

[1] The striking existential and contemporary nature of the Spirit's witness mentioned here will be discussed later.

Holy Spirit in the giving of Scripture is 'accidentally' highlighted—as is the conviction, occasionally evident, that through the word that was written (past tense), God continues to speak (present tense).

This point—the reality of the ministry of the third person of the Trinity in the giving of Scripture—has often been neglected because the chief polemical issues surrounding the doctrine of Scripture have focused not on the agent in inspiration, but on the more general issues of inspiration, authority, or reliability. Yet if the Spirit's role is hinted at in the use of the term *theopneustos* (2 Tim. 3:16), it is elsewhere made explicit:

> Concerning this salvation, the prophets who prophesied about the grace that was to be yours searched and inquired carefully, inquiring what person or time the Spirit of Christ in them was indicating when he predicted the sufferings of Christ and the subsequent glories. It was revealed to them that they were serving not themselves but you, in the things that have now been announced to you through those who preached the good news to you by the Holy Spirit sent from heaven, things into which angels long to look (1 Pet. 1:10-12).

Four things should be noted here:

First, in view here is the central message of the Old as well as the New Testament. Peter's reference to the suffering and glory of the Messiah is reminiscent of Jesus' instruction in which he drew various lines from the Old Testament to show how they converged in himself and in his death, resurrection, and glory (Luke 24:25-27, 32, 44-49).[1]

Second, the revelation that was transmitted through the prophets, though not fully understood by them, was sourced in the ministry of the Holy Spirit, who is one and the same as 'the Spirit of Christ'.

Third, the ultimate source of old covenant (and therefore 'Old Testament') written revelation[2] was one and the same as the source of the gospel, since the apostles preached the new covenant message 'by the Holy Spirit sent from heaven'.

---

[1] 'Moses and all the Prophets' (verse 27); 'in all the Scriptures' (verse 27); 'the Law of Moses and the Prophets and the Psalms' (verse 44); 'the Scriptures' (verse 45).

[2] The revelation was 'written' because, as the text makes clear, the prophets understood they were to serve a future generation, not merely speak to their contemporary generation, implying the permanence of the revelation they received and passed on.

Fourth, the preached word and the written word are both attributed to the Holy Spirit. The written word is simply the preached revelation written.

What is stated *en passant* elsewhere is here stated dogmatically, and indeed further elaborated by Peter:

> No prophecy of Scripture comes from someone's own interpretation. For no prophecy was ever produced by the will of man, but men spoke from God as they were carried along by the Holy Spirit (2 Pet. 1:20-21).[1]

Peter's choice of verb is significant. The authors of Scripture *wrote* (or dictated to an amanuensis) the text of Scripture. But Peter's verb is *spoke*. Here, speech and writing share a common character. In this communicative act, the authors were 'carried along' by the Spirit.

This is a particularly striking statement since it refers not simply to the *quality* of the Scriptures as Spirit-given, or God-breathed, but also to the *mode* by which this giving took place. The Spirit 'bore' the authors. The verb *pherō* is used four times in verses 17-18 (twice) and verse 21 (twice). The voice of God on the Mount of Transfiguration carried from heaven to earth (verses 17-18); prophecy is not borne from the will of man, but 'men spoke from God as they were carried along [borne] by the Holy Spirit'. The same verb is used of a ship being carried along by the wind (Acts 27:15, 17). The ship 'sails', but its ability to do so depends on, and is resourced by, the wind. There are analogies here to the manner in which Scripture is given: the penmen wrote, but in their writing they were 'carried along' by the Spirit.

We inevitably ask further questions: How did this happen? What did the authors experience? But Peter's words are not porous at this point, and answers will not be found by dogmatic deduction from these texts, but only by a broader observation of the testimonies found in Scripture

---

[1] The significance of verse 20 has been much discussed: does 'no prophecy ... comes from someone's own interpretation' refer to (1) the experience of the prophet who speaks the word or (2) the hearer who receives and understands the word? For (1), see R. Bauckham, *Jude, 2 Peter, Word Biblical Commentary* (Waco, TX: Word, 1983), pp. 229-33; for (2), see Thomas Schreiner, *1, 2, Peter, Jude, The New American Commentary* (Nashville: Broadman & Holman, 2003), pp. 322-23. Either interpretation is consistent with the point made here with reference to verse 21.

itself. The modes are varied (*polutropōs*), as the author of Hebrews notes (1:1).

In fact, some few parts of Scripture come to us by a form of divine dictation. This is not to claim the much-maligned 'dictation theory' of inspiration—an analogy characteristically used to describe the *result* of inspiration (the very words God wished), but frequently abused as though it referred to the *mode* of inspiration. This misrepresentation notwithstanding, when God said, 'Write', the biblical authors wrote what they were commanded (e.g. Exod. 34:27; Rev. 2:1, 8, 12; 3:1, 7)!

Scripture indicates various other modes were employed by the Spirit: visions, dreams, ongoing application of the covenant law, expositions of earlier promises, meditations on God's glory, remembering what Jesus said, doing careful research, and so on. These phenomena alert us to the fact that the inspiration of Scripture is the fruit of the multi-dimensional activity of the Holy Spirit. It includes, but is not confined to, the existential moment of penning the original *autographa*.[1] In particular, we observe here a ministry of preparation of the authors and one of superintendence of their writing.

This should not surprise us, insofar as the giving of the Scriptures is an aspect of the overarching providence of God in history. In this respect, the classical term *inspiration* can prove to be more misleading than illuminating if it conveys the impression that inspiration is a kind of existentially experienced divine afflatus rendering the biblical authors wholly passive and in a virtually trance-like condition in relation to the actual composition of the text. Rather, inspiration has an organic as well as an immediate dimension. This is an important aspect of the

---

[1] Two comments are in order here. It is recognized, of course, that the 'original' of some parts of Scripture may predate their inclusion in a book of Scripture. The 'faithful sayings' in the Pastoral Epistles predate the writing of these letters. Their 'inspiration' is a function of their inclusion in the text Paul wrote or dictated. It should also go without saying that 'inspiration' attaches to the *autographa*. Indeed, this is virtually a truism for the simple reason that it is the text undergirding our copies that constitutes the 'divine original'. Unfortunately, much unnecessary academic fussing has taken place over this concept—paradoxically by authors who might well be quick to point out to their publishers that they have found 'errors' in the published versions of their manuscripts, such that the manuscripts do not represent *what they originally wrote*!

doctrine of Scripture that has been emphasized especially by Reformed theologians.[1]

Inspiration—two dimensions[2]

When we say that Scripture is 'inspired' as the result of the ministry of the Holy Spirit, we do not mean that the Spirit makes every sentence in it *inspiring*. Many are, but some are mundane; they are 'inspiring' only when read within the larger context of Scripture's grand narrative. For instance, 'I left Trophimus, who was ill, at Miletus' (2 Tim. 4:20) is not particularly 'inspiring', nor does it carry the weight of a statement such as 'Christ Jesus came into the world to save sinners, of whom I am the foremost' (1 Tim. 1:15). Yet, set within the larger context of the Pauline mission, it can 'inspire'. However, when Paul wrote that all Scripture is 'inspired by God' (2 Tim. 3:16 NASB),[3] he was not thinking about its *effect on us* (inspiring), but about its *source in him* ('God-breathed').[4]

Warfield explains:

> It is very desirable that we should free ourselves at the outset from influences arising from the current employment of the term 'inspiration'. ... This term is not a biblical term, and its etymological implications are not perfectly accordant with the biblical conception of the modes of the divine operation in giving the Scriptures. The biblical writers do not conceive of the Scriptures as a human product breathed into by the divine Spirit, and thus heightened in its qualities or endowed with new qualities; but as a divine product produced through the instrumentality of men. They do not conceive of these men, by whose instrumentality Scripture is produced, as working upon their own initiative, though energized

---

[1] Notably by Warfield, e.g., 'Inspiration', *Revelation and Inspiration, Works*, I:101, and especially Bavinck, *Reformed Dogmatics*, I:435-48.

[2] I am following here, and employ, my discussion in *From the Mouth of God*, pp. 9-17.

[3] 2 Tim. 3:16 is the only text in which, strictly speaking, the Scriptures are described as 'inspired'.

[4] He describes its effect or usefulness later in the verse when he explains the ways in which Scripture is 'profitable', or useful, in our lives—to 'inspire' us to receive its teaching, feel its rebukes, be corrected and transformed, and to be equipped for service!

by God to greater effort and higher achievement, but as moved by the divine initiative and borne by the irresistible power of the Spirit of God along ways of his choosing to ends of his appointment.[1]

Warfield's reticence about the term is well founded. The Bible is not a book *into which* God breathed, *breathing into* ('in-spiring'[2]) what men had already written, but something that God himself 'breathed out'. 'Inspiration' actually involved God *breathing out* his word ('ex-spiration'). This is why, in the New Testament, the expressions 'God says', 'the Holy Spirit says', and 'Scripture says', are seen as virtually interchangeable. If Scripture states it, then (since Scripture is God-breathed) we can say: *God, through the Holy Spirit, has said it.*[3]

But how does this take place?

Concurrence

Undoubtedly the human writers of Scripture were conscious that they were expressing their own thoughts as they wrote. But at the same time, they were under the sovereign direction of the Spirit. Theologians call this two-dimensional reality 'concurrence'.[4] It is a characteristic of divine providence. God acts to bring about his purposes, but he does so through human means in a way that maintains human activity and responsibility.[5] He is active in the event in a 'God manner', while we are active in the same event in a 'human manner'.[6] We cannot collapse these two dimensions into one and apportion, say, fifty percent of the event to the action of God and fifty percent to man. While this is a common

[1] B. B. Warfield, 'Inspiration', *Revelation and Inspiration, Works*, I:99.
[2] From the Latin verb *spiro*, 'to breathe', and the preposition *in*, meaning 'in or into'.
[3] See Gal. 3:8 and Rom. 9:17, where 'Scripture' is really the equivalent of 'God'; and Matt. 19:4-5 (quoting Gen. 2:24), Heb. 3:7 (quoting Psa. 95:7), and Acts 4:24-25 (quoting Psa. 2:1), where what 'Scripture says' is regarded as equivalent to what 'God says'.
[4] From the Latin verb *concurrere*, 'to run together', from which we get our English word concurrent, that is, events that take place simultaneously.
[5] As the *Westminster Confession of Faith* notes, in relation to sovereign divine ordination, 'nor is violence offered to the will of the creatures, nor is the liberty or contingency of second causes taken away, *but rather established*' (III.1).
[6] Outstanding illustrations of this principle are found in Gen. 50:20 and Acts 2:23.

perception, it is a misapprehension that carries disastrous theological and practical implications.

There is mystery here, of course, but it is in the nature of the case. God is God; we are not. But while this is so, the concept of concurrence prevents us from employing mistaken logic and concluding that if God is active in an event, then, to that extent, man must be inactive. It is this fundamental *theological* error that leads people to an automaton view of inspiration, in which the Spirit is perceived as rendering the writer wholly passive, perhaps even wholly inactive at the cognitive level.

But only unthinking readers of Scripture have ever held this view.[1] And only prejudiced theologians imply that this is the 'conservative' or 'traditional' (or worse, 'fundamentalist') view of divine inspiration. Paradoxically, theological critics sometimes commit the opposite error, concluding that if human authors were actively involved in the writing of Scripture, then it must by definition be fallible and errant. To make such an *a priori* claim is to imply that the divine action was limited by the human engagement.

Here, the Christological parallel proves to be helpful. The Son of God assumed real humanity in the womb of the (sinful) Virgin Mary. He was genuinely of the seed of David (and of Abraham, and ultimately of Adam; Matt. 1:1; Luke 3:23-38). Gabriel said to Mary, '*You will conceive in your womb*' (Luke 1:31), yet only because '*the Holy Spirit will come upon you*, and the power of the Most High will overshadow you' (verse 35). Thus, 'that which is conceived in her is from the Holy Spirit' (Matt. 1:20), and 'therefore the child to be born will be called holy—the Son of God' (Luke 1:35). Here is both concurrence (the Spirit overshadows; Mary conceives) and a Spirit-guaranteed holiness (the 'child to be born will be called holy'—a moral 'inerrancy'), preserving Jesus from the sinfulness that is characteristic of fallen humanity (but not definitive of humanity as such).[2]

[1] A more careful reading of the theologians who have used metaphors—such as Scripture coming through the authors as music comes from a lute—usually indicates that, set in the broader context of the authors' work, the metaphors refer to the product of inspiration rather than to the mode.

[2] It is therefore inadequate to parrot, 'To err is human, to forgive is divine', since, strictly speaking, erring is not a function of human nature as such but of *fallen people*.

Rather than say, 'The Spirit was fifty percent active, while Mary accomplished the other fifty percent', or, 'If Mary conceived in her womb, the child must, by definition, have been fallen, sinful, and errant', Scripture teaches us that both deity and humanity were involved, and that the Spirit secured the moral inerrancy of the humanity of the Saviour.

In a parallel way, the inspiration of the Bible is a special example of concurrence. God fulfilled his purpose by means of secondary causation.[1] The Spirit of God was one hundred percent engaged in *breathing out* his word; the human authors were one hundred percent active in *writing out/dictating* that word. The Scriptures came from or by (*apo*) the Spirit, but also through (*dia*) the human author.

The early church clearly understood this. Thus, for example, when they quoted from Psalm 2:1-2, they understood these words to entail God speaking by the Holy Spirit through the mouth of King David (Acts 4:24-26). David spoke/wrote, but as he did, the Spirit governed his life so that all David wrote was in keeping with God's purposes.

There were, therefore, two elements involved in the inspiration of the Scriptures. God (1) overruled the lives of those who wrote the Bible, in ways that would prepare them to write it, and (2) God also superintended them as they wrote.

Same Spirit, a variety of ways of working

Scripture's claim to be Spirit-borne should not be seen to create any real tension with the diversity of styles, thought patterns, linguistic preferences, or descriptions of personal experiences in the authors. This diversity—it is hard to imagine Jeremiah preaching Isaiah's sermons, or the author of Chronicles writing the Song of Solomon, or Paul writing 1 John—is an illustration of Paul's principle that in the exercise of spiritual gifts, there is a diversity of operations, yet one and the same Spirit at work (1 Cor. 12:4-6). Again, Warfield pointedly (and in his day, somewhat controversially) described what this means:

[1] The *Westminster Confession of Faith* well expresses the idea: 'Although, in relation to the decree of God, the first cause, all things come to pass immutably and infallibly; yet by the same providence, he ordereth them to fall out according to the nature of second causes, either necessarily, freely, or contingently' (V.2). The same principle can be seen in Paul's description of the process of sanctification in Phil. 2:12-13.

If God wished to give his people a series of letters like Paul's, he prepared a Paul to write them, and the Paul he brought to the task was a Paul who spontaneously would write just such letters.[1]

One result of this is that the nature of the Spirit's work in giving Scripture cannot be deduced from the mere statement of the fact that he does work. It must be expounded in terms of the nature of the Scriptures themselves. Its contents were composed in very different ways. A few parts of it came in the context of unusual mystical experiences. The book of Psalms was composed over an extended period of time. In places (such as the book of Job), it contains reflections on the activity and even the character of God that flow from the author's theological and spiritual malfunctions. 'Inspiration' turns out to have been a complex phenomenon because it was embedded in the historical process.

Take another New Testament example: how did the Spirit 'inspire' Luke's Gospel? The author tells us:

> It seemed good to me also, having followed all things closely for some time past, to write an orderly account for you, most excellent Theophilus, that you may have certainty concerning the things you have been taught (1:3-4).

Luke was not an eyewitness of the events he describes, nor was he the penman of a mystical revelation. Rather, he was a careful researcher. The Spirit shaped him with gifts and opportunities to do this, then superintended his activity.

The book of Revelation provides a further illuminating illustration of the Spirit's activity in the production of Scripture. No New Testament book sits closer to mystical experience. John received the revelation from Jesus when he was 'in the Spirit on the Lord's day' (1:1, 10). Yet John himself frequently described what *he himself saw* (e.g., 1:12; 5:1; 6:9; 7:1; etc.).[2]

It is clear that the lenses through which John 'saw' were crafted according to a prescription filled with Old Testament imagery and

---

[1] B. B. Warfield, 'Inspiration', *Revelation and Inspiration, Works*, I:101. This is not meant to deny divine superintendence.

[2] Thus, while there is some 'dictation' in Revelation (chaps. 2–3), the dominant verb is 'see' (vision), not 'write' (dictation).

language. He did not make up the vision. Yet he could not have described what he saw in the terms he did unless his mind was *already* deeply imbued with a profound knowledge of the Old Testament Scriptures.[1]

Here is a vivid, yet essentially simple and obvious, proof of Warfield's point. John 'sees' the book of Revelation during the period he describes himself as being 'in the Spirit on the Lord's day' (that is, within the time constraints of a Sunday!). But in order for him to 'see' and be the penman of this part of Scripture, it was necessary for the Spirit to have prepared John in advance to see what he would see. His whole life, of necessity, had required the Spirit's superintendence of his lifelong study and absorption of the Old Testament in order to enable him both to recognize the imagery he would see and to describe it in terms of its Old Testament connections. The way in which the Spirit gave us the text of the book of Revelation thus provides an illustration of how inscripturated revelation as a whole comes to us, through long-term providential preparation and under the immediate superintendence of the Holy Spirit in the actual writing of the text.[2] In this sense, the Spirit

---

[1] Sometimes, in an effort to demonstrate connections to the Old Testament in the text of Revelation, commentators fall into the trap of describing the biblical allusions as though John were consciously piecing together the vision itself from the Old Testament. The more encyclopedic commentaries become in their inclusion of every inter-textual hint, the more likely it is that this way of expressing things will occur. But—at least for those who hold to a biblical doctrine of the Spirit's work in inspiration—it is of considerable importance to make clear that John describes what was actually 'there' in his vision; that is to say, it was because of his superlative knowledge of the Old Testament that he was able to describe the visions God gave him in their appropriate terms. Put otherwise, a person without John's knowledge of the Old Testament would have described the same things differently. Without the appropriate categories in his mental equipment, he would not have been able to 'see' and therefore 'write' what was actually 'there'. Think of a child's answer to the question, 'What do you see?' Answer: 'A bird.' 'Describe it for me please.' 'It has a small head, a soft covering, two feet, two eyes, and wings with which it flies.' Then contrast the answer a leading ornithologist would give to the same question. The ornithologist has the categories in his mental equipment to explain the significance of what the child sees, and so he does so more fully, in greater detail. Both 'see' the same object, but they do not perceive the same things. That said, in describing what he sees, the ornithologist is not 'making it up', but more fully exegeting the same perceived reality.

[2] If C. H. Spurgeon could say of John Bunyan, 'Prick him anywhere—his blood is

has embedded in the text he has 'inspired' clues to how 'inspiration' took place.

There is a further, and often neglected, dimension to the Spirit's work. The apostles were empowered by the Holy Spirit to fulfil the Great Commission.[1] Insofar as this commission was originally given exclusively to the apostles (as Matthew specifically states in 28:16), a question arises: How were they to accomplish this? While it may not seem to be a necessary deduction from Jesus' command, the apostolic band realized that a *de facto* requisite for this commission to be accomplished to the ends of the earth *and* to the end of the age was a written form of the gospel message—in a word, new Scriptures, what we know as 'the New Testament'.

If there is a hesitation to see this as a *necessary* logical conclusion of Christ's commission, it is important to realize that Christ gave such a responsibility to the apostles in the context of his Upper Room Discourse (John 13:1–17:26).

Links in a chain of inspiration
The discourse begins with our Lord's dealings with Peter and Judas, and continues by explaining how the disciples will be helped and strengthened through the coming of the Spirit. This is set in the midst of Jesus' remarkable revelation of the interaction of the three persons of the Trinity. Here we find a strand of teaching that illuminates his specific purposes in sending his Spirit to the apostles:

> But the Helper, the Holy Spirit, whom the Father will send in my name, he will teach you all things and bring to your remembrance all that I have said to you (John 14:26).

> When the Spirit of truth comes, he will guide you into all the truth, for he will not speak on his own authority, but whatever he hears he will speak, and he will declare to you the things that are to come.

Bibline', we can surely say of John, 'Look into his eyes and you will see their colour is Old-Testamentine!'

[1] John 20:21-23 contains parallels to what is also in view in Matt. 28:18-20. The responsibility of the apostles to teach others everything Christ commanded them, and the horizons of this task ('all nations' and 'the end of the age'), seem to require something beyond the *vivae voces* of the apostles themselves.

He will glorify me, for he will take what is mine and declare it to you. All that the Father has is mine; therefore I said that he will take what is mine and declare it to you (John 16:13-15).

Here are three promises about what the apostles would experience through the coming of the Spirit. They would (1) remember the words of Christ, (2) understand the mystery of Christ, and (3) receive revelation regarding the future fulfilment of his kingdom. All this would be the end result of a divine dynamic. In the discourse itself, this involves the Son receiving from the Father, and the Spirit in turn receiving from the Son and the Father, and taking that which he has received to the apostles (16:14-15).

This becomes even clearer when Jesus prays for the apostles and for all who will later come to faith:

- He had received the words he spoke from his Father. His words were his Father's words. The Father had granted him a 'power of attorney' in the world to act and speak on the Father's behalf and with his authority (17:7-8).

- Jesus then had given these words to the apostles. They had received and believed them. Now, in turn, he grants them a 'power of attorney'. This will take place through the ministry of the Spirit, who, having received from Christ what he in turn has received from the Father, will communicate it to the apostles (17:14).

- The apostles' task is now to give those words to others who will come to believe in Jesus (17:20).

The new word of God for the new age thus comes through these links:

Father → Son → Spirit → apostles → whole church.

In this way, *inter alia*, the promise of Jesus will be fulfilled:

When the Helper comes, whom I will send to you from the Father, the Spirit of truth, who proceeds from the Father, he will bear witness about me. And you also will bear witness, because you have been with me from the beginning (15:26-27).

Here, in the teaching of Jesus, we hear a striking prophecy of divine
and human concurrence. The Spirit, who has been with Jesus 'from the
beginning' (i.e., from the beginning of the incarnation, and, in a deeper
sense, from all eternity), and the apostles, who have, in a lesser sense,
been with Jesus 'from the beginning' (i.e., the beginning of his ministry),
together will bear witness to him. We see this given a first fulfilment on
the Day of Pentecost. But Pentecost is not the *terminus ad quem*.[1] As is
clear from the extension of Jesus' prayer to those who believe in him
through the apostles' word (17:20), this witness will be borne everywhere
men and women come to believe through the apostolic testimony. By
implication, the New Testament is in view. For if we ask, 'Where do we
find all these promises of the Spirit's ministry coalescing?' the answer,
surely, is 'In the New Testament!'

Here Jesus was specifically preparing his apostles through the coming
ministry of the Spirit to give the New Testament to the church.[2] This was
what he had in view when he promised that the Spirit would remind
them of his words, lead them into the truth, and reveal the things that
were still to come.

The apostles' 'word' thus became the contents of the New Testament:
Gospels (what Jesus said and did); *Epistles* (the truth about Jesus); and
Revelation (the things still to come[3]). In these ways—memory of things
said and done, understanding of the gospel, a sense of future things, and
the ability to articulate the revelation—God would 'breathe out' through
them the New Testament Scriptures to add to the Old Testament, which
they, with Christ, received as the Spirit-breathed word of God.

[1] The point at which something ends or finishes; an aim or goal.
[2] It is worth noting here in passing, by way of caveat, the common modern tendency
to apply Jesus' words in John 14:26 and 16:13 (especially the latter: '[The Spirit] will
guide you into all the truth') directly to ourselves. But we were not present in the
upper room. These words were not spoken to or about us. Their fulfilment is found
in the ministry of the apostles. If they have any application to us, it involves our
searching the Scriptures where the apostles recorded the truth into which the Spirit
thus led them.
[3] One wonders if the apostle John reflected on what he had written in John 16:12-15
after he had completed the book of Revelation!

Links in a chain of illumination

There is a further work of the Spirit, however, which Paul implies when he speaks about the communication of the word of God (1 Cor. 1:18–2:16).[1]

Paul eschewed the style of the classical orators ('lofty speech or wisdom'). Instead, he employed the rhetoric of the cross. Neither was his disposition one of self-assurance based on his talents and training, but of 'weakness … fear and much trembling'. Yet his speech and message were 'in demonstration of the Spirit and of power, so that your faith might not rest in the wisdom of men but in the power of God' (1 Cor. 2:3-5).

Here Paul is describing the Spirit's concursive operation: 'my speech and my message … in demonstration of the Spirit' (verse 4). This wisdom of God had been '*revealed* … through the Spirit' (verse 10), but God had also given him the Spirit so that he 'might *understand* the things freely given us by God' (verse 12). Paul experienced the Spirit's work of superintending the 'inspiration' of the apostolic word as illumination. The communication of this revelation led, in turn, to the hearers' illumination.

Notice that the dynamic pattern here is reminiscent of that in the Upper Room Discourse: the Father had given the Son his words; he, through the Spirit, had given the words to the apostles; and they had received them and would go on to speak them with the authority of the Father and the Son. This they would be enabled to do only when the Father and the Son sent the Spirit to them.

The Spirit who gave the revelatory word is the same Spirit who illumines the hearers' or readers' understanding by the saving and transforming reception of the word. The Spirit has now come with a full divine power of attorney. He 'searches everything, even the depths of God' (verse 10). Paul has been commissioned into this 'chain of revelation and illumination', for the wisdom of God has been 'revealed to [him] through the Spirit' (verse 10). Now he can impart it to others 'in words … taught by the Spirit' (verse 13). The result is a 'demonstration of the Spirit and of power, so that your faith [the Corinthians', but surely

---

[1] Here it is a safe assumption that whether the word is spoken or written, the same dynamic is operative.

ours also] might not rest in the wisdom of men but in the power of God'
(verses 4-5).

The Spirit gave Scripture to us through his servants. There was
concursive activity in the *donation*. But there also needs to be concursive
activity in the *reception*, for apart from the Spirit's work, 'the natural
person does not accept the things of the Spirit of God, for they are
folly to him, and he is not able to understand them because they are
spiritually discerned' (verse 14).

In the presence of the inscripturated word, we are by nature in the
same position as was Nicodemus in the presence of the incarnated
Word—we can neither see nor enter the kingdom (John 3:3, 5). We are
spiritually dead, blind, and deaf. How, then, can we receive the word
of the gospel contained in the Scriptures? We can do so only when the
Spirit works in us with and by the word itself to open our eyes and
ears to see, hear, and respond to the illumined word. In Paul's words to
Timothy, when we 'think over' the apostolic word, 'the Lord will give …
understanding' (2 Tim. 2:7).

This is exactly what the Thessalonians experienced. By grace they
'received the word of God … [and] accepted it not as the word of men
[merely] but as what it really is, the word of God, which is at work in
you believers' (1 Thess. 2:13). How so? Because the 'gospel came … not
only in word, but also in power and in the Holy Spirit and with full
conviction' (1:5). The joint testimony of the Spirit with the word reaches
into the hearts of hearers/readers with the result that they are enabled to
see the kingdom although they have been blind, and to hear the voice of
Christ although they have been deaf.

In this way, in a Lazarus-like phenomenon, it is the word that Christ
speaks in the power of the Spirit that makes those who are in fact deaf
actually hear! Herein lies the mystery: words that Lazarus was not able
to hear effected in him the ability to hear those very words! Similarly,
illumination takes place not by the apostolic word *apart from the Spirit*,
nor by the Spirit *apart from the apostolic word*, but through the Spirit and
the word operating together, concursively.

Thus, as in our understanding of *inspiration*, so in our understanding
of *illumination* we find an analogy in Christ. His word enables the deaf

to hear, the blind to see, the lame to walk, the leper to be cleansed, and the dead to live (Matt. 11:4-5). He spoke to those who were 'foolish' and 'slow of heart', and his words caused their hearts to 'burn' (Luke 24:13-35). He later 'opened their minds to understand the Scriptures' (verse 45). He still does. And the point he underlines in the Upper Room Discourse is that what he did during his earthly ministry will be continued by *allos paraklētos*, 'another Helper' like himself, who will come in his place to continue and consummate his ministry (John 14:16).[1]

What Christ did then through his personal presence on his resurrection day, he now does throughout the last days by the Spirit's illumination of the word. Thus, in the words of William Cowper (1731–1800):

The Spirit breathes upon the word,
And brings the truth to light.[2]

Of course, Cowper was describing the experience of illumination from the perspective of appearance and experience—it seems as if something has happened to the Bible. But it would be both inconsistent and anachronous to think he was adopting a neo-orthodox view of Scripture![3] Theologically, of course, it would be truer to say that it is on the reader/hearer that the Spirit breathes through and with the word, thus giving illumination of the word through the word itself. We *hear* something that has been there all the time—in his word, the Father is always 'addressing' us (*present* tense; Heb. 12:5).

This is the ministry that John Calvin well described as the *internum testimonium Spiritus Sancti*, and we can do no better than listen to his words:

The highest proof of Scripture derives in general from the fact that God in person speaks in it. ... We ought to seek our conviction in

[1] The distinction between the Greek words for 'another'—*allos*, another of the same kind, and *heteros*, another of a different kind—may not always have been sustained, but certainly in this context Jesus is underlining for the disciples the intimacy of the relationship between himself and the Spirit, and his presence and that of the Spirit.

[2] The opening line of the hymn 'The Light and Glory of the Word', in *Olney Hymns* (1779; repr., Olney: The Cowper and Newton Museum, 1979), Book II, hymn LXII, p. 255.

[3] That is, that Scripture is not so much in itself the word of God, but 'becomes the word of God' to us existentially.

a higher place than human reasons, judgments, or conjectures, that is, in the secret testimony of the Holy Spirit. …

The testimony of the Spirit is more excellent than all reason. For as God alone is a fit witness of himself in his word, so also the word will not find acceptance in men's hearts before it is sealed by the inward testimony of the Spirit. The same Spirit, therefore, who has spoken through the mouths of the prophets must penetrate into our hearts to persuade us that they faithfully proclaimed what had been divinely commanded. Isaiah very aptly expresses this connection in these words: 'My Spirit which is in you, and the words that I have put in your mouth and of the mouths of your offspring, shall never fail' (Isa. 59:21). Some good folk are annoyed that a clear proof is not ready at hand when the impious, unpunished, murmur against God's word. As if the Spirit were not called both 'seal' and 'guarantee' (2 Cor. 1:22) for confirming the faith of the ungodly; because until he illumines their minds, they ever waver among many doubts![1]

This, then, is how we *hear* the word of God as the word of God. This is how the Father addresses us and how the Son speaks to us—when the Spirit engages us through Scripture.

Implications for inerrancy?

These pages have provided something of an overview of the role Scripture *specifically* attributes to the Holy Spirit in relationship to Scripture. Insofar as the Spirit is in some senses the executive person of the Trinity, what can be said about inerrancy in general can also be said of the Spirit and his ministry. But within the confines of this particular study, several implications for inerrancy can be derived *specifically* from the exposition above.

1. *The possibility of inerrancy.* In his ministry of sanctifying believers, the Spirit clearly works in and through sinful humanity without as yet perfecting it. Few Christians have doubted that they remain sinners and continue to err, although indwelt by the Spirit. But the Spirit is not constrained by our sinfulness. Mary was sinful, yet she bore the inerrant Son of God; the humanity of Christ was derived from Mary,

---

[1] Calvin, *Institutes*, I.vii.4.

yet 'sanctified, and anointed with the Holy Spirit above measure'.[1] In a similar way, Scripture is sanctified and preserved by his power.

2. *The theological argument for inerrancy.* When God speaks, what he says is expressive of his character and is by implication therefore inerrant. Since Scripture comes to us through the work of the Spirit, we may say that it is the special work of the Spirit to accomplish this. He is himself divine and also the person of the Trinity who effects in the world the purposes of God. Consistently in the New Testament, the new word and words that accompany and interpret the incarnation of Christ are said to be the fruit of the Spirit's ministry. This divine testimony bears its own divine character, namely, inerrancy. Men and women may lie to the Holy Spirit, and do so (cf. Acts 5:3). But he does not lie to them.

3. *The integrity of the Spirit.* Whenever the Holy Spirit is mentioned in relation to Scripture, the absolute integrity of what he says there is implied and assumed, never doubted, and certainly never contradicted or accused of error. The ease with which this truth is recognized carries with it the assumption that the verbal integrity characteristic of the person of the Spirit is manifested in the Scriptures the Spirit gives. Thus, it is no aberration when Luke virtually concludes the Acts of the Apostles with a quotation from Isaiah 6:9-10 introduced by Paul's comment, 'The Holy Spirit was right in saying …' (Acts 28:25).[2]

4. *The reliability of the Spirit's work.* Peter attributes God's carrying of the prophetic word to its divinely intended destiny specifically to the Holy Spirit. This implies that we are given in Scripture precisely the revelation God intended us to receive. Again, therefore, it is to be received as expressive of his character. This is not to adopt a naive view of inerrancy,[3] but to say that the Spirit who gives Scripture expresses his

---

[1] *Westminster Confession of Faith*, VIII.3.

[2] Paul uses *kalos* here in the sense of 'correct, in a manner free from objection'; literally, 'Right was the Holy Spirit…'!

[3] One of I. H. Marshall's criticisms of the concept is that there are statements in Scripture in which to ascribe inerrancy is, essentially, a category mistake. For instance, whereas John 11:18, 'Bethany was near Jerusalem, about two miles off', may be true or false, inerrant or errant, Jesus' command, recorded later in the chapter, 'Take away the stone' (verse 39), can be neither inerrant nor errant. *Biblical Inspiration* (Grand Rapids: Eerdmans, 1982), p. 54. But the point of claiming inerrancy is not to suggest that all biblical statements are truth claims, but that God has breathed

holy character in it in a manner analogous to the way he sanctified the human nature assumed by God's Son.

In this sense, we can have the same confidence in the Spirit's ministry in relationship to Scripture as we have in relationship to his Son. In both, he commits himself to historical realities, indeed to the historical process; in both, he preserves the integrity of his gracious gifts.

The inerrancy of Scripture is a confession of faith. In the very nature of the case, we are not able to prove *a posteriori* that every statement in the Bible is error-free. Nor can we have absolute confidence in Scripture unless it is confirmed by an authority equal to or greater than itself. In this, too, the Spirit who has given us Scripture remains faithful by giving his own testimony to Scripture by the way he illumines it to us in its true light. He who carried the word of Scripture into history continues to minister to us in our place in that same history so that as we read the word he has brought to us, we recognize it for what it really is—the inerrant word of the inerrant God, breathed out to us through the one who is to him as his own breath, the Holy Spirit.

Thus, when it is said, 'This is the word of the Lord', we know we can trust it without reservation, and therefore we say, 'Thanks be to God!'

---

out his word in a way that preserves its truthfulness and integrity. In addition, clearly there are 'errors' in Scripture. We meet one as early as Gen. 3:4, in the lie of the serpent. The point, however, is that it is indeed true that this was the form the first lie took.

CHAPTER TWENTY-TWO

WHAT IS BIBLICAL THEOLOGY?

WHAT is relatively familiar territory in one part of the evangelical world is sometimes discovered by, and then promoted vigorously, in another. In the late twentieth and early twenty-first century that became true of biblical theology. Within the distinctively Reformed tradition—paradoxically often thought of as dominated by dogmatic theology—biblical theology had long been familiar territory. In very large measure that was due to the influence of Geerhardus Vos. He was almost certainly the first in the English-speaking world appointed specifically to be Professor of Biblical Theology. But those aware of Reformed theology's history were conscious that—to the surprise of many—its approach was already present in the thinking of Jonathan Edwards, in some of the Puritan pastor-theologians of the seventeenth century, and was deeply embedded in the work of some of the sixteenth-century Reformers.

But what, exactly, is *biblical theology*? The expression can mean different things to different people, and indeed different things to the same person at different times. By way of personal illustration, I was reared as a Christian in a culture in which it was emphasized that we need a *biblical* theology—by which was meant little more than that we should believe and live by the teaching of Scripture. Wider study then introduced me to what was known as 'the biblical theology movement' which, to some extent could be traced to the impact of theologians such as Karl Barth, with his strong and reactionary emphasis on the centrality of the word of God. Somewhat humorously, I recall being asked in what turned out to be an interview for a teaching position, 'What do you think of *Biblical Theology*?' and answering the question as though it sought my opinion on that movement when, in fact, as I realized from the questioner's somewhat surprised response, that he was actually wanting to find out if Geerhardus Vos's landmark book *Biblical Theology* had made any impact on my theological development!

It is with this last sense—we might even call it 'the Vosian sense' of biblical theology—that we are concerned here. We can explore it under five headings, creeping up slowly to our theme: (1) Theology and its task; (2) The history of the term 'biblical theology'; (3) Illustrations of the nature of biblical theology; (4) The contribution of biblical theology to theology as a whole; and (5) The goal of biblical theology.

1. Theology and its task

The word 'theology' is a Greek compound from *theos*, God, and *logos*, meaning a word, the expression of inward thought or reasoning, Thus, *theologos* is a person who thinks and speaks about God or divine things, someone (to use the modern parlance) who engages in 'God-talk'.

These terms, 'theology', 'theologian', have developed historically through several stages which we can roughly classify as follows:

(1) A pagan term

The word *theologos* was applied first by Greek-speakers to poets such as Homer and Hesiod—authors who wrote about the gods or interpreted them. A *theologos* was thus someone who spoke about the divine nature, or the activity of the gods, often using poetic language and structure. Thus 'theology' could mean the study and interpretation of that poetry— and eventually its specific study and interpretation by philosophical thought, resulting in knowledge—*scientia*—hence the long-held view that theology was the queen of the *sciences*.

Aristotle (384–322 BC), in his *Metaphysics*, distinguished between theoretical or speculative philosophy and practical and moral philosophy. Speculative philosophy or *scientia* examines the very roots and founda-tions of reality, and itself falls into several categories. Notes Aristotle:

> If there is anything eternal, immutable, and existing separately, it must be studied by a speculative science. Not by physics (which is concerned with mutable objects), nor by mathematics, but by

one that is prior to both; for physics deals with objects which exist separately but are not immutable, while some branches of mathematics deal with objects which, though immutable, do not exist separately.

Now all first causes must be eternal, especially those immutable causes which act upon what is visible of the divine. Hence there are three speculative sciences: mathematics, physics, and what we may call theology. The highest science must deal with the highest genus; so that the speculative are the highest of the sciences, and 'theology' the highest of all these.[1]

(2) The early church

The term *theologia* does not appear in the New Testament—although a few manuscripts of Revelation describe it as 'The Revelation of John *ho theologos*' (traditionally in English, 'John the divine'). Through its use by the early Apologists of the second century, the term increasingly came to mean speech about God. But interestingly this was understood not so much in the broad sense of engaging in thought and speech about God but rather in the narrow sense of the exposition of the deity of Jesus Christ—i.e. of Christ as *theos*. For example, Gregory of Nazianzus, who with Basil the Great and Gregory of Nyssa constituted the famous theological triumvirate of the Cappadocian Fathers of the fourth century, was known as 'the Theologian' because of his defence of the deity of Christ. Thus, the expression *theologein Iesoun* implied not merely engaging in what today we would call 'Christology' in a general sense, but doing so in the context of a specific recognition of the deity of Jesus of Nazareth.

As theological discussion continued and issues of the implications of the identity of Jesus for the nature of God developed, *theologia* came to have a broader significance within a further distinction between *theologia*, with its focus on the identity and character of the triune God, on the one hand, and *oikonomia* on the other (cf. Eph. 1:10; 3:2, 9), denoting the economy or external activity of God, his so-called *opera ad extra*, or engagement with the *cosmos* he created and its inhabitants.

---

[1] Aristotle, *Metaphysics*, edited and translated by John Warrington, with an introduction by Sir David Ross (London: J. M. Dent and Sons, 1956), p. 154.

(3) Theology as God-talk in general

It was by a process of osmosis therefore that 'theology' came to mean, as it now does, the broader idea of the study of, and speech about, Christian doctrines in general—not only 'theology proper' (the personal being of God), but what we now know as *systematic* or *dogmatic* theology covering the entire range of Christian thought. Certainly, by the time of the sophisticated discussions that developed in the medieval monasteries and the new universities of the Middle Ages, this was how the term *theologia* was understood. As such it applies to every discipline in the theological encyclopedia—man as well as God, the application of redemption as much as the mystery of the Trinity.

In this connection, it is worth remembering that it was only in the sixteenth and seventeenth centuries that the discrete theological disciplines with which we are familiar (biblical exegesis, systematic theology, historical theology, practical theology) began to emerge. The explosion of knowledge and its communication through the printed page and the inevitable collapse of the possibility of the 'Renaissance man' with a knowledge of all known things, inevitably led to a degree of specialization. Before that, Thomas Aquinas, Martin Luther, John Calvin—all thought of as *theologians* by us—were in fact professors of Bible and only in their written work what we would call *systematic* theologians. It is not nearly well enough known (perhaps especially by his detractors!) that Thomas Aquinas left behind a remarkable corpus of lectures of biblical exposition, as of course did Luther and especially Calvin. These men were not, nor did they think of themselves as being, systematic theologians in distinction from other kinds of theologians. To them theology was still a unified discipline in which each theologian sought to master all the elements. It is inevitably one of the challenges of being an academic or school 'theologian' today that the mastery of the literature on single passages of Scripture can be almost beyond an individual, far less an encyclopedic understanding of the whole of theology.[1]

---

[1] In this connection, I can still 'hear' the groans of a New Testament specialist colleague telling me, just as his commentary was soon to go to press, that he had just seen a multi-hundred-page new work with a focus on some eleven verses in the biblical book on which his commentary had been written!

So much, in general, for the use of the term 'theology'. We turn now to the question: What is it about biblical theology that makes it different from systematic theology, and why does it merit the adjective 'biblical'?

2. Biblical theology—and its distinctives

By systematic theology we simply mean theology which is expounded and expressed in a systematic, coherent form which contains and expresses its own inner logic, and arranges itself into an integrated whole in a topical fashion. As Agatha Christie's most famous male creation, Hercule Poirot, would say, the concern here is with 'order and method'. This, of course, is not to say that, for example, Old Testament theology or New Testament theology, or for that matter biblical theology, lacks logic, arrangement, order, or method—but simply that their organizing principle is different.

The distinction between the two disciplines of biblical theology and systematic theology was famously expressed by Geerhardus Vos in these wise and balanced words:

> There is no difference in that one would be more closely bound to the Scriptures than the other. Nor does the difference lie in this, that the one transforms the biblical material, whereas the other would leave it unmodified. Both equally make the truth deposited in the Bible undergo a transformation: but the difference arises from the fact that the principle by which the transformation is effected differs in each case. In biblical theology, this principle is one of historical, in systematic theology it is one of logical construction. Biblical theology draws a *line* of development. Systematic theology draws a *circle*. Still it should be remembered, that on the line of historical progress there is at several points already a beginning of correlation among the elements of truth in which the beginnings of the system-atizing process can be discerned.[1]

Vos was never known for pandering to intellectual laziness, as the dense style of his *Biblical Theology* and his other works demonstrates.[2]

---

[1] Geerhardus Vos, *Biblical Theology* (Grand Rapids: Wm. B. Eerdmans, 1948), pp. 24-25.

[2] One thinks here of the comments of the young J. Gresham Machen written to his mother during his student days at Princeton Seminary: 'We had this morning

The paragraph just quoted, however, is a model of clarity and simplicity. But it is also weighted with profundity in every sentence, and seems to me to be an exceedingly important and salutary statement indeed. Paying close attention to it would save us from many false steps.

Here the modern father of biblical theology makes it clear that the common criticism of *systematic* theology on the grounds that (unlike *biblical* theology!) it is *systematic* and therefore *transforms* the pure biblical material, is self-falsifying. For *biblical* theology is also systematic. Responding to this perspective—which in some circles has naively become a point of orthodoxy—I have sometimes suggested to students that they take any work of Old or New Testament theology and, censor-like, black out any statement that moves from a strict restating of what the text of Scripture says to the *collating* of texts, or making a statement about what author X teaches about subject Y. They will be left with a virtually unreadable and certainly incomprehensible book. For in its very nature, thought is coherent, thinking is systematic in character. Moreover, as Vos insisted, biblical theology is no more a mere parroting of the text of Scripture than systematic theology is. In fact, systematic theology is supplied by, builds upon, and gives expression to the resources provided by biblical theology, and indeed, as a systematic understanding, in turn probes the verity, lucidity, and coherence of statements of biblical theology. The two are sisters, not opponents.

Gabler

The use of the term 'biblical theology' is often associated, historical-ly, with the name of Johann Philipp Gabler (1753–1826) and with his inaugural professorial lecture at Altdorf in 1787, entitled: 'On the Proper Distinctions between Biblical and Dogmatic Theology and the Right Determination of the Boundaries.'[1] Gabler himself did not write a

---

one of the finest expository sermons I have ever heard. It was preached by Dr Vos … and rather surprised me. He is usually rather too severely theological for Sunday morning. Today he was nothing less than inspiring. … Dr Vos differs from some theological professors in having a better-developed bump of reverence.' N. B. Stonehouse, *J. Gresham Machen: A Biographical Memoir* (Grand Rapids, 1954; repr., Edinburgh: Banner of Truth Trust, 1987), p. 72.

[1] The lecture is widely available on the Internet.

biblical theology, but in his inaugural address he sought to establish the principle that biblical theology was a descriptive discipline; systematic or dogmatic theology a normative discipline. But Gabler was clearly not creating something *ex nihilo* although the prominence of his name and the fame of his lecture can easily give that impression. In fact, the tradition of biblical theology has a much older pedigree.

Forerunners

Elements of engaging in theology in a distinctively biblical-historical way can in fact be traced back to within the New Testament itself. It should go without saying that Paul gives expression to biblical theology in this sense. He can employ as the organizing principle of a piece of theological reasoning the historical flow of redemptive history. Thus his argument in Galatians 3 is a piece of biblical theology placed in service of his systematic theological arguments.

Similarly, the work of the great second-century theologian Irenaeus of Lyons (*c.* AD 130–200) displays touches of biblical theology, not least in the way in which he operates with the deeply biblical Adam–Christ parallel principle and expounds the way in which Jesus Christ recapitulates in himself, and reverses in his work, the history of Adam.[1]

Similarly, Augustine, in the *City of God*, written in the context of the sack of Rome by the Goths in AD 410, and the implied defeat of the city of God, seeks to respond not simply by systematic theology, by an appeal to the doctrines of divine sovereignty and providence, but by way of biblical theology. And so, in Books XII to XVIII he traces the story of the city of God/heavenly city set (since the fall) against the city of this world/earthly city from the beginning through to the end of the world.

Elements of this kind of thinking would later emerge in different ways in the writings of the sixteenth-century Reformers, especially Calvin and Bullinger. But the following century would see a wholescale attempt to expound theology in this way emerging in the writings of the Dutch theologian Johannes Cocceius (1603–69)—not to be confused with the Roman Catholic theologian with whom the Reformers had to wrestle, Johannes Cochlaeus (1479–1552); 'The Cock' as Calvin calls him!

---

[1] For example, in *Against Heresies*, Book V, chapter 21.

In 1648 Cocceius published his *magnum opus* under the title *Summa Doctrinae de Foedere et Testamento Dei* (*A Summary of the Doctrine concerning the Covenant and Testament of God*). In it he self-consciously distanced himself from the way in which Protestant orthodoxy was engaging in the theological task. Cocceius somewhat controversially sought to order his work along biblical-theological rather than logical-topical lines. Later, a *via media* would be found in Herman Witsius's 1677 publication *De Oeconomia Foederum Dei Cum Hominibus* in which he sought to pull the covenantal-historical and the systematic-theological together.

There are also pre-Gabler illustrations of a more biblical theological approach to 'doing theology' in the English-speaking world. Hidden away for many years in Latin, and only partly translated into English until the late twentieth century, lay John Owen's *Theologoumena Pantodapa* (*Theology of Every Kind*). Finished in 1661 this is a work full of various digressions (Owen obviously never worked with a modern editor!); it contains an exposition of the various epochs and stages of theological knowledge from Adam through Noah to Abraham, Moses and Christ.

A century later, in 1774, Jonathan Edwards Jr published his father's 1739 sermons *A History of the Work of Redemption*, with its subtitle *Containing outlines of a body of Divinity including a view of Church History—in a method entirely new*. Edwards was clearly excited by approaching the whole message of the Bible from a redemptive-historical perspective and not exclusively using a *locus* method of arranging his thinking. But he did not live to develop the 'outline' into a full version. One can only wonder what the impact might have been if he had.

But we should not assume that the remainder of theological literature was redemptive-historically silent. It is an all too frequently made mistake, for example, to assume that the authors of *locus* method confessions of faith (such as that written by the Westminster divines[1]) were advocates of a proof-text methodology. In fact, they were opposed to adding 'proof-texts' because a mere list of passages could not indicate

---

[1] *The Confession of Faith* (London, 1647).

the theological thinking that connected them.[1] An examination of some
of the writings of those most intimately involved in framing the various
chapters of the Confession makes clear their ability to handle passages
of Scripture within their redemptive-historical context. A noteworthy
illustration of this can be seen by comparing the Confession's chapter
on the law (XIX) with Anthony Burgess's work *Vindiciae Legis.*[2] Particularly noteworthy in Burgess is the way in which he grounds the multi-
dimensional character of the Mosaic Law not in a Thomistic *a priori,* but
in careful exposition of the text of the Pentateuch.

All this said, theological training and writing from the post-Reformation period onwards tended to be dominated by system theology. In
the nature of the case there is a certain inevitability about this. No Old
Testament department in any theological seminary known to me has the
ambition to work with exegetical detail through the text of the entire
Old Testament with a view to then being able to construct a comprehensive biblical theology. When that is the case 'whole Bible theology' is
likely to be left to the teachers of systematic theology.

Geerhardus Vos

For our purposes, May 8, 1894 then becomes a significant date in
the story of biblical theology as a discipline, and consequently as an
approach to reading and expounding Scripture taught to, and adopted
by, the teachers and preachers of the church. On that date, to the gathered assembly in the First Presbyterian Church of Princeton, Geerhardus
Vos took up the newly created Chair of Biblical Theology at Princeton
Seminary, and delivered his inaugural lecture: 'The Idea of Biblical Theology as a Science and as a Theological Discipline'.[3] Here biblical theology was now being seen as a discrete theological discipline. In his lecture,
Vos articulated the thoughts that would come to fuller expression in his
Biblical Theology:

[1] It is often forgotten (or worse, not known) that the proof-texts were added by
order of the English Parliament. The divines themselves opposed the action and
submitted the texts reluctantly. The Assembly was, in essence, a large advisory
committee to Parliament, and not in any strict sense a church assembly.
[2] Anthony Burgess, *Vindiciae Legis* (London: Thomas Underhill, 1647).
[3] Reprinted in Gaffin, *Redemptive History and Biblical Interpretation.*

The specific character of biblical theology lies in this, that it discusses both the form and contents of revelation from the point of view of the revealing activity of God himself. … In biblical theology both the form and contents of revelation are considered as parts and products of a divine work. In systematic theology, these same contents of revelation appear, but not under the aspect of the stages of a divine work; rather as the material for a human work of classifying and systematizing according to logical principles. Biblical theology applies no other method of grouping and arranging these contents than is given in the divine economy of revelation itself. …

Biblical theology, rightly defined, is nothing else *than the exhibition of the organic progress of supernatural revelation in its historic continuity and multiformity.*[1]

Notice the 'big ideas' in these last words: (i) Organic; (ii) Progress; (iii) Supernatural revelation; (iv) Historic continuity; and (v) Multiformity.

Biblical theology in Vos's view is always the fruit of exegesis, but exegesis then gathered into a whole in the context of historical continuity. Thus, in distinction from systematic theology, biblical theology asks not 'What does Scripture as a whole say, and what is to be believed about X?', but 'What is the knowledge of God received by revelation throughout the history of that revelation and received at the time of Moses or David or John the Baptist, or Paul?' It should be clear, however, that these two approaches are intimately related. For in the latter there is the discovery of systematic theological constructions *in nuce*, in the former its full development.

In his oft-cited illustration, in Vos's view biblical theology draws a line, systematic theology draws a circle.

This, then, is the view of biblical theology Vos introduced into the bloodstream of English-speaking evangelical theology. Later in the twentieth century, a movement known more broadly as 'the biblical theology movement' came to prominence. Its perspective and agenda were, however, very different from those of Vos. It was in part the fruit of the critical approach to Scripture which destroyed its unity, and in undercutting specifically verbal revelation, placed its focus not on the word of God as speech-revelation, but on the acts of God, which lay somewhere

---

[1] Gaffin, *Redemptive History and Biblical Interpretation,* 6-7, 15 (emphasis original).

behind it, as revelation. It rested on an uncertain foundation, however, because it put asunder what God had united, by tacitly assuming that God's acts are self-interpreting from our perspective. But revelation is not constituted of 'brute facts or events' which we are capable of accurately interpreting; it comes to us as *interpreted* events. Jesus died—that is a 'brute fact'; but it is no more revelation than the statement 'Julius Caesar died'. In and of itself there is no gospel in the brute fact. But 'Christ died for our sins in accordance with the Scriptures' (1 Cor. 15:3)—that is revelation. It is an interpreted fact: the gift of God with God's interpretation of that gift. This constitutes revelation.

Vos clearly recognized this. And in addition, coming to Princeton as someone who himself had taught systematic or dogmatic theology,[1] he knew that 'It were useless to deny that it [biblical theology] has been often cultivated in a spirit more or less hostile to the work in which systematic theology is engaged.' In sharp contrast, he responded:

> I desire to state most emphatically here, that there is nothing in the nature and aims of biblical theology to justify such an implication. For anything pretending to supplant dogmatics there is no place in the circle of Christian theology.[2]

Thus, biblical theology is the friend and accomplice, not the opponent, of systematic theology. In his own words, 'Dogmatics is the crown which grows out of all the work that biblical theology can accomplish.'[3]

Vos believed that biblical theology contributed to the discipline of systematic theology in several specific ways:

• Biblical theology keeps systematic theology rooted in objective knowledge, found in the historical biblical revelation. Theology, in Aristotle's categories, is speculative. But Christian theology is not. For God has taken special care to make himself known and understood in an objective and historical way and provides us with the interpretation of his self-manifestation in creation and history.

---

[1] His lectures, given originally in Dutch, have now been published in five volumes: Geerhardus Vos, *Reformed Dogmatics*, translated and edited by Richard B. Gaffin, Jr (Bellingham, WA: Lexham Press, 2014–16).

[2] *Biblical Theology*, p. 23.

[3] *Biblical Theology*, p. 24.

- Biblical theology preserves systematic theology (when informed by it) from falling into the trap of, and from the common accusation that it is in fact, 'theology by proof-texting'. Anchored to the fruit of biblical theology it will become clear that dogmatics grows organically out of the stem of revelation.

- Biblical theology enables systematic theology to stay in contact with the historical realities of revelation, and not to become abstracted from the realities of life in an historical setting.

Perhaps the best single biblical summary of this vision for theology is found in Hebrews 1:1-4:

> Long ago, at many times and in many ways, God spoke to our fathers by the prophets, but in these last days he has spoken to us by his Son, whom he appointed the heir of all things, through whom also he created the world. He is the radiance of the glory of God and the exact imprint of his nature, and he upholds the universe by the word of his power. After making purification for sins, he sat down at the right hand of the Majesty on high, having become as much superior to angels as the name he has inherited is more excellent than theirs.

Jesus Christ, the divine *Logos*, is the central point and the climax of all redemptive history. He is the one through whom all things were created, and in whom they subsist (John 1:3; Col. 1:16-17; Heb. 1:2-3). He is the Mediator of creation and providence. Fittingly, he is also the Mediator of the recreation and restoration in order that at the last he might hand over the kingdom to the Father after he has destroyed all dominion, authority, and power (1 Cor. 15:24). The one through whom all things were created became (as the church Fathers believed, 'fittingly') the one through whom they would be redeemed, restored, and brought to full and final perfection in the *eschaton*.

In other words, the one by whom we come truly to know God, by special redemptive revelation, is the one who displayed his glory in general revelation. Consequently, when we come to know him through this special, redemptive revelation, our minds and hearts are illumined to receive, appreciate, and enjoy general revelation. As George Wade

Robinson puts it in his hymn 'Loved with Everlasting Love',

> Something lives in every hue
> Christless eyes have never seen.[1]

Hebrews 1:1-3 brings to the fore a whole series of structural ideas that enable us to think of the flow of biblical theology through the eyes of Scripture itself, by emphasizing the following:

1. *The fundamental diversity in the revelatory process.* God spoke (i) in different times or epochs and (ii) in different ways. These include dreams, visions, historical research, meditation on his word, and yes, even on occasion by a form of dictation (e.g. in the book of Revelation: 'To the angel of the church in Ephesus, write: "The words of him who holds the seven stars …"' [Rev. 2:1]). In this way, God's word always addresses the mind, but at the same time appeals to the whole person in a variety of modalities.

2. *Given this diversity, God's redemptive revelation possesses an underlying unity and continuity.* It is one and the same God who revealed himself in times past who has revealed himself in these last days. Moreover, the one through whom he created all things is the one through whom he effects his redeeming work.

3. *The historical character of, and development within, special redemptive revelation.* There is clear development from the forefathers to the community addressed by the author of Hebrews. Formerly God revealed himself in many and various ways, but now he does so in a single way. This development moves from the fragmentary to the complete, from the preliminary to the final.

4. There is a Christological dimension to the whole. From beginning to end, from the promise of Genesis 3:15 to the consummation in the book of Revelation, there is a dynamic forward thrust towards Christ. His anticipated coming shapes all that precedes it.

5. *The revelation in Christ not only shapes the whole, but as its telos also stands in contrast with all that leads up to it.* For Christ is *sui generis*. In

---

[1] Some hymnbook compilers have felt it necessary to change the wording 'lives in every hue', presumably concerned lest the former wording be understood to be a pantheistic, or at least a panentheistic statement. But perhaps this is no more necessary than adjusting the more famous words of 'Immortal, Invisible, God Only Wise' ('In all life Thou livest, in both great and small').

the past God spoke by means of prophets (*en tois prophētais*) who spoke words. But now he has spoken in a language which was hitherto only hinted at—'by his Son' (*en huiō*). 'Son' here (*huios*) is anarthrous,[1] not in order to indicate that he is one among many sons, but that revelation in the 'Son' incarnate is a new mode of revelation altogether, both complete and personal.

6. *The epochal character of special redemptive revelation.* Earlier, Old Testament revelation was given at different epochs. But in essence there are only two epochs, or 'times': the past days and the last days; there is the present age, and there is the inbreaking of the new age in Christ which currently intersects the present age and one day will supersede it entirely.

7. *The covenantal character of special redemptive revelation.* The term 'covenant' (*diathēke*) does not appear in these verses. But Hebrews, as Geerhardus Vos himself well expressed it, uniquely is the epistle of the *diathēke*.[2] Thus, once we have read Hebrews as a whole, we are likely to return to these opening verses with fresh vision and perhaps especially notice that the first thing that is said about the revelation of the Son is *not* that he is the Creator of all things, but that he has been appointed *heir* of all things. This, surely, echoes the call given to the first Adam at creation (Gen. 1:26-28) to subdue and fill all things, and the promise given to Abraham that all the nations would be blessed through his seed. In this sense, Christ brings to fulfilment the whole pattern of covenantal revelations which punctuate the various epochs of the Old Testament.

8. *The finality of special redemptive revelation in Christ.* Revelation moves from preamble to consummation. God spoke formerly through frail and sinful men. The one in whom he now speaks his final word is (a) the radiance of his glory; (b) the exact imprint of his nature; (c) the upholder of the universe; (d) the one who has made purification for our sins; and (e) the exalted promised King and Son now seated at the Father's right hand.

---

[1] That is, it lacks the definite article.

[2] *Redemptive History and Biblical Interpretation*, pp. 161-233 (originally published as two extensive articles in *The Princeton Review*, 13 (1915): pp. 587-632; and 14 (1916): pp. 1-61.

In the light of this, biblical theology recognizes that revelation comes historically, progressively, epochally, cumulatively, teleologically, and moves towards Christ until it is completed in him. It enhances systematic theology by encouraging it not only to ask: 'What does Scripture as a whole say about X or Y?' but also to pose the question: 'How is the drama of redemption unfolded in the pages of the Bible?' Christ, the climax and conclusion of the drama, does not stand in contrast to the plot line but he both explains and consummates it.

Perhaps it is helpful for us here to pause and reflect now not on what biblical theology is, but on what it looks like in specific terms. Often the value of a concept or way of doing things is best seen by actually doing it.

3. Illustrating biblical theology

The basic questions in theology are: Who is God?—and what are the implications of this?

An exploration of biblical theology leads to the answers: God is as he reveals himself in this history, to these people, and in these ways, and, since we were created in or as his image (Gen. 1:26), our 'chief end' is to reflect and seek his glory: herein lies our enjoyment. The whole narrative of the Bible tells us how this all began, what has happened since, and how the story will be consummated. We can explore this briefly in a biblical theological way in terms of two connected themes that run through Scripture to an *omega* point in Christ.

(1) The name of God

In a nutshell, biblical theology tells the story of the significance of the *name* (and therefore the *character*) of God as he reveals himself. He makes himself known through his name.

Virtually from the beginning of the Bible he is identified as *Yahweh*. Genesis 1 reveals him as *Elohim* the Creator of the cosmos; but we have scarcely begun to read Genesis 2 before we encounter the covenant name of Yahweh (Gen. 2:5, 7, 8, 9, 15, 16, 18, 19, 21, 22), the name revealed to Moses in the wilderness (Exod. 3:13-18). It is the Exodus Redeemer who was also the Creator.

As is well known, orthodox Jews never pronounce this name, and whenever they read the Hebrew Bible they substitute the word *Adonai*.

Thus, one of the paradoxes of history is that no one now can be certain how the covenant name was originally pronounced. Nevertheless, from the beginning of the Old Testament narrative to the end of the Gospels, Yahweh is the high, sacred name for God.

What we find here, in the flow of redemptive history, provides us with what we might call 'theological depth perception'. We are brought to see that the teaching of our Lord Jesus Christ did not take place in either a verbal or a doctrinal vacuum. When he tells his Father 'I have manifested your name to the people whom you gave me out of the world' (John 17:6), he is indicating that his ministry is both the summation and the climax of a programme of revelation that has been in place since the beginning of time. At the climactic midpoint, the full possible extent of the knowledge of the divine name is gained exclusively by revelation in and through Christ.

As the Gospel narrative ends a dramatic development in revelation takes place. Jesus reveals to his disciples a yet more sacred, richer, and fuller pronunciation of this name. Yahweh is 'Father, Son, and Holy Spirit' (Matt. 28:19)—one name, three persons. It is impossible to put into words just how significant this moment is, immediately preceding Jesus' ascension.

It signifies the dawning of a new epoch in revelation, when God is to be known, as we might put it, by his *Christian* name. Only in Christ do we, ultimately, learn how correctly to pronounce the name of God which nevertheless was made known in earlier epochs of redemptive history.

Jesus the Son alone knows the Father, and so he alone can reveal the Father to us (Matt. 11:25-30). When we see him we see the Father (John 14:8-11). This is why, among the contrasts between the old and new covenants of redemptive history, none is more striking than the way in which new covenant believers address Yahweh as 'Abba, Father'.[1]

---

[1] A simple comparison of the paucity of direct address to God as 'Father' in the sense of personal fellowship with him (in distinction from his work in creation, the creation of the nation of Israel, and the use of the term in the form of a simile ['as a father pities his children …']) with the frequency of the appeal to God as Father within the three chapters of the Sermon on the Mount in Matthew 5-7 makes this point with great force. It is set out in redemptive historical terms in Gal. 4:1-7.

When we move beyond this climactic point of revelation in Christ to its *omega* point in the consummation of redemption in the beatific vision, this name is not only *revealed to* God's people, but actually *written on* them: 'I will write on him the name of my God ... and my own new name', says the Lord (Rev. 3:12); 'They will see his face, and his name will be on their foreheads' (Rev. 22:4).

Setting this in its broader biblical context brings us to another important illustration of the importance of biblical theology and its significance for systematic theology. The context in which this revelation of the divine name takes place has a fundamentally covenantal or federal structure.

So, within our discussion of biblical theology we need to learn the importance of the central role of the covenant.

(2) The covenant relationship

The Old Testament word for covenant (*berith*) occurs almost 300 times in the Hebrew Bible. It is employed of both human and divine covenants. Unlike the idea of 'contract' with which it has often been theologically confused, it does not mean a negotiated settlement—an agreement in that sense. Especially in the case of divine–human relations, covenants are sovereignly disposed by God, not negotiated by the two parties involved. God's covenants always have a unilateral dimension (sovereign engagement by God) as well as a bilateral character (the covenants have two parties, God and man).

In general terms, everything that is recorded in Scripture is set within a covenant context. Not to recognize this or to be conscious of it, however subliminally, is likely to lead to a lack of 'theological depth perception' as the Bible is read and expounded.

The first specific reference to a covenant is in Genesis 6:17-18. The choice of verbs here is significant. The normal 'formula' for making a covenant employs the verb *karath*, to cut. There is a kind of 'sacramental union' involved between the symbolism of the bond and the language describing its formation. This is vividly reflected in the dramatic covenant-making rite we find in Genesis 15:1-21. Although the term *berith* is not used anywhere in the chapter the event is clearly enough portrayed as covenant engagement symbolism.

But in the case of the Noahic covenant, the language used is not *karath berith* (*cut* a covenant) but a causative form of the verb *qum*, to confirm or establish. Critical scholarly orthodoxy of the late nineteenth and twentieth centuries saw this difference as essentially the language of choice of the 'Priestly' ('P') and the 'Jahwistic' ('J') streams of tradition.[1] But a good case can be made out for seeing the choice of verb not as merely a variant, but as an indication that what is in view is the confirmation, ratification, even recovery of a covenant commitment already in existence.[2] This seems to be its nuance later in Genesis as well as elsewhere.[3] The implication of this is that the covenant with Noah confirms, makes stand up again, a covenant relationship already in place but somehow marred, disfigured, and prostrated.

If we ask, from the standpoint of Genesis 1–11, what covenant might have been already in place, the text provides us with a series of notes within the Noahic covenant which echo the original created relationship. These are so many hints that in fact the original relationship in which God made man as his image was a covenantal relationship, even although it was not specifically spelled out as such:

Genesis 6:18-22 echoes the language of Genesis 1:20-22:

> 'But I will establish my covenant with you, and you shall come into the ark, you, your sons, your wife, and your sons' wives with you. And of every living thing of all flesh, you shall bring two of every sort into the ark to keep them alive with you. They shall be male and female. Of the birds according to their kinds, and of the animals according to their kinds, of every creeping thing of the ground, according to its kind, two of every sort shall come in to you to keep them alive. Also take with you every sort of food that is eaten, and store it up. It shall serve as food for you and for them.'
> Noah did this; he did all that God commanded him.

---

[1] Thus, for example, Gerhard Von Rad notes: 'Going beyond the Yahwist's representation, the Priestly document now speaks of a *covenant*' (Gerhard Von Rad, *Genesis*, tr. John H. Marks, London: S.C.M. Press, 2nd edition, 1963), p. 129.

[2] See especially William J. Dumbrell, *Covenant and Creation* (Exeter: Paternoster Press, 1984), pp. 26-43.

[3] Cf. 17:7, 19, 21. Also Deut. 9:5 (confirm earlier words); Num. 30:14 (confirm earlier vows); 2 Sam. 7:25 (confirm earlier promises).

Genesis 8:10-12 echoes the seven-day pattern of Genesis 1:

> He waited another seven days, and again he sent forth the dove
> out of the ark. And the dove came back to him in the evening, and
> behold, in her mouth was a freshly plucked olive leaf. So Noah
> knew that the waters had subsided from the earth. Then he waited
> another seven days and sent forth the dove, and she did not return
> to him anymore.

Genesis 9:1-3 echoes the wording of Genesis 1:28-29:

> And God blessed Noah and his sons and said to them, 'Be fruitful
> and multiply and fill the earth. The fear of you and the dread of you
> shall be upon every beast of the earth and upon every bird of the
> heavens, upon everything that creeps on the ground and all the fish
> of the sea. Into your hand they are delivered. Every moving thing
> that lives shall be food for you. And as I gave you the green plants,
> I give you everything. …'

Not only so, but already in Genesis 2–3 we find the divine name
Yahweh, revealed to Moses as the covenant name of God, used repeatedly,
indeed almost twenty times. How can this be since, according to Exodus
6:2-3, 'by my name the Lord I did not make myself known to them'
(i.e., Abraham, Isaac, and Jacob)? The simplest explanation remains the
best: Genesis 1–3 was not written contemporaneously with the events
it describes, but within the context of the Exodus events. An historian
today would not be faulted for referring to 'the days when President
Reagan was Governor of the State of California' without misleading us
(it was the same *Governor* Reagan who *later* was to be known as *President*
Reagan). In the same way, the use of the divine name Yahweh in the early
chapters of Genesis is a hint to us that the divine subject of the creative
action recorded 'in the beginning' was none other than the covenant
Lord. As such he *always* acts in a covenantal fashion.

In this sense, Robert Rollock was surely right to say that 'God speaks
nothing to man without the covenant.'[1] This in itself suggests that the
created relationship was of a covenantal nature.

---

[1] In his *Tractatus De Vocatione Efficaci* (*Treatise on Effectual Calling* [1597]); tr.
Henry Holland, London (1603); in *Select Works of Robert Rollock*, ed., William Gunn
(Edinburgh: Wodrow Society, 1849), I:33.

In many ways, the 'plot-line' in biblical theology resembles that of a novel. Indeed, the blueprints for novels, dramas, perhaps even operas, as well as many other *genres* of literature and music are embedded already in the pages of the Old Testament. In a crime (sin) novel it is often only as the denouement occurs that we realize that we have been given clues without noticing their real significance.

So, in Scripture, these clues from Genesis 8 and 9 suggest that a covenant was in fact already present in Genesis 1–3 (promises, threats, penalties, visible representations of the covenant). It should not be too surprising therefore that biblical scholars have detected certain similarities in the opening section of Genesis to ancient Near East suzerain treaties—for in one sense we are looking here at the *original* treaty drawn up by Yahweh the Great King![1]

Covenants, as O. Palmer Robertson has put it, are 'life-and-death bonds'—they promise life, but the alternative is death. Adam will enjoy life as he lives enjoying the munificent provision of God ('you may surely eat of every tree of the garden' [Gen. 2:16]) but will taste death if he breaches the perimeter fence of loving obedience ('but of the tree of the knowledge of good and evil you shall not eat, for in the day that you eat of it you shall surely die' [Gen. 2:17]). This principle is also worked out in a different terminology. The Lord sets Adam within a context of blessing (Gen 2:3) which he will enjoy in trust and obedience to the Lord's word. But rebel against him and he will find himself living under conditions no longer of blessing but curse. Alas, 'Adam ... transgressed the covenant' (Hos. 6:7). The entail is tragic: 'cursed is the ground because of you ...' (Gen. 3:17).

These alternatives of blessing and cursing then run through the whole of Scripture like railway tracks on which the entire story travels forwards. From Genesis 3 onwards the long narrative unfolds as a story of God bringing blessing where the curse has reigned. Each unfolding chapter in the grand covenantal narrative promises blessing to faith, while exposure to the curse is the consequence of unbelief and disobedience.

Here we have an illustration of the principle that a redemptive-historical approach to Scripture provides 'theological depth perception'

[1] Notice that the *divine* covenant is theological, not the suzerain treaties.

to the way we read it. Thus, the words 'bless' and 'blessing' carry far greater weight in Scripture than they do in our ordinary usage where they signify little more than 'good things happening'.

Paradoxically, and usually unrealized, the closest we come to using this language with anything approaching its biblical significance is when we say 'Bless you!' to someone who sneezes. A well-known children's nursery rhyme and game may shed light on this for us:

> Ring-a-ring o' roses,
> A pocket full of posies,
> A-tishoo! A-tishoo!
> We all fall down.

A well-acknowledged origin of the rhyme is that it depicts the world of the plague: the roses cover the terrible stench of death; sneezing was one of the symptoms of the plague; to 'fall down' in the rhyme is to die. And therefore to say 'Bless you!' is tantamount to a prayer that instead of the plague (seen as a divine curse) the recipient of the greeting may taste the saving power of God.

So, when we read in the Gospels that Jesus 'blessed' the children we ought not to think of this merely as a lovely gesture on his part (contrasted with the mean-spirited disciples), any more than when we read Paul say that God has 'blessed us in Christ with every spiritual blessing' (Eph. 1:3) we would respond in a blasé fashion by saying 'That's very nice.' No, what we have here is the covenant Lord coming in grace and mercy to bring us salvation! And ultimately this is possible only because 'Christ redeemed us from the *curse* of the law by becoming a *curse* for us ... so that in Christ Jesus the *blessing* of Abraham might come to the Gentiles, so that we might receive the promised Spirit through faith' (Gal. 3:13-14).

If, then, Genesis 1–2 represents God's covenant bond, from the very beginning God is represented as a Lord of covenant generosity and man is called to respond in trust and obedience. The covenant life is from the beginning a life of faith (trust) bearing fruit in good works (obedience), the latter always flowing from the former. Genesis 3 then describes the repudiation of the blessing through (1) a rejection of God's covenant word and (2) a distortion of God's gracious and generous covenant character—the serpent insinuates that God has grievously restricted them ('Did God actually say, "You shall not eat of any tree in the garden"?' [Gen. 3:1]). Although one cannot always be dogmatic about textual details, it is surely significant that while the covenant name Yahweh is used so frequently in Genesis 2, it *never* occurs on the lips of the serpent. Of course not, because it is exactly God's covenant character that he seeks to distort.

Insofar as Genesis 3:15 represents a promise of deliverance, it takes place through the divine curse falling on the serpent whose head will be crushed by the seed of the woman. The structure of the words suggests an ongoing conflict that will come to a denouement in a personal one. There is first enmity between the serpent and the woman; there is then enmity between the seed of the serpent and the seed of the woman. But the climax involves the bruising of the head of the serpent himself while he is in the process of crushing the heel of the seed of the woman— the balancing nature of the three statements suggests that 'seed' in this final clause is singular: Seed versus Serpent is the final conflict in view. Certainly, from the New Testament's viewpoint this promise points to and is fulfilled in Christ.[1] It is God himself who guarantees that the Serpent-Crusher will come.

There is reason to believe that Noah was viewed by his parents as the hoped-for fulfilment of this covenant promise, the one who would end the curse. His father Lamech 'called his name Noah, saying, "Out of the ground that the LORD [Yahweh] has cursed this one shall bring us relief ..."' It was not to be. Ultimately only Jesus Christ can bring rest. But while Noah was not the longed-for Saviour, the covenant made with Noah was nevertheless essential to that salvation. It enshrined the promise that God would not destroy the earth. That preservation of a world under his curse was essential if it were ever to be a world in which God's blessing and salvation could be experienced.

Much could be said about this, but it will suffice here simply—in the context of the covenant blessing of rest—to draw attention to the words of Jesus, 'Come to me, all who labour and are heavy laden, and I will give you *rest*' (Matt. 11:28). Here again our biblical theology gives us 'depth perception'. For now we can no longer read these 'comfortable words' of

[1] See Rom. 16:20; 1 John 3:8; Rev. 12:9-10.

Christ as though we had to guess what the significance of the promise of 'rest' might be. It means that, in Christ, God's covenant promise finds its *yes* and *amen* (2 Cor. 1:20). Isaac Watts was right. Because of Christ's fulfilment of God's covenant we can sing:

> No more let sins and sorrows grow,
> Nor thorns infest the ground;
> He comes to make His blessings flow
> Far as the curse is found.[1]

The promise itself is then furthered in the promissory covenant made with Abraham, that in his seed the nations of the earth would be blessed (Gen. 12:1ff.), which further points to Christ (cf. Gal. 3:7ff.). It is then developed in greater detail in the context of the revelation of the covenant name to Moses in Exodus 3 and 6. Here covenant continuity and redemption are stressed (cf. Exod. 3:6, 15-16; 6:2-8; 20:1-2; Ezek. 16:1ff.). The Mosaic covenant, with all its specifically legal aspects, contains and develops rather than abrogates the promise (as Paul argues in Gal. 3).

In the Davidic covenant, this design is taken one step further. Now we further learn that the promised Messiah will be not only in the Abrahamic line in general but in the Davidic line in particular. In David too there is more than the promise. He himself embodies in typological fashion the way in which the covenant promises of God will reach their fulfilment in Jesus Christ. Into his story is written rejection and suffering, death and resurrection, defeat and victory. His kingdom is glorious, and as such adumbrates the glory that is to come in the Messianic kingdom which will be inaugurated by Christ. He points forwards to the true and last Adam whose dominion will know no end (Pss. 2; 8; 110).

All that is added by the promise of the new covenant in Jeremiah 31:31ff. is the notion that this promise of God will be brought to its applicatory consummation through the mediation of one. Thus it will no longer be necessary for prophets, priests, or kings, to say, 'Let me pass on to you the knowledge of the Lord'. For in the one mediator Jesus Christ and by the ministry of the Holy Spirit (cf. 1 John 2:27), all have

---

[1] From the hymn written by Isaac Watts, 'Joy to the World! the Lord Has Come'.

the same access to the eternal life which consists in knowing the Father
whose name the Son has manifested to us (John 17:3, 5). And this is
but the beginning of that ever-increasing satisfaction that will fully and
finally be consummated when the name of the Lord revealed to us in
Christ is actually written upon us (Rev. 3:12; 22:4). Eden will then not
only be restored but glorified. And God's people will have access to the
tree of life (Rev. 22:1-4).

There is of course much more to these two themes than this. And
there is much, much more to biblical theology than these two themes.
They serve here only as illustrations of this 'depth perception' to which
biblical theology leads. Without it the Bible will seem like the dots on
the page of a child's drawing book—still waiting to be 'joined up' so that
the picture presently hidden may be fully revealed. Yet, while there is
much more to biblical theology than we can explore here, perhaps this
is enough to indicate that the discipline constitutes the backbone and
the basic ground plan and architecture on which all Christian doctrine
is to be built.

4. The contribution of biblical theology to theology as a whole

In the light of this survey, then, we may say that biblical theology hands
over certain strategic principles to systematic theology which the latter
in turn employs.

First, biblical theology expresses the unity of the biblical message. A
coherent biblical theology is possible only on the basis of the unity of
revelation. Without this at best we would have simply so many biblical
theologies (plural). While we can legitimately speak of 'the theology of
Moses' or 'the theology of Isaiah', an overall theology, yes in all its multi-
facetedness, requires a single plot-line. This, in turn, makes possible a
systematic theology of the whole. A circle, to resort to Geerhardus Vos's
metaphor, is, after all, a single line. Without such unity there can be no
truly coherent system.

Second, biblical theology is Christ-centred. Jesus saw the whole of
the Old Testament bearing witness to his own coming and its significance; the New Testament both records and expounds the inner significance of that coming and the resultant building of the church. This

fact challenges students of system theology to endeavour to relate all points in the system to the actual person of Christ. Engaging in the task of systematic theology involves not only forming the straight line of biblical theology into a circle, but, to tweak the metaphor a little, taking the track on which redemptive history runs and turning it into the circumference of a wheel, in which each of the *loci* of systematic theology serves as a spoke, all related to one another because they move from the circumference into the centre, and all held together by the hub, Jesus Christ. The constant danger of systematic theology is abstraction. And the danger of abstraction is a kind of reductionism that equates description or definition with reality. At the end of the day, theology is about persons (God and humans) and their relationship to creation.

Put in other words, biblical theology summons systematic theology, in all its systematizing, not to allow the cognitive to lose touch with the historical, not to allow the principial to take on a life of its own that is not anchored in the particularity of divine revelation. This in turn means that systematic theology will always remain connected to pastoral theology. The Scottish theologian James Denney, despite his doctrinal drift, was surely right to say that he had little interest in a theology that could not be preached.

Third, biblical theology also, by its very nature, has an eschatological character from the beginning. The narrative of Genesis 1–3 points forwards to a consummation—the *eschaton* is implied in the *proton*. In the past century this has often been expressed in terms of a formula of 'already and not yet'. That tension permeates the entire biblical narrative from Genesis 3:15 onwards: the promise is *already* given, but it is *not yet* fulfilled. In one sense the development of the plot-line involves the clarifying, filling out, and moving forwards of the *already*. In Christ, in the metaphor used by Oscar Cullman, 'D-Day' has arrived: the critical battle has been fought; 'V-Day' is still to come:[1] in the light of Christ's coming and revelation, we are *already* living in the time when full and final victory has been guaranteed, although it has *not yet* been realized. Biblical theology therefore requires systematic theology to share this eschatological character.

[1] O. Cullmann, *Christ and Time*, tr. F. V. Filson (London: SCM, 1962), p. 84.

Fourth, biblical theology also hands over to systematic theology its inbuilt trinitarianism. The unfolding of the divine name, which we have seen is a *leitmotif* throughout Scripture, is the story of the disclosure of God's triune being, character, and works. It was legitimate for Moses to use the covenant name Yahweh when describing events that took place long before that name was revealed to him. Revelation had progressed, but God had not changed. In a similar way, it is proper for us to see the presence and activity of the Trinity in the biblical revelation even in those epochs in which his trinitarian being and character were veiled to those contemporaneous with them. Here of course the progressive and accumulative character of revelation should preserve us from doing this on the grounds of a narrow exegesis. This was a mistake some of the early apologists committed when claiming *simpliciter* that 'Let *us* make man' (Gen. 1:26) was itself proof that God was Trinity. At best it was logically an indication that some form of plurality inhered in him, as Tertullian, to whom we owe the term 'Trinity', realized. At the same time systematic theology is right to see God the Trinity as the author and agent of creation, providence, redemption, and consummation.

Fifth, in addition, biblical theology hands over to systematic theology its evangelical or covenantal grammar. With the covenant Lord the structure of revelation and of redemptive history is always that the imperatives of obedience are rooted in the indicatives of grace. This was true from the beginning, which is why many early Reformed theologians spoke about the created, as well as the redeemed, relationship as one of grace: God supplies loving bounty, man is called to faithful and joyful obedience. After the fall that 'grace' has a super-added dimension: it is expressed in costly sacrifice, in forgiveness, restoration, and renewal, and ultimately in the incarnation, death, resurrection, heavenly session, and return of Jesus Christ. Biblical theology therefore is the grammar book of systematic theology: reverse its basic structure and our theology will distort the message of the Bible in general and the nature of the gospel in particular.

Sixth, because biblical theology is *covenantal* in nature, it also dictates a style and approach for systematic theology that exudes humility. The same may be said of the systematic theologian. The first requirement is to be humble-minded. Since it is God who initiates the revelation and disposes the covenant, we are to learn to 'think his thoughts after him'. Because he is infinite and we are finite, he is original while we are image, our theology requires analogical thought and speech. The difference between God and man is not simply quantitative; it is qualitative. The revelation to Moses underscores this. The answer to his question of God 'Who are you?' leads to a sense of humility, even inadequacy expressed in his response to God's calling on his life, 'Who am I to ...?' Revelation is given history by the God whose own theology is immediate, infinite, and original. This means that our theology is mediated, finite, and a miniature copy. In addition, we cannot force the disclosure. None of us can know the Father unless the Son reveals him (Matt. 11:27). That is true of the giving of revelation in Scripture; it remains true of the illumination of believing theologians throughout history.

The covenant relationship teaches us that we always—and ever—do theology as creatures, as servants. Thankfully, we do it as children, as image bearers. But in both dimensions of the relationship, our approach is always that of dependents.

What, then, is the goal of biblical theology?

5. The goal of biblical theology

Calvin begins his *Institutes*:

> Nearly all the wisdom we possess, that is to say, true and sound wisdom, consists of two parts: the knowledge of God and of ourselves.[1]

Calvin is here implying that theology, in the sense of our thought, speech, and knowledge of God, lies at the very core of all human existence. Man (in the generic sense) was made as God's image (Gen. 1:26-27). Consequently, both the ground and true direction of our lives are to be found in the God in whom we live, move, and have our being.

To be fully and truly human means to be both theo-dependent and theological beings. But even when we are egocentric and anthropocentric, rather than theocentric in our thinking or in our lifestyle, we can never be anything but *theological* creatures. Either positively or

[1] Calvin, *Institutes*, I.i.1.

negatively, our lives are determined by how we relate to God in every dimension and aspect of our lives.

Clearly, then, theology is vitally important to us, because we were made for theology, to know God. This is what Augustine means when he says so eloquently at the beginning of his *Confessions*: 'You have made us for yourself, and our hearts are restless, until they find their rest in you.'[1]

It should not surprise us, then, to discover that the goals of biblical theology reflect the goal of revelation as a whole: *the knowledge of God.*

This general thesis can be further developed in a series of basic propositions for all Christian theologians:

(1) The knowledge of God at the heart of biblical theology is our greatest privilege.

None of us is to boast in wisdom, strength, or riches (Jer. 9:23). Yet the instinct for boasting in something reflects the fact that we were made to be worshipping creatures, to boast in God. To boast of wisdom, strength, or riches, however, is to turn the truth of God into a lie, to worship and serve the creature rather than the Creator. Boasting must be reserved: 'Let him who boasts boast in this, that he understands and knows me, that I am the LORD' (Jer. 9:24). These words are as true of New Testament Christianity and theology as they are of Old Testament faith, as Paul makes clear by citing them in 1 Corinthians 1:31.

We have no higher privilege, then, than knowing the Lord. It is what we were created for. It is the goal of all theological thinking.

(2) The knowledge of God at the heart of biblical theology is covenantally grounded.

We have argued that the whole biblical revelation, and therefore all knowledge of God, is always covenantally grounded. The covenant relationship between God and his people lies at the very heart of biblical teaching. True, the fulfilment of his covenant brings forgiveness and pardon, according to Jeremiah 31:34: 'I will forgive their iniquity, and I will remember their sin no more.' But we must also remember that such forgiveness is ultimately a means to an end, not the end itself. The end in view is:

[1] Augustine, *Confessions* (Harmondsworth: Penguin Books, 1961), I.1.

And no longer shall each one teach his neighbour and each his brother, saying, 'Know the LORD', for they shall all know me, from the least of them to the greatest, declares the LORD (Jer. 31:34).

The same principle appears earlier, in Jeremiah 24:7, where restoration to covenant blessing—expressed in terms of return to the land—is contingent upon a more fundamental restoration in the promise: 'I will give them a heart to know that I am the LORD.'

We should notice here, that this promise of the knowledge of God in the new covenant does not imply an antithesis between not knowing God under the old covenant, and knowing him under the new covenant. That would be—and often is—a mistaken exegesis and application. Rather these words denote a difference in *the content of the knowledge* and in *the way we attain it* in the age of fulfilment. The undergirding difference is between:

(i) The medium of the knowledge of God in the Old Testament era (prophets, priests, and kings) and

(ii) The anointing of all believers with the Messianic Spirit in the New Testament era so that now all believers have equal access to the secrets of the one prophet, priest, and king, Jesus Christ, in whom the knowledge of the Lord is revealed. It is in this specific sense that we now do not need anyone to 'teach' us (1 John 2:27). Clearly in a letter in which John is *teaching* his readers he does not mean that the new covenant church has no teaching office. Rather his statement is an application of the promise through Jeremiah that the one Mediator of the new covenant is the fulfilment and consummation of the many mediators of the old. It is their ministry that those who have the Spirit of Christ will no longer need in the new age. But while there is epochal advance in the *character* of this covenantal knowledge of God, central to both dispensations of the covenant relationship (whatever the medium) is the common theme: *knowing God.*

This is why the Messianic age is viewed as the age of the universal expansion of the knowledge of God, as Isaiah testifies. The *telos* of the ministry of the one on whom the Spirit of the Lord will rest is that 'the earth shall be full of the knowledge of the LORD as the waters cover the sea' (Isa. 11:9). The knowledge of the Lord is therefore the epicentre of all the covenant blessings.

Already this was true for the people of God in the old covenant. By contrast with the surrounding peoples, the psalmist can say, 'In Judah God is known; his name is great in Israel' (Psa. 76:1). This is a foretaste of the knowledge of God given in the Messianic era that Christ inaugurates.

3. The knowledge of God in biblical theology focuses on salvation in Christ.

To say this is simply further to elucidate what we have already hinted at under the previous heading. But it is worth emphasizing.

What is the heart of salvation? Jesus provides answers in Matthew 11:25-30. We are to come to him to learn from him (verse 29). But what will we learn? He tells us in verse 27: 'No one knows the Son except the Father, and no one knows the Father except the Son and anyone to whom the Son chooses to reveal him.' This whole well-known section of the Gospel teaches us about the need for revelation. But it also tells us what the content of revelation and salvation is: *knowing the Father through the Son.* Knowledge of God is not additional to salvation; it is the core of salvation.

Thus, while in evangelical theology we rightly emphasize the need for forgiveness and new life, it is important to emphasize that in Scripture these blessings, however remarkable in themselves, are means of bringing us into the knowledge of God. The knowledge of God, then, is not an 'added extra' to salvation—a kind of theological dessert for people who like their Christianity to be intellectually orientated. Indeed, this knowledge cannot be limited to or contained within the activities of the mind. It is salvation. It is, as Jeremiah again describes it, having a heart to know God (Jer. 24:7).

This notion is in fact spelled out both by John and by Paul:

(i) For both psychological and theological reasons, we would expect that in his 'High Priestly Prayer' (John 17), our Lord would focus on the central burdens on his heart. He does indeed. He prays about the way in which he has been given authority to give his disciples eternal life which he describes, if not defines, in terms of the knowledge of God: 'And this is eternal life, that they know you the only true God, and Jesus Christ whom you have sent' (John 17:3). Here, eternal life or salvation means knowing God.

(ii) We find a similar perspective in Paul. For him, becoming a believer is coming to know God. Conversely, not to be a believer is not to know God. Unbelief, or preconversion, is described in precisely these terms by Paul: 'in the wisdom of God, the world did not know God through [its] wisdom' (1 Cor. 1:21).

Again, Paul speaks of those 'who do not know God' (1 Thess. 4:5). Thus, for all the knowledge inherent in his Jewish background, his own conversion involved a coming to know God: 'God, who said, "Let light shine out of darkness", has shone in our hearts to give the light of the knowledge of the glory of God in the face of Jesus Christ' (2 Cor. 4:6).

Perhaps the most striking illustration of this antithesis between unbelief and faith as essentially one between ignorance of God and knowledge of him is found in Galatians 4:8-9. Formerly we were slaves. We were in bondage. What was the reason? Paul explains: 'Formerly, when you did not know God, you were enslaved ... But now that you have come to know God, or rather to be known by God ...' Notice the intriguing way in which Paul expresses a great theological principle: our coming to know God is based on God's knowledge of us: being *known by God*. It cannot exist independently of him; mutuality is one of its essential characteristics. It is this that was lost in the fall. Rather than seek God, Adam hid from him. Now all this is thrown into reverse gear for the believer and in our theology.

Paul's words are apposite here:

> For now we see in a mirror dimly, but then face to face. Now I know in part; then I shall know fully, even as I have been fully known (1 Cor. 13:12).

These words form a fitting conclusion to a lecture honouring the Vos family and expressing gratitude for the labours of Johannes Vos in particular.[1] The preface to his father's *Biblical Theology*, which he so lovingly edited, contains words which are usually attributed to Thomas Aquinas: *Theologia a Deo docetur, Deum docet, ad Deum ducit*—Theology

---

[1] The substance of this chapter was originally given at Geneva College, Beaver Falls, PA, where Johannes Vos (1903–83) taught from 1954 to 1973.

is taught by God, teaches us about God, and leads us to God. Although the Angelic Doctor is thought of today as a systematic theologian in the scholastic mould, throughout his working life he was for all practical purposes a professor of sacred Scripture, and many of his lectures are extant. Geerhardus Vos, by contrast, is universally known as a biblical exegete and theologian. But he came to his chair of biblical theology in Princeton Seminary on the back of teaching systematic theology from 1888 to 1893 at the Theological School of the Christian Reformed Church (now Calvin Seminary). He stood, therefore, in a great tradition of Christian thinkers who understood the deep relationship between biblical theology and systematic theology. This, after all, was the tradition in which John Calvin stood. He served as professor of Old Testament in the Academy in Geneva, although he is better known today as the author of *The Institutes of the Christian Religion*, one of the truly great works expressing Christian theology in a systematic way. To a greater or lesser extent each managed to marry together the two disciplines and understand the ways in which they interpenetrate. Certainly, in this sense Geerhardus Vos pursued, and his son Johannes Vos helped to communicate, the basic message enshrined so magnificently in the challenge and promise of the first question of the *Shorter Catechism*. Our chief end is to glorify God and to enjoy him forever. All theological pursuit must begin here, all biblical theology leads us here; and all systematic theology should end here.

We are therefore debtors to those who have kept that vision before us, and not least for the contribution of the Vos family.

CHAPTER TWENTY-THREE

'HALLOWED BE THY NAME':
THE HOLINESS OF THE FATHER

THE seventeenth chapter of John's Gospel takes us to a holy place where Christ introduces us to his holy Father:

When Jesus had spoken these words, he lifted up his eyes to heaven, and said, 'Father, the hour has come; glorify your Son that the Son may glorify you, since you have given him authority over all flesh, to give eternal life to all whom you have given him. And this is eternal life, that they may know you the only true God, and Jesus Christ whom you have sent. I glorified you on earth, having accomplished the work that you gave me to do. And now, Father, glorify me in your own presence with the glory that I had with you before the world existed. ... All mine are yours, and yours are mine, and I am glorified in them. And I am no longer in the world, but they are in the world, and I am coming to you. Holy Father, keep them in your name, which you have given me, that they may be one, even as we are one. ... Sanctify them in the truth; your word is truth. As you sent me into the world, so I have sent them into the world. And for their sake I consecrate [or sanctify] myself, that they also may be sanctified in truth. I do not ask for these only, but also for those who will believe in me through their word, that they may all be one, just as you, Father, are in me, and I in you, that they also may be in us, so that the world may believe you have sent me. ... Father, I desire that they also, whom you have given me, may be with me where I am, to see my glory that you have given me because you loved me before the foundation of the world. O righteous Father, even though the world does not know you, I know you, and these know that you have sent me. I made known to them your name, and I will continue to make it known, that the love with which you have loved me may be in them, and I in them' (John 17:1-5, 10-11, 17-21, 24-26).

In many ways, it would be much easier to write about the holiness of God, about which the Scriptures have a great deal to say, than to address the subject of the holy Father. If the truth be told, we are not really accustomed to thinking specifically of the holiness of the Father *as Father*. This itself underlines the fact that often when we speak about the holiness of God we are still thinking in a man-centred fashion in this sense: we speak of him as being 'separate from us'. But we may then still be thinking thoughts centred in ourselves rather than in him.

When, however, we speak about the holiness of the Father *as Father*, we must begin with God the Trinity. The holiness of the Father is not an attribute he adopts, as it were, only when he creates. If he is the holy Father, he is ever so, and indeed must have been so before all worlds in the ineffable mystery of the eternal in-being and fellowship of the Trinity. The Fathers of the church expounded this relationship in terms of what they called the divine *perichōrēsis* (from the Greek verb *perichōreō*, 'to go around, come around, go to in succession'). The Father, the Son, and the Spirit are always engaged in mutually dynamic relationships and fellowship within the unity of their threeness. Within that relationship, each person is 'holy'. It is attractive to think that the seraphim are in such constant awe in the presence of God because they are privileged to sense this mystery—yet feel they are not fit to gaze on it without winged protection—so they cry, 'Holy, holy, holy is the LORD of hosts' (Isa. 6:3).

It is part of the mystery of the incarnation, as John expresses it in the prologue to his Gospel, that this fellowship remains unbroken throughout our Lord's earthly ministry. The *Logos* (Word) is always 'at the Father's side' (literally 'in the Father's bosom') and 'has made him known' ('he has exegeted him', John 1:18). This is underlined in John 17:11 by the only occurrence of the words 'holy Father' in the entire New Testament.

It would be challenging enough to ask, 'What would *we* mean if we addressed God in prayer as "holy Father"?' But to ask, 'What did *Jesus* mean?' is to enter what is, for most of us, uncharted territory and to feel that we have a privilege hitherto reserved for seraphim. John 17 is indeed holy ground, and, at least metaphorically, we need to take off our shoes if we are to walk on it.

Our Lord's prayer here comes not only at the high point theologically in the Gospel, but also the deepest point emotionally and affectionally in his life and ministry. In a sense, he is, as he says here, 'no longer in the world' (verse 11). The die is cast. He is going to the cross and to the Father. The apostle John records words here that he does not record Jesus saying anywhere else as he sets before us the poignant scene in which Jesus pours out his soul before his heavenly Father, desiring his glory in his Father's presence, requesting the blessing and salvation of his beloved disciples, and expressing his last will and testament: that the whole church, which he will purchase with his blood, will see him in his glory (17:24).

With heightened intensity, the Lord prays. Six times he addresses God as Father. But only once do the words 'holy Father' form on his lips. This is what the grammarians call a '*hapax legomenon*', a word or statement that is made once in a body of literature and does not appear again.

It is challenging to us mentally and spiritually to grasp what Jesus means when he addresses God in this way. Perhaps the sheer immensity of this title is indicated by the fact that in your personal prayer and in corporate prayer conducted by the leadership in your church, this may be the least frequently (if ever) used mode of address to God—'O holy Father'. It behooves us, therefore, to come up gently on this title, as though we were conscious that we are little boys and girls about to explore something so intimate, so sacred, that we are endangered—as indeed we are endangered—by exploring what it meant for Jesus to say 'holy Father', and then to invite us to pray in like language: 'When you pray, say: "Our Father in heaven, Hallowed be your name"' (Luke 11:2, NKJV).

Unfolding mysteries

We are helped to do this when we understand that the Gospel of John divides neatly into two halves. Scholars debate as to exactly where the division comes. But there comes a point in the twelfth chapter when Jesus withdraws from the world and does no more signs, except the manifestation of his great name, the 'I AM'. Thus ends what some commentators have described as the 'Book of the Signs' (chapters 1–12), as Jesus withdraws to disclose the intimate truths of grace to his disciples in what is likewise sometimes called the 'Book of Glory' (chapters 13–21).

Every reader of the Gospels is conscious of a difference in style between the first three Gospels (often called 'Synoptic' because they share a common approach and viewpoint) and the Gospel of John. John Calvin sums this up cleverly when he writes that although all the Gospels 'had the same object, to show Christ, the first three exhibit his body, if I may be permitted to put it like that, but John shows his soul'.[1]

This emerges from John 13 onward. In Jesus' pre-Passover tutorial he unfolds mysteries the disciples struggle to grasp. Even then, he says, 'I still have many things to say to you, but you cannot bear them now' (16:12). But while that is true, he begins to bring them, in fellowship and in ministry, to a deeper knowledge of the ineffable mystery of God the Trinity.

This—at least for me—is the ultimate evidence that for John the Trinity is not the most speculative and most impractical doctrine, as it often seems to be for Christians today. In fact, if this is what Jesus teaches his disciples when he—and they with him—stand under such great stress, then this must be the *least speculative* doctrine in the Bible, and, at the end of the day, it must be the *most practical*. After all, if they love him they will not only want to keep his commandments (14:21), they will also want to know him better. He thus brings them to understand the ministry of the Holy Spirit, through whom this intimate knowledge will be theirs. He not only brings them in to understand the identity of the heavenly Father, but also to appreciate his own relationship with him. 'In that day', he says, with reference to Pentecost, 'you will know that I am in my Father, and you in me, and I in you' (14:20).

If the language had not been abused elsewhere, we would probably write as a heading over John 13-17, 'The sacred heart of Christ'. If you want to know Jesus Christ, then you must have at least a basic working knowledge of what he teaches his disciples in this farewell discourse.

---

[1] John Calvin, *Comm. John*, I:6.

Fascinatingly, this discourse begins with a parable of descent, as Jesus rises from supper, disrobes, and stoops down to wash his disciples' dirty feet. Knowing that he has come from the Father and is going to the Father, he gives his disciples an acted parable of his gracious work of atonement (13:1-17). But the whole section also ends with a parable of ascent, or better, a prayer of ascent, as Jesus comes to the Father, praying that he will be able to glorify his Father's name and that his Father will glorify him (John 17). Here we are able to eavesdrop on things that are almost illegitimate for man to utter.

Marvellously, then, Jesus prays that the disciples, who are about to see him in his abject humiliation, will be kept by the holy name of the Father to see him in his magnificent glory: 'Father, I desire that they also, whom you have given me, may be with me where I am, to see my glory that you have given me because you loved me before the foundation of the world' (verse 24). His desire is that those he knows and loves best, and who—despite all their failings—love him best in return, although they now realize he is 'despised and rejected by men; a man of sorrows, and acquainted with grief' (Isa. 53:3), should see him exalted, crowned, glorified—home. Only when he has prayed thus does he go out to fulfil the atoning work of his death and resurrection.

Here is the link to us: when he rises in the early morning of his resurrection day, he charges Mary Magdalene, 'Go to my brothers and say to them, "I am ascending to my Father and your Father, to my God and your God"' (20:17). Although his words are sometimes interpreted as though Jesus were making a distinction between his relationship with the Father and our relationship with the Father, the reverse is almost certainly the truth. In and through his resurrection, he is, as it were, beginning to gather children, from all the ends of the earth, into the worldwide, eternity-long family of God. And he is inviting us similarly, as we shall see, to come to God and say far more frequently than we are wont to do, 'O holy Father'.

An eternal address

What does it mean for the Lord of glory to come to the Father and say 'holy Father'? The eternal Word, the Son of God, has, from all eternity, in all eternity, and through all eternity, always addressed the Father as 'holy Father'. What does that mean? What does it mean that from all eternity in the blessed Trinity there has been this response of the eternal Son to his eternal Father—a response to the Father's person in which the Son's instinct has been to address him, as he does at this high point of emotion, as holy?

For something to be an essential divine attribute, it must have been exercised before all worlds. In fact, for something properly to be called an attribute of God, it must have been expressed and experienced in its most intense and dynamic form among the three persons of the Trinity—when nothing else existed.[1]

In this sense, technically speaking, the wrath of God is not an essential attribute of God. God indeed expresses wrath in history. But this is the manifestation of his eternal attribute of righteousness coming into contact with the temporal context of the fall and human sinfulness. Thus wrath is not itself an eternal attribute. It had no place in the inner communion among the three persons of the eternal Trinity. We can say 'God is, in himself, in his in-being, love'; but we can never say 'God is, in his in-being, wrath.' It had no existence in the persons and relations of the Trinity. By contrast, holiness did.

But the holiness of God *did* come to expression. God is admired in sinless glory for his holiness. So when Jesus says 'holy Father', what he says here on earth expresses the heart of the Son who has gazed on the face of his blessed Father from all eternity, revealing that his instinct has been to praise him, to admire him, and to love him because of his perfect holiness.

That means that whatever the semantics of the biblical terms for holiness may be, the *meaning* of holiness cannot be 'separation'. With respect to the creation and especially the human creature, the meaning of holiness implies separation from the creation and from the sinner. But within the blessed fellowship of the divine Trinity, the meaning of 'holy' must be, shall we say, purity of love, perfect devotion. Scholars have seen the notion of the numinous, the awe-inspiring, bound up with this idea.

[1] The theological point here is that if God is 'holy' when there is neither creation nor sin, his holiness should not be defined in relation to them. This is a different distinction from the commonly made one between God's communicable and his incommunicable attributes.

454

Perhaps we could even say it involves 'intensity'. In the Father, holiness is a purity of an infinite intensity of love and beauty that creates a sense of devotion and wonder in the spectator, but also within the participants.

Though we are almost driven to think in terms of divine attributes as entities in themselves (thus we see love, righteousness, and holiness as abstractable qualities), the truth is that God is simple in his being. He is all that he is in everything he is. Thus, divine holiness is his infinitely intense three-personal devotion as the God whose nature is simplex. His holiness is his love, righteousness, and faithfulness—the infinite intensity of all that he is in the unity of his fatherly being with reference to his beloved Son, so that as his Son looks on him, his Son's response is to say, 'O holy Father'. To both the Son and the Spirit, the Father is truly awesome. In a human relationship, a man might see his wife appearing after readying herself for a formal social event and find that the sight of her takes his breath away in admiration and love. To be 'awestruck' in this sense is not the sign of being an inferior being or person, but rather that sense of wonder at beauty and dignity that is enhanced by the very fact that the husband knows that this woman belongs to him and has a love for him that is unique. It is in this way, surely magnified greatly, that there is a sense of profound personal awe when our Lord breathes the words 'holy Father'.

This is a place we can scarcely go. We turn to Isaiah 6 and see the prophet responding to the expressions of the divine holiness as he feels himself undone. As we read through Isaiah 5 into Isaiah 6, we find a very specific pattern emerging: Isaiah pronounces a series of woes on sinners. There are six of them (5:8, 11, 18, 20, 21, 22). Given the biblical fascination with the number seven, we are led to expect that a final woe is yet to come. But we have no way of anticipating against whom it will be pronounced. So it is to our astonishment that the prophet pronounces it *on himself.* 'Woe is me! For I am lost' (Isa. 6:5). Catching a glimpse of the true worship of the Holy One overwhelms him and undoes him. Correspondingly, the reason we are not undone is not because we are purer than God's prophet; it is because we have so little sense of whom we address when we take on our lips the words 'holy Father'.

The truth is we know we are not fit to say 'holy Father'. But when we consider the seraphim of Isaiah's vision, we find something possibly even more unexpected. These seraphim, who have never sinned, who are holy, as they sense the intensity of God's attributes being expressed toward them out of the heart of the divine being, are constrained to veil their faces and cover their feet. Although perfectly holy, they dare not look directly on the intensity of the holiness of the heavenly Father without danger, if not certainty, of disintegration.

It is in stark yet glorious contrast to this that we find John opening his Gospel by saying, 'In the beginning was the Word, and the Word was with God' (*pros ton theon*—literally 'toward God').

Do you see the picture here? If the Son is 'toward God', he must be face to face with him[1]—alone (with the Spirit) able to bear the intensity of the Father's gaze. That face is all-consuming love; nothing can bear it that is not itself perfect love. Thus, he gazes on his Son. All creatures must cover their faces or avert their eyes. Only the Son (always in and with the Spirit) is able to love in return with an intensity that preserves him from being consumed by the holiness of the Father.

According to the biblical revelation God has made us not only to have communion with him, but in such a way that we can grasp and appreciate what that communion is like. This is in measure the meaning of the biblical doctrine of our creation as the image of God. But further, embedded within this are further echoes of the in-being of God in the mutual being of man and woman.

By far my most intimate human relationship is with my wife. No one else should lock eyes with my wife and gaze at her the way I am privileged to do and say, 'I love you with all of my being.' Doubtless we use the word 'holy' in a weakened sense, but it is nevertheless employed in a real sense when we speak about 'holy' matrimony. It is the sphere in which there can exist an almost devouring intensity of desire to possess and be possessed (but never one without the other). Unless the love is both holy and mutual, the desire on the part of the one will destroy the relationship.

But there is a further dimension to this analogy. Those who thus love are capable of spending extraordinary amounts of time with each other

[1] A translation suggested by William Hendriksen, *The Gospel according to John* (Grand Rapids: Baker, 1963), p. 70.

456

doing 'little more' than enjoying one another's company—whether few or many words are exchanged. Love in its most heightened relationships is satisfied by and with the beloved in and for himself or herself.

The holiness of love that flows between the Father and the Son in the Spirit is infinitely greater than the most intense human devotion and holy passion. The blessed Son is able to gaze into the eyes of the holy heavenly Father and bear in his being, in the mystery of his own person, the intensity of the Father's holy love for him and desire for fellowship with him so that 'the deep things' of God (1 Cor. 2:10 KJV) with respect to each person are fully unveiled and enjoyed. That is the intensity of the Father's desire to have fellowship with him.

As is well known, Augustine in his *Confessions* tells of a questioner demanding to know, 'What was God doing before he made heaven and earth?' He is content to say that he does not know, although he admits he is familiar with the more famous and facetious answer, 'He was preparing hell for people who pry into mysteries.'[1] Apparently Calvin found the answer more apt than his master.[2]

But surely—if a cat may look at two kings—neither of them provided the right answer. The answer is that he was enjoying his Son in and with the Spirit. That which the image—male and female—may experience intensely in the wonder of mutual devotion and satisfaction, the Eternal One knows within the inter-personal relationships of the Trinity.

Seeing the Father in the Son

John records our Lord speaking of the nature of his relationship with the Father as being 'in' the Father: 'you, Father, are in me, and I in you' (John 17:21). This is the ground of our union with the Father.

These words of our Lord unveil great depths of truth while simultaneously underlining that while we can grasp this we cannot comprehend it all. The Father is in the Son and the Son is in the Father. As the incarnate Son, Jesus gives expression to the relationship that he has with the Father. He longs, as he says in verse 24, to return from his state of humiliation to his state of exaltation. He longs also that we may be there

[1] Augustine, *Confessions*, XI.12.
[2] Calvin, *Institutes*, I.xiv.1.

to see him as he is, to stand, as it were, on the sidelines and observe and taste the glory.

Since no man can see God and live, the only way we can do this (for that matter, the only way the seraphim can ever do this) is by indirect means—by seeing the glory of God in the face of Jesus Christ. We cannot look into the eyes of the Father and hold our gaze, as though we had access to his eternal being. Rather, we must, as it were, stand on the circumference and watch the eyes of the God-man Jesus Christ as he gazes on his heavenly Father. In this we are like those who take the greatest delight and pleasure in seeing two lovers 'made for each other' engaging in a human *perichōrēsis* of mutual affection, admiration, and devotion that is marked by open self-giving to one another and total satisfaction in each other. When we see the face of the Father reflected in the eager eyes of his Son incarnate, then we find ourselves worshipping and ever crying with the seraphim, and with all the choristers of heaven, 'Holy, holy, holy is the LORD of hosts', as though we were witnessing the display of a trillion laser beams of light, pure and intense.

Sometimes we mistakenly think that what most causes awe and reverence before God is the terror of his holiness, the fear of his law, and the threat of judgment and condemnation. But it is not so. Pure and intense love has more power to effect awe, even gracious fear, than all terror.

Have you ever felt that someone cared so much that you should be the best you can be that you needed to turn away? Often, as a student, spending time with someone who cared deeply that I should belong without reservation to Christ, honour him throughout my life, and use whatever gifts I might have for the glory of God, I found myself experiencing a strange paradox—leaving the person's presence with a longing to be in it again and yet inwardly running lest all this prove so costly that my life would no longer be under my own sway.

That is a pale reflection of our experience of God. We cannot gaze directly on the Father—but, says Jesus, 'Whoever has seen me has seen the Father. ... Do you not believe that I am in the Father and the Father is in me?' (John 14:9, 10). As the Lord Jesus comes to his heavenly Father, he reveals the extraordinary intimacy between the Father and Son as he looks on him and says, 'holy Father'. He invites us to taste this.

Perhaps the simplest analogy is this. You are a young student who has just fallen in love. You return to your dorm. Your friends, who know the name of the girl you were with, want to know where you have been and what you have been doing for the past four hours. You say, 'We haven't actually been doing anything.' Then they say, 'You can't spend four hours not doing anything.' But to yourself you say: 'I have never experienced anything quite like this! I feel I could explore her mind and soul without intermission. And even then I feel there would be more to know and adore.'

Think of it. We are finite, distorted human beings, but in the exploration of one another, we find such amazing temporal satisfaction. If that can be true of the image God created male and female, how much more true of God himself? He thus provides us with a simple, yet astonishingly common, analogy of that which is beyond our comprehension.

Incidentally, Scripture underlines for us that *being* is fundamental to *doing*. But we have reversed that in our day. For us, doing has become the more important thing. People sometimes ask me, 'What do you and your wife like to do?' I always say: 'We don't do anything much. We just like to be together.' They will say, 'But what do you *do* when you're together?' 'Well', I say, 'we sometimes talk and we sometimes sit in silence.' Again they'll inquire, 'But what do you *like* to do?' The truth of the matter is that I just like to look at my wife and ponder how it can be that she has devoted her life to me.

In considering what Jesus meant when he said 'holy Father', we do well to follow Calvin, who said, 'When [God] sets an end to teaching … stop trying to be wise.'[1] Rather than stand in perplexity and say, 'I cannot understand this', let it suffice us that we can overhear the words of our Lord Jesus Christ and be lost in wonder, love, and praise that we have had a glimpse of this ineffable relationship between the Father and his Son, and are invited into that fellowship (1 John 1:3).

---

[1] *Institutes*, III.xxi.3.

A glorious new relationship

It is against this background that John's Gospel then introduces us to what the relationship between the Father and the Son must have been in all eternity and continues to be today.

Throughout his ministry, the Son remained in the bosom (perhaps even 'in the lap') of his Father. The amazing thing is that he became flesh. The Word, who was face to face with God, in the bosom of the Father, became flesh in the womb of his mother. Why? Let the answer bring a sense of awe to our hearts: he became flesh to bring us into the same relationship to the holy Father that he experienced and enjoyed in the finitude and weakness of the flesh in which he was incarnated.

Of the many wonderful insights John's Gospel gives us into this relationship, two seem especially marvellous.

The *first* is in John 5:19-20. Here, Jesus is speaking about his relationship with his Father and says, 'Truly, truly, I say to you, the Son can do nothing of his own accord, but only what he sees the Father doing.' This shows us the way he lived as a Son. We can imagine that Jesus lived this way with Joseph, watching his adoptive father making the yoke for the oxen or tables for the neighbourhood homes, and learning to be a carpenter.

The *second*, expressed from the other side of the relationship (that is, from the perspective of the Father's attitude to the Son), is in John 10:17, when Jesus speaks about giving his life for the sheep. 'For this reason', he says, 'the Father loves me, because I lay down my life that I may take it up again.'

Luke tells us that Jesus, the Incarnate One, actually grew in favour with the holy Father (Luke 2:40). Indeed, unless our Jesus is a Jesus who grew physically, grew in wisdom, *but also grew in favour with his heavenly Father*, our Jesus is not the Jesus of the New Testament. As the pressures mounted and became the more challenging and demanding, and as he had opportunity to demonstrate increasingly costly submission until he was obedient unto death, even the death of the cross, Jesus gave hints of the inner mystery of his relationship to his Father. Even when he was under the judgment of his heavenly Father—no, *especially* when he was under the judgment of God—his heavenly Father was surely singing,

> My Jesus, I love thee, I know thou art mine; …
> *If ever I loved thee, my Jesus, 'tis now.*[1]

Is it not almost unbearable to think of such devotion on the part of the Son to his beloved Father—and of the Father's heart-breaking admiration and love for his Son?

All of this was accomplished to bring us—lost, broken sinners—into fellowship with God so that we can say, as John says, in essence, in his first letter, 'Here is the mystery of the blessing of the gospel, that our fellowship is in the power of the Spirit, through the Son, with the holy Father' (see 1 John 1:1-3). As our Lord Jesus leads us and gives us access to the presence of God, we want to hide behind Jesus. But he says, 'Now, my child, come from behind me, and watch my eyes as I gaze into the eternal heart of my Father and say, "Holy Father, here am I, and the children you have given me"' (see Heb. 2:13).

The privileges of the relationship

That is our privilege, because, of course, the Scriptures teach us that we have been brought into God's family. So what does it mean for us as the people of God to be able to come to him in the name of the Lord Jesus and say to him 'holy Father'?

Notice three very simple things:

(1) *First*, if we say 'Our holy Father' when we pray, that means that *the church, which he purchased with his own blood, is the holy family.*

On Sunday night in the church I served in Glasgow, Scotland, I was preaching on the Trinity, and halfway through the service, a whole crowd of people from the Near East trooped into the gallery of the church. I remember thinking: 'Help—Muslims are here because they know I am preaching on the Trinity. Perhaps I will be here for a long time afterwards engaged in debate and defence!' If I remember rightly, all of the late arrivals were from Egypt. They were educators sent over by the Egyptian government. Half of those in the group were, in fact, Muslims, but those who had come to the service were Coptic Christians.

Afterwards, one of them asked me eagerly and proudly, 'Did you know the holy family came to Egypt?' 'Yes', I replied. 'I know they went

---

[1] From the hymn 'My Jesus, I Love Thee' by William R. Featherstone (emphasis added).

461

to Egypt. We read of this in Matthew's Gospel. Indeed we know they went to Egypt.' But I also wanted to say: 'Dear friend, *this congregation here is the holy family.*'

We see this in the early chapters of the Acts of the Apostles. One of the great paradoxes in Acts is that the holiness of the Father so dawns on the early believers as to fill the community with such awe that (we are told) nobody dared join the church (Acts 5:13). Do you belong to a church like that—a church that some people avoid not because people within the church are angular, but because God is in the midst of his people as the holy Father? Yet, astonishingly, the very next verse says, 'And more than ever believers were added to the Lord' (Acts 5:14). That is what it means when a congregation of the Lord becomes the holy family. There is something about their community that expresses the holiness of the Father, and that makes outsiders feel 'there is no way I could be worthy to be part of that'. Yet, at the same time, they wish with all their hearts they could be part of such a family.

(2) *Second*, this understanding should *permeate our worship*. Some of us are good at 'family'; others of us feel we are better at what we take to be 'holiness'. But not many of our churches are good at being holy families. Yet when we begin to reflect the fatherhood of God together, that is what we become. So when we come to God, we say, 'Our Father in heaven, hallowed be your name' (Matt. 6:9). Since he is the holy Father, he gives his children the Holy Spirit, who 'bears witness with our spirit that we are children of God' (Rom. 8:16). With this assurance, we cry out, 'Abba! Father!' (Rom. 8:15). That is not a cry reserved for the greatest and the most sanctified, but given to the most deeply hurt. He wants us to know especially as we cry out to him in distress that he is our Father and that he cares for us.

(3) *Third*, since he is the holy Father, *he has set his heart on making all of his children like his holy Son*. Because he has given his Son to death in order that that might take place, he will keep us

> till all the ransomed church of God
> be saved to sin no more.[1]

---

[1] From the hymn 'There Is a Fountain Filled with Blood' by William Cowper.

The privilege of this dawns on us only when we remember how much it cost Jesus to enable us to say 'holy Father' and to provide for us the clearest evidence of the sheer intensity of the Father's holiness. That came to clearest expression when he appeared before his Father, bearing our sins in his own body on the tree, and said, 'Holy Father, smite the Shepherd.' In the intensity of his admiration for his holy Son—'If ever I loved thee, my Jesus, 'tis now'—he smote the Shepherd, in order that the sheep might be gathered through him who was 'wounded for our transgressions … crushed for our iniquities; upon [whom] was the chastisement that brought us peace, and with [whose] stripes we are healed' (Isa. 53:5).

What a privilege it is, therefore, to say 'holy Father'!

CHAPTER TWENTY-FOUR

CHRISTUS VICTOR ET PROPITIATOR: THE DEATH OF CHRIST, SUBSTITUTE AND CONQUEROR

WHAT was the reason the Son of God appeared? In what sense did the cross put authorities to open shame? Why did the Son of God share in our humanity?

Hidden within these questions are, of course, phrases from texts of the New Testament that provide us with the answers: 'The reason the Son of God appeared was to destroy the works of the devil' (1 John 3:8); 'He disarmed the rulers and authorities and put them to open shame, by triumphing over them in him' (Col. 2:15); 'Since therefore the children share in flesh and blood, he himself likewise partook of the same things, that through death he might destroy the one who has the power of death, that is, the devil, and deliver all those who through fear of death were subject to lifelong slavery' (Heb. 2:14-15).

The Reformed tradition

Theologians of an anti-supernatural bent will immediately dismiss such statements as mythological—modern man could hardly be expected to believe that the work of Christ terminated in any sense on the devil.

For a variety of reasons, however, even systematic theologians in the Reformed tradition, who resolutely believe in the supernatural, have given relatively little attention to this aspect of Christ's work. The standard textbooks from Francis Turretin through Charles Hodge to Louis Berkhof[1] do not explore it in any detail, despite the insistence of

[1] Turretin, in his exposition of the work of Christ in *Institutio Theologiae Elencticae*, topic 14, does not concern himself with the issue. Charles Hodge divides the

the apostle John that the destruction of the devil's works is a key reason for the incarnation.

There are at least three identifiable causes of this lack of interest:

1. The first is that the agenda for discussing the work of Christ was already settled in the twelfth century following the benchmark interpretations of the atonement by Anselm of Canterbury in his *Cur Deus Homo* (around 1090) and in the early twelfth century by Peter Abelard in his controversial response in his exposition of Romans 3:19-26.[1]

Anselm stressed that the atonement was a satisfaction of God's honour. Abelard, on the other hand, argued that the cross is the supreme manifestation of God's love. The dialectic thus set up has dominated theological discussion ever since, and interpretations of the meaning of Christ's death have therefore tended to argue that its effect terminates either on God or on man, the so-called objective and subjective views of the atonement. Post-Reformation controversies over the atonement have also been waged within these parameters, and the theme of Christ's defeat of Satan has been largely neglected.

2. In the Reformed thinking of the seventeenth century, some development of interest is apparent. Often this was expressed within the

---

'theories' of the atonement into five groups (*Systematic Theology*, 3 vols [New York, 1872–73], II:563-91), but deals with the effect of the atonement on Satan only under the heading 'The Doctrine of Some of the Fathers'. In this he is followed by B. B. Warfield (*The Person and Work of Christ* [Philadelphia: Presbyterian and Reformed, 1950], pp. 356ff.), as well as by Berkhof, who lists seven views of the atonement, including the 'Ransom-to-Satan' view; but his own exposition makes no reference to the effect of the cross on Satan (Louis Berkhof, *Systematic Theology* [Grand Rapids: Eerdmans, 1939], pp. 384-99). The *Westminster Confession of Faith*, albeit briefly, does note in its chapter 'Of Christ the Mediator' that the *protevangelium* is a reference to Christ's victory over the devil, 'wherein he was revealed and signified to be the seed of the woman, which should bruise the serpent's head' (VIII.6).

[1] Abelard's understanding is expressed in powerful eloquence. But even when it is recognized that the criticisms of Abelard's teaching, which begin with Bernard of Clairvaux, wrongly accuse him of holding an exemplary view of the atonement *simpliciter*, his exposition of Rom. 3:19-26 makes redemption take place through the effect of divine love itself rather than by the payment made in love of the penalty of sin. See *A Scholastic Miscellany: Anselm to Ockham*, ed. and tr. E. R. Fairweather (Philadelphia: Westminster, 1956), pp. 276-87, for an accessible translation. For a modern treatment of Abelard, see R. E. Weingart, *The Logic of Divine Love: A Critical Analysis of the Soteriology of Peter Abelard* (Oxford: Clarendon, 1970).

context of a shift of focus from *historia salutis* (history of salvation) to *ordo salutis* (order of salvation). That, in my judgment, is too simple an analysis.[1] But it is certainly true that there developed in the seventeenth century a sophisticated pastoral theology that gave greater attention to expounding the Christian's conflict with, and victory over, Satan than it did to Christ's triumph over him, albeit rooted in the latter. Titles such as John Bunyan's *The Holy War*, Thomas Brooks's *Precious Remedies against Satan's Devices*, and William Gurnall's *The Christian in Complete Armour* provide a commentary on this transition, as do the words of many later evangelical hymns (perhaps even more potent shapers of evangelical piety).

3. The third and probably most important reason is the discrediting of the early Fathers' view of how it is that Christ's work was a conquest of the devil.

The early Fathers

The teaching that the work of Christ was a conflict with, and conquest of, Satan is found in some of the greatest of the early Christian Fathers such as Justin Martyr[2] and Irenaeus.[3] The latter particularly saw the work of Christ as a recapitulation of Eden, a re-run of the conflict between the serpent and Adam and Eve. His ingenious development of Romans 5:12-21 and 1 Corinthians 15:20-49, in which he traced parallels not only between Adam and Christ but also between Eve and Mary, was to provide the basis for many later developments, not always with happy consequences.

It fell to Origen—Origen of the allegorical hermeneutic and the universal restoration—to develop the theme of Christ's death as a

---

[1] It ignores, for example, the solid expositions of the person and work of Christ that are found in the writings of the seventeenth-century Reformed divines, particularly, but by no means exclusively, Thomas Goodwin and John Owen.

[2] Justin writes of the righteous reversal of the fall in a style that would become beloved of the Fathers: 'He became man by the Virgin in order that the disobedience which proceeded from the serpent might receive its destruction in the same manner in which it derived its origin.' See *Dialogue with Trypho* 100, in *Ante-Nicene Fathers*, ed. A. Roberts and J. Donaldson, rev. A. C. Coxe, I:249 (cf. also 45:4; 49:8; 85:1; 103:6; 125:4).

[3] See *Adversus Haereses* III.22.3-4, in *Ante-Nicene Fathers*, I:455, and for his working out of the Eve–Mary parallel, V.19.1; I:547.

ransom paid to Satan. He rightly saw the death of Christ in Johannine terms as 'the first blow in the conflict which is to overthrow the power of that evil spirit the devil, who had obtained dominion over the whole world'.[1] But, as in other areas, Origen went astray because he gave the wrong answer to profoundly difficult and important questions. Lesser theologians would give more acute answers than did Origen. In fairness to him, however, it should be said that he did seek to distinguish between the catholic faith (i.e., the orthodox teaching confessed by the whole church) and his own speculations.

The classic exposition of the 'ransom to Satan' view, and the one most easily caricatured, is to be found in Gregory of Nyssa (c.335–395), the youngest of the three Cappadocian Fathers.[2] In his *Great Catechism* he describes how Satan accepted the incarnate Christ as a ransom for the souls of men, but did so without taking account of the fact that Christ's humanity concealed his deity. Like a ravenous fish, Satan gulped down the flesh of Christ, only to discover that with that flesh he had swallowed the hook of indestructible deity by which he himself would be destroyed! Thus he was both deceived and defeated.[3]

Although the problem of the righteousness of such deception troubled even his friend Gregory Nazianzus,[4] Gregory of Nyssa rejoiced in its fittingness. After all, this was the *lex talionis* par excellence: an eye

---

[1] Origen, *Contra Celsum* 7.16, in *Ante-Nicene Fathers*, IV:617. Origen affirms that the devil was deceived by the cross. At the same time, however, Christ also was a spotless sacrifice that served as a propitiation before God. Origen thus seems to have grasped the necessity of both propitiation to deal with guilt and a redemption price to set us free from bondage, but failed to see the actual nature and logic of the inner connection between propitiation and liberation.

[2] Basil of Caesarea and his younger brother, Gregory of Nyssa, along with their friend Gregory Nazianzus.

[3] See his *Great Catechism*, chaps. 22–26 (*Ante-Nicene and Post-Nicene Fathers*, 2nd series, V:492–509). The idea of deception was by no means original to Gregory. Traces of it can be found as early as Ignatius of Antioch, *To the Ephesians*, 19.

[4] Gregory was cautious about over-extending the ransom idea to the point of identifying a recipient. The idea that it was paid to the devil he believed was 'outrageous'. 'But if the price is offered to the Father, I ask first of all, how? For it was not the Father who held us captive. ... What remains to be said shall be covered with reverent silence.' *Second Oration on Easter*, 22, in *Ante-Nicene and Post-Nicene Fathers*, 2nd series, VII:431.

for an eye! How fitting that in overcoming the one who himself had used deceit to entrap Eve in the garden of Eden, God himself proved to have more guile than even the serpent! By way of an *apologia pro Deo*, as it were, Gregory argues that just as two persons may mix poison with food for different motives—one to murder, the other as an antidote to bring healing—so, since this deception is the antidote to the fall, it is altogether righteous.

In any event, Gregory of Nyssa's case was in his own eyes somewhat ameliorated by his sharing with Origen (and Clement of Alexandria before him)[1] the expectation of a universal salvation, Satan included. The deceived deceiver would also in the end be undeceived and redeemed.

This ransom tradition recurs in Ambrose of Milan and Rufinus.[2] In it Augustine also stood,[3] albeit giving it a more sophisticated and acceptable interpretation. It endured until the time of Anselm and Abelard, but thereafter largely, although by no means entirely, disappeared.[4]

Aulén's Christus Victor

In a famous series of lectures delivered in 1930, later to be published as *Christus Victor*,[5] the Swedish Lutheran theologian Gustav Aulén (1879–1977) sought to rehabilitate the Patristic view, purged of its excesses. He argued that historical theology was in error to see either the Anselmic or the Abelardian theories, the so-called objective and subjective views, as the classical interpretations of the work of Christ. On the contrary, he argued that the 'dramatic view'—Christ's work viewed as the conquest of the powers of darkness—was the truly classical teaching. This, he maintained, was in fact the view of Martin Luther.

Aulén stated that his only interest in this question was historical and not apologetic. But it seems clear enough from the theological construction in his later systematic study *The Faith of the Christian*

---

[1] See his *Stromateis* (Miscellanies) 1.17, in *Ante-Nicene Fathers*, II:319-20.

[2] Ambrose saw the hungering of Christ in the desert as a deliberate snare set to catch the devil. For the views of Rufinus, see his *Commentary on the Apostles' Creed* 16, in *Nicene and Post-Nicene Fathers*, III:550.

[3] See, for example, *On the Trinity* 13.13-15.

[4] Interesting examples of its reluctance to die can be found in such figures as Lancelot Andrewes (1555–1626) as well as in the Puritan evangelical tradition.

[5] Gustav Aulén, *Christus Victor*, tr. A. G. Hebert (London: SPCK, 1931).

Church[1] that he operated within his own theological agenda. In arguing that Luther held to the dramatic view, he was denying that Luther's view was merely a continuation of the Anselmic view. The implication was that later orthodoxy, with its emphasis on the idea of satisfaction, was neither the view of historic Christianity nor that of the founder of Lutheranism. The net effect of Aulén's exposition, then, was to deny that penal substitution is the classical atonement doctrine of the Christian church as a whole.

In arguing thus, Aulén was surely mistaken on several counts. In particular he missed the key point in the Patristic teaching. Curiously, Charles Hodge grasped this point well, although he dismissed the teaching as such. (Indeed, Hodge confuses Gregory of Nyssa with Gregory Nazianzus in the process, a further indication of his lack of real interest in the theme.) But Hodge nevertheless recognized a key point: the Patristic view 'was intended only as a solution to the question *how Christ delivers us from the power of Satan*'.[2]

The Fathers, therefore, had asked a correct and important question, to which they gave an imperfect answer. Hodge, as I think we shall see, actually knew the right answer, but did not show sufficient interest in the question. Aulén, by contrast, for all the benefits of his drawing attention to this theme, did not well state the right question and failed to elicit the biblical answer to it.

Against this background I want to explore this important dimension of Christ's work by examining (1) the Gospel record of Christ's conflict with Satan and (2) the apostolic understanding of his victory, before drawing (3) some brief but important conclusions.

1. The Gospel record of Christ's conflict with Satan
In the Gospels, the whole of Christ's ministry is seen as a conflict with Satan. This is obviously true of the Synoptic Gospels, where the multi-dimensional conflict motif is a dominant theme.

---

[1] Gustav Aulén, *The Faith of the Christian Church*, tr. E. H. Wahlstrom (Philadelphia: Muhlenberg, 1948).
[2] Hodge, *Systematic Theology*, II:565, my emphasis.

(1) The Synoptic Gospels

All three Synoptics open their accounts of our Lord's public ministry by reference to his baptism and temptations. In his baptism he is anointed with the Spirit for Messianic ministry. Immediately he is driven out into the wilderness to be tempted by the devil.

Geerhardus Vos has rightly commented here that in interpreting Christ's temptations the mistake has frequently been made of viewing them primarily as analogous to our own.[1] But whatever exemplary lessons may be appropriately learned (and there are many), it must be emphasized that this event is *sui generis*—of a unique kind. It is deliberately set before us as a recapitulation and a rerun of the Eden temptation.

This is evident from various signals in the narrative. In Luke the baptism of Jesus as Messiah, climaxing with the words from heaven, 'You are my beloved Son' (Luke 3:22), leads to the temptation narrative by way of his genealogy. This significantly traces Jesus back to Adam, who is also seen as 'the son of God' (Luke 3:38). The setting of this *last Adam's* temptations—in the wilderness, surrounded by wild beasts (Mark 1:13), starving from forty days without nourishment—not only echoes the testing of Moses and Elijah in the wilderness, but points up the stark contrast between the conditions in which this man faces Satan and those in which the *first Adam* was confronted by him. The hiss of the tempter's 'Take, eat' is set in a context a diameter removed from Eden.

What is even more striking is the Synoptic writers' stress on the fact that Jesus, as the man full of the Spirit, was driven into the desert *by the Holy Spirit* (Luke 4:1). Temptation does not merely 'come' to him; he goes to it. He attacks it. 'He entered the lists in the name of his whole church', writes Calvin.[2] He appears as the divine champion, as it were, entering into enemy-occupied territory under the guidance of the Spirit as the director of spiritual intelligence. Miss this, and we miss the point of the narrative: it is a declaration of war, an attack on the one who claims to be the ruler of this world (Luke 4:6). Rather than overcome Jesus, Satan is comprehensively defeated, and in sovereign

---

[1] Vos, *Biblical Theology*, p. 358.
[2] Calvin, *Harmony of the Gospels*, I:135.

manner dismissed by his conqueror with the words, 'Away from me, Satan!' (Matt. 4:10 NIV).

This is Jesus' first step in binding the strong man. He is armed in order that he may systematically despoil him of his goods (Matt. 12:29) and 'undeceive' the nations (Rev. 20:3), although the final victory will not be won without continued opposition (Luke 4:13). The heel of the Seed must be crushed before the head of the serpent is (Gen. 3:15).

These three Gospels also give us hints of the reverberations Christ's victory caused in the kingdom of darkness. The fact that the wilderness conflict is soon followed in each of the Synoptics by the widespread manifestation of the presence of demons and the exorcism of them is surely significant here. This is the sign that the kingdom of God has come (Matt. 12:28; Luke 11:20). The demons know who Jesus is (Luke 4:41) and react in terror in the consciousness that he has already won a signal victory and plans to finalize it. They know, fear, and confess that he has come to destroy them (Mark 1:24; 5:7; Luke 4:34; 8:28).

This preview of Christ's final victory is probably the most coherent explanation for the extraordinary measure of demonic activity that seems to have taken place during our Lord's ministry. It is not essential for a legion of demons to indwell a man in order to destroy him. One is sufficient. But Legion experiences multiple indwelling because it is Christ and his kingdom, not simply Legion as an individual, who is the object of satanic assault (Mark 5:1-20). Yet even here we are given only fleeting glimpses of the nature of this conflict. In Luke 10:18, for example, Jesus tells his disciples who are rejoicing in the power they have exercised over the demons, that he had seen 'Satan fall like lightning from heaven'.

What is sometimes overlooked in this connection is that the Gospel narratives give us two signals which at first sight—but only at first sight—seem to be in tension with each other.

The first signal is that Satan's efforts, through various means, appear to be geared *to preventing Jesus from going to the cross*. Is it reading too much into the text to see the hand of Satan behind the infant pogrom instituted by Herod? John's words in Revelation 12:4, 'And the dragon stood before the woman who was about to give birth, so that when she bore her child he might devour it', suggest such a view. Another such effort is the wilderness temptation in which Satan seeks to divert Christ from the way of the cross as an act of obedience to his Father. Later Satan speaks again, this time through the lips of Simon Peter, seeking to divert Jesus from the path of the Suffering Servant Messiah (Mark 8:33).

The second signal paradoxically reveals Satan's activity in actually *seeking to bring the cross to pass*, but now as an act of his satanic will rather than an act of Jesus' obedience. This he does through human instrumentality, doubtless including the religious leaders, but specifically through Judas Iscariot, into whose heart, Luke tells us, Satan comes to complete his malevolent work (Luke 22:3).

In both of these aspects Satan is intent on opposing the solemn resolve of Christ to give his life as 'a ransom for many'. This in itself should have prevented the Fathers from the excesses of their 'ransom-to-Satan' theory. The truth is, the Gospels view Satan as opposing the payment of a ransom.

It is clear, then, in the Synoptic Gospels, that the whole of Jesus' ministry is one of conflict. Here two quotations from my own New Testament teachers are apposite: 'In acting as the bringer of the kingdom of God', wrote I. Howard Marshall, 'Jesus placed himself in total opposition to the kingdom of Satan. ... The task of Jesus was to dethrone "the prince of this world". ... From this point of view the whole of the ministry of Jesus was a campaign against satanic power.'[1] In a similar vein are the words of A. M. Hunter:

> The emergent picture of the chief figure in the campaign, so far from being that of a high-souled teacher patiently indoctrinating the multitudes with truths of timeless wisdom, is rather that of the strong Son of God, armed with his Father's power, spear-heading the attack against the devil and all his works, and calling men to decide on whose side of the battle they will be.[2]

What is not so fully expressed in the Synoptics, however, is an explanation of the means by which Christ overcomes Satan. To this question we will return. But we ought not to lose sight of it as we consider the conflict theme as it is traced in John's Gospel.

[1] I. H. Marshall, *The Work of Christ* (Exeter: Paternoster, 1969), p. 31.
[2] A. M. Hunter, *Introducing New Testament Theology* (London: SCM, 1945), pp. 17-18.

SOME PASTORS AND TEACHERS

(2) John's Gospel

The Gospel of John is sometimes divided into two sections or volumes: chapters 1–12, the Book of Signs; chapters 13–21, the Book of Glory.[1] Significantly the first volume ends with a focus on the conflict motif, which will be developed in volume 2: the time for 'the judgment on this world' had come. Here is a development of the Synoptics' driving back of Satan in the wilderness. Jesus now advances further, saying, 'Now will the ruler of this world be cast out' (John 12:31).

Here too, consistent with the testimony of the Synoptics, the final denouement of the conflict focuses on the activity of Judas Iscariot. In John 13:2 we are told that Satan had already put it into his heart to betray Jesus. By 13:27, Satan has entered him—a satanic indwelling, set significantly in the very context in which Jesus will speak about his indwelling of his disciples by the Spirit (John 14:20). But just as in the Synoptics our Lord regally dismissed Satan and his demons from his presence, so in the same way in John he gives the sop to Judas and sovereignly dismisses him to his task: 'What you are going to do, do quickly' (John 13:27). He is in as complete control of the situation here as he had been in the temptations. He chooses the moment when the conflict will reach its ultimate climax.

In this context C. H. Dodd's interpretation of John 14:30-31 is theologically attractive, although it does not seem to have found favour among other New Testament commentators as a solution to the puzzling setting of the words: 'The ruler of this world is coming. He has no claim on me, but I do as the Father has commanded me, so that the world may know that I love the Father. Rise, let us go from here.' As the narrative stands, the disciples do not appear to go anywhere until 18:1. 'When Jesus had spoken these words, he went out' has, as its most natural antecedent of place, the same location as the entire previous conversation (from 13:1). Dodd makes the suggestion that the words *egeiresthe agōmen* ('Rise, let us go from here') be understood in a quasi-military sense. According to Dodd, the verb *agō* is used in extra-biblical sources of marching, of advancing.[2] Interestingly, the same words occur in a conflict context in

[1] For example, by Raymond Brown, *The Gospel according to John*, I:ix-xii; II:ix-x.
[2] C. H. Dodd, *The Interpretation of the Fourth Gospel* (Cambridge: Cambridge University Press, 1953), pp. 407-9.

Mark 14:41-42: 'The Son of Man is betrayed into the hands of sinners. Rise, let us be going [*egeiresthe agōmen*]; see, my betrayer is at hand.' The picture is of Jesus advancing to meet his oncoming human enemy, not as a hapless victim but as one who has 'found new resources of arms. … He advances of his own accord to meet death', as Calvin finely says.[1] C. F. D. Moule agrees, if with less vivid expression: 'Jesus sees the situation as a great campaign—the battle of the kingdom of God. His friends are summoned to "advance" like soldiers entering battle. But it is a battle in which Jesus will not use physical force but only the weapon of loyalty to God's will.'[2]

In John, however, it is not simply Judas whom Jesus goes to meet. He goes to do battle with Satan: 'The ruler of this world is coming. … Rise! Let us advance to meet the enemy!'

We have now seen that in the Synoptics Satan suffers defeat in the wilderness, is repelled on later occasions, and finally enters into Judas (Luke 22:3). But his purposes are resisted and overcome by Jesus. No further exposition is offered to us to explain the mechanism of his defeat.

On the other hand, while omitting the wilderness temptations, John does provide such added exposition. The judgment and driving out of Satan will take place not simply by Jesus' refusal of Satan's temptations and his storming of the positions that the demons have occupied. Rather it will be specifically when the Son of Man is lifted up on the cross (John 12:31-32). It is in the event of his going to the Father *by way of a death thus interpreted* that Jesus arises and advances to meet and defeat his enemy (John 14:31).

In John that triumphant military advance begins when Judas appears with a detachment of soldiers carrying weapons (John 18:3). In response to Jesus' lordly *ego eimi*, I am! (his words echo—indeed more than echo—Exodus 3:14: Jesus is Yahweh!), the advancing forces draw back and fall to the ground (John 18:5-6). As in the last day, so now, Christ's human enemies are 'destroyed'—blown away as it were by the breath of his divine mouth (cf. 2 Thess. 2:8)! But the supernatural enemy himself must be faced in the agony of death.

[1] Calvin, *Harmony of the Gospels*, III:155-56.
[2] C. F. D. Moule, *The Gospel according to Mark*, 2nd ed., *Cambridge Bible Commentary* (Cambridge: Cambridge University Press, 1969), p. 118.

This lends special significance to the words 'It is finished' (John 19:30; cf. 17:4). Following them, in regal dignity, Christ 'bowed his head and gave up his spirit' (John 19:30). Thus, in John, Satan is driven out as the King is exalted.

John therefore advances the insight given to us in the Synoptics. By means of the complex of actions involved in his crucifixion Christ judges, condemns, and casts out Satan. But again we are forced to probe more deeply into the question: How? By what means does the death of Christ thus affect Satan?

It should now be a little clearer why it was possible for the early Fathers of the church to give a misleading answer to this question. Christ is set forth in the Gospels as one who conquers Satan. But there is little reflection on precisely how he does so. In the proclamation of the gospel the fact of Satan's downfall is of greater immediate moment than the precise mechanism by which it takes place.

But when we turn to the rest of the New Testament, we receive more specific light on this aspect of the work of Christ.

2. The apostolic understanding of Christ's victory
In the Epistles the nature of Christ's conquest of Satan is more fully explored. Here we may focus on the three key biblical statements with which we began.

(1) 1 John 3:8
John says that 'the reason the Son of God appeared was to destroy the works of the devil'. This statement is paralleled by 1 John 3:5: 'He appeared in order to take away sins, and in him there is no sin.' What lies behind these words is explained in 1 John 4:10: God 'sent his Son to be the propitiation for our sins'. Interestingly, 1 John 3:5 is also reminiscent of Jesus' statement in John 14:30 that 'the ruler of this world is coming. He has no claim on me.'

For John, then, the work of Christ has these two aspects: (i) it is a propitiatory sacrifice made by the sinless one; (ii) in addition, in that same act, the devil's work is destroyed by the one in whom he could find no foothold. The altar of propitiation of God is at one and the same time the arena of conflict against, and victory over, Satan. In essence then, for John, since it is by the cross that Satan is defeated, it is through the propitiatory character of Christ's sacrifice that this is accomplished.

(2) Hebrews 2:14-15

This hypothesis is strengthened by the teaching of Hebrews 2:14-15. Here the author underlines that it is not only by Christ's incarnation, viewed narrowly as his assuming of our flesh, but particularly and specifically by his death, that the devil, the one who has the power of death, is destroyed or disarmed.

There is an echo in these words of the principle enunciated first in Genesis 3:15—whether one sees that promise as a specific prophecy of Christ, as the Fathers did, or, as Calvin seems to have done, as a more general prophecy that is in fact consummated in Christ. The serpent[1] crushes the heel of the seed of the woman; but the seed of the woman crushes the head of the serpent. Victory is gained only through injury; it is in being crushed that Christ crushes Satan. The prince of death is defeated by means of Christ's 'defeat'. As Johann Bengel somewhere noted, 'Jesus, who suffered death, conquers; the devil, who wields death, succumbs to it.'

But how is it that Christ's death is thus the means for Satan's overthrow? The answer lies in the book of Hebrews' understanding of the nature of that death. The constant appeal of Hebrews to the sacrificial system of the Old Testament underlines that Christ's death is a sacrifice for the guilt of sin. Man is destined to die and face judgment because death implies guilt, and guilt evokes condemnation and condign punishment. This is why Christ was 'offered once to bear the sins of many' (Heb. 9:28; cf. Isa. 53:12). He has made purification for our sins (Heb. 1:3) as the sacrifice that has turned aside God's wrath, making 'propitiation for the sins of the people' (Heb. 2:17).

The death that overthrows Satan is specifically the Godward sacrificial and propitiatory death of Jesus for the guilt of his people. The result is that his blood cleanses their guilty consciences (Heb. 9:14). Believers

---

[1] It is surely significant here that it is the serpent himself, not the seed of the serpent, who crushes the heel of the seed of the woman. The antithesis at this point is not the seed of the serpent against the seed of the woman, but the serpent ('you') against the seed of the woman.

now have confidence to enter into the presence of God, by his blood (Heb. 10:19). This boldness, or confidence, in approaching God is the antithesis of the fear of death that the guilt of sin and the knowledge of judgment had engendered (Heb. 2:14-15).

For the author of Hebrews, this death not only cleanses guilty consciences but also liberates from fear because it destroys ('renders ineffectual') the one who held the power of death (Heb. 2:14-15). It must therefore be Christ's death as a propitiatory sacrifice that renders powerless the one who has brought humanity into captivity to fear.

It is the older exegetes who tend to provide serious reflection on this dual aspect of Christ's work. Here is a sample from the Puritan genius John Owen:

> When the sinner ceaseth to be obnoxious unto death, the power of Satan ceaseth also. And this every one doth that hath an interest in the death of Christ: for 'there is no condemnation unto them that are in Christ Jesus', Rom. 8:1; and this because he died. He died for their sins, took that death upon himself which was due unto them; which being conquered thereby, and their obligation thereunto ceasing, the power of Satan is therewith dissolved.
>
> (1) The first branch of his power consisted in the bringing of sin into the world. This is dissolved by Christ's 'taking away the sin of the world', John 1:29; which he did as 'the Lamb of God', by the sacrifice of himself in his death, typified by the paschal lamb and all other sacrifices of old.
>
> (2) Again, his power consisted in his rule in the world, as cast under sin and death. From this he was cast out, John 12:31, in the death of Christ. When contending with him for the continuance of his sovereignty, he was conquered, the ground whereon he stood, even the guilt of sin, being taken away from under him, and his title defeated. ...
>
> (3) Nor can he longer make use of death as penal, as threatened in the curse of the law, to terrify and affright the consciences of men: for 'being justified by faith' in the death of Christ, 'they have peace with God', Rom. 5:1; Christ making peace between God and us by the blood of his cross, Eph. 2:14-15; 2 Cor. 5:19-21; the weapons of this part of his power are wrested out of his hand, seeing

death hath no power to terrify the conscience, but as it expresseth the curse of God.

(4) And, lastly, his final execution of the sentence of death upon sinners is utterly taken out of his hand by the death of Christ, inasmuch as they for whom he died shall never undergo death penally. And thus was Satan, as to his power over death, fully destroyed by the death of Christ.[1]

(3) Colossians 2:14-15

This is confirmed in the third passage, Colossians 2:14-15. Here, forgiveness through the cross coalesces in Paul's thought with the disarming of Satan. Through the cross sins are forgiven (Col. 2:13); by his death Christ disarms Satan and triumphs over him. A similar combination of ideas is found in Colossians 1:13-14. In Christ the saints are rescued from the dominion of darkness and brought into Christ's kingdom; in Christ we have redemption through the forgiveness of sins. Thus the work of Christ which brings forgiveness effects redemptive deliverance and does so precisely because it brings forgiveness.

But how does the propitiation which effects forgiveness simultaneously effect release from Satan?

It was here that many of the Fathers took their wrong turn, assuming that if the work of Christ terminated on Satan and the ransom effected deliverance from Satan, then the ransom itself must have been paid to Satan. They did not give careful enough attention at this point to the reasons why Satan is able to exercise his tyrannical dominion over the human race, or to the biblical witness that Christ triumphed over Satan by removing the guilt and dominion of sin that made his reign possible.

Few commentators explore this aspect of the theological (in distinction from the grammatical) significance of Colossians 2:14-15. One who did in a previous generation was George Smeaton (1814–89), Professor of Exegetical Theology in New College, Edinburgh. He comments on this passage in a way that reminds one of Owen before him and, as we shall see, John Murray after him:

> How did the cross effect the results recounted in the three several clauses [that Christ disarmed the powers and authorities, made a

[1] Owen, *Comm. Hebrews*, *Works*, XIX:450ff.; numeration added for clarification.

public spectacle of them, and triumphed over them in the cross]? I answer: Sin was the ground of Satan's dominion, the sphere of his power, and the secret of his strength; and no sooner was the guilt lying on us extinguished, than his throne was undermined, as Jesus himself said (John 12:31). When the guilt of sin was abolished, Satan's dominion over God's people was ended; for the ground of his authority was the law which had been violated, and the guilt which had been incurred. This points the way to the right interpretation; for all the mistakes have arisen from not perceiving with sufficient clearness how the triumph could be celebrated on his cross. … It was on God's part at once a victory and a display of all God's attributes, to the irretrievable ruin, dismay, and confusion of satanic powers.[1]

'Paul with good reason, therefore', writes Calvin, 'magnificently proclaims the triumph that Christ obtained for himself on the cross, as if the cross, which was full of shame, had been changed into a triumphal chariot.'[2]

That it is by Christ's propitiation and expiation that Satan is conquered and people are set free is both confirmed and uniquely portrayed in the vision of John in Revelation 12. Here the evil one is named and described in the sinister multifaceted nature of his work: as the ancient serpent who has now grown into the dragon (12:3-4, 7-9) who sought to destroy the Christ, but failed; as Satan, the prosecuting counsel who accuses believers; as the devil, who hurls his fiery darts of temptation against them; and as the accuser of the brethren who fills his diary with a record of their sins in order to blackmail them (12:9-10).

Yet the brethren overcame him. How? 'By the blood of the Lamb', said the loud voice in heaven, 'and by the word of their testimony, for they loved not their lives even unto death' (Rev. 12:10-12). This is the sacrificial blood of the Lamb slain (Rev. 5:6), by which they were freed from their sins (Rev. 1:5).

Thus, through his death as it dealt with our guilt and its implications in relationship to God, Christ disarms him who had the power of death,

---

[1] George Smeaton, *The Apostles' Doctrine of the Atonement* (Edinburgh: T&T Clark, 1870), pp. 307-8.
[2] Calvin, *Institutes*, II.xvi.6.

and releases his people from their lifelong bondage to the fear of death (cf. Heb. 2:15).

This explains how those who, by Christ's blood, overcame Satan did not love their lives so much as to shrink even from death (cf. Rev. 12:11). From fear of it they had been most gloriously delivered! Here, then, the theology and the experience of the early Christians were one.

3. Implications of Christ's victory

In the light of this, we may briefly draw attention to four implications of the victory of Christ.

(1) Theology

Any adequate understanding of the atonement must include within it this aspect of Christ's disarming of the powers of darkness. It is personally gratifying in this context to be able to quote some apt words from the late Professor John Murray:

> Redemption from sin cannot be adequately conceived or formulated except as it comprehends the victory which Christ secured once for all over him who is the god of this world, the prince of the power of the air. ... It is impossible to speak in terms of redemption from the power of sin except as there comes within the range of this redemptive accomplishment the destruction of the power of darkness.[1]

A comprehensively biblical exposition of the work of Christ recognizes that the atonement, which terminates on God (in propitiation) and on man (in forgiveness), also terminates on Satan (in the destruction of his sway over believers). And it does this last precisely because it does the first two.

In this respect, Aulén's view was seriously inadequate. He displaced the motif of penal satisfaction with that of victory. But, as we have seen, in Scripture the satisfaction of divine justice, the forgiveness of our sins, and Christ's defeat of Satan are not mutually exclusive but complementary. Each is an essential dimension of Christ's work. Each is vital

---

[1] Murray, *Redemption*, p. 50.

for our salvation, and each provides an aspect of the atonement from which the other aspects may be seen with greater clarity and richness. Moreover, these aspects are interrelated at the profoundest level. For the New Testament the dramatic aspect of the atonement involves a triumph that is secured through propitiation. Aulén therefore failed to recognize that in setting the dramatic view over against the penal view of the atonement he inevitably enervated the dramatic view of its true dynamic.

(2) Doxology

Worship is theology set to music. The praises of Christ are Christology in song since we praise him for who he is and for what he has done. Praise is therefore energized and expanded by an increased vision of his accomplishments, and correspondingly limited whenever it fails to show forth the totality of his work.

The fact that Christ's death terminated on Satan and delivers us from him needs to be recovered in our spirituality and our worship. Here, *ordo salutis* concerns appear to have dominated our hymnology, to the neglect of *historia salutis*. To a degree that is true even of Luther's great hymn 'A Mighty Fortress Is Our God'. Although it does speak of 'the Right Man on our side' fighting for us, the emphasis is on the present aspect of his kingly ministry rather than on his already accomplished triumph. True, Christ exercises his kingly office on behalf of his people. But even more fundamentally, he has already fought for us in his life, death, and resurrection, and gained the victory.

The motif of Christ's conflict and victory is more often expressed in the ancient Catholic tradition, and in more modern guise in John Henry Newman's hymn 'Praise to the Holiest in the Height', theologically deficient though it may be in other respects:

> O loving wisdom of our God!
>   When all was sin and shame,
> A second Adam to the fight
>   And to the rescue came.
>
> O wisest love! that flesh and blood,
>   Which did in Adam fail,

> Should strive afresh against the foe,
> Should strive and should prevail.
>
> O generous love! that He who smote
> In man, for man, the foe,
> The double agony in Man
> For man should undergo.[1]

We surely need to rekindle this classical theme in our praises today.

(3) Ministry

The significance of Hebrews 2:14-15 for pastoral counselling can hardly be overestimated. The thesis of the author is that through the fear of death men and women are subject to lifelong bondage. Our deepest fear, the fear of death, is a mother phobia which gives birth to all the phobias of life. 'An overdose of fear', writes Calvin again, with insight, 'comes from ignorance of the grace of Christ.'[2] The angst of man, and many of the spiritual neuroses of our day, must therefore be analysed in these terms as aspects and symptoms of bondage to Satan, or as aspects of his malevolent efforts to hinder Christian believers and to rob them of their joy in Christ. The ministry of the word, and the work done confidentially in pastoral counselling, must accordingly be sensitive to this whole dimension of Christian life and warfare, and provide 'precious remedies against Satan's devices'.[3]

Christ is not offered to us in the gospel as a panacea for our fears. But he is a deliverer from that bondage to Satan which engenders the fear of death and gives rise to all manner of other fears. Pastoral counselling must always therefore have the one great fear in view, and Jesus Christ the Deliverer as the divinely appointed remedy. We need to appreciate at the deepest level the fact that the words 'fear not' were so frequently on his lips.

---

[1] From his poem 'The Dream of Gerontius', written in 1865 and later set to music by Edward Elgar for his oratorio of the same name.

[2] Calvin, *Comm. Hebrews*, p. 31 (on Heb. 2:15).

[3] The allusion is to the book of this name by the Puritan author Thomas Brooks.

(4) Missiology

There is a final implication of Christ's victory over Satan. Through the judgment of Satan and his being cast out, all men are now to be drawn to the Saviour—that is, men and women from every tribe and tongue and people and nation. In some definitive sense we can say that since Christ has finished his work, and in the light of his death, resurrection, ascension, and the gift of the Spirit, Satan is already bound and the undeceiving of the nations has begun (Rev. 20:2-3). This is implied in the wording of the Great Commission. All authority in heaven and earth is now Christ's; we are to penetrate 'all nations' with the gospel (Matt. 28:18-20). Satan has been overcome. Jesus has asked the Father for the nations as his inheritance in accordance with the promise of Psalm 2:8. He has poured out the Spirit on all flesh to bring it to pass, and now waits for his enemies to be made his footstool.

No doubt what Richard B. Gaffin Jr has, in another connection, called 'the staging principle that marks the coming of the kingdom of God'[1] is operative here also, and we must continue to pray, 'Your kingdom come … Deliver us from [the] evil [one].' But in a profound sense, surely, the kingdom has already been established. Christ has already bound the strong man armed and is even now, through the sword that issues from his mouth (that is, the word in the hands of the Spirit whom Christ has breathed out on us), spoiling his goods.

In the light of their sense of Christ's victory over Satan and the powers of darkness, the early disciples went into the world proclaiming Christ the Redeemer and Conqueror. If we share their appreciation for Christ's triumph, we will also share their passion to proclaim it. For we live in the light of this fact: Jesus has triumphed over Satan.

We too may therefore ask the questions Paul does in Romans 8:31-35. Here, significantly, in the light of the cross seen as a triumph over Satan, Paul uses the personal interrogative pronoun. Does he have Satan specifically in mind? *Who* can be against us? *Who* will bring any charge against those whom God has chosen? *Who is he* that condemns? *Who* shall separate us from the love of Christ?

---

[1] Richard B. Gaffin Jr, *Perspectives on Pentecost* (Phillipsburg, NJ: Presbyterian and Reformed, 1978), p. 40.

Satan certainly cannot; for by his death Christ disarmed him of the weapons that would otherwise enable him to do so. Christ has conquered!

No, in all these things we are more than conquerors through him who loved us. For I am sure that neither death nor life, nor angels nor rulers, nor things present nor things to come, nor powers, nor height nor depth, nor anything else in all creation, will be able to separate us from the love of God in Christ Jesus our Lord (Rom. 8:37-39).

Christus Victor indeed!

CHAPTER TWENTY-FIVE

SOLA FIDE

J USTIFICATION by grace alone (*sola gratia*) through faith alone (*sola fide*) has stood at the centre of evangelical theology ever since Martin Luther's famous insistence that the church stands or falls with this doctrine. While his younger contemporary, John Calvin, employed the concept of *faith-union* with Christ as a theological organizing principle, he too could write of justification:

> This is the main hinge on which religion turns, so that we devote the greater attention and care to it. For unless you first of all grasp what your relationship to God is, and the nature of his judgment concerning you, you have neither a foundation on which to establish your salvation, nor one on which to build piety toward God.[1]

Thus, Reformed theology has echoed Luther's judgment that justification is ours *sola fide*. Indeed, defending Luther's emphasis on the *sola*, Calvin wrote with vigour against Rome, 'Not only by a false but by an obviously ridiculous shift they insist upon excluding this adjective [i.e., *alone*].'[2]

But what does it mean that we are justified by faith alone? To unpack this, we need to reflect on both the nature of justification and the character of faith.

The nature of justification
The Westminster divines declared that justification is 'an act of God's free grace, wherein he pardoneth all our sins, and accepteth us as righteous

---

[1] Calvin, *Institutes*, III.xi.1.
[2] *Ibid.*, III.xi.19.

in his sight, only for the righteousness of Christ imputed to us, and received by faith alone.'[1]

Spelling this out more fully, justification involves both a *negative* aspect (sins not counted) and a *positive* aspect (being counted righteous by God). This righteous standing is, according to the New Testament, eschatological (i.e., it is the judgment of the Last Day brought forward into the present) and final (i.e., it will never be reversed). It becomes ours in and through Jesus Christ, whom God has made our sin, and in whom we become the righteousness of God (1 Cor. 1:30; 2 Cor. 5:21). His righteousness is imputed, or counted, to us; in his righteousness we are righteous before God. We are thus 'justified by his [God's] grace as a gift, through the redemption that is in Christ Jesus, whom God put forward as a propitiation by his blood, to be received by faith … so that he might be just and the justifier of the one who has faith in Jesus' (Rom. 3:24-26).

How does this take place? Paul explains that Jesus Christ rose again for our justification (Rom. 4:25). The resurrection vindicates or justifies Jesus Christ as one counted righteous by God. In Paul's later statement, that Christ 'was manifested in the flesh, vindicated [justified] by the Spirit, seen by angels, proclaimed among the nations, believed on in the world, taken up in glory' (1 Tim. 3:16), the resurrection is similarly viewed as a vindication or justification by the Spirit. As the last Adam, the second man, he was made sin for us, bore our guilt, sustained our punishment, and exhausted sin's power. He died to sin once for all and now is freed or justified from it (Rom. 6:10; cf. 6:7). In the resurrection, God indicated that he counted Jesus righteous—how could he right-eously do anything else?—since his Son was indeed righteous!

The implication of this for those who are 'in Christ' is as startling as it is obvious: united to Christ as our substitute-representative, we share in his justification. We too are justified, counted as righteous before God. Indeed, to put it boldly, we are as righteous before God as Jesus Christ himself is because it is in him, and with his righteousness, that we are righteous. Our righteousness is his righteousness; his righteousness is our righteousness!

To appreciate the significance of this we must explore the idea of justification a little more fully.

---

[1] *Westminster Shorter Catechism*, Q. 33.

Biblical background

In the Old Testament, central to the idea of righteousness (*tsedeq/ tsedaqah*) is its covenant orientation. God's righteousness is his complete consistency with himself in the glory of his perfect being, and is expressed in the consistency between all his acts and the covenant declarations in which he has described and pledged himself to his people. Righteousness is his absolute integrity to his own character and to the covenant in which he expresses it. This covenant context explains why his righteousness can be expressed in either condemnation or salvation.[1]

Against this background, the righteous person is one who is rightly related to God through his covenant—a covenant that implies judgment on the unfaithful, but gracious and merciful provisions for sinners who trust in God's promises. Since all are sinners (Rom. 3:20ff.), the righteous man is not someone who is morally impeccable, but someone who, through these covenant provisions, has a right standing, status, and relationship with God. This explains Luther's vivid notion that the Christian is *simul justus et peccator* (righteous and yet at the same time a sinner).

Elijah is an obvious Old Testament illustration. His fervent prayers were effectual because he was a righteous man (James 5:16, 17). Elijah was by no means sinless, but his relationship with God was grounded in the provisions of covenant grace and came to expression in his trust in God's covenant word and his obedience to his covenant commands. His praying was an expression of his faithfulness to the covenant promises and trust that God would bring to pass his covenant threats.[2]

The same was true of Abraham, who was accounted righteous by faith (Gen. 15:6; James 2:23). But James can also speak of the fulfilment of that 'justification' in the way that Abraham was '*considered righteous* [justified] for what he did when he offered his son Isaac on the altar' (James 2:21 NIV). In that act of obedience, Abraham acted in a righteous way, that

---

[1] Cf. Daniel 9, in which, within a covenant context (9:4), the righteousness of God serves as the foundation for his judgment, but also as the ground on which an appeal for mercy is made.

[2] In essence, Elijah's prayer that it would not rain was an expression of his conviction that God would keep his covenant promises and threats (e.g., Deut. 28:24), and it was a confident (faith) request that he should do so.

is, in a manner consistent with absolute trust in the covenant God and his promise (cf. Rom. 4:20-24). James' point is not that Abraham's justification was rooted in his obedience, but that the obedient act of a justified man is in fact righteous (covenantally consistent), and thus that Abraham was appropriately 'considered righteous' in doing it.

Therefore, when the Bible speaks about 'justifying', it is not the creating of sinlessness that is in view, but rather the recognizing of a right relationship in the context of the covenant. To legitimate that right relationship with *sinners*, a covering over of sin by substitutionary sacrifice was essential (cf. Rom. 3:25). By means of the sacrifice of an impeccable animal in the Mosaic economy, God pointed his covenant people forward to the reality of an impeccable incarnate sacrifice as alone adequate to bear the weight of the exchange (Heb. 9:6-14; 10:1ff.).

Justification (considering or counting righteous), then, belongs to the world of relationship to God's norm, expressed in his own character-revealing covenantal demands. This sense is most frequently illustrated in biblical usage in the context of legal relationships. Three examples will suffice to make the point:

1. The Old Testament verb *tsadaq*, used in the causative (Hiphil: *hitsdiq*), means 'to justify', and is the antithesis of 'to condemn': 'If there is a dispute between men and they come into court and the judges decide between them, acquitting [justifying] the innocent and condemning the guilty ...' (Deut. 25:1). Here only a declarative, constitutive sense of the verb is appropriate. To condemn is not to create a subjective moral condition of sin, but to constitute a relationship of guilt with respect to the norm (the law).

Similarly, Proverbs 17:15 speaks of God's hatred of justifying the guilty and condemning the innocent. If justification meant moral transformation, then Proverbs would commend, rather than condemn, such activity! To justify someone is, therefore, to constitute a person in a right relationship with respect to the norm (here, the law).

2. *Justify* carries a declarative sense in Job 32:2: 'Elihu ... burned with anger at Job because he justified himself rather than God.' The only possible sense in which God can be envisaged as being justified is in a declarative sense. God is righteous, and he ought to be declared to

be righteous. Similarly, when the tax collectors 'justify' God (KJV), that justification is declarative (Luke 7:29; similarly Psa. 51:4, cited in Rom. 3:4).

3. Scripture uses the language of justification in connection with Christ's resurrection (cf. 1 Tim. 3:16, discussed above). There was, of course, a transformation involved in Jesus' resurrection, but it was not ethical in character. Rather, the physical transformation was itself the divine indication that Christ was declared, counted, or recognized to be righteous by God—not the ground for the justification.

The connection between Christ's justification and ours underlines the significance of this statement. If Christ's justification in the resurrection is the basis for our justification in union with him, then our justification will share the same declarative quality as his.

In passing, it is worth noting here—as Calvin saw so clearly—that the role of union with Christ in our salvation safeguards the Reformation doctrine of justification from the twofold Roman Catholic criticism that the evangelical view of justification is a legal fiction and that it inevitably leads to moral indifference.[1] In fact, this was essentially the accusation levelled against Paul's gospel of justification (Rom. 3:8). But justification takes place *only through union with Christ*, and can never be abstracted from it. Apart from that union, we have no share in his justification. But in that union in which Christ is our righteousness, he is also our sanctification (1 Cor. 1:30). We cannot be united to a half-Christ!

Thus, while justification and sanctification (holiness of life) ought not to be confused with each other, they can never exist apart from each other, because both are the certain and invariable fruits of faith-union with Christ. Justification does not depend on sanctification, yet in union with Christ these are two sides of the same coin, so that to imagine one without the other would be to mutilate Christ. This was clearly Calvin's view:

> It is, indeed, true, that we are justified in Christ by the mercy of God alone, but it is equally true and certain, that all who are justified are called by the Lord to live worthy of their vocation. Let

---

[1] Calvin explains in *Institutes*, III.iii.1 the polemical context in which he expounds union with Christ and the Christian life before dealing with justification.

believers, therefore, learn to embrace him, not only for justification, but also for sanctification, since he has been given to us for both these purposes, that they may not rend him asunder by their own mutilated faith.[1]

This is really to say that faith never exists apart from repentance being concretely expressed in a life of new obedience to God.

But how is the justification of *sinners* possible and morally defensible?

Moral basis

More specifically, the question is not merely 'How *does* God justify?' but 'How *can* God be simultaneously just and the justifier of the ungodly?'

Two elements are involved here:

1. The ungodly are *forgiven*. Justification in their case requires forgiveness or pardon. It is 'an act of God's free grace, wherein he pardoneth all our sins'.[2] Paul stresses this aspect of justification when expounding Psalm 32:1-2 in Romans 4:7-8: 'Blessed are those whose lawless deeds are forgiven, and whose sins are covered; blessed is the man against whom the Lord will not count his sin.'

2. But there is necessarily more to justification than pardon. Pardon alone would produce only a *tabula rasa*, a clean slate. It would bring us back only to the same status as Adam had prior to the fall. The biblical understanding of justification involves a further step. In justification, the ungodly *are constituted eschatologically righteous*. This is the thrust of Romans 5:19, which says that 'by the one man's obedience the many will be made [i.e. constituted] righteous' (epitomizing Rom. 3:21-26). This statement grounds the confidence of Romans 8:1 that condemnation is no longer possible. For not only are we pardoned, but constituted positively, eschatologically righteous, with a righteousness that will be judgment-proof on the Last Day.

This is such a radical reversal of our natural status that we are bound to ask how God remains righteous and yet justifies the ungodly, how he can be 'just' and 'forgive' (1 John 1:9). The answer, of course, is rooted in the work of the Christ to whom we are united. We are justified through the redemption that is in Christ Jesus (Rom. 3:24).

---

[1] Calvin, *Comm. Romans*, p. 167.
[2] *Westminster Shorter Catechism*, Q. 33.

The work of Jesus Christ

In Paul's teaching, the heart of the matter is located in Christ's role as the second man and the last Adam (Rom. 5:12-21; 1 Cor. 15:45-49). He is an *Adam* because he was made like us in every respect, apart from sin, and is also the head of a new humanity. He is *second* because no man between Adam and Christ entered the world without sin. He is second also to remind us that he entered a fallen world, not the pristine world of the first Adam (Rom. 5:16). He is *last* (*eschatos*) because there is not, and need not be, any like him who follows after him, since he reverses what Adam did in his sin and also accomplishes for us what Adam failed to do.

What did the last Adam do? He became one with us in our flesh in order to provide a righteousness in and for our humanity by (1) obeying the law of God perfectly and (2) offering himself as an atonement, life for life, death for death, substituting himself for us under the curse of God (Gal. 3:13). He kept the law on our behalf and paid the penalty for our breach of it. And—here is the genius and importance of union with Christ—since he united himself to us, what is ours by nature became his by assumption, and since by the Spirit we are united to him, what he accomplished in the incarnation becomes ours by faith. His lifelong obedience, his sacrifice, and his 'justification' are ours through what the Reformers called 'the wonderful exchange' (*mirifica commutatio*).

The Gospel narratives make clear that Christ was condemned and died as the innocent substitute for sinners. Over and over again in the Passion narrative, he was declared innocent (cf. Luke 23:4, 14, 15, 22, 40, 41, 47). Yet he was condemned as though guilty of the twin crimes of treason against lawfully constituted authority and blasphemy against the name of God—precisely the crimes of which Adam was guilty in Eden, and of which we are guilty before God. He died in our place:

- *He* was wounded—for transgressions that were *ours*.

- *He* was crushed—for iniquities that were *ours*.

- *He* was chastised—to deal with 'dis-peace' that was *ours*.

- *He* was wounded—to heal the disease that was *ours* (cf. Isa. 53:5).

- *He* who knew no sin was made to be *sin*, so that

493

- *We* who know sin might be made *righteous* in him (cf. 2 Cor. 5:21).

Or, in specifically covenantal language:

- *Christ* became a *curse for sinners.*
- *Sinners* become *blessed* in *Christ* (cf. Gal. 3:13).

So Christ grounds our pardon by bearing our guilt and punishment; he grounds our positive righteousness by providing his own perfect obedience. Consequently, justification not only deals with past guilt, but also secures a complete, eschatological righteousness for us before God.

The character of faith

Reconciliation has been accomplished in Christ. Yet, as Calvin notes, 'as long as Christ remains outside of us, and we are separated from him, all that he has suffered and done for the salvation of the human race remains useless and of no value for us'.[1] Hence, we find in Scripture an invariable relationship between what Christ has done and how we actively appropriate it. Again Calvin says, 'We obtain this by faith.'[2]

The New Testament expresses this relationship between justification and faith in various ways. We are said to be justified 'through faith' (*dia pisteōs*) (Rom. 3:22), 'by faith' (*ek pisteōs*) (Rom. 3:30), and 'by faith' (*pistei*) (Rom. 3:28). But we are never said to be justified 'on account of faith' (*dia ten pistin*), that is, on the basis of faith itself as the ground of justification. Faith is, in the technical terminology of the theologians, the *instrumental* cause, not the *material* cause of justification. Thus, according to the *Westminster Confession*, 'Faith, thus receiving and resting on Christ and his righteousness, is the alone instrument of justification.'[3]

Paul powerfully underlines this in Romans 4:1ff., where he demonstrates that Abraham's justification came not through works (4:1-8), nor by the instrument of sacramental administration (4:9-12), nor by performance of the law (4:13-15), but by faith. He trusted in the God who promised him a seed that would be a blessing to the nations (Gen.

---

[1] Calvin, *Institutes*, III.i.1.
[2] *Ibid.*
[3] *Westminster Confession of Faith*, XI.2.

12:2-3). Again, as Christ is the proper object of our faith, so Christ (as the promised seed) was the resting place of his trust and commitment.

But this raises an important question. Why should faith be the appropriating instrument in justification? At one level, the answer is that since our justification is in Christ, it can be ours only through a personal fellowship with him; and faith introduces us to such fellowship, since we believe 'into' (*eis*) Christ and are thus united to him.

But at another level, the answer is that faith is the appropriate instrument of justification because in its very nature faith is *active* in receiving Christ, but *non-contributory* (in that sense 'passive' or, perhaps better, 'receptive') in relation to the justification we receive. It has no constructive energy; it is complete reliance on another. It is Christ-directed, not self-directed, and Christ-reliant, not self-reliant. It involves the abandoning, not the congratulating, of self.

Consequently, as Paul notes in Romans 3:27, boasting 'is excluded'. His answer to the question 'By what kind of law?' is illuminating. It is not by the law (or the principle) of works. That is true because we do not live up to the demands of the law. But it is true at another level also. The law or the principle of works theoretically leaves room for human achievement, and therefore for boasting. But, Paul says, boasting is excluded '*by the law of faith*'. Why? By definition, faith excludes even the possibility of boasting. 'That is why it depends on faith, in order that the promise [of justification] may rest on grace' (Rom. 4:16). 'By faith' actually implies 'by grace', because of the very nature of faith as a receptor rather than a contributor. *Faith* draws everything from Christ and contributes nothing to him. Faith is simply a shorthand description of abandoning oneself trustingly to Christ, whom God has made our righteousness. Therefore, says Paul, 'Let the one who boasts, boast in the Lord' (1 Cor. 1:31).

Faith thus takes its character and power from its object, not from itself.

These were the biblical considerations that lay behind the Reformation's doctrine of faith, and which enabled the Reformers to pinpoint with new clarity just exactly what was involved in faith in Christ.

The Reformation doctrine of faith

The Reformers' doctrine of faith was worked out against the specific background of the medieval order of salvation. The Roman teaching operated with two important distinctions in relation to faith:

1. A distinction between *fides implicita* and *fides explicita*. The former was 'implicit faith' in the teaching given by the Church, on the basis of the teaching office of the Church.

2. But the medieval theologians and the Church of Rome developed a further distinction, between *fides informis* and *fides formata* (*caritate*), i.e., 'unformed faith' and 'formed faith', or faith that is formed by and issued in love. Unformed faith could be evoked by a fear of divine justice that drove the individual to hope in Christ and to that initial love expressed in contrition. If this contrition was suffused with perfect love and desire for the sacrament, then justification took place. But if that sorrow (*contritio*) was imperfect (i.e., *attritio*), then justification could be attained only through the sacrament of penance, with its climax in absolution. In the earlier institution of penance, satisfaction for sin preceded absolution. In the later sacrament of penance, satisfaction followed absolution and had to do with the mitigation of temporal penalties.

It is not difficult to see what deeply disturbed the Reformers about this teaching. Justification became the goal to which the individual moved, not the foundation on which the whole Christian life was lived. Justification belonged to the 'not yet', whereas in the gospel it belongs to the 'already' of the Christian's life.

It was also at root semi-Pelagian. It was said that we are saved by grace; in fact, Roman theology spoke much about 'grace'. But that grace was so intimately related to our own works of sanctification that its nature was distorted and its true role was obscured. This, in turn, affected the role of faith and the significance of Christ.[1] Hence, the *sola* watchwords we use about the Reformation are intended to spell out the sheer graciousness and unmerited character of grace: *sola fide, sola gratia, sola Scriptura*, and *solus Christus* all related to this teaching.

When we understand this background, we realize that while Rome always taught that salvation was never *without* grace, it denied that it

[1] The statements of the Council of Trent on justification exemplify this perspective. See Schaff, *Creeds of Christendom*, II:89-118.

496

was by grace *alone* and faith *alone*. It thus essentially dis-graced grace. Against that background, it is not difficult to understand the sheer joy of the Reformation's rediscovery of the biblical teaching on faith alone. For the Reformers, faith has three dimensions: *notitia* (or *cognitio*), *assensus*, and *fiducia*. It involves knowledge of God's revelation in general and specifically of his revelation in Jesus Christ.[1] It includes assent to biblical revelation (*sola Scriptura*). And such assent is based on and compelled by the truth of the gospel. It is 'forced' upon us, irresistibly, by the truth of the gospel. As John Murray writes,

> Faith is *forced* consent. That is to say, when evidence is judged by the mind to be sufficient, the state of mind we call 'faith' is the inevitable precipitate. It is not something we can resist or in respect of which we may suspend judgment. In such a case faith is compelled. It is demanded, it is commanded. For whenever the reasons are apprehended or judged sufficient, will we, nill we, faith or belief is induced. Will to the contrary, desire to the contrary, overwhelming interest to the contrary, cannot make us believe the opposite of our judgment with respect to the evidence.[2]

But, supremely, faith is *fiducia* personal trust in Christ, without the mediation of priest and sacrament (*solus Christus*). The believing man trusts directly in Christ. Faith is thus 'a heart trust which the Holy Ghost works in me by the gospel'.[3] Consequently, for the Reformers, faith implies a joyful assurance of salvation in Christ, a 'sure and certain knowledge of God's benevolence towards us',[4] as Calvin put it. The believer is not left in darkness, doubt, and anxiety about his salvation.

Such an exposition of faith emphasizes in biblical fashion the human responsibility involved in believing and at the same time completely preserves the grace of God in the way of salvation. *Cognitio* arises out of the grace of revelation, *assensus* is evoked by the authority of the gospel, and *fiducia* arises, not because of anything in us, but only because of the utter trustworthiness of our Saviour Jesus Christ!

---

[1] This point has been made by theologians as diverse as Calvin (*Institutes*, III.ii.7) and R. Bultmann (*Theological Dictionary of the New Testament*, Kittel & Friedrich eds, VI:227).

[2] Murray, *Collected Writings*, II:237.

[3] *Heidelberg Catechism*, Q. 21.

[4] Calvin, *Institutes*, III.ii.7.

Justifying faith

By way of summary, several things should be emphasized about justifying faith:

1. *Faith contributes no merit.* It is the nature of faith, indeed its very genius, that by it we actively receive justification in Christ without contributing to it. After all, faith is trust in another. It is the antithesis of all self-contribution or self-trust. The promise of salvation is made to faith. Why? So that it might be by grace and be guaranteed to believers (Rom. 4:16). Faith engages grace without meriting it in any way. B. B. Warfield puts it this way:

> The *saving power* of faith resides thus not in itself, but in the Almighty Saviour on whom it rests. ... It is not faith that saves, but faith in Jesus Christ. ... It is not, strictly speaking, even faith in Christ that saves, but Christ that saves through faith. The saving power resides exclusively, not in the act of faith or the attitude of faith or the nature of faith, but in the object of faith. ... We could not more radically misconceive it than by transferring to faith even the smallest fraction of that saving energy which is attributed in the Scriptures wholly to Christ himself.[1]

We are saved by Christ as we believe. There is total engagement of the believer, yet at the same time grace is not compromised.

2. *Faith is a gift of God.* Philippians 1:29 provides an important perspective here: 'For it has been granted to you that for the sake of Christ you should not only believe in him but also suffer for his sake.' Suffering is a gift of grace in Christian experience. So is faith.

This parallel between faith and suffering helps to safeguard us from a misunderstanding of faith as a gift. The gift of suffering is not a commodity we receive as a *fait accompli.* We suffer in the sovereign purposes of God. But it is *we*—not God—who experience the suffering. In the same way, in his grace God gives us faith, but it is exercised by us, not by him. We—not God—are the ones who believe!

Thus, even if the classic text of Ephesians 2:8—'For by grace you have been saved through faith. And this is not your own doing; it is the gift of

---

[1] B. B. Warfield, 'Faith', *Biblical Doctrines, Works,* II:504.

God'—may carry a broader interpretation,[1] Paul confirms that faith is a divine gift later in Ephesians 6:23 when he prays for 'faith, from God the Father and the Lord Jesus Christ'. Whatever comes from God is given in grace. Yet, as Otto Weber well puts it, 'Faith, according to the biblical understanding does not consist of man's being set aside, but of his being involved to the uttermost.'[2]

3. *Faith is capable of 'degrees'.* The New Testament speaks of faith in various ways: little faith (Matt. 14:31), great faith (Matt. 15:28), sincere faith (2 Tim. 1:5), and strong faith (Rom. 4:20). Yet the least faith saves, and ultimately also overcomes (1 John 5:4), because it gives us a great Saviour.

These different 'degrees' of faith have in view the extent to which we respond to God in a manner commensurate with the greatness and trustworthiness of his promise. Weak faith focuses on immediate circumstances; by contrast, great or strong faith is trust that responds in a way consistent with the greatness of its object. Thus, Abraham grew strong in faith as he refused to allow himself to be influenced by the circumstances of Sarah's barrenness and his own age, and instead allowed his faith to be determined by the promise of God, and gave glory to him (Rom. 4:20).

Faith and good works
Salvation, including justification, Paul argues, is by faith, not by works. Yet at first sight there is a paradox here. For the New Testament indicates that we will be judged according to our works: 'For we must all appear before the judgment seat of Christ, so that each one may receive what is due for what he has done in the body, whether good or evil' (2 Cor. 5:10). The works of teachers of the gospel are tested by fire (1 Cor. 3:12-13). Other statements, such as Ephesians 6:8 ('whatever good anyone does, this he will receive back from the Lord'), Colossians 3:24-25 ('from the Lord you will receive the inheritance as your reward. ... For the wrongdoer will be paid back for the wrong he has done, and there is no partiality'), and 1 Peter 1:17 (God 'judges impartially according to each

[1] Since 'this' (*touto*) is neuter, grammar alone cannot determine the antecedent to which reference is made (grace, faith, and salvation are all grammatically feminine).
[2] Otto Weber, *Foundations of Dogmatics*, tr. D. L. Guder (Grand Rapids: Eerdmans, 1981–83), II:261.

one's deeds'), further emphasize the importance of works with respect to divine judgment on our lives.

The clue to interpreting these statements is well expressed by Philip Edgcumbe Hughes:

> It is important to see that the purpose of this tribunal is not positively penal, but properly retributive, involving the disclosure not only of what has been worthless, but also of what has been good and valuable in this life. The judgment pronounced is not a declaration of doom, but *an assessment of worth*, with the assignment of rewards to those who because of their faithfulness deserve them.[1]

The point is that the reality of future judgment according to works in no sense compromises the finality of present justification by faith, to which works make no contribution, but of which they are rather its fruit.

James: a letter of straw?

But when we turn to James 2:14-26, the question arises whether the New Testament's teaching is quite so straightforward. That issue is most pointedly raised by the stark nature of James' conclusion: 'You see that a person is justified by works and not by faith alone' (James 2:24). Is it any wonder that the Luther of *sola fide* thought of the letter of James as an epistle of straw?

It may help here if we notice two things:

(1) The contrast expounded by James

Part of the complexity of James' argument derives from the fact that he is contrasting two different persons, both of whom profess to be genuine believers. We may call them 'Faith A' and 'Faith B'. Each believes his faith is authentic. Hence, James speaks of both as having 'faith'. But he will eventually demonstrate that Faith A is not really saving faith; indeed, it is therefore not 'faith' at all.

---

[1] Philip Edgcumbe Hughes, *Paul's Second Epistle to the Corinthians*, NICNT (Grand Rapids: Eerdmans, 1962), pp. 182-83 (emphasis original).

Faith A is:

> Faith without deeds (verses 14, 18, 20, 26)
>
> Faith in contrast to deeds (verse 18)
>
> Faith in itself, i.e., unaccompanied by action (verse 17)
>
> Faith alone, i.e., isolated from deeds (verse 24)

Faith B is:

> Faith shown by what it does (verse 18)
>
> Faith accompanied by actions (verse 22)
>
> Faith consummated by actions (verse 23)

James asks whether the former, Faith A, can save (verse 14). His logic and grammar anticipate a negative answer.[1]

On what basis does he reach this conclusion? Saving faith always expresses itself in good works. Unless professed faith is working faith, it is not saving faith and therefore cannot be true faith. To borrow Paul's language, true faith, saving faith, always works by love (cf. Gal. 5:6). But Faith A does not work!

James' teaching has often been seen as a potential embarrassment to Paul's gospel, and consequently harmonization has often driven its interpretation. But the proper interpretation of James' words should not be formulated along a Paul–James axis, for example, by suggesting that James is using either or both of the terms *faith* and *justify* in different senses from Paul. Paul is not his conversation partner here; moral indifference is.

In fact, James himself is using *faith* in two quite different senses. He is also teaching that the faith by which a person is considered righteous (James 2:23) will always be expressed by that person acting in a righteous manner. He or she is therefore quite properly considered to be righteous.

(2) The conclusion drawn by James

When James draws his conclusion—'You see that a person is justified by works and not by faith alone' (verse 24)—his logic is shaped by the

---

[1] His words *mē dunatai hē pistis sōsai auton* mean 'Surely his faith cannot save him.'

Abraham narrative. Earlier (in verse 23), James has cited Genesis 15:6, which rests justification instrumentally in faith, having already stated that Abraham was 'justified by works when he offered up his son Isaac on the altar' (2:21). These two statements he sees as complementary, not contradictory. Abraham was justified by faith and was also 'justified' (in the sense of being considered righteous, i.e., rightly related to God in his covenant) for what he did. He was thus later counted righteous because, already accounted righteous by faith, he acted in a righteous way and could thus be accounted righteous. The fruit of justification is always righteousness of life.

James' teaching here in essence is that the man who is righteous by faith will be recognized and therefore counted as righteous through his deeds, just as Abraham was.

The key, then, is verse 18: what a man does is the touchstone of faith. So, true faith, which alone justifies, is expressed by what a man does, not by what he presumes. The man who lives faithfully is the justified man (although he is not justified by living faithfully). Deedless faith cannot save, not because works are the ground of justification, but because the lack of works is an evidence of the absence of real faith.

James' basic logic is that the faith alone by which we are justified is not an abstraction. It unites us to Christ as our righteousness and simultaneously as our sanctification. Expressed otherwise, James teaches that if he who professes faith is not also one whose faith expresses itself in practical works, then he does not believe with a faith that receives justification, and therefore does not believe truly. The one who genuinely believes is united to Christ, in the power of his new life, and such a one is also sanctified in Christ and works for his glory. As John Murray puts it, 'Faith alone justifies but a justified person with faith alone would be a monstrosity which never exists in the kingdom of grace.'[1] Or, as Calvin says,

> We confess with Paul that no other faith justifies but faith working through love. But it does not take its power to justify from that working of love. Indeed it justifies in no other way but in that it leads us into fellowship with the righteousness of Christ.[2]

[1] Murray, *Redemption*, p. 131.
[2] Calvin, *Institutes*, III.ii.20.

This is also what the *Westminster Confession* is at pains to emphasize:

> Faith ... is the alone instrument of justification: yet is it not alone in the person justified, but is ever accompanied with all other saving graces, and is no dead faith, but worketh by love.[1]

Thus wrote Luther in 1522:

> O, when it comes to faith, what a living, creative, active, powerful thing it is. It cannot do other than good at all times ... A man not active in this way is a man without faith ... It is impossible, indeed, to separate works from faith, just as it is impossible to separate heat and light from fire.[2]

That is why faith alone, *sola fide*, is never lonely!

---

[1] *Westminster Confession of Faith*, XI.2.

[2] Martin Luther, Preface to Romans, 1522; *Martin Luther, Selections from His Writings*, ed. *with an introduction by John Dillenberger* (New York: Doubleday, 1962), p. 24.

CHAPTER TWENTY-SIX

ASSURANCE JUSTIFIED[1]

If you have assurance, be careful you do not lose it; keep it, for it is your life. ... Keep assurance. First, by prayer, Psa. 36:10, 'O continue thy lovingkindness.' Lord, continue assurance; do not take away this privy seal from me. Secondly, keep assurance by humility. Pride estrangeth God from the soul; when you are high in assurance, be low in humility. St Paul had assurance, and he baptizeth himself with this name, 'chief of sinners', 1 Tim. 1:15. The jewel of assurance is best kept in the cabinet of an humble heart.

—Thomas Watson, *A Body of Practical Divinity*

I F, as is sometimes said, Paul's letter to the Romans represents the Himalayas of his writings, then Romans 8 is Mount Everest. Standing on its summit, Paul surveys an entire panorama of God's grace. His mind and spirit are raised in triumph. The gospel has placed him on top of the world, in a spiritual sense: 'Those whom [God] called he also justified, and those whom he justified he also glorified. ... Who shall bring any charge against God's elect? It is God who justifies. Who is to condemn? Christ Jesus is the one who died—more than that, who was raised—who is at the right hand of God, who indeed is interceding for us' (8:30, 33-34). Nothing 'will be able to separate us from the love of God in Christ Jesus our Lord' (8:39).

Fundamental to this sense of exaltation is Paul's conviction that the present reality of justification guarantees its future consummation in final salvation. That, Paul says, remains true despite all opposition and

---

[1] Pages 505-14 summarize the ground covered in the previous chapter.

in the face of the menacing powers that are hell-bent on the Christian's destruction. In the last analysis, he argues, nothing can be against us if God is for us (8:31).

However, God's being for us does not carry the simple implications we might naturally prefer. The divine logic is clear enough. Who could ever withstand God? Our problem is the way in which the divine logic expresses itself in our experience—not by removing all opposition to us but by overcoming all obstacles. Paul does not make the mistake of thinking that justification ends all opposition (on the contrary, in one sense it increases it!). Rather his point is that justification stands and lasts no matter what the opposition. To appreciate the significance of this we must explore the idea of justification a little more fully.

Justification—counted righteous

In biblical language, to be justified is to be accounted righteous by God. Scholars have long recognized that in Scripture the idea of righteousness is related to God's covenant with his people. God's personal righteousness is seen in there being an integrity between who he is, what he has promised to be, and what he actually does. As we relate to God, his righteousness comes to expression in either covenant blessing or covenant judgment (cursing).

Against this background, for someone to be righteous means that he or she is rightly related to God through his covenant. The righteous people in Scripture are not, therefore, morally perfect, but those who trust in the God of the covenant, seek to live in the light of it, and therefore—not least because of the provisions made for pardon, restoration, and new life in the covenant—enjoy a right standing, a right status before God.

Elijah is an interesting illustration of this. He was a 'righteous' person (James 5:16). He was not perfect; but he trusted in Yahweh, and in faith his life was aligned with Yahweh's covenant word. He demonstrated that he was righteous (i.e., rightly related to God) by his confidence that God would keep his covenant threats to shut up the heavens and make them like brass and the earth like iron (Deut. 28:23). Elijah's right standing before the Lord gave rise to right living in his power. The latter was an expression of the former. In the Old Testament, to be righteous, then, is to be counted in a right relationship with God by faith through his covenant, so that the life we live in an unrighteous world is an expression of this faith relationship.

Thus the Old Testament's understanding of the verb 'justify' is to account someone to have a right relationship with respect to the law and thus to God himself. In the nature of the case, justification involves both a legal standing and a personal relationship. Living righteously flows from this, never the other way around. Therefore, the use of 'justify' is a statement about a person's status; it is not a statement about the change of a person's inner condition and disposition. Despite the form of the word in English (from Latin *iustus* ['righteous'] and *facere* ['to make']), in the Bible the verb 'justify' means 'to count righteous' not 'to make inwardly righteous'.

This becomes clear when we see that the antithesis of 'justify' is 'condemn', which also refers to a status. Deuteronomy 25:1 illustrates this: 'If there is a dispute between men and they come into court and the judges decide between them, acquitting [justifying or declaring righteous] the innocent and condemning [declaring guilty] the guilty …' Here, clearly, a declarative sense alone is appropriate. To condemn does not involve the creation of a subjective, moral condition, but the accounting of a status (Prov. 17:15; Luke 7:29).[1]

---

[1] There is today a considerable debate, which began in scholarly circles but has since spread, over the question of the precise significance of 'justify'. A number of scholars argue that the justified are simply those who belong to the covenant community. In other words, justification language refers not to how we 'get into' fellowship with God but rather describes those who 'are in' such fellowship. It therefore belongs to the doctrine of the church (ecclesiology), not to the doctrine of how we become Christians (soteriology). The problem that ought to be obvious with this perspective is that it confuses the description of a valid consequence with the explanation of its cause. To say that 'to be justified' means 'to belong to the community' sheds no more light on the exact meaning of the term than, for example, to say that 'to be adopted or reconciled or regenerated' means 'to belong to the community'. Unless these terms have no specific denotation, each one refers to how this comes about. They are not amorphous metaphors all denoting the same thing. While they all refer to the reality of our coming into fellowship with God and his people, they each nuance a different aspect of how this takes place and what the result is. The older understanding rightly safeguarded this nuance.

Perhaps the most arresting use of this language in Scripture is its use in connection with Christ's resurrection (1 Tim. 3:16). This was a divine speech-act in which God was reversing the verdict of the human court that had cried 'guilty ... crucify'. The Father was saying, 'righteous ... resurrect!' He thus reversed the false verdict of humanity on his Son, our substitute.

Justification—Christ's and ours

There is in fact a very close connection between Christ's resurrection-justification and ours (Rom. 4:25). This gives us a further clue as to how justification underpins assurance. If Christ's justification in resurrection is the basis for our justification in union with him, then our justification will share the same declarative quality. Unlike him, however, our justification does not take place simultaneously with our final resurrection. We might say that in our Lord's case, his 'justification' was written all over him in his resurrection. In our case, our real and final justification is hidden from the eyes of the world; it is only partially revealed in our Christian lives. But one day it will be fully manifested in the final resurrection.

When we grasp that our justification is intimately related to that of Jesus, we come to understand something vital about its nature. His justification was once-and-for-all. Being raised from the dead he will never die again. God's verdict on Jesus will be neither reversed nor repeated. It is his last word on the matter. But precisely because we are justified in him—that is, in his justification—our justification is also final and irreversible. Indeed we can be so bold as to say that we are as *fully* justified before God as our Lord Jesus is. We are as *finally* justified as our Lord Jesus is. We are as *irreversibly* justified as our Lord Jesus is. The only justification we have—our only righteousness—is that of the Lord Jesus. We are justified with his justification.

In more technical language we can say that in justification the ungodly are constituted *eschatologically* righteous. That is to say, our righteousness is a complete and final righteousness that endures for all eternity. This evokes the confidence of Romans 8:1 that no condemnation is possible for us; not only are we pardoned, in a neutral position, but Christ's whole righteousness wrought out in his obedience to death *and* his Last-Day vindication in his resurrection have been counted to us. Thus, we are constituted righteous (Rom. 5:19). We are justified by the redemption that is *in him* (Rom. 4:24).

In Paul's teaching, the heart of the matter is located in Christ's role as the second man and the last Adam (Rom. 5:18-21; 1 Cor. 15:45-49). Christ is 'Adam' because he was made like us in every respect, yet without sin. He is 'second' because there is none between Adam and Christ who enters the world without sin. But he is also second in the sense that he came not to the garden in which Adam was placed, but to the wasteland that Adam left behind. He is 'last' because no other Adam is needed. He perfectly accomplished what Adam failed to do, and he reversed what Adam brought about as the consequence of his sin.

But what exactly did this second man and last Adam do? He became one with us in our flesh in order to provide a righteousness in and for our humanity by his perfect obedience to the law of God and by his offering himself as an atonement, life for life, substituting himself for us under the curse of God (Gal. 3:13). He both kept the law on our behalf and paid the penalty for our breach of it. Since we are united to him (and here is the genius and importance of union with Christ), what is ours by nature became his by assumption, so that what was accomplished by him throughout the whole course of his incarnation might become ours by union. His lifelong obedience, his sacrifice, his resurrection—that is, his righteous life, his substitutionary condemnation, and then his justi-fication—all are ours through what the Reformers called 'the wonderful exchange' (*mirifica commutatio*) he makes with us.

He was pierced for transgressions that were ours. He was crushed for iniquities that were ours. He was punished to deal with 'dis-peace' that was ours. He was wounded to heal the disease that was ours (Isa. 53:3). He who knew no sin was made to be sin, so that we who know sin might be made righteous in him (2 Cor. 5:21).

Or in covenant-specific language: Christ became a curse for sinners. We become blessed in Christ (Gal. 3:13). He 'sealed my pardon with his blood'[1] by bearing our guilt and punishment. He grounds our final

---

[1] From the hymn 'Man of Sorows, What a Name!' by Philip Bliss.

righteousness before God by his own perfect obedience. Consequently, justification not only deals with past guilt, but also secures for us a complete and final (or eschatological, to use the technical term) righteousness before God. This is what it means to be justified by faith.

Justification by faith alone

In a daring passage in his *Institutes of the Christian Religion*, John Calvin reminds us: 'as long as Christ remains outside of us, and we are separated from him, all that he has suffered and done for the salvation of the human race remains useless and of no value for us'.[1] Consequently we find in Scripture an invariable relationship between what Christ has done and how we actively appropriate it. Calvin says: 'We obtain this by faith.'[2]

The New Testament expresses this central role of faith in various ways: We are justified *through* faith (*dia pisteōs*, Rom. 3:22) and *by* faith (*ek pisteōs* or *pistei*, 3:28, 30-31). But justification is never said to be *on account of* faith (*dia tēn pistin*). Faith is never the ground or foundation for justification. Faith is always and only the recipient (the instrumental cause, to employ the older language of Calvin and others). Thus, according to the *Westminster Confession of Faith*: 'Faith, thus receiving and resting on Christ and his righteousness, is the alone instrument of justification' (XI.2).

Paul stresses this point in Romans 4, in which he demonstrates in the case of Abraham that justification came not through works (4:1-8), or by the instrument of sacramental administration (4:9-12), or by keeping the law (4:13-15). Then, as now, justification is by way of faith. The important point is that the object of faith is always the covenant promise (in the Old Testament) or its fulfilment, Christ (in the New Testament), and not justification itself.

Why is faith the appropriate instrument in justification? At one level, the answer is that, since justification is in Christ, it can be ours only through personal fellowship with Christ. Faith involves such fellowship since it unites us to Christ. At another level, the answer is that, while faith is actively engaged in receiving Christ, it is in its nature receptive,

[1] Calvin, *Institutes*, III.i.i.
[2] *Ibid.*

non-contributory in relation to salvation. It has no constructive energy of its own. It is complete reliance on another. Faith is Christ-directed, not self-directed; it is Christ-reliant, not self-reliant; it involves self-abandonment, not self-congratulation.

Consequently, as Paul reasons in Romans 3:27: 'Boasting ... is excluded.' He asks: 'By what kind of law' does this exclusion take place? His answer is thought-provoking. It is not excluded by the principle of works. In fact, the principle of works leaves open the possibility of boasting, because the works principle always leaves room for human achievement, at least in theory. Rather, boasting for Paul is excluded on the principle of faith. Why? Because by definition faith excludes the possibility of boasting.

Thus Paul is able to say that 'the promise [of justification] comes by faith, so that it may be by grace' (4:16 NIV). To say 'by faith' implies 'by grace' because of the very nature of faith, for faith draws everything from Christ, and it contributes nothing to him. Faith is simply a shorthand description of those who abandon themselves unreservedly to Christ, whom God has made our righteousness. Therefore, says Paul, 'let the one who boasts, boast in the Lord' (1 Cor. 1:31).

Justification and sanctification

Salvation, including justification, Paul argues is by faith, not by works. Yet, at least at first sight there is a paradox here, if not a problem. It involves the charge that has often been levelled against the Reformation's doctrines of *sola gratia* (by grace alone) and *sola fide* (by faith alone). The accusation is that the justification of sinners by faith alone is a legal fiction and that it leads inevitably to antinomianism.

How are we to respond to this? The groundwork we have established points us in the right direction—the direction that Reformed theology has consistently taken:

1. Justification takes place only in union with Christ and can never be abstracted from that union.

2. In this union in which we are justified, Christ who becomes our righteousness also becomes our holiness or sanctification (1 Cor. 1:30).

3. While justification and sanctification must never be confused, they never actually exist apart from each other. Both are ours in our

faith-union with Christ. We believe into union with Christ.

While justification does not depend on sanctification, it is always coexistent with it. Both become ours immediately and simultaneously through faith in Christ. Since justification is God's Last-Day verdict about us, it is complete and final. It has been marvellously brought forward for us to enjoy in the present day.

On the other hand, holiness in Christ is his present-day work within us, and because it is progressive it will not be completed until the Last Day. The two realities belong to different dimensions: but are united together in Christ. To believe that we could receive justification but not be inaugurated into the process of sanctification would be to imagine that the person and work of the Saviour could be divided into a series of electives from which we can choose. But, as Calvin regularly said, to divide the work of Christ for our justification and sanctification would be to

> rend Christ asunder. ... Let believers, therefore, learn to embrace him, not only for justification, but also for sanctification, as he has been given to us for both these purposes, that they may not rend him asunder by their own mutilated faith.[1]

True faith

Two important passages in the New Testament can help us understand this point.

1. The first passage is James 2. The question arises here whether the New Testament's teaching is either so consistent or so straightforward as we suggest. James appears to stress the importance of works in our salvation. Indeed he says that we are not justified 'by faith alone' (2:24).

But the sharp words of James simply confirm the point we are making: true faith unites us to Christ and therefore does not exist without its fruit in good works; the justified individual is the being-sanctified individual. For James uses the idea of 'faith' to describe two different professing believers, but makes clear that the faith of one does not— indeed cannot—save, for the simple reason that it is not genuine faith. Essentially, James is asking questions about the nature of saving faith. In

[1] Calvin, *Comm. Romans*, p. 167.

order to understand his teaching properly, it may help to outline the two types of faith he is speaking about. Faith A is defined by James as follows:

- faith without deeds (2:14, 18, 20, 26)

- faith in contrast to deeds (2:18)

- faith in itself (i.e., unaccompanied by action; 2:17)

- faith alone (i.e., isolated from deeds; 2:24)

This faith is distinct from Faith B, which is defined as follows:

- faith shown by what it does (2:18)

- faith accompanied by actions (2:22)

- faith consummated by actions (2:23)

Can Faith A save, James asks (2:14)? The form of his question anticipates a negative answer. Why? Because Faith A does not work. But saving faith always works. Unless professed faith is working faith, it is not saving faith and therefore cannot be true faith (Gal. 5:6). Put another way, James is saying that if the person who believes is not also the person who works, then that person does not believe with a faith that is unto justification and, therefore, that person does not believe truly. The person who believes is thereby united to Christ in the power of his resurrection life, and such a person, sanctified in Christ, works for his glory. John Murray puts it this way: while faith alone justifies, 'a justified person with faith alone would be a monstrosity which never exists in the kingdom of grace'.[1] And Calvin teaches:

> We confess with Paul that no other faith justifies 'but faith working through love'. But it does not take its power to justify from that working of love. Indeed it justifies in no other way but in that it leads us into fellowship with the righteousness of Christ.[2]

This is also what the *Westminster Confession of Faith* is at pains to emphasize: 'Faith ... is the alone instrument of justification; yet it is never alone in the person justified, but is ever accompanied by all other saving graces, and is no dead faith, but worketh by love' (XI.2).

---

[1] Murray, *Redemption*, p. 131.
[2] Calvin, *Institutes*, III.xi.20.

2. The second important New Testament passage pertaining to the believer's sanctification is Romans 6, in which Paul argues that the believer cannot go on sinning. Why not? It is simply because the grace that brings about faith reigns through righteousness to eternal life (Rom. 5:21). To go on sinning would be to contradict the style of the reign of grace; it would be to contradict grace itself. Believers are those who have 'died to sin' (6:2). It follows that, if they have died to sin, they cannot go on living in it. Moreover, they have also been raised with Christ into newness of life (6:4-5). There is a double reason why the old way of life is impossible for the justified.

True, we live 'between the times' as Paul's subsequent exhortations make plain (6:12-14). To employ the illustration made famous by Oscar Cullmann and inspired by events that brought World War II to an end, while D-Day has already taken place in the cross and resurrection of Christ, V-Day is yet to arrive.[1] In the meantime, the conflict with sin continues to be real and painful. However, such conflict takes place within the context of the decisive victory having already been won; the final conquest is assured. There may still be bloodletting; but the end result is not in doubt.

Grace reigns through righteousness in us as well as for us. Thus, the *Westminster Confession of Faith* states:

> Although the remaining corruption for a time may much prevail, yet, through the continual supply of strength from the sanctifying Spirit of Christ, the regenerate part doth overcome; and so the saints grow in grace, perfecting holiness in the fear of God (XIII.3).

Justification is a *status*, sanctification a *condition*. They must always be distinguished from each other, but they do not exist *apart* from one another any more than Christ can be divided. But how do justification and sanctification relate to the assurance that the Christian enjoys?

Justification and assurance

Assurance is the conscious confidence that we are in a right relationship with God through Christ. It is the confidence that we have been justified and accepted by God in Christ, regenerated by his Spirit, and adopted

---

[1] Oscar Cullmann, *Christ and Time*, p. 84.

into his family, and that through faith in him we will be kept for the day when our justification and adoption are consummated in the regeneration of all things.

The theology of assurance is simple and logical: justification is final. But experiencing assurance can be complex for the simple reason that we ourselves are deeply complex individuals; there may be much in our natural psyche that militates against assurance. It may take time before we who are loved know that we are truly loved, and it may take time before we who are forgiven understand and enjoy that we are indeed forgiven. Hence the *Westminster Confession of Faith* notes that 'a true believer may wait long, and conflict with many difficulties before he be partaker of it'. Nevertheless he 'may, without extraordinary revelation, in the right use of ordinary means, attain thereunto' (XVIII.3).

It was this conviction—if anything, expressed with even greater vigour—that marked the Reformation in the sixteenth century. Indeed, in some senses, the Reformation was the great rediscovery of assurance. If the gospel was the power of God for salvation, if in Christ we are accounted righteous before the Father—so the Reformers understood—since earthly fathers lavish on their children assurances of their love, protection, and provision, how much more does our heavenly Father lavish on us his love, protection, and provision! Yet in many ways this was a dramatic reversal of both doctrine and experience within the history of Roman Catholicism. It may be helpful in this context to provide a brief overview of church history leading to the Reformation.

Medieval lack of assurance

The leading theologians of the Middle Ages represent a very wide variety of doctrinal and pastoral opinions. At one end of the spectrum, Pope Gregory I, the Great (540–604), from whose time the Middle Ages are usually dated, regarded assurance of salvation as basically impossible and even undesirable. At the other end of the spectrum, Thomas Aquinas (1225–74) was somewhat more judicious. He believed that assurance might come by various means: by special revelation or by signs of grace in an individual's life. But this special revelation was reserved for very few Christians, such as the apostle Paul, and in any case, Aquinas believed, the evidences of the marks of grace are very uncertain indeed.

Assurance was possible—but only in theory. It could not be regarded as the inheritance of every Christian.

Aquinas's position was later confirmed as the orthodox position of Roman Catholicism by the Council of Trent (1545–63): 'No one can know with a certitude of faith … that he has obtained God's grace.'[1] Indeed, Cardinal Robert Bellarmine (1542–1621), who was proclaimed a *Doctor Ecclesiae* in 1931, went so far as to write: 'The principal heresy of Protestants is that saints may obtain to a certain assurance of their gracious and pardoned state before God' (*De justificatione* III.2.3).

Rome seriously misunderstood the teaching of the Reformation. But, in addition, Rome's underlying double fear was that assurance would lead to a libertarian approach in personal morals and ecclesiastical authority. Nevertheless, there was still a more sinister element behind this, for, given the penance-oriented order of salvation of Roman Catholicism, assurance was inevitably and necessarily denied. Any way of salvation that depends on something that we must contribute ('doing what is in you,' in the medieval theological language, or in its modern form: 'heaven helps those who help themselves') can never bring assurance to us, for we can never be sure we have done enough to help.

Reformation breakthrough

The Reformation was born out of this womb. Luther's spiritual experience, and perhaps also Calvin's, can be understood as a search for a truly gospel-centred understanding of the assurance of salvation. How can we be sure of Scripture, of Christ, of grace, of salvation? These were the great Reformation questions to which the slogans we associate with the Reformation reply: Scripture alone (*sola Scriptura*) is sufficient to give the certainty of our salvation that is accomplished by grace alone (*sola gratia*), through faith alone (*sola fide*), Christ alone (*solus Christus*) for the glory of God alone (*soli Deo gloria*).

On this particular issue, Reformed theology at its best and wisest has spoken with one voice: it is possible to have assurance of salvation without extraordinary revelation. The first recipients of Scripture possessed the assurance of salvation; Christians throughout the ages have possessed

[1] Denzinger, *Compendium of Creeds*, p. 379.

assurance; we may have assurance as well. Believers 'may in this life be certainly assured that they are in a state of grace, and may rejoice in the hope of the glory of God'.[1]

Pathway to assurance

As the theologians of the Reformation studied the Scriptures, it became clear to them that the Lord gives assurance to us, his children, as we come to faith in Christ, as we gain a clear understanding of the grace of Christ, as we walk in the way of Christ, and as we experience the witness of the Spirit of Christ (*Westminster Confession of Faith*, XVIII.2).

(i) Faith in Christ

Christ is the source of salvation. Faith is the means by which we draw that salvation to ourselves. Faith is trust in Christ as the one who is able to save. There is already a kind of assurance seminally inherent in such faith. Indeed, faith in its first exercise is an assurance about Christ. The enjoyment of assurance is simply the inner nature of faith bursting out into our conscious awareness of what it means.

(ii) Grace of Christ

Faith seeks understanding (to use the idea of Augustine and Anselm). It is possible, of course, to have little knowledge and considerable assurance, but that is because faith has nourished itself richly even on relatively limited knowledge of a great Saviour. Correspondingly, it is possible to have much knowledge and little assurance; that is because faith has starved itself by failing to feed on the knowledge it has.

The clearer and fuller appreciation we have of the nature of God's grace in Christ and all the spiritual blessings that are ours in him (Eph. 1:3-14), the greater will be our enjoyment and assurance of this grace. Here three chief enemies rear their heads:

(a) We smuggle our own contributions into the foundation of our salvation.

(b) We find it difficult to believe that we are freely justified by the Father who in his love sent his Son for us. We forget that God

---

[1] *Westminster Confession of Faith*, XVIII.1.

the Father is absolutely, completely, and totally to us what he reveals himself to be to us in Christ (John 14:7, 9). Understand this, and faith strengthens while assurance is nourished.

(c) We fail to recognize that justification is both final and complete. Justification is final because it is the final-day, irreversible, divine verdict on our lives pronounced now. Justification is complete because we are as righteous before the Father as Christ himself is, since we are righteous with his righteousness.

(iii) Way of Christ

Low levels of obedience are incompatible with high levels of assurance. If Christ is not actually saving us—producing in us the obedience of faith in our struggle against the world, the flesh, and the devil—then our confidence that he is our Saviour is bound to be undermined, imperceptibly at first perhaps, but nevertheless really. This is why there is a strong link in the New Testament between faithfulness in the Christian walk and the enjoyment of assurance. Obedience strengthens faith and confirms it to us because true faith is always marked by what Paul calls 'the obedience of faith' (Rom. 1:5).

(iv) The Spirit's witness

We are assured of salvation, Paul notes, because 'we cry, "Abba! Father!" The Spirit himself bears witness with our spirit that we are children of God' (Rom. 8:15-16). Paul's point is essentially simple. Our conscious awareness that we are God's children, and therefore assured of his grace, is sometimes obscured in various ways. But the word that issues from our hearts when we are in need and cry out to him—'Father!'—is itself an expression of a deep-down assurance that we are his. In fact Paul employs a verb (*krazō*) that is elsewhere expressive of a cry of need or pain (Mark 15:39 variant reading; Rev. 12:2). Here it is a child's appeal for help to *Abba*, Father!

Assurance, then, is not reserved only for Christians who have attained to the highest and holiest of conditions ('saints' in the Roman Catholic sense); it is for all of God's children ('saints' in the biblical sense), even—indeed, especially—at their weakest and neediest.

Of course, there are obstacles, as we have hinted. We cannot here explore them all. We are prone to confuse the foundation of salvation in grace (justification) with its fruit in our lives (sanctification); we obscure the enjoyment of our privileges by failure to take seriously our responsibilities; we are confused by our afflictions; we fail to appreciate the continuing presence of sin and are destabilized by our own failures; in some instances our natural temperament, our damaged mindset, may be a special hindrance to assurance; an attack of the devil may flood our minds with doubts and fears; our own consciences can hinder assurance by condemning us, and they need to be cleansed. This may all be true. But the seed of assurance that is present in faith will—as it is nourished by the truth of God's promise, the knowledge of his character, the grace of his Son, and the witness of his Spirit—press through even the poor soil of our hearts and grow to full assurance of salvation!

Effects of assurance

We must briefly notice some of the fruits of assurance in our lives. In fact, rather than produce antinomianism and licence (as Rome feared), assurance produces their opposite. Again, the Westminster divines describe this succinctly and wisely. In assurance our hearts are enlarged by grace (1) in peace and joy, (2) in love and thankfulness, and (3) in strength and cheerfulness in duties.[1]

This echoes the joyful confidence of New Testament faith whose enjoyment of assurance produced boldness in witness; eagerness and intimacy in prayer; poise in character in the face of trial, danger, and opposition; and joy in worship. It is worth asking if the absence of these is evidence of a lack of the assurance that produces them. Rather than lead to presumption, assurance actually produces true humility, faithful obedience, joyful worship; for true Christian assurance is not self-assurance and self-confidence, but confidence in the Father, confidence in the Son, and joy in the Spirit. 'Blessed assurance' indeed![2]

---

[1] *Westminster Confession of Faith*, XVIII.3.
[2] From the well-known hymn 'Blessed Assurance, Jesus Is Mine!' by Frances Jane Van Alstyne (Fanny Crosby), the hymn-writer who lost her sight when she was six weeks old.

CHAPTER TWENTY-SEVEN

CHRISTIAN SPIRITUALITY: THE REFORMED VIEW OF SANCTIFICATION

REFORMED theology owes a special debt to the principles of biblical exposition recovered for the church at the time of the Reformation. It is particularly associated with the work of John Calvin, but was later developed by such seventeenth-century Puritans as John Owen and Thomas Goodwin (in England), and Thomas Hooker and John Cotton (in New England). Many later Christians have owed a special debt to the Reformed theological tradition. They include preachers such as George Whitefield, C. H. Spurgeon and D. Martyn Lloyd-Jones; and theologians such as Jonathan Edwards, Charles Hodge, Abraham Kuyper and B. B. Warfield; as well as such influential twentieth-century Christian leaders as J. Gresham Machen and Francis Schaeffer. From one point of view, most evangelical theology in the English-speaking world can be seen as an exposition of, deviation from, or reaction to, Reformed theology.[1]

A cursory glance at the writings and biographies of these men underlines the fact that Reformed theology has always placed special emphasis on the subject of sanctification. Few axioms are more central to Reformed teaching than that theology and practice, doctrine and lifestyle are partners joined together by God. They ought never to be separated.

---

[1] Such statements inevitably involve a subjective reading of history, but note the words of I. Howard Marshall (my own New Testament teacher, and himself a Wesleyan Methodist) to the same effect: 'within conservative evangelicalism the dominant school of thought is Calvinism'. *Kept by the Power of God* (Minneapolis: Bethany, 1975), preface.

Nor is this relationship merely a 'marriage of convenience'. It is one which Reformed theology sees as being 'made in heaven', or more exactly, made in Scripture. A necessary connection between biblical doctrine and holy living is fundamental to the biblical and apostolic way of thinking. That is why Scripture is so full of moral imperatives logically derived from doctrinal indicatives: since these things are true, this is how you should live (compare Matt. 6:32-34; Rom. 12:1-2; Eph. 4:20-25). The title of one of Francis Schaeffer's best-known books grows directly out of this Reformed appreciation of the shape of basic biblical teaching: *How Should We Then Live?* The 'then' is pregnant with significance. It means 'in light of the biblical teaching we know to be true, ...' Indeed, in Schaeffer's case, it meant specifically 'in the light of Reformed theology'.

In fact, this marriage between what we believe and how we live was early illustrated by the *magnum opus* of Reformed theology, John Calvin's *Institutes of the Christian Religion*.[1] It was (and is) a manual to the teaching of Scripture. When Calvin first published it (at the tender age of 27), it bore the significant subtitle: *Containing the whole sum of piety*.[2] In apparent contrast to medieval works which bore the title *Sum of Theology* (*Summa Theologiae*), Calvin sought to engage the reader in an experiential fashion. His purpose was not only intellectual; it was also spiritual. One cannot read the *Institutes* without being impressed by this. Thus, from the beginning, Reformed theology has always emphasized sanctification. It could be said of many Reformed Christians, as it was actually said of John Owen, one of the finest Reformed theologians: 'His aim in life was to promote holiness.'[3]

What, then, are the distinctive features of the Reformed doctrine of sanctification? By definition (*Reformed* means reformed according to

[1] First published in 1536 and revised constantly, the work known in English as the *Institutes* is a translation of the final Latin edition of 1559.

[2] For Calvin 'piety' did not mean what is sometimes connoted by 'pietism' today, that is, a separation of life into sacred and secular and a withdrawing from the latter. Rather, Calvin states, 'I call "piety" that reverence joined with love of God which the knowledge of his benefits induces' (*Institutes*, I.ii.1). For Calvin this governs the whole of life.

[3] David Clarkson, 'A Funeral Sermon on the Much Lamented Death of the Late Reverend and Learned Divine John Owen, DD', *Select Works of David Clarkson*, p. 452. Clarkson was at one time Owen's assistant and was a leading seventeenth-century theologian in his own right.

Scripture), these should also be the leading features of the Bible's own teaching. For this reason there are, thankfully, many points of contact and agreement between Reformed teaching and other perspectives. These should not be minimized; but the function of this essay is to express the chief emphases of the Reformed perspective.

Two features are central to sanctification: (1) Jesus Christ himself is our sanctification or holiness (1 Cor. 1:30); and (2) it is through union with Christ that sanctification is accomplished in us. As Calvin says, 'First we must understand that as long as Christ remains outside of us, and we are separated from him, all that he has suffered and done for the salvation of the human race remains useless and of no value to us.'[1] But the phrase 'Christ, our sanctification' has been variously understood. It is important, therefore, to notice that undergirding Calvin's statement are several strands of New Testament teaching.

Union with Christ

In the New Testament, Jesus is presented as the 'author', 'captain' or 'pioneer' of salvation (Acts 3:15; 5:31; Heb. 2:10; 12:2). The word *archēgos* (author) is notoriously difficult to translate into English.[2] In the case of Jesus (especially in the context of Hebrews) it seems to convey the twin notions of primacy and origin. Jesus is the 'author' of our sanctification, in the sense that he creates it for us, but he is also its 'pioneer' because he does so out of his own incarnate life, death, and resurrection. He is the 'pioneer' of our salvation, because as *the* hero of faith (to be distinguished from the long list of those heroes who bear witness to him, Heb. 12:1), he has endured the cross, despising its shame and the opposition of sinners, and is now seated at God's right hand. He is the first and only fully sanctified person. He has climbed God's holy hill with clean hands and a pure heart (Psa. 24:3-6). It is as the 'lead climber' that he gives the sanctification he has won to others (Acts 5:31). As 'pioneer', Jesus has himself gone ahead of us to open up the way to the Father. By doing so,

---

[1] Calvin, *Institutes*, III.i.1.

[2] 'The noun ἀρχήγος is difficult to translate satisfactorily. It signifies one who is both the source or initiator and the leader (ἀρχή plus ἄγω), one who first takes action and then brings on those on whose behalf he has acted to the intended goal.' Philip Edgcumbe Hughes, *Commentary on the Epistle to the Hebrews* (Grand Rapids: Eerdmans, 1977), p. 100, fn 88.

he brings to the Father in similar obedience all those who are 'roped' to him by grace and faith.

Christ *is* our sanctification. In him it has first come to its fulfilment and consummation. He not only died for us to remove the penalty of our sin by taking it himself; he has lived, died, risen again, and been exalted in order to sanctify our human nature in himself for our sake. This is the significance of his words shortly before the cross, 'Sanctify [the disciples] in the truth. ... As you sent me into the world, I have sent them into the world. And for their sake I sanctify myself, that they also may be sanctified in truth' (John 17:17-19).

Behind this lies a strand of teaching in the New Testament to which evangelicals have sometimes given insufficient emphasis—the notion that the Son of God took genuine human nature, 'in the likeness of sinful flesh' (Rom. 8:3), so that 'Both the one who makes men holy and those who are made holy are of the same family' (Heb. 2:11 NIV). Having sanctified his human nature from the moment of conception by his Spirit in the womb of the Virgin Mary (Luke 1:35), Jesus lived his life of perfect holiness in our frail flesh set in a world of sin, temptation, evil, and Satan. In our human nature, he grew in wisdom, in stature and in his capacity to obey the will of his Father.

As Jesus grew as a man, his human capacities developed, and with them the pressure of temptation (Luke 2:52). In that context he developed in obedience, not from imperfect to perfect, but from infancy to maturity. When he cried out on the cross 'It is finished' (John 19:30; see also 17:4) and with royal dignity committed his spirit into the hands of his Father, he was the first person to have lived a life of perfect obedience and sanctification. In his resurrection his sanctified human life was divinely transformed into what the New Testament calls 'the power of an indestructible life' (Heb. 7:16). Because this has taken place first in Christ our representative, it is possible for it to take place also in us through the Spirit. Christ himself is the only adequate resource we have for the development of sanctification in our own lives.

Sanctification is therefore neither self-induced nor created in us by divine *fiat*. Like justification, it has to be 'earthed' in our world (that is, in Christ's work for us in history) if it is to be more than a legal fiction. To change the metaphor, we can only draw on resources which have already been deposited in our name in the bank. But the whole of Christ's life, death, resurrection, and exaltation have, by God's gracious design, provided the living deposit of his sanctified life, from which all our needs can be supplied. Because of our fellowship (union) with him we come to share his resources. That is why he can 'become for us' sanctification, just as he is also our wisdom, righteousness and redemption (1 Cor. 1:30).

No one has expressed the riches of this biblical teaching more eloquently than Calvin himself:

> We see that our whole salvation and all its parts are comprehended in Christ [Acts 4:12]. We should therefore take care not to derive the least portion of it from anywhere else. If we seek salvation, we are taught by the very name of Jesus that it is 'of him' [1 Cor. 1:30]. If we seek any other gifts of the Spirit, they will be found in his anointing. If we seek strength, it lies in his dominion; if purity, in his conception; if gentleness, it appears in his birth. For by his birth he was made like us in all respects [Heb. 2:17] that he might learn to feel our pain [compare Heb. 5:2]. If we seek redemption, it lies in his passion; if acquittal, in his condemnation; if remission of the curse, in his cross [Gal. 3:13]; if satisfaction, in his sacrifice; if purification, in his blood; if reconciliation, in his descent into hell; if mortification of the flesh, in his tomb; if newness of life, in his resurrection; if immortality, in the same; if inheritance of the heavenly kingdom, in his entrance into heaven; if protection, if security, if abundant supply of all blessings, in his kingdom; if untroubled expectation of judgment, in the power given to him to judge. In short, since rich store of every kind of good abounds in him, let us drink our fill from this fountain, and from no other.[1]

If Calvin is right, then the dynamic for sanctification, indeed for the whole life of the Christian, is to be found in union with Christ

---

[1] Calvin, *Institutes*, II.xvi.19.

The effecting of the union

In Christ's incarnate, crucified, risen, and glorified humanity lies the sanctification I lack in myself. The question therefore becomes: How are his sanctification and my need for it brought together?

According to the New Testament, it is by the ministry of God's Spirit and by the exercise of the believer's faith. Union with Christ is the purpose and one of the *foci* of the ministry of the Spirit. Jesus emphasized that the Spirit 'will glorify me, for he will take what is mine and declare it to you' (John 16:14). This was to be realized when the Father would give the apostles the Spirit, the Counsellor, to be with them forever (that is, on the Day of Pentecost: 'In *that* day you will know that I am in my Father, *and you in me, and I in you*' [John 14:20, emphasis mine]). The coming of the Spirit ('baptism with the Spirit') on the Day of Pentecost is the means by which the disciples are united to Christ.

But this union with Christ does not take place over our heads, as it were. It engages our whole being. Consequently, a second element in it is that of *faith*. In the New Testament's language, we believe *into* Christ (*pisteuein eis*), that is, into union with him. Faith involves trusting in and resting on the resources of Christ as though they were our own.

The first disciples' experience in this context was obviously in some elements unique. They alone belonged to the time before and after Christ. Like other believers of the Old Testament era, they were regenerated before the death, resurrection, ascension, and Pentecost events (and in some sense, united to Christ [compare John 15:3-5; 13:10]). But, like believers in all ages thereafter, they also received the Spirit of the ascended Christ, an event which (in their case necessarily) was chronologically separated from their regeneration. Their entrance into all that union with Christ means to New Testament believers was therefore progressive. By contrast, for Christians after the initial period of overlap between the Old and New epochs of redemption, the experiences of faith, regeneration, and baptism with the Spirit take place simultaneously—a threefold perspective on the one event in which no perspective is simply reducible to either of the other two.

Union and sanctification

How does this union have significance for sanctification? Or are Calvin's eloquent words, cited above, simply a theologian's rhetoric? The fact that union with Christ has profound significance lies on the surface of the New Testament. In the crisis hours before his arrest, Jesus gave his disciples careful instruction on this theme (John 14:20; 15:1-4; 17:23). Similarly, in dealing with pressing pastoral problems, Paul frequently reminds his readers of their union with Christ as the solvent of their situation and the ground of his own exhortations to them (compare Rom. 6:1-14; Gal. 2:20-21; Eph. 2:1-6; Col. 2:6–3:17). On the basis of such passages the *Westminster Confession of Faith*, for example, is able to say:

> They who are effectually called and regenerated, having a new heart and a new spirit created in them, are farther sanctified really and personally, *through the virtue of Christ's death and resurrection.*[1]

The most meticulously logical development of this appears in Romans 6:1-14.

> What shall we say then? Are we to continue in sin that grace may abound? By no means! How can we who died to sin still live in it? Do you not know that all of us who have been baptized into Christ Jesus were baptized into his death? We were buried therefore with him by baptism into death, in order that, just as Christ was raised from the dead by the glory of the Father, we too might walk in newness of life.
>
> For if we have been united with him in a death like his, we shall certainly be united with him in a resurrection like his. We know that our old self was crucified with him in order that the body of sin might be brought to nothing, so that we would no longer be enslaved to sin. For one who has died has been set free from sin. Now if we have died with Christ, we believe that we will also live with him. We know that Christ, being raised from the dead, will never die again; death no longer has dominion over him. For the death he died he died to sin, once for all, but the life he lives he lives to God. So you also must consider yourselves dead to sin and alive to God in Christ Jesus.

[1] 'Of Sanctification', *Westminster Confession of Faith*, XIII.1 (emphasis added).

> Let not sin therefore reign in your mortal body, to make you obey its passions. Do not present your members to sin as instruments for unrighteousness, but present yourselves to God as those who have been brought from death to life, and your members to God as instruments for righteousness. For sin will have no dominion over you, since you are not under law but under grace.

The complexity of Paul's logic in this passage is obvious. He has just been expounding the central fact of redemptive history: what was forfeited in Adam has been regained in the last Adam, Jesus Christ (Rom. 5:12-21). The principle is that where sin increased, the grace of God has abounded all the more (Rom. 5:20). To this there is an obvious retort: 'Shall we continue sinning, therefore? For if increased sin evokes increased grace, does it not follow that our indulgence in sin will promote grace and therefore enhance the glory of God?'

Such a response is a monstrous misunderstanding of the gospel. Paul's reaction is as violent as it is theological. For the forgiveness of sins is not received in a vacuum, but in union with Christ ('In him we have redemption through his blood, the forgiveness of our trespasses', Eph. 1:7). But if we have been united to Christ, we share in him as a crucified and risen Saviour. When he was crucified, he died to sin; when he was resurrected, he was raised to new life with the Father (Rom. 6:8-10). If in becoming Christians we have been united to *this* Christ, it follows that (in some sense) we have died to sin with him and been raised similarly into a new life. This being the case, how can those who have received forgiveness in Christ, and are thus united to him, go on living in sin? They do not. Indeed, Paul's point is that they *cannot* because they have died to sin.

Paul's logic is impeccable:

1. We receive forgiveness of sins through Christ.

2. This reception involves being united to Christ.

3. The Christ to whom we are united, died to sin.

4. Since we are united to him, we also have died to sin.

5. If we have died to sin, we cannot continue living in it.

6. Therefore, we cannot continue in sin that grace may abound.

Justification is received by faith alone, but since that faith unites us to Christ as sanctifier, justification and sanctification can no more be separated than Christ himself can be divided.

Death to sin

While Paul's logic is flawless, his interpreters have found his teaching sufficiently obscure to give rise to a variety of interpretations of it. In particular, his idea of the believer as one who is 'dead to sin' has frequently been abused to suggest various forms of perfectionism. Here even Homer nods, when in his often masterly paraphrase of Romans, J. B. Phillips translates Romans 6:7 as: 'a dead man can safely be said to be immune to the power of sin'. But both Scripture and experience make it abundantly clear that Christians can 'safely' be said *not* to be immune to the power of sin!

Again, it is sometimes suggested that the key to sanctification lies in Paul's command to count oneself 'dead to sin'. Defeat in the Christian life is therefore attributed to a failure to enter into a new stage of experience altogether in which sin is no longer a serious challenge to the Christian. But this is the high road to theological and pastoral, as well as psychological, shipwreck.

The notion that we have died to sin and are alive to God lies at the heart of the biblical doctrine of sanctification. Death to sin and life to God *is* sanctification. But what is the nature of this death and life?

Reformed theology has not answered that question with a completely harmonious voice exegetically; but theologically and pastorally the response has been relatively constant. Even an outline of its chief features underscores the fact that Reformed theology has stressed the cosmic context in which Scripture expounds sanctification.

In the immediate context in Romans, Paul has been expounding the work of Christ and his grace by contrasting them with Adam and his fall. Through Adam, sin and death have come into the world. But such is the divinely instituted relationship between Adam and his posterity, the human race, we all by nature are 'in Adam'. He has acted as our head and representative. Consequently, through his one act of disobedience, all persons in Adam have come under the power of sin and death (compare Rom. 5:12; 1 Cor. 15:22). This is the ultimate foundation for, and explanation of, the fact that humanity is unsanctified before God. 'None is righteous, no, not one ... No human being will be justified in his sight ... for all have sinned and fall short of the glory of God' (Rom. 3:10-23). This situation is encapsulated in Paul's statement that 'sin reigned' (Rom. 5:21).

Throughout Romans 5 and 6, Paul uses the definite article with the word sin (*hē hamartia*), perhaps suggesting that sin is to be thought of as a personified power or as a realm in which humans live. It reigns as a king (5:21; 6:12) and makes people serve it as their master (6:14) so that they are sin's slaves (6:17, 20). It is a warring general who uses people's bodies as his weapons (*hopla*, 6:13); it is an employer who pays wages at the end of the day—but 'the wages of sin is death' (6:23).

Against this background it becomes clearer what death to sin *does not* mean. It does not describe an activity which the Christian must perform (die to sin!), for the verb is in the indicative mood, not the imperative. Paul is not telling us we are to do something; he is analysing something that has taken place.

Nor does death to sin mean that we are no longer capable of committing any acts of sin. Not only would that contradict the teaching of Scripture elsewhere (e.g., 1 John 1:8-10) and run counter to actual experience, it would make nonsense of Paul's urgent exhortations in this very passage to cease sinning. 'Let not sin therefore reign' and 'Do not present your members to sin as instruments for unrighteousness' (Rom. 6:12-13) suggest that the Christian continues to battle with it.

Freed from sin

What, then, does Paul mean? He explains in verse 7: 'For one who has died has been set free from sin.' Two different interpretations of his words have been adopted by Reformed theologians.

First, Paul's words in this verse (*ho gar apothanōn dedikaiōtai apo tēs hamartias*) may be narrowly interpreted to mean: 'For the one who has died is *justified* from his sin.' In this case Paul is saying that sharing in Christ's death for sin means being released from bearing the burden of guilt for sin ourselves.[1]

---

[1] The classic exposition of this view is found in Robert Haldane, *The Epistle to the Romans* (repr. London, 1966), pp. 248-50. Cf. Cranfield, *Romans*, I:311.

Alternatively, Paul's words may mean: 'The one who has died (with Christ) is not merely justified, but has also been set free from the reign, or dominion, of sin.' There are solid reasons for accepting this second interpretation:

1. At this point in the context of Romans 6, Paul is speaking about the dominion or reign of sin; his concern is with the authority of sin over us, not its guilt. The point at issue is whether Christians continue to live under the reign of sin as they formerly did. Since Paul's general argument is that Christians are delivered from the reign of sin (although not its continuing presence), 'set free' from sin is the more relevant concept.

2. Later in the passage (6:18), Paul specifically expounds the significance of union with Christ in terms of freedom from sin: 'you … having been set free from sin, have become slaves of righteousness'. Here the context is clearly one of deliverance from bondage, not alleviation of guilt, and the term Paul uses (*eleutherōthentes*) implies such freedom.

Against this view it is sometimes argued that proper exegesis demands the conclusion that the believer has died to sin in the same sense that Christ is said to have died ('the death he died he died to sin, once for all', Rom. 6:10). Christ could not die to sin except in the sense of bearing its guilt, it is argued.

But Paul has already indicated that sin's reign is expressed in death. Insofar as Christ died for us, we must say that he submitted himself not only to death, but to the reign of sin through death. He too died to sin, in the sense of dying to its reign over him. It may further clarify Paul's thinking here if we remember that for him, the resurrection involved Christ's deliverance (his vindication, or justification) from the reign of sin in death (1 Tim. 3:16). In union with him, we too are delivered from sin's reign as a tyrant-king as well as from sin's guilt. Only because we are free from both are we in any position to resist the remaining presence of sin.

In view of this, Paul says, 'sin will have no dominion over you' (Rom. 6:14). This indicative-mood statement forms the basis for the radical imperatives which Paul issues to those who have thus died to sin and are now alive to God.[1]

We may follow Paul further. Not only is this 'death to sin' deliverance from its dominion—and something which has already been accomplished, rather than an injunction to be obeyed—it is a fundamental and universal principle of sanctification for every Christian. Indeed, it is so true of each and every Christian as to be virtually definitive of being a Christian. 'All of us who have been baptized into Christ Jesus' (all Christians) have thus died to sin. 'We died to sin' (*hoitines apethanomen tē hamartia*) might be more fully rendered: 'We who are the kind of people who died to sin', that is, 'we—who have this as one of our leading characteristics—that we have died to sin'.[2] Therefore we are to act 'as those who have been brought from death to life' (6:13; 'as dead men brought to life' is C. K. Barrett's fine rendering).

This is so because 'we have been united with [Christ] in a death like his' (verse 5). Here again Paul's language is illuminating. His use of *sumphutos* (*sun*, along with; *phuō*, to bring forth, beget, and in the

---

[1] See Murray, *Romans*, I:222; also Ernst Käsemann, *Commentary on Romans*, tr. and ed. G. W. Bromiley (Grand Rapids: Eerdmans, 1980): 'Paul's concern is not with guilt, but with the power of sin', p. 170.

Cranfield's exposition at this point fails to take account of the entire context of Paul's teaching in Romans 6. He says that 'free from sin' (Rom. 6:7) 'must clearly mean "has been justified from sin" rather than "has been freed from sin" … since, while … the Christian is no longer the completely helpless and unresisting slave of sin, he is not in this life actually free from sin' (*Romans*, I:311).

Cranfield shares with other exegetes the nervousness that if Paul affirmed Christians are free from sin he would be guilty of the very perfectionism the New Testament elsewhere denies (compare 1 John 1:5-10) and also of denying the continual warfare in which the Christian is engaged (Gal. 5:17). But the perspective from which Paul speaks in Romans 5–7 is one in which he sees sin as a tyrant-king from whose reign (not presence or even influence) Christ delivers the Christian. Curiously, on 6:18, Cranfield states this without showing his earlier reservations: 'They have already been set free from sin in the sense that they have been transferred from the possession of sin to the possession of a new master and so are now in a position to resist sin's controlling hold upon them' (*Romans*, I:325).

[2] Paul's relative pronoun here (*hoitines*) appears to be equivalent to the Latin *quippe qui* ('seeing that'). The sense is 'which by its very nature'. Compare H. G. C. Moule, *Idiom Book of the New Testament* (Cambridge: Cambridge University Press, 1960), pp. 123-25.

passive, to spring up or grow) suggests that we share one bundle of life with Christ in what he has done.[1] All that he has accomplished for us in our human nature is, through union with him, true *for* us and, in a sense, *of* us. He 'died to sin, once for all'; 'he lives to God' (6:10). He came under the dominion of sin in death, but death could not master him. He rose and broke the power of both sin and death. Now he lives forever in resurrection life to God. The same is as true of us as if we had been with him on the cross, in the tomb, and on the resurrection morning!

We miss the radical nature of Paul's teaching here to our great loss. So startling is it that we need to find a startling manner of expressing it. For what Paul is saying is that sanctification means this: in relationship both to sin and to God, the determining factor of my existence is *no longer my past. It is Christ's past.* The basic framework of my new existence in Christ is that I have become a 'dead man brought to life' and must think of myself in those terms: dead to sin and alive to God in union with Jesus Christ our Lord.

Precisely at this juncture, however, personal experience tends to intrude. As Christians we continue to sin. And the danger is that we may think that the sinful lifestyle is still normative for us. We thus obscure the power of the gospel by focusing attention on the remaining sin in our lives. But for the New Testament, that view of the Christian life is to look at grace through the wrong end of the telescope. No one has expressed this with more accurate eloquence than John Murray:

> We are too ready to give heed to what we deem to be the hard,
> empirical facts of Christian profession, and we have erased the clear
> line of demarcation which Scripture defines. As a result we have
> lost our vision of the high calling of God in Christ Jesus. Our ethic
> has lost its dynamic and we have become conformed to this world.
> We know not the power of death to sin in the death of Christ,
> and we are not able to bear the rigour of the liberty of redemptive
> emancipation.[2]

[1] See *Theological Dictionary of the New Testament*, VII:786, for the view that 'the basic meaning is "native"'.

[2] Murray, *Principles of Conduct*, p. 205.

A similar point was made three hundred years earlier by the great Puritan theologian John Owen. He saw two major pastoral burdens to be: 'To convince those in whom sin evidently hath the dominion that such indeed is their state and condition'; and

> To satisfy some that sin hath not the dominion over them, notwithstanding its restless acting itself in them and warring against their souls; *yet unless this can be done, it is impossible they should enjoy solid peace and comfort in this life.*[1]

A new creation

Union with Christ in his death and resurrection is the element of union which Paul most extensively expounds. But the principle of Romans 6 is a wider one: if we are united to Christ, then we are united to him at all points of his activity on our behalf. We share in his death (we were baptized into his death), in his burial (we were buried with him by baptism), in his resurrection (we are resurrected with Christ), in his ascension (we have been raised with him), in his heavenly session (we sit with him in heavenly places, so that our life is hidden with Christ in God) and we will share in his promised return (when Christ, who is our life, appears, we also will appear with him in glory [Rom. 6:14; Col. 2:11-12; 3:1-4]).

This, then, is the foundation of sanctification in Reformed theology. It is rooted, not in our humanity and our achievement of holiness or sanctification, but in what God has done in Christ, and for us in union with him. Rather than view Christians first and foremost in the microcosmic context of their own progress, the Reformed doctrine first of all sets them in the macrocosm of God's activity in redemptive history. It is seeing oneself in this context that enables the individual Christian to grow in true holiness.

This general approach is well illustrated by Paul's key statements: 'We know that our old self [*anthrōpos*, man] was crucified with [Christ] in order that the body of sin might be brought to nothing, so that we would no longer be enslaved to sin' (Rom. 6:6).

What is here said to be accomplished already is the central element in sanctification (we are no longer slaves to sin, we are servants of God).

---

[1] Owen, *Works*, VII:517 (emphasis added).

It is accomplished by doing away with 'the body of sin'—an expression which may refer in the context of Romans 6 to the physical body, or more generally, to bodily existence as the sphere in which sin's dominion is expressed. In Christ, sin's status is changed from that of a citizen with full rights to that of an illegal alien (with no rights—but for all that, not easily deported!). The foundation of this is what Paul describes as the co-crucifixion of the old man with Christ.

The 'old man' (*ho palaios anthrōpos*) has often been taken to refer to what I was before I became a Christian ('my former self'). That is undoubtedly implied in the expression. But Paul has a larger canvas in mind here. He has been expounding the fact that men and women are 'in Adam' or 'in Christ'. To be 'in Adam' is to belong to the world of the 'old man', to be 'in the flesh', a slave to sin and liable to death and judgment. From this perspective, Paul sees Jesus Christ as the second man, the last Adam, the new man. He is the first of a new race of humans who share in his righteousness and holiness. He is the first of the new age, the head of the new humanity, through his resurrection (compare 1 Cor. 15:45-49). By grace and faith we belong to him. We too share in the new humanity. If we are in Christ, we share in the new creation (2 Cor. 5:17), we are no longer 'in the flesh', but 'in the Spirit' (Rom. 8:9). The life and power of the resurrection age have already begun to make their presence felt in our life.

What is so significant here is the transformation this brings to the Christian's self-understanding. We do not see ourselves merely within the limited vision of our own biographies: volume one, the life of slavery in sin; volume two, the life of freedom from sin. We see ourselves set in a cosmic context: in Adam by nature, in Christ by grace; in the old humanity by sin, in the new humanity by regeneration. Once we lived under sin's reign; now we have died to its rule and are living to God. Our regeneration is an event of this magnitude! Paul searches for a parallel to such an exercise of divine power and finds it in two places: the creation of the world (2 Cor. 4:6; 5:17) and the resurrection and ascension of Christ (Eph. 1:19-20).

Against this background Paul urges radical consecration and sanctification (Rom. 6:11-14). In essence his position is that the magnitude of what God has accomplished is itself an adequate foundation and motivation for the radical holiness which should characterize our lives.

In actual practice, it is the dawning of this perspective which is the groundwork for all practical sanctification. Hence Paul's emphasis on 'knowing' that this is the case (verses 3, 6, 9), and his summons to believers to 'consider' themselves dead to sin and alive to God in Christ Jesus (verse 11). 'Consider' ('reckon', KJV) does not mean to bring this situation into being by a special act of faith. It means to recognize that such a situation exists and to act accordingly.

Sanctification is therefore the consistent practical outworking of what it means to belong to the new creation in Christ. That is why so much of the New Testament's response to pastoral and personal problems in the early church was: 'Do you not know what is true of you in Christ? (Rom. 6:3, 16; 7:1; 1 Cor. 3:16; 5:6; 6:2, 3, 9, 15, 19; 9:13, 24). Live by the Spirit's power in a manner that is consistent with that! If you have died with Christ to sin and been raised into new life, quit sinning and live in a new way. If, when Christ appears, you will appear with him and be like him, then live now in a manner that conforms to your final destiny!'

Spiritual warfare

When the groundwork of sanctification is seen in this light, its progress is inevitably marked by conflict or tension. By contrast with teaching which emphasizes that the chief characteristic of the Christian life is quietness (physical, mental or spiritual), Reformed theology has stressed pilgrimage (*The Pilgrim's Progress*) and conflict (*The Holy War*). Such conflict is not viewed as either an unfortunate malfunction, or the result of a lack of faith or spirituality. Rather, conflict is inherent in the very nature of the glory of what God has already done for us. The magnitude of grace, when it impacts fallen humanity in a fallen world, inevitably produces conflict.

The New Testament provides several perspectives on this conflict which together present a unified picture.

The conflict is the result of our now being *in Christ* and yet, at the same time, living *in the world* (compare 1 Cor. 1:2, 'in Corinth' and 'in Christ Jesus'). Since by nature we were dead in sin and used to live according to the fashions of this world, gratifying our own lusts (Eph.

2:1-3), our new lifestyle in Christ is bound to be on a collision course with the lifestyle of this world. Why else would Paul 'insist ... that [we] must no longer live as the Gentiles do' (Eph. 4:17 NIV)? The goals, motives and energies of our lives now stand in complete contrast to the world around us. That radical difference makes tension, conflict, even stress inevitable (compare 2 Tim. 3:1-9).

A further biblical element in this conflict which Reformed theology has consistently sought to emphasize is Satan's ongoing opposition to Christian growth. What is true of the reign of sin is also true of the dominion of darkness. We have been freed from it, yet its presence is not finally destroyed. Rendered ultimately powerless (Heb. 2:14, where the same verb [*katargeō*] appears as in Rom. 6:6 in connection with the destruction of the body of sin), Satan continues to menace Christians. He seeks, says Calvin in connection with Job, 'to drive the saint to madness by despair'.[1] He is the hinderer, the enemy, the accuser, the tempter, the devourer. He seduces, deceives and tempts us with his many wiles.

Reformed literature therefore contains many serious manuals to serve the Christian soldier.[2] Here again we find the New Testament's emphasis on sanctification taking place in a cosmic context. We have been 'blessed ... in Christ with every spiritual blessing in the heavenly places' (Eph. 1:3, also verse 20). But now that we are united to him we are immediately involved in a conflict which is engaged precisely in the same 'heavenly places' (Eph. 6:12). Our daily lives involve the skirmishes of the eschatological war of the end times. For this reason we need to wear all the armour of God, so that 'in the evil day' we may remain standing (6:13).

But the conflict is not only external and objective; it is internal and subjective—with the flesh as well as with the world and the devil. All that is true *for me* in Christ has not yet been accomplished *in me* by the Spirit. I live in the Spirit, the flesh still lives in me (though I am no

---

[1] Calvin, *Institutes*, I.xviii.1.

[2] Outstanding examples of these are William Gurnall, *The Christian in Complete Armour* (London, 1655–62) and Thomas Brooks, *Precious Remedies Against Satan's Devices* (London, 1652). For a modern exposition in the same tradition, see D. Martyn Lloyd-Jones, *The Christian Warfare* (Edinburgh: Banner of Truth Trust, 1976) and *The Christian Soldier* (Edinburgh: Banner of Truth Trust, 1977).

longer dominated by it, nor a debtor to it). But as I have been delivered from bondage to the flesh, I continue to live my life with a body and mind marred by sin, and in a world and community which remain dominated by the flesh. Although I have been delivered from addiction to sin, its presence remains. I experience withdrawal symptoms and remain weakened by its devastating impact on my life. The desires of the flesh and the desires of the Spirit are contrary to one another. Whatever view I would like to take of my own degree of sanctification, I know that there are times when Paul's words ring true: 'You do not do what you want' (Gal. 5:17 NIV). In microcosm, I experience a reflection of the conflict between the kingdom of God and the kingdoms of this world. Because I am destined for the glory of Christ, so long as I am in the body, I groan, longing for the day when my life as a child of God will be brought to its final consummation (Rom. 8:23).

In this context, especially in more recent years, Reformed exegesis has not been unanimous in its interpretation of Romans 7:14-25. In the post-Reformation centuries, it has been normal, if not normative, to understand Paul's words as a description of a regenerate person. Despite trends to the contrary, my opinion is that this remains the best approach to understanding the passage.[1] It does, however, need to be underlined (as it has not always been in Reformed or any other tradition of interpretation) that while what Paul says in Romans 7:14-25 may be true of him as a believer, *it is not the only way of describing his experience as a believer.* At the heart of Romans 7:14-25 is a profound paradox, both elements of which must be recognized. As G. C. Berkouwer has written:

> Whoever thinks he has been treated [in Rom. 7:14-25] to an intolerable contradiction is probably the victim of the effort to make this duality psychologically transparent. He is a dupe indeed: there is no

---

[1] In recent decades the weight of opinion, under the powerful influence of European scholarship, has largely been committed to some form of the view that Romans 7:14-25 does not describe Paul's personal Christian experience. It is of interest to note the relatively recent expressions of commitment to the 'traditional' Reformed view on the part of three leading English-speaking scholars: J. I. Packer, 'The Wretched Man in Romans 7', *Studia Evangelica* 2 (1964), pp. 621-27; J. D. G. Dunn, 'Rom. 7:14-25 in the Theology of Paul', *Theologische Zeitschrift*, 31 (1975), pp. 257-73; Cranfield, *Commentary on Romans.*

transparency here, only grief over sin, meekness, confession of guilt, and a glory in salvation.[1]

For Paul is viewing himself within a particular context—his continued imperfection when judged by the spiritual standards of the divine law. But whether Romans 7:14-25 in particular is Paul speaking as a Christian or not, *it is a strange Christian who has not at some time realized that everything Paul describes is also experienced by all Christians.*

So long as we are in the body, in this world, we will find ourselves crying out from time to time: 'Wretched man that I am! Who will deliver me from this body of death? Thanks be to God through Jesus Christ our Lord!' (Rom. 7:24-25). Our sanest conclusion about our present status as believers will be: 'I myself serve the law of God with my mind, but with my flesh [*sarx*] I serve the law of sin' (Rom. 7:25). No other interpretation does justice to the remarkable combination of Paul's cry of victory and his recognition of the reality of sin's continuing influence via the flesh in Romans 7:25.[2] Nor is this pessimism. Indeed it is biblical realism. It is the inevitable concomitant of a glorious redemption already inaugurated but not yet consummated. The greater the glory, the greater the contrast with all that has not yet been glorified.

Partly in reaction to such a serious (and dark) emphasis, some have been tempted to stress the way in which the Spirit of God lifts the believer beyond this plane of experience. In response, Reformed theologians have sought to say, graciously but firmly, that while the dispensation of the Spirit is indeed glorious (2 Cor. 3:7-11), it is seriously mistaken to conclude that the presence of the Spirit will keep us from sin. It illustrates the difficulty we have in accepting the tensions produced by the present incompleteness of God's work in us, in view of the completeness of his work for us in Christ. But the biblical response to the view that the Spirit raises God's people above those conflicts is that in fact *it is the presence of the Spirit that produces these conflicts.*

---

[1] G. C. Berkouwer, *Faith and Sanctification, Studies in Dogmatics* (Grand Rapids: Eerdmans, 1952), I:340-70.

[2] Some modern commentators conclude the verse is misplaced, and originally came after verse 23, or that it is a scribal gloss. E. Käsemann adopts the latter position, yet recognizes it is 'against the whole textual tradition'. *Comm. Romans*, p. 211.

It is those who have the firstfruits of the Spirit who groan inwardly as they wait eagerly (note the balance!) for their final redemption (Rom. 8:23). Here 'firstfruits' does not mean that we have only a little of the Spirit and we need more if we are to cease groaning and enter into victory. The Spirit himself is the firstfruits of glory. No one can be possessed by him without being caught up in the contrast between flesh and Spirit.

Necessary mortification

This conflict, inherent in sanctification prior to glorification (final sanctification), in turn provides the proper context for a further feature of the Reformed doctrine of sanctification: the necessity of mortification.

The Latinate nature of the term 'mortification' suggests the world of the medieval, the monastic, and the masochistic. At times Christians have mistakenly resorted to weapons of the flesh rather than the sword of the Spirit to deal with sin. But again at this point, Reformed theology has sought to maintain a biblical balance, recognizing the continuing presence of sin in the believer and Scripture's frequent exhortations to deal with it severely. Wrong views of sanctification can frequently be traced to misunderstanding the nature of sin in the Christian.

In the New Testament, mortification is not a form of legalism (as Col. 2:9-23 emphasizes), but a repercussion of divine blessing. It is those who belong to the kingdom of God as 'beatitude people' (Matt. 5:1-12) who are urged to deal rigorously with sin (Matt. 5:21-48), to cut off or pluck out whatever is a source of temptation. It is those who are united to Christ in his death, resurrection, ascension, session and coming glory who are urged to 'put to death, therefore, what is earthly in you', whether it be mental acts or physical deeds (Col. 3:5-11).

Since Christians have put off the old man and put on the new man, they should live accordingly (Col. 3:9-10). It is those who have received God's promises who should purify themselves 'from every defilement of body and spirit, bringing holiness to completion in the fear of God' (2 Cor. 7:1). It is the person who has the hope that 'when [Jesus] appears we shall be like him, because we shall see him as he is' who 'purifies himself as [Jesus] is pure' (1 John 3:1-3). It is the one who already possesses the Holy Spirit as the gift of God's future kingdom, who by that Spirit is to 'put to death the deeds of the body' (Rom. 8:13). Those 'who belong to Christ Jesus have crucified the flesh with its passions and desires' (Gal. 5:24).

Grace demands mortification. Without it there is no holiness. John Owen writes graphically: 'Let not that man think he makes any progress in true holiness who walks not over the bellies of his lusts.'[1]

Mortification is the outworking of our union with Christ in his death to sin. But that must not be limited to our interior life. There is in the New Testament what Calvin called an internal and an external mortification. Bearing the cross involves crucifying the lusts of the flesh. The providential experiences of life serve a similar function. Just as we put sin to death in order to live (Rom. 8:13), so God sends painful providences in order that new life may arise both in us and in others. This external mortification is described variously. It involves bearing the cross; it is the Father's pruning in order that we may bear more fruit (John 15:2); it is described supremely in Paul's remarkable words in 2 Corinthians 4:7-12:

> But we have this treasure in jars of clay, to show that the surpassing power belongs to God and not to us. We are afflicted in every way, but not crushed; perplexed, but not driven to despair; persecuted, but not forsaken; struck down, but not destroyed; always carrying in the body the death of Jesus, so that the life of Jesus may also be manifested in our bodies. For we who live are always being given over to death for Jesus' sake, so that the life of Jesus also may be manifested in our mortal flesh. So death is at work in us, but life in you.

Union with Christ is not an inner mysticism. It affects the whole person. The silhouette of Christ's life marks all of the Christian's experience. Our personal *Sitz im Leben* becomes the instrument God uses to work out the realities of our union with Christ. Thus, Louis Berkhof has written:

> By this union believers are changed into the image of Christ *according to his human nature*. What Christ effects in his people is in a sense a replica or reproduction of what took place with him. Not only objectively, but also in a subjective sense they suffer, bear the

---

[1] Owen, *Works*, VI:14.

cross, are crucified, die and are raised to newness of life with Christ. They share in a measure the experiences of their Lord.[1]

Imitation and self-evaluation

The ground plan of sanctification, union with Christ, is prophetic of the divine goal in sanctification: renewal in the image of Christ. 'For those whom he foreknew he also predestined to be conformed to the image of his Son, in order that he might be the firstborn among many brothers' (Rom. 8:29). The whole *schema* of redemptive history has this in view. Humans by creation were made as the image of God, and called to express that image as offspring and reflectors of the divine glory. We sinned and fell short of the glory of God (Rom. 3:23). Thus Adam and Eve became prodigals (Gen. 3:24). In Christ, glory and sonship are restored (he was declared to be the Son in power when he was raised from the dead by the glory of the Father [Rom. 1:4; 6:4]). Through Spirit-union with Christ in the epochal events which brought him to the new humanity of the resurrection, we are already being conformed to his image from one degree of glory to another (2 Cor. 3:18).

The corresponding responsibility for the believer is the imitation of Christ. Like mortification, this is a notion which, because of its abuse, has often fallen into disuse among evangelical Christians. But it is thoroughly biblical. Union with Christ for the Thessalonians meant that they 'became imitators ... of the Lord' (1 Thess. 1:6). We are to have the 'mind of the Lord' (1 Cor. 2:16), who left his disciples an example, 'that you also should do just as I have done to you' (John 13:15). When Peter urges slaves to live as Christians, he tells them: 'Christ also suffered for you, leaving you an example, so that you might follow in his steps' (1 Pet. 2:21). Peter is applying to slaves a general principle which governs all Christian living. His language is graphic: *example* (*hupogrammos*, from *hupographō*, to write under, or over) is the word for a written copy. It belongs to the world of elementary education, where the teacher traces out a word and tells the child to copy it by writing over it. Peter is urging Christians to write the biography of their own lives with one eye on the lifestyle which Jesus had written. Imitation of the incarnate Saviour is essential to continuing sanctification.

[1] Berkhof, *Systematic Theology*, p. 451.

Because sanctification involves the imitation of Christ, its goal is true humanity, regained through Christ. That this is the heart of the Reformed doctrine of sanctification cannot be overstressed. Sanctification is radical humanization. It means doing the 'natural' thing spiritually, and the 'spiritual' thing naturally. 'What a redeemed soul needs', wrote Abraham Kuyper, 'is human holiness.'[1] Restoration of the image of God to true humanity is God's ultimate purpose for his people. The model and source for this transformation are both found in the humanity of Jesus Christ, the one truly sanctified human.

It is in this context that the thorny issue of the relationship between sanctification and self-image should be discussed. How we view ourselves has an immense impact on the style of our sanctification. Here, the Reformed perspective prevents us from falling into a common trap in discussions of self-image: reductionism and simplification, which invariably result either in what is often disparagingly referred to as worm theology ('Would he devote that sacred head *for such a worm as I?*'[2]), or alternatively an ego-trip ('God loves me the way I am—period').

The truth of the matter is that now as a Christian I must see myself from two perspectives and say two contrasting things about my life: *in myself* there dwells no good thing by my own creation or nature (Rom. 7:18); and *in Christ* I have been cleansed, justified, and sanctified so that in me glorification has begun (1 Cor. 6:11). Even in final glory, presumably, part of the cause of our praise of Christ will be that we are capable of distinguishing between what we have become because of Christ and what we would have become of ourselves. (The Lamb is forever worthy of praise not only because of his eternal divine person, but because he shed his blood to redeem humanity [Rev. 5:9].)

The New Testament will not allow us to reduce these two polarities to a common denominator. We must say both: God has given me a new identity with a glorious destiny; in myself I am utterly defiled and deserve only death. I belong to a time when the present evil age and the future glory overlap. I must therefore see myself from two perspectives. Miss this and we miss the biblical doctrine of sanctification, for the

---

[1] Abraham Kuyper, *The Work of the Holy Spirit*, tr. H. De Vries (New York: Funk & Wagnalls, 1900), p. 461.

[2] From the hymn 'Alas! and Did My Saviour Bleed' by Isaac Watts.

Christian's self-image is not properly viewed binocularly, reducing two
different perspectives to one, but microscopically, by viewing the variety
of activity involved in growth in holiness.

The means of sanctification

It should now be clear that in Reformed theology sanctification is by no
means a mystical experience in which holiness is ours effortlessly. God
gives increase in holiness by engaging our minds, wills, emotions, and
actions. We are involved in the process. That is why biblical teaching on
sanctification appears in both the indicative ('I, the Lord, sanctify you')
and the imperative ('sanctify yourselves'. Cf. Lev. 20:7).

Here we should be careful not to be misled by wrong deductions
drawn from biblical metaphors. In some expositions of sanctification,
for example, the phrase 'the fruit of the Spirit' or the analogy of the
vine and the branches (Gal. 5:22; John 15:1-8) is taken to suggest that
Christian graces grow effortlessly. Indeed, in such teaching effort is
sometimes seen as a hindrance to sanctification. Christians are exhorted
rather to 'let go, and let God have his wonderful way'. Similarly, the
Christian is encouraged to sing:

> Buried with Christ and raised with him too;
> What is there left for me to do?
> Simply to cease from struggling and strife,
> Simply to walk in newness of life,
> Glory be to God!

But at best this is confusing. At worst the metaphor loses all contact
with the control centre of the rest of Scripture and goes into an orbit of
its own, seriously distorting apostolic teaching. It rends asunder what
God has joined together: indicative and imperative; Christ's work and
our response of faith; God's grace and our duty.

Reformed teaching on sanctification has focused attention on four
areas in which the grace and duties of sanctification coincide. Together,
these constitute what are sometimes called 'means of grace'.

(1) The word

The word of God is the principal means. It is to be hidden in our hearts as the preservative from sin (Psa. 119:11), and those who keep its precepts know the liberty of God's children (verse 45). God's word is the instrument of both the initial cleansing which takes place in regeneration (John 15:3) and the sanctification which continues through the whole Christian life ('Sanctify them in the truth; your word is truth' [John 17:17]).

God uses Scripture. It is the 'sword of the Spirit' (Eph. 6:17). By it our lives are transformed. It is God-breathed for this very purpose, equipping us through its 'teaching, reproof, correction and training in righteousness' (2 Tim. 3:16). It has the power to instruct the mind, introduce clear thinking, inform the conscience and conform us to God's will. At the same time, we are to grab hold of the sword of the Spirit; we have 'purified [our] souls by [our] obedience to the truth' (1 Pet. 1:22); we are to abide in Christ by letting his word take up residence in our lives (John 15:7).

This is why, in Reformed theology, the law of God is seen to play such an important role in sanctification. Its three functions or uses are well known: (i) to convict of sin, (ii) to restrain evildoers and (iii) to instruct believers. A distinctive feature of Reformed theology is that the third use is seen to be the central one:

> The third and principal use, which pertains more closely to the proper purpose of the law, finds its place among believers in whose hearts the Spirit of God already lives and reigns. For even though they have the law written and engraved upon their hearts by the finger of God (Jer. 31:33; Heb. 10:16), that is, have been so moved and quickened through the directing of the Spirit that they long to obey God, they still profit by the law.[1]

Is this legalism? Legalism usually involves seeking salvation on the basis of obedience to the law or believing that every detail of life is covered specifically by some law. But neither of these positions was ever mandated in Scripture, even during the epoch when the Mosaic law governed life in considerable detail.

[1] Calvin, *Institutes*, II.vii.12.

God's law expresses what he intended humanity to be when he made us as his image. That is why the commandments in Exodus 20 can readily be traced back to the ordinances of creation in Genesis 1–3. Further, Jesus himself expounds the continuing relevance of the law in the Sermon on the Mount (Matt. 5:17-48) and the gospel he proclaimed gave rise to his 'new command' (John 13:34; 15:9-17).

For this reason sanctification in the New Testament involves conformity to the moral law. For God by 'sending his own Son in the likeness of sinful flesh and for sin ... condemned sin in the flesh, in order that the righteous requirement of the law might be fulfilled in us, who walk not according to the flesh but according to the Spirit' (Rom. 8:3-4). Rather than contradict law, love is its fulfilment (Rom. 13:8-10). Consequently, the law of God fulfilled in Christ remains the standard of holiness for the New Testament believer. But now (in contrast to what may have been true before becoming a Christian) believers endeavour to fulfil the law, not in order to be justified but because they have already been justified, not in the flesh but in the Spirit, not out of merit-seeking but out of the response of faith which works by love (Gal. 5:6).

This emphasis on Scripture as a means of sanctification also helps to explain why Reformed theology has placed such an emphasis on preaching as an instrument in sanctification. Expository preaching which engaged the minds of the congregation as hearers (in contrast to elaborate liturgy at which the congregation were spectators) was a leading characteristic of all the mainstream reformers, not least of whom was Martin Luther; but it has been in the Reformed churches that this emphasis has been most marked.

Calvin preached several times each week in Geneva, patiently expounding book after book of Scripture. (Indeed, when he returned to the pulpit of St Peter's church after a period of forced exile, he simply carried on expounding from the point at which he had left off![1]) In one form or another such in-depth preaching characterized the later Puritans and other Reformed pastors such as Jonathan Edwards.

---

[1] Various preaching programmes marked Calvin's extended ministry in Geneva, involving him in preaching every day on alternate weeks and twice on Sundays. This marked a decrease in his preaching load from an earlier period of ministry!

What is so striking about their sermons, however, is that they covered the whole word of God and did not limit their preaching either to a few 'evangelistic' texts or necessarily to evangelistically orientated messages. Compare many of these older sermons with much evangelical preaching today and one is struck by the contrast. How much doctrine they taught from Scripture! They believed that the whole Bible was given to make whole Christians.

This emphasis on preaching is grounded in the conviction that God works through it to sanctify his people. Because God's word of grace can 'build you up and … give you the inheritance among all those who are sanctified' (Acts 20:32) and is 'profitable for teaching, for reproof, for correction, and for training in righteousness' (2 Tim. 3:16), it is to be preached (2 Tim. 4:2).

For this purpose God has given gifts to his church to help us to reach full maturity (Eph. 4:11-16). It is interesting in this context that those Paul mentions are all (apparently) ministries of the word. It is equally interesting that the Ephesian church (which received this instruction along with other congregations) had firsthand experience of what Paul had in mind. He had taught them daily in the lecture hall of Tyrannus and from house to house (Acts 20:20; cf. 19:9). This went on for three years, Luke notes. Indeed, one manuscript tradition records that these meetings lasted for five hours each day![1]

This in no way denigrates the private reading and study of Scripture (a phenomenon simply not possible for the first Christians, since even if they had been able to collect the entire canon of the New Testament, the materials required for one copy would have cost a year's wages). But it does emphasize the strategic role which public exposition of Scripture can play in the life of the church, and also the premium which Scripture places on the mind and its activity in sanctification. It is by the renewal of the mind that we are transformed by the Spirit, as we reflect on (or

---

[1] The Western text adds to Acts 19:9 that Paul taught in the lecture hall of Tyrannus 'from the fifth to the tenth hour' (from 11 a.m. to 4 p.m.), on which F. F. Bruce comments, 'A very reasonable guess, if guess it be. Tyrannus no doubt gave his lectures before 11am at which hour public life in Ionian cities, as elsewhere, regularly ended.' *The Acts of the Apostles* (Grand Rapids: Eerdmans, 1953), p. 356.

contemplate) the glory of the Lord in Scripture (Rom. 12:1-2; 2 Cor. 3:18).

(2) The providences of God

The providences of God, not least of which are severe trials and afflictions, are also ordained for the purpose of sanctification. 'These afflictions', wrote John Flavel, with the quaintness characteristic of a seventeenth-century divine, 'have the same use and end to our souls, that frosty weather hath upon those clothes that are laid and bleaching, they alter the hue and make them white.'[1]

This is confirmed by biblical biography and explicit testimony. In most of the key figures in redemptive history we can trace the way in which God's providences moulded their characters. What people or devils intend for evil, God intends for good (Gen. 50:20). Affliction serves as a divine beacon for those who are going astray (Psa. 119:67).

We have already discussed this theme from another point of view in considering the external dimension of mortification. That discussion should serve to remind us that providence yields sanctification only as it is experienced in union with Christ. Only to those who love God and are called (into union with Christ) according to his purpose do all things work together for good (Rom. 8:28). This is because in his foreknowledge God has predestined his people to be conformed to the image of Christ (Rom. 8:29). Because this is the end in view in all the circumstances of life, believers can respond to them positively, knowing that the Spirit of God is employing them in his transforming ministry. In providence, then, the believer looks for God's handiwork and submits to God's severe mercies. Indeed, says Calvin, united to Christ, 'the church of Christ has been from the beginning so constituted that the cross has been the way to victory and death the way to life'.[2] United to Christ, we understand providences in these terms: 'For as we share abundantly in Christ's sufferings, so through Christ we share abundantly in comfort too' (2 Cor. 1:5).

---

[1] Flavel, *Works*, IV:407.
[2] Calvin, *Comm. 1 Peter*, p. 240.

(3) The fellowship of the church

The fellowship of the church is the context in which sanctification matures, and in this sense is also a means for its development. For sanctification involves our attitudes and actions in relation to others. The love which is the heart of imitation of Christ (compare 1 Cor. 13) cannot be isolationist; the death of our inordinate love of self is tested therefore in fellowship. This is the thrust of Paul's exposition of true sanctification in the context of weak and strong sharing the same fellowship: 'We who are strong have an obligation to bear with the failings of the weak, and not to please ourselves. Let each of us please his neighbour for his good, to build him up. For Christ did not please himself ...' (Rom. 15:1-3).

Reformed theology sees the church as a preaching and suffering community. By these means it is sanctified, is thus transformed into Christ's likeness and so bears witness in the world. But several other elements mark the true church. Included among them are the fact that the church is a caring and praying community. These elements in its life are also helps for our sanctification.

The church is a fellowship of pastoral care. Explicit directions are given to those who have specific gifts (Rom. 12:3-8, for example). But exhortation is also given to the whole church to exercise a pastoral ministry: 'To each is given the manifestation of the Spirit *for the common good*' (1 Cor. 12:7, emphasis added). It is 'when each part is working properly' that the whole body in Christ is made to 'grow so that it builds itself up in love' (Eph. 4:16). We 'teach and admonish one another with all wisdom' (Col. 3:16 NIV). The New Testament letters illustrate this regularly, both with extended exposition and with what we might call apostolic one-liners—simple epigrams which are aimed at the mutual encouragement of holy living. If we bear in mind that the recipients of the 'practical' segments in Paul's letters are addressed in the second person plural ('you' is usually plural), his intended impact will become clear. His logic is that these things are to be true of all of us as a church and therefore of each of us as individuals.

By contrast, our logic in the evangelical tradition has tended to be that once these things are true of me individually, and I can gather enough individuals like myself around me, then they will be true of the church. We move from the individual to the corporate, the microcosm to the macrocosm. Paul's teaching moves in the opposite direction. Once that is grasped, the necessity of church association for true sanctification becomes self-evident.

The church is also a community of prayer. Again the sheer weight of the prayers which permeate the apostolic writings confirms this and shames the contemporary church for its mistaken assumption that sanctification can be produced prayerlessly. This is a theme which requires extended treatment beyond the scope of this essay.[1] Here it is sufficient to mention it for the sake of completeness in expressing the Reformed understanding of sanctification.

(4) The sacraments

Finally, it should be noted that in Reformed theology, the sacraments play an important role in sanctification. How they do was a major bone of contention at the time of the Reformation and remains so today, and cannot be expounded in detail here. Simply expressed, in Reformed teaching, the sacraments are communicative signs. They point us away from ourselves to Christ; but they also are a visible, tangible means by which he communicates with us and we with him. They display his grace and our union and communion with him in it. They mark off and remind us of the distinction between the church and the world (Rom. 6:1-4; 1 Cor. 10:16, 21). In doing so, they provide incentives to Christ-likeness and sanctification.

The sacraments can never be separated from the word of God. Nor do the sacraments provide sanctifying grace from Christ which is not available to us in the message of the Scriptures. It is the same grace we receive, because the same Christ is held out to us. Both Scripture and sacraments point to the same Lord. But, as Robert Bruce so well expressed it, while we do not get a better Christ in the sacraments than we do in the word, there are times when we get Christ better.[2] In the

---

[1] I have suggested a Reformed or covenantal approach to prayer in 'Prayer—A Covenant Work', *The Banner of Truth*, 137 (1975), pp. 23ff.

[2] Robert Bruce, *The Mystery of the Lord's Supper*, tr. and ed. Thomas F. Torrance (Richmond, VA: John Knox Press, 1958), pp. 64, 84-85.

words of Horatius Bonar's communion hymn which so well represents the Reformed approach to the Lord's Table,

> Here, O my Lord, I see Thee face to face;
> Here would I touch and handle things unseen,
> Here grasp with firmer hand the eternal grace,
> And all my weariness upon Thee lean.

The sacraments are helps to sanctification precisely because they are means to a fresh realization of our union and communion with Christ. They point us back to its foundation and forward to its consummation in glory (as we have been buried with Christ in baptism, we will be raised with him in resurrection; as we commune with the crucified and risen Christ, we also proclaim him until he comes again [1 Cor. 11:26]). Here we are brought back to the foundation on which the Reformed understanding of sanctification rests: union with Christ. We are baptized into him and share in the virtue of his death and resurrection; as we eat the bread and drink the wine, we are able to say, because of that union, 'I have been crucified with Christ. It is no longer I who live, but Christ who lives in me. And the life I now live in the flesh I live by faith in the Son of God, who loved me and gave himself for me' (Gal. 2:20).

Sanctification is simply the outworking of this communion. We become like those with whom we have the closest communion. Thus, in Reformed theology, sanctification means becoming like Christ.

CHAPTER TWENTY-EIGHT

REFORMED THEOLOGY—
REFORMED LIFESTYLE

T HE topic assigned for these Jung-Am lectures[1] is 'Reformed Theology and a Reformed Lifestyle'. It is a remit any Reformed theologian would accept gladly, because the marriage between theology and lifestyle, which it suggests, is a profoundly biblical one. It is characteristic of the New Testament: expositions of God's revelation—who he is and what he has done for us—always lead to practical application to everyday life. In more technical theological language, the indicatives of grace (what God has done for us) are always linked to the imperatives of gratitude (what we are to become in response).

But, of course, this pattern is not a novelty in the New Testament. It is deeply covenantal in character, and is already present and visible in the Old Testament, if we have eyes to see it. It is there in the opening chapters of the Bible in Genesis 1–2. God has been breathtakingly generous in what he has done as Creator; the only appropriate response is obedience to his wise commands. An identical structure is present in the law of God in general and in the Decalogue in particular: theology—who God is as the Lord who redeems his people from bondage in Egypt—carries implications for life, and for what his people are called to be (Exod. 20:1ff.).

[1] The Jung-Am Lectures were established in 1989 in Seoul, South Korea, under the auspices of the Hapdong Presbyterian Theological Seminary, in memory of Dr Yun Sun Park, one of the most distinguished and influential teachers and writers of the Korean Presbyterian Churches of the twentieth century. The lectures are intended to be popular in nature, but with an audience containing a large number of ministers and theological students. The second series of lectures was given in November 1990 and was originally published in Korean in 1991.

This indicative/imperative structure of God's self-revelation pervades the entire Old Testament: 'Be holy, *for* I am holy' (Lev. 11:44) is, in one form or another, a constant refrain. Biblical theology is meant to produce a biblical lifestyle; covenant grace calls for covenant faithfulness; a holy God must have a holy people. Scripture could not be clearer.

We are to explore this theme in terms of our Reformed theology. In introducing ourselves to that tradition we can surely do no better than draw attention to some of the ways in which the great Reformer John Calvin helps us to see more clearly what it means to know God and to live for his glory.

Theology and piety

In this context, it is worth reminding ourselves that reformation of doctrine has always gone hand in hand with revival of spiritual life and vitality. This was certainly true in the Reformation period. Calvin's biographers describe his brilliant participation in the frequent theological debates of the sixteenth century. The dramatic result of his intervention in one of these was that large numbers of priests turned to the Reformed faith, a moral cleansing took place among the local populace, a new spirit of godliness took hold of many people, and true religion began to flourish.

Sometimes this inviolable connection between what Scripture calls 'sound [healthy or health-giving] words' (2 Tim. 1:13) and the transformation of life is seen in quite dramatic ways; on other occasions in a less spectacular manner. But whether dramatic or quiet in its effects, true Reformed theology can never be coldly academic. If it is, it ceases to be either biblical or Reformed.

This point is well illustrated by an interesting footnote to Calvin's *magnum opus*. When the first edition of the *Institutes of the Christian Religion* was published in 1536, it carried the revealing subtitle: '*Containing the whole sum of piety.*' Whether the words were written by Calvin himself, or by some anonymous copy-editor (in a day when the publisher's 'blurb' appeared on the title page, and not on the back cover of the book!), they are highly significant, especially in their Latin form, *summa pietatis*. They stand in marked contrast to the great (and in its own way, noble) tradition of scholastic theology with its focus on intellectual understanding rather than personalized knowledge.

The high point of theology in the Middle Ages was Thomas Aquinas's *Summa Theologiae* (*Sum*, or *Survey*, *of Theology*). But Calvin did not write a *summa theologiae*; he wrote a *summa pietatis*, a survey of piety. He was concerned not merely with the instruction of the intellect, but with the engagement of the heart and the whole person in devotion to the Lord. His work well illustrates his personal motto: 'I offer my heart to you, Lord, readily and sincerely.'

Because of this, as Calvin's *Institutes* developed through its various re-writings (from 1536 until 1559) into the large work we are familiar with today, its central theme was always the same: the true, evangelical knowledge of God, and how that affects and transforms our lives. He therefore constantly seeks to draw the reader into a personal appreciation of what is being expounded. Piety, devotion to God, not merely intellectual understanding, is always his goal since eternal life means knowing God, in Christ, through the Spirit (John 17:3). People who are daunted by the thought of reading Calvin are usually amazed to discover how straightforward, practical, and devotional his writing is.

True wisdom and knowledge

The opening words of the *Institutes*, little changed from the great statement which readers of their first edition encountered when they opened the much smaller six-chapter work in 1536, are these: 'Nearly all the wisdom we possess, that is to say, true and sound wisdom, consists of two parts: the knowledge of God and of ourselves.'[1] As Calvin scholars have often pointed out, the sentiment is an echo of Augustine who, many centuries before, had recorded in his *Soliloquies*: 'O God, who art ever the same, let me know myself and thee. That is my prayer.'[2] The same idea underlies the even more famous words of the opening section of his *Confessions*: 'You have made us for yourself, and our hearts are restless until they find their rest in you.'[3]

[1] Calvin, *Institutes*, I.i.1.
[2] Augustine, *Soliloquies*, II.i.1.
[3] Augustine, *Confessions*, I.1.

Reformed theology, then—or at least the only Reformed theology John Calvin would have recognized—is about knowing God in such a way that we come to know ourselves and our world more fully. We learn not only to 'think God's thoughts after him', but also to live our lives as his moral image in 'true righteousness and holiness' (Eph. 4:24).

Such knowledge of God is, according to Scripture, our greatest privilege. It is the heart of eternal life, says Jesus: 'This is eternal life, that they know you the only true God …' (John 17:3). It is the fulfilment of the promise of the new covenant: 'I will give them a heart to know that I am the LORD' (Jer. 24:7). Says Jeremiah again, 'Thus says the LORD: "Let not the wise man boast in his wisdom, let not the mighty man boast in his might, let not the rich man boast in his riches, but let him who boasts boast in this, that he understands and knows me, that I am the LORD who practises steadfast love, justice, and righteousness in the earth"' (Jer. 9:23-24). Such knowledge of God is the experience Paul prays for the Colossians:

> We have not ceased to pray for you, asking that you may be filled with the knowledge of his will in all spiritual wisdom and understanding, so as to walk in a manner worthy of the Lord, fully pleasing to him, bearing fruit in every good work and increasing in the knowledge of God (Col. 1:9-10).

Here again we see that in all biblical thinking, theology, the knowledge of God, and lifestyle are inseparable.

How, then, is this worked out from Scripture, for example, by John Calvin and the other great teachers in the Reformed tradition? What is involved in knowing God?

As is well known, Calvin speaks of a *duplex cognitio Dei*, a twofold knowledge of God as Creator and as Redeemer. Logically we begin by speaking of God as Creator; but we must recognize that we do not now come to know him as Creator unless we have come to know him as Redeemer.

The knowledge of God the Creator

God is the Creator of all things. Everything, whether visible or invisible to us, comes from his hand and displays his handiwork. The heavens declare his glory (Psa. 19:1). In what he has made he has clearly revealed himself (Rom. 1:20). The whole of creation carries his autograph and reveals his attributes. Furthermore, he has created man in, or as, his very image and likeness. Man, as created, is therefore himself a further, fuller, clearer revelation from God, and indeed, of God.

This biblical teaching has two implications. The *first* shows us how to think about the nature of creation; the *second* about the experience of humanity.

Metaphors

Calvin gives us three metaphors to help us think about creation and its Creator:

(i) The first is that creation is a *theatre*. Calvin actually calls it a 'dazzling theatre' and a 'beautiful theatre' in which the glory of God is marvellously displayed.[1] We have been placed in the world to contemplate the works of God and to be spectators of his majesty. We are to be an audience which responds to his glory. This, of course, has profound implications for the spirit in which we live as believers: it suggests that the wonders of creation are meant to give rise to the praise and applause in the human heart.

(ii) The second metaphor is that creation is a *mirror*. God himself cannot be known by us as he is known to himself, immediately and directly, apart from the medium of his self-revelation in the created order, in history, and in Christ. More than once Calvin emphasizes that it is only a fool who seeks thus to know the divine essence.[2] No, God is known only by means of his revelation. His character is revealed in his deeds. We see him in them as in a mirror, by reflection. We see the 'immense riches of God's wisdom, justice, goodness and power' in creation 'as in mirrors'.[3]

This metaphor also carries practical implications for us: we can never understand (and must never view) the created order as though it were a closed system and therefore explicable in its own terms. We are meant to study it, to explore it and to love it, not as a thing in itself, but as a reflection of the glorious attributes of God.

---

[1] Calvin, *Institutes*, I.v.8; I.xiv.20.
[2] Calvin, *Comm. Romans*, p. 31 (on 1:19).
[3] Calvin, *Institutes*, I.xiv.21.

(iii) The third metaphor Calvin uses for creation is that of a *garment*. God is invisible in his being. He is the invisible God (Col. 1:15). How then can we see and know him? Answer: because he accommodates himself to us and, as it were, clothes himself in the garments of creation. Thus, in Paul's words, the visible things reveal the invisible attributes of God (Rom. 1:20): his eternity, his power, his deity, and his marvellous creatorhood. The great Dutch theologian Herman Bavinck puts all this beautifully when he says: 'According to Scripture, the entire universe is a creation and therefore a revelation of God. Nothing is atheistic in the absolute sense of the term.'[1]

Eternity in our hearts

There is a further significant implication for our experience in the manner of God's work as Creator. He has made man as his image. The whole creation reflects God's glory, but man, supremely, is a mirror-reflection of God. He is the finest and clearest element of creation-revelation since, like God, he is a rational and volitional being, and one who is capable of fellowship with God.

We are not only surrounded by divine revelation. We are also invaded by that revelation. Man is part of God's revelation; indeed, the apex of it. We cannot escape from the truth which our very being proclaims. This, as Ecclesiastes well says, is the burden God has placed upon us; he has set the need for the eternal in our hearts (Eccles. 3:11)! Again it is a Dutch theologian who best expresses this. Abraham Kuyper writes: 'If the cosmos is the theatre of revelation, in this theatre man is actor as well as spectator.'[2]

Consequently we cannot escape from the presence and power of God, as David indicates in Psalm 139. There is 'nowhere' we can go to hide from his presence. As his image-bearers, we are inescapably haunted by what Calvin calls the *sensus divinitatis*, a sense of God. We possess what he terms the *cognitio dei insita*, an implanted knowledge of God such

---

[1] Herman Bavinck, *The Doctrine of God* (1951; repr. Edinburgh: Banner of Truth Trust, 1977), p. 42.

[2] Abraham Kuyper, *Encyclopaedia of Sacred Theology*, tr. J. H. de Vries (London: Hodder & Stoughton, 1899), p. 264.

that, 'No one can look upon himself without immediately turning his thoughts to the contemplation of God in whom he lives and moves.'[1]

In the nature of the case, we may not be able to give a logically adequate account of this knowledge of God, or explain the psychological mechanism by which we know that he *is*. But this should not surprise us, for it is doubtful if we can provide such an account of our general knowledge and awareness of the world and of ourselves. The Christian believer need not feel philosophically threatened by this limitation on his or her analytical powers. We are, after all, *creatures*.

This emphasis on the richness and clarity of the revelation of God's person and attributes is one of the most characteristic emphases of Reformed theology. It is rooted in Paul's important teaching in Romans 1:18-32—a passage which, incidentally, has sometimes been thought to have played a key role in Calvin's own conversion from Rome to the Reformation, from the false to the true knowledge of God. It has a very important implication for our Christian witness.

What is this implication? It is as Paul says in Romans 1 that, surrounded and invaded by this sense of deity, mankind seeks to stifle and repress it. Consequently individual men and women seek to reject at the conscious cognitive level what they know to be true in the depth of their being.

Recognizing this has given lasting stability and confidence to the witness of Reformed Christians. We know something about unbelievers concerning which they themselves are often in a state of denial: they are on the run from the God with whom they have to do, but they cannot escape from his revelation. They are engaged in a programme of self-deceit. Our task is to be instruments of the Spirit's work of unmasking them. Knowing these things gives us great confidence in our witnessing and in our apologetics.

In a word, then, the doctrine of the knowledge of God as Creator has important implications both for our true spiritual enjoyment—we live in a theatre in which God has displayed his many attributes and his marvellous glory—and for the confidence and fruitfulness of our witness to others.

---

[1] Calvin, *Institutes*, I.1.1.

But in speaking of witnessing to others and of the apologetic implications of the knowledge of God the Creator, we have already run ahead of ourselves. For why are witnessing and apologetics necessary? The answer of Reformed theology, following Scripture, is: we have all sinned and fallen short of God's glory. We have rejected him. Now, in a fallen world, if we are to come to a living knowledge of God as Creator, we must be brought back to him, and first come to know him, as God the Redeemer.

In thinking of the knowledge of God as Redeemer, four elements are central in the theology which Calvin expounded. They are: (1) the tragic consequences of man's rebellion; (2) the necessity of Scripture; (3) the centrality of Christ's redemption; and (4) the nature of regeneration.

(1) The tragic consequences of man's rebellion

From one point of view, sinful man cannot escape from his knowledge of God. But that knowledge is a rebellious knowledge, possessed now only in the context of man's attempts to reject it. It is no longer an obedient or covenantal knowledge of God, a knowledge-in-fellowship with God. Hence Paul, who can say in one place that men 'knew God' (Rom. 1:21), can also, without contradiction, characterize unbelievers as those who do not know God (as in 1 Cor. 1:21; Gal. 4:8; 1 Thess. 4:5). They suppress the knowledge they possess and exchange the truth about God for a lie (Rom. 1:18, 28).

For Reformed theology, the strong active language of this last statement of Paul has special significance: men have exchanged the truth about God for a lie. Behind all that the apostle says in Romans 1:18-32 lies the shadow of Genesis 1–3. The 'lie' here is, of course, an allusion to the narrative of Genesis 3, and the falsehood by which Eve was ensnared and deceived: 'You will not surely die' (Gen. 3:4, 13). But it goes further than that. For the motive of Satan in deceiving Eve was not simply to deny the authority of God's word; it was to distort the revelation, and therefore the character, of God himself.

God had said that the man and woman could eat from any tree in the garden except one (Gen. 2:16-17). But the serpent's words distorted that generous freedom: 'Did God actually say, "You shall not eat of any tree in the garden"?' (Gen. 3:1). The lavish kindness of God was thus maligned. Satan was implying: 'Has God set before you this vast display of treasures only to tell you that you may have none of them? What kind of God would do that?'

The 'lie' which was substituted in the garden of Eden for 'the truth about God' involved the defamation of his character. Having accepted the lie, man has a distorted view of God, as well as a heart that rebels against him.

What, then, is our condition? It is this: we cannot escape from being aware of God's revelation—it surrounds us and inwardly haunts us; we cannot avoid being religious—we are made to worship; but we have repudiated the generous revelation of God in creation, twisted the character of God, and rejected his word. There is no greater or more poignant tragedy than this.

In this context, one of the strengths of Reformed theology is the way it stresses the multifaceted character of man's fallen condition in order to underline the depth of human perversity. We often think of the fall as a rebellion against God's law, and indeed it is. But it is also a rejection and denial of God's love and his generous provision—one might even say his grace, since Reformed theologians have not limited that term to the demonstrations of God's love to us in our fallen condition. Man is not only unfaithful to God's word and disobedient to God's command, he is also ungrateful for God's lavish love. His ingratitude is both monstrous and blasphemous (2 Tim. 3:2).

This complex character of man's sinful condition, and especially the recognition that the fall was a rejection of the kindness and generosity of God, gives rise to an important implication. The natural man often professes that his God is 'a God of love'. But biblical theology recognizes that he does not—indeed he cannot—really believe that. He does not, because he has accepted the lie; he cannot, because part of the lie he has accepted is the way it presents God as malign and sinister in character.

The evidence that this is the case is plain for all of us to see. The natural man who makes this empty profession about believing in a God of love does not trust himself to that God; he does not pray joyfully to him; he does not worship him in songs of praise; he does not seek or love fellowship with him; he refuses to allow himself to be 'known' by him (Gal. 4:9). His lips claim one thing; his heart believes something quite different. Instead, as Calvin puts it, his mind 'is a perpetual factory of idols';[1] he will worship any god rather than the living and true God of Scripture.

Such is the tragic, perverse, ruined creature man has become. This conviction lies therefore at the heart of Reformed theology: sin needs to be taken with the utmost seriousness.

How, then, does the gospel provide a remedy for this condition? Because the effects of the fall are so diverse and complex, Reformed theology does not provide a simple, one-sentence answer to the question *How does God restore man to fellowship with himself?* Since the fall has intellectual, moral, and psychological as well as social consequences, the remedy for it must also be manifold. It involves the gift of the Scriptures, the work of Christ, and the ministry of the Spirit in regeneration.

(2) The necessity of Scripture

The intellectual effect of the fall means that although he is surrounded by divine revelation, man no longer appreciates it as a garment God wears to make his attributes visible, nor as a theatre of his glory, nor as a mirror reflecting his presence. Instead, Calvin says, we are at best like 'old or bleary-eyed men and those with weak vision [who], if you thrust before them a most beautiful volume, even if they recognize it to be some sort of writing, yet can scarcely construe two words'.[2]

This is evident to the believer on every hand. He or she studies, perhaps, at a great institute of learning, and there encounters teachers with deep and wide scholarship. Yet, as Calvin unceremoniously puts it, when it comes to the true knowledge of God, they are as blind as bats. They cannot make spiritual sense of anything.

It is in such a context, Calvin says, that God has given to us the book of Scripture in addition to the book of nature. Just as those 'bleary-eyed men … with the aid of spectacles will begin to read distinctly; so Scripture, gathering up the otherwise confused knowledge of God in our minds, having dispersed our dullness, clearly shows us the true God'.[3]

[1] Calvin, *Institutes*, I.xi.8.
[2] *Ibid.*, I.vi.1.
[3] *Ibid.*

Scripture provides the lenses we need to know God again. Naturally, this should not be taken in isolation either from the work of Christ or from the ministry of the Spirit to cleanse our hearts and to give us spiritual illumination. But within that context, Calvin says the Scriptures are like spectacles; they bring everything into proper focus and order, because in them God reveals himself and his ways.

In order to do this, it is essential that Scripture should be *breathed out by God* and possess his *authority.* The Scriptures are truly recognized by us only when we give to them the kind of reverence we give to God, because there his living voice is heard.[1] In the same spirit, the Scottish Reformers, led by John Knox, in composing the *Scots Confession* in 1560, refer to Scripture as the 'mouth of God' (Matt. 4:4). Its origin lies in God.

This is not to say that Reformed theology denies what is nowadays called the humanity of Scripture; far from it, as Calvin's *Commentaries* everywhere indicate. But the chief concern, as must be the perennial concern of every Christian, is to recognize their divine character.

Not only is there divine authority in Scripture, but it also possesses the attribute of *sufficiency.* Nothing additional is needed for equipping the man of God, says Paul to Timothy (2 Tim. 3:16-17)—a point worth bearing in mind whenever the sects appear urging on us the importance of an additional book of revelation. More generally, the Reformed appreciation of the all-sufficiency of Scripture safeguards us against the errors of those who tell us that we cannot be complete Christians unless we have access to the 'truth' which some new piece of literature purveys.

The implications of this doctrine of Scripture are very far-reaching for the Christian lifestyle; but that is a subject for another occasion. Here we must underline that Reformed theology does not teach that it is the Scripture itself that saves. Consequently we must give attention to a third element in the knowledge of God the Redeemer.

(3) The centrality of Christ's work

If we are to be restored to a living knowledge of God, what has been broken must be repaired and what has been lost in the fall must be restored. This is the work of the Mediator, Jesus Christ.

---

[1] Calvin, *Institutes*, I.vii.1.

The central way in which Calvin and the Reformed tradition have described the work of Christ in restoring us to fellowship with God is in terms of his threefold office as Prophet, Priest and King.

Adam was created to be the image of God and, in a sense, to serve him in three ways: (i) As God's appointed prophet he was to speak God's word and give God's direction to the whole creation. Thus, for example, Adam was to name the animals (Gen. 2:19-20). (ii) As God's appointed priest he was to give intelligent expression to the worship of the whole of God's creation, as the conductor of an orchestra of nature, each creature playing its appropriate part in a grand symphony of praise. (iii) As God's appointed king he was to have dominion over all things and govern them as God's representative on earth so that the whole creation might be ordered for God's glory.

By his sin, Adam became apostate and therefore incapable of fulfilling any of his ministries. Since we share in his fall, we too are apostate prophets, priests and kings. But, as the Old Testament hints, when the Christ came—the one anointed by God not with oil but with the power of the Holy Spirit—he would fulfil each of these ministries in our place. Not only so, but he would bear the judgment the first Adam and his seed deserved for sin.

The heart of the gospel, then, in the theology of the Reformation, is found in what Calvin (and Luther before him) called 'the wonderful exchange'. Christ took our flesh in the incarnation in order to take our place and bear our sins on the cross at Calvary. He lived a life of whole-hearted obedience to his Father for our sakes, and then at Calvary bore our judgment. Christ, as Calvin puts it, took on 'the person' of a sinner. He received what was ours, while by faith we receive what is his; he experienced desolation and alienation from God on the cross so that we might be welcomed into the bosom of the Father.

This is the testimony of such passages as 2 Corinthians 5:21: Christ who knew no personal sin became sin (or a sin-offering) for us, so that in him we might become the righteousness of God. Calvin himself believed that this was the significance of the way in which the Gospels describe the judgment and suffering of Christ. He notes, in his brilliant and poignant exposition of the passion narrative, how frequently in his trial and crucifixion our Lord was declared by all parties to be utterly innocent, yet he was still executed as though he were guilty. This, he argues, is not accidental. God so governed the events of his Son's incarnation that they displayed his personal innocence. He died as if he were a sinner, only and precisely because he was dying in the place of sinners.

Other Reformed theologians have seen this vividly illustrated in the events of the night of Jesus' betrayal. In the upper room, he took the cup of fellowship with God in the Passover, and gave it to his disciples; he said he would not drink of the cup until he drank it anew in his Father's kingdom (Mark 14:23-25). In exchange, in Gethsemane he received from his Father's hand a cup from which he naturally shrank back. This was the cup described in the prophets as a cup of judgment and dereliction, the cup of God's condemnation of sin; the cup sinners should have drunk for themselves (Mark 14:33-36; cf. Isa. 51:17, 22; Jer. 25:15, 17; Hab. 2:16). But Christ took it, and he drank its last bitter dregs.

Christ, then, has died to bear our guilt. Penal substitution, as Calvin saw, is the very core of the work of Christ.

But here Reformed theology provides us with a further important insight. Although it sees penal substitution as the heart of the matter, it does not limit its exposition of the atonement to one 'theory'. As evangelical students of historical theology, we affirm the Anselmic-Reformed doctrine of the necessity of satisfaction and reject the so-called Abelardian view which reduces Christ's work to revealing the overwhelming character of the love of God which therefore exerts its powerful influence on us. But we must not lose sight of the fact that, according to Scripture, the cross is the great demonstration of the love of God, as such biblical statements as John 3:16, Romans 5:8 and 8:32 amply demonstrate.

Why is this significant? Because it explains why the message of the cross brings us to an understanding of, and appreciation for, the character of the God it reveals. Yes, the cross displays his holiness; but the cross is also the place where 'heaven's love and heaven's justice meet'.[1] Christ's death deals with our guilt, but it also undoes the twist that sin has produced in our thinking. It is the remedy for the terrible distortion

---

[1] From the hymn 'Beneath the Cross of Jesus' by Elizabeth Clephane.

of the character of God which we have seen took place in the fall. It brings us to believe what creation had in fact proclaimed: God is love!

But only through interpreting the death of Christ *as a penal substitution* do we come to believe this. The love of Christ compels us only because we understand that on the cross Christ died in our place (as Paul indicates in 2 Corinthians 5:14, 21). Here it is appropriate to underline a principle which has carried great weight in our Reformed theology, and one which has important ramifications for us as Christians. Christ did not die in order to persuade the Father to love us; he died *because* the Father loved us. The great Puritan theologian John Owen put it thus, recognizing that even Christians may think of God the Father 'with anxious, doubtful thoughts':

> What fears, what questionings there are of his good-will and kindness! At the best, many think there is no sweetness at all in him towards us, but what is purchased at the high price of the blood of Jesus.[1]

It is essential to understand the point Owen is making. If the cross reveals God, it reveals the love of the Father as *antecedent* to the cross. The atonement is not a work in which the loving Son persuades the Father to be gracious; rather, it demonstrates the quality of the love the Father already has for sinners. He 'so loved the world that he gave'. When this is grasped these fears and doubts which lie deeply embedded in our thinking and feeling about God begin to be dissolved. But they are so only through Christ's *atoning* death.

In this way the message of the cross not only answers the need for the burden of our guilt to be removed, but also for the distortion in our view of God to be remedied. Once again we can become prophets, priests and kings—boldly proclaiming the gospel; joyfully engaging in heartfelt worship, praise and prayer; reigning in life through Jesus Christ our Lord.

This, in turn, leads us to a fourth consideration:

---

[1] Owen, *Works*, II:32.

(4) The necessity of regeneration by the Spirit
God has given special revelation to us; he has given Christ on the cross
for us; but in addition, it is essential for our restoration that he work
inwardly on us by his Spirit. We need to be united to Christ if we are
to experience new life. Without this, Calvin says, everything that Christ
has done for us is of no avail to us.[1]

The heart of this work is divinely-wrought regeneration. Here the
sovereignty of God in salvation stands out in clearest relief, for God's
work of regeneration is parallel to his original work of creation: for the
'God, who said, "Let light shine out of darkness," has shone in our hearts
to give the light of the knowledge of the glory of God in the face of Jesus
Christ' (2 Cor. 4:6). This is sovereign divine monergism *par excellence*.

Regeneration takes place against a background of human helplessness;
we cannot contribute to our own salvation. We are no more capable of
bringing ourselves to new birth than we were of bringing ourselves to
natural birth. New creation can be achieved only by the sovereign work
of the Spirit who—like the wind—blows where he wishes (John 3:8).

In the history of Reformed theology the term 'regeneration' has been
used to connote different aspects of this renewing work of the Spirit.
More recently it has been used of the momentary action of God in
which new life is inaugurated. Calvin, however, employed it in a very
broad sense, to describe the whole process of transformation into the
image of Christ from beginning to end (this explains the otherwise
Arminian-sounding title to *Institutes* III.iii—'Our Regeneration by
Faith: Repentance'!).

In either usage, however, the central feature of this work of the Spirit
is that in it he unites us to Jesus Christ as the one in whom all the
blessings of God are to be found.

Paul speaks of this in the opening chapter of Ephesians (which,
incidentally, seems to have been Calvin's favourite epistle) when he traces
the inward work of grace back beyond even the sovereign regenerating
work of the Spirit to the sovereign electing work of God (Eph. 1:3-14).
In the context of expounding the expansive riches of our salvation,
the apostle tells us that every spiritual blessing is ours in Jesus Christ.

---

[1] Calvin, *Institutes*, III.i.1.

The fruit of regeneration, and its authenticating mark in our lives, will therefore be that we live in fellowship with him. We must therefore look to no other source for our spiritual blessing than Christ and Christ alone.

Nowhere does Calvin speak with greater eloquence than here, and in doing so he reminds us that Reformed theology is, at its best, always Christ-centred. Here is the Reformer at his most lyrical:

> We see that our whole salvation and all its parts are comprehended in Christ. We should therefore take care not to derive the least portion of it from anywhere else. If we seek salvation, we are taught by the very name of Jesus that it is 'of him'. If we seek any other gifts of the Spirit, they will be found in his anointing. If we seek strength, it lies in his dominion; if purity, in his conception; if gentleness, it appears in his birth. ... If we seek redemption, it lies in his passion; if acquittal, in his condemnation; if remission of the curse, in his cross; if satisfaction, in his sacrifice; if purification, in his blood; if reconciliation, in his descent into hell; if mortification of the flesh, in his tomb; if newness of life, in his resurrection . . . In short, since rich store of every kind of good abounds in him, let us drink our fill from this fountain, and from no other.[1]

This, then, in brief, is the heart of Reformed theology and the foundation for a biblical, Reformed lifestyle. It reminds us that knowing God is our greatest privilege, and our highest calling. It accuses us of our rejection of God's good revelation of himself. It underlines the importance of the Scriptures as the divinely given spectacles by which we come clearly to see and know God and his works and ways in the world. It gives much of its creative energy to elucidating the grace of our Lord Jesus Christ who became poor that we might become rich (2 Cor. 8:9). It speaks of the work of the Spirit in regeneration and illumination.

Thus Reformed theology reminds us that all creation is for the glory of God alone (*soli Deo gloria*); that salvation is possible only by his grace (*sola gratia*); that we can come to know God only with the aid of the Holy Scriptures (*sola Scriptura*); that the path to justification is by faith alone (*sola fide*); and that all this is possible in Christ alone (*solo Christo*).

---

[1] Calvin, *Institutes*, II.xvi.19.

We will turn later to explore the various implications of this for the Christian's lifestyle. But, for the moment, it is enough to remind ourselves of these great Reformation watchwords: God's glory, God's grace, God's word, God's Son, God-given faith—alone, yet never one without the others. And let us also remind ourselves of both the emblem and the motto of the father of Reformed theology, John Calvin, and make them our own. The emblem is a heart held out in the palm of an open hand; the motto: 'To you, O Lord, I offer my heart, readily and sincerely.' Having received God's grace in Christ, there is no other way in which we can worthily respond.

We have already stressed the importance of rightly handling the word of God if we are to make consistent progress in living the kingdom of God. This leads us to consider two further principles which are foundational to the Reformed lifestyle.

Union with Christ as the means of conformity to his image
The doctrine of union with Christ lies at the heart of the Christian life, and since the time of Calvin has been central to Reformed theology. All that Christ has done for us, says Calvin, is of no benefit to us so long as we remain outside of Christ.[1] Only when we are united to him do we receive his saving benefits.

Calvin learned the importance of union with Christ from the teaching of the Gospels and the Epistles. In the writings of the apostle Paul the phrase 'in Christ' or its equivalent is definitive of what it means to be a Christian: to be united by the Spirit to Jesus Christ.

Paul learned this when he was still the persecutor, Saul of Tarsus. He thought he was only persecuting Christians. But when Jesus spoke to him on the Damascus Road, he said, 'Saul, why are you persecuting me?' (Acts 9:4). In that moment Saul had his first lesson in the doctrine of union with Christ: Jesus' followers were so united to him that to persecute them was to persecute Jesus himself! To be a Christian means to be 'in Christ'. Thus, when, in Romans 16:7, Paul speaks of two of his kinsfolk, Andronicus and Junias, who were 'in Christ' before he was, he simply means that they became Christians before he did.

[1] Calvin, *Institutes*, III.i.1.

But what are the implications and consequences of this union? Two of them deserve special attention:

(1) Union with Christ in his death and resurrection

Union with Christ means that we come to share in his death to sin and his resurrection to new life. By uniting us to Christ, God the Father means to conform us to the image of his Son. This is the destiny he has in store for us (Rom. 8:29).

Again it is Calvin who expounds this with greatest depth, doubtless because in the doctrine of union with Christ he had discovered a key biblical grid within which he could interpret his own Christian experience. He tells us that as those who are united to Christ we experience both an *inward* and an *outward* mortification and vivification, a dying and a rising with our crucified and resurrected Saviour.

Inwardly, in Christ we have died to sin and are no longer under its dominion (Rom. 6:1ff.); inwardly we are raised with Christ and walk in newness of life through his risen power. This does not mean we are sinless. But since Christ reigns in grace where sin formerly reigned, we have been set free from the dominion, the domination, the tyranny of sin. We are no longer its slaves. This is a vitally important thing for us to know if we are to live the Christian life joyfully and triumphantly.

The great Puritan, John Owen, saw the importance of this, when he said that all pastoral problems involve either persuading those who have never been converted that they are dead in trespasses and sin, and that sin reigns over them; or persuading those who are true believers and have therefore died to sin in union with Christ, that they have died to sin and are no longer under its dominion. They are now alive to God.

But union with Christ in his death and resurrection also affects us in important ways outwardly. For throughout this life we have to bear the cross as disciples of Jesus Christ. But, like Christ's, our sufferings are shaped by God to bear spiritual fruit. Paul speaks of this in 2 Corinthians 4:10-12, when he says that he always carries around in his body the dying of the Lord Jesus, so that the life of Jesus may also be revealed in his mortal body: 'death works' in the apostle, so that 'life works' in others.

Doubtless Paul learned this as he reflected on his own conversion. The structure of Acts 7:58–8:3 suggests a connection between Stephen's death and Saul's subsequent conversion, as though to say: Stephen's death was not a waste but an investment; death worked in Stephen with the consequence that life worked in Saul of Tarsus. Stephen carried around in his body the dying of Jesus, so that the life of Jesus might be produced in Saul. The blood of the martyrs is the seed of the church.

It is almost out of place for a Western Christian to remind Korean Christians of this principle. I recall a seminar at Westminster Seminary on Calvin's theology of the cross when one of our Korean students told us how reading the Reformer's teaching in the *Institutes* on 'life under the cross' had given him renewed appreciation of his family inheritance: 'You see,' he explained, 'my grandfather was martyred for Christ.' As Calvin says, commenting on 1 Peter 1:11, God has fashioned the church from the beginning in such a way that the cross is the way to victory and death the way to life.

But we not only share outwardly in Christ's death; we will also share outwardly in his resurrection. We look forward to that day when he will raise our mortal remains from the dust, and these bodies of humiliation will be changed to become like the body of his glory (Phil. 3:20-21). Indeed, our outward mortification serves to encourage us to look forward to, and long for, that great day.

This is why what Calvin calls 'meditation on the future life' is a central part of the Christian lifestyle. He advises us in this context to beware of the this-worldly horizon of the radical premillenarian view of the ancient Chiliasts that Christ will come and reign for a thousand years. For such teaching Calvin reserves some of his harshest words: it is a 'fiction ... too childish either to need or to be worth a refutation'.[1] Here, following Augustine, Calvin calls on us to fix our eyes not on this world, but on the world to come.

Calvin held that the Mosaic administration of the Sabbath Day pointed believers to Christ's death and resurrection and to their fellowship in them. That Mosaic symbolism has now been fulfilled. But we still use the Sabbath to order our worship and regulate our lives. Yet we do so as those who already enjoy the union with Christ to which it formerly pointed forwards. That is why the Christian's Lord's Day is

[1] Calvin, *Institutes*, III.xxv.5.

the day of resurrection, the first day of the week. We already experience communion with our crucified and risen Lord and carry it into every day of the week.

It is not possible to expound this theme at greater length in one brief study. Suffice it to commend Calvin's own rich exposition of it in Book III of his *Institutes*. Those who have never read Calvin before, and find that even the mention of his name daunts them, are often amazed and then overjoyed to discover the wonderful combination of depth and simplicity in his exposition of this theme in particular.

(2) Union with Christ implies adoption as sons

Union with Christ means that we are brought into God's family as his adopted sons and daughters. The one who chose us in Christ also adopts us into his family through him (Eph. 1:4-5), 'in order that he might be the firstborn among many brothers' (Rom. 8:29). In many ways this is the highest of our present privileges as Christian believers. John Murray eloquently called it 'the apex of redemptive grace and privilege'.[1]

It was not until the *Westminster Confession of Faith* of 1647 that the doctrine of adoption was given its proper place in the church's confessions. But it is interesting to notice, as one reads through Calvin's writings, that the word *adoptio* (adoptive sonship) appears with great frequency. For Calvin it conveys the essence of the Christian life, so much so that he calls the title 'the Spirit of adoption' (Rom. 8:15) 'the first [i.e. supreme] title' for the Holy Spirit.

This sonship is the key to Christian assurance—to know that God loves us as a Father, and that he accepts and rejoices in our works of service and labours of love. It is a great encouragement to intercession: in our petitions we ask our Father to do what he has promised in his word. Because we are his sons and daughters, we can be bold and joyful in approaching him.

Our adoption is also the key to understanding many of our experiences in the Christian life. Fathers train their children and discipline them. This pattern sheds light on the trials and difficulties of the Christian life (as Heb. 12:7 reminds us). Thus, another great Puritan pastor, John Flavel, tells us that afflictions act like the sun on garments

[1] Murray, *Collected Writings*, II:233.

hung out to bleach.[1] They cleanse the children of God and make them holy in their Father's service.

We have seen that Reformed lifestyle is guided by the Scriptures; it is also lived in union with Christ in which we are more and more being made like him. Now we must consider how Christians are:

Called to glorify God as the chief purpose of life

What is to be the attitude of the Christian to the present world order? Our natural instinct is to seek a simple answer to this question. And there is one: we are called to glorify God in the world. But that, in turn, is really a multifaceted statement. For the Reformed Christian (again following Calvin), it consists of three elements:

(1) The Christian is called to develop a healthy contempt for this present world insofar as it is under the reign of sin.

We are by nature inclined to have what Calvin calls a 'slavish' and a 'brute-like' love of this world. We lose our senses in it, and discover that we are no longer able to use it as our servant. It becomes our master and spoils our appetite for spiritual realities and for the world to come. We become sluggish in our pursuit of the knowledge of God.

In this respect the Christian is called to be radically different from his contemporaries. He sees the world in its fallenness and corruption, on the one hand; and on the other he has caught sight of the glorious majesty of God, and of what John Newton called the 'solid joys and lasting treasures'[2] of the world to come. He knows that at God's right hand there is fullness of joy; pleasures for evermore are found in his presence (Psa. 16:11). He cannot look at this world with the same desires and fascination the ungodly man or woman has. We no longer live for ourselves, but for him who loved us and gave himself for us (2 Cor. 5:15).

(2) But the Christian has also been set free to explore this world because God, his Father, is its Creator.

We have already seen that the knowledge of God the Redeemer does not mean that we ignore his creation, but rather that we are restored to

---

[1] See Flavel, *Works*, IV:407.
[2] From the hymn 'Glorious Things of Thee Are Spoken' by John Newton.

the knowledge of him as Creator. This was an important point made by the Reformed theologians of the sixteenth century. There were radical reformers who despised all knowledge of the arts and sciences, believing that the people of God should have nothing to do with a fallen creation. That tradition is still alive in Christendom. It is, unfortunately, creation-denying as well as world-denying in the pejorative sense. But when we come to see, with Calvin, that this world was made by God to be a theatre for his glory, a mirror of his character, a garment to make visible his invisible attributes, then we not only read the book of Scripture, but also the book of nature in order to observe his ways. Of course, only in the light of the book of Scripture (the divinely given spectacles) can we read the book of nature aright. But by doing so we discover, as George Wade Robinson put it, that:

> Something lives in every hue
> Christless eyes have never seen.[1]

Thus, Christians discovered in the wake of the Reformation that they had nothing to fear as they engaged in the hard sciences. Indeed, as has often been pointed out, there seems to be an important connection between the discovery of this teaching and the enormous impetus that was given to scientific research in the post-Reformation period. We know this is our Father's world, and we are confident that by exploring it in the light of his word we will see more of his wonders and be able to say that the heavens themselves declare the glory of God (cf. Psa. 19:1).

The same is true for those who study what we call the humanities, in various ways examining the activities of God's most ingenious (and now, sadly, perverse) creation: man; his history, his literature, his psychology. Here the believer alone is able to penetrate fully to what lies behind and explains humanity's great artistic, musical, and literary achievements. They are the result of God's creating love and now his sustaining and restraining common grace to his fallen and marred image. No wonder man thinks, creates, says, and writes marvellous things. He is the image of God. No wonder too, now that he is fallen and rebellious, that he also creates and writes foul and evil things; *corruptio optimi pessima*—the worst is always the corruption of the best, as the old Latin proverb says.

---

[1] On occasion 'lives' has been altered lest it be misunderstood in a pantheistic sense.

(3) The Christian is also free to use God's world for God's glory, and to enjoy it.

Because the Christian is not enslaved to the world, and is careful not to allow the world to spoil his appetite for the things of God, his taste buds are not dulled to the blessings God has already given in this world. We find this biblical balance well expressed by Calvin in the way he handles the words of 1 Corinthians 10:31 ('whatever you do, do all to the glory of God'). In his sermon on this text, he reminds us that God has given us not merely the essentials, the bare necessities only; rather he has lavished on us an abundance of good things, for us richly to enjoy. In this sense, all things are ours (1 Cor. 3:21). In his commentary on the same passage he sweetly underlines the way in which Paul teaches that 'there is no part of our life or conduct, however insignificant, which should not be related to the glory of God'.[1]

Calvin was astute enough to recognize that it was possible to exercise a mistaken rigour in this world, as well as an erroneous laxity. In this he differed from Augustine, whose experience as a Manichaean no doubt influenced him towards the more ascetic view, that while we may use things in this world, we should avoid enjoying them.

But how can we escape falling into one or other of these two harmful extremes of over-scrupulous rigorism on the one hand and licence and laxity on the other? Here is Calvin's answer:

> Let this be our principle: that the use of God's gifts is not wrongly directed when it is referred to the end to which the author himself created and destined them for us, since he created them for our good and not for our ruin. Accordingly, no one will hold to a straighter path than he who diligently looks to this end.[2]

God's creation, Calvin concludes, is full of wonders; these are not only useful for us, but attractive to us. We have a marvellously generous Father! But how, then, can we live with this world's goods without being ensnared by them? Here is the great Reformer's answer, expressed in a series of four principles. They are well worth remembering:

---

[1] Calvin, *Comm. 1 Corinthians*, p. 224.
[2] Calvin, *Institutes*, III.x.2.

(i) Recognize God as the source of every good gift. If we do, our lusts will be restrained, since we cannot simultaneously express gratitude to God and display unrestrained greed in consuming his provision. Thankfulness to him will enable us, as Paul teaches, to use the blessings of this world as though we did not possess them (1 Cor. 7:29-31).

(ii) When you have few of this world's goods, learn contentment with your heavenly Father and with his present provision. Unless desires for 'more' are curbed when we have little, we will be incapable of a proper stewardship if we should ever have an abundance. We must always remember that everything we have is a stewardship. It is not the abundance of our possessions but the quality of our stewardship that is of cardinal importance. All we possess is his, not ours. Only those who have learned contentment when abased will experience that contentment if they later abound (Phil. 4:11-13).

(iii) Remember what your calling in life really is. You have been called to live in God's presence and for his glory. If you do this, you will never be ensnared by the unruly passions of the flesh or by the pride of life.

(iv) Learn to live calmly in God's world because you believe in God's gracious sovereignty and you know that he is your Father.

The anchor of such a Reformed lifestyle is found in Paul's words in Romans 8:28-29. We know that God works everything together for the good of those who love him, who are called according to his purpose, which is, ultimately, to conform us to the likeness of Christ. Christians know that they live in a world full of darkness and danger. But it is not dark to their Father; therefore it cannot, ultimately, be dangerous for them. For their God works everything together for their good.

Only the person who believes in a genuinely sovereign God can have that confidence. That is what underpins a Reformed lifestyle. It means to know, and to be able to make your own, the answer to the first question of the *Shorter Catechism*: 'What is the chief end of man? Man's chief end is to glorify God, and to enjoy him for ever.'

The great American Reformed theologian B. B. Warfield tells a story which wonderfully illustrates the practical effects of all that we have been considering. It serves as a fitting conclusion to our review of the relationship between Reformed theology and the lifestyle it produces.

> We have the following bit of personal experience from a general officer of the United States Army. He was in a great western city at a time of intense excitement and violent rioting. The streets were over-run daily by a dangerous crowd. One day he observed approaching him a man of singularly combined calmness and firmness of *mien*, whose very demeanour inspired confidence. So impressed was he with his bearing amid the surrounding uproar that when he had passed he turned to look at him, only to find that the stranger had done the same. On observing his turning the stranger at once came back to him, and touching his chest with his forefinger, demanded without preface: 'What is the chief end of man?' On receiving the countersign, 'Man's chief end is to glorify God and to enjoy him for ever'—'Ah!' said he, 'I knew you were a Shorter Catechism boy by your looks!' 'Why, that was just what I was thinking about you', was the rejoinder.[1]

Such Christian character is the rich fruit of biblical teaching. Let us long, pray, and labour that by God's grace we may see it in ourselves and in others. For the acid test of Reformed theology is precisely that it produces this quality of Reformed lifestyle!

---

[1] B. B. Warfield, *Selected Shorter Writings*, 2 vols, ed., J. E. Meeter (Phillipsburg, NJ: P&R Publishing, 2001), I:383-84.

CHAPTER TWENTY-NINE

THE REFORMED DOCTRINE OF SONSHIP

I N his famous William Cunningham Lectures for 1864, entitled 'The Fatherhood of God', R. S. Candlish expressed his purpose in these words:

> My object is chiefly a practical one. It is to bring out the import and bearing of the scriptural doctrine respecting the fatherhood of God as an influential element in Christian experience.[1]

The purpose of this essay is to look at the same relationship between Christian experience and the fatherhood of God, but to do so from a different perspective, namely from the standpoint of the Christian's sonship. Four areas will be discussed briefly: (1) the development and demise of the doctrine in Christian theology; (2) the centrality of the doctrine in biblical theology; (3) its usefulness as a perspective on the nature of salvation; (4) the illumination it yields for our relationship with God.

1. Sonship: development and demise of a doctrine

If one paints the history of theology with a broad brush, it is clear that neither the early nor the medieval church expressed much interest in the idea of the Christian life as a life of *sonship*. The controversies of both periods lay elsewhere. Furthermore, the methods of biblical interpretation adopted were virtually incapable of isolating sonship as a central theme in biblical theology. In the case of medieval theology, with its development of an elongated *ordo salutis*, its distinction between unformed faith and faith formed by love (*fides informis*; *fides formata*

---

[1] R. S. Candlish, *The Fatherhood of God* (Edinburgh: Lorimer & Gillies, 1865), p. 103.

caritate) and its emphasis on penance, purgatory and the place of indulgences, the doctrine of the ordinary Christian as a child of God entitled to all the privileges and joys of fellowship with a loving Father would have had devastating effects.[1]

Devastating effects did occur, of course, in the Reformation. But it was Luther's doctrine of justification by faith which produced them. However, in the context of this essay, it needs to be said that Luther's stress on justification was at the expense of emphasizing the privilege of sonship. Sonship, insofar as it is discussed, is subservient to justification. At best it is the *seal* of justification. The recognition that sonship is 'the apex of redemptive grace and privilege',[2] higher in nature than justification, is one to which Luther would probably not have warmed!

It was left to the Reformed theological tradition, following the lead of Calvin, to recover this biblical emphasis. Even within that tradition, the emphasis has appeared somewhat spasmodically.

Students of Calvin's theology have too rarely recognized how important the concept of sonship was to his understanding of the Christian life. (We do not readily adjust to the notion that the young man who was known by his classmates as 'the accusative case' later revelled in the idea of being God's child!) While there is no separate chapter on sonship in the *Institutes*, *adoptio* (sonship) is one of the expressions by which he most frequently designates the idea of being a Christian. He does not treat sonship as a separate *locus* of theology precisely because it is a concept which undergirds everything he writes.

Calvin's *Institutes* began life as what the title page called a *summa pietatis* (sum of piety). But for Calvin, piety meant recognizing that our lives are 'nourished by God's *fatherly* care';[3] it meant knowing oneself to be a child of God. Similarly, Calvin saw the purpose of the incarnation and atonement to be the adoption of Christians.[4] Consequently, the 'first title' of the Spirit is 'Spirit of adoption'.[5] The knowledge of

---

[1] Still a valuable popular introduction to this is to be found in T. M. Lindsay, *History of the Reformation* (Edinburgh, 1906), I:216-27.
[2] Murray, *Collected Writings*, II:233.
[3] Calvin, *Institutes*, I.ii.1 (emphasis added).
[4] *Ibid.*, II.xii.2; cf. II.xiv.5-6.
[5] *Ibid.*, III.i.3.

adoption is the believer's consolation in suffering.[1] It is no surprise then, to the reader of the *Institutes*, to encounter Calvin at his most eloquent when he comes to expound the phrase 'Our Father' in the Lord's Prayer.[2] As Emile Doumergue has succinctly expressed it, for Calvin 'it is the knowledge of his fatherly love that is the true knowledge of God'.[3]

Despite occasional claims to the contrary, this emphasis of Calvin was kept alive within the Puritan tradition. William Ames's famous lectures in Leyden in 1620–22, later to be published as his *Marrow of Sacred Divinity*,[4] contained an entire section on adoption, and in characteristically Puritan fashion offered a series of twenty-seven different points of exposition. Further discussion took place in the writings of other Puritans, perhaps most notably in the sensitive exposition of the Independent theologian, John Owen.[5] Significantly, for Owen, the doctrine of adoption was intimately related to the idea of communion with God.

Paradoxically to those who regard the *Westminster Confession of Faith* as a document breathing all too little of the fresh air of Calvin's theology, it is in the *Westminster Confession* (followed by its cousins, the Independent *Savoy Declaration of Faith and Order* and the Baptist *London* or *Philadelphia Confession of Faith*) that the doctrine of adoption is given a separate chapter in a confession of the Christian church. Perhaps more than anything else it is the presence of this brief chapter which has kept alive within Presbyterianism (particularly in Scotland and the Southern Presbyterian Church in the USA) the significance of sonship in the life of faith.

The doctrine of adoption suffered considerable demise in later years. The view that it was simply the 'positive side' of justification—Luther's rather than Calvin's view—never really died. It is to be found in some of the classical expositions of theology in the Reformed tradition. Charles

---

[1] Calvin, *Institutes*, III.viii.8.

[2] *Ibid.*, III.xxi.7.

[3] Emile Doumergue, *Jean Calvin: Les hommes et les choses de son temps* (Lausanne, 1910), IV:90-91. It is significant that Doumergue devotes several pages in his exposition of Calvin's doctrine of God to the idea of God as Father.

[4] The Latin edition appeared in 1623 and was later followed by an English edition in 1638.

[5] Owen, *Works*, II:207-22.

Hodge remains silent on the theme of adoption in his *Systematic Theology*.[1] The Southern Presbyterian R. L. Dabney (right-hand man to none other than 'Stonewall' Jackson!) devoted some twenty-two lines only to it in his *Lectures in Systematic Theology*.[2] Despite the efforts of Candlish in Scotland and such Southern Presbyterians as J. L. Girardeau, in his *Discussion of Theological Questions*, and R. A. Webb, in his somewhat disappointing *Reformed Doctrine of Adoption*, adoption was denied the place in systematic theology which biblical teaching would suggest it merited.

The reason for its demise in the Reformed theological tradition may be traced back to the profound influence on English-speaking Reformed theology of Turretin's monumental *Theological Institutes*. Turretin did give consideration to the question of sonship, but only by posing the question 'What is the adoption which is given to us in justification?'[3] The form in which the question was asked assured the continuing subservience of adoption to justification, and its secondary rather than climactic position in theological thinking. Turretin answered his own question in these terms:

> Adoption is included in justification as a part which, with the remission of sins, constitutes the whole of this benefit: nor can justification be distinguished from adoption.[4]

Turretin did have the great merit of linking Christian liberty to the idea of adoption, but the formulation he gave to the relation between justification and adoption became the benchmark for most later expositions.

This long-standing tradition, linked with the influence of nineteenth-century liberalism's emphasis on the universal fatherhood of God and the corresponding universal sonship and brotherhood of man, might have seemed to sound the death-knell of the doctrine of adoption. Evangelical

[1] Hodge, *Systematic Theology*, III.
[2] Dabney, *Lectures in Systematic Theology*, p. 627. Cf. also L. Berkhof, *Systematic Theology*, pp. 513-16.
[3] F. Turretin, *Opera* (Edinburgh, 1847), II. p. 585: '*Quod sit adoptio quae nobis in justificatione datur? I. Altera pars justificationis est adoptio.*'
[4] *Ibid.*

teaching in general fought shy of the employment of language which had become hallmarks of liberalism and universalism.

Voices have, however, cried in the wilderness. In addition to Candlish, Girardeau, and Webb, honourable mention must be made of the two Baptist theologians John Gill[1] and James Petigru Boyce.[2] More recently John Murray[3] and J. I. Packer[4] have lent their weight to a recovery of the doctrine of sonship. Perhaps more than any other influence, the impact of biblical theology on systematic theology has demanded a reorientation of soteriology towards the concept of sonship. The doctrine may therefore be on the verge of a long-awaited reinstatement to the position it occupied in Calvin's thought, one which pervades the whole ethos of the Christian life.[5]

2. *The centrality of sonship in biblical doctrine*

There are two ways in which the centrality of sonship is evident in Scripture.

(1) In the programmatic texts of the New Testament it is commonplace to discover an emphasis on sonship. When the writers discuss the flow of God's plan, from election through the flow of the history of redemption, the purpose of the incarnation and the accomplishments of the atonement, sonship is a central focus. The new covenant introduces the church to a new experience of sonship; the work of the Spirit in conforming us to Christ has sonship in view—Christ is to be the firstborn among many brothers (see, for example, Gal. 3:26–4:7; Eph. 1:3-6; Rom. 8:28-31; Heb. 2:10-18).

(2) In the wider context of biblical theology, sonship is stressed in three distinct ways:

(i) Sonship is the *focus of creation*. Reformed theologians and exegetes have debated whether Adam in creation was a son of God or was intended to be adopted as a son following a period of testing in Eden.

---

[1] John Gill, *Body of Divinity* (London, 1769–70), VI.9.

[2] James Petigru Boyce, *Abstract of Systematic Theology* (1887). See especially his judicious criticisms of other Reformed theologians on pp. 404-9.

[3] Murray, *Redemption*, pp. 132-40; *Collected Writings*, II:223-34.

[4] J. I. Packer, *Knowing God* (London: Hodder & Stoughton, 1973), pp. 223-57.

[5] As indeed it has since 1986 when these words were first written.

The state of the question has rested a good deal on whether Luke 3:38 gives positive encouragement to think of Adam as the *created* son of God. More recently J. Jeremias has underlined the significance of the Adam–Christ parallel which follows the announcement of Luke 3:38, as the last Adam is exposed to the wilderness temptations as the Son of God. The case for thinking of Adam's relationship to God as *filial* in nature is strengthened by two considerations: the lavishness of the provision made for him, in Genesis 2 (a father's love expressed for his son); the intimate connection between sonship and image in Genesis 1:26-28 and Genesis 5:1-3.

In either case—whether Adam was created as a child of God or to enter into the enjoyment of sonship—the filial relation lies at the heart of God's creating purposes.

(ii) Sonship is the *pattern of redemption*. When God redeems his people in the Old Testament, it is the filial model which most eloquently describes the relationship between the Lord and his people. Moses tells Pharaoh that God's word is 'Israel is my firstborn son, and I say to you, "Let my son go that he may serve me." If you refuse to let him go, behold, I will kill your firstborn son' (Exod. 4:22-23). The basis for Moses later upbraiding the people is precisely this: 'Is not he your father, who created you, who made you and established you?' (Deut. 32:6). Again the Father son metaphor appears in the exquisite picture of the exodus in Deuteronomy 1:31: 'you have seen how the LORD your God carried you, as a man carries his son, all the way that you went until you came to this place'.

This is what Paul refers to as 'the adoption' (Rom. 9:4). Adoption is not itself an Old Testament concept.[1] But the Roman legal metaphor which Paul borrowed from the world in which he lived admirably summarized the *nature* of the sonship unveiled by the Old Testament and brought to fulfilment in Jesus Christ. Yet even the Old Testament pictures the salvation of God's people in language which is tantamount to adoption:

[1] See F. Lyall, *Slaves, Citizens and Sons: Legal Metaphors in the Epistles* (Grand Rapids: Zondervan, Academie Books, 1984), pp. 67-99.

Thus says the Lord GOD to Jerusalem: 'Your origin and your birth are of the land of the Canaanites; your father was an Amorite and your mother a Hittite. And as for your birth, on the day you were born your cord was not cut, nor were you washed with water to cleanse you, nor rubbed with salt, nor wrapped in swaddling cloths. No eye pitied you, to do any of these things to you out of compassion for you, but you were cast out on the open field, for you were abhorred, on the day that you were born.

'And when I passed by you and saw you wallowing in your blood, I said to you in your blood, "Live!" I said to you in your blood, "Live!" I made you flourish like a plant of the field. And you grew up and became tall and arrived at full adornment. Your breasts were formed, and your hair had grown; yet you were naked and bare.

'When I passed by you again and saw you, behold, you were at the age for love, and I spread the corner of my garment over you and covered your nakedness; I made my vow to you and entered into a covenant with you, declares the Lord GOD, and you became mine.'

Ezekiel 16:3-8

Salvation is God taking the foundling child and bringing it into a new family relationship altogether. It is adoption into the covenant of love.

(iii) Sonship is also the *goal of restoration*. The entire process of sanctification, leading to the final restoration of glorification, is intended to bring to perfection our sonship to the Father. We are being transformed into the likeness of Christ in order that he might be the firstborn of many brothers (Rom. 8:29). This is the 'one, far-off, divine event, to which the whole creation moves' (Tennyson). But it is not so far-off from the biblical point of view. Already we are sons of God (1 John 3:1-3). It does not yet appear what we shall be. But even now the creation 'stands on tiptoe' waiting to see the sons of God 'come into their own' (Rom. 8:19; cf. J. B. Phillips translation). The process of sanctification is, in essence, the reproduction of the family likeness in the people of God; it involves us being transformed to be more and more like the elder brother, because he is the express likeness of the Father.

We might therefore summarize the grace of the gospel by saying that it involves adoption into the family of God, with the corresponding process of ridding us of the influences of our former family and more and more remaking us to conform to the incarnate Son.

3. Sonship as an organizing principle for understanding salvation

The question of the most appropriate model by which to understand salvation has been much debated in Reformed theology. It has been characteristic, for example, for Reformed theology to make considerable use of the idea of ordered experience (*ordo salutis*). As we have already noted, characteristic of Lutheran theology has been the principle of justification.

It is probably an error of some magnitude to insist that only one principle should be employed to unify one's understanding of the nature of salvation. Scripture provides us with various models, of which justification is but one. Sonship may well be proposed as another.

Any organizing principle for the doctrine of salvation must meet certain important biblical tests: Does it convey the covenantal perspective of the Bible? Does it arise out of the flow of redemptive history? Is it eschatological in nature (that is, does it express the 'already/not yet' tension which is so characteristic of the New Testament's view of present Christian existence)? Does it centre on Jesus Christ?

Sonship meets each of these tests in a satisfactory manner. It is a covenantal concept. Simply expressed, biblical covenants bind individuals to the family. God's covenant binds men and women to his family as his children. It is a blood covenant making Christians 'blood-brothers'. Notice the extent to which the events surrounding the covenant of the exodus are described in terms of God establishing the Father–son relationship (Deut. 1:31; Jer. 31:9; Hos. 11:1, etc.).

But sonship is also a concept through which the development of salvation in biblical history is encapsulated. It does not 'flatten out' the contours of redemptive history. In the Old Testament period (until Pentecost), God's people are indeed his children. But they are as yet under age; they have not been brought to mature sonship. They are heirs in their minority. But now, by contrast, we have 'come of age' in the era of the Spirit of sonship. This is the trend of thought in Paul's argument in Galatians 3:23–4:7. Not only so, but we look forward to yet fuller dimensions of the experience of sonship (1 John 3:1-3). It does not yet appear what we shall be!

Consequently, sonship is characterized now by the tension between what has *already* been accomplished for us in Christ and what is *yet to be* accomplished. We already possess the adoption as sons and the presence of the Spirit of adoption. But precisely because of that, we long for its consummation. Those who have the Spirit of adoption (the 'firstfruits of the Spirit') *groan*, says Paul (Rom. 8:23). Why? Because enjoying the privileges of sons now, we anticipate the glorious liberty of sons in the future when we receive the 'adoption as sons' which Paul describes variously as 'the redemption of our bodies' and 'the freedom of the glory of the children of God' and being 'glorified with him' (Rom. 8:23, 21, 17).

Sonship, then, has a retrospective and a prospective dimension. It recognizes what has already been accomplished: we have been adopted into God's family and experience the access and liberty of grace. But it also recognizes that more is still to be accomplished: we look forward to eschatological adoption, and the access and liberty of glory. The omega-point of Christian experience has not yet come for us. But it will; the fact that we are already children of God is the guarantee.

Sonship, however, is also centred in Jesus Christ. It is because he has entered our family that we enter the family of God (Heb. 2:5-18). Only because he is not ashamed to call us brothers may we call his Father, 'our Father' (cf. John 20:17). Indeed it can be argued that in Pauline thought the resurrection of Christ is viewed as his 'adoption'[1]— not in the sense that he became Son of God in the resurrection, but insofar as he was 'declared to be [marked out as] the Son of God in power ... by his resurrection' (Rom. 1:4). He was 'firstborn from the dead', brought into the family of the new age by resurrection. Through union with Christ, in which we are 'raised into newness of life', we too are adopted into that family. It is, therefore, only in Christ, in the family fellowship we have with him, that we are adopted children of God. He has not left us as orphans, after all (John 14:18). He has given us the Spirit of adoption as sons (Rom. 8:15).

---

[1] R. B. Gaffin Jr, *The Centrality of the Resurrection* (Grand Rapids: Baker, 1978), pp. 117-19.

The biblical doctrine of sonship, therefore, well summarizes the whole of the life of the Christian in relation to God.

4. Sonship and the character of God

R. S. Candlish spoke of the doctrine of the fatherhood of God as an 'influential element in Christian experience'. We, likewise, studying the same relationship from the opposite end as it were, may say that sonship is an influential element in understanding the character of God. The New Testament reasons *both* ways: God is your Father, therefore ... *and* you are God's children, therefore ...

What are the implications inherent in the idea of sonship? To paraphrase the apostle John, we may say: 'Look, you are the children of God; do you not realize the degree to which this shows how much God loves you (1 John 3:1)?' In fact John calls this love 'amazing'. It is the size and unexpectedness of it which he finds so remarkable.

By contrast we have grown somewhat accustomed to the love of God; we do not find it so very amazing. But the recognition that what we are is 'family' in relation to God, that we are his sons and daughters, and that we (of all people!) are his children, is calculated to produce a new and true appreciation of God as our Father. There is no higher self-image that the Christian can have, and no doctrine which will more readily help him or her enjoy the life of faith.

The pastoral implications of this may best be summarized by setting down, side by side, the words of the elder brother in Jesus' Parable of the Waiting Father, and the words of the apostle John. The elder brother symbolizes one to whom all the privileges of God's grace have been extended, but never received. John's words express the amazed joy of one who has begun to appreciate that the gospel makes us sons and daughters of God:

> Look! (said the elder brother)] All these years I've been slaving for you (Luke 15:29).

> Look! (said John) Of what a size is the love the Father has lavished on us, that we should be called the children of God (1 John 3:1).

Of these words, John Cotton, the renowned Old and New England Puritan, quaintly wrote:

This reproves men's squint looking. They do not look at God's love, but at themselves and at their own corruptions and affections. It is a wonder that God's children should pore only upon their corruptions, and not consider what love it is for God to discover them and pardon them.[1]

The doctrine of sonship helps to correct our spiritual squint. It enables us to see ourselves more clearly, because it helps us to see the grace of God more clearly. The doctrine of sonship undergirds the high privileges of Christian experience.

[1] John Cotton, *A Practical Commentary or Exposition upon the First Epistle of John* (1657), on 1 John 3:1.

CHAPTER THIRTY

SOME REFLECTIONS ON
THE 'FIRST TITLE' OF THE HOLY SPIRIT

I N his discussion of the ministry of the Holy Spirit in *The Institutes of the Christian Religion*, John Calvin surprises the reader by noting that 'Spirit of adoption' is the 'first title' of the Holy Spirit.[1] Calvin was biblical scholar enough to know that this was not true in a chronological sense. Nor can he have meant this in any statistical sense, since the title is *hapax legomenon* in Scripture, occurring only in Romans 8:15.

What Calvin evidently has in view is that 'Spirit of adoption' is the supreme description of the Spirit's identity in terms of his ministry to the Christian. In all likelihood this reflects both his use of *adoptio* as the most comprehensive New Testament description of what it means to be a Christian, and also his sense that, to use an expression of John Murray, adoption itself is 'the apex of grace and privilege'.[2]

From the early centuries Christian theologians have insisted that the so called *opera ad extra Trinitatis* (the works of God the Trinity beyond his own in-being) are always the actions of the whole Godhead, each person being involved in some dimension or aspect. This is doubtless also true of our adoption into God's family: it takes place in Christ, and is the fruit of the Spirit's work in us. But adoption itself is an act specifically appropriated to himself by God the Father. He is the one who adopts. Like justification it is a legal act—the individual's status is

---

[1] *Institutes*, III.i.3 (*Primo vocatur Spiritus adoptionis*).

[2] Murray, *Redemption* (repr., 2009), p. 127. Cf. the comments by James Buchanan: 'The privilege of adoption presupposes pardon and acceptance, but is higher than either.' James Buchanan, *The Doctrine of Justification* (1867; repr. London: Banner of Truth Trust, 1961), p. 263.

changed. But this transition is not now from condemnation to justification by the pronouncement of a judge. It is a transition from being
a child of wrath and Satan to being regarded as a child of God—it is a
familial action accomplished only by a Father.

The individual believer's adoption as a son (*huiothesia*: literally, 'being
placed as a son') is a distinctively New Testament privilege. Jewish law
did not quite possess this concept, since in some senses all that adoption
might effect for the benefit of a child was already built into the nature
of Old Testament family relationships. It is probable, therefore, that
Paul derived his metaphor from Roman law where the concept did
exist.[1] Significantly the occurrence of the term in the New Testament
is restricted to letters written to Rome and Romanized areas, such as
Galatia and Ephesus.

This said, Paul does see adoption as a lens through which the old
covenant community as a whole can be described. To his kinsmen, the
Israelites, 'belongs the adoption' (Rom. 9:4). In fact, it is mentioned first
in the list of blessings they have received. And while it is the communal
adoption of the people as a whole Paul has in view here,[2] it may well be
that he uses it as a summation of all the blessings of God's people Israel.
But the realization of individual adoption as such, with all of its privileges, awaited the full revelation of God in his triune nature as Father,
Son, and Holy Spirit.[3] Only when the Father is known through the Son
by the Holy Spirit is adoption a fully coherent notion.[4]

Paul speaks about the 'Spirit of adoption'[5] as such in only one place,
Romans 8:14-17. But in Galatians 4:5-6 there is a clear parallelism to his

---

[1] Cf., among others, Lyall, *Slaves, Citizens and Sons*, pp. 81-99.

[2] Cf. the picture Ezekiel paints in Ezekiel 16:1ff.

[3] It is noteworthy that the few references to adoption (Rom. 8:15, 23; Gal. 4:5; Eph.
1:5) are all set within the context of letters and are not only addressed to areas under
Roman rule, but are set within deeply trinitarian contexts.

[4] A simple contrast supports this distinction. The three chapters of Matthew
comprising the Sermon on the Mount contain many more references to the believer
knowing God as his or her heavenly Father than the entire Old Testament.

[5] 'Sonship' (NIV) not because of any gender prejudice on the part of Paul, but
because in antiquity—and indeed until relatively recently in English law—it was
only sons (not daughters) who inherited, as the underlying plot-line of Jane Austen's
famous *Pride and Prejudice* indicates.

later thought. If there is a difference it is that in Romans Paul's perspective deals with experiential situations and needs while in Galatians 3 and 4 his perspective is redemptive-historical.

Here we have space for only a few suggestive reflections.

1. The Spirit of adoption and the Spirit of slavery

The Spirit of adoption is contrasted with the 'spirit of slavery' in Romans 8:15. The text presents several exegetical issues: (1) Is the reference to *pneuma* (spirit) the same in both expressions? (2) Are either or both references to the human spirit or to the Holy Spirit? In the Reformed tradition a considerable number of earlier pastor-theologians assumed that the reference was to the Holy Spirit (or at least to the fruit of his ministry) in both instances: the Spirit brings conviction of sin (the 'spirit of slavery') and then freedom in the new sense of sonship enjoyed by the regenerate. Before an individual becomes a believer the '(S)pirit of slavery' prevails: the internal disposition of the individual in relationship to God is one of fear and restrictiveness. It is well illustrated in different ways in each of the sons in the Parable of the Prodigal Son: first in the case of the younger son, in his rehearsed speech, 'I am no longer worthy to be called your son. Treat me as one of your hired servants' (Luke 15:19). He sees slavery as his destiny, but is granted sonship as a gift. Similarly, the elder brother complains, 'Look, these many years I have served you ['all these years I've been slaving for you' NIV] ... yet you never gave me ...' (Luke 15:29). Despite the fact that everything the father had to offer was his, he knew only a 'spirit of slavery'.

However this issue is resolved, in the act of adoption the believer is introduced into a wonderful new status in Christ and receives 'the Spirit of adoption'. Through the Spirit (by way of analogy with Gal. 4:6) believers cry, 'Abba! Father!'

But what are the implications of the Spirit's ministry to us in this capacity?

The cry 'Abba! Father!'

Some commentators take the believer's cry 'Abba! Father!' to be a reference to a corporate liturgical or charismatic moment in the life of the Christian assembly, suggesting that it is expressive of an ecstatic outbreak of praise, an outburst of response to the gospel, or even a saying of the Lord's Prayer, the 'Our Father'.

But Paul gives us an important clue to an interpretation more suited to the context. It lies in his use of the onomatopoeic verb *krazein*, expressing a loud cry, a sharp cry of pain and need. It is thus used in the Septuagint,[1] for example, in Psalm 34:6: 'This poor man cried, and the LORD heard …' It is later used in the Gospels of the cries for mercy of blind men (Matt. 9:27) and of our Lord's own loud cry on the cross (Matt. 27:50). Its context is certainly not limited to the liturgy of the church but extends to the experiences of misery, pain, shock, and need that may characterize the individual Christian life.

What Paul here underlines is that the consciousness that we are the children of God, which comes to expression in this filial cry of need, is not reserved for outstandingly mature believers at the height of their spiritual powers, but for *all* believers, and it comes to expression not only in experiences of spiritual ecstasy but in the depths of their need. It is a cry *de profundis* (from the depths), which wonderfully, if paradoxically, expresses a subconscious, 'deep-down' awareness of the heights of privilege and honour—'I am a child of God and call out to him as my Father!'

The significance of this aspect of the Spirit's ministry should not be lost on us. Paul is here pointing to a deep experiential anchor of the believer's assurance. Just as a little boy who has tripped and fallen painfully, instinctively cries, 'Daddy!' because of the deep consciousness of his relationship to his father, so it is with the believer. The emergence of the cry 'Abba! Father!' is the supreme illustration of the deep-down knowledge the Christian has of his or her true status in Christ.

The non-Christian may be capable of reciting the Lord's Prayer, but will never instinctively cry out, 'Abba! Father!' in times of stress and pressure, of sorrow and pain. At best the words 'O God', or the like, form on his lips. In this sense, John Murray was right to say,

> The consciousness of the believer differs by a whole diameter from that of the unbeliever. At the lowest ebb of faith and hope and love

[1] The ancient Greek translation of the Old Testament.

his consciousness never drops to the level of the unbeliever at its highest pitch of confidence and assurance.[1]

The reason is that God is the redeeming and adopting Father of the former and has a fatherly desire for his children to be conscious of the gracious relationship they have with him. Rather than break the bruised reed or quench the dimly burning wick (Matt. 12:20), the Lord grants an assurance—a consciousness that cannot be erased or finally destroyed by trials. And this consciousness comes to the surface precisely in the midst of trials in the manner in which the Christian's deepest cry of need gives clearest expression to his awareness that he is nothing less than a son of the heavenly Father.

2. *The witness of the Spirit*
Paul provides a further analysis of this cry. In it the Spirit is bearing witness with our spirits that we are God's sons. Two interpretive issues arise here.

(i) *Who is said to cry, 'Abba! Father!'?*
In Galatians 4:6 Paul states, 'And because you are sons, God has sent the Spirit of his Son into our hearts, crying, "Abba! Father!"' Here it appears that the cry 'Abba! Father!' is uttered by the Spirit. In the parallel passage in Romans 8:15 it is clearly the believer who cries, 'Abba! Father!': 'you have received the Spirit of adoption as sons, by whom we cry, "Abba! Father!"'

Are there then two different cries? Or is there a resolution to this paradox? In my own view a hint towards the solution lies in Paul's parallel thinking in connection with our confession of Christ.

'No one can say "Jesus is Lord" except in the Holy Spirit' (1 Cor. 12:3). In this context the believer's confessional cry 'Jesus is Lord' is possible only through the concursive ministry of the Spirit in him or her. The Spirit bears his witness to Jesus as Lord (John 16:13-14), but I am the one who cries, 'Jesus is Lord'. The witness of the Spirit is not distinguishable from my witness.

In the same way, the implicit confession 'I am your child' expressed in the cry 'Abba! Father!' is made by believers, but only through the

---

[1] Murray, *Collected Writings*, II:265.

concursive operation of the Spirit in their hearts. As Benjamin B. Warfield well puts it, 'Distinct in its source, it is yet delivered confluently with the testimony of our human consciousness.'[1]

Commentators have rightly noted the background to Paul's statement may lie in the principle that testimony needs to be established in the mouth of two witnesses if it is to be allowed in court.[2] The spirit of the believer and the Spirit who indwells the believer give conjoint testimony in the single cry of the believer, 'Abba! Father!' It is this that then confirms for the believer the assurance of being a child of God.

(ii) Does the Spirit bear witness 'with' or 'to' our spirits?
Some commentators have argued vigorously that Paul must here be thinking of the Spirit's witness *to* our spirits. That, after all, is the assurance we need—a testimony: 'I authenticate you as a genuine child of God.' Among modern scholars no one has argued this position more forcefully than C. E. B. Cranfield. He argues that the witness of the Spirit is not conjoint *with* our own witness but is a witness given *to* our spirits by God's Spirit. He seems to view this exegesis as being theologically confirmed by his answer to the question: 'What standing has our spirit in this matter? Of itself it surely has no right at all to testify to our being sons of God.'[3]

But this surely confuses two things, namely (a) the authority of God by whom alone an individual is counted a son of God, and (b) the consciousness the believer has, on the basis of the gospel, that he or she is in fact a son of God. For if the believer has a properly grounded consciousness he is a son of God, and a recognition that this status is not based on his opinion but on God's promise, then he has in fact the God-given privilege of expressing this consciousness in saying, in whatever words, 'I am a son of God.' Indeed one might say that not to do so would be more an expression of unbelief than of faith.

Furthermore, throughout this section of Romans 8 Paul uses a series of compound words with the prefix *sun* (together with): *sunklēronomoi*

---

[1] B. B. Warfield, *Faith and Life* (1916; repr., Edinburgh: Banner of Truth Trust, 1990), p. 185.
[2] Deut. 19:15. Hence the significance in Jesus' trial of Matt. 26:60 and Mark 14:59.
[3] Cranfield, *Comm. Romans*, I:403.

(verse 17: 'heirs together with'); *sustenazei kai sunōdinei* (verse 22: 'groaning together in the pains of childbirth'—'groaning and travailing together'); *sunantilambanetai* (verse 26: 'helps together with'); verse 28: *sunergei* ('works together'). It is likely therefore that this refrain of things happening or being accomplished 'together with' should influence our understanding of the Spirit's witness and *summarturei* (verse 16: 'bears witness with') should be translated 'witnesses *along with*' and not 'witnesses *to*'. Yes, our spirit's testimony may be shaky at times, especially in moments of stress and pain. But in situations of deepest weakness this cry 'Abba! Father!' is both a summons for help and an expression of the deep-down conviction, 'I am a child of the heavenly Father.'

John Owen well captures what this means in practice when he writes:

> Now, sometimes the soul because it hath somewhat remaining in it of the principle that it had in its old condition, is put to the question whether it be a child of God or no; and thereupon, as in a thing of the greatest importance, puts in its claim, with all the evidences that it hath to make good its title. The Spirit comes and bears witness in this case.
>
> An allusion it is to judicial proceedings in points of titles and evidences. The judge being set, the person concerned lays his claim, produceth his evidences, and pleads them; his adversaries endeavouring all that in them lies to invalidate them, and disannul his pleas, and to cast him in his claim. In the midst of the trial, a person of known and approved integrity comes into the court, and gives testimony fully and directly on the behalf of the claimer; which stops the mouths of all his adversaries, and fills the man that pleaded with joy and satisfaction. So it is in this case. ... When our spirits are pleading their right and title, he comes in and bears witness on our side; at the same time enabling us to put forth acts of filial obedience, kind and childlike; which is called 'crying, Abba, Father.'[1]

[1] Owen, *Works*, II:241-42. Interestingly Owen goes on in this context to compare the Spirit's witness to Jesus' action in stilling the storm on Galilee, described in Matthew 8:25-27. This was the very passage which had been the means of his own assurance through the sermon of an unknown preacher who had substituted for the great Edmund Calamy whom he had gone to hear preach at Aldermanbury Chapel in London.

And Charles Hodge, although he slips in stating that the Spirit is called Spirit of sonship 'because he adopts', is surely right to say, 'How this is done we cannot fully understand, any more than we can understand the mode in which he produces any other effect on our mind.'[1]

3. The Spirit of the Son and the Spirit of adoption

A final reflection is worth offering here. We have noted that Galatians 4:1-6 and Romans 8:14-17 are in several respects parallel to each other:

Galatians 4:1-6	Romans 8:14-17
We were *enslaved*	The *spirit of slavery* to fall back into fear
God has sent the Spirit of his Son	*You have received* the Spirit of adoption as sons
The *Spirit of his Son* crying, *'Abba! Father!'*	The *Spirit of adoption as sons,* by whom *we cry,* *'Abba! Father!'*

Of interest here in these parallels is a further distinction: in Romans the Spirit is described as 'the Spirit of adoption as sons' while earlier in Galatians Paul had called him 'the Spirit of his Son'. Through the Spirit of adoption/the Spirit of his Son comes the cry 'Abba! Father!'

For Paul, it seems, the Spirit of adoption is to be thought of precisely as the Spirit of the Son. In other words, the Spirit of adoption in the believer who brings him a consciousness that he is a child of God is one and the same Spirit as the Spirit who exercised an indwelling and empowering ministry in the life of the Lord Jesus. Set against the background of the New Testament's insistence that there is 'one Spirit', this, surely, is a truth of staggering proportions. He who enabled the Son to cry, 'Abba, Father' is the one who indwells believers as they cry, 'Abba! Father!' He is not merely sent from the Son; he comes to us in his specific identity as the Spirit of the Son.

What is implied here is that the Spirit who indwells believers is the one who first indwelt the incarnate Son, being constantly present with him from the moment of his conception (Luke 1:35), through his growth

---

[1] Charles Hodge, *Commentary on Romans* (1864; repr., Edinburgh: Banner of Truth Trust, 1986), pp. 266-67.

in wisdom (Luke 2:52, cf. Isa. 11:1-2), his baptism (Luke 3:22), temptations (Luke 4:1), ministry in word and deed (Luke 4:18-19), in his joy (Luke 10:21), and empowering his miracles (Luke 11:20, 'the finger of God' = the Spirit [Matt. 12:28]). To this catena of Lukan passages we may add testimony to the Spirit's empowering in Jesus' death (Heb. 9:14) and his resurrection (Rom. 1:4).

This is the Spirit Jesus promised to send from the Father in order that his disciples would not be left as 'orphans' (John 14:18). The new covenant identity of the Spirit, and therefore the specific identity and capacity in which he comes to believers now, is that he is the Spirit of the incarnate, crucified, risen, reigning Son. Christ was not only empowered by him, but on his ascension specifically asked the Father that he might be sent to us (John 14:16), and, in perhaps the least emphasized aspect of the work of Christ, 'Being therefore exalted at the right hand of God, and *having received from the Father* the promise of the Holy Spirit, he has poured out this that you yourselves are seeing and hearing' (Acts 2:33).[1] The Son's final 'transaction' in fulfilling the mandate of his incarnation was to ask for, and to receive, the giving of his own Spirit, his incarnation-companion, for all believers. We are therefore able to cry, 'Abba! Father!' as he did, because we are possessed by the Spirit who possessed, and was possessed by, the Son. There is no deification implied here, but rather a glorious indwelling in which the believer's individual identity is never lost and the Creator–creature distinction never transgressed.

Earlier in Romans 8:9-11 Paul had set up the parameters of his thinking:

- You, however, are not in the flesh but in the Spirit, if in fact the Spirit of God dwells in you.

- Anyone who does not have the Spirit of Christ does not belong to him.

- But if Christ is in you, although the body is dead because of sin, the Spirit is life because of righteousness.

---

[1] Emphasis added. Doubtless here there is also a fulfilment of Psa. 2:8: 'Ask of me, and I will make the nations your heritage, and the ends of the earth your possession.' But our interest here lies in the other aspect of the Pentecost event.

• If the Spirit of him who raised Jesus from the dead dwells in you, he who raised Christ Jesus from the dead will also give life to your mortal bodies through his Spirit who dwells in you.

The Holy Spirit is the Spirit of God. As such he is the Spirit of the Father. He is also the Spirit of Christ the Son. As the Spirit of the one who raised Jesus from the dead he indwells us. This is one and the same reality as Christ indwelling us.[1]

Paul is not here confusing the persons of the Trinity, but rather indicating that the intimacy of the relationship between Christ and the Spirit in the course of the incarnation means that the Spirit who indwells the believer does so in a manner that is economically indistinguishable from the indwelling of Christ.

Moreover, he is the 'one Spirit'. There are not two Spirits, the one who indwelt the Son and the one who indwells believers. One Spirit indwells all. No, our spirits are one with Christ (1 Cor. 6:17) through the bond of union effected by the indwelling of the Spirit of the Son in those he has made sons and joint heirs with him (Rom. 8:17).

Again, there are not many Spirits, the one who indwells one believer and the many who indwell other believers. This is why we are not only sons of God, brothers of Christ (John 20:17), but also in the deepest sense members of one another, children in the same family, indwelt by the Spirit by whom each of us cries, 'Abba! Father!'

Here, then, is the reason why the title 'Spirit of adoption' is truly 'the first title' of the Holy Spirit. This is why we can sing with Charles Wesley, whose brother John was taught by their dying father, 'The inward witness, son, the inward witness; this is the proof, the strongest proof, of Christianity':[2]

> My God is reconciled;
>   His pardoning voice I hear;
> He owns me for His child;
>   I can no longer fear:

[1] Further, it seems to be this that Christ has in view when he says, 'If anyone loves me, he will keep my word, and my Father will love him, and we will come to him and make our home with him' (John 14:23).
[2] John Wesley, letter to John Smith, March 22, 1748, in *The Works of the Rev. John Wesley* (London: Wesleyan Conference Office, 1872), XII:98.

> With confidence I now draw nigh,
> And 'Father, Abba, Father', cry.[1]

And with Henry Francis Lyte:

> Think what Spirit dwells within thee,
> What a Father's smile is thine,
> What thy Saviour died to win thee,
> Child of heaven, should'st thou repine?[2]

---

[1] From the hymn 'Arise, My Soul, Arise' by Charles Wesley.
[2] From the hymn 'Jesus, I My Cross Have Taken' by Henry Francis Lyte.

CHAPTER THIRTY-ONE

REPENTANCE, RECOVERY, AND CONFESSION

F EW events in post-apostolic history are better remembered by confessing evangelicals, or apparently more honoured, than that All Saints' Eve in 1517 when Martin Luther posted his Ninety-five Theses to the door of the Castle Church at Wittenberg.

'*Apparently* more honoured'? Do evangelicals in general perhaps exercise a strange kind of implicit faith with respect to these famous theses? Probably only a minority have any idea what they contained. In the immortal perspective on history expressed by *1066 and All That*,[1] whatever Luther's theses were exactly, we assume they were 'a good thing'.

They were much more than 'a good thing'; the truth is that they contained statements of church-shattering importance, and none more so than the first thesis. Although provoked by the indulgences peddled by Johannes Tetzel, the very first proposition that Luther offered for public debate put the axe to the root of the tree of medieval theology:

> When our Lord and Master, Jesus Christ, said 'repent', he meant that the entire life of believers should be one of repentance.

From Erasmus' Greek New Testament, Luther had come to realize that the Vulgate's rendering of Matthew 4:17 by *penitentiam agite* ('do penance') completely misinterpreted Jesus' meaning. The gospel called not for an act of penance but for a radical change of mindset and an equally deep transformation of life. Later Luther would write to Staupitz about this glowing discovery: 'I venture to say they are wrong who make more of the act in Latin than of the change of heart in Greek.'[2]

---

[1] W. C. Sellar and R. J. Yeatman, *1066 and All That* (London: Methuen, 1930) is a satirical survey of English history.

[2] Roland Bainton, *Here I Stand* (1950; repr. Nashville: Abingdon, 1978), p. 67.

Is it not true that we have lost sight of this note that was so prominent in Reformation theology? We could well do with a Luther *redivivus* today. For a number of important reasons evangelicals need to reconsider the centrality of repentance in our thinking about the gospel, the church, and the Christian life.

The nature of repentance

Even for relatively well-instructed Christians today the centrality of repentance to the gospel needs to be underlined. While it is not the instrument of justification, as the *Westminster Confession* reminds us, 'none may expect pardon without it'.[1]

The Scriptures have an extensive and, in places, lively vocabulary to describe repentance. In the Old Testament various metaphors are used, such as ploughing and circumcising, to make its meaning both clear and vivid. On occasion there is a focus on the emotion that characterizes repentance, namely, that of grief and regret (*nāham*). But the central Hebrew verb for repent (*šûbh*) is one of the dozen most common verbs in the entire Old Testament. As W. L. Holladay has noted, it occurs well over one hundred times in the specific context of God's covenant dealings with his people.[2] This is especially true in the Book of Jeremiah. To repent is to return to the provisions and prescriptions of God's bond.

The verb *šûbh* is, interestingly, also the verb used to describe the return of God's people from geographical exile (e.g., Isa. 10:21-22), and in many ways this provides us with a helpful metaphor to understand what repentance is. Restoration from exile means returning geographically from the far country to the sphere where God has covenanted to fulfil his promise of blessing. Repentance from sin means returning from the far country of bondage in sin and guilt to the place where God has promised to fulfil his covenanted blessings—and all based on the promise of God's free mercy and grace (cf. Deut. 30:11).

It is, of course, precisely this Old Testament idea that Jesus turns into an entire parable of God's grace in conversion in the story of the son who showed such prodigal indifference to his father and ended up in 'the far

---

[1] *Westminster Confession of Faith*, XV.3.

[2] W. L. Holladay, *The Root Šûbh in the Old Testament: With Particular Reference to Its Usages in Covenantal Contexts* (Leiden: E. J. Brill, 1958), pp. 1, 116-55.

country' only for the knowledge of the supplies in his father's house to first bring him to himself, and then home to his father (Luke 15:11-32).

Biblical repentance, then, is not merely a sense of regret that leaves us where it found us; it is a radical reversal that takes us back along the road of our sinful wanderings, creating in us a completely different mindset: we come to our senses spiritually (cf. Luke 15:17). No longer is life characterized by the demand 'give me' (Luke 15:12) but now by the request 'make me' (cf. Luke 15:19).

It is this that lies on the surface of the New Testament's vocabulary, which rather clearly distinguishes between the emotional epiphenomena that may accompany true repentance and true repentance itself. Paul neatly expresses these two things (regret and repentance, *metamelomai* and *metanoeō*) when he speaks about the genuine godly sorrow of a repentance we need never regret (2 Cor. 7:10). Involved in this is a change of mindset (*metanoeō*) which is accompanied by a lifelong moral and spiritual turnaround (*epistrephō*).

This twofold character of genuine biblical repentance is well captured by the way Paul uses both ideas when he speaks about the conversion of the Thessalonians, who 'turned to God from idols to serve the living and true God' (1 Thess. 1:9). It is this combination and simultaneity of turning away from and turning toward that marks genuine biblical repentance. According to Paul it involves the radical crucifixion of the flesh and yet at the same time a radical reclothing with Christ (Gal. 5:24; 3:27). It leads to an ongoing putting to death of the works of the flesh and a simultaneous putting on of the graces of Christ (Col. 3:5-11, 12-17).

Herein, then, lies the importance of Luther's statement. Repentance does not merely begin the Christian life; according to Scripture the Christian life is repentance from beginning to end. So long as the believer is *simul justus et peccator* it can be no other way.

No doubt there is a vividness of language, a drama of presentation, in Luther that is quite unique. In nailing this first thesis to the Castle Church door he simultaneously 'nailed' the gospel of Christ into the heart of the church. Who could match this?

> Repentance which is occupied with thoughts of peace is hypocrisy. There must be a great earnestness about it and a deep hurt if the old

man is to be put off. When lightning strikes a tree or a man, it does two things at once—it rends the tree and swiftly slays the man. But it also turns the face of the dead man and the broken branches of the tree itself toward heaven.[1]

But while Luther's vocabulary and imagery may be uniquely vivid, his emphasis on the radical and lifelong character of repentance is the common testimony of the Reformers.

This can be readily documented in the post-Reformation catechisms of various traditions. From the *Heidelberg Catechism* (1563) to the Westminster Assembly's *Shorter Catechism* (1648) there is a common emphasis on the absolute necessity and centrality of repentance.

But not only is there general agreement between Lutheran and Reformed teaching on the importance of repentance. We may go further and say that there is a special thoroughness in Calvin's exposition of it. Standing on Luther's shoulders he says things that we need to hear in our own time.

For Calvin, repentance is really the personal, concrete expression of divine regeneration and renewal. He defines regeneration as repentance.[2] But more than that, he provides us with a deep exegesis of what repentance is in the New Testament. It can never be separated from faith, although it should never be confused with it. It involves a threefold cord: 'denial of ourselves, mortification of our flesh, and meditation on the heavenly life'.[3]

This understanding of repentance means that it can never be reduced to a single act that stands alone at the beginning of the Christian life; nor can it be understood superficially and one-dimensionally. Calvin sees that true repentance arises in the context of grace and faith, and therefore in the context of union with Jesus Christ. Indeed, since its goal is the restoration of sinners into the image of Christ, by necessity it involves the outworking of our union with Christ in his death and resurrection—what Calvin calls *mortification* and *vivification*.[4]

---

[1] Cited in Bainton, *Here I Stand*, p. 48.
[2] See chapter title of *Institutes*, III.iii.1.
[3] Calvin, *Comm. Acts*, II:176.
[4] *Institutes*, III.iii.3.

Faith in Christ as crucified and resurrected thus leaves a stamp on the character of the whole of our lives. This union is not only the ground plan for the Christian life, but the mould by which the Christian life is shaped. He was crucified and lives; we share in his sufferings, bear around in our bodies his dying, and are conformed to his death—all in order to share in his resurrection power and to be transformed into his likeness and glory (2 Cor. 4:10-12; Phil. 3:10-11, 20-21).

Not only my life as an individual is thus repentance-shaped; this is true of the church as a whole community united to Christ by the Spirit. Repentance in the fullest sense of restoration to God is worked out both inwardly and outwardly among us. Thus, notes Calvin, '[Peter] teaches us that the government of the church of Christ has been so divinely constituted from the beginning that the cross has been the way to victory, death the way to life.'[1] Repentance, therefore, for Calvin, *is* the Christian life.

Of course, this emphasis we find in our forefathers was set against the background of medieval theology and medieval lifestyle. But rather than render their teaching irrelevant, this context may well provide part of the key to its relevance, because we ourselves once again need to proclaim this full-orbed doctrine of repentance within an evangelical context that has begun to manifest alarming symptoms of the medieval sickness.

The need for repentance

While it is with a measure of biblical authority that we can stress both the nature and centrality of repentance, it is with reticence that we draw attention to what we might call the incipient medievalizing of the evangelical church. For one thing, the present author cannot claim expertise of any kind in the sociology of church history; in addition, we all ought to have a healthy suspicion of Jeremiads if they are unaccompanied by tears (cf. Jer. 9:1, 18; 14:17; Lam. 2:11).

One of our great needs is for the ability rightly to discern some of the directions in which evangelicalism is heading, or, perhaps more accurately, disintegrating. We desperately need the long-term perspective that the history of the church gives us.

---

[1] Calvin, *Comm. 1 Peter*, p. 240.

Even within the past half-century or so there has been a sea-change in evangelicalism. Many 'positions' that once were standard evangelical teaching are now regarded as either reactionary or even prehistoric.

If we take an even longer-term view, however, we face the alarming possibility that there may already be a medieval darkness encroaching upon evangelicalism. More perplexing yet is the fact that many of its features are welcomed as though they were fresh light. But if the light within be darkness, how great is that darkness!

Can we not detect, at least as a tendency, dynamics within evangelicalism that bear resemblances to the life of the medieval church? The possibility of a new Babylonian or (more accurately, following Luther) the Pagan Captivity of the Church looms nearer than we may be able to believe.

Consider the following five features of medieval Christianity that are evident to varying degrees in contemporary evangelicalism.

1. Repentance has increasingly been seen as a single act, severed from a lifelong restoration of godliness.
There are complex reasons for this—not all of them modern—which we cannot explore here. Nevertheless, this seems self-evident. Seeing repentance as an isolated, completed act at the beginning of the Christian life has been a staple principle of much modern evangelicalism. Sadly that evangelicalism has often despised the theology of the confessing churches. It has spawned a generation who look back upon a single act, abstracted from its consequences, as determinative of salvation. The 'altar call' has replaced the sacrament of penance. Thus repentance has been divorced from genuine regeneration, and sanctification severed from justification.

In the USA especially there have been long-standing disagreements about 'the carnal Christian' and recently 'the Lordship controversy'. These controversies have deep and sophisticated theological and historical roots—deeper perhaps than some of its participants may have realized. But there is little doubt what a Martin Luther or a John Calvin would make of it: the idea that it is possible to receive justification without sanctification, to trust in a Saviour who is not our Lord, to receive a new birth that does not actually give new life, or to have a faith that is not ongoingly repentant despite uniting us to a crucified and risen Christ, simply did not compute in their theology. For them Paul had spelt this out with perfect clarity: 'those who belong to Christ Jesus have crucified the flesh with its passions and desires' (Gal. 5:24). To fail to live thus is, as Calvin vividly pointed out, to 'rend [Christ] asunder by … mutilated faith'.[1]

At its darker edges this is the gospel of tele-evangelicalism (doubtless not all equally erroneous theologically) that Tetzel-like peddles its wares on the small screen, implying, if not actually openly suggesting, that the divine blessing can be purchased financially rather than received only in faith and repentance.

Almost six hundred years ago, medieval theology at its worst gave rise to the famous ditty:

> As soon as the coin in the coffer rings
> The soul from purgatory springs.

But there is a contemporary version found nowhere except in evangelicalism:

> As soon as the cheque in my pocket arrives
> An increase in blessing will be your surprise.

This has become endemic; its influence is pervasive. It is not historic evangelicalism; it is incipient medievalism. Would to God a Martin Luther might arise within it and cry, 'Enough! When our Lord Jesus Christ said "repent" he meant that the whole of the Christian life should be one of repentance.'

2. The canon for Christian living has increasingly been sought in a 'Spirit-inspired' living voice within the church rather than in the Spirit's voice heard in Scripture.

Again, we need to underline that what we are speaking about here is a tendency. It is not confined to the charismatic or pentecostal wing of Christendom.

Our concern is not to drag ourselves through the cessationist/non-cessationist controversy. Whatever our view of that, it is perspicuous

---

[1] Calvin, *Comm. Romans*, p. 167.

that within large sectors of evangelicalism, charismatic and non-charismatic, continuing 'revelation' is welcomed. In a previous generation this came to clearest expression in those who expected to find guidance by 'listening to the Spirit'.

The Reformers and Puritans, including the likes of Calvin and John Owen, were familiar with such 'spirituals'. Adding to, or bypassing, the voice of the Spirit in Scripture, they claimed to hear his voice directly. Then, as now, some of them claimed to believe in the infallibility of the Scriptures, although they seemed to know little about the doctrine of the sufficiency of Scripture. Sadly, as Calvin experienced already at the Reformation, it is impossible to discuss the meaning of Scripture with those who claim the direct intervention of the Spirit.

What was once little more than a mystical tendency has become a flood. Is it far from the mark to suggest that those who hold to the Reformers' doctrine of the absolute sufficiency of the voice of the Spirit in Scripture illumined by the work of the Spirit in the heart are a decreasing breed? Both in academic theology as well as at the grassroots level such a position is becoming increasingly regarded as reactionary if not deviant because minority in subscription!

But what has this to do with the medieval church? Just this: the entire medieval church operated on the same principle, even if expressed in a different form. The Spirit speaks outside of Scripture; believers cannot know the detailed guidance of God if they try to depend on their Bible alone. The living voice of the Spirit in the church is essential.

Not only so, but once the 'living voice' of the Spirit has been introduced it follows by a kind of psychological inevitability that it is this living voice which becomes the canon for Christian living.

This equation—inscripturated word plus living voice equals divine revelation—lay at the heart of the medieval church's fumbling in the dark for the power of the gospel. Now we are on the verge—and perhaps more than the verge—of being overwhelmed by a parallel phenomenon. The result then was a famine of hearing and understanding the word of God—all under the guise of what the Spirit was still saying to the church. What of today?

3. The divine presence was brought to the church by individuals with sacred powers deposited within them and communicated by physical means.

As the Council of Trent underlined, the medieval doctrine of orders (ordination) imprinted an indelible character on the priest.[1] Through mystical powers the words of the Mass, *hoc est corpus meum*, could change bread and wine into the body and blood of Jesus. While the 'accidents' of bread and wine remained, the 'substance' became the body and blood of the Lord. With his hands the priest could put Jesus into the believer's mouth.

Today an uncanny parallel is visible wherever cable television can be seen. Admittedly it is no longer Jesus who is given by priestly hands; now it is the Spirit who is bestowed by physical means, apparently at will by the new evangelical priest. Special sanctity is no longer confirmed by the beauty of the fruit of the Spirit, but with signs that are predominantly physical.

The Reformers were not unfamiliar with similar phenomena. In fact, one of the major charges made against them by the Roman Catholic Church was that they did not really have the gospel because they lacked miraculous phenomena.

What we ought to find alarming about contemporary evangelicalism is the extent to which we are impressed by performance rather than piety. In the midst of the plethora of claims to the physical manifestations of the Spirit, will no one raise a voice to cry that it is not physical manifestations but knowing and being known by Christ in a life of sheer and unquestioned godliness that is the only real evidence of the power of the Spirit?

4. The worship of God is increasingly presented as a spectator event of visual and sensory power, rather than a verbal event in which we engage in a deep soul dialogue with the triune God.

The mood of contemporary evangelicalism is to focus on the centrality of what 'happens' in the spectacle of worship rather than on what is heard in worship. Aesthetics, be they artistic or musical, are given prior-

---

[1] *Canons and Decrees of the Council of Trent*, 'On the Sacraments in General', Canon IX.

ity over holiness. More and more is *seen*, less and less is *heard*. There is a sensory feast, but a hearing famine. Professionalism in worship leadership has become a cheap substitute for genuine access to heaven, however faltering. Drama, not preaching, has become the *didache* of choice.

This is a spectrum, of course, not a single point. But most worship is to be found somewhere on that spectrum. Time was when four words brought out goose-bumps on the necks of the congregation—'Let Us Worship God.' Not so for twenty-first-century evangelicalism. Now there must be colour, movement, audio-visual effects. God cannot be known, loved, praised, and trusted for his own sake or in unvarnished simplicity.

We have lost sight of great things—the fact that Christ himself is the true sanctuary of the new covenant people; that the true beauty is holiness; that when the Lord is in his holy temple all are transfixed with a heart of silence before him.

We have also more subtly lost sight of the transportability of new covenant worship. By comparison with old covenant worship, which depended on the temple, the new was simple *and therefore universalizable*. That was part of the vision that drove on our evangelical forefathers; but much of our worship has become *dependent* on place, size, and, alas, even technology.

Here, as 'confessing evangelicals', we cannot smugly point the finger of scorn and derision at evangelicals who have sold their reformational and confessional heritage for a mess of modern pottage. In how many of our churches is the glory due to the aesthetics rather than to the sheer power of the Spirit and the word? In how many of our services is there such a sense of God's overwhelming presence that outsiders fall on their faces saying, 'God is really among you' (1 Cor. 14:25)?

Of course we must offer our very best to God in corporate worship. But 'confessing evangelicals' do that by a regulative principle even when they differ on its exact import. They do not think that true worship is a spectator event, where we luxuriate in what others do. It is a *congregational* event, in which Christ mediates our prayers, conducts and leads our praise, and preaches his word to us. He alone is the God-ordained worship leader, the true *leitourgos* of the people of God, the minister in the sanctuary (Heb. 8:2). We dare not obscure this Christ-centred and congregational character of worship, nor make it dependent on anything else than approaching God in the Spirit through Christ with clean hands and a pure heart. Such the Father seeks to worship him!

The tragedy of medieval worship was precisely this: when God was no longer heard with penetrating clarity in the exposition of Scripture—when the sense of the Spirit's presence was no longer a reality—what was substituted for it was ritual rather than true liturgy; mystery (Latin!) rather than plain speaking; colour rather than clarity of doctrinal understanding; and drama (the medieval plays!) rather than the doctrine that would give them the knowledge of God, nourish their souls, and make them morally and spiritually strong. A spiritual vacuum was created; collapse was inevitable. For years we have been on this slippery slope to neo-medievalism.

In 1978 I had one of the high privileges of my life: speaking at a conference of ministers in Wales with the great Welsh preacher Dr Martyn Lloyd-Jones. One of his addresses on that occasion was entitled 'Extraordinary Phenomena in Revivals of Religion'. It was an extraordinary phenomenon in itself: ninety minutes in length, it seemed like fifteen. I was gripped and fascinated to hear of incidents—largely in Wales!—which eyewitnesses had described to him.

Inter alia Dr Lloyd-Jones mentioned a relatively recent and well-known Welsh evangelist whose 'trade mark' was the fact that he himself played an instrument during the evangelistic meetings he conducted. His father on one occasion urged him to lay it aside—his generation of ministers had not needed it. 'No, Dad,' came the reply, 'but *you had the Holy Spirit.*' Thus we are condemned out of our own mouths.

The tragedy here is that in our worship we are in grave danger of producing a generation of professing Christians who are spiritual infants—feeding them emotionally with what temporarily produces stimulation but never builds them up.

Dr James Montgomery Boice well expressed this once in the context of introducing congregational prayer for Sunday-school teachers at Tenth Presbyterian Church, Philadelphia. He noted that from the beginning the children were taught small portions of Scripture on which they built until (for example) they were able to recite such chapters of the Bible as Romans 8. Hymns (yes, *hymns!*) were sung and learned because of their power to teach doctrine (yes, *doctrine!*). Why this stark contrast with, if not opposition to, the trends of the time? Here, as I recall, is what Dr Boice gave as the rationale: 'We are living in a time when adults, including Christians, want to behave like children. Here, in our Sunday school, we are training our children to grow up to be Christian adults.'

How smug we evangelicals have become—we who know too much about child psychology to care about the catechism! But, alas, many of today's seminary graduates and ministers know less Christian doctrine than a child in Calvin's Geneva, know less of the misery of sin and the way to the joy of salvation than a boy in Ursinus's Heidelberg, have only half the grasp of man's chief end that a girl in some remote fastness of seventeenth-century Scotland might have had, and also know far less about how to overcome sin than a teenager in John Owen's Oxford.

It should not surprise us, therefore, to discover what books evangelicals have been reading of late. Some of those that have been given cult status ('You haven't read _____? My dear, where have you been?' we are asked, with a look of blank amazement!) have more to say about how we think of ourselves than they do about what God thinks.

5. The success of ministry is measured by crowds and cathedrals rather than by the preaching of the cross, by the quality of Christians' lives, and by faithfulness.
It was the medieval church leaders—bishops and archbishops, cardinals and popes—who built cathedrals, ostensibly *soli Deo gloria*. But all this was to the neglect of gospel proclamation, the life of the body of Christ as a whole, the needs of the poor, and the evangelism of the world. The 'mega-church' is not a modern, but a medieval phenomenon.

Ideal congregational size and specific ecclesiastical architecture thankfully belong to the *adiaphora*. That is not really the central concern here. Rather it is the almost endemic addiction of contemporary evangelicalism to size and numbers as an index of the success of 'my ministry'—a phrase that can itself be strikingly oxymoronic.

Here, too, there is something reminiscent of the Middle Ages. How much indulgence-buying goes on in contemporary church life? How much of the medieval desire for a *kathedra* (throne!) for the leader(s) comes to expression in the staggering buildings we erect 'for the glory of God'?

This is not a plea for a new evangelical iconoclasm; smaller is not necessarily more beautiful. But it is to raise the question of reality, depth, and integrity in church life and in Christian ministry. The lust for 'bigger' makes us materially and financially vulnerable. But worse, it makes us spiritually vulnerable. For it is hard to say to those on whom we have come to depend materially: 'When our Lord Jesus Christ said "Repent!" he meant that the whole of the Christian life is repentance.' And then, what will we make of Thesis 92?

> Away, then, with those prophets who say to Christ's people, 'Peace, peace', where there is no peace.

Or, again, what do we make of the spine-chilling Thesis 93?

> Hail, hail to all those prophets who say to Christ's people, 'The cross, the cross', where there is no cross.

And can I respond to Thesis 94 with a clear conscience?

> Christians should be exhorted to be zealous to follow Christ, their head, through penalties, deaths, and hells.

Or Thesis 95?

> And let them thus be more confident of entering heaven through many tribulations rather than through a false assurance of peace.

We may well wish that Luther's Theses had been left in the Latin in which he first penned them and kept within their original arena of academic dispute! But only where these notes ring through our churches can we be sure that we are building Christ's church with gold, silver, and costly stones, and not wood, hay, and stubble. And only what we build thus will last to eternity. Everything else will be burned by fire (1 Cor. 3:10-15).

The grace of repentance

If repentance is the lifelong process of the restoration of sinners, it is, as we have seen, an inescapable, ongoing, and permanent necessity. But how is it to be produced?

Here it is vitally important for us not to write our agenda merely in terms of what is wrong with evangelicalism today. That exercise may be necessary, but it is only partial. It is less than apostolic. For what gives repentance power is not the guilt evoked by the law alone (Rom. 7:7), but the grace proclaimed to us in the gospel of our Lord Jesus Christ: it is the *kindness* of God that leads to repentance (Rom. 2:4); it is because there is forgiveness with God that we live lives of penitential fear (Psa. 130:4). Repentance is a gift of the ascended Christ in his glorious office as Mediator. As the Westminster divines put it:

> Repentance unto life is an evangelical grace. ... By it, a sinner, out of the sight and sense not only of the danger, but also of the filthiness and odiousness of his sins, as contrary to the holy nature, and righteous law of God; *and upon the apprehension of his mercy in Christ to such as are penitent*, so grieves for, and hates his sins, *as to turn from them all unto God, purposing and endeavouring to walk with him in all the ways of his commandments.*[1]

Wherever we see repentance in the Scriptures, this is the pattern: the revelation of divine holiness in the law and commandments of God creates the guilt-burden; yet through the weakness of the flesh, law as command cannot save sinners. But, thank God, what the law could not do has been accomplished in the incarnation, death, resurrection, and coronation of our Lord Jesus! The kingdom has come; grace enables the guilt-burdened and heart-broken to repent. Repentance is possible only because it is motivated by the promise of grace. Only then do we cry through our tears:

> Have mercy ...
> according to your steadfast love ...
> according to your abundant mercy ...
> Purge me ...

---

[1] *Westminster Confession of Faith*, XV.1, 2.

> Wash me ...
> Let me hear joy and gladness ...
> Hide your face from my sins ...
> Blot out all my iniquities ...
> Create in me a pure heart ...
> Renew a right spirit within me ...
> Restore to me joy ...
>
>   (Psa. 51:1-12)

The way to the true *theologia gloriae* is by way of the *theologia crucis*! In this God is magnified in the salvation of sinners so that his glory (*kabod*—he is not weightless![1]) bows us down in humble worship as those whose mouths have been shut and reopened with songs of praise.

But this happens only when we hear the cry, 'the cross! the cross!'

Sadly, just here, evangelicalism has become like a latter-day Jonah. It seeks prestige as a power-player in the nation, prophesying the only way for the nation's boundaries to be enlarged to fulfil divine destiny (was this the only 'prophecy' of Jonah's ministry that anyone could remember?—2 Kings 14:23-25). It seeks to preserve its own *kudos* among its own kind. It sings, but does not find that grace is 'amazing' or the cross 'wondrous'; it wears, but does not bear, the cross. The evangelical church offers literature and seminars largely *on what we can accomplish*, rarely on *what Christ has accomplished* because we cannot. (When did you last read a book or attend a seminar on the cross and on cross-bearing?) It offers having-your-life-together-successfully, heedless of the Christ who cannot thus be tamed, house-trained, and thoroughly domesticated. We fear the chaos God may sovereignly create in order to reorder our lives, eschewing the other-worldliness that alone enables us to make a lasting impact on the present world.

But in the purposes of God the way up is the way down. Only as humbled under the mighty hand of God can there be exaltation. We need first to see—Jonah-like—how far down we have sunk; to see our need of grace and the cross; and to find forgiveness and restoration.

As with Jonah, the word of the Lord comes to us with great clarity (cf. Jon. 1:2). We believe in the perspicuity of Scripture:

---

[1] *Kabod*, the Hebrew word for *glory*, is also the word for *weight*.

> Those things which are necessary to be known, believed, and
> observed, for salvation, are so clearly propounded and opened in
> some place of Scripture or other, that not only the learned, but the
> unlearned, in a due use of the ordinary means, may attain unto a
> sufficient understanding of them.[1]

Our problem does not lie in the parts of Scripture we find difficult to
understand! Like Jonah, we turn from the word of the Lord that we *do*
understand. We do not read it, we do not love it, we have become almost
incapable of meditating upon it; we are careless, if not actually callous,
about submitting to it.

That we have done so is evidenced, as it was with Jonah, in the way we
run from the presence of God (Jon. 1:3, 10). We cannot sit either still or
silent before him. Prayer has become the hardest thing in the world for
evangelicals to do. Worship together in his presence has been conformed
to our convenience mentality.

One of the most obvious evidences of this is the way in which behind
all manner of extraordinarily spiritual excuses, the majority of evangelicals leave God in peace even on Sunday after the noon hour strikes!
Under the guise of our fear of being black-balled as 'Sabbatarians' we
rob the Lord. As a result we taste less of the cumulative blessing of the
worship of the people of God on the Lord's Day. We still honour our
evangelical saints, but we find practically incomprehensible their desire
to squeeze every last moment out of congregational foretastes of eternal
glory.

Have you never, in the dying embers of a Sunday night, rested your
head on the pillow with wet eyes because the day of congregating in the
presence of God does not yet last forever? Are we in danger of so being
squeezed into this world's mould that Christ has this against us: we have
lost our first love? Or do we still believe *here and now* that in his presence
is fullness of joy and at his right hand pleasures for evermore?

Poor Jonah: he ran away from the presence of the Lord. Where was
the blessedness he knew when first he saw the Lord? But then, what
about my 'soul-refreshing view' of the presence of Jehovah-Jesus and his
word (William Cowper)?

[1] *Westminster Confession of Faith*, I.7.

Recovery

Is there a way back? Do we still have a future? Yes, there is a way back. There is the sign of Jonah: the cross. And God has his ways of preparing winds to pursue us, great fish to swallow us, dark bellies which—as Calvin says—become hospitals to heal us of our deathly sickness. But we may well need 'distress' as a community to make us call on the Lord (Jon. 2:2) and turn back to his presence and his word.

It is an amazing, if revealing, *faux pas* when liberal Old Testament scholars have suggested that the prayer of Jonah 2 is simply a smart piece of authorial creativity because it is virtually a catena of quotations from the Psalms. (Have they never attended a church prayer meeting?) But that is precisely the point. The man could not get enough of Scripture. Like all who deeply repent he devoured them, turned them into prayer, wanted to bathe in, and feed upon, them, and longed to put into practice everything they commanded. What he had vowed he would make good (Jon. 2:9).

And, inevitably, he sought the presence of God and the worship of God. Banished in exile, he wanted his captivity to end. He wanted to be in the temple (Jon. 2:4, 7)—where the portrayal of forgiveness could be found, where the praise of God could be heard, where the people of God could be met, where encouragement to keep his vows could be received.

When Jonah thus repented, it was inevitable that his heart would be moved with compassion for the lost who 'pay regard to vain idols [and] forsake their hope of steadfast love' (Jon. 2:8). But that happened only when he realized the grip the idols of his own heart had on him (Ezek. 14:3, 4, 7), and how tightly he had gripped them. Only then did it dawn on him that 'Salvation belongs to the LORD!' (2:9). When that happens to us, true evangelical repentance becomes the sweetest pain in the whole world.

Would we had a baptism of it!

Clearly this has the most general application. But if we are cut to the heart by the need for repentance, how are we to learn to live to God's glory?

By God's grace we need, first of all, to be better men and women. We need to be godly, not merely efficient. We need to resolve that we will never defile ourselves in the city of this world with Babylonian meat and believe that the bread and water of the city of God will make us spiritually fat and healthy and fill us with the wisdom of heaven. We need to be more heavenly-minded, more Christ-centred, more ready to bear the cross; we need to be more sin-mortifying and Christ-imaging men and women. It is as simple as that. But how?

Evangelicalism is a noble tradition. Shall we not learn from our fore-fathers? They determined to live in the presence of God; they gathered to seek his presence and to listen to his voice in the exposition and application of Scripture; they built communities of Christ with precious stones hewn at great cost from deep quarries; they eschewed wood and hay and stubble. They knew they would stand before the judgment seat of Christ to receive what was due them for the things they had done in the body (2 Cor. 5:10)—and so they lived and laboured, prayed and built for eternity. And so must we.

They prayed, and asked for divine blessing. And they were heard. Alas, we do not have, because we do not ask; and even when we ask, it is too often to spend it on our ungodly passions (cf. James 4:2-3).

What must we do? We must feel the weight of the truth that the kingdom has come in Jesus Christ; we must repent and believe the gospel.

Confession

This chapter focuses on *Repentance, Recovery, and Confession*. Thus, we come, in conclusion, to *confession*—to homologating the judgment of Almighty God upon our lives and ministries.

Unlike our forefathers, we do this with great infrequency, for evangel-icalism has tended to individualize and privatize. Moreover, who of us is capable of bearing the weight of being the mouthpiece of the confession of such sins as ours? We all need to *be led* in confessing sin and failure, for we are neophytes in this matter. But perhaps again our forefathers can come to our aid.

The Confession and Catechism drawn up by the Westminster Assembly between 1643 and 1648 are well known. Less well known is the fact that four years later the ministers of the Church of Scotland, having embraced these grand doctrinal statements, recognized their need not only to confess the doctrines of the faith but also the sins of their lives as an essential beginning point for ongoing repentance.

Those were critical, but by no means wholly barren days spiritually, any more than our own days are wholly barren. There were many evidences of God's preserving goodness; there were numerous ministries of outstanding godliness, grace, power, and fruitfulness. Those were days when Puritan giants could be met in the streets of London, Oxford, and many other places. Indeed, in 1650 an English merchant returning from a visit to Scotland was able to say:

> Great and good news! I went to St Andrews, where I heard a sweet majestic-looking man [Robert Blair], and he showed me *the majesty of God*. After him I heard a little fair man [Samuel Rutherford] and he showed me *the loveliness of Christ*. I then went to Irvine, where I heard a well-favoured proper old man with a long beard [David Dickson] and that man showed me *all my heart*.[1]

Yet it is surely evidence of the stirrings of God that such Christian leaders corporately confessed their faults. We may learn from their example what it is that the Lord requires of us. What follows is part of their confession of their sins *as Christian leaders*. It is applicable to all Christians. For as the *Westminster Confession* notes, each of us is called 'to repent of his particular sins particularly'.[2] So they confessed:

> Ignorance of God, want [lack] of nearness with him, and taking up little of God in reading, meditating and speaking of him; exceeding great selfishness in all that we do; acting from ourselves, for ourselves, and to ourselves.
>
> Not caring how faithful and negligent others were, so being it might contribute a testimony to our faithfulness and diligence, but being rather content, if not rejoicing, at their faults.
>
> Least delight in those things wherein lieth our nearest communion with God; great inconstancy in our walk with God, and neglect of acknowledging him in all our ways. In going about duties, least careful about those things which are most remote from the eyes of men. Seldom in secret prayer with God, except to fit for

[1] Thomas M'Crie, *The Story of the Scottish Church* (London: Blackie & Son, 1875), p. 248.
[2] *Westminster Confession of Faith*, XV.5.

public performance; and even that much neglected, or gone about very superficially.

Glad to find excuses for the neglect of our duties. Neglecting the reading of Scripture in secret, for edifying ourselves as Christians. ... Not given to reflect upon our own ways, nor allowing conviction to have a thorough work upon us; deceiving ourselves by resting upon absence from and abhorrence of evils from the light of a natural conscience, and looking upon the same as an evidence of a real change of state and nature. Evil guarding of and watching over the heart, and carelessness in self-searching; which makes much unacquaintedness with ourselves and estrangedness from God.

Not esteeming the cross of Christ and sufferings for his name, honourable, but rather shifting sufferings from self-love.

Not laying to heart the sad and heavy sufferings of the people of God abroad, and the not-thriving of the kingdom of Jesus Christ and the power of godliness among them.

Refined hypocrisy; desiring to appear what, indeed, we are not. Studying more to learn the language of God's people than their exercise. Artificial confessing of sin, without repentance; professing to declare iniquity, and not resolving to be sorry for sin. Confession in secret much slighted, even of those things whereof we are convicted.

Readier to search out and censure faults in others than to see or deal with them in ourselves. Accounting of our estate and way according to the estimate that others have of us.

Estimation of men, as they agree or disagree from us.

Fruitless conversing ordinarily with others, for the worse rather than for the better. Foolish jesting away of time with ... useless discourse.

Slighting of fellowship with those by whom we might profit. Desiring more to converse with those that might better us by their talents than with such as might edify us by their graces.

Not studying opportunities of doing good to others. Shifting of prayer and other duties when called thereto ... loving our pleasures more than God. Taking little or no time to Christian discourse with young men trained up for the ministry. ...

Not praying for men of a contrary judgment, but using reservedness and distance from them; being more ready to speak of them than to them, or to God for them. Not weighed with the failings and miscarriages of others, but rather taking advantage thereof for justifying ourselves. Talking of and sporting at the faults of others, rather than compassionating of them. Carelessness in employing Christ, and drawing virtues out of him, for enabling us to preach in the Spirit and in power. In praying for assistance we pray more for assistance to the messenger than to the message which we carry, not caring what becomes of the word, if we be with some measure of assistance carried on in the duty.

Exceeding great neglect and unskillfulness to set forth the excellencies and usefulness of (and the necessity of an interest in) Jesus Christ. ... Speaking of Christ more by hearsay than from knowledge and experience, or any real impression of him upon the heart. ... Want of sobriety in preaching the gospel; not savouring anything but what is new; so that the substantials of religion bear but little bulk.

Not preaching Christ in the simplicity of the gospel, nor ourselves the people's servants, for Christ's sake. Preaching of Christ, not that the people may know him, but that they may think we know much of him. ... Not preaching with bowels of compassion to them that are in hazard [danger] to perish.

Bitterness, instead of zeal, in speaking against malignants, sectarians and other scandalous persons. ... Too much eyeing our own credit and applause; and being pleased with it when we get it, and unsatisfied when it is wanting. ... Not making all the counsel of God known to his people.[1]

There is more; and there is surely much more we need to confess. Ought we not to make a beginning now? For in the broadest sense it remains true: unless we repent, we will all—evangelicals, confessing evangelicals, Reformed, Lutheran, Baptist, and Congregationalist alike—likewise perish.

[1] Drawn up in 1651, this confession is accessible in Horatius Bonar, *Words to Winners of Souls* (Boston, 1860; repr. Phillipsburg, NJ: Presbyterian and Reformed and the den Dulk Foundation, 1995), pp. 25-34.

From depths of woe I raise to Thee
   The voice of lamentation;
Lord, turn a gracious ear to me
   And hear my supplication:
If Thou iniquities dost mark,
   Our secret sins and misdeeds dark,
O who shall stand before Thee?

To wash away the crimson stain,
   Grace, grace alone availeth;
Our works, alas! are all in vain;
   In much the best life faileth:
No man can glory in Thy sight,
   All must alike confess Thy might,
And live alone by mercy.

Therefore my trust is in the Lord,
   And not in mine own merit;
On Him my soul shall rest, His word
   Upholds my fainting spirit:
His promised mercy is my fort;
   My comfort and my sweet support;
I wait for it with patience.

What though I wait the live-long night,
   And till the dawn appeareth,
My heart still trusteth in His might;
   It doubteth not nor feareth:
Do thus, O ye of Israel's seed,
   Ye of the Spirit born indeed;
And wait till God appeareth.

Though great our sins and sore our woes
   His grace much more aboundeth;
His helping love no limit knows,
   Our utmost need it soundeth.
Our Shepherd good and true is He,
   Who will at last His Israel free
From all their sin and sorrow.

   (Based on Martin Luther's rendering of Psalm 130)

V. THE PASTOR
AND
PREACHING

CHAPTER THIRTY-TWO

THE BIT, THE BRIDLE, AND THE BLESSING: AN EXPOSITION OF JAMES 3:1-12

OUR focus in this study is the teaching of James 3:1-12:

Not many of you should become teachers, my brothers, for you know that we who teach will be judged with greater strictness. For we all stumble in many ways, and if anyone does not stumble in what he says, he is a perfect man, able also to bridle his whole body. If we put bits into the mouths of horses so that they obey us, we guide their whole bodies as well. Look at the ships also: though they are so large and are driven by strong winds, they are guided by a very small rudder wherever the will of the pilot directs. So also the tongue is a small member, yet it boasts of great things.

How great a forest is set ablaze by such a small fire! And the tongue is a fire, a world of unrighteousness. The tongue is set among our members, staining the whole body, setting on fire the entire course of life, and set on fire by hell. For every kind of beast and bird, of reptile and sea creature, can be tamed and has been tamed by mankind, but no human being can tame the tongue. It is a restless evil, full of deadly poison. With it we bless our Lord and Father, and with it we curse people who are made in the likeness of God. From the same mouth come blessing and cursing. My brothers, these things ought not to be so. Does a spring pour forth from the same opening both fresh and salt water? Can a fig tree, my brothers, bear olives, or a grapevine produce figs? Neither can a salt pond yield fresh water.

James 3:1-12 contains the single most sustained discussion in the New Testament on the use of the tongue. I take the author of this little book to have been James, the half-brother of our Lord Jesus.[1] It is clear that he is steeped in the wisdom literature of the Old Testament Scriptures and also in the teaching of the Lord Jesus, to which his own teaching has many parallels. Both the book of Proverbs and our Lord Jesus spoke with searching clarity about the nature and use of the tongue. James walks in their footprints. Much of what he says is a powerful exposé of the sin and failure that mar our speech.

In this way James' words exemplify the central purposes of the teaching and preaching of God's word. The resulting effect will be to 'reprove, rebuke, and exhort' (2 Tim. 4:2). But James' message also exemplifies what Paul calls the profitability or usefulness of sacred Scripture: 'teaching ... correction ... [child-]training'.

In a word, the immediate focus of James' teaching—one might say the same of all apostolic teaching—is to bring Christian believers to maturity. Here, as well as in other places, he is completely in harmony with the way the apostle Paul employed all his God-given powers: 'Him we proclaim, warning everyone and teaching everyone with all wisdom, that we may present everyone mature in Christ. For this I toil, struggling with all his energy that he powerfully works within me' (Col. 1:28-29).

In fact, this is one of James' burdens also. His five chapters constitute an extended piece of pastoral preaching, laced as it is with words of wisdom and warning. All along his goal is to lead his readers and hearers—men and women who were possibly once under his direct pastoral care but are now widely scattered—to full spiritual maturity, so that their whole being, without reservation, should be wholly Christ's.

We find that this motif runs through the entire book. As we come upon it in chapter 3, he has already shown (1) how spiritual maturity *develops through response to suffering*, and (2) how spiritual maturity is *enhanced by response to the word*. Now he goes on to show that (3) spiritual maturity is *evidenced by the use of the tongue*. The mastery of it is one of the clearest marks of a whole person, a true Christian. Tongue-mastery is the fruit of self-mastery. It is essential to gospel ministry.

[1] The author does not identify himself beyond revealing that he is 'James' (1:1). The view of the earliest church tradition is that this is James the (half-) brother of the Lord, and this is certainly in accord with what evidence of authorship there is in the letter, and of what we know of James.

We will examine this teaching in order to accomplish three goals: (1) to 'walk' through James 3:1-12 in order to feel the weight of his appeal; (2) to set this teaching in the context of the whole book of James to discover that it is, in effect, only the tip of the iceberg of what he has to say about our speech; (3) to place these words in the broader gospel context expressed in the book of James.

1. James 3:1-12 and its teaching on the tongue

As we make our way into James 3:1-12, we notice it has a variety of basic driving principles.

The difficulty of taming the tongue

James issues a special word of wise counsel to those who aspire to be teachers: 'Not many of you should become teachers, my brothers, for you know that we who teach will be judged with greater strictness' (3:1).

Why should this be? Teachers should be conscious of the weight and potential influence of what they say because words lie at the heart of the teaching ministry. To have an unreliable tongue is likely to provide a destructive model for those who are taught. The potential for multiplication of influence requires a canon of judgment that takes the measure of both responsibility and opportunity into account.

But James does not write as one who has 'arrived'. He is conscious of his own shortcomings: 'For we all stumble in many ways' (3:2). He has no false perfectionism. Perhaps he remembers how he misspoke about Jesus, demeaning him during the days of his ministry. Was James among those who said, 'He is out of his mind' (Mark 3:21)? Was this one reason why our Lord visited him, in particular (as he did Simon Peter), after the resurrection (1 Cor. 15:7)?

But James' words are applicable far beyond those who are called to teach. We all use our tongues. If the mastery of the tongue is a sign of maturity, it is so for all Christians. So James 3:1-12 has general as well as specific application. How we use our tongues provides clear evidence of where we are spiritually.

When I was a child, our family physician used to ask us to stick out our tongues. (That was the only circumstance in which I was ever permitted to do this!) He seemed to be able to tell a great deal about our health by looking into our mouths. That is a parable of spiritual reality. What comes out of our mouths is usually an accurate index of the health of our hearts. Jesus said: 'For out of the abundance of the heart the mouth speaks' (Matt. 12:34). So here, as a spiritual physician, James engages in a rigorous tongue analysis. James 3:1-12 is a veritable pathology laboratory in which analysis and diagnosis take place.

Notice James' axiom: the mature person is able to 'bridle' his tongue. The person who can do this is master of the whole body.[1] The spiritual guides of the past understood this to have a double reference. The control of the tongue has both negative and positive aspects. It involves the ability to restrain the tongue in silence. But it also means being able to control it in gracious speech when that is required. Sanctification in any area of our lives always expresses this double dimension—a putting off and a putting on, as it were. Silence and speech, appropriately expressed, are together the mark of the mature.[2]

Nor is this James' first reference to speech. He had already noted that for a professing Christian to fail to bridle the tongue is to be guilty of self-deception (1:22-25), and the hallmark of a person whose religion is worthless (1:26). One might think here of the ease of speech but super-ficial use of words in the life of John Bunyan's Mr Talkative. He was all talk but no control, all words but without weight.

But with all of this said, James is forced into a confession. Nobody—Jesus excepted—has succeeded in mastering the tongue! Our only hope as we pursue the discipline of self that leads to mastery of the tongue is that we are Christ's and that we are being made increasingly like him. But this battle for vocal holiness is a long-running one, and it needs to be waged incessantly, daily, hourly.

Are we fighting it? We must seek to do so for a very important reason.

---

[1] Some scholars take 'body' here to refer to the church, arguing that this makes sense of the context (teachers), and also of the reference to 'members' in 4:1 (see ESV footnote translation) understood not as physical members but as church members. For a judicious assessment, see Dan G. McCartney, *James*, BECNT (Grand Rapids: Baker Academic, 2009), pp. 181-83. While carefully outlining the case for seeing 'body' as a reference to the church, he concludes against it.

[2] One of the clearest illustrations of this is Colossians 3:1-17; note the exhortations in verse 5 ('Put to death therefore …') and verse 12 ('Put on then …').

The disproportionate power of the tongue

In James 3:3-5, James uses two commonplace but very vivid illustrations. *The tongue is like the bit in the mouth of a horse.* This tiny appliance controls the enormous power and energy of the horse and is used to give it direction. James may well have been familiar with this picture from common experience in daily life. He had seen powerful Roman military horses and had probably heard stories of chariot races. The point, however, is the extraordinary power and influence concentrated in one small object. So it is with the tongue.

The tongue is also like the rudder in a boat. Large ships were not unknown in the ancient world. The ship that originally was to transport Paul across the Mediterranean en route to Rome held 276 people (Acts 27:37). We know that a large ship like the *Isis* could carry 1,000 people. Yet such a capacious and heavy vessel was directed simply by a turn of the rudder! So it is with the tongue. The tongue is small. But its power, both for good and for ill, is out of all proportion to its size. 'A fool's tongue', Bruce Waltke wryly notes, 'is long enough to cut his own throat.'[1]

Why does James speak this way? Presumably out of both biblical knowledge and personal experience. The tongue carries into the world the breath that issues from the heart.

Alas, we do not realize how powerful for evil the tongue is because we are so accustomed to its polluting influence. En route to give this address, I rode the hotel elevator with several others. On one floor the elevator stopped, the doors opened, and a woman entered the confined space. The doors closed, and I suspect everyone in the elevator almost instantaneously had the same thought: 'She has been smoking!' In this confined 'smoke-free' environment her breath could not be disguised.

So, says Jesus, the tongue projects the thoughts and intentions of the heart. It is from within, 'out of the heart', that the mouth speaks (cf. Matt. 12:34; 15:18-19). But like smokers, so accustomed to the odour, the atmosphere in which they live, the person with polluted speech has little or no sense of it—no sense that they exhale bad breath every time they speak.

---

[1] Bruce K. Waltke, *The Book of Proverbs: Chapters 1-15*, NICOT (Grand Rapids: Eerdmans, 2004), p. 102.

Yet there is another side to this, a wonderfully encouraging side. Scripture teaches us that the breath by which we express our deepest desires, instincts, and opinions may produce helpful and pleasing fruit. Writes the wise man of Proverbs:

> The tongue of the wise brings healing (Prov. 12:18).
> A gentle tongue is a tree of life (Prov. 15:4).

So James sees that the tongue is an instrument of extraordinary power, out of all proportion to its size. Whatever its anatomical connections, its most significant connection is to the heart—whether hardened by sin or recreated by grace.

At this stage James is chiefly concerned that we should have a sense of the convicting power of his teaching. For this reason he began by addressing *the difficulty of taming the tongue*. It is a word spoken primarily to bring conviction of sin. For the tongue is difficult, indeed impossible, to tame naturally, because, as we have also seen, *it exercises power out of all proportion to its size*.

The destruction caused by the tongue

Now, third, a series of vivid pictures flashes rapidly across James' mind as he thinks about the power of the tongue.

A fire (3:6). A small fire can destroy an entire forest; all it takes is an uncontrolled spark. So it is with the tongue. A sharp word, a loose sentence, a callous aside can cause a conflagration that cannot be extinguished. Words can consume and destroy a life.

James is very specific about the energy source for such destruction. The tongue that sets on fire is set on fire itself by hell. He employs the biblical term *Gehenna*—the background reference being to the Valley of Hinnom on the southern outskirts of Jerusalem. It served as the city dump, which presumably constantly burned there to destroy garbage— hence the reference to fire.[1] Was this the place to which our Lord's body would have been taken were it not for the thoughtfulness of Joseph of Arimathaea? If so, it is difficult not to share with James a sense of disgust. It is from such a hell that destructive words arise. Remember

---

[1] Dan McCartney reports that it continued to be thus used through 1996 and beyond. *James*, p. 190.

that imagery whenever similar words seek to force their way out of your mouth.

A world (3:6). The tongue is 'a world of unrighteousness'. I remember reading a picture quiz in an in-flight magazine many years ago. Various things photographed from unusual angles were presented, and the challenge was to guess what the objects actually were. One seemed to be a striking photograph of the moon with all its craters—a dark world of death. Turning to check the answers I was astonished to find it was in fact a photograph of a human tongue! How appropriate that, when photographically magnified, it would appear like an entire world of death and darkness, full of dangerous craters.

A stain (3:6). The tongue is 'set among our members, staining the whole body'. How careful you are as you get dressed for a wedding, especially if it is your own! How nervous about that new silk tie during dinner. The spot need only be a small one, but it ruins everything. So it is with the tongue and its words. No matter what graces you may have developed, if you have not gained tongue-mastery, you can besmirch them all by an unguarded and ill-disciplined comment. Graces are fragile; therefore guard your tongue lest it destroy them.

A restless evil (3:8). The unregenerate tongue roams the wilds, quick to defend itself, swift to attack others, anxious to subdue them, always marked by evil. It mimics Satan in this respect, who, having rebelled against the God of peace, can never settle. He goes to and fro throughout the earth (as in Job 1:7; 2:2), like a roaring lion seeking someone to devour (1 Pet. 5:8). The tongue that is under his lordship always shares that tendency. It has an inbuilt need to guard its own territory, to destroy rivals to itself, to be the king of the beasts.

A deadly poison (3:8). James shares the perspective of Paul and, before him, of the psalmist. The 'venom of asps' is under the lips of sinners, 'Their throat is an open grave; they use their tongues to deceive' (Rom. 3:13; Psa. 5:9). Whether suddenly or slowly, life is eaten away and destroyed. Perhaps here there is an echo of Genesis 3 and the deadly deceit of Eve by the serpent—with all its deadly and hellish consequences.

James, however unbelieving he might have been during Jesus' early ministry, has clearly absorbed his half-brother's teaching and has been led by it to the multitude of Old Testament word pictures about the power and destructive ability of the tongue. If the pen is mightier than the sword, it is equally true that we can destroy a man as easily with the words we use as with a physical weapon (Matt. 5:21-22).

Of course, all this is naturally true of the unregenerate man. The tragedy is—and it is this tragedy that surely concerns James here—that the same destructive powers may be released within the believing community.

Do you ever wonder if this is a distinctively evangelical sin? Of course it is by no means exclusively so. But how commonplace it seems to be to hear a fellow Christian's name mentioned in some context or other, and the first words of response demean his reputation, belittle him, and distance him from acceptance into the fellowship, although this is a brother for whom Christ died!

The saintly Robert Murray M'Cheyne was surely nearer the mark when he resolved that when a fellow Christian's name was mentioned in company, if he could not say anything good about him, he would refrain from all speech about him. Better that, surely, than to be careless with fire and 'destroy a brother for whom Christ died' (Rom. 14:15; 1 Cor. 8:11).

The young Jonathan Edwards penned a number of his 'Resolutions'[1] around this theme. They are worth noting:

31. *Resolved*, Never to say anything at all against any body, but when it is perfectly agreeable to the highest degree of Christian honour, and of love to mankind, agreeable to the lowest humility, and sense of my own faults and failings, and agreeable to the golden rule; often, when I have said anything against any one, to bring it to, and try it strictly by, the test of this Resolution.

34. *Resolved*, In narrations never to speak anything but the pure and simple verity.

---

[1] See Sereno E. Dwight's *Memoirs of Jonathan Edwards* in *The Works of Jonathan Edwards*, 2 vols, ed. E. Hickman (1834; repr. Edinburgh: Banner of Truth Trust, 1974), I:xxi-xxii.

36. *Resolved*, Never to speak evil of any, except I have some particular good call to it.

70. Let there be something of benevolence in all that I speak.

How easily the failure to master the tongue can destroy the effect of every grace that has taken years to build into our lives! Introduce poison here and we endanger everything.

A seminary colleague once told me how, because of flight delays, he arrived late and very weary at a hotel where he had booked a room. The young desk clerk could find no reservation under his name. My weary friend, who had had a miserable day, lost some self-control and started a small verbal blaze around the unfortunate employee, as if the problem were of the young man's making. Having found him a room the clerk invited him to fill in the guest form. My colleague included the name of the theological seminary at which we both taught. As the clerk looked at the form he gasped; 'Are you from *the* Westminster Seminary?' he asked, and then said excitedly, 'This is amazing. I have just recently become a Christian. I have heard about your seminary! How amazing, and marvellous to meet you! Wow, are you really from Westminster Seminary?'

The story could so easily have ended on a different note: a stain inflicted on a young man by a mature believer—a stain that might have proved impossible to wash out. We have all seen or caused moments like this. The tongue can be the most powerful, destructive member in the entire body.

In this connection it is salutary to remember the thrust of Paul's most basic and powerful presentation of our need for the gospel. 'Whatever the law says it speaks to those who are under the law, *so that every mouth may be stopped*' (Rom. 3:19).

I still recall the shivers that went down my spine on first reading, in 1970, D. Martyn Lloyd-Jones's exposition of these words:

> Paul now points out ... that when you realize what the Law is truly saying to you the result is that 'every mouth shall be stopped'. You are rendered speechless. You are not a Christian unless you have been made speechless! How do you know whether you are a Christian or

not? It is that you 'stop talking'. The trouble with the non-Christian is that he goes on talking … .

How do you know whether a man is a Christian? The answer is that his mouth is 'shut'. I like this forthrightness of the gospel. People need to have their mouths shut, 'stopped'. … You do not begin to be a Christian until your mouth is shut, is stopped, and you are speechless and have nothing to say.[1]

There is a 'something', almost indefinable, about the person who has clearly been converted to Christ. Dr Lloyd-Jones surely put his finger on the essence of it—the humbling of the proud, self-sufficient heart, the breaking of our native arrogance. Our tongues are so often the most obvious index of that ungodly drive at the centre of our being. But the slaying of inner pride and the illumination of our minds in regeneration create a new disposition and affection. The true convert will have a Jacob-like limp in his speech as well as in his walk—because in spiritual anatomy (as distinct from physical anatomy), the heart and the tongue are directly connected to each other. The subduing of the heart leads to the silencing of the tongue; humility within leads to humility expressed. Only when we have been thus silenced are we in any position to begin to speak. And when we do, by God's grace, we speak as those who have first been silenced.

The deadly inconsistency that plagues the tongue
James is not yet finished with his devastating analysis of the tongue. He draws attention to a fourth characteristic as the analysis now rises to a crescendo of exposure:

No human being can tame the tongue. … With it we bless our Lord and Father, and with it we curse people who are made in the likeness of God. From the same mouth come blessing and cursing. My brothers, these things ought not to be so. Does a spring pour forth from the same opening both fresh and salt water? Can a fig tree, my brothers, bear olives, or a grapevine produce figs? Neither can a salt pond yield fresh water (James 3:8-12).

[1] D. M. Lloyd-Jones, *Romans, Exposition of Chapters 3:20–4:25: Atonement and Justi-fication* (Edinburgh: Banner of Truth Trust, 1970), p. 19. Although not an exposition of the first section in Romans, this was the first volume in the series to appear in print.

I am reminded of the old 'cowboy-and-Indian' movies my parents used to take me to when I was a child. There is only one line I recall a Native American ever speaking, but it was so frequently repeated it became engraved as one of my earliest memories of childhood: 'White man speak with forked tongue.' It was meant as, and really was, a damning indictment.

James shared that perspective but brought to it a more profound analysis: 'Forked tongue connected to forked heart.' Such speech is a mark of the 'double-minded man' who is 'unstable in all his ways' (1:8). It is not an amiable weakness. It expresses a damnable contradiction in our very being. It is an 'ought not to be', like a spring that spouts forth both fresh and salt water. It is more contradictory than anything we find in nature, like a fig tree bearing olives, a grapevine producing figs, a salt pond yielding fresh water.

Notice the power of James' own words. Do not try to parry the blow. His words are intended to be a sharp two-edged sword 'piercing to the division of soul and of spirit, of joints and of marrow, and discerning the thoughts and intentions of the heart' (Heb. 4:12).

We were created as the image of God to bless God. It is blatant hypocrisy, double-mindedness, and sin to bless God and then casually curse those who have been made as his very likeness. But the forked tongue of the double-minded person enslaves him or her. He or she thinks the unthinkable and speaks unspeakable contradictions. James is blood-earnest as he rips up the consciences of his contemporary readers, many of whom were, perhaps, once members of his dear flock in Jerusalem before being scattered abroad (Acts 8:1; 11:19).

If such words could be spoken to professing Christians serious enough in their faith to experience persecution and suffer privation in a world that was becoming increasingly inhospitable to the followers of the Way—how much more devastating are they when addressed to pampered, often self-indulgent professors of Christianity in the early twenty-first century?

But now that our consciences have been, to use Puritan language, 'ripped up', a question arises. Why does James apparently give no practical counsel about how we are to deal with the tongue? Are we left to go to the local Christian bookstore, or attend a seminar or conference, in order to know how to sanctify the use of the tongue? Isn't James a 'practical letter'? Why is there no practical counsel?

But in fact there is—if we will only stay with James long enough to hear it. Indeed, whenever there is such analysis in the New Testament letters there is ordinarily practical counsel written into the teaching itself. True, it may not be immediately evident, but if we keep our minds and spirits in the passage long enough and learn to wait patiently on the Lord in his word, it will become clear. Even where there are no obvious imperatives to tell us what to do next, they are almost invariably implied in the text, woven as it were into its very warp and woof, underlining for us that it is by *the word itself* and not by ourselves that we are sanctified. Did not James' half-brother pray, 'Sanctify them in [or by] the truth; your word is truth' (John 17:17)?

In order to enable us to grasp how James does this, it will be helpful, further, to consider how this teaching fits in with the rest of the book.

2. James 3:1-12 in the context of the entire book

We are told in the sacred record that when Job felt himself to be under special pressure in his sufferings (and, unknown to him, under the specific assault of the devil to destroy his enjoyment of God) he made 'a covenant with [his] eyes' in order thus to bind on his heart the pattern of holiness he needed to develop (see Job 31:1ff.). Guarding the eyes implied guarding eyes in the heart as well as in the head.

Temptation, and therefore spiritual compromise, often find their easiest access route to the heart via the eyes. By the same token, sin may find its easiest exit route from our hearts via the mouth. The exhortation of Proverbs to 'Keep your heart with all vigilance' is immediately followed by an exhortation to 'Put away from you crooked speech, and put devious talk far from you' (Prov. 4:23-24). Guarding the heart involves guarding the tongue. To apply Job's principle to our present subject, we need to learn to say, 'I will make a covenant with my tongue.'

Rather wonderfully, this is what James helps us to do throughout his letter. Perhaps we may be permitted to take a leaf out of Jonathan Edwards's *Resolutions* and express the burden of the practical exhortations implicit in James in a similar fashion.

Here, then, are twenty resolutions on the use of the tongue to which the letter's teaching gives rise:

(1) *Resolved: To ask God for wisdom to speak and to do so with a single mind.*

If any of you lacks wisdom, let him ask God, who gives generously to all without reproach, and it will be given him. ... in faith, with no doubting. ... For that person must not suppose that he will receive anything ... he is a double-minded man, unstable in all his ways (James 1:5-8).

(2) *Resolved: To boast only in my exaltation in Christ or my humiliation in the world.*

Let the lowly brother boast in his exaltation, and the rich in his humiliation, because like a flower of the grass he will pass away (James 1:9-10).

(3) *Resolved: To set a watch over my mouth.*

Let no one say when he is tempted, 'I am being tempted by God,' for God cannot be tempted with evil, and he himself tempts no one (James 1:13).

(4) *Resolved: To be constantly quick to hear, slow to speak.*

Know this, my beloved brothers: let every person be quick to hear, slow to speak, slow to anger (James 1:19).

(5) *Resolved: To learn the gospel way of speaking to the poor and the rich.*

My brothers, show no partiality as you hold the faith in our Lord Jesus Christ, the Lord of glory. For if a man wearing a gold ring and fine clothing comes into your assembly, and a poor man in shabby clothing also comes in, and if you pay attention to the one who wears the fine clothing and say, 'You sit here in a good place,' while you say to the poor man, 'You stand over there,' or, 'Sit down at my feet,' have you not then made distinctions among yourselves and become judges with evil thoughts? (James 2:1-4).

(6) *Resolved: To speak in the consciousness of the final judgment.*

So speak and so act as those who are to be judged under the law of liberty (James 2:12).

(7) *Resolved: To never stand on anyone's face with words that demean, despise, or cause despair.*

If a brother or sister is poorly clothed and lacking in daily food, and one of you says to them, 'Go in peace, be warmed and filled' without giving them the things needed for the body, what good is that? (James 2:15-16).

(8) *Resolved: To never claim a reality I do not experience.*

If you have bitter jealousy and selfish ambition in your hearts, do not boast and be false to the truth (James 3:14).

(9) *Resolved: To resist quarrelsome words as marks of a bad heart.*

What causes quarrels and what causes fights among you? Is it not this, that your passions are at war within you? (James 4:1).

(10) *Resolved: To never speak evil of another.*

Do not speak evil against one another, brothers. The one who speaks against a brother or judges his brother, speaks evil against the law and judges the law. But if you judge the law, you are not a doer of the law but a judge (James 4:11).

(11) *Resolved: To never boast in what I will accomplish.*

Come now, you who say, 'Today or tomorrow we will go into such and such a town and spend a year there and trade and make a profit'—yet you do not know what tomorrow will bring. What is your life? For you are a mist that appears for a little time and then vanishes (James 4:13-14).

(12) *Resolved: To always speak as one who is subject to the providences of God.*

Instead you ought to say, 'If the Lord wills, we will live and do this or that' (James 4:15).

(13) *Resolved: To never grumble, knowing that the Judge is at the door.*

Do not grumble against one another, brothers, so that you may not be judged; behold, the Judge is standing at the door (James 5:9).

(14) *Resolved: To never allow anything but total integrity in my speech.*

But above all, my brothers, do not swear, either by heaven or by earth or by any other oath, but let your 'yes' be yes and your 'no' be no, so that you may not fall under condemnation (James 5:12).

(15) *Resolved: To speak to God in prayer whenever I suffer.*

Is anyone among you suffering? Let him pray (James 5:13).

(16) *Resolved: To sing praises to God whenever I am cheerful.*

Is anyone cheerful? Let him sing praise (James 5:13).

(17) *Resolved: To ask for the prayers of others when I am sick.*

Is anyone among you sick? Let him call for the elders of the church, and let them pray over him, anointing him with oil in the name of the Lord (James 5:14).

(18) *Resolved: To confess it whenever I have failed.*

Therefore, confess your sins to one another (James 5:16).

(19) *Resolved: To pray for others in need when I am with them.*

Pray for one another, that you may be healed (James 5:16).

(20) *Resolved: To speak words of restoration when I see another wander.*

My brothers, if anyone among you wanders from the truth and someone brings him back, let him know that whoever brings back a sinner from his wandering will save his soul from death and will cover a multitude of sins (James 5:19-20).

Will we so resolve?

Finally, we turn to consider this passage in the context of the gospel.

3. James 3:1-12 in the context of the whole gospel

When we take one step back from James 3:1-12 and read it in the context of the entire letter, we discover that James' searing analysis is surrounded by the most practical counsel to enable us to master the tongue and to speak well for God.

When we take another step back and view his words through the wide-angle lens of the biblical gospel, we are able all the more clearly to understand and appreciate what James is 'doing' when he speaks as he does.

As is well known, in his early days as a reformer, Martin Luther thought that James was 'an epistle full of straw':

> In sum the gospel and the first epistle of St John, St Paul's epistles, especially those to the Romans, Galatians, and Ephesians; and St Peter's first epistle, are the books that show Christ to you. They teach everything you need to know for your salvation, even if you were never to see or hear any other book or hear any other teaching. In comparison with these, the epistle of St James is an epistle full of straw, because it contains nothing evangelical.[1]

---

[1] From Luther's 1522 preface (to the New Testament), cited from *Martin Luther, Selections from His Writings*, p. 19. It should be remembered that Luther's Ninety-five Theses published only five years before in 1517 had radically deconstructed the authority of a church that had, for all practical purposes, claimed to be the judge of what should be in the canon of Holy Scripture. With the removal of the Church's authority for what they believed, the early reformers found themselves in the unenviable situation of having to reconstruct orthodox Christianity. That included making decisions about the most basic issues such as how to recognize the canon of Scripture. To his credit, Luther admitted that the judgment of one man cannot be treated as if it were infallible. Later experience with antinomianism would clarify his thinking on the importance and value of James's perspective.

He would later think better of it. For the truth is that James' teaching cannot be rightly interpreted without realizing that it is rooted in the teaching of, and energized by, the grace of 'faith in our Lord Jesus Christ, the Lord of glory' (James 2:1).

In that light we can discern a profoundly gospel-centred pattern in what James is seeking to accomplish as a pastor of the souls of his readers. His gospel method encourages us to take three steps.

(1) Realize that the depth of your sin, the pollution of your heart, and your need of saving grace are all evidenced in your use of the tongue.

This is the method of grace from beginning to end. It is nowhere more starkly illustrated than in the experience of Isaiah. There is no more powerful passage in the Old Testament than Isaiah 6; but it is often read as if it were detached from Isaiah 1–5. By reading it in isolation we inevitably miss a very clear pattern into which it fits.

Isaiah has been ripping up the consciences of his sinful contemporaries. He does so in a series of six woe pronouncements (Isa. 5:8, 11, 18, 20, 21, 22). God's holy anger burns against them (5:25). Like a shepherd whistling for his dogs to come to tend the sheep, Yahweh will call on the nations to come as his servants, with their arrows sharpened, with horses' hoofs like flint, with roaring like a lion. Darkness and distress will ensue—the terrible judgment of the Holy One of Israel (Isa. 5:26-30). But for the sensitive Bible reader the appearance of six woes creates an expectation that a *climactic* seventh woe is about to be pronounced. Against whom will Isaiah pronounce the ultimate woe?

The answer follows in chapter 6. The prophet meets with the exalted God whose majestic presence seems to flood the temple. Isaiah sees creatures who are perfectly and perpetually holy cover their faces before the glory of the one who is eternally, infinitely, inherently, uncreatedly holy. Everything around Isaiah seems to be disintegrating. Everything within him seems to come apart. He is 'lost', or 'ruined' (Isa. 6:5). The language expresses the stunned silence felt in the presence of major disaster or death.[1] This is Isaiah's 'Twin Towers' day, the 9/11 moment in his spiritual experience. From his assumed security he had pronounced

---

[1] Cf. J. A. Motyer, *The Prophecy of Isaiah* (Downers Grove: InterVarsity, 1993), p. 77.

six devastating maledictions. Now he realizes that the last and climactic woe must be pronounced against—himself! And why? 'Woe is me! For I am lost; for *I am a man of unclean lips*, and I dwell in the midst of a people of unclean lips; for my eyes have seen the King, the LORD of hosts!' (Isa. 6:5).

Can you not—in your imagination—see Isaiah as he staggers into the house of his friend Benjamin later that day, ashen-faced, shaken to the roots by his experience? He blurts out fragmentary details of his vision of the Holy One of Israel (the title that hereafter will be his preferred way of describing the Lord). He has discovered he is a 'man of unclean lips'.

And can you hear dear Benjamin reply sympathetically? He is worried that his friend of many years is becoming unstable: 'Not you, Isaiah; you are the last person of whom that is true. You are our most prominent and most eloquent preacher.'

Can you not hear Isaiah's response? 'You do not understand. I have seen the King. I have felt the pollution on my tongue. The light has exposed the darkness in its every crevice. Alas for me, it is in the very instrument God has called me to use, in the very area of my life in which others call me "gifted", that sin has most deeply entangled itself. I am a wretched man! Woe, woe, woe is me!'

We naively assume that our real struggles with sin are in the areas where we are 'weak'. We do not well understand the depth of sin until we realize that it has made its home far more subtly where we are 'strong', and in our gifts rather than in our weaknesses and inadequacies. It is in the very giftedness God has given that sin operates in its most perverse and subtle ways!

But when we are brought to see this, stripped bare of our layers of self-deceit, and led to repentance, then God may make something of us.

Many—even if you do not number yourself among them—seem to find speech easy. Recent generations have, after all, been educated to be able to speak, to contribute to discussion and debate, to express themselves by the spoken word rather than by writing (as was true of my generation—at least in my native land of Scotland).

It rarely seems to strike us that it is precisely here, therefore, in our speech, that sin is most likely to abound.

Only when we have been brought to such a recognition do we realize how dangerous and destructive our tongues have been. Only then do we cry out to God in repentance and run to him with tears to seek forgiveness in the gospel.

Then we need to grasp a second principle.

(2) Recognize that you are a new creation in Christ.
At the beginning of his argument, James had urged his hearers, 'You need to recognize that you are part of a new creation in Christ Jesus, indeed a kind of firstfruits of his creation' (cf. James 1:18). I may not yet be that mature man I want to be. But thank God that I am not the old man that I once was!

What a great way to think about an ordinary Christian life! We live in a created order marred by sin. That sin has twisted and polluted our speech. But God has begun his work of new creation and has inaugurated aspects of it that will be consummated when Jesus Christ returns. Then in the 'regeneration' of all things (Matt. 19:28, NASB),[1] every tongue will confess that Jesus Christ is Lord.

But notice carefully how God regenerates us: 'Of his own will he brought us forth by the word of truth, that we should be a kind of firstfruits of his creatures.' Regeneration is a sovereign work of God, yes; but it does not ordinarily take place in a vacuum. Since it involves having our eyes opened to see the kingdom of God (John 3:3), God ordinarily regenerates us in the context of the truth of the gospel illuminating our minds. Truth in the mind forms truth in the heart, the very thing for which David prayed (Psa. 51:10), and which he realized would lead in turn to transformed speech:

> Then I will teach transgressors your ways,
>   and sinners will return to you.
> Deliver me from bloodguiltiness, O God,
>   O God of my salvation,
>   and my tongue will sing aloud of your righteousness.

[1] The translation 'the new world' (ESV) is a rendering of the Greek *palingenesis*, which elsewhere is translated 'regeneration'. Our personal renewal in regeneration is best seen as a present participation in the final, cosmic transformation that will take place at the return of Christ.

> O Lord, open my lips,
>> and my mouth will declare your praise (Psa. 51:13-15).

How important for us to recognize the power of new birth to create new affections, which in turn come to expression in the new speech patterns of the gospel!

(3) Continue in the word

The work of the word inaugurates the Christian life, but it also sustains its progress. My tongue is ongoingly cleansed and transformed by (if we may so express it) what comes from God's tongue. As the heart hears with open ears the word of God again and again, it is renewed and begins to produce a transformed tongue. The principle is this: what comes out of our mouths is more and more determined by what has come out of 'the mouth of God'. The sanctification of the tongue is a work in us that is driven by the word of God coming to us as we hear it and indwelling us as we receive it.

This was the 'secret' of the Lord Jesus' own use of his tongue. Matthew sees him as fulfilling the prophecy of the first of the Servant Songs in the second half of the prophecy of Isaiah:

> He will not quarrel or cry aloud,
>> nor will anyone hear his voice in the streets;
> a bruised reed he will not break,
>> and a smouldering wick he will not quench
>>> (Matt. 12:19-20, quoting Isa. 42:2-3).

If we ask how this was true in his life, the answer is found in the third Servant Song:

> The Lord God has given me
>> the tongue of those who are taught,
> that I may know how to sustain with a word
>> him who is weary.
> Morning by morning he awakens;
>> he awakens my ear
>> to hear as those who are taught.

> The Lord God has opened my ear,
>   and I was not rebellious;
>   I turned not backward.
> I gave my back to those who strike,
>   and my cheeks to those who pull out the beard;
> I hid not my face
>   from disgrace and spitting (Isa. 50:4-6).

The most important single aid to our ability to use our tongue for the glory of Jesus is allowing the word of God to dwell in us so richly that we cannot speak with any other accent. When we do, the result is 'teaching and admonishing one another in all wisdom, singing … And … in word or deed, do[ing] everything in the name of the Lord Jesus, giving thanks to God the Father' (Col. 3:16-17).

That, incidentally (although it is *not* an incidental matter) is why it is so important to be under a ministry of the word where the Scriptures are expounded with the grace and power of the Holy Spirit. It is by this means—yes, with private study—that the word of God begins to do its own spiritual work in us. As words that have been formed in God's mouth are digested as the bread of life by us, they begin to shape our thinking, affections, and volitions in a wonderful way.

Too many Christians fall into the trap of believing that God gives regeneration and justification, but then we are essentially left to our own efforts to do the rest. We need to see that we live by every word that comes out of God's mouth. God's word sanctifies us. The more I awake in the morning and feed myself with the Scriptures and the more I am saturated with the word under a biblical ministry, the more the word of Christ will do the sanctifying work in me and on me, and consequently the more Christ will train my tongue as his word moulds and shapes me. Yes, there needs to be rigorous activity—but it is in order to let the word of Christ dwell in us richly. It is a receptive activity!

In this, as Isaiah's song teaches us, our Saviour is our exemplar. But he is not only, nor is he first of all, an exemplar. To be that, he needed first to become our Saviour. All this is part of the grand vision of Isaiah's Servant Songs (so influential in Jesus' own reception of God's word). The Father opened the ear of his Son; the Son was not rebellious. He was willing to be 'oppressed and afflicted'. As he experienced this in his trial and condemnation, 'he opened not his mouth' (Isa. 53:7).

Why was Jesus silent? Is there more to this than meets the eye? Indeed there is! He was silent because of every word that has proceeded from your lips; because of every word that provides adequate reason for God to damn you for all eternity, because you have cursed him or his image. The Lord Jesus came into the world to bear the judgment of God against the sin of our tongues. When he stood before the high priest and the judgment seat of Pontius Pilate, he accepted a sentence of guilt. But that was my guilt. He bore in his body on the tree the sins of my lips and my tongue.

Do you wish you could control your tongue better? Do you want to follow the example of Jesus? Then you need to understand that he is Saviour first, and then he is example. You need to come, conscious of the sin of your lips, and say:

> God, be merciful to me, a sinner.
> I thank you that you came and were silent
> in order that you might bear the penalty
> of all my misuse of my tongue.

And when you know that he has taken God's judgment and wrath against your every sinful word, you cannot but say:

> O, for a thousand tongues to sing
> My great Redeemer's praise.

He is able to answer that prayer, and its companion petition:

> Be of sin the double cure,
> Cleanse me from its guilt and power.

All the guilt can be cleansed away! Christ can deliver you from the misuse of the tongue. And when you come to him conscious of that sin, you discover what a glorious Saviour he is. Delivered, albeit not yet perfected and glorified, your tongue now shows forth his praises. Taken out of the pit and from the miry clay, on your lips is now a new song of praise to your God (Psa. 40:2-3). Then people not only hear a different vocabulary, but they hear you speak with a different accent. That is what leaves the lasting impression of the power of Christ and the transformation of grace in your life.

My native land is Scotland. I have had the privileged status of being a resident alien in the United States, carrying a green card. But people often remind me, 'You have an accent.' (That said, it is one of the wonderful things about the presence and work of Christ's Spirit in preaching that, fifteen minutes into the exposition, it is possible that others cease to notice the accent and hear only *his* accent.) Being 'afflicted', therefore, with an 'accent', brief elevator rides—and the usual brief conversations that ensue there—often provide a certain mischievous pleasure. As the doors open at my floor and I step out, someone will occasionally call, 'You have an accent. Where do you come from?' As I watch the doors begin to close, I say with a smile, 'Columbia, South Carolina', and watch the puzzled faces whose expression says, 'Come on! You're not from there … are you?'

That is surely a parable of what it is possible for the people of God to become in the way we use our tongues, as by God's grace we learn to speak with a Jesus-like accent.

At the end of the day, it may not be so much what people say to you when you are in a room that is the really telling thing about your speech as a Christian. Rather it may be the questions people ask when you leave the room. 'Where does he come from?' 'Do you know where she belongs?'

Do you speak like someone who 'sounds' a little like Jesus because, broken in your consciousness of your sinful tongue, you have found pardon and renewal in Christ, and now his word dwells richly in you?

At the end of the day, that is what spiritual maturity looks like—or better, sounds like—because of the transformation of our use of the tongue.

May that be true of us more and more!

CHAPTER THIRTY-THREE

EXEGETICAL PREACHING

W HAT is exegetical preaching? From one perspective all preaching that is truly Christian preaching is exegetical in nature. Exegesis is the explanation, or exposition, of a sentence, a word, an idea. As an exercise it depends on the prior existence of materials. It may be a creative discipline; but it does not create *ex nihilo*. In this sense the preacher is always an exegete simply because he is a herald, or ambassador, of Christ.

The preacher creates the sermon he does not create the message. Rather he proclaims and explains the message he has received. His message is not original; it is given to him (2 Cor. 5:19). Consequently, whether he preaches a topical, doctrinal, or textual sermon; whether he deals with a passage, preaches through a book, or on a topic, the exegetical principle will always be present: he is explaining and expounding the message that has already been given. Therein lies his authority and his confidence in the promise of God's help and blessing. The sermon is not the preacher's word; it is God's word.

When we speak about 'exegetical' or 'expository' preaching, however, we customarily think not of preaching in general, but of a particular style of preaching.[1] In exegetical preaching the explanation of Scripture forms the dominant feature and the organizing principle of the message. *All* preaching should be based on the apostolic *kerygma* and *didache*. Exegetical preaching is governed by the goal of expounding the meaning and significance of this 'faith once-delivered' in terms of the actual way in which it has been delivered, namely the structure and content of

---

[1] Although the terms 'exegetical' and 'expository' can carry differing nuances, in this context they belong together and are used as virtual synonyms.

the biblical revelation, in which truth is revealed not in the form of a series of theological or topical *loci* (God, sin, justification, sanctification; war, money, social ethics, etc.), but through history, parable, narrative, argumentation, poetry, and so on. Exegetical preaching therefore sees as its fundamental task the explanation of the text in its context, the unfolding of its principles, and, only then, their application to the world of the hearers. As William Taylor, a notable expository preacher of a former generation, well expressed it, exposition is 'the honest answer which the preacher gives, after faithful study, to these questions: What is the mind of the Holy Spirit in this passage? and What is its bearing on related Christian truths, or on the life and conversation of the Christian himself?'[1]

Two caveats need to be entered at this juncture.

1. The first is that *exegetical preaching should not be confused with a homiletical running commentary on the text.* The function of the exegetical sermon is not limited to furnishing information. Rather, it is dominated by a message, and is intended to produce action as well as to impart instruction. Indeed, precisely because this is a function of the teaching of Scripture (grace leads to faith, indicatives lead to imperatives), it is also necessarily a dimension of exegetical preaching. The words of Jonathan Edwards about his own preaching are equally applicable to exegetical and to textual preaching:

> I should think myself in the way of my duty, to raise the affec-
> tions of my hearers as high as I possibly can. ... such preaching has
> been thought to have the greatest tendency to answer the ends of
> preaching. ... Our people do not so much need to have their heads
> stored, as to have their hearts touched; and they stand in need of
> that sort of preaching which has the greatest tendency to do this.[2]

Exegetical preaching seeks to do this precisely because it is biblical preaching and recognizes that, as such, it will speak to the whole man, not exclusively to man as a cerebral being.

---

[1] William Taylor, *The Ministry of the Word* (Grand Rapids: Baker Book House, 1975), p. 157.

[2] Jonathan Edwards, *Some Thoughts Concerning the Present Revival of Religion in New England* (1742), *Works*, I:391.

2. The second caveat is that *exegetical preaching is not merely systematic preaching in the sense of preaching a course of sermons on a book of Scripture.* Historically, many expository preachers have adopted the method of following the text of Scripture to the logical conclusion of preaching through entire books of the Bible. Here one may think of Chrysostom and Augustine, of Luther and Calvin, of Joseph Caryl and Thomas Manton, of Alexander MacLaren and D. Martyn Lloyd-Jones. It would therefore be relatively easy, particularly for a younger preacher, to assume that by preaching on the previous passage the previous week and the following passage the following week, he was expounding Scripture. But the core of expository preaching is not the connecting link between sermons; rather it is the style and content of a particular sermon. It is actually engaging in exegetically controlled exposition this week, not preaching on the following verses next week! It may be of the *bene esse* of preaching that it should be systematic as well as expository, but it is the *esse* of preaching that it should unfold the meaning and significance of the biblical text. It is this particular exercise that is the focus of our attention.

Systematic, exegetical preaching has many advantages. Indeed, such are its advantages that it ought to be the staple (if not exclusive) diet of the preacher's ministry.[1] For one thing, it teaches the congregation how to read the Bible for themselves. Most Christians tend to use in their own Bible study the style of study presented to them in the pulpit. Models of study are necessary, and exegetical preaching is the best way to teach Christians exegetical reading of Scripture.

Furthermore, we live in an age (as did Chrysostom and Calvin) when the primary need is for our people to be instructed in the teaching and application of Scripture. Exegetical preaching serves that purpose,

[1] Some great preachers like C. H. Spurgeon have, of course, expressed a strong antipathy for such systematic exposition. Note also W. G. T. Shedd's remark—which today seems overly sanguine: 'The expository sermon should be occasionally employed. There is somewhat less call for this variety than there was before the establishment of Sabbath schools and Bible classes.' *Homiletics and Pastoral Theology* (New York: Charles Scribner and Co., 1867), p. 137. Compare Pierre Charles Marcel's more recent remarks in which he lists ten reasons why systematic expository preaching is vital. *The Relevance of Preaching*, tr. R. R. McGregor (Grand Rapids: Baker Book House, 1977), pp. 74-75.

bringing the hearers under the influence both of the *content* of God's word, and the *spirit* in which God's word has come to us.

Moreover, it is chiefly by the exegetical method of preaching that the individual pastor is most likely to grow as a student of Scripture, a man of God, and a preacher. One of the rather sad features of the community of preachers is that so few of us seem to exhibit continuing growth *as preachers* (1 Tim. 4:11-16). Our congregations are little conscious that we increasingly love God's word and feed on it, or that we are bringing from it 'things old and new' with an excitement born of continued preparation for exegetical preaching.

This is not to say that the endorsement of a conviction about exegetical preaching will overnight revolutionize our pulpits. For such preaching is not the creature of a night. It is not the easiest or most natural of disciplines in which to engage. Nor should we ever forget that it is men sent from God (cf. John 1:6), more than methods devised by these men, that God employs to build his kingdom.

The elements of expository preaching

There are six primary elements in the preparation for and preaching of exegetical sermons. They may be described as selecting, understanding, crystallizing, structuralizing, concretizing, and delivering.

1. Selecting

How are we to select a text or passage of Scripture for exposition? We have already noted that many expositors adopt a systematic form of preaching. To an extent this system obviates the need for selection, at least on a week-by-week basis. Indeed that is one of its main attractions to the preacher—he spends his preparation time studying the text rather than searching for one! But, unless the preacher is committed to series that last for years, exposition still requires selection. It takes place less frequently when entire books are to be expounded. But these also must be selected—and, once selected, the commitment is one of months rather than minutes. The choice of book (text) to be expounded systematically is therefore of immense importance to the preacher and in a profound sense to the whole ethos of the congregation's life. A *series* that 'fails' may have far more disastrous consequences for the congregation than one sermon that 'fails'! A right choice is therefore a matter of singular importance.

Our first principle must be to recognize (whether we preach from a single section, or through an entire book of the Bible) that the preacher operates with two horizons: (1) the text of Scripture, and (2) the people of God and their environment in the world. He ought not normally to make his selection without consciously bringing these two horizons together. That, in the last analysis, is what all of his preaching is intended to do. His thinking must therefore begin here. The preacher's task is to communicate the whole counsel of God to his people. Over the period of his ministry the preacher must endeavour to discharge this responsibility faithfully. That is one horizon toward which he will work. The preacher must ask himself several questions: Am I covering the whole range of biblical teaching—Old and New Testament, historical and theological, poetic and prose, exhortatory and denunciatory? Am I covering the whole range of biblical doctrines—God and man, Christ and Spirit, sin and grace, heaven and hell? Am I dealing with all the applications of the gospel message—to individual, home and family, business and pleasure, man and woman, church and society, personal and civil? The expositor will be a man who engages in this kind of analysis of his own ministry, so that one element in his choice will always be that he is operating within the total framework of biblical revelation and doctrine.

Within that context the preacher will also, by necessity, be a biblical theologian.[1] He will be concerned to provide biblical depth as well as breadth. He will see his responsibility to focus on teaching that forms a central part of biblical teaching. He should not be deluded by the notion that his people need to hear the so-called 'deeper truths' of the faith. Those truths in Scripture are none other than the fundamental truths of the faith, with all their implications rightly grasped.

But alongside this objective exercise, there is an exercise in spiritual sensitivity also required in the selection of preaching material. The preacher is not a systematic theologian whose exclusive task is to expound an inwardly coherent account of the Christian faith. He is a pastor, whose major task is to feed the flock of God. The context of the

[1] I am thinking here of the comment that Calvin became a theologian in order to become a better pastor.

congregation therefore plays a major role in the selection of his material. Where are they in terms of the Christian pilgrimage? What are their situations, needs, lacks, and their pressures? Of course our preaching is not to be need-determined, but it must be *people-oriented*, as Jesus Christ's was (cf. John 16:12).

At this point we see something of the value of systematic theology, when that theology enables us to see the interconnections between Christian truths. For those connections are not always the ones preachers tend to make. To give an obvious illustration: we find ourselves called to preach to people whose chief characteristic is lack of assurance. How does this govern our selection of biblical material? The natural instinct is to reply, 'Preach a series of sermons on the nature of true assurance.' But to do this is not only pastorally a questionable response; theologically it is a confused response. Why? Because assurance is not received by knowing about assurance so much as it is by knowing about Christ! In other words, the selection of material in such a context should be governed not by the nature of the problem so much as by the shape of the gospel, what Paul calls 'the form of teaching to which you were entrusted' (Rom. 6:17 NIV). This is a principle of selection that lends itself to wide application.

One or two further general comments may be in place at this juncture. It is the present writer's conviction that under all ordinary circumstances an expository series should not be unduly prolonged. In this gifts and hearers differ very considerably. There are men who have such ability as preachers and find themselves in such circumstances that long series of expositions may be justified. But such men and circumstances are rare. It ought to be remembered in this context that the great series of sermons preached by Chrysostom, Luther, Calvin, and others generally included several sermons preached each week-day, so that the entire series was not prolonged to many years. People need breadth and variety in their spiritual diet, which is not necessarily the same thing as superficiality and novelty.

In connection with the exposition of individual passages, it is a commonplace observation that what first impresses us is most likely to make an impression on others through us. This should not, however, be taken to mean that we should preach on those texts which have made most recent impressions on us. There may be occasions when that is wise. But often younger preachers are tempted to make this the major rule of text selection. They in particular need to remember that there is a difference between our ability to hear the word clearly and our gifts and experience in preaching that same word clearly. Often the composition of a message from a text or passage that has meant a great deal to us will involve the passage of many months, even years, before we are able to use the material in such a way that we edify God's people rather than simply drag them through our own spiritual experience.

2. *Understanding*

Having made the selection of the book or passage to be expounded, we are now faced with the task of working with that text. What is our primary duty? Here we are faced with a fundamental issue that often sets apart theological education from the actual practice of ministry. For it is tempting for those involved in theological education to say, 'The first step is to reach for the Hebrew Bible, or the Greek Testament.' At the other end of the spectrum, it seems likely that some preachers enter their pulpits Sunday by Sunday not only not having consulted their original texts, but perhaps not even knowing where in the muddle of their studies their original language tools are to be found! It is tempting for them to say (and many have eager, well-instructed congregations large enough to confirm the conviction) that they are perfectly able to expound God's word to their people from the English text.

To an extent this intramural debate between scholars and practitioners often centres on the wrong issue, for all practical purposes. On the one hand, perhaps not many men gain a sufficient mastery of the original texts while at seminary to be encouraged to make regular use of them. Seminaries need to ask themselves, How is it that we train men for two or three years in the text of Scripture, yet fail to prepare them adequately? But on the other hand, it will not do for those of us who are practitioners to operate on the basis that an English text is altogether adequate for the task of exposition. We, for our part, should be asking, Should I not make use of all the tools available to me to give my very best to my people?

This focus on language skills *simpliciter*, however, is a mistaken one in the current situation. Rather our concern should be the broader one of understanding the text. Such an understanding demands some kind of appreciation of the language in which that text is written, however and wherever that appreciation is gained. Consequently, whether we are capable readers of the original text, or whether we have simply enough grasp of the original tongues to proceed slowly through concordances, lexicons, grammars, theological wordbooks, and technical linguistic commentaries, our primary task is always the same—coming to an understanding of the meaning of the text to the best of our ability. Language skills alone are of limited help for the composition of a sermon, but they are of fundamental help if it is our concern to interpret Scripture correctly. Furthermore, because of the very nature of language as a form of communication of concepts, the use of the original tongues and such aids as help us to read in them can sometimes be astonishingly illuminating. Sir Edwyn Hoskyns spoke wisely of burying oneself in a dictionary and coming up in the presence of God. One does not need to be a language expert to share that experience. But, if we share it, our hearers will undoubtedly be enriched as well.

It would be inappropriate in this context to proceed by listing a series of principles that should govern our exegesis. What should be recognized, however, is that our exegesis of Scripture must serve the ultimate goal of preaching. Our exegesis as preachers is not completed when we have analysed the text. For that reason, it should not be limited to a grammatical exercise. As important—in some ways of greater importance—is engaging in an exegesis that uncovers both what the text *said* to the first readers, and what it *meant* to them. Out of the exegesis emerge the context and circumstances in which this word from God was first spoken. It is here that the exegete is also the man of imagination. He does not 'imagine' a context *de nouveau*; but he must 'image' the context in such a way that what is being said in the text takes on a three-dimensional significance. He sees that *this* text addresses itself to *that* situation. In a word the preacher-exegete grasps the dynamics that form the context of the text, statement, or passage.

Frequently this element in exegesis makes the difference between what one might call a surface exposition and a dynamic exposition in which hearers are caused to say, 'So that is what this passage is saying; it is so clear to me now that I wonder why I never noticed it before.' This may be called 'depth exegesis', so long as we are aware that we are speaking here about the actual dynamics of the text, and not some spiritual, esoteric, allegorical sense that bears little relationship to the fundamental meaning of the passage.

Some illustrations may help to underline this point. Two of Jesus' parables will serve to illustrate—partly because the material being expounded is so familiar that one might think it impossible for anyone to say, 'So that is what the passage means; why did I not see that before?' The parables are those known customarily as the Good Samaritan and the Prodigal Son and are instances in which careful exegesis is obviously a larger discipline than merely the use of original languages.[1]

The Good Samaritan (Luke 10:25-37)

The 'punch-line' of this parable is 'You go, and do likewise' (Luke 10:37). Accurate exegesis will take this to be the determining element in the structure of our exposition. Hearers are to be urged to imitate the Good Samaritan. But on what basis?

Christ's words emerge from the question he poses at the end of the parable: 'Which of these three, do you think, proved to be a neighbour to the man who fell among the robbers?' (Luke 10:36). Notice that our Lord's question answers the original *questioner*, but *not the original question*. The original question was 'Who is my neighbour?' (verse 29). For that reason Jesus' answer is often taken to mean that whoever is in need is my neighbour. But that is not what he says. The neighbour in the story is not the man who fell among robbers, but the Samaritan. Jesus answers the question 'Who is my neighbour?' by saying: *You are the neighbour.* So long as I can answer the question 'Who is my neighbour?', I can draw limits to my responsibilities. But that is the very reverse of

---

[1] Modern scholarship has emphasized the importance of recognizing that parables have one main point. That, generally speaking, may be true; but it must be remembered that their one point is the consequence of a build-up of a variety of points essential to the parable. Cf. V. S. Poythress's review of Robert H. Stein, *An Introduction to the Parables of Jesus* (Philadelphia: Westminster Press, 1981) in the *Westminster Theological Journal*, 44 (Spring 1982), pp. 158-60.

what Jesus is saying. He is saying, there are no limits to your responsibilities, for *you* are the neighbour.

Here, then, we have an example of how careful exegesis of the text throws the dynamics of Christ's conversation and the resulting emphasis of our exposition into an entirely new light. It is not difficult to see that this presents us with a message at once more demanding and more revolutionary to our thinking than we would otherwise recognize. What at one level is an encouragement to 'neighbourliness' in the sense of seeing needs in others, is transformed into a challenge as to our own identity in relationship to the principles that govern the kingdom of God—namely to unreserved abandonment to the kingdom lifestyle.

The Prodigal Son (Luke 15:11-32)
In this parable it is abundantly clear that the 'one point per parable' principle preserves us from allegorization. But this principle also needs to be employed in such a way that not one of the nuances of Jesus' teaching is lost. Thus, the unity of the parable is not broken by the recognition that the figures—Father, Pharisee, sinner—are all equally recognizable, and that something is said here about each of them.

With that in mind, the details of the parable become highly significant. Take, as an illustration, the inability of the younger son really to believe that the father loves him and welcomes him as a son, rather than as a slave. Engraved in the prodigal's mind is his utter unworthiness to be a son any longer. By contrast, engraved in the elder brother's mind is the notion that his sonship has meant slavery (cf. Luke 15:29 vividly expressed in the NIV, 'All these years I've been *slaving* for you …'). While the younger son, even when his father falls on his neck in forgiveness, weeps, and kisses him, cannot believe that he is accepted, the older son has an altogether mistaken idea of what sonship is. There is a sense in which these two brothers share something in common. Neither of them has grasped who the father is. Ultimately this is Jesus' own condemnation of the Pharisees. They dis-graced God, the Father; they barred themselves from his kingdom, and would have barred others also.

For those of us who are not particularly gifted as illustrators, or who lack that quality of imagination present in outstanding teachers and preachers, exegesis carefully done is our salvation! For here, in the dynamic of Scripture, in the imaginativeness of revelation properly expounded, is the arresting word of God, which bears fruit as it instructs, searches, and challenges the minds of our hearers. Just as those who engage in academic teaching tell students that the answers in the exams lie in understanding the questions—if you understand the significance of the question you have the materials to answer it—so with preaching. If we understand the meaning of the passage, we have already the heart of the exposition and application.

3. Crystallizing

The third stage of preparation for exposition is what we may call 'the process of crystallizing'. Crystallization is the process by which bodies with orderly arrangements of atoms, ions, or molecules are formed or enlarged, generally from the liquid state. The metaphor is appropriate, for what is involved in expository preaching, as we have already noticed, is more than the production of sound exegetical commentary. Rather, at this stage we are moving from exegesis to the orderly arrangement of a single message. In exposition the principal concern is that of *unity*. That is a basic principle of all rhetoric, and certainly, as our Lord himself indicates by his own example, of sacred rhetoric.

The question we are now asking, therefore, is, What is the *point* of this passage? Unity of course does not imply uniformity. The fact that the fundamental message of the passage is to be underlined does not mean that this message will be monotonously expressed. The crystallizing process may produce one large and beautiful crystal, but it is that, in turn, because it is composed of other crystals. We are therefore investigating the relationship between the parts and the whole, and seeking to bring those parts (furnished by our *exegesis*) together legitimately in relationship to the whole (the *message*).

For the expositor this is a very demanding but extremely fruitful discipline. Again, an example may make the point more lucidly than a prolonged discussion of the principles involved. One of the chief themes of Ephesians 3:1-13 is that of the wisdom of God. In discussing his own ministry, Paul sees that at the heart of it lies God's purpose to make known 'through the church the manifold wisdom of God' (Eph. 3:10). But how does this theme crystallize in the context of the entire passage?

It is fascinating to recognize how Paul speaks of various manifestations of God's wisdom in this context. As we hold the level of this passage up to the light, we recognize its multifaceted beauty. For God's wisdom is seen here in three ways. First, God's plan to reveal his wisdom has been displayed *in Christ* (verse 11). But Paul also says that it is revealed *through the church* (verse 10). But notice that this little section ends with an application that at first glance is totally dislocated from the general context of wisdom. Paul encourages the Ephesians, on the basis of what he has already said ('So', verse 13), not to lose heart. How does what he has already said carry that implication? Precisely because they have learned about the 'manifold' (*polupoikilos*—multi-coloured) wisdom of God in Christ and through his people. *That same wisdom* they may expect to see displayed in the life of the apostle Paul also.

God's wisdom is therefore to be seen in three places: (1) in Christ, (2) in the church, and (3) in the sufferings of God's servants ('what I am suffering for you, which is your glory' [Eph. 3:13]). Interestingly, in another (prison) epistle, Paul indicates this principle in a very concrete fashion. To the Philippians he writes: 'I want you to know, brothers, that what has happened to me has really served to advance the gospel, so that it has become known … that my imprisonment is for Christ. And most of the brothers, having become confident in the Lord by my imprisonment, are much more bold to speak the word without fear' (Phil. 1:12-14). Multi-coloured wisdom indeed!

What is the basic principle involved in this kind of movement from the general teaching of the passage to the recognition of a specific theme? It is the recognition of the principle of unity. Only practice enables us to be properly sensitive to the extent and limits of this principle. Yet it is not an esoteric principle. It is the principle of our ordinary speech. We say *something*. So too do portions of Scripture. We are therefore able to isolate what that 'something' is, and recognize how it is built together as a unified 'something'. That is of advantage to us not only in the stage of crystallizing our message, but also in the stage that immediately follows.

4. Structuralizing

Thus far the pattern of our activity has been that of unpacking the text to be expounded and arranging it in its component parts. It is just at this point that an expository message requires different disciplines from those employed in a 'running-commentary homily'. For in expository preaching the material of the text is not only examined, it is also restructured in order to become a sermon. Whereas before the text was dismantled in order to unveil the heart of the matter, it is now brought together again on the basis of a new set of principles, the principles of sound rhetoric and communication governed by the identity of our hearers. To put the same point in different words, in preaching we translate the material we have gathered into a different medium from that in which it came to us. It was the word of God *written*; it becomes the word of God *preached*. We are no longer limited to the horizons of original exegesis— the horizon of the original speaker and that of the original hearer. Rather we are concentrating our attention on a third horizon, the contemporary hearer, in order to translate and interpret what was originally given to a different world altogether, and yet to do so without diminution or exaggeration of the message being preached.

How is this accomplished? The best way to accomplish it is along the lines already suggested. In the process of crystallizing the message we saw that the heart of the exposition was a composite centre. We have already examined those various elements. Whereas earlier we brought them together to discover the essential message, we must now separate them once again in order to designate in our exposition the divisions of thought through which the core of the message is to be grasped. The analysis of how these parts are connected to the whole provides us with the division of thought involved. Again perhaps an illustration serves better than a series of vague principles.

Let us suppose we have chosen to expound Psalm 121. In our basic preparation we will have noticed a number of things. It bears the title 'Song of Ascents'. That title is shared by all the Psalms from 120 to 134; yet no other psalm bears this title. Our investigations set the actual use of this psalm probably in the pilgrim festivals of the Old Testament church. Although we may not know in precisely what context it was written, we do know that it served as instruction for the pilgrim. This in turn sheds light on the context of the psalm's use. Here we have what seems to be a younger, inexperienced pilgrim, facing his pilgrimage with some sense of apprehension, and receiving counsel either from the collective wisdom of others, or perhaps from the individual whose counsel is recorded in the rest of the psalm. The younger pilgrim is anxious about the dangers and hazards of the pilgrimage (verse 1): attacks from bandits, the possibility of sunstroke, the fear of lunacy ('the moon by night'). He wants to know where he can apply for help and strength. The answering voice points to the character and operation of God as the source of security and peace.

Now, our basic spadework, along with the more detailed questions of exegesis and etymology, has been intended to take us to the meaning of the text. But as in a carpenter's workshop there are pieces of materials lying around as the result of the cutting process, which he can use in the more creative process of his carpentry, so with exposition. Now our aim is not to put the material back the way we found it, but to create out of it something shaped for our own particular hearers. Out of these materials we may build the structure of the message.

There are several ways this can be done in Psalm 121. In any event, the psalm has a twofold division, in terms of the two speakers. We may choose a twofold division therefore for our message:

(1) The Assertion of Untried Faith ('My help comes from the LORD …') and

(2) The Assurance of Well-Tried Experience ('He will not … the LORD is your …').

Again, focusing on the material from a different angle, we might restructure the psalm in terms of

(1) The Fears of a New Pilgrim (What about my feet slipping, the noon-day sun blazing, the robbers, the moon, etc.?) and

(2) The Encouragements of an Experienced Pilgrim ('God is *a*, *b*, *c*'; 'God does *x*, *y*, *z*').

Similarly we might more directly speak of the fears of the disciple and the sufficiency of God, or the weakness of the disciple and the strength of the Lord. But in any of these divisions the principle is the same: we have restructured the psalm in a fashion specifically geared to communicate its message clearly and simply in stages to our hearers.

How we deal with those stages is often a matter of personal choice. We may lay out divisions very clearly; we may move along from one to another with less obvious division; we may build up a logical argument out of the materials. As we grow as preachers so we ought also to grow in variety of approaches.[1] But the underlying principle will be that of restructuring for the purposes of communication.

5. Concretizing

The next stage of preparation is one of the most important and difficult for expository ministry; but it pays rich rewards. We have been largely engaged in the process of analysis and synthesis thus far. Now we have reached the vital stage where we must bring together the biblical horizon with the horizon of the early twenty-first century. We have to ask, What does *this* (e.g. Psa. 121) have to say to these (Mr X, Miss Y in my congregation)? For this stage we may employ the metaphor of setting in concrete. It is the final stage in relating biblical exegesis to the hearer. It involves making concrete in our world what we have 'melted down' from the world of Scripture and then crystallized by careful analysis.

What is the process by which this is done? We begin with the biblical text and explore its message. From its message we have brought out a number of basic principles. It is these basic principles that we must now take and translate into our own world. Yet we cannot abandon biblical controls at this point. We must also ask of the passage, *What was the biblical writer doing with these principles?* We cannot simply unravel the principles and then employ them in any fashion that appeals to us. Such exposition would have abandoned proper biblical controls. Instead we must endeavour to use these basic principles in a fashion that remains faithful to the actual use of the original writer. Can we do for our context what he did for his context?

While this is a rigorous procedure, it is not merely an academic one. For the question, 'What was the author doing with these principles in his time?' will itself be highly suggestive for the exposition and application we may also make in our own time. The danger at this point is to leave the text and turn to applications *that do not arise directly out of the exposition*. In Pauline terms the 'therefore', which links exposition to

---

[1] In this connection, a study of Jesus' various preaching 'styles' is illuminating.

application, is absent; the application does not arise *directly* out of the exposition. But if we follow this more rigorous effort to pursue application along the lines of the application inherent in the passage, the effect will increasingly be that our application is not merely an appendage or an interesting personal observation, but actually arises out of the word of God itself. The consequence will be that the hearer will the more clearly sense the weight, thrust, and light of *God's* word.

Although perhaps Psalm 121 is of too general a nature to illustrate this principle most pointedly, 'concretizing' may nevertheless be demonstrated from such a passage. We noticed that the psalm contains a tacit acknowledgment of the weaknesses and fears of the young pilgrim-believer. Those are clothed in the context and lifestyle of a young disciple in the ancient Near East. But what do his fears amount to? What are the fundamental fears which, in his case, have taken *Near Eastern* flesh and blood? Judging by the response of the second voice in the psalm, the younger pilgrim is afraid

(1) that God may desert him;

(2) of various dangers on the way (sun, moon, robbers)—fear of circumstances, fear of the night; and

(3) that he may not be able to make it home from his journey—he may lack the perseverance to overcome the obstacles.

It does not take much imagination to see that the horizons of Psalm 121 and those of twenty-first-century converts are not so far apart. Similarly, the counsel needed will point in the same direction: God is the covenant Father ('LORD') of his people; God is the one who watches and keeps. God is the one who rules over circumstances; God is the one who governs both our beginning and our ending. The answer to the pilgrim's anxiety then, as now, is to be found in the revelation of, and trust in, the character of God. Indeed, in this short psalm we may even pick up leads that will help our less imaginative spirit to preach in the imaginative power of the Spirit in Scripture—God as the guardian of the slipping foot, the watching parent, the shade of protection, the bodyguard of his people.[1]

---

[1] In preaching on a psalm we must also consider (a) How Jesus would have understood (and sung) it, and (b) how it is part of the whole-Bible revelation of Christ.

This is not to say that the use of other biblical material, or even extra-biblical material, for illustration is wrong. Rather it underlines the fact that when we stick to the text with the most rigorous expository intention, we will find more than enough material for exposition, illustration, and application. The more rigorous we are initially with ourselves at this point, the more likely we are to be encouraged with a sense of the absolute adequacy of Holy Scripture for the work of expository preaching. It is this, perhaps supremely, which leads to a style of expository preaching of which it can be said, as John 'Rabbi' Duncan did of Jonathan Edwards's ministry, that *his doctrine is all application* and *his application is all doctrine.*

6. Delivering
When Demosthenes was asked what he regarded as the chief element in rhetoric, he reputedly responded, 'First, delivery; second, delivery; third, delivery.' At first sight it might seem that the connection between exposition and delivery is fairly tenuous. After all, expository preaching is a form of communication rather than a definition of the style of delivery. But precisely because it is biblical exposition, the content of the preaching has an influence on the manner in which we deliver it.

Paul twice described his preaching as *phanerōsis*; that is, there was an *unveiling* or *exposing* of the message in its inherent reality and power. In Colossians 4:4 he appealed for help in prayer that he might thus preach. In 2 Corinthians 4:2, he contrasted deceitful preaching with 'the open statement [*phanerōsis*, 'exposition'] of the truth'. Although he did not preach *himself,* but *Christ* (2 Cor. 4:5), by such exposition, he did commend himself to every man's conscience in the sight of God (2 Cor. 4:2). He was thinking about his motives in the delivery of God's word. But notice that those motives were intertwined with the manner of delivery. It is an open manifestation and exposition of the truth. By this he commended himself as one whose ministry was controlled not only by a particular preaching style, but by the message itself. His exposition of it dominated his presentation of it. The content of the gospel dominates the style and the spirit in which the gospel is preached. To this extent, the medium is part of the message 'heard' by others.

See the comments in the following chapter on 'Preaching Christ from the Old Testament'.

This, supremely, should be the hallmark of expository preaching. It should express a spirit that has been led captive to the truth expounded. For lack of this, congregations may be sent away from the regular diets of worship still hungry, even though the word is, indeed, formally expounded. For God has so ordained it that his people should be fed and nourished by the exposition of his truth through the lips, lives, and personalities of his human servants. It is precisely in this way that he ministers to whole men and women, and makes broken men and women whole. It is for lack of this—a spirit that is dominated by the teaching expounded and is in harmony with it—that the needs of men and women are not met.

We can never rest content with exposition that is formally 'correct'. Unless exposition breathes the Spirit of the truth expounded, it is incorrect and itself needs healing and correction. It may be that this, among other reasons, is a chief cause of the preaching–counselling tension so current in North American churches today. In many instances spiritual health could be preserved at a much earlier stage were preaching directed to whole men from whole men whose disposition and whose message were intertwined.

CHAPTER THIRTY-FOUR

PREACHING CHRIST FROM
THE OLD TESTAMENT SCRIPTURES

THE discipline of biblical theology has only slowly but surely found a place in modern evangelical preaching.[1] As a result, it has now become a commonplace in the teaching of homiletics to stress that we must preach Christ *in all the Scriptures* in a manner that takes account of the flow of redemptive history. In particular we must learn to preach Christ from the Old Testament without falling into the old traps of an artificial exegesis.

But how do we legitimately preach the text of the Old Testament as those who stand on this side of Pentecost? What difference does it make to expound Genesis or Psalms as believers in Jesus Christ? Or, to put it in a more graphic way, how can we reconstruct the principles of Jesus' conversations in Luke 24:25-27, 45, and learn to follow his example of showing how all the Scriptures point to him so that hearts are 'strangely warmed' and begin to burn? In particular, how may we do this without lapsing into what we (sometimes a little too cavalierly) deem to be either patristic allegorizing or post-Reformation spiritualizing? If only we had heard how Jesus did this on the Emmaus Road, in the upper room during the forty days between his resurrection and his ascension, we might grasp the principles by which it is done, so that we too could

---

[1] This is true despite the fact that the great Princeton scholar Geerhardus Vos was already appointed to teach biblical theology (in this sense of the discipline) in the last decade of the nineteenth century and gave his inaugural lecture on that subject in 1894; see R. B. Gaffin, Jr (ed.), *Redemptive History and Biblical Interpretation: The Shorter Writings of Geerhardus Vos* (Phillipsburg, NJ: Presbyterian and Reformed, 1980), pp. x, 3-24.

genuinely preach the text of the Old Testament as Christian preachers and not as rabbis!

Yet we must also preach the Scriptures without denuding them of the genuine historical events they record and the reality of the personal experiences they describe or to which they were originally addressed. How, then, do we preach Christ and him crucified without leapfrogging over these historical realities as though the Old Testament scriptures had no real significance for their own historical context?

In discussing the pre-Christ revelation of God as Trinity, B. B. Warfield describes the Old Testament as a richly furnished but dimly lit room. Only when the light is turned on do the contents become clear. That light has been switched on in Christ and in the New Testament's testimony to him. Now the triune personal being of God becomes clear.[1] To read the Old Testament with the light switched off would be to deny the historical reality of our own context. On the other hand, we would be denying the historical reality of the text and its context if we were to read and preach it as though that same light had already been switched on within its own pages. Thus our task as Christian preachers must be to take account of both. Fulfilling that task drives us back into the basic hermeneutical question for the Christian exegete: How do we relate the Old Testament to the New Testament? The longer we labour in ministry, the more we ask that question. The more we know about the answer to it, the more we realize there is so much more left to explore. It is a lifelong pursuit. Here we can make only a few comments and suggest some principles that are generally applicable and may be specifically helpful to the preacher.

Preaching Christ must become instinctive, not formulaic

Young preachers are often told, 'You must preach *Christ* from the Old Testament.' But having just finished preaching on, for example, Psalm 121, and realizing that we have said little or nothing about Jesus (perhaps not explicitly mentioned his name!), we may be in great agitation, and search desperately for a magic formula that will help us to preach Christ from the Old Testament.

[1] B. B. Warfield, 'The Biblical Doctrine of the Trinity', *Biblical Doctrines, Works*, II:141-42.

It would be possible, of course, to provide a kind of formula, a kind of homiletical version of Thomas's five ways, such as: Point to Christ by showing: (1) the passage is a direct prophecy of him; or (2) the passage shows why Jesus is needed; or (3) the passage speaks about something that reminds us of Jesus; or (4) the passage speaks about something that could not be accomplished without Jesus; or (5) the passage shows us an individual/group unlike Jesus.

The point here is not to comment on whether or not these five ways are helpful so much as the inherent danger in the approach. It is likely to produce preaching that is wooden and insensitive to the rich contours of biblical theology. Its artificiality would lie in our going through the motions of exegeting and expounding the Old Testament and then, remembering the formula, tidying our notes in order to align them with it. The net result over an extended period of time might be akin to that produced by sermons for children: the intelligent child soon recognizes that the answer to the speaker's questions will always be one of the following: God; Jesus; Sin; the Bible; Be Good!

Of course we need to work with general principles as we develop as preachers; but it is a far greater desideratum that we develop an instinctive mindset and, corresponding to that, such a passion for Jesus Christ himself that we will find our way to him in a natural and realistic manner rather than a merely formulaic one.

This is a much bigger issue than how we preach Christ from the Old Testament, for at least two reasons.

First, because (if my own assessment is correct) many sermons from the *Gospels*—where the focus is explicitly on the person of Jesus—are far from Christ-centred, never mind sermons from the Old Testament.

How is this possible? The preacher has looked into the text principally to find himself and his congregation, not to find Christ. The sermon is consequently about 'people in the Gospels' rather than about Jesus Christ who is the gospel. The real question the preacher has been interested in asking and answering is not 'How do we find *Christ* in this Gospel?' but 'Where am *I* in this story? What have *I* got to do?' Even though an entire series of such sermons on a Gospel is preached (as in the *lectio continua* method), we will not necessarily have communicated the basic life of Jesus. Instead we have been given an exploration of the human condition.

So there is an *a priori* approach here that raises a deeper question than 'Is there a formula that helps us to preach Christ from the Old Testament?' The more fundamental issues are as follows: What am I really looking for when I am preaching on any part of the Bible? Am I really looking to tell people what they are like and what they must do—that is, am I really stressing the subjective and the imperative—or am I talking about Jesus Christ himself and the gospel? Do I stress the objective and the indicative of the gospel in the light of which the subjective and imperative are to be considered? After all, it is not the subjective (my condition) or the imperative (Respond!) that saves or transforms people's lives, but the objective and the indicative of God's grace received subjectively in the light of the imperatives of the gospel.

In evangelicalism at large there has been a Schleiermacher-like retreat into the subjective. Luther's *bon mot* that the gospel is 'entirely outside of us' has become an axiom strange to our ears. It badly needs to be recovered.

A *second* observation worth noting in this connection is that many (perhaps most) outstanding preachers of the Bible (and of Christ in all Scripture) are so intuitively. Ask them what their formula is and you will draw a blank expression. The principles they use have been developed unconsciously, through a combination of native ability, gift, and experience as listeners and preachers. Some might struggle to give a series of lectures on how they go about preaching. Why? Because what they have developed is an *instinct*; preaching biblically has become their native language. They are able to use the grammar of biblical theology without reflecting on what part of speech they are using. That is why the best preachers are not necessarily the best instructors in homiletics, although they are, surely, the greatest inspirers of true preaching.

Most of us probably develop the instinct for biblical-theological and redemptive-historical preaching by the osmosis involved in listening to those who do it well. It is always wise to listen to such preachers and their preaching as though we had two minds—one through which the preaching of the word nourishes us, the other through which, simultaneously or on later reflection, asks: 'Why did this exposition nourish me in that way? What dynamics and principles were operative?' Seeing how the hidden principles work out in practice is the best way to make those principles our own, so that they become the grammar of our preaching.

Christ is the prism where all light converges

Given that we are not to become 'method' preachers applying a pro-grammatic formula for biblical preaching, there are nevertheless very important principles that help us to develop Christ-centred expository skills. As we work with them, and as they percolate through our thinking and our approach to the Bible, they will help us develop the instinct to point people to Christ from the Old Testament Scriptures.

The most general principle is one for which we might coin the expression *fillfulment*: Christ fulfils or '*fills full*' the Old Testament. He came not to abolish the Law or the Prophets but to fulfil them (Matt. 5:17). As Christians standing within the light of New Testament revelation and looking back on the Old Testament, Christ himself acts as a hermeneutical prism. Looking back through him, we see the white light of the unity of the truth of Jesus Christ broken down into its constituent colours in the Old Testament (see Heb. 1:1-2). Then, looking forwards, we see how the multicoloured strands of Old Testament revelation converge in him. When we appreciate this we begin to see how the constituent colours unite in Christ and are related both to each other and to him. In this way we see how the Old Testament points forward to him. We see how sometimes one 'colour', sometimes another, or perhaps a combination of them, points forward to Jesus Christ, is related to Jesus Christ, and is fulfilled by Jesus Christ.

Principles for preaching Christ from the Old Testament

We want to develop an instinct to preach Christ. This is the general principle, but it can be broken down into at least four subordinate principles.

Principle 1. The relationship between promise and fulfilment
Genesis 3:15 is in a sense the most basic text in the whole Bible: God puts
enmity between the seed of the serpent and the seed of the woman; the
seed of the woman will bruise the head of the serpent, and the serpent
will crush the heel of the woman's seed. In view here is the ultimate cosmic conflict between our Lord Jesus Christ and Satan and the powers of
darkness. The ongoing conflict of the generations moves towards a final
conflict of the Serpent itself against the Seed.

Of course, Satan is not mentioned by name in Genesis 3—a point
of some hermeneutical interest in itself—but when Paul writes that 'the
God of peace will soon crush Satan under your feet' (Rom. 16:20), and
John sees in Revelation 12:9 that the serpent has grown into a dragon,
it is clear that the New Testament writers thought of Genesis 3:15 as a
reference to the coming Messiah, and to his conflict with Satan. The
war about which the book of Revelation speaks then merely climaxes an
antithesis and antagonism that has run through the whole of Scripture.
It is a Library of Military History, with Genesis 3:15 and Revelation
12:9–20:10 as the opening and closing volumes. It follows that the whole
of the Old Testament scriptures trace the outworking of this promise
of God until it is consummated in Jesus Christ, and finally publicized
throughout the universe in his triumphant return. Jesus' programmatic statement, 'I will build my church, and the gates of hell shall not
prevail against it' (Matt. 16:18) speaks of this cosmic-conflict context,
represents its high point and promises victory in it. Everything between
Genesis 3:15 and Matthew 16:18 can, in one way or another, be tied to the
fulfilment of that promise. Every twist and turn in redemptive history
following Matthew 16:18 expresses that conflict, flows onward to its
denouement, and to that extent can be pinpointed on the historical atlas
of redemptive revelation.

This is the story of the building of the kingdom of God in all its various
stages, over against the kingdom of this world. The promise that the
kingdom/reign of God/heaven will come/is near/has arrived is therefore
a structural key to redemptive history. From Genesis 3:15 to the end, the
Bible is the story of the Warrior King coming to the aid of his people in
order to deliver them from the dominion of darkness and to establish

his reign among, in, and through them. This is what gives weight to the words of John the Baptist that 'the kingdom of heaven is at hand' (Matt. 3:2). Breaking the prophetic silence of the centuries, his message was of God's impending eschatological war-triumph. Judgment-wrath represented by the judgment axe was, for John, the inevitable implication on the dark side; forgiveness and the reign and kingdom-blessing of God was the good news for all who repented.

This kingdom-conflict-conquest-victory theme can be traced in the various narrative perspectives and dimensions of Old Testament revelation. The central point is to see the Old Testament as intimately (although of course not exclusively) connected to this fundamental idea that there is a radical antithesis driving through the whole of redemptive history, between the building of the kingdom of God by his king, and the efforts of the powers of darkness to destroy that kingdom. Recognize this and much of Old Testament Scripture can readily be understood in terms of its position in the central nervous system of divine revelation. It should be possible to move from all of these different points to this backbone promise that runs through the whole of the historical narrative to Jesus Christ.

This is an essential hermeneutical tool with which to relate historical developments in the Old Testament back to the promise of God and forward to the coming of Christ. At the same time we are able to treat these incidents (and the people involved in them) as real in their own right. For one of the dangers inherent in biblical-theological preaching is to minimize historical actuality in our anxiety to preach Christocentrically. The result can be as damaging to the integrity of our handling of the text as was patristic allegorizing. Sensitivity to the war in the heavenly realms being played out in history enables us to expound the concrete-historical and individual experiences of God's people, yet simultaneously to interpret and place them within the big picture, the meta-narrative of the whole Bible. The historical is thus taken seriously for its own sake, while at the same time it is preached as part of the story of the all-conquering Christ.

This—it needs to be underlined—is not the only principle to be employed. But it does not require great imagination to see how events in Old Testament history illustrate it: the narrative of Adam and Eve against the serpent, the story of Cain and Abel, of the city of God and the tower of Babel, Israel and Egypt, David and Goliath. The book of Job is simply a dramatic microcosm of this. The conflicts and the miracles of Elijah and Elisha need to be read within this perspective. A submerged axehead or a poisoned stew are trivial problems, the miraculous reduced to a Harry Potter piece of magic, unless we recognize that these events take place in the context of a deadly conflict with eternal significance for the kingdom of God. Daniel's life story and his apocalyptic visions are to be read through the same lenses. Indeed, the opening words of the book of Daniel indicate that we are entering a conflict narrative. There is war between two kingdoms. Here we have both the onslaught of the powers of darkness and this world ('Nebuchadnezzar king of Babylon came to Jerusalem and besieged it' [Dan. 1:1]) and the righteous purposes of God through which his kingdom will continue and prevail ('the Lord gave Jehoiakim king of Judah into his hand ...' [Dan. 1:2]). Under fierce attack it requires extraordinary miracles to preserve the kingdom (now a remnant of four, exposed to destroying fire and the mouths of lions, Daniel 3; 6). In the midst of this the kingdom (and king!) of this world is seen to be temporary, and it and we are given intimation that it is the rock cut without human hands that will grow and fill the whole earth. Only those who see history this way (Daniel and his three friends) can sing the Lord's song in a foreign land, in enemy-occupied territory (Psa. 137).

In a similar way the opposition to the rebuilding of Jerusalem in the days of Ezra and Nehemiah is part of the unfolding of Genesis 3:15. These books provide conflict narratives in the confined space of God's chosen city, illustrating that the exhortations of Ephesians 6:10-20 are as relevant in fifth-century-BC Jerusalem as in first-century-AD Ephesus.

We stand on the other side of the empty tomb; what was 'not yet' for Ezra and Nehemiah is 'already' for us. But there is also a 'not yet' for us; the conflict in the mopping-up operations of war is as bloody and potentially fatal as in the decisive battle. We too, in the light of what Christ has accomplished, live in the 'not yet-ness' of the completion of the final Jerusalem. This world is as full of the Tobiahs, Sanballats and

Geshems of Nehemiah's day as it is of the Mr Talkatives and the Giant Despairs and Vanity Fairs of John Bunyan's *Pilgrim's Progress*.

Understanding the principle of promise and fulfilment in terms of an ongoing kingdom-against-kingdom cosmic-conflict helps us to apply the message of the Old Testament as Christian preachers today.

Principle 2. The relationship between type and antitype

As the principle of promise and fulfilment (in Christ) develops, we see how the rest of redemptive history functions as a kind of footnote to Genesis 3:15.

However, we also discover that the promise itself is developed both progressively and cumulatively; its implications become clearer as redemptive history unfolds. At particular stages in history God gives hints of what is to come (as a great artist's sketches point towards the final work). So embedded into redemptive history are illustrations of the pattern of working which God will employ in his masterwork—types that will be fulfilled in the work of Christ the antitype. Paul views the relation between Adam and Christ as the supreme illustration of this patterning; Adam, viewed as a real historical figure, is the *tupos* of the Coming One (Rom. 5:14), albeit the analogy is both positive and negative (Rom. 5:12-21).

The Mosaic ceremonial and sacrificial system functions similarly, a prominent theme in the theology of the author of Hebrews. There is a real priesthood, real sacrifice, and real blood. But these, while real, also signify a greater reality that accomplishes what they can only portray. Hebrews suggests that a genuine Old Testament believer, with the stench of the sacrificial blood clogging his nostrils, could deduce from the fact that the priests ministered in this way day after day that these could not be the sacrifices that bring forgiveness. He must look beyond this (and was able to), to that of which these sacrifices were a type—namely to God's covenant promises yet to be fulfilled, and therefore (as Hebrews makes so clear), to Jesus Christ himself (see Heb. 10:1-18).

But this principle of type and antitype operates in another, less technical sense, in what we could call the divine patterning of redemptive history. When we put 'the Christ event' under the microscope we see that there are basic patterns expressed which are first seen in the Old Testament. In the light of that discovery, when we re-read the Old Testament wearing the lenses of the New, we see these Christ-patterns more opaquely. The divine footprints are already visible.

An interesting illustration of this is the use of Hosea 11:1 in Matthew 2:15: 'Out of Egypt I called my son.' These words, Matthew says, are fulfilled in Christ. But is this not either an esoteric or naive approach to reading the Bible? Hosea is talking about the historic event of the people of God coming out of Egypt in the exodus, not about Jesus going to, and returning from, Egypt in his infancy. So what is going on in Matthew's mind? Is he saying Hosea 11:1 is fulfilled in Jesus just as Isaiah 53 is? Yes; but not in the same sense.

Rather Matthew, writing in the light of the incarnation, death, and resurrection of Jesus Christ, and under the guidance of the Holy Spirit, recognizes that the divine pattern in the exodus (delivered from Egypt, led through the wilderness, given the covenant bond and kingdom code) constitutes a *pattern* to be used in the experience of the true Israelite, Jesus Christ. In doing this Matthew provides us with a key to reading and expounding the entire exodus narrative in a Christocentric way, and also to seeing his own narrative against a background that enriches our understanding of Jesus' identity and ministry.

Another example of this kind of pattern-repetition in redemptive history is that of Elisha healing the son of the Shunammite woman (2 Kings 4:8-37). The miracles worked through Elisha demonstrate God's intimate care for ordinary people—the humble poor, the widow, and the barren woman. The healing of the Shunammite's son echoes later in the town of Nain, where Jesus too healed a widow's son (Luke 7:11-17). Luke surely means his readers to empathize with the mindset of the people in Nain who knew well that it was in their little community that the miracle had been accomplished through Elisha (who followed Elijah, the one whose return was promised, Mal. 4:5, and fulfilled in John the Baptist, Matt. 11:14). Nain was near the site of Old Testament Shunem. Even the reaction of the people of Nain to Jesus echoes with allusions to this distant event: 'A great prophet has arisen among us! God has visited his people!' It is as if they are saying, 'Something like this happened here before; and ever since Elisha, we have been looking forward to something even better still to come—*the* prophet himself. Could this be he?' (see Deut. 18:15).

So we are meant to see pattern-repetition, which comes to its fullness in the person of Jesus Christ, the great prophet who heals not merely through delegated authority from God, but on his own authority, without rituals or prayers, but with a simple word of power. Here is the great God and Saviour of Israel in the flesh, whose person is both the origin and consummation of all the patterns and echoes which have prophesied this grace to his people all down the long ages of their history. Yes, God *has* visited his people, at last, in the person of his Son. But clearly this sheds light backwards on the function of Elisha. Now we see the significance of his healing within both the micro-reality of his personal context, and also within the macro-reality of his significance in the patterns of redemptive history. There is a path from Elisha to Jesus!

As we work intimately with the two Testaments, we will increasingly recognize the echoes of the Old Testament. And as we become sensitive to these patterns and allusions, lines from the Old Testament to Christ will become clearer to us and easier to draw.[1]

Principle 3. The relationship between the covenant and Christ
In the New Testament Jesus himself embodies all that the covenant signified in the Old Testament. His is the blood of the new covenant (Luke 22:20). He fulfils all the covenant promises of God. 'For all the promises of God find their Yes in him' (2 Cor. 1:20).

The covenant promises of God form the scaffolding that God was putting in place as he directed redemptive history towards the coming of Jesus Christ. The scaffolding in the Old Testament is therefore built around the person and work of our Lord Jesus Christ and shaped by him. We can see this in two ways.

First, there is the principle that in the covenant relationship the imperatives of God (his laws and commands) are always rooted in the indicatives of his grace. That is how the covenant works: 'I will be your God; you will be my people.' This is scaffolding shaped around Christ

---

[1] A basic manual in this context is the 'Index of Allusions and Verbal Parallels' printed in the corrected 3rd edition of *The Greek New Testament* (United Bible Societies, 1983), ed. K. Aland *et. al.*, pp. 901-11.

and the gospel. For this is how the gospel works: 'I will die for you; therefore trust in and obey me.' The dynamic of the Old Testament covenant was shaped with a view to the coming of Jesus Christ.

We can go further to say this: that which was promised by God in the covenant at Sinai, and demanded by God in terms of its imperatives, did not have a sufficiently strong foundation to effect what it commanded. Geographical relocation is not an adequate support to provide the dynamic for Decalogue-style moral holiness (cf. Rom. 8:3-4). A geographical resettlement may motivate, but it cannot cancel the guilt of sin or empower morally. Thus the Sinai covenant—in its weakness— was always prophetic of a greater and fuller deliverance through God's redeeming grace. '*I* am the LORD your God, who brought you out of the land of *Egypt* ... You shall have no other gods before me' (Exod. 20:2-3, emphasis added) was always a statement that looked forwards as well as backwards. Written into the way in which the old covenant works is an implied expectation, even necessity, that the indicatives of God's grace will find a better consummation and the imperatives a better foundation—in Jesus Christ (see Heb. 3:1–4:13).

Second, the shape of Christ's work is expressed in the covenant principle of blessing and cursing.

Today our appreciation of much of the Bible's language has become very threadbare. There is a tendency to think that the words 'blessing' and 'cursing' function in a relatively trivial manner, equivalent to a kind of divine 'boo-hurrah' approach to morality. When someone sneezes, we say 'Bless you!' Few people set this within the historical context of the pre-modern world when sneezing was a symptom of the plague. It was therefore seen potentially as a sign of the displeasure of God. One prayed that the person sneezing would receive the blessing of God and *therefore not perish*. That is much nearer the Bible's understanding of blessing and cursing than our usage is.

Blessing is not 'Have a nice day!' nor is cursing 'You are a bit of a pain in the neck.' Rather, here is God's covenant; when we respond to it in faith, he showers upon us the blessing he promised when he made it with us. And when we respond in unbelief, we are exposed to curses (cf. Deut. 27–30). The gospel is that Christ took the curse of the covenant in order that the blessings of the covenant (promised to Abraham) might come to us (Gal. 3:13). Paul's thinking here is both redemptive-historical and biblical-theological. He recognizes that all of this covenantal outworking of blessing and cursing in the Old Testament is inextricably tied to the fulfilment of God's covenant purpose and promise in Jesus Christ (2 Cor. 1:20).

This principle of Christ as the heart of the covenants of God, with respect to their blessing and cursing, helps us expound and apply the Old Testament as a covenant-focused message in the light of the fulfilment of both blessing and cursing in Christ. The consequences bound up in the covenant blessing and cursing point us forwards inexorably, if typologically, to the eternal consequences of acceptance or rejection of the gospel. The contents of biblical history and wisdom literature, prophecy and the psalms all reveal this covenant dynamic. Insofar as this is true, we are able to relate them to the ultimate fulfilment of that dynamic in Christ and the gospel.

Principle 4. Proleptic participation and subsequent realization
Despite the continuing influence within evangelicalism of various brands of dispensationalism, it lies on the surface of the apostolic writings that the majority of illustrations of salvation in the new covenant era are actually drawn from the old! Of course the apostles recognize the substantial discontinuity between old and new. Pentecost is indeed a quantum leap forward. But that notwithstanding, when Paul wants to illustrate how the gospel works, he goes back to the Old Testament figures of Abraham and David and says, '*This* is how the gospel works.' A seismic shift took place after Pentecost so that the least in the kingdom is greater than the greatest of the prophets (John the Baptist [Matt. 11:11]). Men and women of faith do not come to perfection apart from new covenant believers who experience better things (Heb. 11:40). Nevertheless Abel, Enoch, Noah, Abraham, Isaac, Jacob, Joseph, Moses, Rahab, Gideon, Barak, Samson, Jephthah, David, Samuel, and the prophets are examples of faith (Heb. 11). We receive salvation 'better', but not a better salvation. If you want to know what the Christian life looks like, then there is much to be learned from the Old Testament! What

right-thinking Christian has not aspired to experience the whole-souled faith and worship of the Psalms?

But how could Old Testament believers experience grace and the fruit of the Spirit? They experienced *proleptic participation* in what would be consummated in Jesus Christ, and then subsequently realized in its fullness in post-Pentecost Christian believers.

Orthodox evangelical Christians employ the principle of proleptic participation with respect to justification. Were Old Testament saints justified by grace, and if so, how? Yes, of course—by faith in the promise of the Saviour. We who are as far removed in time as Abraham was from Christ are justified because we believe in the once-promised Christ now come. But through the promise of God, Abraham experienced in proleptic fashion what we now experience in the light of the actuality of the incarnation.

But exactly the same principle operates in the area of sanctification—both *definitive* (the once-for-all separation from the dominion of sin which takes place in regeneration) and *progressive* (the ongoing overcoming of the presence and influence of sin which takes place throughout the Christian life). For justification and sanctification, while distinguishable, are not separable in either old or new covenant realities. Saints in the Old Testament were justified in the light of what Christ would do; they were sanctified in the same way: their lives were shaped and formed in the light of what Christ would do. An example of that is seen in Hebrews 10:39: 'But *we* are not of those who shrink back and are destroyed, but of those who have faith and preserve their souls.' But from what source does the author illustrate this principle of the grace of perseverance? From the Old Testament! Old Testament saints were commended for their faith, yet none of them had received what had been promised. God had planned something better for us and only together with us would they be made perfect. What they experienced then was a proleptic, anticipatory form of the reality we better experience in its fullness, namely the working out of union and communion with Jesus Christ.

It is the perspective of the New Testament that from the moment an individual becomes a believer, his or her life is shaped providentially by God and pressed into a mould which takes its form from the dying and rising of Jesus, and is shaped by his crucifixion and resurrection, his death bringing new life. In sanctification God transforms us into the likeness of his Son, so that reminiscences of Jesus Christ crucified and resurrected appear in us, and the pattern of death and resurrection shapes our lives—these are the genuine biblical *stigmata* in which all believers share.

But this pattern is also present in the lives of Old Testament saints. Admittedly the fascination with typology in some evangelical groupings has been unfortunate and without controls; but nevertheless a Christ-shape and a Christ-pattern appear clearly in a variety of Old Testament saints, and must ultimately be analysed as a shadow in their lives created by the projection backwards into history of the work of Christ.

There are so many illustrations of this that we can confidently say that there is not an Old Testament historical-biographical account of any length that does not involve dying and rising, humiliation and exaltation, being brought down and being raised up, experiencing opposition and then deliverance, suffering want and then experiencing extraordinary provision. This is not merely the form of good storytelling, it is the embodiment of the gospel pattern.

Joseph is a classic case: the story of his life is shaped unmistakably by the pattern of death and resurrection. A pattern is written large in him: *humiliation* (rejected and stripped of his glory-robe, becoming a slave, being made of no reputation) → *exaltation* (being highly exalted at Pharaoh's right hand) → *provision* (for the needs of the whole world) → the *ingathering* of his people. This, at the end of the day, is the Christ-pattern in sketch-like form. The pattern of meant-for-evil → producing good, the salvation of many (Gen. 50:20) is fulfilled in the one crucified by the hands of wicked men—yet according to the plan of the God who raised him from the dead for the salvation of the nations (Acts 2:23). That same pattern, while written large in Joseph, appears throughout the Old Testament. It connects the Old Testament saints to Christ, and underlines that we do not fully understand their experience apart from this template.

Developing a Christ-centred instinct

If these principles hold good, then it must be possible along different lines, sometimes using one, sometimes using a combination, to move from any point in the Old Testament into the backbone of redemptive history which leads ultimately to Christ, its fulfilment and consummation. In this way, the context and destination for all our preaching will be Jesus Christ himself, Saviour and Lord.

These are general principles; they do not constitute a simple formula, an elixir to be sprinkled on our sermons to transform them into the preaching of Christ. There is no formula that will do that. We never 'arrive' or 'have it cracked' when it comes to preaching Christ. But as we come to know the Scriptures more intimately, as we see these patterns deeply embedded in the Bible, and—just as crucially—as we come to know Christ himself more intimately and to love him better, we shall surely develop the instinct to reason, explain, and prove from all the Scriptures the riches of grace which are proclaimed in Jesus, the Christ, the Saviour of the world. The ability to do that will itself be adequate reward for the hard work involved in learning to preach in a way that takes the Old Testament seriously within its own context, but also recognizes that that context is not complete apart from Jesus Christ.

CHAPTER THIRTY-FIVE

THE PREACHER AS THEOLOGIAN

WHEN I was a student, I came across some words of (I think) Jean-Daniel Benoît about the Genevan Reformer John Calvin: he 'became a theologian in order to be a better pastor'. That may strike us as either interesting (a new slant!) or odd. If so, it is because a principle that all of the Reformers (in England, Scotland, and throughout Europe) held with great conviction began to fall increasingly into disuse from about the end of the seventeenth century: all biblical theology is ultimately pastoral, and all pastoral ministry is ultimately theological.

Think of the sixteenth and seventeenth centuries. Most of the theologians whose names we know were working preachers, pastors, or bishops in some context or another. But then, for a variety of reasons we need not go into here, a dichotomy between the two functions of theologian and pastor-preacher began to develop. This has sometimes (mistakenly in my view) been justified by the apostle Paul's reference to 'pastors *and* teachers' (Eph. 4:11), as though these were two radically separated offices, not one. Thus we find ourselves in the situation in which it can be said of somebody, 'It is just as well he is teaching in a theological college, because he would be a disaster as a pastor.' Or, similarly, we say things such as: 'It would be a waste for him to go into the pastorate because he has so much to offer as a gifted theologian.' Of course our colleges, seminaries, and other training institutions need our best minds; but not on the basis that theology is for the academy whereas ministry is for the church!

It is rare, however, to hear it said: 'It would be a disaster for you to go into pastoral ministry because you have no expertise in theology.' Yet we expect our doctors, dentists, optometrists to have expertise in their fields. While not narrow specialists, we expect them to have expertise far beyond that of the layperson's. Could it be that the relative lack of respect there is for Christian ministers among professional people (even those who are themselves Christians) derives in part from the fact that Christian ministers are all too rarely experts in the very field in which they ought to be, namely theology?

Why do I say that? *First*, because as pastors our whole ministry is necessarily related to being a theologian. But *second* (and here I speak for myself—but perhaps also for others), because our theological colleges never taught us that principle, nor believed it. Consequently being a theologian has not been regarded as a good thing. Sadly, many of my generation came into the Christian ministry having to do a quick crash course in teaching ourselves theology. The result is that there has been a great dichotomy in our thinking between what it means to be a minister of a congregation, a pastor of a flock, an expositor of Scripture on the one hand, and on the other hand, a theologian. But this is a dichotomy that is not present in the Scriptures. The apostle Paul well understood as he handled the gospel, often as a pastor of a particular congregation (as in Ephesus or Corinth), that you cannot be a pastor without simultaneously being a theologian. Indeed, strictly speaking, you cannot be a Christian (or, ultimately, a human being!) without being a theologian. For the whole adventure and process of growing as an expositor of Scripture necessarily involves a very delicate relationship between two things: on the one hand, the system of truth that you have already discovered has emerged from Scripture (your doctrinal framework), and on the other, the fresh light that God is shedding upon that body of truth from the very Scriptures that you are constantly expounding.

Framework and text

We can put it this way: there should have come a point in your life if you are called into pastoral ministry when, in a sense, you have 'bought the house' within which your Christian thinking will take place, develop, and mature. The substructure of your understanding of the gospel is laid down, and the superstructure built. It has a certain shape, and is clearly recognizable as a dwelling to live in. You have the framework of your theology. But for the rest of your life, you will find yourself saying things such as: 'We will need to change the curtains because they don't really fit.' Then, when you have changed the curtains you need to rearrange the furniture, and later you may want to renew the kitchen, and so on. The basic house, the system of theology, is still in place, but the whole process of living in the house involves an ongoing process of rearranging things in such a way that gradually your theology becomes increasingly coherent and self-consistent for you as the occupant. In this way our theology is constantly being reformed by the Scriptures themselves.

There are various ways in which we can see this at work in Scripture itself, particularly in the apostle Paul.

Unity of Scripture

First of all, it is implied by the principle of the unity of Scripture. The moment you go beyond considering a biblical text, to in any way demonstrating how Scripture is a unity, you have moved from the narrow exegesis of the text of Scripture to a theological formulation drawn from it. What you are doing is recognizing that there is a structure within Scripture that is coherent, that has its own inner logic and therefore provides its own inner system. Exegesis and theology, or theology and exposition, are going hand in hand.

Primary and secondary in Scripture

Secondly, there is a more obvious example of this from Paul at the beginning of 1 Corinthians 15. He says there that some things belong to the first rank in the gospel; they are 'of first importance', and he lays them out for the Corinthians (1 Cor. 15:3ff.). But that statement implies that there is a systemic understanding of the gospel in the mind of the apostle Paul so that he can say, within the consistent system of Scripture, 'Here are the things that are absolutely primary and principal; here are other truths that are equally inspired, but are not so close to the centre and the inner fundamental logic of the gospel.' This is not the thinking simply of an exegete of a text working through the grammar; it is the thinking of somebody who recognizes that Scripture throws up for us its own theology, its own system of truth.

Paul clearly assumes that it is against the background of that system of truth that we understand how we relate one part of Scripture to another, and the whole of Scripture within itself.

Romans: a theological exposition

A third illustration of this principle is found in the way in which the apostle Paul expounds Habakkuk 2:4 in his letter to the Romans. He does a great deal more in Romans 1:18ff. than simply give a grammatical exegesis or a running commentary on Habakkuk 2:4. What he does do is relate this text to the whole of Scripture and to the revelation of God in Jesus Christ. In fact the whole letter approximates to a full exposition of the theology contained in and implied by this verse, and this is what serves as the whole backcloth to the way in which he understands and proclaims the gospel.

The gospel pattern

This point is so important and neglected that it may be worth the danger of repeating it almost *ad nauseam*, so here is a fourth illustration. When Paul writes to Timothy towards the end of his life a new note is injected into his teaching. You cannot really understand the pastoral epistles without grasping it: Paul is conscious that he has come to a hinge point in the history of the Christian church where it will no longer be possible for the people of God to turn to living apostles and ask, 'What is the word of the Lord for us?' In this context he urges Timothy to 'follow the pattern of the sound words' (2 Tim. 1:13-14). Note this: he is not to follow the sound words merely (though that would be true). He is to follow the *pattern*. Here *tupos* refers to the mould, the shape, of the sound words which in turn leaves its mark and character on our thinking and living.

In the process of doing this Timothy will guard the good deposit of the gospel in faith and love. What is Paul saying? As Timothy preaches the word (the principle to which he comes at the end of chapter 3 and the beginning of chapter 4) he must do so in such a way that his preaching is in every particular instance consistent with the good deposit, with the totality of 'the pattern of the sound words'. So Paul seems to be suggesting that there is an intimate, intricate relationship between my understanding of the framework, the pattern, the consistent system of truth to which the Scriptures themselves give expression, and my ability to expound the Scriptures accurately and fully so that what they are *for*—'for teaching, for reproof, for correction, and for training in righteousness' (2 Tim. 3:16)—may be exhibited in how we preach them—'reprove, rebuke, and exhort—with complete patience and teaching' (2 Tim. 4:2—the chapter division between 2 Timothy 3 and 4 must be one of the least helpful in the Pauline corpus).

I have used the word *theology* here in a rather comprehensive sense. Characteristically we think about theology in a multifaceted way, the separate disciplines taught in our colleges and in the books in our libraries. In connection with our preaching we think particularly, perhaps, of biblical theology and systematic theology. In using the word *theology* as above I mean it primarily in both these senses: the teaching of Scripture seen along the axis of redemptive history and revelation (biblical theology as a *terminus technicus*); the teaching of Scripture co-ordinated in a coherent, topical and logical order (systematic theology as a *terminus technicus*).

It is clear, for example, that in his reasoning in Galatians 3 and 4 the apostle Paul is working, writing, thinking as someone who has a great grasp of systematic thinking rooted in biblical theology. For him redemptive history (biblical theology) is a hand-maiden to the coherent ordering of truth (systematic theology) and this gives rise to application in the way in which he deals with the Galatian problem (pastoral theology).

This point—that the apostle Paul thinks as a systematic theologian to enable him to expound and apply the revelation of God to contemporary church life—presents us with a paradigm worth pursuing.

Theology: the expositor's essential anatomy and physiology

An analogy may help us here. We can put it in the form of an axiom: *theology is to the expositor of Scripture what anatomy is to the doctor in his consulting room.*

When you go to the health centre and describe your symptoms to the doctor, his ability to bring healing does not depend merely on reaching out to the current edition of *The British National Formulary* to find the appropriate drug. No, the physician's ability to bring healing where there

689

is dysfunction (and herein lies part of the analogy with the pastoral task of providing spiritual medicine for the soul's ills) is intimately related to, and dependent on, a knowledge of the life-system that lies underneath your flesh. Furthermore, this life-system works in all kinds of interesting ways, because the good physician recognizes that if you come with a pain in one part of your body the original source of the problem may lie elsewhere.

I remember going to my dentist one day because I had some discomfort in one side of my mouth. As I tried to relax (!) extended on his chair, he began to poke around in the other side of my mouth. Now, I had known my dentist many years, so once he had the tools of his trade out of my mouth I said, 'It is actually over here on this side I'm feeling the pain.' He replied that I had already told him that, but said that it could very well be a problem of *referred* pain—feeling the pain on one side, when the actual cause of the pain could be traced to the other side of the mouth. He knew that, given the complexity and interrelatedness of the anatomy of the head, the manifestation of dysfunction could be caused by a problem at some distance from, yet connected to, the place where the pain presented itself. Because the physician understands how the physical body is connected and unified, how it 'works', it becomes possible for him to provide an accurate diagnosis and to employ the correct remedy to bring healing.

Diagnosis and treatment of spiritual dysfunction

While this illustration has its limitations, it nevertheless serves our purpose well. When you present your symptoms to the doctor, you assume that he knows his anatomy and physiology well enough to be able to diagnose your problem and make possible the process of healing. Indeed if he or she lacked that acceptable level of expertise you would look elsewhere.

Should not Christian congregations have a similar confidence in us, their pastor-teachers, that we have a sufficiently clear grasp of the anatomy of the gospel, how it works, what spiritual sickness arises when we misunderstand it, distort it, are ignorant of it, or are simply disobedient to it? To extend the analogy a little, they should be confident that we have a solid working understanding of the 'body of divinity' and how it functions so that we can use the remedies of Scripture to deal with spiritual dysfunction and foster spiritual health in the body of Christ.

This, again, is something that can be illustrated clearly in Paul. His letters, in the main, were written specifically to deal with one dysfunction or another in the churches in his care. His task is to bring to bear on this dysfunction the truth of God as it is revealed in Jesus Christ.

The diagnosis of division

The letter to the Philippians is an example. What is the dysfunction? It seems clear from 2:1ff. and 4:2 that the body of Christ in Philippi was beginning to present symptoms of a combination of divisiveness and self-seeking.

Paul understands the system of Christian truth well enough to see that it is simply not adequate to say, 'You people shouldn't be falling out with each other; that's very naughty, you know; you really ought to do better.' He does not preach moralistically to them, and simply command them what to do—to be united.

But that is often our reaction as preachers and pastors, is it not? We pinpoint the problem, and seek to bring redress to that specific area. We are heavy on noting the dysfunction and quick to recognize the proper function. We connect them by issuing a series of imperatives ('Do this, and this ...'). Necessary although this is, it is not medicine, because it is not gospel. It does not heal the problem at the root. And it is not what Paul does here. He employs theological anatomy and physiology. He traces the spiritual sickness to its real source. He understands the deep structure of the gospel and how it provides the remedy which will bring healing. In this instance the symptom of divisiveness presenting itself in the body of Christ in Philippi is traceable to the problem of *pride*. In that sense disunity is referred pain; pride is the root of the disease. Pride must be dealt with first, not disunity.

In addition, Paul also recognizes that the gospel solution to the problem of disunity with its roots in pride must be found in the cultivation of humility. Thus in his thinking he has already moved from divisiveness not merely back to its antithesis in the principle of unity but to the remedial principle of humility. But then he moves on again, as it were, down through the anatomy, understanding that the source of humility in the life of the Christian believer is rooted in union with the self-humbled Christ and the imitation of him to which it gives rise as its necessary corollary.

Thus, the apostolic prescription for a return to spiritual health is a hefty dose not first of exhortation to work harder at church unity, but primarily of the exposition of the person of Christ, exalted in his divine being, humbling himself to death, even the humiliating death of a Roman cross. The cure for disunity is Christology! And so, in the context of squabbles in this little church, a perennial prescription is written for Christ's people—a prescription which contains the most costly of pharmaceuticals: Christ's self-sacrifice in his incarnation, life, and shameful death, and glorious exaltation.

In this way Paul has done much more than simply give us the grammatical exegesis of the Philippians' divisiveness and then tell us it is an evil to be avoided. That would have been true, but neither adequate nor gospel. Rather he has taken his exegesis of their failures and placed this within the context of his understanding of the framework of how the gospel works. He has shown how spiritual dysfunction of this kind is inimical to the gospel. Then he answers the problem with the grace of God in the gospel. He is dealing with the situation as a pastoral theologian, preaching not moralism but grace.

The root cure for legalism and antinomianism

There is another dysfunction that is as common with us as it was with the apostle Paul. It is the dysfunction of legalism and/or its apparently antithetical dysfunction of antinomianism. In one form or another this accounts for perhaps fifty percent or more of the pastoral problems we face. These problems may not surface with these labels, but in reality this is what is involved. In their relationship to God Christian people frequently fall back, in the most general sense, into thinking of their acceptance with God now being dependent on their performance. Or, on the other hand, burdened perhaps by a sense of failure and the promise of freedom, they throw aside the commandments of God and the necessity of doing the good works that God has ordained for us (Eph. 2:10) in order to escape 'that kind of legalism'.

How does Paul respond here? If he operated simply at the level of symptoms he might well say: 'Oh, we've got some legalism here. We're against that, and to provide a spiritual balance we will need a mild dose of antinomianism.' Or, correspondingly, if faced with antinomianism: 'What we need here is a brief course of the law and its commands.'

Often throughout history that is exactly the way the Christian church has operated. 'Aha! *Antinomianism*: we need to tighten up a bit.' Or, 'Your problem is *legalism*: what you guys need to do is loosen up a bit; it is not so vital after all.' But that solution would be Freudian rather than Pauline! How, then, does the apostle Paul deal with legalism and antinomianism? Interestingly, he deals with both dysfunctions in exactly the same way: by treating both maladies with the only lasting remedy for either legalism or antinomianism. This he finds in his understanding of the nature of grace, and the dynamic of the way in which it operates.

Take for instance the case of antinomianism, which he alludes to in Romans 3:8. Paul was himself accused of it and addressed it head-on in Romans 6:1ff. His response, if rightly understood, may strike us as sharply as a cold shower in the morning.

If someone in our congregation is a little 'fast and loose' in their Christian life, clearly not living a life of consistent obedience to the commandments of God, would we go to such a person and say by way of prescription: 'You have been baptized!'?

Are we not more inclined to go to them and say, 'You need to cut this out'? But in doing so we become like cheats in Monopoly—we try to get past 'Go' without going round the rest of the board. We try to deliver them from spiritual dysfunction without reference to the remedy that was given to deliver us from it. We thus indicate our poor grasp of theological anatomy and physiology, of the structure of the gospel, and of the dynamics of its operation.

What Paul does in Romans 6, by contrast, is to take his readers back to the significance of their baptism, and the meaning of our union with Christ. He argues that all those who have been baptized (= Christians, Christ-ones, those united to Christ) have died to sin and been raised to newness of life. Certain implications follow from understanding the logic of this grace, and Paul expounds them: they are to love out of their new identity in Christ.

So where we may be inclined to take a short cut—after all, is not Romans 6 difficult to teach? It seems so alien to the way we think today—the apostle Paul does not. He goes deep into the structure of the gospel in order to provide a permanent cure at the very root of the dysfunction—which is a failure to understand the truth ('Do you not *know*', Rom. 6:3, 6) and to think it through into our mindset ('*Consider yourselves* dead to sin', Rom. 6:11). Notice the importance of the mind in Paul's teaching (both as to its content and its style). Understanding the radical nature of what has happened to us through union with Christ by God's grace is essential for the Christian; this in turn implies that the pastor-teacher must thoroughly understand it.

The remedy for lack of assurance

Let me provide a third example. Perhaps it is not so true elsewhere, but one of the great problems historically among Christian people in Scotland has been lack of assurance. Perhaps today we might be forgiven for thinking that there is not enough lack of assurance! Be that as it may, lack of assurance causes all kinds of harmful side-effects in our Christian lives.

How would Paul deal with that? I think our native instinct would be to respond to it by talking about the doctrine of assurance. But the apostle Paul would probably have done that in only one case out of a hundred because he recognized that the problem—a lack of assurance and joy in the Christian life—is not necessarily caused by a flaw in our doctrine of assurance or our doctrine of joy. Rather, lack of assurance is almost always caused by an inadequate understanding of the free justification we have received in Christ and of the final standing before God that free justification guarantees to believers.

So Paul would not go to someone suffering from a lack of assurance and hand them a book about assurance; that might be an almost fatal mistake! He would preach the gospel to them: preach the freeness and the fullness of justification in Jesus.

Growing as pastors and theologians

Throughout Paul's letters, then, there is always operative in the way he responds to dysfunctional situations a profound understanding of the anatomy and physiology of the gospel.

Remarkably, if we deleted from the Pauline corpus all the sections of gospel teaching drawn out of him by either dysfunctional understanding or lifestyle his letters would disintegrate. He seems to have spent much of his time as apostle-pastor-teacher dealing with dysfunction. It is likely that pastors and teachers today will find themselves doing the same thing both in public and private. We therefore must learn to do our exegesis of the text of the Scriptures within the broader context of a constantly symbiotic relationship, in which exegesis feeds our theology and our theology enables us to expound Scripture in depth. Thus we grow as pastors as we grow as theologians. We grow as theologians as we grow as exegetes, and we grow as exegetes as we grow as theologians. And all this is in order that our preaching, our exposition of the Scriptures, may be truly pastoral and, in the biblical sense, theological. You cannot be a preacher without being a theologian, just as—in the truest sense—you cannot be much of a theologian unless you are, at heart, a pastor. How could it be otherwise if the chief end of our lives is to glorify God and enjoy him forever, and if the chief end of our preaching is that others should come to glorify him and to enjoy him forever? And who would doubt that this is the chief end of our lives and of our preaching?

CHAPTER THIRTY-SIX

PREACHING THE ATONEMENT

I N the apostolic church, the doctrine of the atonement always led to the preaching of the atonement. The 'word of the cross is ... the power of God ... we preach Christ crucified ... the power of God and the wisdom of God' (1 Cor. 1:18, 23-24). And so it should be today as well. In this area of theology particularly, there is much to be said for sharing James Denney's sentiment. He said he had no interest in a theology that could not be preached. Thus, clarity of thinking about the biblical teaching on the atonement is not only an intellectual desideratum; it is vital for the integrity of the Christian faith, for the proclamation of the gospel and for the health of the church.

Critics regularly remind us that we are justified not by any interpretation or 'theory' of the atonement but by Christ himself. But even to say that 'Christ died for our sins' (1 Cor. 15:3) is already to provide an interpretation of his death (a 'theory'). And if the biblical interpretation of the cross becomes muted or transmuted, the result is a view of Christ's death that renders it non-atoning and empties the cross of its power (cf. 1 Cor. 1:17). At least part of the church's malady today must surely be traced to this poisoned spring. Too concerned lest we commit the twenty-first-century sin of dogmatism, we nullify the concrete claims of biblical teaching that stress that Christ saves us by sacrificial atonement, victory, and reconciliation. These so-called 'models' delineate what the atonement is. And without atonement we have no gospel.

A right understanding of the doctrine of the atonement, therefore, is as essential for the pastor-teacher as it is for the academic theologian— perhaps even more essential since the pastor-teacher ordinarily deals directly in his calling with the proclamation of the gospel. The word of the cross is the power of God, and preaching the gospel is preaching the cross: preaching Christ crucified (1 Cor. 1:17; 2:2). Of first importance in the gospel, and therefore in our preaching, is that 'Christ died *for our sins* [i.e., as an atonement for sin] in accordance with the Scriptures' (1 Cor. 15:3).

Two questions arise in thinking about the doctrine of the atonement and the preaching of the cross, one contemporary and the other perennial. The (briefer) answer to the first sets the context for, and provides the motivation to discover, the (longer) answer to the second.

Question 1: Do we preach the cross?

Do we what? Surely the cross is the undergirding, frequently emerging, central theme in all evangelical preaching, as it was for Paul? The question may seem absurd in the light of the force of Paul's description of his own focus. For evangelicals—gospel and Bible people—the answer is surely self-evident. At least until one critically (and, if need be, self-critically) analyses the output of the evangelical world in terms of books, magazine and journal articles, sermons, seminars, and conferences.

During the past decades evangelicals (by far the major purveyors of Christian resources) have inundated the market with literature and teaching opportunities on a wide variety of themes from the creational to the eschatological. But when did you last go to a Christian conference that had the cross of Christ as its theme and focused your attention on the meaning and significance of Jesus' death? Many (perhaps even most) pastor-teachers' bookshelves groan with works answering the question 'How can I?' but are light on works which answer the question '*How did he?*'

This question becomes even more pointed when we ask it in connection with preaching. Most evangelical ministers preach or speak somewhere between one and two hundred times during the course of a year. Most committed church members are likely to hear a half or more of these messages. But how confidently could we say of contemporary evangelical preachers that they 'decided to know nothing among [us] except Jesus Christ and him crucified' (1 Cor. 2:2)?

To ask the question is, sadly in many cases, to answer it. The cross may be assumed and presupposed, but it is hidden. There is a scandal in the late-twentieth- and early-twenty-first-century pulpit: the veiling of the cross. And perhaps the most important contribution of an essay with practical-pastoral-homiletic orientation to the atonement is simply to ask the question: *Is this true—do we explore and defend the orthodox understanding of the atonement theologically but rarely preach the cross?* How essential is it, then, to encourage preaching that is Christ-centred and cross-centred! Here we can, perhaps, begin to do that by reflecting on Paul's seminal statement in 2 Corinthians of what is involved in preaching the cross.

Question 2: How should we preach the cross?
The Corinthian church had, it seems, fallen prey to teachers with a different spirit and motive from that of Paul—'super-apostles' who demeaned him (2 Cor. 11:5; 12:11). Weighty as a correspondent he might seem to be, but in fact as a preacher he was—so they claimed—unimpressive (2 Cor. 10:10). Thus in 2 Corinthians 2:14–7:4, in what Paul Barnett well describes as his 'defensive excursus',[1] Paul gives an open-hearted insight into both the message and the experience of an apostolic minister. This is a section of Scripture of which every preacher of the gospel should have a working knowledge.

Preaching grid
Paul hints in this context at a multidimensional preaching grid with which he seems to have operated. One ought not to think of such things as slick inventions of twenty-first-century professors of homiletics! In embryonic form they can be traced back through William Perkins to John Calvin, and behind them to Jesus and Paul.[2] In any and every age, the preacher must be self-consciously aware of the spiritual condition of the audience in order to address the gospel to them pointedly and relevantly.

---

[1] Paul Barnett, *The Second Epistle to the Corinthians* (Grand Rapids: Eerdmans, 1997), p. 210. Cf. 2 Cor. 6:11.

[2] William Perkins, *The Art of Prophesying* (1606; repr. Edinburgh: Banner of Truth Trust, 1996); John Calvin, *Sermons on 1 and 2 Timothy and Titus* (London, 1579), 933-45 (sermon 24 on 2 Timothy); Jesus in his Parable of the Sower (Matt. 13; Mark 4; Luke 8); Paul in 2 Timothy 3:16–4:5.

Paul presents us with his own basic analysis of those to whom he preaches. They are (1) spiritually blind, (2) under the influence of the god of this age, (3) summoned to stand before the judgment seat of Christ, and (4) destined to perish (2 Cor. 4:3-4; 5:10). In a word, those to whom we preach the gospel are spiritually alienated from God and need to be reconciled to him. According to Paul, this is the situation whether people recognize it or not—indeed, whether they recognize God himself or not. For even in the professing atheist that alienation, rebellion, and hatred cannot be forever drowned out of the conscience, as the following instance vividly demonstrates.

On October 22, 1996, in the church of St Martin-in-the Fields in central London, a congregation of some two hundred people, described the next day by the quality British newspaper *The Daily Telegraph* as 'admirers', gathered to celebrate the life of the famous twentieth-century English novelist Sir Kingsley Amis. The paper described it as 'a secular service: no hymns or prayers, just a lot of laughter'.[1] During the service, the late Sir Kingsley's son, the novelist Martin Amis, told the following story, recalling a conversation his father had with the Russian poet and novelist Yevgeni Yevtushenko. Yevtushenko, perhaps having mistakenly assumed all Englishmen were Christians, asked Amis if it was true that he was an atheist. 'Well, yes,' said Sir Kingsley, and then added, 'But it's more than that. *I hate him.*'[2] Here, then, was a quintessential atheist, displaying such remarkable blindness that he could shoot his own atheism in the foot without even feeling the pain. What clearer testimony could one hope to find to Scripture's claim that those who are by nature enemies of God, seek to suppress and deny the truth they know (Rom. 1:18-25)? This is the blindness into which we are called to preach the gospel.

But why is Paul's 'preaching grid' relevant to our thinking about the proclamation of the atonement? Because it underscores why our preaching must involve 'the open statement of the truth' (2 Cor. 4:2)— expounding it in the power of the Spirit in such a way that it exposes both the spiritual condition of the hearer and the divinely given remedy

---

[1] *The Daily Telegraph*, October 23, 1996.
[2] *Ibid.* (emphasis added). Born in 1933, Yevtushenko died in 2017.

for it in the work of Christ. And if we see this as our task in preaching, then we are less likely to 'lose heart' in our ministry (2 Cor. 4:1, 16). When our gaze is focused on the real goal of our preaching—opening the eyes of the blind so that they see, understand, and respond to the word of the cross—and when we are clear about the opposition that the preaching of Christ crucified will encounter, we are less likely to cave in to the pressures.

But what are we to preach about Jesus Christ and him crucified? Paul answers at length in 2 Corinthians 5, a passage noteworthy for the fact that while addressing Christians, he does so in the language in which he preached the gospel to unbelievers in Corinth. As B. B. Warfield puts it, 'We have here the phrases in which Paul was accustomed to give expression to the heart of his gospel.'[1] To a world alienated from God, the gospel comes as the message of reconciliation. In outlining his message, Paul also gives us a basic education in what is involved in preaching it.

The source of the gospel

God the Father is himself the fountain from which the gospel flows. It is God who reconciles us to himself. He is the architect of the work of Christ and of the reconciliation he accomplished (2 Cor. 5:19), the source of the evangelists' commission (2 Cor. 5:19), the one issuing the evangelistic appeal (2 Cor. 5:19-20). Implied here is the perfect harmony within the Trinity, sustained precisely in connection with the death of Christ, which effects our reconciliation. Jesus did not die in order to persuade the Father to love those for whom he died. No, the Father himself in love planned and enabled the death of Christ for us: 'God so loved ... that he gave his only Son' (John 3:16). He appeals (2 Cor. 5:20).

This may seem to be a truism. But it is often overlooked that it has important implications for the ethos and spirit of our preaching. Evangelical preaching too often falls into the trap of suggesting that the Father loves sinners only because Jesus has died for them. A wrathful Father is persuaded to have mercy by a loving Son. This in turn has a tendency to breed a deep-down suspicion of God. Thus, the great

---

[1] B. B. Warfield, *The Saviour of the World* (1916; repr., Edinburgh: Banner of Truth Trust, 1991), p. 136.

Puritan John Owen could be heard lamenting in his own seventeenth century that many Christians tend to have a distorted view of the Father:

> How few of the saints are experimentally acquainted with this privilege of holding immediate communion with the Father in love! With what anxious, doubtful thoughts do they look upon him! What fears, what questionings are there, of his good will and kindness! At the best, many think that there is no sweetness at all in him towards us, but what is purchased at the high price of the blood of Jesus. It is true, that alone is the way of communication; but the free fountain and spring of all is in the bosom of the Father.[1]

Doubtless this is due partly to a natural fallen instinct that makes us suspicious of God. Injecting such a spirit seems to be partly in view in the original temptation.[2] But it is also due to a failure to understand the harmony of the Trinity and the nature of the atonement as the ultimate demonstration of the Father's love (Rom. 5:8), and therefore of the divine unity. This failure emerges in different ways, not least when the cross of Christ and his atoning death are preached in such a manner that the God who is presented in our preaching appears to be reluctant to save, while Jesus seems eager to do so. Such a dichotomy between the motivations of the Father and the Son destroys a basic element in the gospel. For it suggests that God the Father is not truly revealed in Jesus Christ. Behind the Saviour stands—it is feared—an ogre God, who is other than love. That doctrinal error leads to deep psychological-spiritual mistrust. This in turn begins to poison the Christian's sense of pardon, stability, and joy, which are grounded in the knowledge that Christ is truly and fully the revelation of the Father.

---

[1] Owen, *Of Communion with God the Father, Son and Holy Ghost* (1657), *Works*, II:32.

[2] 'Did God actually say, "You shall not eat of any tree in the garden"?' (Gen. 3:1) casts doubt not only on God's word, but also on his character ('Did he set this abundance before you and then so sullenly restrict you?').

The nature of the gospel message

Paul speaks about the gospel as a message or word of reconciliation.[1] This reconciliation has both an *objective* and a *subjective* side to it. In the grammar of the gospel, all subjective experience of reconciliation depends on, and is shaped by, the objective accomplishment of that reconciliation in Christ. The importance of this for preaching can scarcely be overstressed. Sadly, however, evangelical preaching can sometimes (perhaps often) either ignore it or appear to be ignorant of it.

This last statement may appear reactionary and even hypercritical. Yet it is commonplace for evangelical preaching to give the impression that the gospel is a message of salvation and justification by regeneration or by the indwelling of Christ. But the basis for our justification is not Christ *indwelling us* or our *being born again*. Rather it is that Christ *has died for us*. In Martin Luther's apt statement: the gospel is entirely *outside of us*.

Our times are not alone in falling into this confusion of the *subjective effects* with the *objective foundation* of the gospel. Preachers like George Whitefield in the eighteenth century and D. Martyn Lloyd-Jones in the twentieth century shared a similar misunderstanding of the gospel in their early ministries. They had to learn the lesson that we are not justified by regeneration, or by Christ indwelling, but by the objective work of Christ on the cross and in his resurrection. We must learn that lesson too.

The failure to grasp this gospel grammar—*Christ for us* the foundation, *Christ in us* the realization of the gospel—has reached epidemic proportions in some segments of contemporary evangelicalism. We see that the gospel-enervating entail of Schleiermacher's attempt to rescue the Christian faith from the Enlightenment has now come home to roost in, of all places, evangelicalism. Although assuming that they are preaching the gospel, many are in danger of preaching little more than personal subjective experience, bypassing the gospel's foundation in the cross. If anything, this has increased since the halcyon days of the 'born-again' movement of the late twentieth century. But being 'born again' is not the gospel. It is the *fruit* of the gospel. To confuse it with the gospel is to

[1] *tes katallagēs* (2 Cor 5:19).

turn the gospel on its head, and to do so in such a way that the cross of Christ is no longer central and essential; it is emptied of its significance and marginalized in preaching. What is the remedy for such a malady? Paul provides us with the answer.

The Great Exchange, Dimension 1: The Finished Work of Christ— Reconciliation Accomplished

How does Paul preach the gospel as a message of reconciliation? He does so by stressing the finished work of Christ: 'In Christ God was reconciling the world to himself' (2 Cor. 5:19). Reconciliation is not first and foremost a subjective condition in us, but it is an objective provision made by God for us in his Son. But how is this so?

At the root of the language used for reconciliation (*katallagē*) is the idea of a change or an exchange taking place;[1] one set of circumstances giving way to, and being exchanged for, another. The point is expressed perfectly in Paul's great statement about Christ: God 'made him to be sin who knew no sin, so that in him we might become the righteousness of God' (2 Cor. 5:21). Despite attempts to show the contrary,[2] the apostle is speaking here about what lies at the heart of the gospel, namely *a double exchange*: our sin was imputed to Christ; Christ's righteousness is imputed to us.

Finished work

Our sin is not imputed to us: 'God was reconciling the world to himself, not counting their trespasses against them' (2 Cor. 5:19). 'Exactly,' says John Doe—'I have always believed in a God who doesn't count our sins!' In fact, however, God does count our sins. But not against us! Rather, he counts them against Christ. In the exchange described in 2 Corinthians 5:21, he has taken what is ours in our fallen human nature (he was made sin) in order that we might become by grace what is his in his human nature (we become the righteousness of God).

---

[1] See Kittel & Friedrich, eds, *Theological Dictionary of the New Testament*, I:258.

[2] The rejection of a *double* imputation on the grounds that the righteousness of a person is an attribute and cannot therefore be imputed to another fails to take account of the fact that *sin* is also a personal attribute. To reject double imputation on these grounds therefore eviscerates the heart of the gospel.

This is what a former generation referred to as 'Christ's finished work'. It does not take place *because* we believe or *after* we believe; it took place *on the cross*. There my sins were imputed to him; there God dealt with the objective grounds for his alienation from me. He has done the reconciling. The task of the preacher now is to publish this message of reconciliation accomplished for us by Christ, offered to us by God through the preacher, and made ours by faith.

Effectual work

This aspect of the work of Christ is thus completed already; moreover, it is efficacious—God was reconciling the world to himself in Christ, not counting humans' sins against them—this has happened. That is the good news—it has already taken place at the cross—and this is the message we are to preach. But this carries a biblical and logical implication: those for whom Christ died will be saved by his atoning work. There is no double jeopardy. In A. M. Toplady's words:

> If Thou hast my discharge procured,
> And freely in my room endured
> The whole of wrath divine;
> Payment God cannot twice demand,
> First at my bleeding Surety's hand,
> And then again at mine.[1]

This is the doctrine of *effectual atonement*, sometimes described in terms of its most controversial implication, *limited* or *definite atonement*.[2] It bears mentioning that it is an aspect of what Paul is teaching in 2 Corinthians 5:14. Here, in a passage frequently assumed to be the clearest description of gospel preaching in Paul's letters, he makes a universal statement that has long puzzled exegetes: 'we have concluded this: that one has died for all, therefore all have died'.

Paul does not say what he is sometimes misunderstood to say, either: one has died for all, *therefore all do not need to die*; or that one has died

---

[1] From his hymn 'From Whence This Fear and Unbelief?'
[2] A doctrine long and ably defended and expounded by the late Roger Nicole to whom this essay was originally dedicated. See *Standing Forth: Collected Writings of Roger Nicole* (Tain, Ross-shire: Christian Focus Publications, 2002), pp. 283-318.

for all, *therefore all must learn to die* (to self). But rather he says one has died for all, *therefore all have died*. He uses the aorist tense in the indicative mood (*apethanen*). The death has been completed. This is not a continuing activity or a command to activity (which would have required either the present tense or the imperative mood).

But in what sense have 'all died'? In the same sense as Paul teaches in Colossians 2:11-12 and 3:3, with Christ in his death, emblematized in our baptism: all have died *to sin*, in Christ's death to sin (Rom. 6:2, 6-8). We died with Christ, in the death of Christ, because he died that death as our representative-substitute. If Christ died for us, we died in Christ. Those of whom the former is true are those of whom the latter is also true. But not all can be said to have 'died with Christ' in his death. The implication is that he therefore died effectually for those who may be said to have died with him in his death.[1]

Consequently, as those who have died in and with Christ to the old Adamic order, the implication follows that we should no longer live for ourselves but live for Christ (2 Cor. 5:15). Thus, the work of Christ is (1) objective, (2) finished, (3) efficacious, and (4) life-transforming. Each of these aspects presents the preacher with rich veins of gospel gold waiting to be mined in the ministry of the word.

Real suffering

But the atonement is not to be preached as a merely symmetrical mathematical arrangement, as though the pardon of sin were akin to some great divine problem solved by God's perfect algebra or by a commercial transaction. Paul would hardly have become passionate about divine arithmetic, as he evidently was about the gospel (2 Cor. 5:20).

In preaching, then, the question must be asked and answered: Why this passion? Because the exchange Christ made has a terrible element in it: *the Father* counted humanity's sins against his *Son*. The transaction in the atonement is *personal*; it involves the persons of the Godhead and their interpersonal relationships. If we miss this, we miss the power and also the attraction of the gospel.

---

[1] See the classic treatment in Owen, *The Death of Death in the Death of Christ* (1647), in *Works*, X:350-52; Smeaton, *Apostles' Doctrine of the Atonement*, pp. 210-14.

The exchange adumbrated in Isaiah's fourth Servant Song was realized in the personal experience of Jesus. He 'was pierced ... crushed ... upon him was the chastisement ... the Lord has laid on him the iniquity of us all' (Isa. 53:5-6). On the cross he became the scapegoat of the Day of Atonement (Lev. 16:6-10, 20-22), bearing our guilt out into the uninhabited desert space between heaven and earth, God and humanity—isolated from the latter and feeling abandoned by the former (Matt. 27:45-46). The price of our reconciliation was Christ's alienation.

Exchange lies at the heart of the action of the passion narrative. In the upper room Jesus gives his disciples the cup of blessing.[1] In Gethsemane he takes from his Father the cup of judgment (Mark 14:36), which he drinks to the bitter dregs on the cross. The Old Testament prophets described that cup as containing the most appalling potion. It is 'the cup of his wrath ... the cup of staggering' (Isa. 51:17); the '"cup of the wine of wrath ... They shall drink and stagger and be crazed ..." So I took the cup from the Lord's hand, and made all the nations to whom the Lord sent me drink it ... to make them a desolation and a waste, a hissing and a curse' (Jer. 25:15-18). It is a 'cup that is deep and large; you shall be laughed at and held in derision ... you will be filled with drunkenness and sorrow. A cup of horror and desolation' (Ezek. 23:32-33). So, according to Habakkuk 2:16, 'You will have your fill of shame instead of glory. ... Drink, yourself, and show your uncircumcision! The cup in the Lord's right hand will come around to you, and utter shame will come upon your glory!'

No wonder, then, as these prophecies unfold almost literally in the passion narrative, the Gospels are compelled to press language to the limits to express Jesus' experience of deep distress as he looked toward Calvary. The soul of the cross-bearing Saviour began 'to be greatly distressed and troubled ... very sorrowful, even to death' (Mark 14:33-34). Mark's verb *adēmonein* ('troubled') 'describes the confused, restless, half-distracted state, which is produced by physical derangement, or by mental distress, as grief, shame, disappointment'.[2] This vivid, poignant, but profoundly realistic portrayal of Christ's sin-bearing humanity,

---

[1] Cf. 1 Cor. 10:16, *to potērion tēs eulogias*.

[2] J. B. Lightfoot, *Saint Paul's Epistle to the Philippians* (London: Macmillan, 1913), p. 123.

facing the dissolution of his life on the cross with a holy revulsion, is, surely, part of the apostolic preaching that Paul describes as a 'public portrayal' of Christ crucified before the very 'eyes' of the Galatians (Gal. 3:1).

When Christ's atonement is preached thus, it becomes clear that we do not believe we are saved by a mere mathematical equation (or by a theological 'theory'), but by the all-demanding, all-consuming, Son-in-the-flesh-forsaking activity of the God of grace. In the very act of proclaiming this, 'the love of Christ controls' the preacher (2 Cor. 5:14). For it not to would be tantamount to unbelief in the reality we proclaimed. 'We are ambassadors for Christ, God making his appeal through us. We implore you ... be reconciled to God' (2 Cor. 5:20). This objective exchange—he takes our sin and gives us his righteousness—is the heart of the atonement.

Polyvalent atonement
But the great exchange is not the only aspect of Christ's work. For the atonement is multidimensional, polyvalent. In the context of 2 Corinthians 2:14–7:4, Paul does not major on the other dimensions. But they are implicit in his teaching. While the aspect of reconciliation is central here, the necessity of forensic justification is also implied ('we must all appear before the judgment seat of Christ', as 2 Cor. 5:10 states), as is the principle of redemptive deliverance from bondage. Unbelievers are held in the grip of Satan (2 Cor. 4:4). Only once delivered from the cavernous maze in which the evil one imprisons them can they ever be brought out into the light of Christ. Implied, then, in Paul's teaching is the *Christus Victor* motif that he spells out in Colossians 2:14-15. But here, as there, it is the atoning exchange of our guilt for his righteousness as the basis for reconciliation that simultaneously grounds both forensic justification and spiritual emancipation.

Person and work
In addition, it needs to be stressed that in our preaching the work of Christ must never be abstracted from the person of Christ. We do not preach 'the atonement' as such, or 'salvation', 'redemption', or 'justification' as such, but '*Jesus Christ* and *him* crucified'. These blessings

were accomplished by Christ and are available only in Christ, never abstracted from him. We must learn to avoid the contemporary plague of preaching the benefits of the gospel without proclaiming Christ himself as the benefactor in the gospel. We do not offer people abstract blessings (peace, forgiveness, new life) as commodities. Rather we preach and offer Christ crucified and risen, in whom these blessings become ours and not otherwise. We preach the person in the work, never the work and its blessings apart from the Saviour himself.

Yet, having thus emphasized the objective character of the gospel, we must not lose sight of the fact that the objective exchange that has taken place in the work of Christ produces a radical subjective exchange in the lives of those who receive it.

The Great Exchange, Dimension 2: The Continuing Work of Christ— Reconciliation Applied

Laying down our arms, surrendering in faith to God in Christ, responding to the exhortation to 'be reconciled to God' (2 Cor. 5:20) means trusting in Christ crucified. But Paul no more divides the message of Christ the Saviour from Christ the Lord than he separates the benefits (salvation) from the benefactor (Christ). For Christ is one Christ, Saviour and Lord. He does not save other than in his identity as Lord; he is not trusted as Saviour if his lordship is postponed for a later response.

Saviour and Lord

Jesus himself spells out the implication of this: to belong to him by faith involves taking up the cross. Woven into his dying is our dying. This is the point Simon Peter resisted so stubbornly. He had an instinctive sense that Jesus' death and his dying to himself were two sides of a coin. As he would later see with great clarity, Christ's death, while unique in its atoning character, is also paradigmatic for the shape of the Christian life of every future disciple (1 Pet. 2:21).

Preaching the atonement must therefore include expounding its implications in our lives. The objective exchange is radically applied in the ongoing exchange it effects in believers. For Paul did not preach effectual atonement without spelling out its actual effects. He describes this in terms of a series of concentric exchanges.

The epicentre of these lies in the way the old creation order is exchanged for the new: 'if anyone in Christ—new creation' (2 Cor. 5:17, literally). In view is not so much that 'I am a new creature in Christ' but that I have entered into a new order of reality. In the death of Christ as second man and last Adam (1 Cor. 15:45-47), my connection with the old order of humanity in Adam has been dissolved; in his resurrection, the new order of humanity has emerged in Christ. To be in Christ means the exchanging of the old for the new.[1] In regeneration/conversion the old person was stripped off, the new person embraced (Col. 3:9-10; cf. Eph. 4:22-24). Again we should note the spiritual vigour in the strong objectivity of the apostle Paul. He does not think of conversion in terms of adding to what we already are; rather, it involves entering into what we are not, getting 'into' (*eis*) Christ. We are no longer 'in' Adam, but we are 'in' Christ (cf. Rom. 5:12-21). This radical exchange of the old for the new then works itself out in a variety of ways.

(i) Exchanging the old view of Christ for a new and true view of him

Like Paul, we 'once regarded Christ according to the flesh [*kata sarka*]' (2 Cor. 5:16); we judged him from the perspective of the blind men and women of this age (cf. 2 Cor. 4:3-4). Now we know him as he really is, the Son of God, the Saviour, the Lord of glory (1 Cor. 2:8). Paul himself is a vivid illustration of this exchange. Peter also serves us by way of example. He viewed Christ *kata sarka*, resisting with a stubborn passion the notion that Jesus could be Christ only as the Suffering Servant, the crucified one. But *kata pneuma* ('according to the Spirit') he comes to see that the new order of reality emerges out of a cross-shaped mould (cf. 1 Pet. 2:21, 24; 4:1, 12-14).

(ii) Exchanging the old attitude toward others for a new attitude toward them

We 'regard no one according to the flesh [*kata sarka*]' (2 Cor. 5:16). Such a new view involves a recognition of their present condition (spiritually blind and perishing [2 Cor. 4:3-4]) and their appointed destiny ('we must all appear before the judgment seat of Christ, so that each one may receive what is due for what he has done in the body, whether good or

---

[1] A fact emblematized by baptism, Col. 2:12.

evil' [2 Cor. 5:10]). This creates a great sense of awe in Paul's heart in the light of that judgment. In turn, this becomes a major motivation in his life as he tries to persuade people of their need for, and the power of, the gospel of Christ (2 Cor. 5:11).

(iii) Exchanging the old way of life for a new way of life
Formerly, unbelievers lived 'for themselves'; they do so 'no longer'. Now they live 'for him who for their sake died and was raised' (2 Cor. 5:15). The result of the atonement is that believers' lives become externally focused, not self-critically devoted; no longer egocentric, but Christo-centric.

Two implications
But this question 'How should we preach the atonement?' has further dimensions. For the apostles the nature of the atonement, the substance of their message, carried implications for the way in which its heralds announced it. Two aspects only can be touched on here.

(i) The free offer of the gospel
We have stressed that the atonement is both completed (and therefore perfect) and efficacious (it actually saves). The implication of this is that *all those for whom Christ died will be reconciled.* Unless one is a universalist (holding that Christ died for all and therefore all will be reconciled whether they hear and believe the gospel or not) this implies both a definiteness and a limitation of a certain kind to the atonement. Its corollary is that Christ died efficaciously for the elect alone (whatever impact his atoning work may or may not make on others).

The alternative, of course, is not an unlimited atonement, but an atonement limited in another way, namely in its efficacy. This involves holding that while Christ died for all, that death does not actually accomplish reconciliation for anyone, but only the *potential* of recon-ciliation for everyone. For all practical purposes, this implies that faith completes the saving character of Christ's work.

This latter view inherently carries potentially disastrous consequences. It weakens the atonement's efficacy. (If Christ died for some who are not saved, in what sense can his atonement itself be said to be *saving?*)

In addition, it cuts the nerve of assurance of salvation based on the atonement. For if Christ's atonement was made for someone who is never saved by it, how can I look to it *with confidence* that I will be 'saved by his precious blood'?

Nevertheless, this view of the atonement—the Reformed view—has often been seen to carry with it the insurmountable problem of limiting to the elect alone the offer of the gospel and the command to faith and repentance. This is a serious issue that has long dogged the heels of churches that are Reformed. It continues to do so to this day and therefore requires at least brief comment.

We have already seen that the preaching of the atonement is the preaching of Christ crucified—this, better *he*, is the word of the cross. In Calvin's beautiful expression, we preach 'Christ … as he is offered by the Father: namely clothed with his gospel'.[1] We do not offer merely the benefits of Christ's work to the elect; we offer Christ himself to all, the person himself, the Saviour, believing that 'he is able to save to the uttermost those who draw near to God through him' (Heb. 7:25). When we understand that to preach the gospel is to preach Christ as Saviour, not to preach his benefits, then, with the high Calvinist Samuel Rutherford, we are set free in our preaching of the gospel, knowing that even 'reprobates have as fair a warrant to believe in Christ as the elect have'.[2]

In fact, it is this view of the atonement—Pauline, apostolic, Reformed, confessional—that creates confidence in the preaching of the gospel. It is the means by which God brings into his kingdom those whom he gave to his Son before the foundation of the world, and for whom his Son shed his precious and effectual blood.

(ii) The preacher of the gospel

When the gospel is preached in the power of the Holy Spirit, there is a symbiotic relationship between proclamation and preacher, which Paul eloquently describes in his *apologia pro sua vita* in 2 Corinthians 2:14–

[1] Calvin, *Institutes*, III.ii.6.

[2] Samuel Rutherford, *Christ Dying and Drawing Sinners to Himself* (London, 1647), p. 442. For a fine popular statement, see J. I. Packer, *Evangelism and the Sovereignty of God* (Downers Grove, IL: InterVarsity Press, 1961) and also his sturdy introductory essay to Owen, *The Death of Death in the Death of Christ*, pp. 3-25, esp. pp. 15ff.

7:4. Especially in 2 Corinthians 5:11-21, the characteristics of the authentic preacher of the cross can be virtually lifted off the page seriatim.

(a) *The preacher of the cross is marked by the fear of the Lord.* This injects such urgency into the preacher's life that every effort is made to 'persuade others' (2 Cor. 5:11). We do not often regard godly fear as a central motive for evangelistic preaching, but it was clearly one for Paul. His emotions were akin to those of Robert Murray M'Cheyne who wrote in his diary toward the end of a life of only twenty-nine years:

> As I was walking in the fields, the thought came over me with almost overwhelming power, that every one of my flock must soon be in heaven or hell. Oh, how I wished that I had a tongue like thunder, that I might make all hear; or that I had a frame like iron, that I might visit every one, and say, 'Escape for thy life!'[1]

Behind and beyond everyone to whom we preach lurks the shadow of a future judgment before Christ's throne. With such a perspective (no longer *kata sarka*, since 'From now on, therefore, we regard no one according to the flesh', according to 2 Cor. 5:16) the heart is melted with a sense of compassion, and the conscience is gripped by a sense of responsibility.

There is another side to this 'knowing the fear of the Lord' (2 Cor. 5:11), however. For Paul recognized that believers will also be assessed by Christ ('we must all appear before the judgment seat of Christ' [2 Cor. 5:10]). The *fear* here is of a different complexion: filial fear and awe—the fear of disappointing one who has so signally loved us, a fear caused by the knowledge of grace. For the principle on which Christ exercises his judgment on the works, service, witness, and ministry of his people is one of grace as well as absolute integrity.

Jesus illustrates this in his parable of the minas (Luke 19:11-27). To those who have—those who have grace—more will be given (Luke 19:26)! In the parable, one servant is faithful in his stewardship of his master's mina by making ten more. In the judgment he experiences, there is an integral connection between what he has done with what he received and the reward he is given. Having made ten minas, he is

---

[1] *Memoir and Remains of R. M. M'Cheyne*, ed. Andrew A. Bonar (1844; repr. London: Banner of Truth Trust, 1960), p. 148.

put in charge of ten cities. The correlation of service and assessment is expressed numerically.

But what is the relationship between making ten minas (the equivalent of two-and-a-half years' wages) and being made mayor of ten cities? Surely there is disproportion here? What did the servant do to deserve such largesse? But this is the whole point! The reward is a reward of grace, not of inherent merit. This master, whom one servant feared to the point of paralysis, faithlessly describing him as 'a severe man' (Luke 19:20), is in fact generous beyond calculation. Having given his Son for his people, he will stop at nothing to lavish his blessings on them (Rom. 5:10; 8:32). The preacher who has grasped that Christ is thus immeasurably gracious to his people from first to last will soon be driven by a passion to persuade others to trust such a gracious Saviour.

(b) *The preacher of the cross is stripped of a desire for human position or admiration.* A further *bon mot* of James Denney was an adage now inscribed behind many pulpits in his native country of Scotland: 'No man can show at one and the same time that he himself is wise and that Christ is mighty to save.' The only legitimate ambition that can accompany preaching the cross is the desire to live with a clear conscience before God and humanity. Such preachers care little if their commitment is so radical that those whose perspective is *kata sarka* regard them as having lost the place (2 Cor. 5:12-13).

This is what it means to glory in the cross (cf. Gal. 6:14 KJV). For Paul it was a profound reality with implications that ran through the core of his being and gave shape to his entire life. He describes these implications poignantly (notice the significant chiastic structure of his words, expressing the chiastic structure of his experience):

(a^1) We always carry around in our body the *dying* of Jesus,

(b^1) so that the *life* of Jesus may also be revealed in our body.

(b^2) For we who are *living*

(a^2) are always being given over to *death* for Jesus' sake,

(b^3) so that his *life* may be revealed

(a^3) in our *mortal* body.

(a^4) So then, *death* is at work in us,

(b^4) but *life* is at work in you (2 Cor. 4:10-12).

As Paul preaches the cross, God providentially creates a cruciform structure in his life. Of course, he literally bore on his body 'the marks of Jesus' (Gal. 6:17). In that he was distinctive. But the shape of the cross was true of the underlying rhythms of his life: preaching Christ as a cross-bearer meant that he too shared in afflictions, trials, opposition, misunderstandings, privations, loneliness, and rejection—as well as in fruitfulness, joy, and the triumphs of grace. The life of the preacher is *death-and-resurrection* shaped.

If, as Phillips Brooks's definition claims, preaching is (among other things) 'the bringing of truth through personality',[1] then the lives of the preachers of the cross will be marked by the cross: they will be cruciform, themselves 'Christophers'—*Christ-bearers*—in life, and Christ crucified placarders as they try to 'persuade others' (Gal. 3:1; 2 Cor. 5:11).

The preacher of the cross is compelled to preach by the love of Christ (2 Cor. 5:14). Paul's logic here is significant: it is not simply Christ's death, but his death *interpreted as a sacrifice* that grips us ('The love of Christ controls us because we have concluded this: that one has died *for* all, therefore all have died'). The love of Christ crucified as atonement is preached with integrity only by those who have been gripped by that love and left with no choice but to say with Paul, 'Woe to me if I do not preach the gospel!' (1 Cor. 9:16). Paul's point is essentially the one famously expressed by Isaac Watts:

> When I survey the wondrous cross,
>   On which the Prince of glory died,
> My richest gain I count but loss,
>   And pour contempt on all my pride.
>
> Were the whole realm of nature mine,
>   That were an offering far too small;
> Love so amazing, so divine,
>   Demands my life, my soul, my all.

When the preaching of the cross has become the power of God to us personally, and the cross itself the demonstration of God's love for us (Rom. 5:8; Gal. 2:20), an obligation arises to go and preach the gospel to every creature. As John Owen once noted:

---

[1] P. Brooks, *Lectures on Preaching*, p. 5.

A man preacheth that sermon only well unto others which preacheth itself in his own soul. ... If the word do not dwell with power *in* us, it will not pass with power *from* us.[1]

When we are thus gripped and controlled by the love of Christ at the heart of the 'word of the cross', then the aspiration of Charles Wesley will also become our lifelong ambition too:

> Happy, if with my latest breath
> I might but gasp His name;
> Preach Him to all, and cry in death:
> Behold, behold the Lamb![2]

---

[1] Owen, *The True Nature of a Gospel Church*, *Works*, XVI:76.
[2] From Charles Wesley's hymn 'Jesus! The Name High over All'.

CHAPTER THIRTY-SEVEN

PREACHING TO THE HEART

N
O more poignant or instructive description of the work of the minister of the gospel exists than Paul's 'defensive excursus'[1] in 2 Corinthians 2:14–7:4. Every Christian preacher should aim to possess a good working knowledge of this seminal part of the New Testament, in which Paul simultaneously describes and defends his service as an apostle of Jesus Christ and a minister of the new covenant. He uses this language explicitly when he affirms that God 'has made us competent to be ministers of a new covenant' (2 Cor. 3:6). In what follows, he takes us from the outside of his ministry to its deep internal roots:

> Therefore, having this ministry by the mercy of God, we do not lose heart. But we have renounced disgraceful, underhanded ways. We refuse to practise cunning or to tamper with God's word, but by the open statement of the truth we would commend ourselves to everyone's conscience in the sight of God. And even if our gospel is veiled, it is veiled to those who are perishing. In their case the god of this world has blinded the minds of the unbelievers, to keep them from seeing the light of the gospel of the glory of Christ, who is the image of God. For what we proclaim is not ourselves, but Jesus Christ as Lord, with ourselves as your servants for Jesus' sake. For God, who said, 'Let light shine out of darkness,' has shone in our hearts to give the light of the knowledge of the glory of God in the face of Jesus Christ.
>
> But we have this treasure in jars of clay, to show that the surpassing power belongs to God and not to us. We are afflicted in every way,

---

[1] The expression is that of Paul Barnett, *The Second Epistle to the Corinthians* (Grand Rapids: Eerdmans, 1997), p. 210.

but not crushed; perplexed, but not driven to despair; persecuted, but not forsaken; struck down, but not destroyed; always carrying in the body the death of Jesus, so that the life of Jesus may also be manifested in our bodies. For we who live are always being given over to death for Jesus' sake, so that the life of Jesus also may be manifested in our mortal flesh. So death is at work in us, but life in you.

Since we have the same spirit of faith according to what has been written, 'I believed, and so I spoke,' we also believe, and so we also speak, knowing that he who raised the Lord Jesus will raise us also with Jesus and bring us with you into his presence. For it is all for your sake, so that as grace extends to more and more people it may increase thanksgiving, to the glory of God.

So we do not lose heart. Though our outer self is wasting away, our inner self is being renewed day by day. For this light momentary affliction is preparing for us an eternal weight of glory beyond all comparison, as we look not to the things that are seen but to the things that are unseen. For the things that are seen are transient, but the things that are unseen are eternal (2 Cor. 4:1-18).

The title of this chapter is 'Preaching to the Heart'. All truly biblical preaching is preaching to the heart. Therefore, it is important that we have a clear idea of what 'preaching to the heart' means.

The heart

In Scripture, the word *heart* only rarely denotes the physical organ. It characteristically refers to the central core of the individual's being and personality: the deep-seated element of a person that provides both the energy and the drive for all of the faculties (e.g., Deut. 4:9; Matt. 12:34). It denotes the governing centre of life.

Interestingly, of the 858 occurrences of the Hebrew terms that are translated as 'heart' (*leb* and *lebab*) almost all have reference to human beings (in distinction from either God or other creatures). Indeed, 'heart' is the Old Testament's major anthropological term.[1]

---

[1] H. W. Wolff, *Anthropology of the Old Testament*, tr. M. Kohl (London: SCM Press, 1974), pp. 40-55.

Modern Westerners tend to think of the heart as the centre of a person's emotional life (hence its use as the symbol of romantic rather than volitional love). But the Hebrew conceptualization placed the emotional centre lower in the anatomy and located the intellectual energy centre of a person in the heart. Hence, the word *heart* is frequently used as a synonym for the mind, the will, and the conscience, as well as (on occasion) for the affections. It refers to the fundamental bent or characteristic of an individual's life.

In this sense, when we think about speaking or preaching to the heart, we do not have in view directly addressing the emotions as such. In any event, as Jonathan Edwards argued with such force, the mind cannot be so easily bypassed. Rather, we are thinking of preaching that influences the very core and centre of an individual's being, making an impact on the whole person, including the emotions, but doing so primarily by instructing and appealing to the mind. Such a focus is of paramount importance for preachers because the transformation and the renewal of the heart are what is chiefly in view in their proclamation of the gospel (cf. Rom. 12:1-2).

This, in fact, is already implied in Paul's description of himself and his companions as 'sufficient to be ministers of a new covenant' (2 Cor. 3:6). Built into the foundation of the new covenant is the promise of a transformed heart: 'I will sprinkle clean water on you, and you shall be clean from all your uncleannesses, and from all your idols I will cleanse you. And I will give you a new heart ... I will remove the heart of stone from your flesh and give you a heart of flesh' (Ezek. 36:25-26).

No matter what the circumstances under which we preach the word of God, no matter to whom we are speaking, insofar as we too are called to be competent ministers of the new covenant, our preaching must always have the heart in view.

Threefold openness
Paul speaks more fully here about his own preaching ministry than anywhere else in the New Testament. One of the keynotes he strikes is that his preaching to the heart was marked by a threefold openness:

1. It involved an openness of Paul's being, a transparency before God. 'What we are', he says, 'is known to God' (2 Cor. 5:11).

2. It also implied an opening out of the love that filled his heart towards the people to whom he was ministering: 'We have spoken freely to you, Corinthians; our heart is wide open' (2 Cor. 6:11).

3. Within that twofold context—his own heart opened vertically toward God and horizontally toward those to whom he was seeking to minister—Paul's preaching to the heart was also characterized by a disclosing (an opening up) of the truth. He expresses this in an illuminating way when he describes it as 'the open statement of the truth' (2 Cor. 4:2), what the King James Version describes more graphically as 'the manifestation of the truth'.

Thus, just as he is (1) an open book in the sight of God, similarly the preacher (2) lays open the integrity of his life to the consciences and hearts of his hearers as though he were a letter to be read by them (cf. 2 Cor. 3:2). But these characteristics are never isolated from (3) the way in which we handle the Scriptures, opening up and laying bare their message in both exposition and application. The Corinthians had seen these hallmarks in Paul's ministry. They were a large part of the explanation for its power and fruit. They are no less essential to the minister of the gospel today, if he is to preach with similar effect on the hearts of his hearers.

Preaching to the heart, then, is not merely a matter of technique or homiletic style. These things have their proper place and relevance. But the more fundamental, indeed, the more essential, thing for the preacher is surely the fact that something has happened in his own heart; it has been laid bare before God by his word. He, in turn, lays his heart bare before those to whom he ministers. And within that context, the goal he has in view is so to lay bare the truth of the word of God that the hearts of those who hear are opened vertically to God and horizontally to one another.

Paul had reflected on this impact of God's word in 1 Corinthians 14, in the context of his discussion of tongues and prophecy in the Corinthian church. Prophetic utterance always possesses an element of speaking 'to the heart' (Isa. 40:2).[1] Through such preaching, even someone who

---

[1] 'Speak tenderly' (Isa. 40:2 ESV) is, literally, 'speak to (or, upon) the heart' (cf. Gen. 34:3; Hos. 2:14).

comes in from the outside finds that 'the secrets of his heart are disclosed, and so, falling on his face, he will worship God and declare that God is really among you' (1 Cor. 14:24-25).

In the last analysis, this is what preaching to the heart is intended to produce: inner prostration of the hearts of our listeners through a consciousness of the presence and glory of God. This result distinguishes authentic biblical preaching from any cheap substitute; it marks the difference between preaching *about* the word of God and preaching *the* word of God.

The presence of this threefold openness, then, is the *desideratum* in preaching. When there is the exposition of the Scriptures, an enlarging and opening of the preacher's heart, and the exposing of the hearts of the hearers, then the majesty of the word of God *written* will be self-evident and the presence of the Word of God *incarnate* will stand forth in all his glory.

Man small, God great

There is a widespread need for this kind of preaching. We have an equal need as preachers to catch the vision for it in an overly pragmatic and programmatic church culture that believes it is possible to live the Christian life without either the exposing of our own hearts or the accompanying prostration of ourselves before the majesty of God on high.

It is just here that one notices a striking contrast between the biblical exposition one finds in the steady preaching of John Calvin in the sixteenth century and preaching in our own day. It is clearly signalled by the words with which he ended virtually every one of his thousands of sermons: 'And now let us bow down before the majesty of our gracious God. ...' True biblical exposition elevates God and abases man. By contrast, much modern preaching seems to have the goal of making man feel great, even if God himself is made small.

So a leading characteristic of preaching to the heart will be the humbling, indeed, the prostration of hearts before the majesty of God on high. This is simultaneously the true ecstasy of the Christian, and therein lies the paradox of grace: the way up is always the way down.

But if, through the preaching of the gospel, we want to see people prostrated with mingled awe and joy before God, the essential prerequisite is that we ourselves be prostrated before him. John Owen's words still ring true even after three and a half centuries: 'a man preacheth that sermon only well unto others which preacheth itself in his own soul. ... If the word do not dwell with power *in* us, it will not pass with power *from* us.'[1]

Preaching to the heart—through whatever personality, in whatever style—will always exhibit the following characteristics:

1. A right use of the Bible

Preaching to the heart is undergirded by our familiarity with the use of sacred Scripture. According to 2 Timothy 3:16-17, all Scripture is profitable (*ōphelimos*) for certain practical functions: 'for teaching, for reproof, for correction, and for training in righteousness, that the man of God may be competent, equipped for every good work'.

If it were not for the fact that a chapter division appears in our Bibles at this point (giving the impression that Paul is now changing gears in his charge to Timothy), we would not so easily miss the point implicit in what he goes on to say. In 2 Timothy 4:1-2, Paul takes up these same uses of Scripture (teaching, rebuking, correcting, encouraging in godly living) and applies them. In effect, he says to Timothy, 'Use the God-breathed Scriptures this way in your ministry!'

Those who love the richer, older theology of the Reformation and Puritan eras, and of Jonathan Edwards and Thomas Boston, may be tempted to look askance at the modern professor of preaching as he hands out copies of his 'preaching grid' to the incoming class of freshmen taking 'Homiletics 101'. But the fact is that here we find Paul handing out the last copy of his own 'preaching grid' to Timothy! This is by no means the only preaching grid to be found, either in Scripture or in the Reformed tradition,[2] but it certainly is a grid that ought to be built into our basic approach to preaching.

Thus informed, we come to see that preaching to the heart will give expression to four things: instruction in the truth, conviction of the

---

[1] Owen, *Works*, XVI:76.

[2] I am thinking here of our Lord's 'grid' in the parable of the sower and the soils (Mark 4:1-20), and of the seminal work of the early English Puritan William Perkins, *The Arte of Prophecying* (Latin 1592, English 1606).

conscience, restoration and transformation of life,[1] and equipping for service.[2] Let us not think that we have gained so much maturity in Christian living and service that we can bypass the fundamental structures that the apostles give us to help us practically in these areas.

Preaching, therefore, involves *teaching*—imparting doctrine in order to renew and transform the mind. It implies the inevitable rebuke of sin, and brings with it the healing of divine correction. The language of 'correction' (*epanorthōsis*) is used in the Septuagint for the rebuilding of a city or the repair of a sanctuary.[3] Outside of biblical Greek, it is used in the medical textbooks of the ancient world for the setting of broken limbs. It is a word that belongs to the world of reconstruction, remedy, healing, and restoration.

This brings us to another characteristic of the apostle Paul: a masterful balance between the negation of sin and the edification of the Christian believer, 'that the man of God may be competent, equipped for every good work'. If we are going to preach to the heart, then our preaching will always (admittedly in different kinds of balance) be characterized by these four marks of authenticity.

But such preaching must first be directed to the mind. When we preach to the heart, we are not engaged in rebuking the conscience or cleansing the emotions directly. Rather, preaching to the heart addresses the understanding first, in order to instruct it; but in doing so it also reaches through the mind to inform, rebuke, and cleanse the conscience. It then stirs the affections and touches the will in order to reform and transform life and equip the saints for the work of ministry (Eph. 4:12).

When we preach to the heart, the mind is not so much the terminus of our preaching, but the channel through which we appeal to the whole person, leading to the transformation of the whole life.

---

[1] *Epanorthōsis*, 'correction', here carries the positive connotation of 'restoration'.

[2] *Exērtismenos*; the same root (*artizō*) is used of the goal of the ministry of the word in Ephesians 4:12 and of the disciples washing and mending their nets in Mark 1:19.

[3] See C. Spicq, *Theological Lexicon of the New Testament*, 3 vols, tr. and ed. J. D. Ernest (Peabody, MA.: Hendrickson, 1994), II:30-31.

2. *Nourishment of the whole person*

There is an important balance to be pursued here—the balance of ministering to the understanding, affections, and will. It is very easy to lose sight of this. Its significance may perhaps best be underlined by means of a personal illustration.

I once visited a church several times as a guest preacher. During this period (and with no connection between these events!), the pastor of the church received and accepted a call to serve elsewhere. Friends whom I made during these occasional visits confided in me some time after the departure of their pastor (to whom they were extremely loyal): 'As we have sought to assess the impact of these last years of ministry on our lives, we have come to this conclusion: while we were thoroughly well instructed, we were poorly nourished.'

There is a difference between a well-instructed congregation and a well-nourished one. It is possible to instruct, yet fail to nourish those to whom we preach. It is possible to address the mind, but to do so with little concern to see the conscience, the heart, and the affections reached and cleansed, the will redirected, and the whole person transformed through a renewed mind. By contrast, in the picture of preaching first painted for Timothy, Paul is teaching us how to preach to the heart in a way that will nourish the whole person.

One of the characteristics of such preaching is pathos, the stimulation in us of a sense of sadness, even broken-heartedness. Pathos is not mere emotion for its own sake, certainly not the kind of emotionalism that tends to descend into an insincere expressiveness. In preaching, it is, rather, the communication and evoking through our words of the responsive 'mood' appropriate to sinners listening to the gospel being preached. In this way, our hearers become aware of the power of the truths we are preaching about human sin, divine grace, and glory.

The great Welsh preacher Dr D. Martyn Lloyd-Jones once made a fascinating and illuminating (to me, at least) self-critical comment on what he felt had been a weakness of his own preaching ministry. He thought it had lacked in at least one particular aspect—pathos.[1]

[1] D. M. Lloyd-Jones, *Preaching and Preachers* (London: Hodder & Stoughton, 1971), p. 92.

Christians of an earlier time sometimes spoke of sermons as 'pathetic'. We, of course, would not cross the street to hear preaching if it was 'pathetic' in the modern sense of the word! But our forefathers meant something quite different by this expression, namely, preaching that leaves its hearers with melted hearts. The preaching that does this comes from a similarly broken and melted heart that already has placed itself under this fourfold applicatory grid of Scripture: the preaching heart has been instructed by the truth of Scripture; the conscience rebuked by the holiness of Scripture; and the spirit nourished by the correction, healing, and restorative power of Scripture, so that the man of God, the preacher, is competent, equipped to relay God's word from his own heart to our hearts.

3. An understanding of the condition of the hearers

Preaching to the heart always reflects an awareness of the actual condition of our hearers. In one form or another, most preaching manuals underscore this point. The preacher emerges from the world of the biblical text to speak in the name of Christ to the world of his hearers.

One of the hidden snares in systematic biblical preaching is that we may become so taken up with the task of studying and explaining the text that we forget it addresses the contemporary world. One distinctively Reformed manifestation of this is that our love for the works of the past (coupled with their ready availability today)—our discovery, for example, of the depth of Puritan preaching by comparison with contemporary preaching—may suck us into the very language and speech patterns of a past era, thus making us sound inauthentic to our own generation.

By contrast, preaching to the heart will not be encrusted with layers of ill-digested materials from the past, however relevant these were in their own day. Those preaching helps must rather be thoroughly digested, made our own, and applied to people today in contemporary language. That is what it means to bring the truth to bear upon men, women, boys, and girls in such a way that it opens up and penetrates their hearts.

In this sense, biblical exposition must speak to the people sitting today in the pews, not to those who sat in them hundreds of years ago. This, in fact, is one of the cardinal principles expounded by William

Perkins in his great work *The Arte of Prophecying* (*sic*), the original Puritan manual on preaching. Perkins argues that we have to understand the *soul-condition* of those to whom we preach, and address them in an appropriate and relevant way.

We always preach to people in a variety of spiritual conditions. Perkins realized that if he was going to touch people with the truth of the gospel, then he must—always in a manner consistent with the gospel—explain and apply his text. Only then would it serve as a sharp instrument that the Holy Spirit, the divine surgeon, might use to cut open the hearts of the people and bring healing to their diseased spirits. In that sense, the way we explain the Scriptures can never be abstracted from the characteristics, personality, and maturity level of those to whom we preach.

Perkins's own grid is inherently interesting and valuable, if one employs it in a way that makes it genuinely one's own. He suggests that preaching should be shaped to seven categories of hearers:

- Non-Christians who know nothing about the gospel and have unteachable spirits.

- Non-Christians who know nothing about the gospel but who are teachable.

- Those who know what the gospel is but who have never been humbled to see their need of a Saviour.

- Those who have been humbled, some of whom are in the early stages of seeing their need, and others who see that they need salvation.

- Genuine believers who need to be taught.

- Backsliders, either because of a failure to understand the gospel clearly or a failure to live consistently with it.

- Congregations made up of both believers and unbelievers.

As Perkins acknowledged, most preachers will serve mixed congregations. In other words, they will generally preach simultaneously to all seven types of hearers.[1]

[1] Perkins, *The Arte of Prophecying*, in *The Works of William Perkins* (London, 1617), II:665-68. For an edited and modernized version, see *The Art of Prophesying*, ed. Sinclair B. Ferguson (Edinburgh: Banner of Truth Trust, 1996), pp. 56-63.

But we do not need to appeal to the Puritans for the authority to operate with this type of 'preaching grid'; our Lord Jesus did so himself. On at least one occasion, he divided his hearers into four categories and likened them to different kinds of soil distinguished by their receptivity to the seed of the gospel: the hard-packed soil of the pathway, the rocky soil, the weed-infested soil, and the good soil (Mark 4:1-20).

It would make a fascinating academic study of the ministry of Jesus to take this parable of the sower, the seed, and the soils as a lens through which to examine, categorize, and analyse his preaching. For preachers, too, it is a fruitful exercise to consider the ways in which he applied his message to the four spiritual conditions to which he saw himself speaking.

Is it because expository preaching is such a demanding activity, and we are so consumed by its demands, that some of us pay so little attention (or at least too little attention) to the spiritual condition of those to whom we are preaching? If so, we need to reconsider our approach.

If it is important that we know the condition of the hearts of our hearers, the best place to begin is, of course, with our own hearts. If we apply the word there, we soon will learn to be like surgical attendants: our exposition of the text will become like sterilized knives, perfectly tooled, that we hand to the Spirit for the precise spiritual surgery that our people need.

A further feature that characterized our Lord Jesus' preaching was that 'the common people heard him gladly' (Mark 12:37 KJV). We ought not to dismiss this with the cheap comment that they soon changed their tune. They immediately and instinctively recognized the difference between the book-learning and authority-citing style of the scribes and the applied biblical wisdom and heart knowledge displayed in Jesus' preaching. The scribes and teachers of the law spoke about the Bible in a manner removed from daily experience. Jesus, in stark contrast, seemed to speak from inside the Bible in a way that addressed their hearts.

Sadly, some of our preaching carries with it the atmosphere of being 'about the Bible' rather than conveying a sense that here the Bible is speaking, and indeed God himself is speaking. This will be changed only when we come to Scripture in the spirit of the Servant of the Lord:

'The Lord GOD has given me the tongue of those who are taught, that I may know how to sustain with a word him who is weary. Morning by morning he awakens; he awakens my ear to hear as those who are taught. The Lord GOD has opened my ear, and I was not rebellious; I turned not backward' (Isa. 50:4-5).

4. The use of the imagination

Preaching to the heart is aided by our recognition of the true nature of our task. The great question is: How, through the work of the Spirit, can I best get the word of God into the hearts of the people?

Those who do this with the greatest fruitfulness and success are marked by many gifts and characteristics, often very diverse. But one thing all of them seem to have in common is imagination—an imaginative creativity that bridges the distance between the truth of the word of God and the lives of those to whom they speak.

In some preachers, this is most evident in the imaginative power of their illustrations. George Whitefield's use of illustrations was sometimes so vivid that people thought they were actually caught up in the events he was describing, confusing what they were hearing with reality. By contrast, the congregation of St Peter's Church in Geneva listened to John Calvin preach an average of five forty-minute sermons a week during the course of his lengthy ministry, but with virtually no stories or illustrations of that kind.

Like most of us, Calvin did not possess Whitefield's imaginative power (or his magical voice). Nevertheless, his sermons *lived* and had the power to stir young men to be willing to suffer martyrdom for Christ, for Calvin had an ability to use language with such imaginative power that his preaching bridged the gap between life in ancient Judah and Israel and life in sixteenth-century Geneva, Switzerland. He expressed and applied the truth in a way that was saturated in the language of the daily life of his hearers, bringing the word of God right into the nitty-gritty practicalities of their experience.

Similarly, Richard Baxter preached in such a way that his sermons so connected with life in seventeenth-century Kidderminster, England, that the truth he spoke exploded during the week like time bombs planted in his congregation's memories.

The Spirit is able to use different sets of imaginative skills employed in different contexts but producing similar effects. But clearly the ability to imagine the word being taken from the Scriptures and implanted into the minds of the hearers is common to all lively exposition.

Scripture itself employs different metaphors to help us grasp how important it is to 'see ourselves into' the hearts and situations of those to whom we preach. Here are some drawn simply at random: the preacher is a sower of seed; a teacher of students; a father of children; a mother giving birth; a nurse feeding infants; a shepherd caring for his flock; a soldier engaging in warfare; and a builder constructing the temple of God.

We need only to think of ourselves in terms of these metaphors to see what is involved in bringing the word of God to bear upon the hearts and consciences of those to whom we are preaching. What does a farmer do? He ploughs the ground and sows the seed, then prayerfully waits for the fruition of his work. What does a builder do? He clears a building site and erects the building. What does a shepherd do? He feeds and protects his flock. How, then, can I get the seed into this soil? How can I clear the site and chisel this stone into shape? How can I prepare this meal for these people?

In these different ways, we come to recognize what it means to be a preacher. Our own imagination is fired and we begin to learn how to preach to the heart.

5. Grace in Christ

The fifth key to fruitful preaching to the heart is the preacher's own grasp of the principle and the reality of grace. This needs to be set within the multifaceted context of a growing familiarity with the uses of sacred Scripture, an awareness of the actual condition of our hearers, and a conscious recognition of the preacher's task. But always the melody line of preaching to the heart lies in our own grasp of the principle of grace. That is what makes preaching 'sing', and it applies to two aspects of our preaching.

(i) First, it applies to the content of our preaching.
Only the preaching of grace can open the sinful heart. Unaided law, imperatives without indicatives, cannot pry open locked hearts. It is grace, and, yes—the preaching of the law in the context of grace, expounding the grace of law—that brings conviction of sin. This is the very point John Newton so famously made in the best-known of his Olney Hymns, 'Amazing Grace!':

> 'Twas grace that taught my heart to fear,
> And grace my fears relieved.

Paul stressed this to the Corinthians. The heart and soul of his ministry was this commitment: 'For I decided to know nothing among you except Jesus Christ and him crucified' (1 Cor. 2:2). Through such preaching, there was a *phanerōsis*, an open statement ('a manifestation' [2 Cor. 4:2]) of the truth, a making known of what Paul calls 'the light of the gospel of the glory of Christ, who is the image of God' (2 Cor. 4:4). For when 'Jesus Christ as Lord' is thus manifested in preaching, God again shines 'in our hearts to give the light of the knowledge of the glory of God in the face of Jesus Christ' (2 Cor. 4:6).

A caveat is in order here, which is particularly relevant to a time like our own when the ancient patristic and Reformation style of consecutive exposition (the *lectio continua* method) has undergone something of a revival. We must never make the mistake of thinking that any system of consecutive exposition of Scripture absolutely guarantees the preaching of Christ. It is possible to naively assume that because we are preaching systematically through books of the Bible, we are inevitably preaching Christ and him crucified. That *ought* to be the case, but it is *not necessarily* so. Sadly, one may preach in a consecutive way through the Bible without truly preaching Christ-centred sermons.

In addition, we may major on the theme of grace in a way that is disconnected from Christ himself, treating it as a commodity and losing sight of the fact that it can be found only through a person.

There is a centre to the Bible and its message of grace. It is found in Jesus Christ crucified and resurrected. Grace, therefore, must be preached in a way that is centred and focused on Jesus Christ himself. We must never offer the benefits of the gospel without the Benefactor himself. For many preachers, however, it is much easier to deal with the pragmatic things, to answer 'how to' questions, and even to expose and denounce sin than it is to give an adequate explanation of the source of the forgiveness, acceptance, and power we need.

It is a disheartening fact that evangelical Christians, who write vast numbers of Christian books, preach abundant sermons, sponsor numerous conferences and seminars, and broadcast myriad TV and radio programmes, actually write few books, preach few sermons, sponsor few conferences or seminars, and devote few programmes to the theme of Jesus Christ and him crucified. We give our best and most creative energies to teaching God's people almost everything except the person and work of our Lord and Saviour. This should cause us considerable alarm, for there is reason to fear that our failure here has reached epidemic proportions.

We need to return to a true preaching to the heart, rooted in the principle of grace and focused on the person of the Lord Jesus Christ. Then people will not say about our ministry merely, 'He was an expository preacher', or 'That was practical', or even 'He cut open our consciences.' Instead they will say: 'He preached Christ to me, and his preaching was directed to my conscience. It was evident that he gave the best of his intellectual skills and the warmth of his compassion to thinking about, living for, and proclaiming his beloved Saviour, Jesus Christ.' This is what will reach the heart! And when you have experienced such preaching, or seen its fruit, you will know what true preaching is. And you will agree that its fruit lasts for all eternity.

(ii) Second, this principle of grace in Christ applies to the manner of our preaching.

Even today, long after their death, when we read the memoirs or the sermons of preachers such as Robert Murray M'Cheyne, we can still feel the power that must have gripped people as their preaching reached into their hearts. While Robert M'Cheyne lay dying, a letter of gratitude for what turned out to be the last sermon he ever preached reached him. It was left unopened on his desk, and he never read the words of a grateful listener who commented, 'It was not so much what you said *as your manner of speaking* that struck me. I saw in you a beauty in holiness that

I never saw before.'[1] This is a major key to reaching the heart. For while preaching involves bringing the world of the Bible to bear upon the world of our contemporaries, it also involves bringing the message-in-words of the Scriptures through the message-in-manner of the preacher.

There needs to be a marriage between the message and the manner; therein lies the heart of the mystery of preaching. As our hearts are opened wide to the grace of God in the gospel, and simultaneously opened wide to our hearers, the power of the gospel is set on display (see 2 Cor. 6:11). Paul expresses this memorably in 2 Corinthians 4:5: 'For what we proclaim is not ourselves, but Jesus Christ as Lord.' But there is a corollary to this: '… with ourselves as your servants for Jesus' sake.' The evidence that I preach Jesus Christ as Lord is found not so much in my declarations as it is in the manifestation of the lordship of Christ in my life and preaching—when I, his bondslave, am willing to be and actually become in my preaching the bondslave of others for Jesus' sake.

In the last analysis, preaching to the heart is preaching Christ in a way that reminds people of Christ, but also manifests Christ to them, and draws them to him. If, among other things, preaching is (as Phillips Brooks's famous description claims) 'the bringing of truth through personality',[2] then the personalities of the preachers of the cross must be marked by the cross. So we are called to be cruciformed (shaped by the cross), 'Christophers' (bearing the Christ of the cross), and Christ-placarders (setting Christ and him crucified on display, cf. Gal. 3:1) in our preaching as we 'persuade others' (2 Cor. 5:11).

Perhaps such preaching of Christ is less common than we assume. If so, it is because we do not yet know him nearly well enough.

Let us then resolve, above all other ambitions, to know him, the power of his resurrection, and the fellowship of his sufferings (Phil. 3:10). Let us also decide to know nothing except Jesus Christ and him crucified (1 Cor. 2:2), so that, as we preach to the heart, God himself will speak to his people heart to heart.

---

[1] Alexander Smellie, *Robert Murray M'Cheyne* (London: National Council of Free Evangelical Churches, 1913), pp. 203-4 (emphasis added).

[2] P. Brooks, *Lectures on Preaching*, p. 5.

CHAPTER THIRTY-EIGHT

PREACHING AND THE REFORMED THEOLOGICAL TRADITION

I F we were to date the Reformed tradition somewhat arbitrarily from the first edition of Calvin's *Institutio* in 1536, it covers almost 500 years of history. If we then viewed it in terms of theological output, it would require entire library buildings to hold the research material, and if we thought of it geographically, we would find ourselves roving from one side of the planet to the other.

Given that breadth, it is natural that the phrase 'the Reformed theological tradition' is itself open to more than one nuance, and one would need to recognize that these words might well mean somewhat different things to different people. It may therefore be helpful if we revisit that tradition nearer rather than further away from its origin. Indeed, the further away one moves from the origin the more doubtful becomes the use of the definite article and the singular noun.

This brief study will limit itself to two major aspects of the topic. First, those elements of Reformed theology which have formed the foundation and have been the theological engine that has driven Reformed preaching. Second, the homiletical principles this has produced in the preaching of the Reformed churches.

I. Principal theological convictions

When we think of the best Reformed preaching we are reminded of James Denney's oft-cited *bon mot* that he had no interest in a theology that could not be preached. It is certainly one of the hallmarks of the Reformed tradition that many of its best theologians have also had a passion for preaching and been preachers of note. That tradition began, of course, with Calvin himself, and has continued in an almost unbroken line of descent ever since. But it is also true that a characteristic of Reformed preaching has been its conviction that all true theology is for all of the people of God, since every Christian believer is a theologian. Thus Reformed preaching, perhaps more than any other, has—or ought to have—a tendency to range over the whole corpus of Christian theology. Within that broad corpus, however, several key *loci* stand out as essential even to a brief summary of the theology which undergirds the Reformed preaching tradition.

1. The role of theology proper
Fundamental to Reformed preaching is the reality of the Trinity, and the revelation of the character of God.

The heart and goal of preaching is the knowledge of God. Calvin makes that clear in the famous opening words of his *Institutes*. These had a deep lineage traceable back to Clement of Alexandria and Augustine, and they remained relatively little changed through all the revisions Calvin made of his great work: 'Nearly all the wisdom we possess, that is to say true and sound wisdom, consists of these two things: the knowledge of God and of ourselves.'[1] It is against that background that, for all the developments in the *Institutio* from 1536 until 1559, as Calvin's knowledge of the history of theology increased, and as the powerful impact of Romans more and more influenced his thought patterns, its fundamental trinitarian structure remained constant.

Why was this so important for preaching? Because the trinitarian God is an inwardly communing and communicating God, even before all worlds. And whatever is, actually is because this communicating God reaches out from within his threefold communion to communicate beyond himself. For Calvin, he does this by speaking his word at creation, by sending the Word in redemption, by expressing his word in the Scriptures and having that word expounded in the assembly of his people, the church. In each case, whatever the Father speaks through his Word, the Holy Spirit accompanies in an executive capacity, applying and bringing to consummation the divine purpose. *Opera ad extra*

---

[1] Calvin, *Institutes*, I.i.i.

trinitatis sunt indivisa: the external activities of the Trinity engage each person of the Trinity. For the Reformed fathers, then, preaching exists, and makes sense, only within this matrix of the reality of the Trinity. One of the most obvious effects of this is the extent to which Reformed preaching has been marked by a sense of the majesty and tenderness, glory and love of God, and has been redolent with a sense of Trinity. Reformed preaching, as Aquinas wrote about theology generally, *a Deo docetur, Deum docet, ad Deum ducit*—is taught by God, teaches God, and leads us to God. No more than Luther was Calvin prepared to tolerate Erasmus' God who was 'too man-like'.

This, it might be said, stands as a healthy corrective to some modern preaching which washes ashore on the church as a spent wave from the ocean of the Reformed tradition and speaks chiefly about man and society exclusively from a horizontal, non-revelational perspective. In this connection one of those remarks of Karl Barth that one wished one had first thought up oneself is *à propos*: speaking of the theology of Schleiermacher he noted that one cannot say God by shouting 'Man' with a loud voice. We must begin with God and see everything in the light of his triune being. All the springs of our world-and-life view must find not only their origin but their centre in him.

Without this, preaching is destined to suffer from what David Wells has shrewdly called the 'weightlessness' of God in the church in the West.[1]

Reformed theology, and therefore Reformed preaching, by contrast, is marked by a sense of the weight of the glory of God. It gives rise to what John Newton, who stood in a centrist Anglican way in the Reformed tradition, calls 'solid joys'. It is not entirely tongue in cheek that we may say that in the Reformed tradition the ultimate joy of communion with God the Trinity is too substantial a business to smile about!

Be that as it may, a second element needs to be added to this emphasis on the doctrine of God.

---

[1] D. F. Wells, *God in the Wasteland* (Grand Rapids: Eerdmans, 1994), pp. 88-117.

2. The significance of anthropology

In Reformed theology a major role has been given to the doctrine of the *imago Dei*.

It is often claimed today by biblical theologians that systematic theology has built a mountain out of a molehill at this point, in view of the paucity of explicit references to the image of God in Scripture. But perhaps it may be said by way of defence that in fact the idea is much more pervasive in the Bible itself than the mere statistics of the *terminus technicus* might suggest, informing Christology as much as anthropology.

But why should this doctrine be important for Reformed preaching? Because it suggests that God has created man as an appropriate receptor of his personal revelation in creation, history, and inscripturation. God may be *totaliter aliter* to use the technical jargon—'wholly other'—but man is not *totaliter aliter*. Rather he has been made like God, for God, to experience communion with God, and communication from him. He is a rational personal being; like God, but not God. Therefore both the mode of revelation of the Scriptures and the mode of their exposition in preaching are coherent vehicles for the true knowledge of God.

Ultimately, this principle of the *imago Dei* would become part of Reformed theology's response to the Kantian dilemma that the phenomenal can never disclose the noumenal, and that we cannot penetrate beyond the phenomenal to true knowledge of the noumenal without that knowledge exploding into a cloud of contradiction. But not only so, for, of course, Reformed theology recognized that there is a sting in the anthropological tail: *sin*. Even in the fallen condition of humanity the *imago Dei* persists, but—and this is true however the concept is defined—in an alienated and perverted fashion. In terms of the older faculty psychology employed by earlier theologians, the understanding is distorted, the heart perverted, the will crippled. Reformed theology at this point grasped the implication of Jesus' words that if the light in us is darkness, how great that darkness must be! Sin, within this theology, was not seen as an aberration in contemporary man, but a revelation of his true condition. Furthermore, this situation is not only bad for man, but dangerous for him, because it is a condition of moral perversity for which he is responsible. It evokes the crisis of the judgment of God and issues of eschatological magnitude. This injected a note of apostolic urgency into Reformed preaching.

Reformed theology saw the implications of this for preaching in two ways, recognizing that: (a) it underlined the necessity of preaching as a central means of communicating God's truth, because the Scriptures supplied the spectacles which clarified vision, and (b) paradoxically, that preaching, handing the spectacles to sinners (i.e., in the preaching of the gospel), was total folly because they were spiritually dead and blind. This is why a third locus of theology became so essential to preaching:

3. The vital importance of soteriology
The Christological must always undergird the soteriological or our understanding of the application of the gospel will go to seed. It is sometimes said that the Reformed theological tradition has contributed nothing to Christology. But in one or two significant ways, Calvin brought to a new level of self-consistency the church's understanding. That is true of his exposition of the unoriginated deity of the Son, with respect to the formulation of the doctrine of the Trinity. It can also be argued that in his *Harmony of the Gospels* Calvin gave the church its finest, most theologically consistent and exegetically sensitive exposition of the humanity of Christ. Interestingly these emphases, not least the stress on the true and full humanity of Christ, found important exposition in the preaching of the next century, although that has been much obscured.

In Reformed theology in general, then, and in Calvin in particular, the Christological and the soteriological are correlative. Or, more fundamentally, the Christological and the Pneumatological—the Saviour and the Spirit—are. It is fitting, therefore, that being so closely associated with the exposition of the three-fold office of Christ, Calvin should also be worthy of the title bestowed on him by B. B. Warfield: 'The theologian of the Holy Spirit'.

Calvin opens Book III of the *Institutes* with the striking statement:

> First, we must understand that as long as Christ remains outside of us, and we are separated from him, all that he has suffered and done for the salvation of the human race remains useless and of no value to us.[1]

[1] Calvin, *Institutes*, III.i.i.

The 'in Christ' must go hand in glove with the 'Christ for us'. The role of the Holy Spirit, therefore, is to get us out of ourselves and into Christ. The manner in which he does this involves both the mystery of regeneration and the reality of the response of intelligent individuals as through the Spirit they are convicted of sin, illuminated with respect to Christ, and regenerated by the Spirit working through the word.

There is no avoiding the fact that Calvin himself asked 'how' questions just at this very juncture. It is not our purpose here to enter into the ongoing debate about the relationship between Calvin and his successors in the formulation of the application of redemption and the issue of the so-called *ordo salutis*. Suffice it to say that the problem here lies not with the question of whether there is an *ordo salutis* or not, but with the model we employ to formulate it. For myself I believe we are safer with the 'in Christ model' of the New Testament than the golden chain model which tends to be associated with the names of Beza and Perkins, although both of them held it together in a more Christocentric way than was often true later in the Reformed tradition.[1]

Calvin's own theology thrust upon him as a pastoral theologian the question: By what means am I to bring those who are outside of Christ into Christ, and those who are in Christ to realize all that this may mean for them? A full answer to that question is not to be found so much in his *Institutes* or commentaries as it is in his sermons.[2]

How, then, did this Calvinian theological undergirding feed into the preaching which came to characterize the Reformed churches and answer such questions?

II. Principal homiletical methods

What Reformed theology highlighted was that the basic need of humanity is for communication from God; since this has been given in Christ and is recorded in the Scriptures, in practical terms the greatest need of all—while not denying other needs—is for the exposition of the

[1] Cf. Sinclair B. Ferguson, *The Holy Spirit* (Leicester: IVP, 1996), pp. 93-113.

[2] Ronald S. Wallace's extended catena of materials remains an excellent starting place for pursuing such a study. See his *Calvin's Doctrine of the Christian Life* (Edinburgh: Oliver & Boyd, 1959), *passim*.

Scriptures. A hallmark of the Reformed churches, therefore, has been the centrality of biblical exposition. That has taken different forms and it is salutary to notice some of them.

1. *Approaches to preaching*

(i) *Calvin's method*

Calvin, as is well known, returned to the practice of some of the great Fathers such as Augustine and Chrysostom, and encouraged in Geneva constant public exposition, at times himself preaching typically between four and seven times in the week. At the peak of his ministry, from his early forties to fifties, he preached from the Old Testament several days during the week, the New Testament on Sunday mornings, and Psalms on Sunday afternoons. Thus, for example, on weekdays from 1552 until 1561 he preached 174 sermons on Ezekiel, 159 on Job, 300 on Deuteronomy, 352 on Isaiah—all around 35-40 minutes in length.

That formula, systematic expository preaching, became the bedrock pattern of the Reformed homiletical tradition. Paradoxically in the present day when preaching is very much at a discount both outside and increasingly inside the church, it is probably practised in more pulpits worldwide than at any previous time in the history of the church. But it is by no means the only formula the Reformed tradition has employed with fruitful results.

(ii) *The 'Ordinary'*

Alongside this, certainly throughout the sevententh and eighteenth centuries, we find the widespread use of the so-called 'ordinary'—a text or passage of Scripture which would be expounded not only in detail, but in terms of its manifold connections with a whole range of biblical and doctrinal motifs and themes. Thomas Boston, some of whose unpublished manuscript sermons are held in the archives of King's College,[1] serves as an outstanding example.

---

[1] This lecture was delivered at King's College, the University of Aberdeen.

(iii) Catechetical preaching

Particularly in the continental Reformed churches, under the influence of the deeply engaging experimental character of the Heidelberg Catechism, a third style of preaching developed, and was frequently employed in tandem with the first two: catechetical preaching. In this way, often at the second service on Sundays, congregations were given—following the model of Calvin's understanding of the relationship between his *Institutes* and his *Commentaries*—a framework of reference in which to grasp, frame, and retain the expository teaching they received at other times. In many ways the employment of a lectionary served a similar function.

Perhaps it should be said here, as an aside, that something of this order is probably greatly needed in our own age, in order to encourage Christians to develop a genuinely coherent framework of thought and, indeed, to help them have the necessary mental Velcro®-strips upon which what they hear in preaching will stick. Most Christians today are far less familiar than their forefathers with the Christian faith as a coherent world-and-life view. The value of the catechism and of preaching on it lay in large measure in the unity of thought it provided, and in the ability it created to ask the right questions of both Scripture and the world.

It would be foolish to argue that any of these formulae guaranteed a faithful exposition of the text of Scripture. We will return later to an important caveat that was developed to meet this problem. But for the moment, we should notice that two things drove this emphasis on ongoing, cumulative, biblical exposition.

The first was the conviction that the gospel is truth, and that it is by addressing truth to the mind that the Spirit works to illumine our darkened understanding. Reformed theology always kept returning to the model of the apostles who reasoned out of the Scriptures in contexts where the Scriptures were available and known. As is well known, the magisterial Reformers fought battles on two fronts in order to maintain this word and Spirit/Spirit and word principle: on the one hand, against Rome's obscuring of the word and replacing the Spirit's ministry of uniting us to Christ by the virtually *ex opere operato* nature of the sacraments; on the other hand, against the so-called 'Spirituals' who, as Calvin said, could scarcely utter a couple of sentences without referring to their knowledge of the Spirit's leading—in a way that was divorced from, or above, the word. No, argued Calvin, since the Spirit is the author of the word, he is consistent with himself when he speaks through the word.

The second was that in this act of preaching, the Spirit operated in sovereign and indeed mysterious ways in order to individualize the exposition. The response of the Reformed tradition to the contemporary horror with preaching as an extended monologue would have been to draw attention to their conviction that preaching is always dialogical. In and through it, God speaks to the soul, and the soul responds to, struggles with, resists, submits to, trusts in, or rejects the word of the Lord. Every sermon is an internal, personal, Jacob-like wrestling with the messenger of God at the Wadi Jabbok. Nothing, then, is more characteristic of the Reformed view of preaching than this: it is an event, a divine–human encounter. That principle, incidentally, influenced not only the content but also the length of sermons which was *de rigueur* in the past. Those who experienced such encounters of the soul with God wanted them to be relatively extensive for other reasons than the lack of alternative entertainment!

This brings us to the question of *method*, which is one of the most interesting of the many features we could discuss: on what homiletical principles was the Reformed tradition of preaching crafted? Again we must, of necessity, be selective here and limit ourselves to two examples:

2. Calvin

We have noticed that Calvin's basic approach was that of systematic exposition through entire books, expounding them section by section.

This principle he famously illustrated on his return from his Genevan banishment when he simply picked up the exposition where he had left off more than three years earlier. But there was more to Calvin's expository preaching than the consecutive principle, and since there has been a renaissance of consecutive preaching in our own day it is important to underline it. Calvin's whole approach was governed by his understanding of 2 Timothy 3:14–4:2.

(i) The function of Scripture is to make us wise for salvation through faith in Christ Jesus. He never tired of emphasizing that Christ is its *scopus*. This implied, along the lines of Luke 24:27, 44, that since all Scripture led to Christ, all preaching should bring us to Christ. That was by no means guaranteed by the simple expedient of preaching on consecutive passages, but only by properly expounding each particular passage within the context of the flow of redemptive history, and by seeing the person and ministry of Christ as the fulcrum around which all Scripture and ultimately every sermon must move. Consequently preaching must be *both* Christ-centred and Christ-full.

(ii) But in addition to this, Calvin's preaching is evidently shaped by the statements which follow where the usefulness of Scripture is stressed. Second Timothy 3:16 stresses not only the basic *theopneustic* character of Scripture, but also—to coin an expression on the basis of the biblical term here—its *ophelimostic* nature, its practical usefulness.

Paul's contention is that all Scripture is useful for teaching, reproving or convicting, correcting and restoring, and training in righteousness. Here the traditional chapter divisions fail us because they obscure the interconnectedness between these words and the exhortation which follows which, essentially, says: 'Since this is what Scripture is for, let it fulfil its proper task in your preaching of the word in season and out of season.' The imperative to Timothy to 'reprove, rebuke, and exhort, with complete patience and teaching' (2 Tim. 4:2) is rooted in the indicative of the statement already made in 3:16 about the actual nature and function of Scripture.

Calvin himself did this—as those who have read any of his sermons realize—by means of a running exposition of the text which gave rise in various ways to underlining doctrine, rebukes to the conscience, points of encouragement, and correction in the restorative sense in which the term is used in 2 Timothy 3:16. To a remarkable degree he sought to marry together the form and content of the passage on which he was preaching within a twofold biblical preaching grid which underlined that Christ is the destination of every sermon, and that teaching, reproving, transforming, and equipping are its effects. Earnestness, sharpness, force, and power are the terms he uses to describe what is needed in addition to the act of speaking and teaching.

What is particularly impressive about Calvin's preaching is that it was Calvin's own. The basic model fits a variety of personality. Calvin fitted *himself* into it, exemplifying Phillips Brooks's (1835–93) later motto that preaching is *truth through personality*. All really great preachers, indeed all great communicators, have been men of imagination, in the sense that they have been able to get themselves into the world of their hearers and express their message accordingly. Thus, the last thing Calvin seems to have been—unlike his German counterpart Luther!—was a good storyteller.[1] But he was an extraordinarily shrewd observer with his own imaginative powers. And these he used constantly to draw his hearers into the fact that this ancient text from God impacted day-to-day life in sixteenth-century Geneva. Patient reading of his sermons, especially out loud, will quickly confirm that point. Random sampling will underline the vividness of his language. Casually opening his sermons on 2 Timothy at Sermon 25 (yes, 25!), for example, we are told: 'the world holds us back, and we are tied here by the teeth, as it were'. It was not only Luther whose language touched the senses of his hearers. The fact that so many young people were prepared to become martyrs for Christ after sitting under his ministry speaks volumes for its power and effect.

Calvin's approach has remained a constant feature of the Reformed tradition, but I think it would be accurate to say that while its substance has continued its form has undergone important reconstruction, and did so within fifty years of his death. Let me turn, therefore, to say something about the development of what came to be known as 'the plain style'.

3. *The plain style*

The description is virtually self-explanatory. The so-called 'plain-style' preaching began where Calvin left off. It was developed in sharp contrast to 'witty' preaching which employed the fashions and devices of human eloquence and classical oratory. It sought to conform to the apostolic formula of preaching marked by great 'plainness of speech' (2 Cor. 3:12 KJV). Unfolding and applying the text of Scripture in a straightforward and simple, yet vigorous and direct style of speech and manner were its hallmarks.

[1] By way of contrast with Luther, we have no *Table Talk* from Calvin!

This should not be misunderstood. Plain-style preaching was not lacking in wit or in the powerful use of the imagination or appropriate illustration.[1] But the employment of these was always aimed at the mind in order to affect the conscience, and not merely to impress and delight aesthetic taste by clever oratory or a display of education and learning. In the plain style, spiritual taste was everything; only those who possessed it appreciated the 'pure spiritual milk' of biblical teaching.

William Perkins

The development of the plain style is usually associated with the name of William Perkins, who exercised an enormously influential ministry in Cambridge during the last quarter of the sixteenth century.

Concern for biblical preaching of the gospel was not innate in William Perkins. While himself a student at Christ's College he was far from Christ and seems to have dabbled in the occult as well as in the fruit of the vine. According to tradition Perkins's awakening took place when he overheard a woman threatening her son, 'Hold your tongue, or I will give you to drunken Perkins yonder.' Converted, he began to preach, first to condemned prisoners in the castle jail. Later he would exercise his considerable gifts from the pulpit of Great St Andrews, where he continued to minister until his death.

The impact of Perkins's ministry was remarkable. When the young John Cotton heard the church bell tolling for Perkins's death he inwardly celebrated because now his conscience would no longer be smitten by the preacher's sermons! Ten years or so later when the twelve-year-old Thomas Goodwin came up to Cambridge in 1613, 'the town was then filled with the discourse of the power of Mr Perkins's ministry, still fresh in most men's memories'.[2]

---

[1] See, for example, R. B. Jenkins, *Henry Smith, England's Silver-Tongued Preacher* (Macon, GA: Mercer University Press, 1983). Smith (*c.* 1560–93) who was profoundly influenced by the major early Puritan figure Richard Greenham of Dry Dayton, was one of the most popular Puritan preachers of the Elizabethan period. Yet Jenkins's title accurately reflects the quality of his rhetoric, albeit placed in tribute to the message he preached.

[2] *Memoir of Thomas Goodwin, D.D.* Composed out of his own papers and memoirs, by his son. *Works*, II:lxvii.

The form of the plain style appears to have been influenced as much by the impact of the Sermon on the Mount as by any other part of Scripture. The preaching portion, be it text or passage, was presented in its context; the doctrine, or central teaching, of the passage was explained clearly and concisely; and then careful application to the hearers followed in further exposition of the 'uses'. Within this simple formula, the message of the Scriptures was brought home in personal and practical, as well as congregational and societal applications to the hearers. What does Scripture teach? How does this apply to us today? What are we to do in response? How does Scripture teach us to do it? These became the issues handled with seriousness and vigour in the pulpit.

This perspective came to expression in his work, published in English only after his death: *The Art of Prophesying*. The title alone is enough to attract attention in the contemporary church scene and it may therefore be necessary to explain exactly what Perkins means. For Perkins *prophesying* is the task of the minister of the gospel as he stands in the great succession of biblical prophets and apostles who expounded God's word and prayerfully stood between God and the people. It can be divided into two elements, *preaching* and *prayer*. For this role the *sine qua non* is a clear understanding of the message of Scripture and an ability to explain and apply it to the people. Perkins therefore sets out to provide a survey of the nature and contents of Scripture, and of the principles by which we may rightly handle and interpret it. While not providing a complete system of biblical interpretation, he supplies us with a little handbook of instruction on how to study the Scriptures. But as one might expect from Perkins, the distinctive element in *The Art of Prophesying* is the attention he gives to the application of Scripture and the use of it in public preaching.

One of the most interesting features of this is the way in which he consciously adds to Calvin's preaching grid for *expository* preaching what one might call an additional grid for *applicatory* preaching. Perkins divided hearers into seven categories:

1. Ignorant and unteachable unbelievers.

2. Ignorant but teachable.

3. Knowledgeable but unhumbled.

4. The humbled—either partly or thoroughly.

5. Those who are already believers.

6. Backsliders—of various kinds.

7. Congregations containing a mixture of believers and unbelievers.

Perkins believed that preaching should 'rip up the hearts' of those who heard it; but by the same token he saw the preacher as a spiritual apothecary whose knowledge of biblical remedies enabled him to bathe the wounds and heal the spiritual sicknesses of God's people with the grace of Christ. As the pages that follow demonstrate clearly, Perkins realized that the application of God's word must be made to a wide variety of spiritual conditions. He recognized that this was possibly the most demanding aspect of preaching, but also potentially the most significant. What is worth underlining here is not so much the details of Perkins's division (although every preacher ought to know that he has all seven categories listening to him!); rather that, while he was far from being needs-orientated in his preaching, he clearly shaped his application to the specific conditions of his hearers.[1]

Ramist influence?

This is not the place to enter the historiographical debate about the extent to which Perkins and his successors were influenced in their spiritual rhetoric by the work of Petrus Ramus, the French logician who was murdered in the wake of the St Bartholomew's Day massacre in Paris in 1572. It is one of the oddities of historiography that scholars who delight in bemoaning the Aristotelianism of seventeenth-century Reformed theology also bemoan the Ramist structures of its preaching in view of Ramus' dissertation on Aristotle's work which today might well be published under the title 'Aristotle is Bunk'! Be that as it may, Ramus emphasized the role of logic in the context of rhetoric, on the principle of analysis and division as a mode of understanding, and this

---

[1] Perkins's fascinating little work is available in a modernized edition: *The Art of Prophesying* (Edinburgh: Banner of Truth Trust, 1996).

undoubtedly had a major impact on the preaching which emerged in the seventeenth century, marked as it was—unlike Calvin's—by divisions and sub-divisions.[1] Perhaps the finest exposition of this is to be found in the two-page summary of what preaching should be, published in 1645 as part of the Westminster Assembly's *Directory for the Publick Worship of God.*

As we have seen, three features had come to mark the Puritan sermon by the mid-seventeenth century. First the text was 'opened'—explained in its context in Scripture. Second it was 'divided' and the basic doctrine of the text was set on display. Thirdly, the practical question was asked and answered: How does this apply to me? This aspect of exposition the Westminster divines described as most 'painful'[2] for preachers; for it demanded the greatest knowledge of, and sensitivity to, the human heart and its foibles. It also challenged their ability to act as Christ's bride-getter and to 'woo' the hearts of their listeners to Christ (as they put it). It was at this point evident to the hearers of such preachers that—at least in imagination—these ministers had placed themselves in the pew, and listened to their own exposition for themselves and also for others.

Guidelines from the Westminster Assembly

Specific guidelines were suggested by the Westminster divines as a help in such ministry. They framed their instruction in a way that is applicable to a whole range of preaching methods and styles (a range illustrated throughout the tradition they helped to create). These fundamental principles were, in their view, equally applicable to preaching from one text, an entire passage, a key doctrinal statement, or systematically through a section or entire book of Scripture. They further note:

---

[1] It may be worth reflecting here more critically on the standard contemporary impatience with the Ramist fascination with learning by analysis and division. A glance at, e.g., a standard first-year university text book on psychology will reveal that a not dissimilar analysis and division is alive and well in the social (as well as the 'hard') sciences. Indeed the teacher or preacher who announces in the course of a lesson, lecture, or sermon that, e.g., 'there are three things to understand here …', is likely to find his hearers reaching for their pens (or fingering their computer notebooks) with a heightened degree of interest!

[2] That is, requiring the taking of pains, painstaking.

This method is not prescribed as necessary for every man, or upon every text [he is likely to be homiletically disadvantaged who has not heard powerful sermons which seem to break most homiletical rules!]; but only recommended, as being found by experience to be very much blessed of God, and very helpful for the people's understandings and memories.

In particular the following principles were considered fundamental:

1. What is taught must be biblical truth. In addition it must be clearly drawn from the text or passage so that people can see for themselves that it is biblical and learn how they themselves can draw that truth from the same Scripture. Most Christians read the Bible privately using the hermeneutical principles and doctrinal framework of the preaching they hear. They learn these principles of interpretation by osmosis. That is why accurate exposition is essential to the integrity of pastoral preaching and central to the whole ethos of a congregation's life.

2. The teaching on which the passage focuses should then be highlighted, expounded and illustrated, and honest and relevant difficulties (intellectual or practical) dealt with. In general, whatever is not edifying the preacher should not be expounding.

3. Stage three is the most demanding of all: having expounded the text, the preacher is to

> bring it home to special use, by application to his hearers ... a work of great difficulty to himself, requiring much prudence, zeal and meditation, and to the natural and corrupt man ... very unpleasant; yet he is to endeavour to perform it in such a manner, that his auditors may feel the word of God to be quick and powerful, and a discerner of the thoughts and intents of the heart; and that, if any unbeliever or ignorant person be present, he may have the secrets of his heart made manifest, and give glory to God.

This preaching left deep impressions on its hearers. One thinks here, for example, of the New England preacher Thomas Hooker who, it was said, seemed to grow so large when he was preaching that one would have thought he might 'pick up a king and put him in his pocket'!

This, then, was the plain-style 'method' which in a variety of ways has, alongside, or mixed with Calvin's method, tended to dominate the Reformed tradition. It placed great demands on preachers. As the Westminster divines observed, it required—

(i) A commitment to the hard work of studying, meditating on, and applying to oneself the truth of Scripture.

(ii) A concern to speak God's truth to all of God's people, however simple they might be. The great Reformed preachers were well-educated and highly intelligent ministers who placed their learning in tribute to Christ in their ministry, seeking to be servants of others (2 Cor. 4:5).

(iii) Wisdom in teaching and applying the word of God, as well as the grace of God in the very spirit of the preaching passage and without 'passion or bitterness'.

(iv) A sense of the *gravitas* which ought to characterize a servant of God—which will in turn influence both physical demeanour and even voice and speech. The preacher is neither joker nor trifler. But nor is he lugubrious or censorious. 'Zeal for the glory of God, love for the Lord Jesus Christ, and a desire for the salvation of men' were prerequisites.

(v) All this must be backed up by a life which is consistent both in private and in public with the message that is preached.

Who, indeed, is sufficient?

It should be said here, however, that throughout the first four hundred years of this preaching tradition, from Calvin's work in Geneva onwards, it was assumed that this public exposition formed part of the threefold cord of preaching, family worship, and catechizing. In that sense it was never isolated from what today we might call personal and small-group ministries. It is little less than astonishing to find Richard Baxter explaining what convinced him of the necessity of this, in the course of his monumental work *The Reformed Pastor*:

> For my part, I study to speak as plainly and movingly as I can … and yet I frequently meet with those that have been my hearers eight or ten years, who know not whether Christ be God or man, and wonder when I tell them the history of his birth and life and death, as if they had never heard it before. And of those who know the history of the gospel, how few are there who know the nature of that faith, repentance, and holiness which it requireth, or at least, who know their own hearts. … I have found by experience,

that some ignorant persons, who have been so long unprofitable hearers, have got more knowledge and remorse of conscience in half an hour's close disclosure, than they did from ten years' public preaching.[1]

We cannot linger on the story of what followed. Suffice it to say, however it is done (and the extraordinary small-group spread of evangelistic Bible studies underlines both the point and the need), it was never the intention of the Reformed tradition to place its emphasis on preaching *over against* the need for personal and communal study and fellowship.

This study has been almost entirely descriptive in character. In many ways, however, even a brief descriptive account of the early Reformed tradition of preaching is cathartic, if not already prescriptive. But we ought not to conclude without asking: What specifically should we learn? Here we can note only a few answers.

1. Ours is not the first age in which preaching has been set at a discount both inside and outside of the church. The days which we have briefly revisited here may seem to have been a golden age *of* preachers, but they were by no means a golden age *for* preachers. Scotland's Thomas Boston serves as a prime example. 'For the Sabbath's sermons', he writes in his *Memoir*, 'they were but coldly enough received … they seem to have little desire for the gospel: the most weighty truths look as nauseous to them.'[2] Something new happened, in the medieval world, that had discovered that the visual cannot satisfy the needs of the heart. It is not impossible for that to happen again. Preachers should take heart.

2. The overwhelming demands of preaching, if taken seriously, require the highest degree of commitment as well as giftedness: personal godliness; some measure of expertise in handling biblical, systematic, and pastoral divinity, surely at least on a par with the expertise expected in the contemporary world of engineers, physicians, and lawyers; ability to communicate, and much else. Who, indeed, is sufficient for these

---

[1] Baxter, *Reformed Pastor*, p. 196.
[2] See *Memoirs of Thomas Boston* (1776), edited with an introduction and notes by G. H. Morrison (Edinburgh: Oliphant, Anderson & Ferrier, 1899), pp. 215, 220.

things (2 Cor. 2:16)? In an age of mediocrity in public utterances about temporal matters, who will rise beyond it to speak of eternal matters?

3. Our generation of preachers needs most of all the conviction which the Reformed fathers shared: we have something not only worth saying, but a message which must by all means be heard.

There is a perennial need for preaching that does everything Paul urged on Timothy. Today, people turn to hard-pressed family physicians, to analysts and psychiatrists, to the daily astrology column, and to quacks for the exorcism of the demons of the mind and for the freeing of the conscience from the guilt that sears it. But sedatives and 'forgiving ourselves', or our family, or society, or even, *mirabile dictu*, God himself, are not the same as being forgiven.

Perhaps the most basic conviction of preaching in the Reformed theological tradition is this. It is against God that we have sinned (Psa. 51:4), and he alone can forgive us. The need to know forgiveness is endemic in our society. It is widely reported that many of those who belong to 'Generation X', or are 'Millennials', are caught in a vortex of hopelessness, and many self-confessedly feel themselves to be 'beyond redemption'. But this should not take by surprise anyone who understands that alienation from God produces manifold subsidiary alienations. Now is not the hour for the church to lose its grip on the instrument by which God's forgiveness in Christ has been declared to millions throughout the world.

The Reformed church has always been driven at this point by the apostolic conviction: How can they hear [that there is forgiveness with God] without a preacher (Rom. 10:14)? May it continue to be so driven!

CHAPTER THIRTY-NINE

A PREACHER'S DECALOGUE

L ISTENING to or reading the reflections of others on preaching is for most preachers inherently interesting and stimulating (whether positively or negatively). The reflections that follow, then, are offered in the spirit of the Golden Rule!

It is many years now since my first sermon in the context of a Sunday service. Five decades is a long time to have amassed occasions when going to the church door after preaching is the last thing one wants to do—even if one loves the congregation (sometimes precisely *because* one loves the congregation and therefore the sense of failure is all the greater!). How often have I had to ask myself, 'How is it possible to have done this thousands of times and still not do it properly?'

Yes, I know how to talk myself out of that mood! 'It's faithfulness, not skill, that really matters.' 'How you feel has nothing to do with it!' 'Remember you're sowing seed.' 'It's ultimately the Lord who preaches the word into people's hearts, not you.' All true! Yet we are responsible to make progress as preachers, indeed evident and visible, or at least audible, progress (1 Tim. 4:13, 15 is an instructive and searching word in this respect!).

All of this led me while travelling one day to reflect on the question: What ten commandments, what rules of preaching-life, do I wish someone had written for me to provide direction, shape and ground rules, that might have helped me keep going in the right direction and gaining momentum in ministry along the way?

Once one begins thinking about this, whatever ten commandments one comes up with, it becomes obvious that this is an inexhaustible theme. An editor could easily run a journal for a year with a whole series of 'My Ten Commandments for Preaching'. I offer these ten, not as infallible, but as the fruit of a few minutes of quiet reflection on a plane journey.

1. *Know your Bible better*

Often at the end of a Lord's Day, or a conference, the thought strikes me again: 'If you only knew your Bible better you would have been a lot more help to the people.' I teach at a seminary whose founder stated that its goal was 'to produce experts in the Bible'. Alas, I was not educated in an institution that had anything remotely resembling that goal. The result? Life has been an ongoing 'teach yourself while you play catch-up'. At the end of the day seminaries exist not to give authoritative line-by-line interpretations of the whole of Scripture but to provide tools to enable its graduates to do that. That is why, in many ways, it is the work we do, the conversations we have, the churches we attend, the preaching under which we sit, that make or break our ministries. This is not 'do it yourself', but we ourselves need to do it.

As an observer as well as a practitioner of preaching, I am troubled and perplexed by hearing men with wonderful equipment, humanly speaking (ability to speak, charismatic personality, and so on), who seem to be incapable of simply preaching the Scriptures. Somehow God's word has not first invaded and gripped them.

I must not be an illiterate. But I do need to be *homo unius libri*—a man of one book. The widow of a dear friend once told me that her husband wore out his Bible during the last year of his life. 'He devoured it like a novel,' she said. Be a Bible-devourer!

2. *Be a man of prayer*

I mean this with respect to preaching—not only in the sense that I should pray before I begin my preparation, but in the sense that my preparation is itself a communion in prayer with God in and through his word. Whatever did the apostles mean by saying that they needed to devote themselves 'to prayer and to the ministry of the word' (Acts 6:4)—and why in that order?

My own feeling is that in the tradition of our pastoral textbooks we have over-individualized this. The apostles (one may surmise) really meant 'we'—not 'I, Peter' or 'I, John' but 'We, Peter, John, James, Thomas, Andrew … together'.

Is it a misreading of the situation to suspect that preachers hide their desperate need of prayer for the preaching and their personal need? By contrast, reflect on Paul's appeals. And remember Spurgeon's *bon mot* when asked about the secret of his ministry: 'My people pray for me.'

Reflecting on this reminds me of one moment in the middle of an address at a conference for pastors when the bubble above my head contained the words 'You are making a complete and total hash of this.' But as my eyes then refocused on the men in front of me, those men seemed like thirsty souls drinking in cool refreshing water, and their eyes all seemed to be fixed on the water carrier I was holding! Then the above-the-head-bubble filled with other words: 'I remember now, how I urged the congregation at home to pray for these brethren and for the ministry of the word. They have been praying!'

Alas for me if I don't see the need for prayer or the need for encouraging and teaching my people to see its importance! I may do well (a sinister voice whispers 'You have!'). But not with eternal fruit.

3. Don't lose sight of Christ

Me? Yes, me! This is an important principle in too many dimensions fully to expound here. One must suffice. Know and therefore preach 'Jesus Christ and him crucified' (1 Cor. 2:2). That is a text far easier to preach as the first sermon in a ministry than it is to preach as the final sermon.

What do I mean? Perhaps the point can be put sharply, even provocatively, in this way: systematic exposition did not die on the cross for us; nor did biblical theology, nor even systematic theology or hermeneutics or whatever else we deem important as those who handle the exposition of Scripture. I have heard all of these in preaching … without a centre in *the person of the Lord Jesus*.

Paradoxically, not even the systematic preaching through one of the Gospels guarantees Christ-crucified-centred preaching. Too often preaching on the Gospels takes what I whimsically think of as the 'Find-Waldo-Approach'. The underlying question in the sermon is 'Where are *you* to be found in this story?' (Are you Martha or Mary, James and John,

Peter, the grateful leper …?) The question 'Where, who, and what is Jesus in this story?' tends to be marginalized.

The truth is, it is far easier to preach about Mary, Martha, James, John, or Peter than it is about Christ. It is far easier to preach even about the darkness of sin and the human heart than to preach Christ. Plus my bookshelves are groaning with literature on Mary, Martha … the good life, the family life, the Spirit-filled life, the parenting life, the damaged-self life … but most of us have only a few inches of shelf-space on the person and work of Christ himself.

Am I absolutely at my best when talking about *him*? or about *us*?

4. Be deeply trinitarian

Surely we are? At least in some of our churches, not a Lord's Day passes without the congregation confessing one God, Father, Son, and Holy Spirit. But as is commonly recognized, Western Christianity has often had a special tendency to either an explicit or a pragmatic Unitarianism, be it of the Father (liberalism, for all practical purposes), the Son (evangelicalism, perhaps not least in its reactions against liberalism), or the Spirit (charismaticism, with its reaction to both of the previous).

This is, doubtless, a caricature. But my concern here arises from a sense that Bible-believing preachers (as well as others) continue to think of the Trinity as the most speculative and therefore the least practical of all doctrines. After all, what can you 'do' as a result of hearing preaching that emphasizes God as Trinity? Well, at least inwardly if not outwardly, fall down in prostrate worship that the God whose being is so ineffable, so incomprehensible to my mental math, seeks fellowship with us!

I sometimes wonder if it is failure here that has led to churches actually to believe it when they are told by 'church analysts' and the like that 'the quality of your church's morning worship is excellent … small groups, well, you need to work on that … .' Doesn't that verge on blasphemy? (Verge on it? There is surely only *One* who can assess the quality of our worship. This approach confuses aesthetics with adoration.)

John's Gospel suggests to us that one of the deepest burdens on our Lord's heart during his last hours with his disciples was to help them understand that God's being as Trinity is the heart of what makes the gospel both possible and actual, and that it is knowing him as such that forms the very lifeblood of the life of faith (cf. John 13–17). Read Paul with this in mind, and it becomes obvious how profoundly woven into the warp and woof of his gospel his understanding of Father, Son, and Holy Spirit is.

Our people need to know that, through the Spirit, their fellowship is with the Father and with his Son, Jesus Christ. Would they know that from my preaching?

5. Use your imagination

Does this not contradict the immediately preceding observations that the truth of the Trinity should not be thought of as speculative metaphysics? No. Rather it is simply to state what the preaching masters of the centuries have either explicitly written or, at least by example, implied. All good preaching involves the use of the imagination. No great preacher has ever lacked imagination. Perhaps we might go so far as to say it is simply an exhortation to love the Lord our God with all of our ... mind ... and our neighbour as ourselves.

Scripture itself suggests that there are many different kinds of imagination—hence the different *genres* in which the word of God is expressed (poetry, historical narrative, dialogue, monologue, history, vision, etc.). No two biblical authors had identical imaginations. It is doubtful if Ezekiel could have written Proverbs, for example!

What do we mean by *imagination*? Our dictionaries give a series of definitions. Common to them all seems to be the ability to 'think outside of oneself', 'to be able to see or conceive the same thing in a different way'. In some definitions the ideas of the ability to contrive, exercising resourcefulness, the mind's creative power, are among the nuanced meanings of the word.

Imagination in preaching means being able to understand the truth well enough to translate or transpose it into another kind of language or musical key in order to present the same truth in a way that enables others to see it, understand its significance, and feel its power—and to do so in a way that gets under the skin, breaks through the barriers, and grips the mind, will, and affections, so that they not only understand the word preached but also feel its truth and power.

Luther did this by the sheer dramatic forcefulness of his speech. Whitefield did it by his use of dramatic illustration (overdid it, in the view of some). Calvin—perhaps surprisingly—did it too by the extraordinarily earthed-in-Geneva-life language in which he expressed himself. So an overwhelming Luther-personality, a dramatic preacher with Whitefieldian gifts of story-telling and voice (did David Garrick not say he would give anything to be able to say 'Mesopotamia' the way George Whitefield did?), a deeply scholarly, retiring, reluctant preacher like Calvin—all did it, albeit in very different ways. They saw and heard the word of God as it might enter the world of their hearers and convert and edify them.

What is the secret here? It is, surely, learning to preach the word to oneself, from its context into our context, to make concrete in the realities of our lives the truth that came historically to others' lives. This is why the old masters used to speak about sermons going from their lips with power only when they had first come to their own hearts with power.

All of which leads us from the fifth commandment back to where we started. Only immersion in Scripture enables us to preach it this way. Therein lies the difference between preaching that is about the Bible and its message and preaching that seems to come right out of the Bible with a 'Thus says the Lord' ring of authenticity and authority.

This is, surely, a good place to end the 'first table' of these commandments for preachers. Now it is time to go and soak ourselves in Scripture to get ready for the 'second table'.

6. Speak much of sin and grace

In his exposition of Paul's letter to the Romans, Martin Luther insightfully uses the words of Jeremiah's call (Jer. 1:10):

> The sum total of this epistle is to destroy, root out, and bring to naught all carnal wisdom. ... All that is in us is to be rooted out, pulled down, destroyed, and thrown down, i.e., all that delights us because it comes from us and is found in us; but all that is from outside of us and in Christ is to be built up and planted.

758

If that is true of Paul's 'preaching' in Romans, it ought to be true of ours as well. Sin and grace should be the downbeat and the upbeat that run through all our exposition.

But there are some cautions. Preaching on sin must unmask the *presence* of sin, and undeceive about the *nature* of sin, as well as underline the *danger* of sin.

This is not the same thing as hammering a congregation against the back wall of the 'sanctuary' with a tirade! That requires little more than high levels of emotion. A genuine, ultimately saving, unmasking and undeceiving of the human heart is more demanding exegetically and spiritually. For what is in view here is the skilled work of a surgeon—opening a wound, exposing the cause of the patient's sickness, cutting away the destructive malignancies, all in order to heal and restore to life.

Doubtless people need warnings against the evils of contemporary society (abortion, apostasy in the visible church, etc.). But we cannot build a ministry, nor healthy Christians, on a diet of fulminating against the world. No, rather we do this by seeing the Scriptures expose the sin in our own hearts, undeceive us about ourselves, root out the poison that remains in our own hearts—and then helping our people to do the same 'by the open statement of the truth' (2 Cor. 4:2).

There is only one safe way to do this. Spiritual surgery must be done within the context of God's grace in Jesus Christ. Only by seeing our sin do we come to see the need for, and the wonder of, grace. But exposing sin is not the same thing as unveiling and applying grace. We must be familiar with, and exponents of, its multifaceted power, and know how to apply it to a variety of spiritual conditions.

Truth to tell, exposing sin is easier than applying grace; for, alas, we are more intimate with the former than we sometimes are with the latter. Therein lies our weakness.

7. Use 'the plain style'

This is a familiar enough expression in the history of preaching. It is associated particularly with the contrast between the literary eloquence of the High Anglican preaching tradition and the new 'plain style' of the Puritans in the sixteenth and seventeenth centuries. William Perkins's *The Art of Prophesying* served as the first textbook in this school.

But this seventh commandment is not insisting *per se* that we should all preach like the Puritans. Indeed, acquaintance with the Puritans themselves would underline for us that they did not all preach as if they had been cloned from William Perkins! But they did have one thing in common: plain speech, which they believed Paul commended and should be a leading characteristic of all preaching (2 Cor 6:7; cf. 4:2).

There are many ways this principle applies. Do not make eloquence the thing for which you are best known as a preacher; make sure you get the point of the passage you are preaching, and that you make it clear and express its power. True evangelical eloquence will take care of itself. Despite Charles Hodge's reservations, Archibald Alexander was in general right in urging students to pay attention to the power of biblical ideas and then the words used in preaching will take care of themselves.

The 'masters' of clear style can teach us here. Paradoxically, in this context, two of them were themselves Anglicans. C. S. Lewis's counsel on writing applies equally to preaching:

1. Always try to use language so as to make quite clear what you mean and make sure y[ou]r sentence couldn't mean anything else.

2. Always prefer the plain direct word to the long, vague one. Don't *implement* promises, but *keep* them.

3. Never use abstract nouns when concrete ones will do. If you mean 'More people died' don't say 'Mortality rose.'

4. In writing. Don't use adjectives which merely tell us how you want to *feel* about the thing you are describing. I mean, instead of telling us a thing was 'terrible', describe it so that we'll be terrified. Don't say it was 'delightful'; make *us* say 'delightful' when we've read the description. You see, all those words (horrifying, wonderful, hideous, exquisite) are only like saying to your readers 'Please will you do my job for me.'

5. Don't use words too big for the subject. Don't say 'infinitely' when you mean 'very'; otherwise you'll have no word left when you want to talk about something *really* infinite.[1]

In a similar vein, here is J. C. Ryle's counsel: Have a clear knowledge of what you want to say. Use simple words. Employ a simple sentence

[1] C. S. Lewis, *Letters to Children* (London: William Collins, 1985), p. 64.

structure. Preach as though you had asthma! Be direct. Make sure you illustrate what you are talking about.[1]

Of course, there are exceptions to these principles. But why would I think I am one? A brilliant surgeon may be able to perform his operation with poor instruments; so can the Holy Spirit. But since in preaching we are nurses in the operating room, our basic responsibility is to have clean, sharp, sterile scalpels for the Spirit to do his surgery.

8. *Find your own voice*

'Voice' here is used in the sense of personal style—'know yourself' if one can Christianize the wisdom of the philosophers.

That being said, finding a voice—in the literal sense—is also important. Few of us have good voices. But the good preacher who uses his voice badly is a *rara avis* indeed. Clearly, affectation should be banned; nor are we actors whose voices are moulded to the part that is to be played. But our creation as the image of God, creatures who speak—and speak his praises and his word—really requires us to do all we can with the natural resources the Lord has given us.

But it is *voice* in the metaphorical sense that is really in view here— our approach to preaching that makes it authentically *our* preaching and not a slavish imitation of someone else. Yes, we may—must—learn from others, positively and negatively. Further, it is always important when others preach to listen to them with both ears open: one for personal nourishment through the ministry of the word, but the other to try to detect the principles that make this preaching helpful to people.

We ought not to become clones. Some men never grow as preachers because the 'preaching suit' they have borrowed does not actually fit them or their gifts. Instead of becoming the outstanding expository preacher, or redemptive-historical, or God-centred, or whatever our hero may be, we may tie ourselves in knots and endanger our own unique giftedness by trying to use someone else's paradigm, style, or personality as a mould into which to squeeze ourselves. We become less than our true selves in Christ. The marriage of our personality with another's preaching style can be a recipe for being dull and lifeless. So it is worth taking the

---

[1] See J. C. Ryle, *Simplicity in Preaching* (Edinburgh: Banner of Truth Trust, 2010).

time in an ongoing way to try to assess who and what we really are as preachers in terms of strengths and weaknesses.

9. Learn how to transition

There is a short (two pages) but wonderful 'must-read' section for preachers in the Westminster Assembly's *Directory for the Publick Worship of God*. *Inter alia* the divines state that the preacher 'In exhorting to duties … is, as he seeth cause, to teach also the means that help to the performance of them'. In contemporary speech this means that our preaching will answer the 'how to?' question. This perhaps requires further explanation.

Many of us are weary of the pandemic of 'how-to-ness' we find in much contemporary preaching. It is often little better than psychology (however helpful) with a little Christian polish; it is largely imperative without indicative, and in the last analysis becomes self- and success-orientated rather than sin- and grace-oriented. But there is a Reformed and, more importantly, biblical, emphasis on teaching how to transition from the old ways to the new way, from patterns of sin to patterns of holiness. It is not enough to stress the necessity, nor even the possibility, of this. We must teach people how this happens.

Years ago I took one of our sons for coaching from an old friend who had become a highly regarded teaching golf professional. My son was not, as they say, 'getting on to the next level'. I could see that but I no longer had (if I ever had!) the golfing *savoir faire* to help. Enter my friend, and within the space of one coaching session, the improvement in ball-striking was both visible and audible (there is something about the sound of a superbly struck shot—or home run, for that matter!).

This is, in part, what we are called to effect in our handling of the Scriptures—not 'this is wrong … this is right'—but by our preaching to enable and effect the transition from one to the other.

But how? For all its criticism of the pragmatism of evangelicalism, Reformed preaching is not always skilled in this area. Many are stronger on doctrine than on exegesis and often stronger on soul-searching than on spiritual up-building. We need to learn how to expound the Scriptures in such a way that the very exposition empowers in our hearers the transitions from the old patterns of life in Adam to the new patterns of life in Christ.

How do we do this? To begin with, by expounding the Scriptures in a way that makes clear that the indicatives of grace ground the imperatives of faith and obedience and also effect them. This we must learn to do in a way that brings out of the text the way the text itself teaches how transformation takes place and how the power of the truth itself sanctifies (cf. John 17:17).

This usually demands that we stay down in the text longer, more inquisitively than we sometimes do, asking the text, 'Show me how your indicatives effect your imperatives.' Such study often yields the surprising (?) result: depth-study of Scripture means that we are not left scurrying to the Christian bookshop or the journal on counselling in order to find out how the gospel changes lives. No, we have learned that the Scriptures themselves teach us the answer to the 'What?' questions and also the answer to the 'How to?' question.

Do we—far less our congregations—know 'how to'? Have we told them they need to do it, but left them to their own devices rather than model it in our preaching?

Some years ago, at the end of a church conference, the local minister, whom I knew from his student days, said to me, 'Just before I let you go tonight, will you do one last thing? Will you take me through the steps that are involved so that we learn to mortify sin?'

I was touched—that he would broach what was obviously a personal as well as pastoral concern with me, but perhaps even more so by his assumption that I would be able to help. (How often we who struggle are asked questions we ourselves need to answer!) He died not long afterwards, and I think of his question as his legacy to me, causing me again and again to see that we need to exhibit what John 'Rabbi' Duncan of New College said was true of Jonathan Edwards's preaching: 'His doctrine was all application, and his application was all doctrine.'

The ministry that illustrates this, and that understands what is involved in how preaching transitions its hearers from the old to the new, will have what Thomas Boston once said about his own ministry, 'a certain tincture' that people will recognize even if they cannot articulate or explain why it is so different and so helpful.

10. Love your people

John Newton wrote that his congregation would take almost anything from him, however painful, because they knew 'I mean to do them good.'

This is a litmus test for our ministry. It means that my preparation is a more sacred enterprise than simply satisfying my own love of study; it means that my preaching will have characteristics about it, difficult to define but nevertheless sensed by my hearers, that reflect the apostolic principle:

> What we proclaim is not ourselves, but Jesus Christ as Lord, *with ourselves as your servants for Jesus' sake* (2 Cor. 4:5).

> We were ready to share with you not only the gospel of God *but also our own selves, because you had become very dear to us* (1 Thess. 2:8).

In Jesus Christ, the church's *one true preacher*, message and messenger are one. He is *the* preacher, and also *the* message. That is not true of us. But, in union with Christ (and we preach 'in Christ' as well as live and die 'in Christ'), a coalescence of a lesser sort takes place: the truth of the message is conveyed by the preacher whose spirit is conformed to the grace of God in the message. How can it be otherwise when preaching involves 'God making his appeal through us' (2 Cor. 5:20)? 'A preacher's life', wrote Thomas Brooks, 'should be a commentary upon his doctrine; his practice should be the counterpanc [counterpart] of his sermons. Heavenly doctrines should always be adorned with a heavenly life.'

Conclusion

A 'Preacher's Decalogue' might be helpful, but at the end of the day we are nourished not by the commands of law but by the provisions of God's grace in the gospel. It is as true of our preaching as of our living, that what law cannot do, because of the weakness of our flesh, God accomplishes through Christ, in order to fulfil his commands in us by the Spirit. May it be so for us! Then we will be able truly to sing with Charles Wesley:

> Happy, if with my latest breath
> I might but gasp His Name,
> Preach Him to all and cry in death,
> 'Behold, behold the Lamb!'

EPILOGUE

DOXOLOGY

Praising God is one of the highest and purest acts of religion. In prayer we act like men; in praise we act like angels.[1]

—Thomas Watson

TO set the scene for the conclusion to this book, let me invite you to take a simple word-association test. The usual procedure for such a test is that the administrator says a word and the subject responds with the first word that comes to mind. Thus, the word *horse* might immediately prompt the word *cart* from some people, but *race* (as in *horse race*) from others.

Here, then, is the word-association test:

Calvinism _____

Did the noun *doxology* or the adjective *doxological* come to mind? If so, would it have come to mind apart from the title of this chapter? The terms *Calvinism* and *doxology* are not ordinarily associated with each other, even by Christians. Yet it is the overall contention of both this volume as a whole, and of this conclusion in particular, that Calvinism is *always* doxological—otherwise it cannot be either truly biblical or truly Calvinistic, and therefore, at the end of the day, cannot be true theology. For true theology always leads to doxology.

Doxology is a word or words of praise or glory. Doxologies punctuate the Bible because they punctuate the life of faith.[2] This at least was Paul's understanding of the life of Abraham: 'he grew strong in his faith as he

---

[1] Quoted in I. D. E. Thomas, *The Golden Treasury of Puritan Quotations* (Chicago: Moody Press, 1975), p. 209.

[2] See, for example, Gen. 24:27; Exod. 18:10; 1 Chron. 29:10-13; Luke 1:68; Rom. 9:5; 2 Cor. 1:3-4; Eph. 1:3; Rev. 5:12.

gave glory to God' (Rom. 4:20). The rhythm of the Christian's life is always determined by the principle that when the revelation of God in his glory is grasped by faith, the response is to return all glory to God.

Paul himself summarizes this truth at the climax of three chapters of the most tightly woven theology found anywhere in Scripture. In Romans 9–11, he traces God's ways in faithfulness to his word, in divine election, and in distinguishing grace (chap. 9); in gospel proclamation (chap. 10); and in sovereign, divine providence toward Jew and Gentile (chap. 11). Then he draws the conclusion: 'For from him and through him and to him are all things. To him be glory forever. Amen' (Rom. 11:36).

What is being underlined here is, surely, that the knowledge of the sovereignty of God, exercised in all of these spheres, leads to a single response from the heart of faith: 'Glory to God forever', or, in the familiar Latin words by which the teaching of the Reformation is often summarized, *soli Deo gloria*—to God alone be the glory!

These considerations notwithstanding, the expression *doxological Calvinism* may seem strange to many people—an oxymoron or straightforward contradiction in terms. Whether one thinks of the so-called five points of Calvinism (in terms of their origin, more accurately labelled 'the five corrections to Arminianism'), or of the much larger vision of John Calvin himself, or of the teaching of his followers, such as John Knox and the Puritans, *doxology*, *praise*, *worship*, and *adoration* may not be words that come to mind in any word-association test.

But if with B. B. Warfield we consider Calvinism to be no more and no less than biblical theology expressed in its fullest and richest way, we readily see that the effect of such theology will indeed be doxology. That is true because Reformed theology emphasizes doxology-evoking *biblical teaching*, it is illustrated in the expressions of Calvinistic singing we find in church history, and it is evident in the *Christian experience* of those who have embraced the Reformed faith and lived it out as a lifestyle.

Biblical teaching

Perhaps the historically best-loved gospel invitation in the New Testament is found in the so-called 'comfortable words' of Christ: 'Come to me, all who labour and are heavy laden, and I will give you rest. Take my yoke ... you will find rest for your souls' (Matt. 11:28-29). Here is rich grace; here is an open-hearted genuine invitation to all in need to come to Christ. Here, too, the Lord Jesus is God's yes and amen to all his promises (2 Cor. 1:19-20); the rest in God that was symbolized (but rarely experienced) in the old covenant is now realized in the shed blood of Jesus himself in the new covenant.

But what lies behind these words? Surprisingly to those who are familiar with these words only apart from their context in Matthew 11, they follow a most remarkable outburst of praise from the heart of the Lord Jesus: 'I thank you, Father, Lord of heaven and earth ... .' But for what reason does Christ express such worship? It is because

you have hidden these things from the wise and understanding, and revealed them to little children; yes, Father, for such was your gracious will. All things have been handed over to me by my Father, and no one knows the Son except the Father, and no one knows the Father except the Son and anyone to whom the Son chooses to reveal him (Matt. 11:25-27).

Jesus' invitation to trust him emerges from his praise to his Father. That praise is predicated on the distinguishing election of God: in sovereign fashion ('his gracious will', Matt. 11:26), God has hidden his truth from some and revealed it to others; only the electing grace of the Son opens the way to the knowledge of the Father. Here the praise of Jesus presupposes human depravity and helplessness (the Father is not known by men naturally); it rests on a divine choice in which God both hides and reveals; and it affirms God's sovereign good pleasure in irresistible grace. What strikes most readers as so remarkable is that Jesus prays all this within the context of the clearest, sweetest, most gracious invitation to sinners to come to him for rest.

It should be no surprise, therefore, that it was a Calvinist, Horatius Bonar, who penned the famous lines:

I heard the voice of Jesus say,
'Come unto Me and rest;
Lay down, thou weary one, lay down
Thy head upon My breast.'

> I came to Jesus as I was,
>   Weary and worn and sad;
> I found in Him a resting place,
>   And He has made me glad.[1]

The rooting of doxology in divine sovereignty, glory, grace, and freedom—in a word, in God's 'Godness'—is a pattern we find regularly repeated in the New Testament. And it is not in the more recondite texts of the New Testament that we find doxology closely linked with the truths that Calvinists affirm, but in those passages that are the commonly loved property of all believers.

What Christian has never found consolation in the comfort of Romans 8:28—surely one of the all-time-favourite texts of Scripture? All things work together for our good. Yes, but how do we know that everything works together for good for those who love God? We have this assurance: because we are called according to his purpose. And where is that purpose rooted but in the sovereign, supra-temporal disposition of God: 'For those whom he foreknew he also predestined … And those whom he predestined he also called, and those whom he called he also justified, and those whom he justified he also glorified' (Rom. 8:29-30).

Paul's repeated and consistent use here of the aorist tense for his main verbs underscores the certainty and the definitiveness of God's sovereignty; nothing can ultimately resist his will. Moreover, these truths stimulate Paul to speak with a doxological heart and a confident—indeed, exuberant—lyricism in the face of all that might oppose God's work for and in him. These truths are the marrow of Calvinism and give to true Calvinism the same lyrical and doxological spirit.

The point could be illustrated from a variety of other passages. The doxology of Ephesians 1:3ff. ('Blessed be the God and Father of our Lord Jesus Christ … to the praise of his glorious grace … to the praise of his glory … to the praise of his glory') is rooted in the sovereign, loving election of God and in his equally sovereign outpouring of all spiritual blessings on us. Faith receives these blessings, but it is not their cause.

In the same way, the doxology that opens Peter's first letter expresses the praise of those who have been chosen by God. Brought into new life

---

[1] From the hymn 'I Heard the Voice of Jesus Say' by Horatius Bonar.

by sovereign, spiritual new birth, they persevere because God perseveres with them (1 Pet. 1:1-5). Faith grasps this, but is not its origin. Rather, 'by God's power' we 'are being guarded [a present *passive* participle] through faith'.

This point, then, should be beyond dispute. Praise to God in Scripture results from the sense that we are depraved and can contribute nothing to our salvation—yet God has been pleased to save us. He has chosen us; Christ's blood has atoned for us; the Spirit has worked irresistibly in us (despite our initial resistance) to give us new life; and we persevere as saints because of the perseverance of God with us. This biblical teaching is precisely what later came to be described as Calvinism.

Calvinistic singing

The wonderful, albeit absent-minded, 'Rabbi' John Duncan (1796–1870), professor of Hebrew at New College, Edinburgh, once read out the words of Charles Wesley's hymn 'And Can It Be That I Should Gain':

> Long my imprisoned spirit lay
>   Fast bound in sin and nature's night;
> Thine eye diffused a quickening ray;
>   I woke, the dungeon flamed with light;
> My chains fell off, my heart was free;
>   I rose, went forth, and followed Thee.

Duncan commented quizzically, 'Where's your Arminianism now, friend?' The Wesley brothers were indeed Arminian in theology (despite their conviction that many of their views were 'within a hair's-breadth of Calvinism'[1]). But at this point, Charles Wesley's expressions of praise are rooted in a theology borrowed from his Calvinist friend George White-field's preaching on the new birth.

Wesley bids us sing praise to God for his sovereign, liberating, prevenient, divine work on the soul that both awakens us and delivers us. When he does so, he is forced to borrow a Calvinistic frame of reference. A moment's reflection will underline how contradictory it would be to

---

[1] From *Minutes of Some Late Conversations between the Rev. Mr Wesley and Others*, Conversation II, August, 1745, Bristol, in *The Works of John Wesley* (Grand Rapids: Baker, 1979), VIII:284.

sing praise to God for something he had not done. Of course, hymns may be written to parody Calvinistic doctrine, and on very rare occasions one hears songs that celebrate 'free will'. But the great hymns of ages past, like their predecessors in Scripture, praise God for being God, for being sovereign, for being a saving and keeping God. To cast a critical glance sideways at the contemporary evangelical world, it is difficult to imagine what hymns of adoration and praise might be written by Open Theists (whose chief enemy appears to be Calvinism). Do we praise God for being like us in that he is neither sovereign over all things in the present nor aware of what will unfold in our future?

Most of the old hymns underscore the point that Calvinism is in its very nature doxological, and that all doxology, in fact, depends on such biblical theology. Here, for example, is the best-known hymn of Augustus Montague Toplady (1740–78):

> Not the labours of my hands
>> Can fulfil Thy law's demands;
> Could my zeal no respite know,
>> Could my tears forever flow,
> All for sin could not atone;
>> Thou must save, and Thou alone.
>
> Nothing in my hand I bring,
>> Simply to Thy cross I cling;
> Naked, come to Thee for dress;
>> Helpless, look to Thee for grace;
> Foul, I to the Fountain fly;
>> Wash me, Saviour, or I die.[1]

This is Calvinism in poetry: such is our depravity and helplessness that 'Thou must save, and Thou alone'. Only these emphases that are characteristic of Calvinism can give birth to such theology as poetry. Granted, the Calvinism is more pronounced and more deliberately articulated with some hymn-writers. But these same truths come to expression in the more pastoral spirit of a John Newton and his 'Amazing Grace!' What makes grace so amazing is precisely that it sovereignly frees and

[1] From his hymn 'Rock of Ages, Cleft for Me'.

sovereignly saves from first to last. Since every stable doctrine of providence stresses God's absolute sovereignty over the details of life, robust singing on providence is characteristically well rooted in this Calvinistic emphasis.

It is no surprise, therefore, to discover that at the time of the Reformation, while Ulrich Zwingli, despite his own musical accomplishments, resisted singing in worship, Calvin insisted on it. Not only so, but while Calvin was in Strasbourg, he himself put into verse a number of the psalms for congregational singing, and later he encouraged others to do so in Geneva. We still use many of their tunes. Doxology sits comfortably within Reformed theology; in fact, it is required by it as a logical and spiritual necessity.

Christian experience

Calvinistic theology has always placed great emphasis on biblical and doctrinal knowledge, and rightly so. We are transformed by the renewing of our minds (Rom. 12:1-2). This transformation is a prerequisite for our worship, since it is by the Spirit's illumination of our minds through Scripture that we gain understanding of God and his ways. But Calvinism—at least in its consistent forms—has never been merely cerebral. The history of Reformed Christianity is also the story of the highest order of spiritual experience. Calvinistic doctrine expressed in God-exalting words of praise leads to a distinctive Christian experience. The melody that is composed intellectually in Calvinistic theology, and sung enthusiastically in Reformed worship, also can be heard in the lifestyle and experience of Reformed Christians.

The seriousness of the Reformed world-and-life view means that, even when the melody is played in a minor key, it remains a melody. Indeed, to use a metaphor of Calvin, as this melody is played in the church, it becomes a glorious symphony[1] blending the following motifs:

- Trust in the sovereignty of God.

- The experience of the power of God's grace to save hopeless and helpless sinners.

[1] John Calvin, *Comm. Psalms*, V:178.

- An overwhelming sense of being loved by a Saviour who has died specifically and successfully for one's sins.

- The discovery of a grace that has set one free to trust, serve, and love Christ while yet not destroying one's will.

- The quiet confidence and poise engendered by knowing that God has pledged himself to persevere with his people

  'Til all the ransomed church of God
  Be saved to sin no more.[1]

These motifs all conspire to give God alone the glory.

The essence of the Calvinistic life is living in such a way as to glorify God. This, after all, is the burden of the answer to the opening question of the *Shorter Catechism* written by the Westminster Assembly of divines: 'Man's chief end is to glorify God, and to enjoy him for ever.' Here is the ultimate surprise in Calvinism for many people: the glory of God and the enjoyment of man are not antithetical, but are correlated in the purposes of God.

The view that God's glory diminishes man and robs him of pleasure is, in the light (or should one say 'darkness'?) of Genesis 3, the lie about God that was exchanged for the truth (Rom. 1:25). It is Satanic theology that plays God against man.

In sharp contrast, biblical theology that exalts God in his sovereign grace and glory opens the door for man to enter into a quite different order of reality. Here is offered the experience of, and delight in, the rich pleasures of restoration to fellowship with God, transformation into the likeness of Christ, and anticipation of being with Christ where he is in order to see him in his glory (John 17:24). This, at least, was the view of Isaac Watts:

  The sorrows of the mind
  Be banished from the place;
  Religion never was designed
  To make our pleasures less.

[1] From the hymn 'There Is a Fountain Filled with Blood' by William Cowper.

Let those refuse to sing
　　That never knew our God;
But children of the heavenly King
　　May speak their joys abroad.

There we shall see His face,
　　And never, never sin!
There, from the rivers of His grace,
　　Drink endless pleasures in.

Yea, and before we rise
　　To that immortal state,
The thoughts of such amazing bliss
　　Should constant joys create.

The men of grace have found
　　Glory begun below.
Celestial fruit on earthly ground
　　From faith and hope may grow.

The hill of Zion yields
　　A thousand sacred sweets,
Before we reach the heav'nly fields,
　　Or walk the golden streets.[1]

It is surely this outlook that Warfield had in mind when he described the fruits of doxological Calvinism in a story he relates in his essay 'Is the Shorter Catechism Worthwhile?'

> We have the following bit of personal experience from a general officer of the United States army. He was in a great western city at a time of intense excitement and violent rioting. The streets were over-run daily by a dangerous crowd. One day he observed approaching him a man of singularly combined calmness and firmness of *mien*, whose very demeanour inspired confidence. So impressed was he with his bearing amid the surrounding uproar that when he had passed he turned to look back at him, only to find that the stranger had done the same. On observing his turning

---

[1] From the hymn 'Come, We That Love the Lord' by Isaac Watts.

the stranger at once came back to him, and touching his chest with his forefinger, demanded without preface: 'What is the chief end of man?' On receiving the countersign, 'Man's chief end is to glorify God and to enjoy him forever'—'Ah!,' said he, 'I knew you were a Shorter Catechism boy by your looks!' 'Why, that was just what I was thinking of you,' was the rejoinder.[1]

That is doxological Calvinism—a melody played in the midst of a world of chaos, a life lived in the knowledge that God is the Lord, that the Saviour is also the Creator who sustains all things, so that I can be assured

> That I with body and soul, both in life and death, am not my own, but belong unto my faithful Saviour Jesus Christ; who, with his precious blood, hath fully satisfied for all my sins, and delivered me from all the power of the devil; and so preserves me that without the will of my heavenly Father, not a hair can fall from my head; yea, that all things must be subservient to my salvation, and therefore, by his Holy Spirit, he also assures me of eternal life, and makes me sincerely willing and ready, henceforth, to live unto him.[2]

This is doxological Calvinism—and when we see and hear it, we are never in any doubt that we have seen Christianity in its finest flower.

[1] B. B. Warfield, *Selected Shorter Writings*, I:383-84.
[2] *Heidelberg Catechism*, Answer I.

SCRIPTURE INDEX

GENERAL INDEX

SOME PASTORS AND TEACHERS

ACKNOWLEDGEMENTS

The Banner of Truth Trust is grateful to the following for permission to reproduce many of the chapters that have appeared in this book.

Alliance of Confessing Evangelicals
'Repentance, Recovery, and Confession' in *Here We Stand*, ed. James Montgomery Boice and Benjamin E. Sasse (1996) ISBN: 978-0-80101-134-4

Baker Book House, a division of Baker Publishing Group
'John Murray: Biblical Theologian', *Handbook of Evangelical Theologians*, Walter A. Elwell, ed. (1993) ISBN: 978-0-801032-127. Used by permission.
'How Does the Bible Look at Itself', *Inerrancy and Hermeneutic*, Harvie Conn, ed. (1988) ISBN: 978-0-80102-533-8. Used by permission.

Christian Focus Publications
'Manifested in the Flesh: John Calvin on the Reality of the Incarnation' in *The Practical Calvinist*, ed Peter A Lillback (2002) ISBN: 978-1-85792-814-3
'Calvin on the Lord's Supper and Communion with Christ' in *Serving the Word of God*, eds. David Wright and David Stay (2002) ISBN: 978-1-85792-745-1
'Puritans – Ministers of the Word' in *The Westminster Directory of Public Worship* (2008) ISBN: 978-1-84550-427-4
'Introduction' to *The Priesthood of Christ*, John Owen (2010) ISBN: 978-1-84550-599-8
'The Preacher as Theologian' in *The Practical Preacher*, ed. William Philip (2002) ISBN: 978-1-85792-794-8

Christ's College Aberdeen

'Preaching and the Reformed Theological Tradition' in *Northern Accents: Aberdeen Essays on Preaching*, eds. David Fergusson and Alan Main (2001) ISBN: 978-0-95161-364-2

Crossway

'Christus Victor et Propitiator: The Death of Christ, Substitute and Conqueror' in *For the Fame of God's Name*, eds. Sam Storms & Justin Taylor (2010) ISBN: 978-1-4335-0492-1

'The Bit, the Bridle, and the Blessing: An Exposition of James 3:1-11' in *The Power of Words and the Wonder of God*, eds. John Piper & Justin Taylor (2009) ISBN: 978-1-4335-1049-6

Evangelical Press

'John Owen and the Doctrine of the Person of Christ' in *John Owen: The Man and His Theology*, ed. Robert Oliver (2002) ISBN: 0-87552-674-8

'John Owen and the Doctrine of the Holy Spirit' in *John Owen: The Man and His Theology*, ed. Robert Oliver (2002) ISBN: 0-87552-674-8

IVP UK/SPCK

'Preaching Christ from the Old Testament' in *When God's Voice is Heard: The Power of Preaching*, eds. Christopher Green & David Jackman (1995, 2003) ISBN: 978-0-85111-284-8

IVP USA

'The Mystery of Providence by John Flavel' taken from *The Devoted Life* edited by Kelly M. Kapic and Randall C. Gleason. Copyright © 2004 by Kelly M. Kapic and Randall C. Gleason. Used by permission of InterVarsity Press, P.O. Box 1400, Downers Grove, IL 60515, USA. www.ivpress.com

'The Reformed View' taken from *Christian Spirituality* edited by Donald Alexander. Copyright © 1988 by Donald L. Alexander. Used by permission of InterVarsity Press, P.O. Box 1400, Downers Grove, IL 60515, USA. www.ivpress.com

'Preaching the Atonement' taken from *The Glory of the Atonement* edited by Charles E. Hill and Frank A. James III. Copyright © 2004 by Charles E. Hill and Frank A. James III. Used by permission of InterVarsity Press, P.O. Box 1400, Downers Grove, IL 60515, USA. www.ivpress.com

Presbyterian and Reformed Publishing Company
'John Owen and the Doctrine of the Person of Christ' in *John Owen: The Man and His Theology*, ed. Robert Oliver (2002) ISBN: 0-87552-674-8
'John Owen and the Doctrine of the Holy Spirit' in *John Owen: The Man and His Theology*, ed. Robert Oliver (2002) ISBN: 0-87552-674-8
'Sola Fide' in *After Darkness Light*, ed. R. C. Sproul Jr. (2003) ISBN: 0-87552-712-4
'Assurance Justified' in *Assured by God*, ed. Burk Parsons (2006) ISBN: 978- 1-59638-029-5
'Exegesis' in *The Preacher and Preaching*, ed. Samuel T. Logan, Jr. (1986) ISBN: 0-87552-294-7

Reformation Heritage Books
'Calvin the Man: A Heart Aflame' in *Calvin: Theologian and Reformer*, eds. Joel R. Beeke and Garry J. Williams (2010)
'Some Reflections on the First Title of the Holy Spirit' in *The Holy Spirit and Reformed Spirituality*, eds. Joel R. Beeke and Derek W. H. Thomas (2013)

Reformation Trust/ Ligonier Ministries
'Calvin's Heart for God' in *John Calvin: A Heart for Devotion, Doctrine & Doxology*, ed. Burk Parsons (2008) ISBN: 978-1-56769-106-1
'Pastor and Theologian' in *The Trinitarian Devotion of John Owen*, Sinclair B. Ferguson (2014) ISBN: 978-1-56769-403-1
'Scripture and Tradition' in *Sola Scriptura* ed. Don Kistler (2009) ISBN: 978-1-56769-183-2

'"Hallowed be Your Name": The Holiness of the Father' in *Holy, Holy, Holy* (2010) ISBN: 978-1-56769-205-1

'Preaching to the Heart' in *Feed My Sheep* (2008) ISBN: 979-1-56769-107-8

'Doxology' in *Living for God's Glory*, Joel R. Beeke (*et. al.*) (2008) ISBN: 978-1-56769-105-4

Rutherford House

'The Reformed Doctrine of Sonship' in *Pulpit and People* eds. Nigel M. de S. Cameron and Sinclair B. Ferguson (1986) ISBN: 0-94606-819-4

Westminster Conference

'Preaching the Law of God—Reformers and Puritans' in *Puritans and Spiritual Life* (Papers Read at the Westminster Conference 2001)

Westminster Theological Seminary, California

'Christology and Pneumatology: John Calvin, the Theologian of the Holy Spirit' in *Always Reformed*, eds. R. Scott Clark and Joel E. Kim (2010) ISBN: 978-0-98288-050-0.

Other books by Sinclair B. Ferguson
available from the Trust

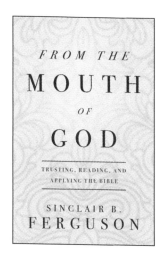

From the Mouth of God:
Trusting, Reading, and Applying the Bible
Sinclair B. Ferguson

224 pp. | paperback | ISBN: 978 1 84871 242 3